Cancer Epigenetics and Nanomedicine

T0269454

Cancer Epigenetics and Nanomedicine
Targeting the Right Player via Nanotechnology

Edited by

Prashant Kesharwani

Department of Pharmaceutics, School of Pharmaceutical Education and Research, Jamia Hamdard, New Delhi, India

Chitra Thakur

Stony Brook Cancer Center, Stony Brook University, Stony Brook, NY, United States

ACADEMIC PRESS
An imprint of Elsevier

ELSEVIER

Academic Press is an imprint of Elsevier
125 London Wall, London EC2Y 5AS, United Kingdom
525 B Street, Suite 1650, San Diego, CA 92101, United States
50 Hampshire Street, 5th Floor, Cambridge, MA 02139, United States

Copyright © 2024 Elsevier Inc. All rights are reserved, including those for text and data mining, AI training, and similar technologies.

Publisher's note: Elsevier takes a neutral position with respect to territorial disputes or jurisdictional claims in its published content, including in maps and institutional affiliations.

No part of this publication may be reproduced or transmitted in any form or by any means, electronic or mechanical, including photocopying, recording, or any information storage and retrieval system, without permission in writing from the publisher. Details on how to seek permission, further information about the Publisher's permissions policies and our arrangements with organizations such as the Copyright Clearance Center and the Copyright Licensing Agency, can be found at our website: www.elsevier.com/permissions.

This book and the individual contributions contained in it are protected under copyright by the Publisher (other than as may be noted herein).

Notices
Knowledge and best practice in this field are constantly changing. As new research and experience broaden our understanding, changes in research methods, professional practices, or medical treatment may become necessary.

Practitioners and researchers must always rely on their own experience and knowledge in evaluating and using any information, methods, compounds, or experiments described herein. In using such information or methods they should be mindful of their own safety and the safety of others, including parties for whom they have a professional responsibility.

To the fullest extent of the law, neither the Publisher nor the authors, contributors, or editors, assume any liability for any injury and/or damage to persons or property as a matter of products liability, negligence or otherwise, or from any use or operation of any methods, products, instructions, or ideas contained in the material herein.

ISBN: 978-0-443-13209-4

For information on all Academic Press publications
visit our website at https://www.elsevier.com/books-and-journals

Publisher: Stacy Masucci
Acquisitions Editor: Linda Buschman
Editorial Project Manager: Michaela Realiza
Production Project Manager: Surya Narayanan Jayachandran
Cover Designer: Greg Harris

Typeset by STRAIVE, India

Working together to grow libraries in developing countries

www.elsevier.com • www.bookaid.org

I would like to dedicate this book to my parents (Mr. Hariom Kesharwani and Mrs. Anguri Kesharwani), my sister (Dr. Punam Kesharwani), and my brother (Er. Pankaj Kesharwani) for believing in me and always being there for me. Equally, the book is also dedicated to the love and sacrifices of my wife (Garima Kesharwani), my kids (Yashsavi and Vidvaan), my nephew (Adhyayan), and my niece (Prisha).

Prashant Kesharwani

This book is dedicated to my parents who have been my biggest strength and inspiration.
The love and support of my kids (Dakshita and Daivik) along with my spouse (Anand) and siblings (Wg Cdr Priya and Alok) have been the driving force behind this work.
I am also deeply grateful for my mentors (Dr. Fei Chen and Dr. K Thangaraj) who have made my scientific journey worthwhile.

Chitra Thakur

Contents

CHAPTER 8 **Metabolic adaptation and epigenetic modulations: Unraveling tumor plasticity under variable tumor microenvironment** **169**

Jowana Obeid and Mehdi Damaghi

Contributors

Somaye Akbari
Textile Engineering Department, Amirkabir University of Technology, Tehran, Iran

Rashi Arora
University Flow Cytometry Resource, University of Minnesota, Minneapolis, MN, United States

Shivani Bhardwaj
ICAR—Central Institute for Research on Buffaloes Hisar, Haryana, India

Sayani Bhattacharjee
NanoString Technologies, Seattle, WA, United States

Prasanthi Chittineedi
Onco-Stem Cell Research Laboratory, Department of Biochemistry and Bioinformatics, GITAM School of Science, GITAM Deemed to be University, Visakhapatnam, India

Mehdi Damaghi
Stony Brook Cancer Center; Department of Biochemistry and Cell Biology; Department of Pathology, Renaissance School of Medicine; Department of Mathematics and Statistics, Stony Brook University, Stony Brook, NY, United States

Rambabu Dandela
Department of Industrial and Engineering Chemistry, Institute of Chemical Technology, Bhubaneswar, Odisha, India

Kamal Dua
Discipline of Pharmacy, Graduate School of Health, University of Technology Sydney, Broadway, NSW, Australia

Siri Chandana Gampa
Department of Biotechnology, GITAM School of Science, GITAM Deemed to be University, Visakhapatnam, India

Sireesha V. Garimella
Department of Biotechnology, GITAM School of Science, GITAM Deemed to be University, Visakhapatnam, India

Monisankar Ghosh
Department of Pathology, Renaissance School of Medicine, Stony Brook University, Stony Brook, NY, United States

Pushparathinam Gopinath
Department of Chemistry, Faculty of Engineering and Technology, SRM Institute of Science and Technology, Kattankulathur, Tamil Nadu, India

Garima Gupta
School of Allied Medical Sciences, Lovely Professional University, Phagwara, Punjab, India

Ashok K. Janakiraman
Faculty of Pharmaceutical Sciences, UCSI University, UCSI Highest, Kuala Lumpur, Malaysia

Rama Kadamb
Department of Cell Biology, Cancer Dormancy and Tumor Microenvironment Institute, Gruss-Lipper Biophotonics Center, Albert Einstein Cancer Center, Albert Einstein College of Medicine, Bronx, NY, United States

Jennifer M. Kalish
Division of Human Genetics and Center for Childhood Cancer Research, Children's Hospital of Philadelphia; Departments of Pediatrics and Genetics, Perelman School of Medicine at the University of Pennsylvania, Philadelphia, PA, United States

Neha Kanojia
Chitkara University School of Pharmacy, Chitkara University, Himachal Pradesh, India

Ananya Kar
Department of Industrial and Engineering Chemistry, Institute of Chemical Technology, Bhubaneswar, Odisha, India

Ritu Karwasra
Central Council for Research in Unani Medicine, Ministry of Ayush, Govt of India, New Delhi, India

Prashant Kesharwani
Department of Pharmaceutics, School of Pharmaceutical Education and Research, Jamia Hamdard, New Delhi, India

Kushagra Khanna
Faculty of Pharmaceutical Sciences, UCSI University, UCSI Highest, Kuala Lumpur, Malaysia

Jatin Kumar
Chitkara University School of Pharmacy, Chitkara University, Himachal Pradesh, India

K.R. Manu
Department of Industrial and Engineering Chemistry, Institute of Chemical Technology, Bhubaneswar, Odisha, India

Yeganeh Modirrousta
Polymer & Color Engineering Department, Amirkabir University of Technology, Tehran, Iran

Akshata R. Naik
Foundational Medical Studies, Oakland University William Beaumont School of Medicine, Rochester, MI, United States

Snehal Nirgude
Division of Human Genetics and Center for Childhood Cancer Research, Children's Hospital of Philadelphia, Philadelphia, PA, United States

Prajakta Oak
Biotech/Scientific Professional, Munich, Germany

Jowana Obeid
Stony Brook Cancer Center; Department of Biochemistry and Cell Biology, Stony Brook University, Stony Brook, NY, United States

Santhi Latha Pandrangi
Onco-Stem Cell Research Laboratory, Department of Biochemistry and Bioinformatics, GITAM School of Science, GITAM Deemed to be University, Visakhapatnam, India

Rajendra P. Pangeni
Institute of Neuro-Immune Medicine, Dr. Kiran Patel College of Osteopathic Medicine, Nova Southeastern University, Fort Lauderdale, FL, United States; Department of Natural and Applied Sciences, Nexus Institute of Research and Innovation, Lalitpur, Nepal

Moumita Roy
Mechanical Engineering, Texas Tech University, Lubbock, TX, United States

Rahul Roy
Centre for Biomedical Engineering, Indian Institute of Technology, New Delhi, Delhi, India

Suchandrima Saha
Department of Pathology, Renaissance School of Medicine, Stony Brook University, Stony Brook, NY, United States

Amirhossein Sahebkar
Biotechnology Research Center, Pharmaceutical Technology Institute; Applied Biomedical Research Center, Mashhad University of Medical Sciences, Mashhad, Iran

Uttara Saran
Department of Genomic Medicine, The University of Texas MD Anderson Cancer Center, Houston, TX, United States

Nitin Sharma
Department of Pharmaceutics, ISF College of Pharmacy, Moga, Punjab, India

Surender Singh
Department of Pharmacology, All India Institute of Medical Sciences, New Delhi, India

Parul Sood
Chitkara University School of Pharmacy, Chitkara University, Himachal Pradesh, India

Ramkanth Sundarapandian
Department of Pharmaceutics, Karpagam College of Pharmacy, Coimbatore, Tamil Nadu, India

Chitra Thakur
Stony Brook Cancer Center, Department of Pathology, Renaissance School of Medicine, Stony Brook University, Stony Brook, NY, United States

Komal Thapa
Chitkara University School of Pharmacy, Chitkara University, Himachal Pradesh, India

Apoorva Uboveja
UPMC Hillman Cancer Center, University of Pittsburgh School of Medicine, Pittsburgh, PA, United States

Nitin Verma
Chitkara University School of Pharmacy, Chitkara University, Himachal Pradesh, India

Priya Wadgaonkar
Department of Pharmaceutical Sciences, Eugene Applebaum College of Pharmacy and Health Sciences, Wayne State University, Detroit, MI, United States

About the editors

Dr. Prashant Kesharwani is presently working as an assistant professor at the Department of Pharmaceutics, Jamia Hamdard, New Delhi, India. He is also a recipient of several prestigious international and national awards, such as USERN Laureate 2023 and SERB-Ramanujan fellowship. Dr. Kesharwani has academic, industrial, and research experience at the international level (including United States, Malaysia, and India). An overarching goal of his current research is the development of nanoengineered drug delivery systems for various diseases. Dr. Kesharwani has more than 300 international publications in well-reputed journals and 23 published international books. His h-index is 76 and i-10 index is 309 (as of May 2024). He is a recipient of several internationally acclaimed awards and research funding from various funding bodies. He has presented many invited talks and oral presentations at prestigious scientific peer conferences, received international acclaim and awards for research contributions, supervised students/junior researchers, and actively participated in outreach and scientific dissemination for the service of the wider community.

Affiliation

Department of Pharmaceutics, School of Pharmaceutical Education and Research, Jamia Hamdard, New Delhi, 110062, India.

Dr. Chitra Thakur is currently working as an assistant professor (research) at the Department of Pathology, Stony Brook Cancer Center, Stony Brook University, New York, United States. As an expert in studying molecular oncology, her research work has unraveled significant epigenetic regulatory mechanisms in lung and breast cancer metastasis. She has specialized in big data analysis in oncology research, transgenic mouse models for human cancers, pathology, biomarker discovery, environmental toxicology in carcinogenesis research, and epigenetics. She sits on the editorial board of several scientific journals, such as *Frontiers in Public Health*, and is actively involved in the editorial peer review process and policymaking. She has served as a scientific reviewer for more than 400 manuscripts submitted to journals, such as *Medicinal Research Reviews*, *Scientific Reports*, and *Toxicology and Applied Pharmacology*. Her research work has contributed toward the discovery of signal transduction pathways, chemotherapeutic drug resistance implicated in human lung and breast cancers, cancer epigenetics, and cancer metabolism, as evidenced by more than 45 scholarly and peer-reviewed articles published in mainstream cancer-oriented scientific journals such as *Seminars in Cancer Biology*, *Frontiers in Oncology*, and *Biomedicine*. As a recipient of internationally acclaimed awards such as the DFG German Excellence Initiative Award, 2007, the NIH-Big Data Training for Translational Omics Research, 2017, and the Junior Scientist Award for the Gloria and Mark Snyder Symposium at the Stony Brook Cancer

Centre in 2023, she is actively engaged in mentoring students, community outreach, and engagement activities toward cancer education and prevention.

Affiliation

Stony Brook Cancer Center, Department of Pathology, Renaissance School of Medicine, Stony Brook University, Lauterbur Drive, Stony Brook, NY 11794, United States.

Preface

Cancer is the leading cause of morbidity and mortality worldwide. Understanding its biology, causes, and mechanisms is crucial for developing effective prevention, diagnosis, and treatment strategies. Cancer research has contributed toward the generation of targeted therapies, immunotherapies, and personalized medicine, which have paved the way for improving the efficacy of treatments while minimizing side effects. Despite significant advancements in this field, the challenges pertaining to metastasis, relapse, and drug resistance still prevail.

Although the field of epigenetics has been intertwined with cancer research for several decades and its understanding has evolved over time, the specific role of epigenetic changes in cancer began to gain significant attention in the late 20th century and has continued to advance since then.

Epigenetics, which studies changes in gene expression that do not involve alterations in the DNA sequence, has strengthened our fundamental knowledge of how genes are turned on or off, influencing various biological processes in homeostasis and cancer. Epigenetics is now recognized as a critical component of cancer biology, influencing gene expression patterns, cellular identity, and response to therapy. Epigenetic modifications are reversible, making them attractive targets for drug development; hence, the dynamic nature of epigenetic changes provides opportunities for the development of novel diagnostic tools and therapeutic interventions in the field of cancer research. Moreover, external factors such as environmental exposures, metabolism, and diet and nutrition have profound influence on epigenetics, where some of the factors also contribute to disease risk.

Therefore, studying cancer research and epigenetics is essential for advancing medical knowledge, improving patient outcomes, and developing innovative strategies for disease prevention and treatment. Combining nanotechnology-mediated drug delivery systems with epigenetic therapy is another promising approach to reaching a high therapeutic index and minimizing the side effects. The interdisciplinary nature of these fields fosters collaboration and the integration of various scientific disciplines to address complex health challenges.

In summary, keeping the above sentiments as the prime focus of this book, we have devised chapters that comprehensively cover the basic attributes of carcinogenesis, immune response, metabolism, and epigenetics, factors affecting epigenetic regulation, and how epigenetic diet and nanotechnology can offer valuable insights toward the development of robust anticancer therapies.

Featuring contributions from field experts and researchers in industry and academia, we provide state-of-the-art information on cancer epigenetics and nanomedicine-mediated approaches to epigenetic therapy. We hope that the readers of this book will find it useful and will stimulate further interest in the areas of cancer epigenetics.

Prashant Kesharwani
Chitra Thakur

Acknowledgments

We sincerely thank all the contributors for offering to write comprehensive chapters within a stipulated tight schedule. This is generally an added responsibility in the hectic work schedules of the researchers. We express our earnest gratitude to the reviewers for their suggestions in framing the chapters and for providing their critical views for the improvement of the book chapters. We also thank Michaela Realiza (Editorial Project Manager, Elsevier), whose efforts during the preparation of this book proved to be very useful.

Prashant Kesharwani
Chitra Thakur

Overview of cancer, internal and external factors associated with cancer

Overview of cancer: Mechanisms of carcinogenesis

Uttara Saran[a] and Chitra Thakur[b]

[a]*Department of Genomic Medicine, The University of Texas MD Anderson Cancer Center, Houston, TX, United States,* [b]*Stony Brook Cancer Center, Department of Pathology, Renaissance School of Medicine, Stony Brook University, Stony Brook, NY, United States*

On occasion, a cell may choose to go its own way ... It is then that we see the much-feared chaos that we call cancer.
Robert Weinberg, One Renegade Cell [1]

Introduction

Cancer is a group of diseases characterized by uncontrolled proliferation and the spread of abnormal cells from the site of origin to other sites in the body, which, if not controlled, can result in death [2]. Cancer is the second leading cause of death worldwide after cardiovascular diseases [3], with the number of deaths from this disease projected to increase in part due to an aging global population [4]. Over 200 types of cancers have been classified to date. The development of cancer involves a complex interplay of genetic and epigenetic alterations that contribute to the initiation, promotion, and progression of malignancy. This chapter provides an overview of the role of epigenetics in cancer and the evolution of cancer theories from the ancient concept of "creeping ulcer" to our current "hallmarks" of cancer that form the basis of our understanding of the complex biology of this disease.

Cancer: A historical perspective

Cancer is not a "modern man-made" disease and has existed in animals since prehistoric times [5]. Albeit its prevalence in the recent decades has significantly increased in unison with rapidly aging populations, increased exposure to dietary and environmental carcinogens, and the adoption of increasingly risky health behaviors [6,7].

Cancer Epigenetics and Nanomedicine. https://doi.org/10.1016/B978-0-443-13209-4.00008-8
Copyright © 2024 Elsevier Inc. All rights are reserved, including those for text and data mining, AI training, and similar technologies.

The earliest evidence of cancerous growth in humans was noted in Egyptian and Peruvian mummies dating back to around 1500 BCE [6]. The oldest descriptions of cancer (although the term cancer was not used) were found in ancient Egyptian manuscripts dating back to the same period, which included descriptions of surgical, pharmacological, and magical treatments for cancerous lesions [7]. The coining of the term "cancer" is attributed to the Greek physician Hippocrates, who described the central body of a tumor and its finger-like projections to resemble the shape of a crab or "*Karkinoma*" (the Greek word for "crab"). This term was later translated into "*cancer*"—the *Latin* word for crab—by the Roman physician Celsus. The term used to describe cancer specialists, i.e., "oncologists," stems from the word "*oncos*" (the Greek for "swelling") coined by Greek physician Galen to describe tumors.

While ancient Egyptian documents regarded cancer as a grave incurable disease that was a "curse of the Gods," Hippocrates and his disciples rejected prevailing views of superstitions as the cause of cancer and instead believed it was initiated by natural causes; thereby proposing the "Humoral Theory" (discussed in the next section), which remained the standard school of thought for over 1300 years [6,7]. This theory was subsequently discarded in the 17th century following the discovery of vascular and lymphatic systems. It was during this period that some physical attributes of cancer began to emerge such as the clinical differences between benign and malignant tumors, which remains largely applicable today. Another key observation that has also held true was the one by Henri François Le Dran (1685–1770), a leading surgeon who suggested that cancer develops locally but could spread through the lymphatic system, thereby becoming inoperable and fatal [8]. A notion was supported by his contemporary, Jean-Louis Petit (1674–1750), who advocated total mastectomy for breast cancer, including resection of axillary glands (lymph nodes), suggesting that this would prevent recurrences [9]—surgical approach that continues to be practiced to date.

Soon prevailing questions of "how cancer begins" and "what its causative factors are" spurred the medical community to search for answers in multiple avenues of cancer-related research. One avenue established was that of "experimental oncology" to confirm or disprove hypotheses related to the causes, nature, growth patterns, and treatment of cancers. One of the pioneers of experimental oncology, Bernard Peyrilhe (1735–1804), refined the concept of cancer being a local disease by suggesting that postsurgical relapses occurred as a result of either local regrowth of the remnant disease or unrecognized dissemination through lymphatic or blood vessels resulting in distal disease "*consequent*" cancer (now known as *metastasis*— a term coined in 1829). A view that was widely embraced by prominent physicians and scholars of the time, including Pierre Paul Broca, whose essay on the pathologic anatomy of cancer provided an empiric foundation for staging and prognostic assessment of cancer that has survived to date [10]. This period also produced the first persuasive empirical evidence of a link between work activity and environment and human disease [11,12] as well as the opening of hospitals specializing in cancer care.

In the late 19th century, improvements in the resolution of microscopes not only helped document and define disease-causing organisms but also made the examination of cells and cellular activity possible, setting the stage for the emergence of new cancer hypotheses (which will be discussed in the next section). Notable discoveries from this period include Robert Remak's (1815–1865) and Louis Bard's (1829–1894) observations on cell division, proposing that cancer was not a "new formation" of cells but rather a "transformation" of normal tissues [13]. Furthermore, their observations correctly proposed that normal cells can develop into a mature differentiated state, whereas cancer cells suffer from developmental defects that result in tumor formation [14]. Together their notions on cell division are significant in providing clues on the genetic origin of cancer and serve as precursors to today's histologic classification of many cancers, a useful stratification to plan treatment and to gage prognosis. Interestingly this period also saw the conception of the cell-based "somatic mutation theory" by Theodor Boveri (1862–1915). However, as this theory proved to be a significant shift from the dominant viewpoint that considered cancer as a tissue-based disease, it was mostly ignored until the emergence of molecular biology and molecular genetics half a century later. Progress in bacteriology and parasitology were also having a profound effect on cancer theory and therapeutics of the 19th century. These theories equated cancer invasion with that of bacterial infections, resulting in the adoption of the bacteria-eradication concept as a model for treating cancer, a notion that still prevails to this day. It would take approximately another 150 years before the bacteria-cancer link (i.e., inflammation and mutagenic bacterial metabolites) were conclusively proven to be able to invoke some cancers. In 1911, Peyton Rous (1879–1970) confirmed a "virus-cancer" link with his momentous discovery of the *Rous sarcoma virus*. Subsequently other viruses such as Hepatitis B or C, Epstein-Barr, and Human papilloma viruses (HPVs) have also been associated with liver, nasopharyngeal, and cervical cancers, respectively. Discoveries of anesthesia [15], asepsis [16], and refinements in surgical techniques between 1842 and 1867 propelled surgery to the forefront of early-stage cancer management and increased cure rates. Similarly, discoveries of X-rays in 1895 [17], uranium, radium, and polonium [18] marked the dawn of modern diagnostic and therapeutic radiology and nuclear medicine.

The middle of the 20th century saw the introduction of innovative research tools that enabled scientists to systematically solve complex problems of chemistry and biology of cancer, leading to incremental progress on many fronts. Notable discoveries include Watson and Crick's discovery of the DNA helical structure. These, in turn, lead to the discovery of cancer-causing chemicals (carcinogens), radiation, and hereditary cancers. The 1970s saw the discovery of two important families of genes, "oncogenes" and "tumor suppressor genes" (discussed in the next section), as well as the regular use of image-guided tools such as ultrasound, computed tomography, magnetic resonance imaging, and positron emission tomography for cancer detection and diagnosis [7]. New methods for cancer treatments, such as combining surgery with chemotherapy and/or radiation, were introduced during the latter half of the 20th century.

Origin of cancer: Theories and drivers of carcinogenesis

Understanding the molecular, genetic, and biochemical changes contributing to carcinogenesis has been the dominating focus of cancer-related research over the last decades. Based on Rudolf Virchow's establishment of the cell as the fundamental building block of living organisms, researchers in the modern era of cancer consider cancer cells as the primary unit of disease. The fundamental question pursued for much of the 20th century has been what drives cancer cells to stop adhering to normal mechanisms of control and expand uncontrollably. In this section, we will discuss the principal theories of cancer origin as well as the principal drivers contributing to the initiation and progression of carcinogenesis.

Theories of cancer origin

Throughout the ages, many theories have attempted to explain the origin and development of cancer. Hippocrates' "Humoral theory" was one of the earliest theories put forward, which suggested that cancer developed due to the excess accumulation of body fluids, particularly black bile in various parts of the body [5,6]. This theory remained popular through the Middle Ages until the discovery of the lymphatic system and the conception of the "Lymph theory." This theory posited that cancer occurred due to the contamination of blood by cancer germs originating from the fermenting and degenerating lymph. This theory prevailed till the 19th century and the conception of Müller's "Blastema theory," which suggested that cancer cells originate from budding elements (blastema) as opposed to the normal tissue. Muller's theory was later partially corrected by Rudolph Virchow's "Chronic irritation theory," which proposed inflammation and chronic irritation as the causes of cancer [7]. Two other theories, the "Parasite theory," where cancer was believed to be contagious and spread via parasites, and the "Trauma theory," which believed that cancer was caused by trauma, were put forward around the 17th to 19th centuries. In 1902, John Beard formulated the "Trophoblast theory of cancer" based on the observation that cancerous cells possessed properties similar to those of placental cells in pregnancy [19].

Currently the two main trends used to explain the mechanisms of cancer development are of genetic and epigenetic origin. Genetic theories suggest that cancer is caused by primary alteration of genetic material in cells, which in turn modulates morphological and phenotypic change [20]. Epigenetic theories, on the other hand, posit that cancer occurs as a result of alterations to the DNA that are not genetic in origin, i.e., caused by DNA methylation, acetylation, or modifications in chromatin proteins (discussed in more detail in "Epigenetics and cancer" section). These theories believe that these molecular mutations are hereditary, and if the change induced is significant, they would subsequently lead to neoplastic transformation [20].

While largely ignored when first proposed, Boveri's "Somatic mutation theory" (SMT) has since become the prevailing one in cancer research [21]. SMT proposes that cancer originates from one somatic cell following the accumulation of multiple

DNA mutations of genes that control cell proliferation and cell cycle, thereby resulting in unbridled proliferation and decreased cell death [22–25]. SMT defines cancer as a clonal, cell-based disease that occurs due to mutations caused by molecular events [20]. The core concept of this theory is that cancer development is driven by mutations of "master genes" (oncogenes and/or tumor suppressor genes) in a single somatic cell.

In 1999, an alternative theory, the "Tissue organization field theory" (TOFT), was proposed by Anderson et al. [26], which defined carcinogenesis as a problem of tissue organization comparable to organogenesis during early development and that proliferation was the default state of all cells [27,28]. SMT and TOFT are in opposition to one another as the former advocates that carcinogenesis occurs at the single-cell level as opposed to the latter's suggestion that this phenomenon occurs at the tissue level [20].

Recently, two additional theories, "The bad luck" [29] and "Ground state" [30] theories, have been proposed that draw concepts from both SMT and TOFT. The "Bad luck" theory, proposed by Tomasetti and colleagues [29,31], extends the SMT by proposing that random mistakes made during DNA replication in stem cells (R-mutations) generate malignant, self-renewing daughters that propagate cancer. This model distinguishes R-mutations from those that are heritable (H-mutations) or caused by environmental carcinogens (E-mutations). One of the main issues with this theory is the assumption that cancer risk is dictated solely by the number of stem cell divisions without taking into consideration that other intrinsic (such as epigenetic states) or extrinsic (such as immune microenvironment) factors can also trigger neoplastic transformation independent of the cell division process [32,33]. Interestingly these shortcomings that are shared by SMT are, in part, the inspiration for TOFT as an alternative. The "Ground state" theory, proposed by Zhu et al. [30], unites elements of the somatic mutation, TOFT, and bad luck theory by focusing on the functional state of the cell (i.e., its ground state) rather than its classification as a stem, lineage-committed progenitor, or other cell type. This concept is important as this theory accords with the notion that intrinsic and extrinsic factors can also trigger neoplastic transformation independent of cell division [27,29–31,34,35]. Thus, this theory builds on principles underpinning both the bad luck and TOFT theories while emphasizing the convergence of extrinsic and intrinsic factors to generate cell states that drive cancer.

Mechanisms of carcinogenesis

Irrespective of whether one adopts a genetic or an epigenetic view of carcinogenesis, it is generally accepted that cancer development occurs in a multistage manner. This section summarizes the acquisition of traits that promote cancer growth and spread, presented in a scheme from the least to greatest complexity, i.e., from genes to cells to tumors.

Endogenous and exogenous factors affecting DNA

Preserving the integrity of nuclear DNA is crucial for the life of a cell, whereby alterations to the cell's DNA could have potentially lethal effects on both the host as well as the entire organism. While DNA mutations are known to enable genetic variation, immunological responsiveness, and species evolution, deleterious accumulation of damage can lead to cancer. Point mutations can occur either randomly during DNA replication or through chemical modification of mutagens. Errors that occur during DNA replication include transition or transversion mutations (resulting from the insertion of the wrong base at the wrong position) as well as insertion or deletion mutations (inclusion or exclusion of one or more extra bases due to slippage of the polymerase complex) [36]. The most common DNA damage caused by endogenous chemical modifications are hydrolysis, oxidative damage, and covalent DNA adduct formation resulting from normal, endogenous metabolic activity. In most cases, majority of these mistakes are corrected by the repair processes active in all cells. Moreover, unrepaired mutations may have little effect on the cell if they occur in the vast noncoding regions of the genome or are genetically silent. Although epigenetic regulation of gene expression mediated by DNA methylation is not considered "mutagenic" (due to the underlying DNA sequence remaining unchanged), the addition of methyl groups to the cytosine at CpG sites is associated with reduced mRNA transcription around the targeted site and consequently leads to decreased translated protein expression [37].

Exogenous factors affecting DNA include chemical, light radiation, and infectious agents that have the ability to bind and disrupt DNA, which, if unrepaired, result in mutations that can promote cancer development. Direct DNA-disrupting mutagens include highly electrophilic compounds with a strong affinity for the negatively charged DNA including alkylating agents, while indirect carcinogens are nucleophilic (proton seeking) or less reactive compounds requiring chemical or enzymatic conversion to their carcinogenic state. Examples of indirect carcinogens include aflatoxins (secondary metabolites produced by *Aspergillus flavus*) [38–40] and compounds released by tobacco smoke [41–44] whose metabolism in the body can lead to mutations in key regulatory genes such as *p53* and *KRAS*. Exposure to ionizing radiation (i.e., X-rays and gamma rays) causes damage at an atomic level, resulting in double-stranded DNA breaks, base oxidations, and DNA-protein cross-links [45]. Some infection agents (viral or bacterial) directly contribute to cell transformation and are required for some cancers (e.g., cervical carcinoma and Kaposi sarcoma) [46–49]. While in the case of others, infection alone cannot initiate cancer, rather malignancy occurs as a result of a combination of other extrinsic cofactors or genetic alterations with the initial infection (e.g., onset of hepatocellular or gastric cancer caused by prolonged chronic infection and inflammatory conditions) [50–54].

DNA repair

The relation between cancer development and inactivating mutations or epigenetic silencing of DNA repair systems has become increasingly apparent over the last few decades [55]. As discussed above, damage to the DNA can be caused by a wide range of normal cellular processes, as well as a host of exogenous insults resulting from external exposures. Such damage can, in turn, induce DNA modifications such as single or double-stranded breaks in the double helix. Chemical modifications and single-stranded breaks are more common and easily repaired using the complementary strand as a template. In contrast, double-stranded breaks are potentially catastrophic to a cell's viability as the coding and regulatory information inherent in the linear sequence can be lost. The simplest form of DNA repair is a direct reversal used to repair O-methyl guanine modifications by the enzyme methyl guanine methyltransferase (MGMT), which does not require either a template or hydrolysis of the phosphodiester backbone [56,57]. A common lesion associated with DNA alkylation involves the addition of the O^6 methyl group to guanine, causing a mispairing with thymine instead of cytosine. MGMT restores the guanine base on the DNA by facilitating the transfer of the methyl group from the DNA strand to a cysteine residue on the protein. This is highlighted by the observation that epigenetic silencing of the *MGMT* gene is a common phenomenon in colorectal and brain cancers [57,58] and that knock-out mice deficient in MGMT become hypersensitive to alkylating agents like temozolomide [56].

Three mechanisms can be utilized to repair single-stranded DNA damage, namely, base excision repair (BER), nucleotide excision repair (NER), and mismatch repair (MMR). As the name suggests this type of damage is restricted to only one strand and these systems use the complementary strand as a template for the repair process. The BER pathway is used to repair small, single-stranded lesions such as nucleotide base deamination, oxidation, or some forms of alkylation, which have not caused major structural disruption to the DNA [59–61]. The MMR system is used to repair insertions or deletions that arise during DNA replication [62,63], while the NER system is used to repair bulky, helix-distorting chemical lesions caused by exposure to tobacco smoke, platinum-based cancer drugs, and/or ultraviolet light [64]. The nonhomologous end joining (NHEJ) [65–67] and homologous recombination (HR) [68] are repair systems used to repair double-stranded breaks in DNA, with HR being considered the more accurate process. As the name suggests NHEJ involves religation of the ends of the broken DNA with little or no homology. While this pathway is essential for genomic stability, NHEJ is also considered to be error prone [69]. In contrast, HR repair requires extensive DNA sequence homology and is restricted to certain times during the cell cycle. Studies have shown that mutations in the *BRCA1* and *BRCA2* genes are caused by defects in the HR DNA repair process [70,71].

Oncogenes and tumor suppressor genes

Oncogenes are mutated forms of normal cellular genes called protooncogenes. Oncogenes function as accelerators of cell growth and division, and their mutations encode proteins (either by hyperactivation or misregulation of the time and/or space of its expression) to equip cancer cells with the capability to grow in the absence of growth signals. Cancer cells can promote growth signals by either autocrine or paracrine signaling. On the other hand, tumor suppressor genes function by slowing down cell growth and division. In essence they serve as negative regulators of oncogenes. They also play roles in cell cycle checkpoint regulation or checkpoints for DNA damage and spindle assembly, as well as stimulating apoptosis [72]. Oncogenes and tumor suppressors work largely through the disruption of 12 signaling pathways the govern three core cellular processes: cell survival (cell cycle/apoptosis, MAPK, TGF-β, STAT, PI3K, RTK/RAS), cell fate (chromatin modification, transcriptional regulation, NOTCH, Hedgehog/Hippo, WNT), and genome maintenance (DNA damage control) [73,74].

Sustained proliferation

Ultimately, what distinguishes a cancer cell is its ability to grow in conditions where normal cells cannot. Cell growth and division cycles are tightly regulated in normal cells to ensure homeostasis of cell number and maintenance of normal tissue architecture and function. Cancer cells, on the other hand, hijack these signals, becoming "masters of their own destinies" [75]. Cancer cells achieve this by harnessing the hallmark capabilities of inducing and sustaining positively acting growth-stimulatory signals as well as being able to circumvent powerful programs that negatively regulate cell proliferation. Cancer cells mediate their effects via both genetic and epigenetic mechanisms. For example, somatic mutations of isocitrate dehydrogenase (*IDH*) are common initiating events in some cancers including gliomas [76]. In gliomas, the resulting formation of the 2-hydroxyglutarate oncometabolite obstructs hydroxylases which are involved in DNA demethylation, resulting in hypermethylated DNA. *IDH* mutations also cause decreased activity of DNA binding protein CTCF (which is responsible for insulating chromatin loops from excessive enhancer stimulation), resulting in hyperproliferation mediated by the activation of oncogene *PDGFRA* due to the loss of CTCF [77]. High-throughput DNA sequencing analyses of cancer cell genomes have revealed that somatic mutations in some tumor types can predict the constitutive activation of proliferative signaling circuits. For example, activating mutations affecting the structure of the B-Raf protein results in the constitutive signaling of the Raf to MAPK pathway [78]. Moreover, defects in the negative-feedback mechanisms that operate within the proliferative signaling circuitry have also been shown to enhance proliferative signaling. For example, loss of function mutations in *PTEN* amplifies PI3K signaling and promotes tumorigenesis in various cancers. Moreover, *PTEN* expression is often lost by promoter methylation [79,80]. In addition to inducing and sustaining proliferation, cancer cells also need to evade powerful programs that negatively regulate cell proliferation. Majority of these programs are dependent on the actions of tumor suppressor genes. *TP53*, which operates as a central control node in the cellular regulatory circuits, is the most prevalently mutated and inactivated gene in cancer cells [81]. *TP53* promoter methylation has also been reported in many cancers including neuroblastomas and melanomas [82,83].

Cell death and resistance

Apoptosis or programmed cell death plays a key role in tumor suppression, and therefore, it is crucial for cancer cells to reduce or eliminate this mechanism during their development [84]. In fact, deregulation of intrinsic apoptosis is a common event during cancer development [85]. Apoptosis can be induced by extrinsic factors mediated by extracellular signals acting through a family of cell surface receptors or by intrinsic pathways requiring intracellular signals (e.g., oxidative stress and DNA damage). The former process involves "death receptors" or the tumor necrosis factor (TNF) receptor family [86], while the latter occurs through the action of the Bcl-2 family [87]. Tumor cells evolve a variety of strategies to limit or circumvent apoptosis. Most common is the loss of TP53, which eliminates this critical damage sensor from the apoptosis-inducing circuitry. Alternatively, tumors achieve similar results by increasing expression of antiapoptotic regulators (Bcl-2, Bcl-xL) or of survival signals (Igf1/2), by downregulating proapoptotic factors (Bax, Bim, Puma) or by short-circuiting the extrinsic ligand-induced death pathway. Bcl-2 chromosomal translocations as well as hypomethylation of the Bcl-2 gene are commonly observed in hematological malignancies. Similarly, deregulated methylation of Bcl-2 (antiapoptotic) and Bax (proapoptotic) has been shown to disrupt apoptotic signaling in glioblastoma [88]. Therapeutic targeting of the apoptotic pathways is a major focus of current cancer therapy. Many chemotherapeutics cause DNA damage with the intent to induce apoptosis through the intrinsic pathway.

Autophagy represents an important cell-physiologic response that can be strongly induced in certain states of cellular stress, the most obvious of which is nutrient deficiency [89,90]. The autophagic program enables the lysosomal degradation and recycling of the cytosolic components for biosynthesis and energy metabolism [91,92]. While excess autophagy can lead to nonapoptotic cell death, paradoxically, cancer cells can activate autophagy as a response to support their survival in stressed, nutrient-limited conditions. Similarly, radiotherapy and certain cytotoxic drugs have also been shown to induce and elevate autophagy levels that confer a cytoprotective effect on cancer cells, as opposed to accentuating the killing actions of these stress inducing situations [93–96]. Severely stressed cancer cells have been shown to shrink to a state of reversible dormancy via autophagy [97], a survival mechanism that may enable the persistence and eventual recurrence of these malignant cells.

Angiogenic switch

Like normal tissues, tumors also need a steady supply of nutrients and oxygen as well as the removal of metabolic waste and carbon dioxide. During embryogenesis, the development of the vasculature involves the birth of new endothelial cells and their assembly into tubes (vasculogenesis) in addition to the sprouting (angiogenesis) of new vessels from existing ones. In adults, normal vasculature remains largely quiescent, with angiogenesis being "switched" on only transiently in response to physiologic stimulus during wound healing and female reproductive cycling. In contrast, the angiogenic switch in tumors is almost always activated to enable a continuous "sprouting" of new vasculature to sustain the expanding neoplastic growth [98].

Moreover, the loose construction of the newly formed endothelial tubes and their attendant pericytes generate "leaky" vessels, a characteristic feature of tumor vasculature that enables the passage of tumor cells into the circulation during metastasis. Targeting angiogenesis by blocking angiogenesis inducers has been suggested as an effective way to block or even reverse tumor growth [99], albeit to date, clinical responses to antiangiogenic therapy have been modest at best. Angiogenesis inducers include nonspecific growth factors (epidermal growth factor [EGF], fibroblast growth factor [FGF], and platelet-derived growth factor [PDGF]) as well as angiogenesis-specific inducers and receptors (vascular endothelial growth factors [VEGF], ephrins, and angiopoietins and Tie receptors). Of the five known VEGF isoforms, signaling via VEGFA and VEGFR2 are the most well-characterized. Their receptor binding activates the RAS-Raf-MAPK pathway as well as PI3K and AKT. This, in turn, leads to the inhibition of apoptosis and increased vascular permeability via increased levels of nitric oxide generated by AKT stimulation of nitric oxide synthase. Expression of the VEGF genes is regulated by a variety of oncogenic proteins (e.g., EGFR and Src) and tumor suppressors (e.g., p53). They are also regulated by the oxygen-sensing protein hypoxia-inducible factor-1 (HIF-1). Hypoxic conditions within tumors stabilize the expression of HIF-1α, which in turn activates a number of genes including VEGF, resulting in increased angiogenesis, enabling the further expansion of the tumor. Angiogenesis can be "switched off" by inhibitors such as angiostatin, endostatin, thrombospondin-1-2, and p53. Increased expression of thrombspondin-1 is, in part, regulated by binding of p53 to its promoter. Thus, mutations in p53 lead to decreased levels of thrombospondin-1 and an increase in the angiogenesis signal. Similarly, loss of tumor suppressor gene Von Hippel-Lindau (VHL) by genetic or epigenetic mechanisms results in the overproduction of VEGF through the accumulation of HIF [100]. Hypermethylation of the VHL promoter is a common event in many cancers [101].

Tissue invasion and metastasis

Metastasis involves the process of tumors migrating from their primary site to a new site throughout the body. While only a small subset of a primary tumor has the potential to become metastatic, this phenomenon is responsible for approximately 90% of patient mortality. Invasion and metastasis are what distinguish benign neoplasms from malignant ones [75,102]. Steps of the metastatic cascade include: (i) disruption of the basement membrane, (ii) detachment of the metastatic cell from the body of the tumor, (iii) invasion of the underlying extracellular matrix (ECM), (iv) entry into the vascular system (intravasation), (v) transport through the vasculature, (vi) arrest and adhesion to the inner surface of the blood or lymphatic vessel, (vii) exit from the vasculature (extravasation), and (viii) colonization of the new tissue and proliferation. Briefly, the initial detachment of tumor cells involves the disruption of cell-cell junctions maintained by E-cadherin (which acts as a tumor suppressor in this context) [103,104] followed by degradation of the basement membrane. Invasion of tumor cells into the surrounding tissues is mediated by the activities of serine and matrix metalloproteases (secreted by the tumor cells). As described above, the vasculature induced by tumor cells is abnormal and displays loose cell-cell junctions. This allows tumor cells to readily pass through the vessel walls and enter the circulation, the process of intravasation. Once inside the vessel the tumor cells travel singly or in clusters with platelets and lymphocytes and are disseminated throughout the body. It is thought that traveling in clusters protects the tumor cells from circulatory shear forces.

It is well established that different tumor types preferentially metastasize to different organs. This phenomenon is partially explained by Paget's "seed and soil" concept [105,106] that certain organs or tissues provide a more favorable environment for the colonization and growth of specific tumor types. An example of this is the CXC-chemokine ligand 12 (CXCL12) [107], which is thought to specifically attract cancer cells expressing the G-protein coupled chemokine receptors CXCR4 and CXCR7. Likewise, the cancer cells migrate to specific sites using these honing signals and adhere to the ECM at the new site after extravasating themselves from the vasculature. From this point, interactions with the cellular microenvironment are what determine if the malignant cells will "take seed and grow," die, or become quiescent. A recent finding demonstrates that one of the preferred sites for some tumor metastases is with the original tumor, which could be a contributing factor to tumor heterogeneity.

Invasion and metastasis of cancer cells are mostly controlled by the epithelial-mesenchymal transition (EMT), a developmental regulatory program [108]. By coopting a process involved in the various steps of embryogenesis and wound healing, cancer cells can concomitantly acquire multiple attributes that enable invasion and metastasis. Both genetic and epigenetic mechanisms have been involved in the activation of EMT [109]. The EMT process is regulated by a set of pleiotropically acting transcriptional factors, including Snail, Slug, Twist, and Zeb1/2, and these regulators have been found to be expressed in a wide range of cancer subtypes. Moreover, EMT directed by histone modifications results in a wide range of transcriptional silencing of epithelial genes and activation of mesenchymal ones [110–114].

The tumor microenvironment

Over the last few decades, it has become abundantly clear that tumors are not just masses of relatively homogeneous malignant cells but are complex "rogue" organs whose complexity could rival and even exceed that of normal healthy tissue [75,115]. It is now well established that the tumor microenvironment (TME) plays a decisive role in tumor initiation, differentiation, invasion and metastasis, immune evasion, and epigenetics [115–117]. The TME consists of nonmalignant cellular components (i.e., stromal cells, fibroblasts endothelial cells, neurons, adipocytes, adaptive, and innate immune cells) surrounding the cancer cells embedded on an altered ECM (noncellular component) [118–120]. Intracellular communication in this space between the malignant and nonmalignant cells is driven by a complex and dynamic network of cytokines, chemokines, growth factors, exosomes, and inflammatory and matrix remodeling enzymes [115]. While the normal tissue microenvironment can constrain neoplastic growth through suppressive functions of immune cells, fibroblasts, and the ECM, malignancy necessitates the evasion of these functions [120]. Cancer cells orchestrate a tumor-supportive environment by recruiting and reprogramming noncancerous host cells and by remodeling the ECM [120]. Notably the unique interplay among cancer cells, immune cells, stromal cells, and the ECM contributes to tumor cell plasticity, leading to metastatic dissemination [121]. Atlases created by computational analysis and modeling using bulk tumor expression profiling, single-cell transcriptomics data, and spatial transcriptomics allow us to obtain a panoramic view of the intricate dialogues between these diverse cellular constituents. Armed with this knowledge, we are gradually becoming better poised to develop interventions that disrupt the supportive TME and weaken the fortress that cancer constructs to ensure its survival.

It also should be noted that within the heart of each tumor resides a mosaic of cellular diversity known as tumor heterogeneity. A phenomenon that underpins treatment resistance, relapse, and therapeutic failures, and herein lies the challenge of attempting to treat the tumor as a monolithic entity while ignoring the multifaceted populations encased within. Using single-cell and spatial sequencing, scientists are now slowly starting to dissect tumors into their distinct populations to unveil their characteristics, vulnerabilities, and interactions. It is with this molecular cartography that researchers are able to navigate the labyrinth of tumor heterogeneity and direct therapies to target specific subclones that would otherwise escape attention.

Hallmarks of cancer

The conceptualization of the hallmarks of cancer was to provide a heuristic tool for understanding the diverse complexity of cancer phenotypes. These hallmarks propose a set of acquired functional capabilities that allow cancer cells to survive, proliferate, and disseminate. This concept was based on the recognition that human cancers develop as products of multistep processes and that the acquisition of these functional capabilities might be mapped in some fashion to the distinguishable steps of tumor pathogenesis. It should also be noted that the hallmarks were selected based on their broad engagement across the spectrum of human cancers.

Initially Hanahan and Weinberg [122] envisioned the complementary involvement of six distinct hallmark capabilities as follows:

- Self-sufficiency in growth signals
- Insensitivity to antigrowth signals
- Evasion of apoptosis
- Sustained angiogenesis
- Limitless replicative potential
- Tissue invasion and metastasis

These hallmarks primarily focused on characterizing distinguishing genes and associated signal transduction pathways mediating their respective activities in malignant cells and tumors. The hallmarks comprise essential alterations that collectively characterize malignant growth and help distinguish tumors from relevant normal tissue. The authors also identified "genomic instability" as an enabling characteristic that generates genetic diversity and expedites tumor progression.

In 2011, Hanahan and Weinberg [75] revisited and refined the organizing principles to incorporate the conceptual progress that had been made over the past decade. One indication of the progress was the renaming of the original hallmarks as follows:

- Sustaining proliferative signaling
- Evading growth suppressors
- Resisting cell death
- Inducing angiogenesis
- Enabling replicative immortality
- Activating tissue invasion and metastasis

The significance of the new terms is that the hallmarks now refer to a *dynamic process* as opposed to a *phenotype*. Moreover two "emerging hallmarks" were added to the original six:

- Deregulating cellular energetics
- Evading immune destruction

The enabling characteristic identified in 2000 was revised as "genomic instability and mutation," and a second enabling characteristic was identified as "tumor-promoting inflammation." It should be noted that "mutation" in the context of carcinogenesis identifies a mechanism through which a chemical carcinogen may cause the emergence of any of the hallmarks, or perhaps of all of them. The second enabling characteristic proposed recognizes inflammation as a causative factor for the emergence of several of the hallmarks, including sustaining proliferative signaling and inducing angiogenesis. The "inflammation" discussed here was primarily focused on the cellular infiltration of cells of both innate and adaptive immune responses.

In 2022, Hanahan [123] presented several prospective new hallmarks and enabling characteristics that could eventually be incorporated as core components to the existing hallmark scaffold. These include the following:

- Unlocking phenotypic plasticity
- Nonmutational epigenetic reprogramming
- Polymorphic microbiomes
- Senescent cells

This review also saw the rebadging of the two enabling characteristics to encompass a broader description: "deregulating cellular metabolism" and "avoiding immune destruction."

Epigenetics and cancer

It has become increasingly clear that the complexity of carcinogenesis cannot be accounted for by genetic alterations alone, but it also involves epigenetic changes [124–129]. Epigenetics is the study of heritable changes that modify gene expression without altering the corresponding DNA sequence [130]. Epigenetic mechanisms comprising DNA methylation, histone modifications, and noncoding RNAs (ncRNAs) affect chromatin structure and regulate gene expression. These mechanisms are essential for normal embryonic development and the maintenance of tissue-specific gene expression in adults [131]. Epigenetic changes are reversible and are influenced by environmental factors. Epigenetic modifications often precede genetic changes and usually occur at an early stage in neoplastic development. Evidence from large-scale cancer genome projects revealed that nearly half of human cancers screened had mutations in chromatin proteins [132,133]. Moreover, malignant cells were shown to contain CpG islands hypermethylation, mostly in tumor suppressor genes, a reduction of total DNA methylation, and progressive histone modification changes [134]. Similarly, other studies have reported that the deregulation of ncRNAs, such as microRNAs (miRNAs) and long ncRNAs (lncRNAs), played a pivotal role in tumorigenesis [135–137]. Dynamic epigenetic changes during oncogenic transformation have also been attributed to tumor heterogeneity, unlimited self-renewal, and multilineage differentiation. These epigenetic changes confer a specific phenotype to cancer cells including uncontrolled proliferation, resistance, and increased invasiveness [138]. Based on the evidence that analogous epigenetic alterations contribute give rise to oncogenic properties that manifest themselves in all the hallmarks of cancer [139], "nonmutational epigenetic reprogramming" was added as a hallmark of cancer in 2022 [123]. Here we will focus on the most investigated epigenetic mechanisms in tumorigenesis, namely DNA methylation, histone modifications, and ncRNA (miRNA and lncRNA) deregulation in cancer and their contributions to the different hallmarks.

DNA methylation in cancer

DNA methylation is the most extensively studied epigenetic mechanism that predominantly occurs in CpG islands (CGIs) [131,140]. About 50%–60% of gene promoters lie within CpG islands, suggesting that these genes are potentially epigenetically regulated [141]. DNA methylation is essential for the maintenance of genome stability and regulation of gene expression [142]. It was the first epigenetic abnormality to be reported in cancer by Feinberg and Vogelstein in 1983 [143]. Cancer cells are often characterized by genome-wide hypomethylation and site-specific CpG island hypermethylation of gene promoter regions [140,144–146]. An example of this is the hypermethylation of the *BRAC1* gene observed in 67%, 55%, and 31% of medullary breast carcinomas, sporadic mucinous breast carcinomas, and sporadic ovarian carcinomas, respectively [147,148]. Most crucial tumor-suppressor gene silencing occurs through epigenetic mechanisms [149], including Rb and p14, p16/inhibitors of CDK4 [150] among others, which favor uncontrolled proliferation [151]. Additionally, studies have reported transcriptional inactivation caused by promoter hypermethylation of genes involved in other major cellular pathways including DNA repair, cell cycle, p53 and Ras signaling, apoptosis, and metastasis, among others [124,152–156]. All of these, in turn, increase genetic instability and confer higher growth advantage and malignant phenotype to cancer cells [124,157]. Similarly, negative feedback signals that inhibit cell proliferation or cell cycle progression may be impaired. For example, PTEN, which counteracts the oncogenic PI3K signaling, is often methylated in some cancers at its promoter region, resulting in the loss of its expression [80]. In cancer cells, hypomethylation is often associated with the gain of functions of oncogenes such as transcription factor c-Myc, a common feature of tumor progression and aggressiveness [158,159]. Moreover, aside from aberrantly activating oncogene expression, hypomethylation at specific promoters can also induce loss of imprinting (LOI). The most common hypomethylation-mediated LOI event reported in a wide range of cancers including breast, liver, lungs, and colon is that of the insulin-like growth factor 2 (IGF2) [160].

DNA methylation can inhibit gene expression via covalent addition of methyl groups from S-adenosylmethionine (SAM) to the C5 position of the cytosine residue [140]. The 5-methylcytosine (5mC) structure can either prevent access of transcriptional factors (TFs) to the binding sites of DNA or recruit methyl-binding domain proteins (MBDs) in association with histone modifications to reconfigure chromatin, thus leading to repressive gene expression. DNA methylation is orchestrated by three DNA methyltransferases (DNMT), namely DNMT1, DNMT3A, and DNMT3B. DNMT1 maintains the preexisting methylation patterns during DNA replication and the pattern during normal and cancer cell replication [161]. DNMT3a and DNMT 3b are de novo methyltransferases [162,163]. Notably, DNMT3A and DNMT3B have been shown to regulate embryonic development, cell differentiation, gene transcription, and cancer cell survival by promoting de novo DNA methylation of previously unmethylated sites [164]. Studies have shown that DNMT plays a paradoxical role in therapeutic response in different tumors. For example, ovarian cancers with elevated DMNT expression were found to be more sensitive to treatment [165], whereas inhibition of DNMT3B was required to sensitize pancreatic cells [166]. Loss of function of DNMT enzymes during cell differentiation and growth has also been correlated to oncogenic transformation, particularly in leukemia and lymphoma. In fact, mutations in DNMT3A resulted in the loss of methylation and promoted AML transformation [167]. DNA demethylation is a reverse action that recovers silenced genes affected by DNMTs. It is catalyzed by a family of 10–11 translocation methylcytosine dioxygenases (e.g., TET1, TET2, and TET3) [168–170]. Gene expression is controlled by the homeostasis between demethylation and methylation of the genome. Unlike genetic changes, the potential reversibility of methyltransferase activity makes it an attractive target for therapeutic interventions.

Histone modifications

Histone modifications are another important epigenetic mechanism of gene expressions. Aberrant reprogramming of histone modifications is often implicated in carcinogenesis, leading to modified chromatin accessibility and altered gene expression [171]. Histones are protein octamers that assist in packaging DNA into the highly organized chromatin structure [172]. The aminoterminal tails of histone proteins are frequently subjected to multivalent posttranslational modifications (PTM) including acetylation, phosphorylation, methylation, and ubiquitination, which alters the degree of local chromatin condensation and, as a result, gene expression and DNA accessibility [173]. Histones can also undergo nonconventional modifications such as citrullination/deamination, sumoylation, formylation, and propionylation [174]. Methylation and acetylation are the most studied histone modifications, but unlike DNA methylation, these histone modifications based on the modification and modified amino acid group can be either an active or repressive epigenetic marker. Histone methylation is frequently observed in lysine (K) and arginine (R) residues and is correlated to both active and inactive transcriptional states [175]. This process is enabled by many enzymes including histone methyltransferases (HMTs) and demethylase (HDM), lysine methyltransferases (KMTs) and demethylases (KDMs, also known as LSD), and protein arginine methyltransferases (PRMTs) [176,177].

Histone acetylation, on the other hand, is usually an epigenetic marker of transcriptional activation [178]. It involves a modification in the lysine amino acid that is catalyzed by histone acetyltransferases (HATs) and histone deacetylases (HDACs). High levels of FGFR2 in cancer cells have been linked to polymorphic sequences with constitutively acetylated histones [179]. HDACs have also been observed to be upregulated in a wide range of cancers including breast, prostate, colorectal, esophageal, cervical, and gastric cancers [112,113,180–182].

While the combination of these modifications is responsible for the maintenance of the chromatin structure and plays a pivotal role in development and cell differentiation, an imbalance of genome-wide histone methylation affects cell growth patterns that may lead to tumorigenesis. Examples of this include the fact that the enrichment of the trimethylation at H3 lysine 9 (H3K9me3) and lysine 27 (H3K27me3), which are repressive epigenetic markers, has been shown to drive tumorigenesis and chemoresistance [183]. Similarly, Enhancer of zeste homolog 2 (EZH2), a member of the polycomb proteins, is often found to be highly mutated in many types of tumors and mediates its effect on downstream target genes by H3K27me3. EZH2 has been shown to promote tumor growth, metastasis, and angiogenesis as it silences antiangiogenic genes [184]. EZH2 is, therefore, recognized as a marker of cancer initiation, progression, and metastasis and is a promising therapeutic target [185]. Dysregulation of HDAC is also often observed in cancers at different progression stages such as differentiation [186], cell cycle [187], angiogenesis [188], apoptosis [189], and autophagy [189]. Considering that HDAC inhibition downregulates the expression of apoptosis-related proteins, targeting HDACs presents an attractive therapeutic target for curtailing abnormal tumor growth and proliferation.

Nucleosome positioning

Nucleosomes function as barriers blocking access of activators and transcription factors to their sites on DNA while simultaneously inhibiting the elongation of the transcripts by engaged polymerases. In fact, the precise position of nucleosomes around the transcription start sites (TSSs) has been shown to play a pivotal role in regulating transcription. Interestingly, nucleosome displacement relative to the TSS by even as few as 30 bp has been shown to alter the activity of RNA polymerase II binding [190]. Moreover, the loss of a nucleosome positioned directly upstream of the TSS was associated with gene activation, whereas its occlusion of the TSS was associated with gene repression [190,191]. Thus, nucleosome positioning not only determines the accessibility of transcription factors to their target DNA sequence but also plays an important role in modulating the methylation landscape [192]. Changes in the nucleosomal occupancy of TSS mediated by promoter hypermethylation in the gene MLH1 were reported in colon cancer [193]. Several families of large macromolecular complexes known as chromatin remodeling complexes have been shown to be able to move, destabilize, eject, or restructure nucleosomes in an ATP hydrolysis-dependent manner. These chromatin remodeling complexes comprise four families, namely SWI/SNF, ISWI, CHD, and INO80, which share similar ATP domains but differ in the composition of their subunits [194]. Mutations in the complex subunits as well as epigenetic-mediated misregulation of these complexes, particularly that of the SWI/SNF, have been reported in various cancers [193,195–199].

Noncoding RNAs

Protein-coding genes represent less than 2% of the human genome, whereas the majority of the regions are transcribed into ncRNAs. Aside from its pivotal role in transcriptional regulation, ncRNAs also influence the translation as components in the protein synthesis machinery and regulate other ncRNA functions in a complex network [200,201]. It is these functions that are now being recognized in both physiological and pathological processes such as development, immune response, stress, and carcinogenesis [202,203]. ncRNA can be broadly categorized into small ncRNA (<200 nucleotides) and long ncRNA (>200 nucleotides).

Small ncRNAs include small nucleolar RNA (snoRNA), PIWI-interacting RNA (piRNA), small interfering RNA (siRNA), and microRNA (miRNA) [204]. Of these ncRNAs, miRNAs are the most widely studied owing to their importance in normal cell physiology, where they have been postulated to regulate the translation of more than 60% of protein-coding genes [205]. Aberrant expression of miRNAs has been observed to induce cell proliferation, invasion, and resistance to death in several cancers by activating oncogenes and silencing tumor suppressor genes [206]. miRNAs can directly target p53 or indirectly through its regulators [207], with over 20 miRNAs being reported to be able to directly target p53 and to reduce its expression. Many of these latter miRNAs are elevated in human tumors, resulting in decreased p53 levels [208]. OncomiR miR-21 is one of the first described miRNAs that is frequently detected as a cancer biomarker. Upregulation of miR-21 was positively correlated to tumor stage [209–211]. Both miR-21 and miR-155 have been shown to be dysregulated in gastric, colon, lung, breast, ovary, and hematologic malignancies [212–216]. Similarly, the miR-17 cluster encodes six miRNAs that function as oncomiRs due to their upregulated expression by c-myc, resulting in cell cycle progression and regulation of E2F [217]. Other examples of miRNA reported to be upregulated include miR-210 and miR-144-3p in renal cell carcinoma (RCC) and miR-141 and miR-375 in metastatic prostate cancer [218,219]. Several miRNAs like miR-17-92 [220] and miR-378 [221] have been shown to regulate VEGF expression and induce angiogenesis in solid tumors. MiR-378, in particular, has been shown to function as an oncogene not only by inducing angiogenesis but also by promoting growth and tumor survival [222]. MiRNA has been shown to play a role in immune checkpoint regulation. Several miRNAs have been shown to target PD-L1 including miR-138-5p, miR-34a-5p, miR-200, miR-513a-5p, and miR-570-3p [136,223], while miR-138 was shown to directly target CTLA-4 [224]. Another miRNA, miR-301a, has been shown to be involved in the regulation of multiple hallmarks such as cell differentiation, apoptosis, inflammatory response, and tumor progression [225–234]. Based on its upregulation in malignancies, Saran et al. [235] observed that this miRNA could be used as a marker to predict the aggressive potential of low-grade prostate cancer at the time of diagnosis. Promoter methylation or histone acetylation has also been shown to epigenetically regulate miRNA expression in cancer [236]. For example, CpG hypermethylation suppresses miR-9-1 in breast cancer and miR-124a in colorectal tumors [237,238]. Similarly, miR-124a which represses the oncogene CDK6 has been found to be frequently silenced in colon cancer, resulting in retinoblastoma (Rb) phosphorylation and inactivation of cyclin D kinase 6, a bona fide oncogenic factor [238]. As miRNA are not specific to a cancer type and can target several molecules simultaneously, understanding miRNA effects in specific pathways particularly as miRNA can target and identifying the most specific and sensitive ones remains challenging [216].

Long noncoding RNAs (LncRNAs) are the most abundant class of ncRNAs in the human genome [239]. Majority of LncRNAs are derived from intergenic regions or are clustered around protein-coding genes, and similar to protein-coding genes, their promoter regions are globally enriched with histone modifications, such as H3K27ac, H3K4me3, and H3K9ac [203,240]. LncRNA modulates gene expression across a complex intracellular network (comprising competing endogenous RNA networks, or ceRNET) through chromatin remodeling, targeting specific sequences at the transcriptional and translational level and participating in PTM [241,242]. Thus, lncRNAs, with their protein- and RNA-based regulation, add additional layer of complexity to the existing myriad of cytoplasmatic posttranscriptional and translational networks orchestrated by miRNAs and proteins [202]. Examples of lncRNA promoting carcinogenesis include overexpression of CCAT2 in colorectal cancer [243]; ANRIL in nonsmall cell lung cancer (NSCLC) and cervical cancer [244]; and SBF2-AS1, DANCR, LINC00239, LINC00319, LINC00265, and LEF1-AS1 in AML [245]. LncRNAs MALATI, treRNA, HOTAIR, HOXD-AS1,

HIF-1A-AS2, and MEG3, among others, have been shown to regulate angiogenesis, invasion, and metastasis [246–252]. HOTAIR has also been shown to be able to sponge miR-148a to reactivate Snail2 to promote EMT in esophageal carcinoma cells [253]. LncRNA has also been related to drug resistance, with oncogenic ncRNAs MACC1-AS1, PVT1, and HAGLR being reported to promote 5-FU resistance in GC cells [254], while lncRNA HOTTIP was shown to contribute to chemoresistance in NSCLC by upregulating Bcl-2 levels [255].

CircRNAs have also been reported to play important roles in cancer growth, metastasis, and resistance to therapy [256]. These ncRNAs are similar in length to lncRNA but lack the $5'$ and $3'$ modifications and are covalently linked, forming a closed circular structure [257]. Cytoplasmic circRNAs act as miRNA sponges that regulate downstream targets or bind proteins, and they can also impart opposing signals based on the miRNA they bind to [258]. In NSCLC, circSNAP47 expression was correlated with metastasis and associated with decreased overall survival, an effect that was mediated through miR-1287/GAGE axis [259]. Upregulation of ciRS-7 expression in colorectal and gastric cancers blocked the suppressive function of miR-7, a crucial tumor suppressor in several cancer types [258,260]. Paradoxically, while circZFR inhibited gastric cancer proliferation through miR-130a/107 targeted PTEN upregulation [261], the same circRNA promoted hepatocellular carcinoma proliferation by modulating miR-1261/4302/3619 [262]. CircRNA also interacts with RNA-binding proteins and regulates RNA transcription, splicing, stability, localization, and translation [263].

RNA modifications as important posttranscriptional regulators of gene expression patterns can be either reversible or nonreversible. The former includes different types of RNA methylation (like cytosine and adenosine methylation), while the latter includes editing and splicing as well as formation of circular RNAs [241]. While RNA modifications are not considered cancer drivers on their own, their ability to modulate several RNA metabolism processes results in the aberrant expression of important genes controlling survival proliferation, self-renewal, differentiation, migration, stress adaptation, and resistance to therapy, all of which are hallmarks of cancer [131].

Recognition of the importance of epigenetics in cancer has propelled this field to the forefront of cancer research over the past decade. Advancements in technology such as third-generation sequencing (enabling simultaneous detection of multiple epigenetic or epitranscriptomic modifications in a single molecule) [264,265] and temporal/spatial DNA and RNA sequencing, have opened new avenues of our understanding of cancer as a whole, upending and adding to long-held perceptions in tumorigenesis and treatment. The dynamic and reversible nature of epigenetic regulation makes it an attractive target for cancer therapy. Nevertheless, while epigenetic therapies have achieved remarkable clinical responses in hematologic malignancies, their success in solid tumors remains modest at best. Another area of future research that remains murky is understanding epigenetic heterogeneity in cancer, a well-recognized feature of tumor masses that continues to challenge the success of effective anticancer therapies.

Conclusion

Over the past decade, a great change has occurred in how we think about cancer. Where once we viewed cancer as an unfathomed black box, now we have pried open the box and cast in the first dim light. Where once we thought of cancer as a bewildering variety of diseases with causes too numerous to count, now we are on the track of a single unifying explanation for how most or all cancers might arise.

JM Bishop, 2003 [266]

Carcinogenesis is a complex, multifaceted process driven by both genetic and epigenetic alterations that disrupt normal cellular homeostasis and promote neoplastic transformation. Technological innovations such as sequencing at single-cell and spatial resolutions, coupled with the combined use of experimental and computationally derived "big data," have allowed us to make great strides in our quest to understand the intricate network of mechanisms underlaying carcinogenesis. Knowledge that will enable us to design and develop better strategies to prevent, detect, and treat cancer. More importantly, we envision significant advances in the coming decades in furthering our understanding of newer "hallmarks" of cancer epigenetic programing, metabolism, immune surveillance, and microenvironment that could hold the key to resolving cancer heterogeneity.

References

[1] R.A. Weinberg, One Renegade Cell, Basic Books, New York, 1998.

[2] L. Pecorino, Molecular Biology of Cancer: Mechanisms, Targets, and Therapeutics, Oxford University Press, 2021.

[3] H. Nagai, Y.H. Kim, Cancer prevention from the perspective of global cancer burden patterns, J. Thorac. Dis. 9 (3) (2017) 448–451.

[4] J.E. Visvader, Cells of origin in cancer, Nature 469 (7330) (2011) 314–322.

[5] S.I. Hajdu, A note from history: landmarks in history of cancer, part 1, Cancers 117 (5) (2011) 1097–1102.

[6] G.B. Faguet, A brief history of cancer: age-old milestones underlying our current knowledge database, Int. J. Cancer 136 (9) (2015) 2022–2036.

[7] A. Sudhakar, History of cancer, ancient and modern treatment methods, J. Cancer Sci. Ther. 1 (2) (2009) 1–4.

[8] W.R. Bett, Historical aspects of cancer, in: R.R. Raven (Ed.), Cancer, vol. 1, Butterworth, London, 1957, pp. 1–5.

[9] J. Petit, Oeuvres Completes, Limoges, 1837, pg 438 (cited in Wolf J. The Science of Cancerous Diseases from Earliest Times to the Present), Science History Publications/USA, Sagamore Beach, MA, 1989.

[10] P. Broca, Mémoire sur l'anatomie pathologique du cancer, Bull. Soc. Anatom. Paris 5 (1850) 45.

[11] B. Ramazzini, De morbis artificum diatriba, Apud Guilielmum van de Water, 1703.

[12] G. Franco, F. Franco, Bernardino Ramazzini: the father of occupational medicine, Am. J. Public Health 91 (9) (2001) 1382.

[13] H. Harris, The Birth of the Cell, Yale University Press, 2000.

[14] L. Bard, Anatomie et classification des tumeurs, Masson, 1885.

[15] C.W. Long, An account of the first use of sulphuric ether by inhalation as an anaesthetic in surgical operations, Surv. Anesthesiol. 35 (6) (1991) 375.

[16] J. Lister, On the antiseptic principle in the practice of surgery, Br. Med. J. 2 (351) (1867) 246.

[17] I. Asimov, Asimov's Biographical Encyclopedia of Science and Technology: The Living Stories of More than 1000 Great Scientists from the Age of Greece to the Space Age, 1964.

[18] N. Pasachoff, Marie Curie: And the Science of Radioactivity, Oxford University Press, 1996.

[19] J. Beard, Embryological aspects and etiology of carcinoma, Lancet 159 (4112) (1902) 1758–1761.

[20] R. Paduch, Theories of cancer origin, Eur. J. Cancer Prev. 24 (1) (2015) 57–67.

[21] C. Sonnenschein, A.M. Soto, Theories of carcinogenesis: an emerging perspective, Semin. Cancer Biol. 18 (5) (2008) 372–377.

[22] C. Nordling, A new theory on the cancer-inducing mechanism, Br. J. Cancer 7 (1) (1953) 68.

[23] T. Boveri, M. Boveri, The Origin of Malignant Tumors, 1929.

[24] A.G. Knudson Jr., Mutation and cancer: statistical study of retinoblastoma, Proc. Natl. Acad. Sci. U. S. A. 68 (4) (1971) 820–823.

[25] P. Armitage, R. Doll, The age distribution of cancer and a multistage theory of carcinogenesis Br, J. Cancer 8 (1954) 1–12.

[26] A.R. Anderson, et al., Tumor morphology and phenotypic evolution driven by selective pressure from the microenvironment, Cell 127 (5) (2006) 905–915.

[27] A.M. Soto, C. Sonnenschein, The tissue organization field theory of cancer: a testable replacement for the somatic mutation theory, BioEssays 33 (5) (2011) 332–340.

[28] D. Thomas, A. Moore, Counterpoints in cancer: the somatic mutation theory under attack, BioEssays 33 (5) (2011) 313–314.

[29] C. Tomasetti, B. Vogelstein, Cancer etiology. Variation in cancer risk among tissues can be explained by the number of stem cell divisions, Science 347 (6217) (2015) 78–81.

[30] L. Zhu, et al., Multi-organ mapping of cancer risk, Cell 166 (5) (2016) 1132–1146 e7.

[31] C. Tomasetti, L. Li, B. Vogelstein, Stem cell divisions, somatic mutations, cancer etiology, and cancer prevention, Science 355 (6331) (2017) 1330–1334.

[32] G. Davey Smith, C.L. Relton, P. Brennan, Chance, choice and cause in cancer aetiology: individual and population perspectives, Int. J. Epidemiol. 45 (3) (2016) 605–613.

[33] A. Jassim, et al., Cancers make their own luck: theories of cancer origins, Nat. Rev. Cancer 23 (10) (2023) 710–724.

[34] L. Riva, et al., The mutational signature profile of known and suspected human carcinogens in mice, Nat. Genet. 52 (11) (2020) 1189–1197.

[35] F. Abascal, et al., Somatic mutation landscapes at single-molecule resolution, Nature 593 (7859) (2021) 405–410.

[36] E. Viguera, D. Canceill, S.D. Ehrlich, Replication slippage involves DNA polymerase pausing and dissociation, EMBO J. 20 (10) (2001) 2587–2595.

[37] X. Gao, et al., Metabolic interactions with cancer epigenetics, Mol. Asp. Med. 54 (2017) 50–57.

[38] A. Magnussen, M.A. Parsi, Aflatoxins, hepatocellular carcinoma and public health, World J. Gastroenterol. 19 (10) (2013) 1508–1512.

[39] S.J. Van Rensburg, et al., Hepatocellular carcinoma and dietary aflatoxin in Mozambique and Transkei, Br. J. Cancer 51 (5) (1985) 713–726.

[40] I.C. Hsu, et al., Mutational hotspot in the p53 gene in human hepatocellular carcinomas, Nature 350 (6317) (1991) 427–428.

[41] M.F. Denissenko, et al., Preferential formation of benzo[a]pyrene adducts at lung cancer mutational hotspots in P53, Science 274 (5286) (1996) 430–432.

[42] S. Rodenhuis, et al., Mutational activation of the K-ras oncogene. A possible pathogenetic factor in adenocarcinoma of the lung, N. Engl. J. Med. 317 (15) (1987) 929–935.

[43] L. Ding, et al., Somatic mutations affect key pathways in lung adenocarcinoma, Nature 455 (7216) (2008) 1069–1075.

[44] Y. Weng, et al., Determination of the role of target tissue metabolism in lung carcinogenesis using conditional cytochrome P450 reductase-null mice, Cancer Res. 67 (16) (2007) 7825–7832.

[45] J.F. Ward, DNA damage produced by ionizing radiation in mammalian cells: identities, mechanisms of formation, and reparability, Prog. Nucleic Acid Res. Mol. Biol. 35 (1988) 95–125.

[46] E.A. Mesri, M.A. Feitelson, K. Munger, Human viral oncogenesis: a cancer hallmarks analysis, Cell Host Microbe 15 (3) (2014) 266–282.

[47] H. Feng, et al., Clonal integration of a polyomavirus in human Merkel cell carcinoma, Science 319 (5866) (2008) 1096–1100.

[48] W. Liu, M. MacDonald, J. You, Merkel cell polyomavirus infection and Merkel cell carcinoma, Curr. Opin. Virol. 20 (2016) 20–27.

[49] L. Giffin, B. Damania, KSHV: pathways to tumorigenesis and persistent infection, Adv. Virus Res. 88 (2014) 111–159.

[50] A. Arzumanyan, H.M. Reis, M.A. Feitelson, Pathogenic mechanisms in HBV- and HCV-associated hepatocellular carcinoma, Nat. Rev. Cancer 13 (2) (2013) 123–135.

[51] H. Higashi, et al., SHP-2 tyrosine phosphatase as an intracellular target of *Helicobacter pylori* CagA protein, Science 295 (5555) (2002) 683–686.

[52] E.M. El-Omar, et al., Interleukin-1 polymorphisms associated with increased risk of gastric cancer, Nature 404 (6776) (2000) 398–402.

[53] A. Saha, et al., Epigenetic silencing of tumor suppressor genes during in vitro Epstein-Barr virus infection, Proc. Natl. Acad. Sci. U. S. A. 112 (37) (2015) E5199–E5207.

[54] D. Martinez-Zapien, et al., Structure of the E6/E6AP/p53 complex required for HPV-mediated degradation of p53, Nature 529 (7587) (2016) 541–545.

[55] S. Bhattacharjee, S. Nandi, Choices have consequences: the nexus between DNA repair pathways and genomic instability in cancer, Clin. Transl. Med. 5 (1) (2016) 45.

[56] B.J. Glassner, et al., DNA repair methyltransferase (MGMT) knockout mice are sensitive to the lethal effects of chemotherapeutic alkylating agents, Mutagenesis 14 (3) (1999) 339–347.

[57] M. Esteller, et al., Inactivation of the DNA repair gene O6-methylguanine-DNA methyltransferase by promoter hypermethylation is a common event in primary human neoplasia, Cancer Res. 59 (4) (1999) 793–797.

[58] M. Esteller, et al., Inactivation of the DNA-repair gene MGMT and the clinical response of gliomas to alkylating agents, N Engl J Med 343 (19) (2000) 1350–1354.

[59] R.W. Sobol, et al., Requirement of mammalian DNA polymerase-beta in base-excision repair, Nature 379 (6561) (1996) 183–186.

[60] Y. Gao, et al., DNA ligase III is critical for mtDNA integrity but not Xrcc1-mediated nuclear DNA repair, Nature 471 (7337) (2011) 240–244.

[61] R.S. Tebbs, L.H. Thompson, J.E. Cleaver, Rescue of Xrcc1 knockout mouse embryo lethality by transgene-complementation, DNA Repair (Amst.) 2 (12) (2003) 1405–1417.

[62] A.A. Larrea, S.A. Lujan, T.A. Kunkel, SnapShot: DNA mismatch repair, Cell 141 (4) (2010). 730.e1.

[63] J.V. Martin-Lopez, R. Fishel, The mechanism of mismatch repair and the functional analysis of mismatch repair defects in lynch syndrome, Fam. Cancer 12 (2) (2013) 159–168.

[64] N. Le May, J.M. Egly, F. Coin, True lies: the double life of the nucleotide excision repair factors in transcription and DNA repair, J. Nucleic Acids 2010 (2010) 616342.

[65] F.W. Alt, et al., Mechanisms of programmed DNA lesions and genomic instability in the immune system, Cell 152 (3) (2013) 417–429.

[66] D.S. Lim, et al., Analysis of ku80-mutant mice and cells with deficient levels of p53, Mol. Cell. Biol. 20 (11) (2000) 3772–3780.

[67] T.I. Ben-Omran, et al., A patient with mutations in DNA ligase IV: clinical features and overlap with Nijmegen breakage syndrome, Am. J. Med. Genet. A 137A (3) (2005) 283–287.

[68] C. Allen, et al., More forks on the road to replication stress recovery, J. Mol. Cell Biol. 3 (1) (2011) 4–12.

[69] J. Budman, G. Chu, Processing of DNA for nonhomologous end-joining by cell-free extract, EMBO J. 24 (4) (2005) 849–860.

[70] A.R. Venkitaraman, Functions of BRCA1 and BRCA2 in the biological response to DNA damage, J. Cell Sci. 114 (Pt 20) (2001) 3591–3598.

[71] A. Ashworth, A synthetic lethal therapeutic approach: poly(ADP) ribose polymerase inhibitors for the treatment of cancers deficient in DNA double-strand break repair, J. Clin. Oncol. 26 (22) (2008) 3785–3790.

[72] C.J. Sherr, Principles of tumor suppression, Cell 116 (2) (2004) 235–246.

[73] B. Vogelstein, et al., Cancer genome landscapes, Science 339 (6127) (2013) 1546–1558.

[74] F. Sanchez-Vega, et al., Oncogenic signaling pathways in the cancer genome atlas, Cell 173 (2) (2018) 321–337 e10.

[75] D. Hanahan, R.A. Weinberg, Hallmarks of cancer: the next generation, Cell 144 (5) (2011) 646–674.

[76] H. Yan, et al., IDH1 and IDH2 mutations in gliomas, N. Engl. J. Med. 360 (8) (2009) 765–773.

[77] W.A. Flavahan, E. Gaskell, B.E. Bernstein, Epigenetic plasticity and the hallmarks of cancer, Science 357 (6348) (2017).

[78] M.A. Davies, Y. Samuels, Analysis of the genome to personalize therapy for melanoma, Oncogene 29 (41) (2010) 5545–5555.

[79] B.H. Jiang, L.Z. Liu, PI3K/PTEN signaling in angiogenesis and tumorigenesis, Adv. Cancer Res. 102 (2009) 19–65.

[80] T.L. Yuan, L.C. Cantley, PI3K pathway alterations in cancer: variations on a theme, Oncogene 27 (41) (2008) 5497–5510.

[81] A.J. Levine, M. Oren, The first 30 years of p53: growing ever more complex, Nat. Rev. Cancer 9 (10) (2009) 749–758.

[82] S.G. Jin, et al., The DNA methylation landscape of human melanoma, Genomics 106 (6) (2015) 322–330.

[83] N.B. Kiss, et al., Quantitative global and gene-specific promoter methylation in relation to biological properties of neuroblastomas, BMC Med. Genet. 13 (2012) 83.

[84] S.W. Lowe, E. Cepero, G. Evan, Intrinsic tumour suppression, Nature 432 (7015) (2004) 307–315.

[85] N. Darwiche, Epigenetic mechanisms and the hallmarks of cancer: an intimate affair, Am. J. Cancer Res. 10 (7) (2020) 1954–1978.

[86] A. Ashkenazi, Targeting death and decoy receptors of the tumour-necrosis factor super-family, Nat. Rev. Cancer 2 (6) (2002) 420–430.

[87] E.H. Cheng, et al., BCL-2, BCL-X(L) sequester BH3 domain-only molecules preventing BAX- and BAK-mediated mitochondrial apoptosis, Mol. Cell 8 (3) (2001) 705–711.

[88] E. Hervouet, F.M. Vallette, P.F. Cartron, Impact of the DNA methyltransferases expression on the methylation status of apoptosis-associated genes in glioblastoma multiforme, Cell Death Dis. 1 (1) (2010) e8.

[89] B. Levine, G. Kroemer, Autophagy in the pathogenesis of disease, Cell 132 (1) (2008) 27–42.

[90] N. Mizushima, Autophagy: process and function, Genes Dev. 21 (22) (2007) 2861–2873.

[91] A.M. Cuervo, Autophagy: many paths to the same end, Mol. Cell. Biochem. 263 (1–2) (2004) 55–72.

[92] A.M. Cuervo, Autophagy: in sickness and in health, Trends Cell Biol. 14 (2) (2004) 70–77.

[93] A. Apel, et al., Autophagy—a double-edged sword in oncology, Int. J. Cancer 125 (5) (2009) 991–995.

[94] R.K. Amaravadi, C.B. Thompson, The roles of therapy-induced autophagy and necrosis in cancer treatment, Clin. Cancer Res. 13 (24) (2007) 7271–7279.

[95] R. Mathew, V. Karantza-Wadsworth, E. White, Role of autophagy in cancer, Nat. Rev. Cancer 7 (12) (2007) 961–967.

[96] Z. Lu, et al., The tumor suppressor gene ARHI regulates autophagy and tumor dormancy in human ovarian cancer cells, J Clin Invest 118 (12) (2008) 3917–3929.

[97] E. White, R.S. DiPaola, The double-edged sword of autophagy modulation in cancer, Clin. Cancer Res. 15 (17) (2009) 5308–5316.

[98] D. Hanahan, J. Folkman, Patterns and emerging mechanisms of the angiogenic switch during tumorigenesis, Cell 86 (3) (1996) 353–364.

[99] J. Folkman, Tumor angiogenesis: therapeutic implications, N. Engl. J. Med. 285 (21) (1971) 1182–1186.

[100] K. Kondo, W.G. Kaelin Jr., The von Hippel-Lindau tumor suppressor gene, Exp. Cell Res. 264 (1) (2001) 117–125.

[101] C.L. Cowey, W.K. Rathmell, VHL gene mutations in renal cell carcinoma: role as a biomarker of disease outcome and drug efficacy, Curr. Oncol. Rep. 11 (2) (2009) 94–101.

[102] B.Y. Reddy, et al., The microenvironmental effect in the progression, metastasis, and dormancy of breast cancer: a model system within bone marrow, Int. J. Breast Cancer 2012 (2012) 721659.

[103] A. Jeanes, C.J. Gottardi, A.S. Yap, Cadherins and cancer: how does cadherin dysfunction promote tumor progression? Oncogene 27 (55) (2008) 6920–6929.

[104] F. van Roy, Beyond E-cadherin: roles of other cadherin superfamily members in cancer, Nat. Rev. Cancer 14 (2) (2014) 121–134.

[105] S. Paget, The distribution of secondary growths in cancer of the breast, 1889, Cancer Metastasis Rev. 8 (2) (1989) 98–101.

[106] A.R. Venkitaraman, Chromosome stability, DNA recombination and the BRCA2 tumour suppressor, Curr. Opin. Cell Biol. 13 (3) (2001) 338–343.

[107] B.A. Teicher, S.P. Fricker, CXCL12 (SDF-1)/CXCR4 pathway in cancer, Clin. Cancer Res. 16 (11) (2010) 2927–2931.

[108] B. De Craene, G. Berx, Regulatory networks defining EMT during cancer initiation and progression, Nat. Rev. Cancer 13 (2) (2013) 97–110.

[109] L. Sun, J. Fang, Epigenetic regulation of epithelial-mesenchymal transition, Cell. Mol. Life Sci. 73 (23) (2016) 4493–4515.

[110] P. Kapoor-Vazirani, et al., Role of hMOF-dependent histone H4 lysine 16 acetylation in the maintenance of TMS1/ASC gene activity, Cancer Res. 68 (16) (2008) 6810–6821.

[111] Y.N. Liu, et al., Regulatory mechanisms controlling human E-cadherin gene expression, Oncogene 24 (56) (2005) 8277–8290.

[112] A. Aghdassi, et al., Recruitment of histone deacetylases HDAC1 and HDAC2 by the transcriptional repressor ZEB1 downregulates E-cadherin expression in pancreatic cancer, Gut 61 (3) (2012) 439–448.

[113] V. Byles, et al., SIRT1 induces EMT by cooperating with EMT transcription factors and enhances prostate cancer cell migration and metastasis, Oncogene 31 (43) (2012) 4619–4629.

[114] M.W. Chen, et al., H3K9 histone methyltransferase G9a promotes lung cancer invasion and metastasis by silencing the cell adhesion molecule Ep-CAM, Cancer Res. 70 (20) (2010) 7830–7840.

[115] F.R. Balkwill, M. Capasso, T. Hagemann, The tumor microenvironment at a glance, J. Cell Sci. 125 (Pt 23) (2012) 5591–5596.

[116] P.I. Ribeiro Franco, et al., Tumor microenvironment components: allies of cancer progression, Pathol. Res. Pract. 216 (1) (2020) 152729.

[117] R. Naser, et al., Role of the tumor microenvironment in cancer hallmarks and targeted therapy (review), Int. J. Oncol. 62 (2) (2023).

[118] R. Baghban, et al., Tumor microenvironment complexity and therapeutic implications at a glance, Cell Commun. Signal. 18 (1) (2020) 59.

[119] Y. Xiao, D. Yu, Tumor microenvironment as a therapeutic target in cancer, Pharmacol. Ther. 221 (2021) 107753.

[120] K.E. de Visser, J.A. Joyce, The evolving tumor microenvironment: from cancer initiation to metastatic outgrowth, Cancer Cell 41 (3) (2023) 374–403.

[121] V. Poltavets, et al., The role of the extracellular matrix and its molecular and cellular regulators in cancer cell plasticity, Front. Oncol. 8 (2018) 431.

[122] D. Hanahan, R.A. Weinberg, The hallmarks of cancer, Cell 100 (1) (2000) 57–70.

[123] D. Hanahan, Hallmarks of cancer: new dimensions, Cancer Discov. 12 (1) (2022) 31–46.

[124] R. Kanwal, S. Gupta, Epigenetic modifications in cancer, Clin. Genet. 81 (4) (2012) 303–311.

[125] Y. Lu, et al., Epigenetic regulation in human cancer: the potential role of epi-drug in cancer therapy, Mol Cancer 19 (1) (2020) 79.

[126] X. Ding, et al., Genomic and epigenomic features of primary and recurrent hepatocellular carcinomas, Gastroenterology 157 (6) (2019) 1630–1645 e6.

[127] G.G. Malouf, et al., Architecture of epigenetic reprogramming following Twist1-mediated epithelial-mesenchymal transition, Genome Biol. 14 (12) (2013) R144.

[128] R. Taby, J.P. Issa, Cancer epigenetics, CA Cancer J. Clin. 60 (6) (2010) 376–392.

[129] C.D. Allis, T. Jenuwein, The molecular hallmarks of epigenetic control, Nat. Rev. Genet. 17 (8) (2016) 487–500.

[130] A.D. Goldberg, C.D. Allis, E. Bernstein, Epigenetics: a landscape takes shape, Cell 128 (4) (2007) 635–638.

[131] P. Costa, et al., Epigenetic reprogramming in cancer: from diagnosis to treatment, Front. Cell Dev. Biol. 11 (2023) 1116805.

[132] J.S. You, P.A. Jones, Cancer genetics and epigenetics: two sides of the same coin? Cancer Cell 22 (1) (2012) 9–20.

[133] H. Shen, P.W. Laird, Interplay between the cancer genome and epigenome, Cell 153 (1) (2013) 38–55.

[134] M. Esteller, Epigenetics in cancer, N. Engl. J. Med. 358 (11) (2008) 1148–1159.

[135] H.J. Ferreira, M. Esteller, Non-coding RNAs, epigenetics, and cancer: tying it all together, Cancer Metastasis Rev. 37 (1) (2018) 55–73.

[136] K. Van Roosbroeck, G.A. Calin, Cancer hallmarks and MicroRNAs: the therapeutic connection, Adv. Cancer Res. 135 (2017) 119–149.

[137] T. Gutschner, S. Diederichs, The hallmarks of cancer: a long non-coding RNA point of view, RNA Biol. 9 (6) (2012) 703–719.

[138] S. Ilango, et al., Epigenetic alterations in cancer, Front. Biosci. (Landmark Ed.) 25 (6) (2020) 1058–1109.

[139] W. Timp, A.P. Feinberg, Cancer as a dysregulated epigenome allowing cellular growth advantage at the expense of the host, Nat. Rev. Cancer 13 (7) (2013) 497–510.

[140] X. Yu, et al., Cancer epigenetics: from laboratory studies and clinical trials to precision medicine, Cell Death Discov. 10 (1) (2024) 28.

[141] E.M. Kennedy, et al., An integrated -omics analysis of the epigenetic landscape of gene expression in human blood cells, BMC Genomics 19 (1) (2018) 476.

[142] S.B. Baylin, DNA methylation and gene silencing in cancer, Nat. Clin. Pract. Oncol. 2 (Suppl 1) (2005) S4–11.

[143] A.P. Feinberg, B. Vogelstein, Hypomethylation distinguishes genes of some human cancers from their normal counterparts, Nature 301 (5895) (1983) 89–92.

[144] S.C. Borinstein, et al., Aberrant DNA methylation occurs in colon neoplasms arising in the azoxymethane colon cancer model, Mol. Carcinog. 49 (1) (2010) 94–103.

[145] M. Ehrlich, DNA methylation in cancer: too much, but also too little, Oncogene 21 (35) (2002) 5400–5413.

[146] C. De Smet, A. Loriot, T. Boon, Promoter-dependent mechanism leading to selective hypomethylation within the 5′ region of gene MAGE-A1 in tumor cells, Mol. Cell. Biol. 24 (11) (2004) 4781–4790.

[147] A. Dobrovic, D. Simpfendorfer, Methylation of the BRCA1 gene in sporadic breast cancer, Cancer Res. 57 (16) (1997) 3347–3350.

[148] M. Esteller, et al., Promoter hypermethylation and BRCA1 inactivation in sporadic breast and ovarian tumors, J Natl Cancer Inst 92 (7) (2000) 564–569.

[149] B. Faam, et al., RAP1GAP functions as a tumor suppressor gene and is regulated by DNA methylation in differentiated thyroid cancer, Cytogenet. Genome Res. 161 (5) (2021) 227–235.

[150] M. Chantre-Justino, et al., Genetic and methylation status of CDKN2A (p14(ARF)/p16 (INK4A)) and TP53 genes in recurrent respiratory papillomatosis, Hum. Pathol. 119 (2022) 94–104.

[151] B. Han, et al., DNA methylation biomarkers for nasopharyngeal carcinoma, PLoS One 15 (4) (2020) e0230524.

[152] B. Jin, K.D. Robertson, DNA methyltransferases, DNA damage repair, and cancer, Adv. Exp. Med. Biol. 754 (2013) 3–29.

[153] A. Nishiyama, M. Nakanishi, Navigating the DNA methylation landscape of cancer, Trends Genet. 37 (11) (2021) 1012–1027.

[154] Y. Kotake, et al., Long non-coding RNA ANRIL is required for the PRC2 recruitment to and silencing of p15(INK4B) tumor suppressor gene, Oncogene 30 (16) (2011) 1956–1962.

[155] I. Koturbash, F.A. Beland, I.P. Pogribny, Role of epigenetic events in chemical carcinogenesis—a justification for incorporating epigenetic evaluations in cancer risk assessment, Toxicol. Mech. Methods 21 (4) (2011) 289–297.

[156] Y. Kaneko, et al., Hypomethylation of c-myc and epidermal growth factor receptor genes in human hepatocellular carcinoma and fetal liver, Jpn. J. Cancer Res. 76 (12) (1985) 1136–1140.

[157] N. Nishida, et al., Unique association between global DNA hypomethylation and chromosomal alterations in human hepatocellular carcinoma, PLoS One 8 (9) (2013) e72312.

[158] H.H. Cheung, et al., DNA methylation of cancer genome, Birth Defects Res. C Embryo Today 87 (4) (2009) 335–350.

[159] C.R. de Souza, et al., MYC deregulation in gastric cancer and its clinicopathological implications, PLoS One 8 (5) (2013) e64420.

[160] R. Kanwal, K. Gupta, S. Gupta, Cancer epigenetics: an introduction, Methods Mol. Biol. 1238 (2015) 3–25.

[161] T. Chen, et al., Complete inactivation of DNMT1 leads to mitotic catastrophe in human cancer cells, Nat. Genet. 39 (3) (2007) 391–396.

[162] L.D. Moore, T. Le, G. Fan, DNA methylation and its basic function, Neuropsychopharmacology 38 (1) (2013) 23–38.

[163] F. Lyko, The DNA methyltransferase family: a versatile toolkit for epigenetic regulation, Nat. Rev. Genet. 19 (2) (2018) 81–92.

[164] M. Okano, et al., DNA methyltransferases Dnmt3a and Dnmt3b are essential for de novo methylation and mammalian development, Cell 99 (3) (1999) 247–257.

[165] M.L. Stewart, et al., KRAS genomic status predicts the sensitivity of ovarian cancer cells to decitabine, Cancer Res. 75 (14) (2015) 2897–2906.

[166] L. Simo-Riudalbas, S.A. Melo, M. Esteller, DNMT3B gene amplification predicts resistance to DNA demethylating drugs, Genes, Chromosomes Cancer 50 (7) (2011) 527–534.

[167] D.H. Spencer, et al., CpG Island hypermethylation mediated by DNMT3A is a consequence of AML progression, Cell 168 (5) (2017) 801–816 e13.

[168] L. Scourzic, E. Mouly, O.A. Bernard, TET proteins and the control of cytosine demethylation in cancer, Genome Med. 7 (1) (2015) 9.

[169] H. Zhao, T. Chen, Tet family of 5-methylcytosine dioxygenases in mammalian development, J. Hum. Genet. 58 (7) (2013) 421–427.

[170] A. Onodera, et al., Roles of TET and TDG in DNA demethylation in proliferating and non-proliferating immune cells, Genome Biol. 22 (1) (2021) 186.

[171] Z. Zhao, A. Shilatifard, Epigenetic modifications of histones in cancer, Genome Biol. 20 (1) (2019) 245.

[172] M. Lawrence, S. Daujat, R. Schneider, Lateral thinking: how histone modifications regulate gene expression, Trends Genet. 32 (1) (2016) 42–56.

[173] C. Demetriadou, C. Koufaris, A. Kirmizis, Histone N-alpha terminal modifications: genome regulation at the tip of the tail, Epigenet. Chromatin 13 (1) (2020) 29.

[174] R.Y. Tweedie-Cullen, et al., Identification of combinatorial patterns of post-translational modifications on individual histones in the mouse brain, PLoS One 7 (5) (2012) e36980.

[175] E.L. Greer, Y. Shi, Histone methylation: a dynamic mark in health, disease and inheritance, Nat. Rev. Genet. 13 (5) (2012) 343–357.

[176] D. Husmann, O. Gozani, Histone lysine methyltransferases in biology and disease, Nat. Struct. Mol. Biol. 26 (10) (2019) 880–889.

[177] X. Wu, et al., A novel cell-free DNA methylation-based model improves the early detection of colorectal cancer, Mol. Oncol. 15 (10) (2021) 2702–2714.

[178] A.J. Bannister, T. Kouzarides, Regulation of chromatin by histone modifications, Cell Res. 21 (3) (2011) 381–395.

[179] X. Zhu, S.L. Asa, S. Ezzat, Histone-acetylated control of fibroblast growth factor receptor 2 intron 2 polymorphisms and isoform splicing in breast cancer, Mol. Endocrinol. 23 (9) (2009) 1397–1405.

[180] M. Nakagawa, et al., Expression profile of class I histone deacetylases in human cancer tissues, Oncol. Rep. 18 (4) (2007) 769–774.

[181] I. Oehme, et al., Histone deacetylase 8 in neuroblastoma tumorigenesis, Clin. Cancer Res. 15 (1) (2009) 91–99.

[182] H. Yang, et al., Overexpression of histone deacetylases in cancer cells is controlled by interplay of transcription factors and epigenetic modulators, FASEB J. 28 (10) (2014) 4265–4279.

[183] J. Torrano, et al., Emerging roles of H3K9me3, SETDB1 and SETDB2 in therapy-induced cellular reprogramming, Clin. Epigenet. 11 (1) (2019) 43.

[184] G.H. Richter, et al., EZH2 is a mediator of EWS/FLI1 driven tumor growth and metastasis blocking endothelial and neuro-ectodermal differentiation, Proc. Natl. Acad. Sci. U. S. A. 106 (13) (2009) 5324–5329.

[185] A. Chase, N.C. Cross, Aberrations of EZH2 in cancer, Clin. Cancer Res. 17 (9) (2011) 2613–2618.

[186] P.A. Marks, V.M. Richon, R.A. Rifkind, Histone deacetylase inhibitors: inducers of differentiation or apoptosis of transformed cells, J. Natl. Cancer Inst. 92 (15) (2000) 1210–1216.

[187] C.C. Wu, et al., HDAC1 dysregulation induces aberrant cell cycle and DNA damage in progress of TDP-43 proteinopathies, EMBO Mol. Med. 12 (6) (2020) e10622.

[188] M.S. Kim, et al., Histone deacetylases induce angiogenesis by negative regulation of tumor suppressor genes, Nat. Med. 7 (4) (2001) 437–443.

[189] C.L. Hanigan, et al., An inactivating mutation in HDAC2 leads to dysregulation of apoptosis mediated by APAF1, Gastroenterology 135 (5) (2008) 1654–1664 e2.

[190] D.E. Schones, et al., Dynamic regulation of nucleosome positioning in the human genome, Cell 132 (5) (2008) 887–898.

[191] B.R. Cairns, The logic of chromatin architecture and remodelling at promoters, Nature 461 (7261) (2009) 193–198.

[192] R.K. Chodavarapu, et al., Relationship between nucleosome positioning and DNA methylation, Nature 466 (7304) (2010) 388–392.

[193] J.C. Lin, et al., Role of nucleosomal occupancy in the epigenetic silencing of the MLH1 CpG island, Cancer Cell 12 (5) (2007) 432–444.

[194] L. Ho, G.R. Crabtree, Chromatin remodelling during development, Nature 463 (7280) (2010) 474–484.

[195] C.A. Jones, W.P. Tansey, A.M. Weissmiller, Emerging themes in mechanisms of tumorigenesis by SWI/SNF subunit mutation, Epigenet. Insights 15 (2022). 25168657221115656.

[196] S. Mulero-Navarro, M. Esteller, Chromatin remodeling factor CHD5 is silenced by promoter CpG island hypermethylation in human cancer, Epigenetics 3 (4) (2008) 210–215.

[197] I. Versteege, et al., Truncating mutations of hSNF5/INI1 in aggressive paediatric cancer, Nature 394 (6689) (1998) 203–206.

[198] N. Sevenet, et al., Constitutional mutations of the hSNF5/INI1 gene predispose to a variety of cancers, Am. J. Hum. Genet. 65 (5) (1999) 1342–1348.

[199] S.R. Naidu, et al., The SWI/SNF chromatin remodeling subunit BRG1 is a critical regulator of p53 necessary for proliferation of malignant cells, Oncogene 28 (27) (2009) 2492–2501.

[200] V.J. Peschansky, C. Wahlestedt, Non-coding RNAs as direct and indirect modulators of epigenetic regulation, Epigenetics 9 (1) (2014) 3–12.

[201] M. Ratti, et al., MicroRNAs (miRNAs) and long non-coding RNAs (lncRNAs) as new tools for cancer therapy: first steps from bench to bedside, Target. Oncol. 15 (3) (2020) 261–278.

[202] M. Aprile, et al., LncRNAs in cancer: from garbage to junk, Cancers (Basel) 12 (11) (2020).

[203] K. Taniue, N. Akimitsu, The functions and unique features of LncRNAs in cancer development and tumorigenesis, Int. J. Mol. Sci. 22 (2) (2021).

[204] Y. Lee, et al., MicroRNA genes are transcribed by RNA polymerase II, EMBO J. 23 (20) (2004) 4051–4060.

[205] M.R. Fabian, N. Sonenberg, W. Filipowicz, Regulation of mRNA translation and stability by microRNAs, Annu. Rev. Biochem. 79 (2010) 351–379.

[206] Y. Peng, C.M. Croce, The role of MicroRNAs in human cancer, Signal Transd. Targeted Ther. 1 (2016) 15004.

[207] J. Liu, et al., MicroRNA control of p53, J. Cell. Biochem. 118 (1) (2017) 7–14.

[208] H. Hermeking, MicroRNAs in the p53 network: micromanagement of tumour suppression, Nat. Rev. Cancer 12 (9) (2012) 613–626.

[209] A. Zhao, et al., Serum miR-210 as a novel biomarker for molecular diagnosis of clear cell renal cell carcinoma, Exp. Mol. Pathol. 94 (1) (2013) 115–120.

[210] N. Lou, et al., miR-144-3p as a novel plasma diagnostic biomarker for clear cell renal cell carcinoma, Urol. Oncol. 35 (1) (2017) 36 e7–36 e14.

[211] H. Tusong, et al., Functional analysis of serum microRNAs miR-21 and miR-106a in renal cell carcinoma, Cancer Biomark. 18 (1) (2017) 79–85.

[212] E. Larrea, et al., New concepts in cancer biomarkers: circulating miRNAs in liquid biopsies, Int. J. Mol. Sci. 17 (5) (2016).

[213] A. Chen, et al., Reduction in migratory phenotype in a metastasized breast cancer cell line via downregulation of S100A4 and GRM3, Sci. Rep. 7 (1) (2017) 3459.

[214] L. Giannopoulou, et al., Liquid biopsy in ovarian cancer: the potential of circulating miRNAs and exosomes, Transl. Res. 205 (2019) 77–91.

[215] R. Kumarswamy, I. Volkmann, T. Thum, Regulation and function of miRNA-21 in health and disease, RNA Biol. 8 (5) (2011) 706–713.

[216] B. Pardini, et al., Noncoding RNAs in extracellular fluids as cancer biomarkers: the new frontier of liquid biopsies, Cancers (Basel) 11 (8) (2019).

[217] K.A. O'Donnell, et al., c-Myc-regulated microRNAs modulate E2F1 expression, Nature 435 (7043) (2005) 839–843.

[218] N.P. Hessvik, K. Sandvig, A. Llorente, Exosomal miRNAs as biomarkers for prostate cancer, Front. Genet. 4 (2013) 36.

[219] R. Samsonov, et al., Lectin-induced agglutination method of urinary exosomes isolation followed by mi-RNA analysis: application for prostate cancer diagnostic, Prostate 76 (1) (2016) 68–79.

[220] M. Dews, et al., Augmentation of tumor angiogenesis by a Myc-activated microRNA cluster, Nat. Genet. 38 (9) (2006) 1060–1065.

[221] Z. Hua, et al., MiRNA-directed regulation of VEGF and other angiogenic factors under hypoxia, PLoS One 1 (1) (2006) e116.

[222] D.Y. Lee, et al., MicroRNA-378 promotes cell survival, tumor growth, and angiogenesis by targeting SuFu and Fus-1 expression, Proc. Natl. Acad. Sci. U. S. A. 104 (51) (2007) 20350–20355.

[223] M.A. Smolle, et al., Noncoding RNAs and immune checkpoints-clinical implications as cancer therapeutics, FEBS J. 284 (13) (2017) 1952–1966.

[224] J. Wei, et al., MiR-138 exerts anti-glioma efficacy by targeting immune checkpoints, Neuro-Oncology 18 (5) (2016) 639–648.

[225] Y. Huang, et al., Endometriosis derived exosomal miR-301a-3p mediates macrophage polarization via regulating PTEN-PI3K axis, Biomed. Pharmacother. 147 (2022) 112680.

[226] G. Cao, et al., Intronic miR-301 feedback regulates its host gene, ska2, in A549 cells by targeting MEOX2 to affect ERK/CREB pathways, Biochem. Biophys. Res. Commun. 396 (4) (2010) 978–982.

[227] L. Cui, et al., Expression of MicroRNA-301a and its functional roles in malignant melanoma, Cell. Physiol. Biochem. 40 (1–2) (2016) 230–244.

[228] X. Huang, et al., miRNA-301a induces apoptosis of chronic myelogenous leukemia cells by directly targeting TIMP2/ERK1/2 and AKT pathways, Oncol. Rep. 37 (2) (2017) 945–952.

[229] Z. Lu, et al., miR-301a as an NF-kappaB activator in pancreatic cancer cells, EMBO J. 30 (1) (2011) 57–67.

[230] F. Ma, et al., Upregulated microRNA-301a in breast cancer promotes tumor metastasis by targeting PTEN and activating Wnt/beta-catenin signaling, Gene 535 (2) (2014) 191–197.

[231] R.K. Nam, et al., MiR-301a regulates E-cadherin expression and is predictive of prostate cancer recurrence, Prostate 76 (10) (2016) 869–884.

[232] W. Shi, et al., MicroRNA-301 mediates proliferation and invasion in human breast cancer, Cancer Res. 71 (8) (2011) 2926–2937.

[233] X.D. Xu, et al., Abnormal expression of miR-301a in gastric cancer associated with progression and poor prognosis, J. Surg. Oncol. 108 (3) (2013) 197–202.

[234] H. Yu, et al., Upregulation of miR-301a correlates with poor prognosis in triple-negative breast cancer, Med. Oncol. 31 (11) (2014) 283.

[235] U. Saran, et al., Diagnostic molecular markers predicting aggressive potential in low-grade prostate cancer, Transl. Res. 231 (2021) 92–101.

[236] Y. Saito, et al., Chromatin remodeling at alu repeats by epigenetic treatment activates silenced microRNA-512-5p with downregulation of Mcl-1 in human gastric cancer cells, Oncogene 28 (30) (2009) 2738–2744.

[237] U. Lehmann, et al., Epigenetic inactivation of microRNA gene hsa-mir-9-1 in human breast cancer, J. Pathol. 214 (1) (2008) 17–24.

[238] A. Lujambio, et al., Genetic unmasking of an epigenetically silenced microRNA in human cancer cells, Cancer Res. 67 (4) (2007) 1424–1429.

[239] F.J. Slack, A.M. Chinnaiyan, The role of non-coding RNAs in oncology, Cell 179 (5) (2019) 1033–1055.

[240] J.J. Quinn, H.Y. Chang, Unique features of long non-coding RNA biogenesis and function, Nat. Rev. Genet. 17 (1) (2016) 47–62.

[241] J.M. Engreitz, et al., Local regulation of gene expression by lncRNA promoters, transcription and splicing, Nature 539 (7629) (2016) 452–455.

[242] R.W. Yao, Y. Wang, L.L. Chen, Cellular functions of long noncoding RNAs, Nat. Cell Biol. 21 (5) (2019) 542–551.

[243] L. Wang, et al., Circulating long non-coding RNA colon cancer-associated transcript 2 protected by exosome as a potential biomarker for colorectal cancer, Biomed. Pharmacother. 113 (2019) 108758.

[244] M. Naemura, et al., Long noncoding RNA ANRIL regulates proliferation of non-small cell lung cancer and cervical cancer cells, Anticancer Res. 35 (10) (2015) 5377–5382.

[245] A.A. Zimta, et al., Long non-coding RNAs in myeloid malignancies, Front. Oncol. 9 (2019) 1048.

[246] J.L. Huang, et al., Characteristics of long non-coding RNA and its relation to hepatocellular carcinoma, Carcinogenesis 35 (3) (2014) 507–514.

[247] T. Thum, J. Fiedler, LINCing MALAT1 and angiogenesis, Circ. Res. 114 (9) (2014) 1366–1368.

[248] K.M. Michalik, et al., Long noncoding RNA MALAT1 regulates endothelial cell function and vessel growth, Circ. Res. 114 (9) (2014) 1389–1397.

[249] Y. Li, et al., HBXIP and LSD1 scaffolded by lncRNA Hotair mediate transcriptional activation by c-Myc, Cancer Res. 76 (2) (2016) 293–304.

[250] A. Khorshidi, P. Dhaliwal, B.B. Yang, Noncoding RNAs in tumor angiogenesis, Adv. Exp. Med. Biol. 927 (2016) 217–241.

[251] K. Gumireddy, et al., Identification of a long non-coding RNA-associated RNP complex regulating metastasis at the translational step, EMBO J. 32 (20) (2013) 2672–2684.

[252] Z.H. Wu, et al., Long non-coding RNA HOTAIR is a powerful predictor of metastasis and poor prognosis and is associated with epithelial-mesenchymal transition in colon cancer, Oncol. Rep. 32 (1) (2014) 395–402.

[253] F. Xu, J. Zhang, Long non-coding RNA HOTAIR functions as miRNA sponge to promote the epithelial to mesenchymal transition in esophageal cancer, Biomed. Pharmacother. 90 (2017) 888–896.

[254] X. Liu, et al., Case report: condylar metastasis from hepatocellular carcinoma: an uncommon case report and literature review, Front. Oncol. 12 (2022) 1085543.

[255] Y. Sun, et al., Long non-coding RNA HOTTIP promotes BCL-2 expression and induces chemoresistance in small cell lung cancer by sponging miR-216a, Cell Death Dis. 9 (2) (2018) 85.

[256] M. Su, et al., Circular RNAs in cancer: emerging functions in hallmarks, stemness, resistance and roles as potential biomarkers, Mol. Cancer 18 (1) (2019) 90.

[257] J. He, et al., Circular RNAs and cancer, Cancer Lett. 396 (2017) 138–144.

[258] S. Nisar, et al., Insights into the role of CircRNAs: biogenesis, characterization, functional, and clinical impact in human malignancies, Front. Cell Dev. Biol. 9 (2021) 617281.

[259] Y. Li, et al., Upregulated circular RNA circ_0016760 indicates unfavorable prognosis in NSCLC and promotes cell progression through miR-1287/GAGE1 axis, Biochem. Biophys. Res. Commun. 503 (3) (2018) 2089–2094.

[260] J. Zhao, et al., MicroRNA-7: a promising new target in cancer therapy, Cancer Cell Int. 15 (2015) 103.

[261] T. Liu, et al., Circular RNA-ZFR inhibited cell proliferation and promoted apoptosis in gastric cancer by sponging miR-130a/miR-107 and modulating PTEN, Cancer Res. Treat. 50 (4) (2018) 1396–1417.

[262] C.Y. Yu, H.C. Kuo, The emerging roles and functions of circular RNAs and their generation, J. Biomed. Sci. 26 (1) (2019) 29.

[263] M.P. Jiang, et al., The emerging role of the interactions between circular RNAs and RNA-binding proteins in common human cancers, J. Cancer 12 (17) (2021) 5206–5219.

[264] V. Khoddami, et al., Transcriptome-wide profiling of multiple RNA modifications simultaneously at single-base resolution, Proc. Natl. Acad. Sci. U. S. A. 116 (14) (2019) 6784–6789.

[265] J. Fullgrabe, et al., Simultaneous sequencing of genetic and epigenetic bases in DNA, Nat. Biotechnol. 41 (10) (2023) 1457–1464.

[266] J.M. Bishop, How to Win the Nobel Prize: An Unexpected Life in Science, Harvard University Press, 2003.

Tumor metabolism and micronutrients: New insights to target malignant tumors

Santhi Latha Pandrangi[a], Prasanthi Chittineedi[a], and Sireesha V. Garimella[b]

[a]*Onco-Stem Cell Research Laboratory, Department of Biochemistry and Bioinformatics, GITAM School of Science, GITAM Deemed to be University, Visakhapatnam, India,* [b]*Department of Biotechnology, GITAM School of Science, GITAM Deemed to be University, Visakhapatnam, India*

Introduction

According to World Health Organization (WHO), cancer is one of the deadliest diseases, followed by ischemic heart disease and stroke [1]. Based on 2013–17 statistics National Cancer Institute demonstrated that the rate of cancer incidence would be 442.4 per 100,000 persons around the world, while the cancer mortality rate might be 158.3 per 100,000 persons [2]. The reason behind the high incidence rate is due to the modern lifestyle such as food habits which include alcohol consumption and smoking, exposure to harmful radiations or chemicals present in cosmetics, and much more [3], while the high mortality rate is due to their late diagnosis, resistance to therapy, and cancer relapse. Cancer could be defined as a cellular impairment disorder where the cells lose their regulation to undergo cell division, leading to continuous cell proliferation, while cell death mechanisms are halted [4]. Each and every cell is tightly regulated by a set of genes that control cell division and cell death process. For instance, proto-oncogenes (cyclins) are genes that regulate cell division by acting as a gatekeeper. These genes control the progression of cells from one phase of cell cycle to another phase of cell cycle [5]. On the other hand, tumor suppressor genes are a set of genes that regulate cell death process when the cell is mutated or damaged. However, a tumor cell loses its regulation where the cell loses its integrity to undergo cell death while proliferating continuously [6]. This occurs due to mutations in proto-oncogenes and tumor suppressor genes, leading to continuous proliferation while the absence of apoptosis or any other cell death mechanism [7].

Cancer Epigenetics and Nanomedicine. https://doi.org/10.1016/B978-0-443-13209-4.00005-2
Copyright © 2024 Elsevier Inc. All rights reserved, including those for text and data mining, AI training, and similar technologies.

Cell cycle regulation plays a crucial role in incidence of cancer. Cell requires a proper set of genes that guide them to either enter into or halt the cell division. Unfortunately, this regulation is impaired in cancer cells, leading to continuous proliferation accompanied by inhibition of apoptosis. Various metabolites (Ca^{+2}, Mg^{+2}, and PO_4^-) and electrolytes (Na^+, K^+, and Cl^-) play an essential role in regulating cell cycle [8,9]. However, these metabolites and electrolytes are imbalanced as a part of cell transformation. These play a key role in regulating various metabolism including cell division, proliferation, and apoptosis [10]. For instance, nuclear factor kappa B (NF-κB), often regarded as cellular homeostasis regulator, which regulates the expression of certain genes involved in inflammation, cell proliferation, and cell death, is upregulated in various malignancies [11]. Interestingly, high Ca^{+2} levels activate NF-κB gene by dissociating IκB from NF-κB. Similarly, Mg^{+2} also plays a major role in regulating cell proliferation by serving as a cofactor for various enzymes; one such enzyme is hexokinase which regulates the first step in glycolysis [12].

Interestingly cancer cells often rely on glycolytic pathways to carry out their metabolic reactions. Studies showed that low levels of Mg^{+2} inhibited DNA and protein synthesis, which led to cell growth arrest and finally apoptosis [13]. In contrast, various other studies have demonstrated that high levels of Mg^{+2} showed an inverse correlation with breast, ovarian, liver, esophageal, and prostate cancer mortality. Besides these ions, PO_4^- is another important ion that regulates various cellular pathways. Nucleotide biosynthesis is of utmost importance for a cell to carry out all other metabolic pathways because DNA is the genetic material that harbors genetic information and regulates the central dogma [14]. Nucleotide is composed of sugar, nitrogen base, and a phosphate group, suggesting that PO_4^- is essential for normal cells as well as for the tumor cells [15]. Additionally, sodium and potassium are also required by the cells to proliferate and inhibit apoptosis. Studies demonstrated that during apoptosis intracellular potassium ions are effluxed in order to protect themselves from apoptosis [16]. Interestingly, intracellular sodium levels have been elevated coupled with decreased potassium levels during the early stage of apoptosis, suggesting that cancer cells have low levels of sodium ions while high levels of potassium ions to abscond apoptosis [17].

Apart from the genes or proteins that regulate cell division, cell also needs to maintain ionic balance within the cellular environment (intracellular as well as extracellular). For example, numerous studies have demonstrated that external calcium controls cell division and proliferation. Similarly, a theory postulated by Harry Rubin entitled "coordinated control of cell proliferation" confers that magnesium might regulate various critical steps of cell division. On the other hand, phosphate ions play a crucial role in regulating cellular homeostasis. Inorganic phosphate plays a vital role in nucleotide biosynthesis and membrane phospholipid synthesis and is also involved in cell signaling pathways by aiding in the process of phosphorylation to either activate or inactivate proteins. All these studies suggest that electrolytes such as calcium, magnesium, and phosphate are essential in regulating cell cycle and promoting proliferation.

Role of micronutrients in targeting malignant tumors

Although numerous antineoplastic drugs are on the market, the rate of cancer incidence and mortality remains constant. This is because of multiple reasons, one among them is acquired drug resistance accompanied by adverse side effects. Also, commercially available antineoplastic drugs target not only tumor population but also healthy cells [18,19]. To overcome this targeting specific components of tumor cells and bulk cancer stem cells (CSCs) is of utmost importance. Cancer cells need bulk micronutrients in order to sustain the inevitable tumor microenvironment and hence targeting these micronutrients might help in overcoming the tumor incidence and mortality rates.

Impact of iron levels on cancer proliferation

Iron is the most copious metal in the human body. No independent life forms on earth could survive without iron [20]. It is hypothesized that iron might play a dual role in cells by both stimulating cell growth and causing cell death. The iron present in the body gets absorbed in the intestinal enterocytes and is utilized for various cellular processes such as nucleic acid synthesis, oxygen transportation, cellular respiration, enzyme activity, heme synthesis, detoxification, immune function, and metabolism. For instance, ribonucleotide reductase is an iron-containing enzyme that catalyzes the synthesis [21].

On the other hand, iron serves as an essential metal in hemoglobin which plays a crucial role in oxygen transport [22]. However, studies suggest that anemic people are at high risk to acquire cancer. This might be due to the fact that anemia characterized by low hemoglobin levels could not deliver the required quantity of oxygen to cells, thereby leading to hypoxic environments [23,24]. It is evident that hypoxic environments act as friends for tumor cells to grow and proliferate. Interestingly numerous studies demonstrate that both cancer cells and CSCs which are termed to be the root cause of tumor relapse/recurrence [25] are characterized by the presence of enormous amounts of iron in the form of ferritin [26].

Ferritin is an iron storage protein that regulates cell proliferation and death under normal homeostasis. Since in malignant tumors this homeostasis is altered, ferritin acts as a barrier for these cells in the hostile tumor microenvironment by preventing them from undergoing cell death which is different from apoptosis [27]. Ferroptosis is a novel mechanism that came into the spotlight in the research world in 2012, which is characterized by targeting the bulk iron reserves [28]. However, tumor cells and bulk CSCs protect themselves from ferroptosis by various mechanisms.

Iron is one of the important ions that regulate cellular metabolism. Dietary iron absorbed in the intestinal epithelial cells is further transported to different cell organelles through an iron exporter called *ferroportin (FPN)* [29,30]. FPN has an affinity toward ferric iron, and hence, the ferrous ion prior to its export is oxidized by the enzymes Hephaestin or ceruloplasmin. Once the ferric iron enters into the circulation, it binds to transferrin [31]. In circulation, transferrin protein exists in two forms: *Holo-Tf* (free from ferric ion binding) and *Apo-Tf* (Tf associated with ferric ion). Ferric ions are endocytosed by *TfR* and are reduced by endosomal *six-transmembrane epithelial antigen of prostate-3 (STEAP-3)* to ferrous iron and enter into *cLIP* of respective cells through *DMT-1* protein [32]. Iron stored in the form of ferritin is used for various pathways. One such pathway is to synthesize nucleotides. Ribonucleotide reductase is an enzyme which requires iron as a cofactor that catalyzes the conversion of ribonucleotides into deoxyribonucleotides. Hence, targeting these bulk iron reserves might lead to a novel approach to induce cancer cell death.

Targeting intracellular iron levels to induce cellular death

Ferroptosis is an iron-dependent regulated necrosis which is independent of caspase activation. Accumulating evidence suggests that both tumor cells and tumor stem cells are rich in ferritin levels which makes these cells sensitive to ferroptosis [33]. Under normal homeostasis ferroptosis is induced by lipid peroxidation which is catalyzed by several enzymes. Initially, plasma membrane comprising lipid bilayer incorporates arachidonic acid and adrenic acid catalyzed by the enzyme that belongs to membrane-bound *O*-acyltransferase family which is referred as *lysophosphatidylcholine acyltransferase 3 (LPCAT-3)* [34]. These lipid molecules are further esterified by the enzyme *acetyl Co-A synthesis long-chain family member-4 (ACSL-4)*, mediated by β-oxidation of polyunsaturated fatty acids (PUFA) biosynthesis [35]. Due to the presence of highly reactive hydrogen atoms that are generated by Fenton reaction, the formed PUFAs are highly sensitive to peroxidation catalyzed by the enzyme lipoxygenase in the presence of ferrous iron as a cofactor, ultimately leading to iron-mediated cell death [36]. Fig. 1 represents the mechanism of ferroptosis.

However, cancer cells dodge ferroptosis by elevating glutathione peroxidase-4 enzyme (GPX-4) levels, which serves as lipid peroxide scavenger by reducing peroxides to alcohols [37]. However, this reaction requires glutathione (GSH) which serves as an electron donor, thereby limiting iron-dependent formation of lipid alkoxy radicals from lipid peroxides [38]. In order to avert ferroptosis, these cells enhance GSH synthesis which is regulated by intracellular cysteine/glutamate levels [39]. The intracellular cysteine/glutamate levels are tightly regulated by sodium-dependent antiporter called xCT system encoded by *SLC7A11* gene. This antiporter imports one cystine (CySS) molecule accompanied by exporting one glutamate molecule [40]. Hence, targeting *xCT* system might play a crucial role in inducing ferroptosis mediated through iron metabolism.

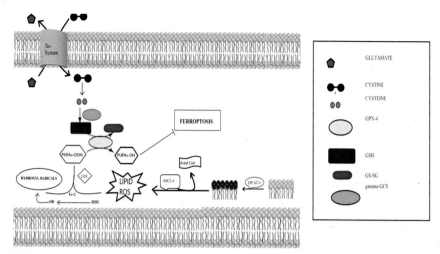

FIG. 1

Mechanism of ferroptosis: Ferroptosis is an iron-dependent cell death pathway that is characterized by the generation of lipid ROS. Initially, the fatty acids present in plasma membrane undergo lipidation followed by acylation, finally combine with hydroxyl free radicals, and form lipid peroxides which are catalyzed by the enzyme lipoxygenase. However, cancer cells/cancer stem cells abscond this cell death pathway by elevating glutathione levels which act as lipid peroxide scavengers by upregulating cysteine-glutamate antiporter system.

Impact of calcium levels on cancer proliferation

It is well known that calcium serves as a second messenger to regulate various metabolic reactions of cells. However, calcium signaling in tumor cells is highly dysregulated in order to sustain the hostile tumor microenvironment [41]. Accumulating evidence suggests the role of calcium signaling in tumor growth, proliferation, and death. Ca^{2+} influx is essential for the inducing cell death program and has been proven by the study in which HT22 cells treated with glutamate did not undergo cell death when Ca^{2+} influx is blocked by $CoCl_2$ or in Ca^{2+}-free medium [42,43]. On the contrary, various studies stated that calcium ions play an important role in cellular proliferation. For instance, in 1995, Yeh et al. attenuated Ca^{+2} influx in the MDA-MD-435 cell line and observed significant cell growth impairment. On the other hand, literature suggests the importance of Ca^{+2} in inducing cell death. Studies evaluated the importance of calcium ions in glutamate toxicity. Under calcium depletion, *xCT* system was overexpressed and resulted in elevated levels of reduced glutathione, thereby promoting cancer cell proliferation [44]. This suggests that calcium ions are important in inducing a novel cell death called oxytosis characterized by glutathione depletion, lipoxygenase activation, reactive oxygen species production, and calcium influx [45].

Additionally, various studies suggest that calcium plays an important role in iron absorption. For instance, Hallberg et al. conducted a series of experiments to evaluate dose-dependent relationship between calcium content and iron absorption [46]. They recommended the volunteer group ingest bread rolls incorporated with calcium chloride. Interestingly, they observed that at 60% calcium dose, 300–600 mg of ferritin has been inhibited [9]. Kletzein et al. observed that ferritin retention and the rate of hemoglobin regeneration were gradually diminished in animal models that were fed with various sources of calcium [47]. Accumulating evidence suggests that both bulk cancer cells and CSCs are characterized by the presence of high ferritin amount which stores excess iron. This suggests that calcium supplementation could inhibit iron absorption, thereby lowering ferritin levels and leading to iron-dependent, calcium-regulated necrosis.

Targeting calcium levels to induce cellular death

Calcium ions play a crucial role in cellular death that is triggered by oxidative glutamate cytotoxicity, formerly called oxytosis, and is defined as a programmed cell death identical to ferroptosis [48]. Oxytosis is characterized by high influx of calcium ions which play a critical role in inducing cell death by executing glutamate oxidation, leading to reduced levels of glutathione (GSH) [37]. GSH serves as a lipid ROS scavenger molecule which inhibits ferroptosis by reducing the activity of lipoxygenase. Several studies have demonstrated the mechanism of how oxytosis is induced. Literature suggests that this type of cell death is characterized by elevated levels of ROS generation associated with GSH depletion which leads to high calcium influx and eventual death, suggesting that reduced levels of GSH serve as markers for inducing oxytosis [49]. Studies suggest that elevated levels of calcium are the key negotiator of glutamate toxicity which is induced by overactivation of ionotropic and metabotropic receptors.

Enhanced intracellular Ca^{2+} concentration interrupts calcium homeostasis and initiates a cascade of signaling pathways, which leads to mitochondrial dysfunction, dysregulation of oxidative phosphorylation, enhanced production of ROS, ER stress, and release of lysosomal enzymes which ultimately leads to calcium-dependent cell death [50]. This suggests that cancer cells are characterized by low intracellular calcium levels and high intracellular ferritin levels. On the other hand, it is evident that activated lipoxygenase (LOX) enhances intracellular calcium uptake. Surprisingly, LOX activation could be triggered by ferric iron. This gives us a clue that when ferritin is degraded into ferric iron, it activates LOX, which elevates intracellular calcium levels [25].

Additionally, *store-operated calcium entry (SOCE-2)* channels permit the entry of calcium ions into the cells which is tightly regulated by LOX [51]. It has been evident that *LOX* activation triggers production of *soluble guanylate cyclase (sGC)*, which in turn activates cGMP, finally leading to the influx of calcium ions

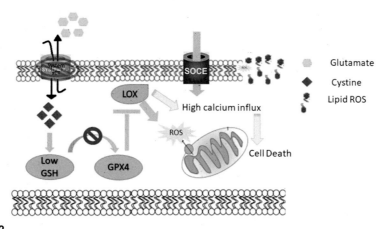

FIG. 2

Mechanism of oxytosis. Oxytosis is a calcium-regulated oxidative glutamate cytotoxicity resulting from calcium accumulation in the cells. Under glutathione deprivation the cell enhances the expression of LOX which activates SOCE. SOCE further activates certain downstream calcium pumps which triggers calcium influx into the cytoplasm.

[52]. Oxytosis is a calcium-mediated cell death pathway which relies on inducing oxidative glutamate toxicity. The critical steps that contribute oxytosis involve glutathione (GSH) depletion, *lipoxygenase (LOX)* activation, and accumulation of ROS, finally leading to Ca^{+2} influx [53]. *Store-operated calcium entry (SOCE)* channels are the calcium influx channels that regulate intracellular calcium levels. Interestingly, *SOCE* mediates calcium influx through *ORAI* and *STIM* proteins which are localized on plasma membrane and endoplasmic reticulum, respectively. Under GSH depletion, *LOX* is activated, which in turn triggers the activation of *SOCE*. Activated *SOCE* triggers *STIM* activation which permits the opening of *ORAI* gate that is localized on the plasma membrane, thereby allowing calcium influx which eventually leads to oxytosis. Fig. 2 represents the mechanism of oxytosis.

Impact of magnesium levels on cancer proliferation

Magnesium is considered to be the second abundant cation that serves as a cofactor for various enzymes that catalyze several reactions involved in maintaining energy metabolism, membrane stability, regulating the central dogma, etc. [54]. It is witnessed that cancer cells rely upon glycolysis and exhibit Warburg effect for rapid ATP synthesis, glucose metabolism, and rapid proliferation. Therefore, cancer cells require bulk quantities of magnesium ions because they serve as cofactors for various glycolytic enzymes. For instance, Mg^{+2} serves as a cofactor for the enzyme phosphofructokinase which is the rate-limiting step for glycolysis. Interestingly, studies demonstrated the positive regulation of glycolysis and hypoxia in the hostile tumor microenvironment, suggesting that enhanced glycolysis results in hypoxia which is regarded as one of the most crucial cellular adaption for the malignant cells. This suggests that magnesium ion chelators might serve as potential targets for malignant tumors through glucose deprivation.

Cellular migration and adhesion are two prominent features of malignant cells which define the invasiveness and metastasis of the tumor. Integrins are an example of cell adhesion molecules that rely on both Ca^{+2} and Mg^{+2} for their proper functioning.

Targeting Warburg effect to induce tumor cell death

Since glucose is bound to provide energy and carbon skeleton, insulin and glucagon have evolved to regulate glucose levels during feeding and fasting states [55]. Under normal homeostasis, glycolysis mediates glucose conversion to pyruvate which is then imported into the mitochondria for ATP generation through electron transport chain (ETC) [56]. To maintain cellular integrity the products such as ATP and carbon skeleton generated by mitochondrial oxidative metabolism and glycolysis, respectively, provide energy. Accumulating evidence emphasizes the prominent role of glycolysis in tumorigenesis and signifies that glycolytic enzyme might be ideal cancer tumor for emerging novel inhibitors [57].

Role of glycolytic enzymes in inducing cancer cell death

Glycolysis is quite a complex metabolic pathway, especially in tumor cells, as it serves as a central energetic resource for the cell. It is well known that breakdown of glucose through glycolysis is a multistep process and requires various enzymes and transporters such as *glucose transporters (GLUTs), pyruvate kinase M2 (PKM2), hexokinase (HK), and lactate dehydrogenase A (LDHA)* [58].

It is known that glycolysis is the key regulator for tumor cells, suggesting that tumor cells are greedy for glucose and import it from the extracellular environment by enhancing the expression of glucose transporters termed *GLUTs. GLUT* transporters allow facilitative transport of glucose across the cell membrane. Hence, targeting *GLUT* transporters might provide novel insights for cancer therapy [59]. For instance, WZB117, a *GLUT1* inhibitor, decreases glucose uptake, intracellular ATP levels, and glycolytic enzymes, yielding poor glycolysis rate accompanied by poor cellular growth. Studies demonstrate that when WZB-117 treated cancer cells were supplemented with exogenous ATP the cells were rescued and continued their proliferation, suggesting that the anticancer effect of WZB117 relies on lowering ATP levels, which is accompanied by induction of endoplasmic reticulum stress, thereby leading to cell cycle arrest. Interestingly WZB117 showed synergistic

Table 1 Various inhibitors targeting cellular metabolism to develop novel cancer therapeutics [58].

Targeted metabolism	Targeted metabolic enzymes	Metabolic inhibitors	Cancer therapeutics	Type of malignancy
Fatty acid	FASN	C75	Trastuzumab	Breast
			5-FU	Breast
		Orlistat	Gemcitabine	Pancreatic
			Adriamycin	Breast
		Cerulenin	Docetaxel	Breast
TCA	PDK	DCA	Sulindac	Lung
			5-FU	Colon
			Omeprazole	Fibrosarcoma
	PDK3	siRNA	Paclitaxel	Cervical
			Cisplatin	Colon
Glycolysis	GLUT-1	WZB117	Daunorubicin	Lung, breast
		Phloretin	Cisplatin	Colon
	HK	3-BrPA	Doxorubicin	Multiple myeloma
			Daunorubicin	Leukemia
			Prednisolone	Leukemia
			5-FU	Colon
		2-DG	Prednisolone	Leukemia
			ABT-263	Cervical, prostrate
			Trastuzumab	Breast
	LDHA	Oxamate	Paclitaxel	Breast
			Trastuzumab	Breast
		FX11	FK866	Lymphoma

anticancer effects when treated in combination with cisplatin and paclitaxel [60]. Table 1 represents various enzymatic inhibitors that target cellular metabolism to induce cancer cell death.

Other metabolic pathways used by tumor cells

Apart from glycolysis, tumor cells use other metabolic pathways, such as glutaminolysis, to provide macromolecules. Glutaminolysis results in generating NADPH, which is regarded as reductive equivalent to ATP [61]. It is well evident that glutamine serves as a conditional amino acid which acts as an essential amino acid under rapid growth and proliferation of cells. This suggests that cancer patients who have high glutamine intake might be subject to a worse prognosis. Because of its important role in providing nitrogen, carbon, and sulfur sources apart from NADPH, tumor cells tend to have glutamate pool [62]. It has also been evident that tumor cells reserve bulk glutamate to protect themselves from ferroptosis. To mediate all these protective metabolic reactions the tumor cells elevate *glutamine synthase (GLS)*, a mitochondrial enzyme that catalyzes the conversion of glutamate to glutamine, which is further used up by the cells for energy generation and protection from lipid peroxidation via synthesizing glutathione, which aids in resistance to oxidative stress associated with a rapid metabolism, DNA-damaging agents, inflammation, etc. [63,64]. Accumulating evidence also suggests that glutamate enhances the enzyme activity of aminotransferase which is required for alanine and aspartate synthesis. Both these amino acids play a vital role in proliferating tumor cells as they aid in protein and nucleotide biosynthesis, respectively.

Apart from its role in intermediary metabolism, glutamine exhibits various other metabolic effects in the proliferating cells that support the growth and development of the cell. Due to their prominent role in anabolic metabolism, tumor cells opt for glutamate-dependent mechanisms in order to maintain continuous cell proliferation via activating various signal transduction pathways [65]. For instance, a recent study demonstrated that the prerequisite for *mTOR* pathway activation is glutamine uptake regulated by *SLC1A5* and its subsequent quick efflux by the cells. Not only for *mTOR* activation, but glutamine is also known to activate the *extracellular signal-regulated protein kinase (ERK)* signaling pathway which is typically characterized in the intestinal epithelial cells. These cells are thought to consume glutamine for their proliferation and survival and are thought to be the major bioenergetic substrate.

Interplay between glutaminolysis and Warburg effect

The interplay between glutamine and glucose consumption by the cells might depend on the particular oncogene/tumor suppressor involved in progression of tumor cells [66]. Various studies demonstrate that myc which is regarded to be an oncogene induces glutaminolysis as well as aerobic glycolysis, while *β-catenin* is thought to activate glutaminolysis only [61]. Since the enzyme glutamate synthetase responsible for conversion of glutamate to glutamine is not expressed in all tumor tissues, rate of glutaminolysis is dependent on metabolic profile of the tumor cells, which varies from cancer to cancer. While glutamate is one of the important metabolites for glutathione synthesis cancer cells use glutamate for glutathione synthesis irrespective of the cancer metabolic prolife to protect themselves from lipid peroxide-induced ferroptosis [67].

Finally, the hostile tumor microenvironment containing supporting host cells such as stroma, fibroblasts, adipocytes, endothelial, muscle, and immune cells plays a prominent role in tumor initiation, progression, metastasis, and therapy resistance

[68]. Numerous studies have highlighted the metabolic crosstalk called the "reverse Warburg effect," which hypothesized that aerobic glycolysis fuels anaplerotic metabolism in stromal cells of malignant tumors. In this two-compartment model, the anabolic malignant cells acquire energy by inducing catabolic processes such as autophagy, mitophagy, and aerobic glycolysis from the surrounding host cells, ultimately leading to the overproduction of various metabolites such as ketone bodies, glutamine, and L-lactate [57]. These metabolites further enter the TCA cycle by converting themselves into acetyl CoA, resulting in ATP generation [62].

Discussion and conclusion

In order to sustain the hostile tumor microenvironment and to meet their bioenergetic and biosynthetic demands tumor cells reprogram their metabolism [69]. Enhanced aerobic glycolysis, fatty acid synthesis, and glutamine metabolism have been associated with therapeutic resistance in numerous malignancies. Due to elevated energy production and metabolic synthesis as a result of deregulated tumor metabolism, tumor cells tend to proliferate abruptly, accompanied by lowering drug-induced apoptosis, conferring resistance to the current anticancer drugs. Enhanced drug efflux, inactivation of drug, intense DNA repair mechanisms, and activation of pro-survival signaling serve as the underlying mechanisms to contribute to chemotherapeutic resistance.

This suggests that tumor cells need more nutrients when compared to healthy cells as they need to proliferate continuously, abscond cellular death pathways, and confer drug resistance. Iron, calcium, and magnesium are believed to be the essential micronutrients required by the body even under normal homeostasis. For instance, iron is one of the essential components of hemoglobin which plays a crucial role in delivering oxygen [22,70]. Calcium, on the other hand, serves as a second messenger in various metabolic reactions apart from its important role in bone formation [47]. Finally, magnesium serves as a key cofactor for various kinase enzymes particularly for glycolysis. It is well known that tumor cells exhibit Warburg effect, and hence, targeting magnesium ions or the glycolytic enzymes makes research one step ahead toward discovering novel cell death strategies [55].

Targeting key metabolic enzymes augments pharmacological efficiency accompanied by enhancement in drug-induced apoptosis of cancer cells. Increased drug sensitization could be achieved by ATP depletion through glycolytic inhibitors, resulting in intracellular drug accumulation [71]. Although the underlying molecular mechanisms by which targeting tumor metabolism could impair chemoresistance is not fully understood, it is believed that combining chemotherapeutic agents with metabolic enzyme inhibitors, micronutrient chelators represent a promising strategy to overcome drug resistance and progress pharmacological efficiency of current chemotherapeutic agents.

Author contributions

Writing the manuscript: PC and SLP; Data compiling: PC; Tables and Figures: PC; Review and Editing: SLP; Conceptualizing the study: SLP. Overall supervision of the study: SLP.

Conflict of interest

None declared.

Acknowledgments

SLP gratefully acknowledges DBT (BT/PR30629/BIC/101/1093/2018), New Delhi; UGC (Ref. No.: No.F.30-456/2018 [BSR]) and SERB (Ref. No.: PDF/2015/000867) for the financial support. PC gratefully acknowledges DBT (BT/PR30629/BIC/101/1093/2018), New Delhi, for the Junior Research Fellowship.

References

[1] C. Mattiuzzi, G. Lippi, Current cancer epidemiology, J. Epidemiol. Global Health 9 (2019) 217–222, https://doi.org/10.2991/jegh.k.191008.001.

[2] R.L. Siegel, K.D. Miller, H.E. Fuchs, A. Jemal, Cancer statistics, 2022, CA Cancer J. Clin. 72 (2022) 7–33, https://doi.org/10.3322/CAAC.21708.

[3] D. Aldinucci, C. Borghese, N. Casagrande, The CCL5/CCR5 axis in cancer progression, Cancers 12 (7) (2020) 1765.

[4] L.G. Carter, J.A. D'Orazio, K.J. Pearson, Resveratrol and cancer: focus on in vivo evidence, Endocr. Relat. Cancer (2014) 21, https://doi.org/10.1530/ERC-13-0171.

[5] T. Ozaki, A. Nakagawara, Role of p53 in cell death and human cancers, Cancers (Basel) 3 (2011) 994–1013, https://doi.org/10.3390/cancers3010994.

[6] K. Mahboobnia, M. Pirro, E. Marini, F. Grignani, E.E. Bezsonov, T. Jamialahmadi, et al., PCSK9 and cancer: rethinking the link, Biomed. Pharmacother. 140 (2021) 111758, https://doi.org/10.1016/J.BIOPHA.2021.111758.

[7] H. Hjalgrim, G. Edgren, K. Rostgaard, M. Reilly, T.N. Tran, K.E. Titlestad, et al., Cancer incidence in blood transfusion recipients, J. Natl. Cancer Inst. 99 (2007) 1864–1874, https://doi.org/10.1093/jnci/djm248.

[8] S.O. Oseni, E. Quiroz, J. Kumi-Diaka, Chemopreventive effects of magnesium chloride supplementation on hormone independent prostate cancer cells, Funct. Foods Health Dis. 8 (2016) 1–15, https://doi.org/10.31989/ffhd.v6i1.229.

[9] P.J. Baney, Calcium: effect of different amounts on nonheme-iron and heme-iron arsorption in humans, J. Nutr. Educ. 23 (1991) 230, https://doi.org/10.1016/S0022-3182(12)81252-0.

[10] S. Elmore, Apoptosis: a review of programmed cell death, Toxicol. Pathol. 35 (2007) 495–516, https://doi.org/10.1080/01926230701320337.

[11] F. Wang, J. Ma, K.S. Wang, C. Mi, J.J. Lee, X. Jin, Blockade of TNF-α-induced NF-κB signaling pathway and anti-cancer therapeutic response of dihydrotanshinone I, Int. Immunopharmacol. 28 (2015) 764–772, https://doi.org/10.1016/J.INTIMP.2015.08.003.

[12] C. Sabu, T.K. Henna, V.R. Raphey, K.P. Nivitha, K. Pramod, Advanced biosensors for glucose and insulin, Biosens. Bioelectron. 141 (2019) 111201, https://doi.org/10.1016/j.bios.2019.03.034.

[13] J.C. Rathmell, C.B. Thompson, Pathways of apoptosis in lymphocyte development, homeostasis, and disease, Cell 109 (2002) 97–107, https://doi.org/10.1016/S0092-8674(02)00704-3.

[14] M. Lakhanpal, L.C. Singh, T. Rahman, J. Sharma, M.M. Singh, A.C. Kataki, et al., Study of single nucleotide polymorphisms of tumour necrosis factors and HSP genes in nasopharyngeal carcinoma in North East India, Tumour Biol. 37 (2016) 271–281, https://doi.org/10.1007/s13277-015-3767-6.

[15] R. Roy, S.V. Garimella, S.L. Pandrangi, Targeting the key players of DNA repair pathways as cancer therapeutics, Res. J. Biotechnol. 17 (5) (2022) 203–210.

[16] P. Karki, C. Seong, J.E. Kim, K. Hur, S.Y. Shin, J.S. Lee, et al., Intracellular K+ inhibits apoptosis by suppressing the Apaf-1 apoptosome formation and subsequent downstream pathways but not cytochrome c release, Cell Death Differ. 14 (2007) 2068–2075, https://doi.org/10.1038/sj.cdd.4402221.

[17] S.L. Pandrangi, P. Chittineedi, S.S. Chalumuri, A.S. Meena, J.A.N. Mosquera, S.N.S. Llaguno, et al., Role of intracellular iron in switching apoptosis to ferroptosis to target therapy-resistant cancer stem cells, Molecules 27 (2022) 3011, https://doi.org/10.3390/MOLECULES27093011.

[18] R. Gulati, M. Naik Ramavath, V. Satya Mahesh Kumar Metta, S. Latha Pandrangi, Exploring the CRISPR/Cas9 system in targeting drug resistant, Cancer Stem Cells 25 (2021) 1583–6258.

[19] P.K. Rambatla, S.L. Pandrangi, S. Rentala, V. Sireesha, A study on the expression of CCL5, CXCR4 and angiogenic factors by prostate cancer stem cells, 25 (2021) 1020–1028.

[20] C. Zhang, Essential functions of iron-requiring proteins in DNA replication, repair and cell cycle control, Protein Cell 5 (2014) 750–760, https://doi.org/10.1007/s13238-014-0083-7.

[21] Y. Wang, L. Yu, J. Ding, Y. Chen, Iron metabolism in cancer, Int. J. Mol. Sci. 20 (2019) 1–22, https://doi.org/10.3390/ijms20010095.

[22] D.M. Frazer, G.J. Anderson, The regulation of iron transport, Biofactors 40 (2014) 206–214, https://doi.org/10.1002/biof.1148.

[23] Y. Chen, Z. Fan, Y. Yang, C. Gu, Iron metabolism and its contribution to cancer (review), Int. J. Oncol. 54 (2019) 1143–1154, https://doi.org/10.3892/ijo.2019.4720.

[24] R.R. Malla, S. Pandrangi, S. Kumari, M.M. Gavara, A.K. Badana, Exosomal tetraspanins as regulators of cancer progression and metastasis and novel diagnostic markers, Asia Pac. J. Clin. Oncol. 14 (2018) 383–391, https://doi.org/10.1111/ajco.12869.

[25] S.L. Pandrangi, R. Chikati, P.S. Chauhan, C.S. Kumar, A. Banarji, S. Saxena, Effects of ellipticine on ALDH1A1-expressing breast cancer stem cells—an in vitro and in silico study, Tumour Biol. 35 (2014) 723–737, https://doi.org/10.1007/s13277-013-1099-y.

[26] S. Recalcati, E. Gammella, G. Cairo, Dysregulation of iron metabolism in cancer stem cells, Free Radic. Biol. Med. 133 (2019) 216–220, https://doi.org/10.1016/j.freeradbiomed.2018.07.015.

[27] J. Yang, S. Hu, Y. Bian, J. Yao, D. Wang, X. Liu, et al., Targeting cell death: pyroptosis, ferroptosis, apoptosis and necroptosis in osteoarthritis, Frontiers in Cell and Developmental Biology 9 (2022) 1–18, https://doi.org/10.3389/fcell.2021.789948.

[28] S.L. Pandrangi, P. Chittineedi, R. Chikati, J.R. Lingareddy, Role of dietary iron revisited: in metabolism, ferroptosis and pathophysiology of cancer, 12 (2022) 974–985.

[29] B.R. Stockwell, J.P. Friedmann Angeli, H. Bayir, A.I. Bush, M. Conrad, S.J. Dixon, et al., Ferroptosis: a regulated cell death nexus linking metabolism, redox biology, and disease, Cell 171 (2017) 273–285, https://doi.org/10.1016/j.cell.2017.09.021.

[30] N. Geng, B.J. Shi, S.L. Li, Z.Y. Zhong, Y.C. Li, W.L. Xua, et al., Knockdown of ferroportin accelerates erastin-induced ferroptosis in neuroblastoma cells, Eur. Rev. Med. Pharmacol. Sci. 22 (2018) 3826–3836, https://doi.org/10.26355/EURREV_201806_15267.

[31] S.M. Elgendy, S.K. Alyammahi, D.W. Alhamad, S.M. Abdin, H.A. Omar, Ferroptosis: an emerging approach for targeting cancer stem cells and drug resistance, Crit. Rev. Oncol. Hematol. 155 (2020) 103095, https://doi.org/10.1016/j.critrevonc.2020.103095.

[32] C.M. Bebber, F. Müller, L.P. Clemente, J. Weber, S. von Karstedt, Ferroptosis in cancer cell biology, Cancers (Basel) (2020) 12, https://doi.org/10.3390/cancers12010164.

[33] B. Proneth, M. Conrad, Ferroptosis and necroinflammation, a yet poorly explored link, Cell Death Differ. 26 (2019) 14–24, https://doi.org/10.1038/s41418-018-0173-9.

[34] W.S. Yang, K.J. Kim, M.M. Gaschler, M. Patel, M.S. Shchepinov, B.R. Stockwell, Peroxidation of polyunsaturated fatty acids by lipoxygenases drives ferroptosis, Proc. Natl. Acad. Sci. USA 113 (2016) E4966–E4975, https://doi.org/10.1073/pnas.1603244113.

[35] S. Doll, B. Proneth, Y.Y. Tyurina, E. Panzilius, S. Kobayashi, I. Ingold, et al., ACSL4 dictates ferroptosis sensitivity by shaping cellular lipid composition, Nat. Chem. Biol. 13 (2017) 91–98, https://doi.org/10.1038/nchembio.2239.

[36] S. Ma, E.S. Henson, Y. Chen, S.B. Gibson, Ferroptosis is induced following siramesine and lapatinib treatment of breast cancer cells, Cell Death Dis. 7 (2016), https://doi.org/10.1038/CDDIS.2016.208.

[37] G. Peng, Z. Tang, Y. Xiang, W. Chen, Glutathione peroxidase 4 maintains a stemness phenotype, oxidative homeostasis and regulates biological processes in Panc-1 cancer stem-like cells, Oncol. Rep. 41 (2019) 1264–1274, https://doi.org/10.3892/or.2018.6905.

[38] P. Jagust, S. Alcalá Jr., B. Sainz Jr., C. Heeschen, P. Sancho, Glutathione metabolism is essential for self-renewal and chemoresistance of pancreatic cancer stem cells, World J. Stem Cells 12 (2020) 1410–1428, https://doi.org/10.4252/wjsc.v12.i11.1410.

[39] J. Liu, M.M. Hinkhouse, W. Sun, C.J. Weydert, J.M. Ritchie, L.W. Oberley, et al., Redox regulation of pancreatic cancer cell growth: role of glutathione peroxidase in the suppression of the malignant phenotype, Hum. Gene Ther. 15 (2004) 239–250, https://doi.org/10.1089/104303404322886093.

[40] P. Koppula, L. Zhuang, B. Gan, Cystine transporter SLC7A11/xCT in cancer: ferroptosis, nutrient dependency, and cancer therapy, Protein Cell (2020), https://doi.org/10.1007/s13238-020-00789-5.

[41] P. Terry, J.A. Baron, L. Bergkvist, L. Holmberg, A. Wolk, Dietary calcium and vitamin D intake and risk of colorectal cancer: a prospective cohort study in women, Nutr. Cancer 43 (2002) 39–46, https://doi.org/10.1207/S15327914NC431_4.

[42] N.J. Satheesh, D. Büsselberg, The role of intracellular calcium for the development and treatment of neuroblastoma, Cancers (Basel) 7 (2015) 823–848, https://doi.org/10.3390/cancers7020811.

[43] S. Latha Pandrangi, S. Shree Chalumuri, P. Chittineedi, S. Garimella, v, leader G., Therapeutic potential of Nyctanthes arbor-tristis on cancer and various diseases, Cell Biol. 26 (2022) 64–74.

[44] T. Finkel, S. Menazza, K.M. Holmström, R.J. Parks, J. Liu, J. Sun, J. Liu, et al., The ins and outs of mitochondrial calcium, Circ. Res. (2015), https://doi.org/10.1161/CIRCRESAHA.116.305484.

[45] P. Maher, A. Currais, D. Schubert, Using the oxytosis/ferroptosis pathway to understand and treat age-associated neurodegenerative diseases, Cell Chem. Biol. 27 (2020) 1456–1471, https://doi.org/10.1016/j.chembiol.2020.10.010.

[46] R. Chikati, L.S. Pandrangi, R. Gundampati, S.H. Vemuri, M. Lakhanpal, S.S. Singh, et al., Molecular studies on evaluation of phytol as cytoskeleton targeting element in cancer, Int. J. Sci. Eng. Res. 9 (2018) 1978–1992.

[47] S.S. Harris, The effect of calcium consumption on iron absorption and iron status, Nutr. Clin. Care 5 (2002) 231–235, https://doi.org/10.1046/j.1523-5408.2002.05505.x.

[48] J. Lewerenz, G. Ates, A. Methner, M. Conrad, P. Maher, Oxytosis/ferroptosis-(re-) emerging roles for oxidative stress-dependent non-apoptotic cell death in diseases of the central nervous system, Front. Neurosci. (2018) 12, https://doi.org/10.3389/fnins.2018.00214.

[49] V. Pandey, F. Arfuso, T. Xie, X. Sui, R. Zhang, S. Liu, et al., RSL3 drives ferroptosis through GPX4 inactivation and ROS production in colorectal cancer, Front. Pharmacol. (2018), https://doi.org/10.3389/fphar.2018.01371.

[50] M.L. Mccullough, A.S. Robertson, C. Rodriguez, E.J. Jacobs, A. Chao, C. Jonas, et al., Calcium, vitamin D, dairy products, and risk of colorectal cancer in the Cancer Prevention Study II Nutrition Cohort (United States), Cancer Causes Control 14 (1) (2003) 1–12.

[51] I. Jardin, J.A. Rosado, STIM and calcium channel complexes in cancer, Biochim. Biophys. Acta Mol. Cell Res. 1863 (2016) 1418–1426, https://doi.org/10.1016/J.BBAMCR.2015.10.003.

[52] S.L. Zhang, Y. Yu, J. Roos, J.A. Kozak, T.J. Deerinck, M.H. Ellisman, et al., STIM1 is a Ca2+ sensor that activates CRAC channels and migrates from the Ca2+ store to the plasma membrane, Nature 437 (2005) 902–905, https://doi.org/10.1038/NATURE04147.

[53] J. Roos, P.J. DiGregorio, A.V. Yeromin, K. Ohlsen, M. Lioudyno, S. Zhang, et al., STIM1, an essential and conserved component of store-operated Ca2+ channel function, J. Cell Biol. 169 (2005) 435–445, https://doi.org/10.1083/JCB.200502019.

[54] S.L. Pandrangi, S.S. Chalumuri, S. Garimella, Emerging therapeutic efficacy of alkaloids as anticancer agents, Ann. Rom. Soc. Cell Biol. 26 (2022) 64–74.

[55] M.G.V. Heiden, L.C. Cantley, C.B. Thompson, Understanding the Warburg effect: the metabolic requirements of cell proliferation, Science 2009 (324) (1979) 1029–1033, https://doi.org/10.1126/SCIENCE.1160809.

[56] L.J. Savic, J. Chapiro, G. Duwe, J.-F. Geschwind, Targeting glucose metabolism in cancer: a new class of agents for loco-regional and systemic therapy of liver cancer and beyond? Hepat. Oncol. 3 (2016) 19–28, https://doi.org/10.2217/HEP.15.36.

[57] S. Ganapathy-Kanniappan, J.F.H. Geschwind, Tumor glycolysis as a target for cancer therapy: progress and prospects, Mol. Cancer (2013) 12, https://doi.org/10.1186/1476-4598-12-152.

[58] Y. Zhao, E.B. Butler, M. Tan, Targeting cellular metabolism to improve cancer therapeutics, Cell Death Dis. 4 (2013) 532, https://doi.org/10.1038/cddis.2013.60.

[59] C. Pecqueur, L. Oliver, K. Oizel, L. Lalier, F.M. Vallette, Targeting metabolism to induce cell death in cancer cells and cancer stem cells, Int. J. Cell Biol. 2013 (2013) 13, https://doi.org/10.1155/2013/805975.

[60] Y. Liu, Y. Cao, W. Zhang, S. Bergmeier, Y. Qian, H. Akbar, et al., A small-molecule inhibitor of glucose transporter 1 downregulates glycolysis, induces cell-cycle arrest, and inhibits cancer cell growth in vitro and in vivo, Mol. Cancer Ther. 11 (8) (2012) 1672–1682, https://doi.org/10.1158/1535-7163.MCT-12-0131.

[61] L. Jin, G.N. Alesi, S. Kang, Glutaminolysis as a target for cancer therapy, Oncogene 35 (2016) 3619–3625, https://doi.org/10.1038/onc.2015.447.

[62] B.J. Altman, Z.E. Stine, C.V. Dang, From Krebs to clinic: glutamine metabolism to cancer therapy, Nat. Rev. Cancer 16 (2016) 619–634, https://doi.org/10.1038/nrc.2016.71.

[63] B. Krümmel, T. Plötz, A. Jörns, S. Lenzen, I. Mehmeti, The central role of glutathione peroxidase 4 in the regulation of ferroptosis and its implications for pro-inflammatory cytokine-mediated, 1867 (6) (2021) 166114, https://doi.org/10.1016/j.bbadis.2021.166114.

[64] S.L. Pandrangi, P. Chittineedi, R. Chikati, J.A.N. Mosquera, S.N.S. Llaguno, G.J. Mohiddin, et al., Role of lipoproteins in the pathophysiology of breast cancer, Membranes (Basel) 12 (2022) 532, https://doi.org/10.3390/membranes12050532.

[65] Q. Meng, S. Shi, C. Liang, D. Liang, J. Hua, B. Zhang, et al., Abrogation of glutathione peroxidase-1 drives EMT and chemoresistance in pancreatic cancer by activating ROS-mediated Akt/GSK3β/snail signaling, Oncogene 37 (2018) 5843–5857, https://doi.org/10.1038/s41388-018-0392-z.

[66] N.S. Akins, T.C. Nielson, H. Le, v., Inhibition of glycolysis and glutaminolysis: an emerging drug discovery approach to combat cancer, Curr. Top. Med. Chem. 18 (2018) 494–504, https://doi.org/10.2174/1568026618666180523111351.

[67] P. Chittineedi, S.L. Pandrangi, G.J. Mohiddin, J.A.N. Mosquera, S.N.S. Llaguno, Concomitant therapy of Aq. Theobroma extract and doxorubicin reduces stemness and induces ferroptosis in therapeutic resistant cervical cancer cells, J. Carcinog. Mutagen. 13 (2022) 1–9.

[68] H. Pelicano, D.S. Martin, R.H. Xu, P. Huang, Glycolysis inhibition for anticancer treatment, Oncogene 25 (2006) 4633–4646, https://doi.org/10.1038/SJ.ONC.1209597.

[69] S.L. Pandrangi, S.A. Raju Bagadi, N.K. Sinha, M. Kumar, R. Dada, M. Lakhanpal, et al., Establishment and characterization of two primary breast cancer cell lines from young Indian breast cancer patients: mutation analysis, Cancer Cell Int. 14 (2014) 1–20, https://doi.org/10.1186/1475-2867-14-14.

[70] J.G. Manis, D. Schachter, Active transport of iron by intestine: effects of oral iron and pregnancy, Am. J. Phys. 203 (1962) 81–86, https://doi.org/10.1152/ajplegacy.1962.203.1.81.

[71] A.F. Abdel-Wahab, W. Mahmoud, R.M. Al-Harizy, Targeting glucose metabolism to suppress cancer progression: prospective of anti-glycolytic cancer therapy, Pharmacol. Res. 150 (2019) 104511, https://doi.org/10.1016/J.PHRS.2019.104511.

The role of one-carbon amino acids in tumor-immune metabolism: From oncogenesis to therapy

3

Suchandrima Saha and Monisankar Ghosh

Department of Pathology, Renaissance School of Medicine, Stony Brook University,
Stony Brook, NY, United States

Introduction

One of the trademark capabilities of malignant cells is proliferative advantage that is demonstrated by rapid growth, and to accommodate their enhanced proliferation, tumor cells enhance their metabolic rate to provide sufficient cellular building blocks (proteins, DNA, RNA, and lipids) and energy [1]. This increased demand for metabolites often involves the activation of prominent oncogenes, including Ras and c-Myc, or loss of tumor suppressors such as PTEN and P53, driving changes in cellular metabolism [2,3]. However, these advantages also highlight vulnerabilities specific to these malignant cells. One of the most important vulnerabilities depicted by cancer cells is an increased demand for amino acids (AAs) and to accommodate them, which often results in a dependency on exogenous sources of AAs or requires upregulation of de novo synthesis. While the tendency of Warburg effect has long been recognized, their dependency on AAs came decades later. Interestingly the dependency of tumor cells toward AAs is not only limited to essential amino acids (EAA), the type that the body cannot synthesize, but also several nonessential amino acids (NEAA) appear to be rate limiting for the growth of tumor cells [4]. Skewed AA metabolism has been recognized as a key determinant of drug resistance in tumors to ultimately satisfy the cellular demands of homeostasis, energy, and biomass production [5,6]. Furthermore, in the context of anticancer drugs and metabolic reprogramming in response to anticancer therapies, a diverse metabolic adaption occurs that is induced by drug-specific resistance and therapeutic pressure [7,8]. Numerous investigations point out that drug resistance mechanisms of cancer cells, tumor heterogeneity, and tumor immune microenvironment inhibit therapeutic efficacy and inhibit the approaches and efforts to overcome drug resistance.

A major determinant of therapeutic interventions and a way to increase their efficacy is not only AA availability but also its impact on immune surveillance [3].

Cancer Epigenetics and Nanomedicine. https://doi.org/10.1016/B978-0-443-13209-4.00007-6
Copyright © 2024 Elsevier Inc. All rights reserved, including those for text and data mining, AI training, and similar technologies.

51

A key criterion to generate effector T-cell function is determined by its ability of clonal expansion and maturation process that requires increased metabolic needs for glucose and AAs. Thus, AA depletion suppresses the antitumor activity of immune cells. Furthermore, cancer cells suppress immune cell function as it competes for specific AAs, and therefore AA depletion strategies might compromise the activity of immune cells [9].

One-carbon metabolism is a series of interlinking metabolic pathways that comprise folate and methionine cycles and support the highly proliferative cancer cells by providing them with nucleotides and methyl groups. AAs like methionine (Met), serine (Ser), and glycine (Gly) are major sources of one-carbon, and their functions in cancer and immune cells have been well studied.

Met is critical for T-cell survival, and Met starvation causes alterations in histone methylation that impair T-cell function [10]. Dietary supplementation of Met can restore those epigenetic alterations and increase T-cell immunity in tumor-bearing mice and patients with colon cancer [10]. Serine is required for T-cell expansion and effector functions even in optimal glucose concentrations that is sufficient to support T-cell activation, bioenergetics, and effector function [11].

Growing literary evidence suggests that modulating AA metabolism and depletion or supplementation of AA availability could be an effective therapeutic strategy [12,13]; however, before AA depletion can be clinically applied, the metabolic signature of a cancer cell type needs to be thoroughly investigated, and extrinsic factors like the immune cells and specific impact on the immune system need to be considered before devising therapeutic interventions.

In this chapter we will discuss evidence from recent studies for the essential roles of AAs driving one-carbon metabolism and how these AAs also impact immune cell function and will summarize the key studies relating to the targeting of AA metabolism in cancer therapy.

One-carbon metabolism

Folate and methionine cycles comprise the one-carbon metabolism, where it provides the cancer cells with nucleotides for rapid proliferative potential and transferrable methyl groups for cellular methylation reactions (Fig. 1). S-Adenosyl-L-methionine (SAM) is an important biological methyl donor that links one-carbon metabolism to the methylation status of the cells, and frequent alteration of methyltransferases and demethylases are observed in cancerous state [14].

Methionine

Methionine is an EAA that is involved in major metabolic pathways, namely protein synthesis, one-carbon metabolism, sulfur metabolism, epigenetic modification, and redox maintenance [15]. It is a precursor for AA cysteine; contributes to polyamine biosynthesis; is indispensable for the generation of SAM; and is the sole methyl

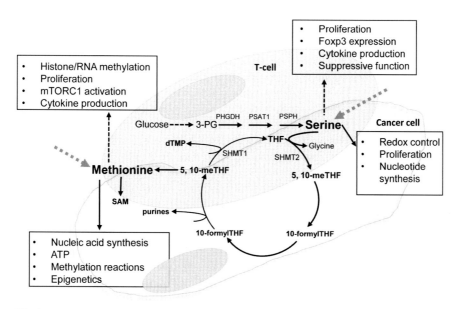

FIG. 1

A diagrammatic representation of one-carbon metabolism where cancer cell and T-cell have been integrated with appropriation of inputs and outputs. The two major nutrient sources, methionine and serine, can be synthesized de novo or could be taken up exogenously and are converted into a variety of outputs such as proliferation, redox balance, methylation, and cytokine production, albeit based on the cell type. Reactions not drawn for intermediates could be considered negligible in this context.

donor for the methylation of DNA, histones, and proteins. Methionine catabolism is highly upregulated in cancer cells as a result of Met adenosyltransferase 2A (MAT2A) upregulation [16], and thus, methionine metabolism is considered to play an important role in malignant transformation. Distal to MAT2A, the methyltransferase nicotinamide N-methyltransferase (NNMT) catalyzes the conversion of SAM into S-adenosylhomocysteine (SAH), and by effectively consuming all available SAM, this enzyme prevents DNA and histone methylation, and changing the epigenetic landscape of cancer cells [17]. Other than the exogenous source, the methionine salvage pathway is another source for methionine availability. The key enzymes of this pathway are methylthioadenosine phosphorylase (MTAP) and Met synthase (MS) [18,19], and because these enzymes are downregulated in cancer cells, MTAP is frequently deleted with the cell cycle regulator CDKN2A [20], rendering cells exclusively dependent on methionine import from the extracellular environment [18,20].

Given its central role in methylation and methionine being an EAA, it is a prime candidate for therapeutic targeting, particularly in tumors that are driven by mutations in epigenetic modifiers and methyl transferases.

Serine

Serine is a NEAA and can be derived from glycine. In healthy individuals, serine is important for brain function, especially the central nervous system (CNS), production of nucleotides, immune system, and fatty acid metabolism. However, enhanced serine metabolism has been reported in multiple tumor types [21,22]. It is a precursor of AAs such as glycine, cysteine, purine nucleotides, and glutathione [23]. Furthermore, serine supports one-carbon metabolism, supplying a carbon source [24]. And while serine can be transported within the cells from the extracellular space, tumor cells synthesize serine from the glycolytic intermediate 3-phosphoglycerate (3-PG) via the three important enzymes known as phosphoglycerate dehydrogenase (PHGDH), phosphoserine aminotransferase 1 (PSAT1), and phosphoserine phosphatase (PSPH) [23]. Serine gets converted to glycine by an enzyme called serine hydroxymethyltransferase (SHMT), and this process generates one additional carbon to tetrahydrofolate, producing CH_2-THF that is required for purine synthesis and made into thymidine (Fig. 1). Additionally, CH_2-THF helps in SAM generation that is required for methylation reactions. Due to its versatile use, serine metabolism or nutrient availability is crucial for cancer cell proliferation [25]. Recent evidence has suggestively explored the relationship between serine and glycine. In the presence of abundant serine availability, cancer cells prefer to uptake serine and excrete glycine and only prefer to take up glycine when serine is not present [26]. This preference is due to the fact that the conversion of serine over glycine gives off an extra one-carbon that the cells use to synthesize nucleotides and, ultimately, for DNA replication.

Another important enzyme that modulates the serine biosynthesis pathway is pyruvate kinase, an enzyme involved in the last step of glycolysis, and its M2 isoform is involved in cancer. Its activity inversely correlates with the endogenous activity of serine synthesis enzymes. Cancer cells decrease pyruvate kinase muscle isozyme M2 (PKM2) activity when there are decreased cellular levels of serine, and thus, the glycolytic flux is directed toward serine synthesis and makes up for the decreased serine levels. Furthermore, decreased PKM2 activity reduces the cancer cell's dependence for oxygen and its potential for increased survival in hypoxic conditions. Another enzyme that is expressed in cancer cells is the serine catabolic enzyme, mitochondrial serine hydroxymethyltransferase 2 (SHMT2), which is upregulated in response to hypoxia. Depletion of SHMT2 modulates the redox potential of the cancer cells to induce reactive oxygen species (ROS) and hypoxia-induced cell death [27].

In colorectal cancer cells, PSAT1 overexpression promoted tumorigenic potential in xenograft mouse model and promoted resistance to oxaliplatin treatment [28]. Additionally, in colorectal cancer cells PSAT1 was highly expressed in cancer tissues and both depletion of both exogenous and endogenous sources of serine inhibited tumor growth and increased the efficacy of 5-FU [29]. In esophageal squamous cell carcinoma (ESCC) tissues, there is increased expression of PSAT1 cancer tissues compared to its nonadjacent counterpart, and it was found to be associated with the disease stage [30]. NRAS harboring melanoma cancer cells exhibit resistance to

MAPK inhibitors, and upregulated expression of PHGDH is responsible for the resistance to MAPK kinase inhibitors. Depleted PHGDH expression with simultaneous administration of MAPK kinase inhibitors modulated cell glutathione levels to combat cellular proliferation [31]. Consistently enhanced expression of PHGDH, PSAT1, and PSPH was seen in v-Raf murine sarcoma viral oncogene homolog B (BRAF) inhibitor-resistant melanoma cells, and depletion of PHGDH sensitizes melanoma cells to BRAF inhibitors [32]. In multiple myeloma cancer, serine biosynthesis is upregulated through PHGDH, leading to increased antioxidant capacity [33]. In hepatocellular carcinoma, PHGDH is responsible for sorafenib resistance. Inactivation of PHGDH modulates the redox capacity of the cells by decreasing the production of α-ketoglutarate, serine, and NADPH, consequently elevating ROS levels and sensitizing sorafenib-resistant cells to treatment [34]. In triple-negative breast cancer (TNBC), PHGDH is upregulated, and depletion of the key enzyme sensitizes cells to doxorubicin-induced oxidative stress [35]. Furthermore, hypoxia induced the expression of PHGDH and SHMT2 in glioma and breast cancer stem cells (CSCs), and knockdown of PHGDH leads to elevated ROS levels to induce apoptosis [36,37]. In EGFR-positive lung adenocarcinomas, depletion of PHGDH or treatment with a PHGDH inhibitor increased ROS stress and DNA damage, to sensitize cells to erlotinib [38].

One-carbon metabolism and T-cell function

As discussed earlier, cellular metabolism is a critical criterion and control mechanism actively proliferating cells, that is, the immune cells and most importantly T-cells [39]. Immune cells that mediate the adaptive immune response are known as the T-cells and are defined by the expression of CD3 molecules on the surface and there are two types of important subsets of T-cells: firstly, the ones that express CD8 surface molecules, and secondly, another important subtype is the helper T-cells or CD4 T-cells that display function that are either proinflammatory or anti-inflammatory that secrete cytokines that help suppressive regulatory T-cell function that are immune suppressive. T-helper cells can also be differentiated by the expression of specific transcription factors, such as TBET for Th1 cells that produce IFN-γ and TNF, GATA3 for Th2 cells that produce IL-4, and RORγT for Th17 cells that produce IL-17 [40]. T regulatory cells, on the other hand, are defined by increased expression of CD25 and the master transcriptional regulator FOXP3 [41]. Although a lot has been studied on the importance of cellular metabolism on T-cell function, it is only recently that one-carbon metabolism in T-cells is appreciated.

Dependency of methionine metabolism in T-cells

Methionine is crucial for T-cell differentiation and activation [42,43], and evidence suggests that activated T-cells have increased expression of genes involved in methionine cycle. Most importantly, these cells do not carry out de novo synthesis of methionine from serine or glucose, and therefore, it has a nonredundant role in activated T-cells [44]. Upon T-cell activation, methionine metabolism is induced, which leads to rapid uptake of methionine. This leads to the transfer of the exogenous methionine group to methyl donor moiety of SAM [45] and maintains H3K4me3 (transactivating) histone methylation in T-cells. Importantly, transactivating H3K4me3 methylation is critically sensitive to varying concentrations of extracellular methionine; however, other types of methylation remain unaffected [45]. In T-helper cells, TCR engagement leads to upregulation of methyltransferases associated with H3K4me3 or H3K27me3 (suppressive) histone methylation [46]. Modulation of extracellular methionine levels leads to changes in histone methylation and could thus result in attenuated cell cycling, proliferation, and cytokine production by both T-helper and T-cytotoxic cells [45,46].

Restriction of extracellular methionine levels limits the expansion of inflammatory Th17 cells and maintains T-cell-mediated inflammation [43]. Essentially important for maintaining the robustness of immunotherapy is to preserve the anticancer efficacy of cytotoxic T-cells in the tumor microenvironment, and competition for methionine between cancer cells and T-cells is a key determinant for prognosis and efficacy of immunotherapy. Of note, cancer cells that overexpress the methionine transporter SLC43A2 outcompete T-cells for methionine [10]. This metabolic competition decreases methionine metabolism and related metabolites in T-cells, resulting in weakened STAT5-mediated anticancer immunity of effector T-cells. Accordingly, T-cells deprived of extracellular methionine depict reduced RNA methylation, as indicated by decreases in N6 adenosine (m6A) and methyl-cytosine (5mc). In mice model of experimental autoimmune encephalomyelitis (EAE), restricting methionine leads to reduced disease severity associated with decreased levels of inflammatory cytokines and pathological T-cells in the brain [45]. These findings imply that one-carbon metabolism and methionine are involved in T-cell function. Evidence indicates that increased extracellular methionine uptake by T-cells is required for T-cell function. Interestingly, methionine supplementation in tumors restored T-cell immunity and reduced tumor sizes [10], and dietary methionine restriction suppressed tumor growth and sensitized tumor cells to chemotherapy [47].

Restricting dietary serine, therefore, indicates a potential side effect where depletion of extracellular methionine might resultantly weaken the T-cytotoxic adaptive immune response during immunotherapy. Also, a recent study showed that dietary methionine restriction had contrasting effects on tumor progression and therapeutic response in immunodeficient and immunocompetent mice [48], where dietary methionine restriction enhanced tumor progression and repressed T-cell activation in an immunocompetent mouse colon cancer model. Furthermore, restriction of dietary methionine affects the gut microbiota, which promotes anticancer immunity [48].

Dependency of serine metabolism in T-cells

As discussed in the previous section, serine is an NEAA that is a major one-carbon source and fuels the one-carbon metabolism by donating one-carbon units. Like methionine, serine also contributes to T-cell proliferation, and numerous literary evidence has suggested that T-cell activation is accompanied by elevated expression of genes involved in one-carbon metabolism [41,49,50]. Activated T-cells have increased expression of SHMT2 [49,51] and inhibition of SHMT2 or extracellular serine and glycine depletion in mouse $CD4^+$ and $CD8^+$ T effector T-cells leads to impaired cell proliferation and survival; however, it does not impact the expression of activation markers or cytokine production upon TCR or antigenic stimulation [41,49]. These studies reinforce the role of serine in one-carbon metabolism as it is important for maintaining redox balance and nucleotide production that is ultimately essential and critical for T-cell proliferation.

Both malignant cells and activated T-cells have the tendency for rapid proliferation; however, they differ in their use of one-carbon metabolism. Cancer cells have upregulated serine synthesis gene expression, which is required even in the presence of abundant extracellular serine, and inhibition of these genes leads to attenuation of major signaling pathways including decreased glycolysis, TCA cycle, and pentose phosphate pathway [52]. Contrastingly, in effector $CD8^+$ T-cells, neither silencing serine synthesis enzymes nor removing extracellular serine affected the expression of T-cell activation lineage markers such as CD44 and CD25 [53]. Serine can be synthesized endogenously using PHGDH, PSAT1, and PSPH or can be imported exogenously using transporters and therefore restriction of both sources is important to restrict cell proliferation. However, in T-cells; restriction of endogenous or exogenous source alone was sufficient to halt T-cell proliferation [53,54]. These results indicate that, in T-cells, any one source of serine that is either de novo serine synthesis or extracellular serine uptake could compensate for the loss of one source of serine availability as long as an optimal level of serine is present for T-cell expansion. Effector $CD4^+$ T-cells cultured without serine/glycine showed a significant reduction in proliferation [41]. Accordingly, in vitro glycine and formate supplementation was able to rescue the T-cell proliferation [54].

Another important regulator of metabolism and cellular redox balance in T-cells is glutathione (GSH) [50,55], and GSH depletion leads to increased ROS production that interferes with T-cell signaling at multiple points [56]. Tregs are deficient for the catalytic subunit of GCL (*Gclc*), which catalyzes GSH synthesis [50], and one-carbon metabolism increases Treg proliferation. Furthermore, the increased need for serine by these cells resulted in increased glycolysis and oxidative phosphorylation. Interestingly, increased serine levels and one-carbon metabolism in Tregs not only increased their proliferation but also activated mTORC1 and reduced Foxp3 expression, leading to impaired Treg suppressive function and promoted autoimmunity [50]. Pharmacologic or genetic inhibition of PHGDH restored glycolysis and suppressive function to the mutant Tregs [50]. These findings highlight the importance of serine regulating one-carbon metabolism and affirm the importance of serine in supporting the expansion and functions of effector T-cells, Tregs, and normal T-cell homeostasis.

Restriction of AAs as therapy

For continued sustenance and rapid proliferation of cancer cells, extreme metabolic demands arise, and therefore, an abundant supply of glucose and AAs is required [57]. The capacity to synthesize NEAA de novo is lost in cancer cells, and contrastingly, this phenomenon is still intact in nonmalignant population, providing a window of opportunity to specifically target the cancer cells, resulting in the development of AA restriction as a viable and effective therapeutic strategy. A number of preclinical and clinical studies have been conducted to exploit this possibility and specifically target the neoplastic population by developing and optimizing strategies that include dietary restriction of AAs and development of pharmacologic or enzymatic inhibitors that target AA availability and/or metabolism. All these strategies highlight the potential and vulnerabilities and open the possibilities to use these strategies in clinic.

Therapeutic restriction of methionine

One of the fundamental hallmarks of cancer is its dependence on methionine metabolism that results in methionine addiction within the cancer cells [58–68]. The proliferative capacity of cancer cells that is dependent on exogenous methionine is known as methionine dependence or Hoffmann effect, where it was demonstrated that neoplastic cells were capable of endogenously high levels of methionine to overall increase their transmethylation reactions and the cause of methionine dependence [62,63,69]. Therefore, modulating methionine levels could affect the nucleotide levels and redox status of cancer cells, and this might induce metabolic vulnerabilities in drug-resistant tumors.

Promising antitumor effects of enzymatic depletion of methionine have been observed using the bacterially derived enzyme L-methionine-gamma-lyase (Methioninase), which was first isolated from *Clostridium sporogenes*, where it converts methionine to α-ketobutyrate and ammonia. Treatment with methioninase successfully inhibited the growth of Walker carcinosarcoma 256 in male Wistar rats [70]. Pancreatic and melanoma exhibit high levels of methionine dependency, and when patient-derived orthotopic xenograft (PDX) mice were treated with recombinant methioninase, there was a reduction in tumor volume [71]. The effects of this enzyme were well studied both in vitro and in vivo in neuroblastoma, colorectal cancer, melanoma, and brain tumors [18,72] and, given the robust potential of methioninase in hampering tumor growth in preclinical models, led to the design and development of both intravenous and oral recombinant methioninase in human clinical trials. In a phase 1 clinical trial that was attributed to assess metastatic breast cancer patients, administration of recombinant methioninase led to a significant decrease in plasma methionine levels [73]. Although this trial did not assess antitumor activity, another study depicted that treatment with oral recombinant methioninase demonstrated a decrease in advanced antigen-specific prostate cancer [74]. Furthermore methioninase showed limited toxicity in phase 1 trials [18].

Another strategy to maximize the efficacy of cancer therapy is to limit dietary methionine as restriction of methionine could possibly alter the histone methylation status that could in turn affect the related epigenetic modifications and one-carbon metabolism. Under dietary methionine restriction, cancer cells are forced to increase methionine production from homocysteine consuming leading the malignant cells to consume intracellular CH_2-THF, resulting in decreased folate cycle-related metabolites and nucleotide biosynthesis [75]. Therefore, methionine restriction could be considered as an attractive treatment option with high feasibility [76].

Indeed in TNBC cells, it has been documented that methionine depletion resulted in reduced proliferation of taxane-resistant TNBC cells with decreased levels of methionine incorporation into SAM and SAH, resulting in DNA hypomethylation [77]. Methionine-free diet not only attenuated TNBC cell growth, but several studies show that it also impacted the growth potential of colorectal cancer, sarcoma, glioma, and mixed-lineage leukemia (MLL)-rearranged leukemia and suppressed concomitant metastasis formation [78,79]. Notably, cellular or in vivo methionine restriction changes intracellular S-adenosyl methionine (SAM) and S-adenosyl homocysteine (SAH) levels and H3K4me3 histone methylation, resulting in altered gene expression and metabolism [80]. In addition, in patient-derived xenograft models of colorectal cancer, dietary methionine restriction sensitizes cancer cells to 5-fluorouracil (5-FU) [47]. Likewise, treatment of MAT2A inhibitor FIDAS-5 reduced SAM and SAH levels in tumor-initiating cells derived from primary NSCLC adenocarcinoma samples, thus altering the tumorigenic potential of tumor-initiating cells [81]. Evidence shows Methionine restriction blocks cyclic GMP-AMP synthase (cGAS) methylation, which is the major cytosolic DNA sensor and activates type I interferon signaling and plays an essential role in antitumor immunity. Blocking cGAS methylation, methionine restriction enhances cGAS-mediated antitumor immunity and suppresses colorectal tumorigenesis [82].

Not just cancer cells, methionine restriction likewise had the potential to affect the stemness of CSCs, resulting in improved treatment outcomes [83]. Indeed, methionine restriction inhibits mammosphere formation and decreases high-CD44- and low-CD24-expressing breast cancer CSC population cells, sensitizing CSCs to inhibition of the enzyme MAT2A, which converts methionine to SAM [84]. Additionally, methionine restriction primes TNBC tumors to TRAIL receptor agonist lexatumumab and induces apoptosis of TNBC cells [85]. To further explore the potential of methionine restriction in clinics, a study showed that dietary methionine restriction is relatively well tolerated over a period of 8–17 weeks, with limited side effects [86].

Therapeutic restriction of serine

Cell proliferation in cancer is shown to be arrested in the absence of serine. Therefore, this phenomenon could be utilized for developing potential antitumor therapies. Serine synthesis enzymes are major contributors to endogenous serine production, and PHGDH catalyzes the first rate-limiting step of serine synthesis to provide one-carbon units for nucleotide synthesis as well as is a critical substrate for protein synthesis. Therefore, targeting this relationship could be used to devise a therapeutic strategy, and indeed, it has been observed that PHGDH expression and activity are higher compared to normal cells [87]. PHGDH inhibitors suppress cancer cell proliferation in vitro and in patient-derived xenograft (PDX) models [88,89]. PHGDH is highly expressed in cancer cells, and in 4% of melanoma and pancreatic cancer cases,

PHGDH gene is amplified and TNBCs have increased PHGDH expression. Thus, PHGDH inhibitors have been developed to interrupt one-carbon metabolism and simultaneously target nucleotide metabolism in cancer [90]. Several PHGDH inhibitors have been generated, like ketothioamides, indole amides, BI-4924, piperazine-1-thiourea-based inhibitors, and allosteric inhibitors that have both in vitro and in vivo efficacy [91–96]. NCT-503 was developed that decreased glucose carbon influx into serine and inhibited incorporation of serine into AMP and dTMP to ultimately hamper nucleotide production. This drug showed an effect on PHGDH-dependent cancer cells and decreased the growth of orthotopic breast tumor xenografts [97]. Another notable PHGDH inhibitor, PH-755 (WO2016040449A1), was able to repress brain metastasis from MDA-MB-231-derived xenografts and increase survival [98]. Although inhibiting PHGDH may seem to be an ideal therapy to inhibit tumor proliferation, unfortunately, low PHGDH expression may cause harmful effects [99]. In mice, PHGDH deletion led to embryonic lethality due to faults in development affecting the CNS. Further studies are required to decipher how PHGDH activity can be limited without harming the brain metabolism of the patient, and potential therapies should aim to develop PHGDH inhibitors that are unable to cross the blood-brain barrier and avoid neurological complications.

Since de novo synthesized serine is converted to glycine by hydroxymethyl transferases, SHMT1 and SHMT2, which produce glycine and generates a methyl group to donate to THF, therapeutic strategy has been devised to target both SHMT1 and SHMT2 [100–103]. Importantly, antifolate inhibitors also significantly reduce the activity of SHMTs. Important inhibitors like pyrrolo[3,2-*d*]pyrimidine AGF347, SHIN1, and SHIN2 target both SHMT1 and SHMT2; project an efficacy against cancer; and are associated with prolonged survival [101,104]. Furthermore a synergism between SHIN2 and methotrexate has been demonstrated. Another drug that is the antidepressant sertraline, previously described to inhibit serotonin reuptake, has been repurposed as an SHMT1 and SHMT2 inhibitor and has been shown to inhibit breast tumor growth [105].

Since cancer cells are dependent on serine and become auxotrophic for serine, restricting serine extracellularly could be a feasible therapeutic approach [88]. It has been documented that TP53-null tumors have repressed growth in the presence of serine depletion [106]. Consistently, several preclinical studies have suggested that combinatorial dietary restriction of Ser and glycine suppresses tumor cell proliferation in mouse models of intestinal cancer and lymphoma [106], as well as in a PDX colon cancer model [106]. Importantly, numerous tumors have been reported to be sensitive to PHGDH loss or inhibition, particularly in the context of serine/glycine deprivation, which suggests that dietary manipulation may affect tumorigenesis [107–109]. The exact mechanistic pathway with which the dietary sources and the availability of serine/glycine affect the tumor microenvironment and alter the one-carbon metabolism remains to be studied; however, studies have revealed promising data which demonstrates that dietary serine starvation in combination with phenformin-enhanced oxidative phosphorylation and prolonged the survival of Eu-Myc lymphoma mice [107]. Similarly, serine starvation and PHGDH inhibition cooperatively curb in vivo tumor growth in various xenograft mouse models [109].

Conclusion and future directions

The broad mutational heterogeneity of malignant cells highlights a growing need for personalized medicine, and the therapeutic strategies that currently exist target the many pathways associated with cancer progression. In spite of the safety profile, patients suffer due to the toxicity of treatment or adaption of cancer cells to manipulations that ultimately lead to chemoresistance. This problem leaves an opportunity for researchers to identify novel signatures and therapeutic interventions to tackle resistance and cancer recurrence. AAs are required for a number of vital signaling processes, and cancer cells display genetic defects that hinder their ability to obtain an adequate supply of the AAs required for progression. Over the years the knowledge regarding the essential roles of AAs in driving metabolism and drug resistance in cancers has increased over the years and this has unlocked the potential to devise strategies for overcoming drug resistance.

Therefore, AA depletion strategies offer a great avenue in the treatment of cancer. A major advantage over other therapeutic regimens is their limited toxicity and their safety profile. However, before AA depletion strategy could be broadly applied to clinic, the dependency and plasticity of the metabolic signature of a particular type of cancer and microenvironment needs to be studied in detail, allowing the specific targeting of the right AA. The biggest challenge is dealing with metabolic plasticity and targeting specific enzymes that are intertwined in various pathways, but looking at passenger deletions or amplification of a particular gene could provide a roadmap for clinical stratification of tumors. AA restriction and enzymatic inhibition of AA metabolism have been successful in preclinical and initial clinical trials as viable strategies against cancer treatment. These approaches have the potential to revolutionize standard therapeutic regimens and practice and could reverse relapse and reoccurrence of many cancers. Importantly, metabolic inhibitors are unlikely to be effective as a single agent, as metabolic plasticity of cancer cells exposed to AA starvation may render cells resistant to the therapy. It is therefore likely that future applications of AA depletion strategies will involve a combination with targeted agents to overcome the phenomenon of resistance. This would imply the use of a multidrug strategy that will simultaneously inhibit different signaling pathways and account for interactions within the tumor microenvironment. Therefore, AA depletion strategies need to be developed that increase the efficacy and durability of the response. Further work in this direction could lead to the biomarker development and design of strategic personalized amino acid modulation that would advance cancer treatment.

References

[1] E.L. Lieu, T. Nguyen, S. Rhyne, J. Kim, Amino acids in cancer, Exp. Mol. Med. 52 (1) (2020) 15–30.
[2] L. Vettore, R.L. Westbrook, D.A. Tennant, New aspects of amino acid metabolism in cancer, Br. J. Cancer 122 (2) (2020) 150–156.
[3] J. Kim, R.J. DeBerardinis, Mechanisms and implications of metabolic heterogeneity in cancer, Cell Metab. 30 (3) (2019) 434–446.

[4] B.H. Choi, J.L. Coloff, The diverse functions of non-essential amino acids in cancer, Cancers 11 (5) (2019) 675.

[5] H.C. Yoo, J.M. Han, Amino acid metabolism in cancer drug resistance, Cells 11 (1) (2022) 140.

[6] N. Muhammad, H.M. Lee, J. Kim, Oncology therapeutics targeting the metabolism of amino acids, Cells 9 (8) (2020) 1904.

[7] E.A. Zaal, C.R. Berkers, The influence of metabolism on drug response in cancer, Front. Oncol. 8 (2018) 500.

[8] Y. Zhao, E.B. Butler, M. Tan, Targeting cellular metabolism to improve cancer therapeutics, Cell Death Dis. 4 (2013) e532.

[9] W. Wang, W. Zou, Amino acids and their transporters in T cell immunity and cancer therapy, Mol. Cell 80 (3) (2020) 384–395.

[10] Y. Bian, W. Li, D.M. Kremer, P. Sajjakulnukit, S.S. Li, J. Crespo, Z.C. Nwosu, L. Zhang, A. Czerwonka, A. Pawlowska, et al., Cancer SLC43A2 alters T cell methionine metabolism and histone methylation, Nature 585 (7824) (2020) 277–282.

[11] E.H. Ma, G. Bantug, T. Griss, S. Condotta, R.M. Johnson, B. Samborska, N. Mainolfi, V. Suri, H. Guak, M.L. Balmer, M.J. Verway, et al., Serine is an essential metabolite for effector T cell expansion, Cell Metab. 25 (2) (2017) 345–357.

[12] M. Butler, L.T. van der Meer, F.N. van Leeuwen, Amino acid depletion therapies: starving cancer cells to death, Trends Endocrinol. Metab. 32 (6) (2021) 367–381.

[13] E. Pranzini, E. Pardella, P. Paoli, S.M. Fendt, M.L. Taddei, Metabolic reprogramming in anticancer drug resistance: a focus on amino acids, Trends Cancer 7 (8) (2021) 682–699.

[14] P. Chi, C.D. Allis, G.G. Wang, Covalent histone modifications—miswritten, misinterpreted and mis-erased in human cancers, Nat. Rev. Cancer 10 (7) (2010) 457–469.

[15] S.M. Sanderson, X. Gao, Z. Dai, J.W. Locasale, Methionine metabolism in health and cancer: a nexus of diet and precision medicine, Nat. Rev. Cancer 19 (11) (2019) 625–637.

[16] Z. Wang, L.Y. Yip, J.H. Lee, Z. Wu, H.Y. Chew, P.K. Chong, C.C. Teo, H.Y. Ang, K.L. Peh, J. Yuan, S. Ma, Methionine is a metabolic dependency of tumor-initiating cells, Nat. Med. 25 (5) (2019) 825–837.

[17] O.A. Ulanovskaya, A.M. Zuhl, B.F. Cravatt, NNMT promotes epigenetic remodeling in cancer by creating a metabolic methylation sink, Nat. Chem. Biol. 9 (5) (2013) 300–306.

[18] H.S. Fernandes, C.S. Silva Teixeira, P.A. Fernandes, M.J. Ramos, N.M.F.S.A. Cerqueira, Amino acid deprivation using enzymes as a targeted therapy for cancer and viral infections, Expert Opin. Ther. Pat. 27 (3) (2017) 283–297.

[19] S. Chaturvedi, R.M. Hoffman, J.R. Bertino, Exploiting methionine restriction for cancer treatment, Biochem. Pharmacol. 154 (2018) 170–173.

[20] Z. Dai, V. Ramesh, J.W. Locasale, The evolving metabolic landscape of chromatin biology and epigenetics, Nat. Rev. Genet. 21 (12) (2020) 737–753.

[21] A.C. Newman, O.D. Maddocks, Serine and functional metabolites in cancer, Trends Cell Biol. 27 (9) (2017) 645–657.

[22] R. Possemato, K.M. Marks, Y.D. Shaul, M.E. Pacold, D. Kim, K. Birsoy, S. Sethumadhavan, H.K. Woo, H.G. Jang, A.K. Jha, et al., Functional genomics reveal that the serine synthesis pathway is essential in breast cancer, Nature 476 (7360) (2011) 346–350.

[23] K.R. Mattaini, M.R. Sullivan, M.G. Vander Heiden, The importance of serine metabolism in cancer, J. Cell Biol. 214 (3) (2016) 249–257.

[24] O.D. Maddocks, C.F. Labuschagne, P.D. Adams, K.H. Vousden, Serine metabolism supports the methionine cycle and DNA/RNA methylation through *de novo* ATP synthesis in cancer cells, Mol. Cell 61 (2) (2016) 210–221.

[25] N. Kanarek, B. Petrova, D.M. Sabatini, Dietary modifications for enhanced cancer therapy, Nature 579 (7800) (2020) 507–517.

[26] C.F. Labuschagne, N.J. Van Den Broek, G.M. Mackay, K.H. Vousden, O.D.K. Maddocks, Serine, but not glycine, supports one-carbon metabolism and proliferation of cancer cells, Cell Rep. 7 (4) (2014) 1248–1258.

[27] J.B. Ye, J. Fan, S. Venneti, Y.W. Wan, B.R. Pawel, J. Zhang, L.W.S. Finley, C. Lu, T. Lindsten, J.R. Cross, et al., Serine catabolism regulates mitochondrial redox control during hypoxia, Cancer Discov. 4 (12) (2014) 1406–1417.

[28] N. Vie, V. Copois, C. Bascoul-Mollevi, V. Denis, N. Bec, B. Robert, C. Fraslon, E. Conseiller, F. Molina, C. Larroque, et al., Overexpression of phosphoserine aminotransferase PSAT1 stimulates cell growth and increases chemoresistance of colon cancer cells, Mol. Cancer 7 (2008) 14.

[29] D.C. Montrose, S. Saha, M. Foronda, E.M. McNally, J. Chen, X.K. Zhou, T. Ha, J. Krumsiek, M. Buyukozkan, A. Verma, et al., Exogenous and endogenous sources of serine contribute to colon cancer metabolism, growth, and resistance to 5-fluorouracil, Cancer Res. 81 (9) (2021) 2275–2288.

[30] B. Liu, Y. Jia, Y. Cao, S. Wu, H. Jiang, X. Sun, J. Ma, X. Yin, A. Mao, M. Shang, Overexpression of phosphoserine aminotransferase 1 (PSAT1) predicts poor prognosis and associates with tumor progression in human esophageal squamous cell carcinoma, Cell. Physiol. Biochem. 39 (1) (2016) 395–406.

[31] M.Q. Nguyen, J.L.F. Teh, T.J. Purwin, I. Chervoneva, M.A. Davies, K.L. Nathanson, P.F. Cheng, M.P. Levesque, R. Dummer, A.E. Aplin, Targeting PHGDH upregulation reduces glutathione levels and resensitizes resistant NRAS-mutant melanoma to MAPK kinase inhibition, J. Invest. Dermatol. 140 (11) (2020) 2242–2252.

[32] K.C. Ross, A.J. Andrews, C.D. Marion, T.J. Yen, V. Bhattacharjee, Identification of the serine biosynthesis pathway as a critical component of BRAF inhibitor resistance of melanoma, pancreatic, and non-small cell lung cancer cells, Mol. Cancer 16 (8) (2017) 1596–1609.

[33] E.A. Zaal, W. Wu, G. Jansen, S. Zweegman, J. Cloos, C.R. Berkers, Bortezomib resistance in multiple myeloma is associated with increased serine synthesis, Cancer Metab. 5 (2017) 7.

[34] L. Wei, D. Lee, C.T. Law, M.S. Zhang, J.L. Shen, D.W.C. Chin, A. Zhang, F.H.C. Tsang, C.L.S. Wong, I.O.L. Ng, et al., Genome-wide CRISPR/Cas9 library screening identified PHGDH as a critical driver for Sorafenib resistance in HCC, Nat. Commun. 10 (1) (2019) 4681.

[35] X. Zhang, W. Bai, Repression of phosphoglycerate dehydrogenase sensitizes triple-negative breast cancer to doxorubicin, Cancer Chemother. Pharmacol. 78 (2016) 655–659.

[36] A.L. Engel, N.I. Lorenz, K. Klann, C. Munch, C. Depner, J.P. Steinbach, M.W. Ronellenfitsch, A.L. Luger, Serine-dependent redox homeostasis regulates glioblastoma cell survival, Br. J. Cancer 122 (9) (2021) 1391–1398.

[37] D. Samanta, Y. Park, S.A. Andrabi, L.M. Shelton, D.M. Gilkes, G.L. Semenza, PHGDH expression is required for mitochondrial redox homeostasis, breast cancer stem cell maintenance, and lung metastasis, Cancer Res. 76 (15) (2016) 4430–4442.

[38] J.K. Dong, H.M. Lei, Q. Liang, Y.B. Tang, Y. Zhou, Y. Wang, S. Zhang, W.B. Li, Y. Tong, G. Zhuang, et al., Overcoming erlotinib resistance in EGFR mutation-positive

lung adenocarcinomas through repression of phosphoglycerate dehydrogenase, Theranostics 8 (7) (2018) 1808–1823.

[39] I. Amelio, G. Melino, C. Frezza, C., Exploiting tumour addiction with a serine and glycine-free diet, Cell Death Differ. 24 (8) (2017) 1311.

[40] J. Zhu, H. Yamane, W.E. Paul, Differentiation of effector CD4 T cell populations, Annu. Rev. Immunol. 28 (2010) 445–489.

[41] M.Y. Fan, J.S. Low, N. Tanimine, K.K. Finn, B. Priyadharshini, S.K. Germana, S.M. Kaech, L.A. Turka, Differential roles of IL-2 signaling in developing versus mature Tregs, Cell Rep. 25 (5) (2018) 1204–1213.

[42] L.V. Sinclair, A.J.M. Howden, A. Brenes, L. Spinelli, J.L. Hukelmann, A.N. Macintyre, X.J. Liu, S. Thomson, P.M. Taylor, J.C. Rathmell, et al., Antigen receptor control of methionine metabolism in T cells, Elife 8 (2019) e44210.

[43] D.G. Roy, J. Chen, V. Mamane, E.H. Ma, B.M. Muhire, R.D. Sheldon, T. Shorstova, R. Koning, R.M. Johnson, E. Esaulova, K.S. Williams, Methionine metabolism shapes T helper cell responses through regulation of epigenetic reprogramming, Cell Metab. 31 (2) (2020) 250–266.

[44] N.N. Pavlova, J. Zhu, C.B. Thompson, The hallmarks of cancer metabolism: still emerging, Cell Metab. 34 (3) (2022) 355–377.

[45] K. DePeaux, G.M. Delgoffe, Metabolic barriers to cancer immunotherapy, Nat. Rev. Immunol. 21 (12) (2021) 785–797.

[46] M. Reina-Campos, N.E. Scharping, A. Goldrath, CD8+ T cell metabolism in infection and cancer, Nat. Rev. Immunol. 21 (11) (2021) 718–738.

[47] M.A. Abid, M.B. Abid, Commentary: dietary methionine influences therapy in mouse cancer models and alters human metabolism, Front. Oncol. 10 (2020) 1071.

[48] M. Ji, X. Xu, Q. Xu, X. Xu, M.A. Azcarate-Peril, X. Wu, J. Liu, J.W. Locasale, J.L. Li, I. Shats, et al., Dietary methionine restriction impairs anti-tumor immunity through gut microbiota, bioRxiv (2021).

[49] R.H. Noga, D. Santos, J.M. Ghergurovich, P.T. Sage, A. Reddy, S.B. Lovitch, N. Dephoure, et al., Mitochondrial biogenesis and proteome remodeling promote one-carbon metabolism for T cell activation, Cell Metab. 24 (1) (2016) 104–117.

[50] J. Muri, M. Kopf, Redox regulation of immunometabolism, Nat. Rev. Immunol. 21 (6) (2021) 363–381.

[51] G.S. Ducker, J.D. Rabinowitz, One-carbon metabolism in health and disease, Cell Metab. 25 (1) (2017) 27–42.

[52] M.A. Reid, A.E. Allen, S. Liu, M.V. Liberti, P. Liu, X. Liu, Z. Dai, X. Gao, Q. Wang, Y. Liu, L. Lai, Serine synthesis through PHGDH coordinates nucleotide levels by maintaining central carbon metabolism, Nat. Commun. 9 (1) (2018) 5442.

[53] E.H. Ma, M.J. Verway, R.M. Johnson, D.G. Roy, M. Steadman, S. Hayes, K.S. Williams, R.D. Sheldon, B. Samborska, P.A. Kosinski, H. Kim, et al., Metabolic profiling using stable isotope tracing reveals distinct patterns of glucose utilization by physiologically activated CD8+ T cells, Immunity 51 (5) (2019) 856–870.

[54] N. Ron-Harel, G. Notarangelo, J.M. Ghergurovich, J.A. Paulo, P.T. Sage, D. Santos, F.K. Satterstrom, S.P. Gygi, J.D. Rabinowitz, A.H. Sharpe, M.C. Haigis, Defective respiration and one-carbon metabolism contribute to impaired naive T cell activation in aged mice, Proc. Natl. Acad. Sci. 115 (52) (2018) 13347–13352.

[55] T.W. Mak, M. Grusdat, G.S. Duncan, C. Dostert, Y. Nonnenmacher, M. Cox, C. Binsfeld, Z. Hao, A. Brüstle, M. Itsumi, C. Jäger, Glutathione primes T cell metabolism for inflammation, Immunity 46 (4) (2017) 675–689.

[56] D.G. Franchina, C. Dostert, D. Brenner, Reactive oxygen species: involvement in T cell signaling and metabolism, Trends Immunol. 39 (6) (2018) 489–502.

[57] A.C. Gonçalves, E. Richiardone, J. Jorge, B. Polónia, C.P. Xavier, I.C. Salaroglio, C. Riganti, M.H. Vasconcelos, C. Corbet, A.B. Sarmento-Ribeiro, Impact of cancer metabolism on therapy resistance—clinical implications, Drug Resist. Updat. 59 (2021) 100797.

[58] K. Booher, D.W. Lin, S.L. Borrego, P. Kaiser, Downregulation of Cdc6 and pre-replication complexes in response to methionine stress in breast cancer cells, Cell Cycle 11 (23) (2012) 4414–4423.

[59] P.L. Chello, J.R. Bertino, Dependence of 5-methyltetrahydrofolate utilization by L5178Y murine leukemia cells in vitro on the presence of hydroxycobalamin and trans-cobalamin II, Cancer Res. 33 (8) (1973) 1898–1904.

[60] D.W. Coalson, J.O. Mecham, P.H. Stern, R.M. Hoffman, Reduced availability of endogenously synthesized methionine for S-adenosylmethionine formation in methionine-dependent cancer cells, Proc. Natl. Acad. Sci. 79 (14) (1982) 4248–4251.

[61] B.C. Halpern, B.R. Clark, D.N. Hardy, R.M. Halpern, R.A. Smith, The effect of replacement of methionine by homocystine on survival of malignant and normal adult mammalian cells in culture, Proc. Natl. Acad. Sci. 71 (4) (1974) 1133–1136.

[62] R.M. Hoffman, Development of recombinant methioninase to target the general cancer-specific metabolic defect of methionine dependence: a 40-year odyssey, Expert. Opin. Biol. Ther. 15 (1) (2015) 21–31.

[63] R.M. Hoffman, R.W. Erbe, High in vivo rates of methionine biosynthesis in transformed human and malignant rat cells auxotrophic for methionine, Proc. Natl. Acad. Sci. 73 (5) (1976) 1523–1527.

[64] R.M. Hoffman, S.J. Jacobsen, Reversible growth arrest in simian virus 40-transformed human fibroblasts, Proc. Natl. Acad. Sci. 77 (12) (1980) 7306–7310.

[65] R.M. Hoffman, S.J. Jacobsen, R.W. Erbe, Reversion to methionine independence in simian virus 40-transformed human and malignant rat fibroblasts is associated with altered ploidy and altered properties of transformation, Proc. Natl. Acad. Sci. 76 (3) (1979) 1313–1317.

[66] J.O. Mecham, D. Rowitch, C.D. Wallace, P.H. Stern, R.M. Hoffman, The metabolic defect of methionine dependence occurs frequently in human tumor cell lines, Biochem. Biophys. Res. Commun. 117 (2) (1983) 429–434.

[67] P.H. Stern, C.D. Wallace, R.M. Hoffman, Altered methionine metabolism occurs in all members of a set of diverse human tumor cell lines, J. Cell. Physiol. 119 (1) (1984) 29–34.

[68] J. Yamamoto, Q. Han, S. Inubushi, N. Sugisawa, K. Hamada, H. Nishino, K. Miyake, T. Kumamoto, R. Matsuyama, M. Bouvet, I. Endo, R.M. Hoffman, Histone methylation status of H3K4me3 and H3K9me3 under methionine restriction is unstable in methionine-addicted cancer cells, but stable in normal cells, Biochem. Biophys. Res. Commun. 533 (4) (2020) 1034–1038.

[69] P. Kaiser, Methionine dependence of cancer, Biomol. Ther. 10 (2020) 568.

[70] W. Kreis, C. Hession, Biological effects of enzymatic deprivation of L-methionine in cell culture and an experimental tumor, Cancer Res. 33 (8) (1973) 1866–1869.

[71] K. Kawaguchi, Q. Han, S. Li, Y. Tan, K. Igarashi, K. Miyake, T. Kiyuna, M. Miyake, B. Chemielwski, S.D. Nelson, T.A. Russell, Intra-tumor L-methionine level highly correlates with tumor size in both pancreatic cancer and melanoma patient-derived orthotopic xenograft (PDOX) nude-mouse models, Oncotarget 9 (13) (2018) 11119–11125.

[72] A.G. Maynard, N. Kanarek, NADH ties one-carbon metabolism to cellular respiration, Cell Metab. 31 (4) (2020) 660–662.

[73] Y. Tan, J. Zavala Sr., M. Xu, J. Zavala Jr., R.M. Hoffman, Serum methionine depletion without side effects by methioninase in metastatic breast cancer patients, Anticancer Res. 16 (6C) (1996) 3937.

[74] Q. Han, Y. Tan, R.M. Hoffman, Oral dosing of recombinant methioninase is associated with a 70% drop in PSA in a patient with bone-metastatic prostate cancer and 50% reduction in circulating methionine in a high-stage ovarian cancer patient, Anticancer Res. 40 (5) (2020) 2813–2819.

[75] X. Gao, S.M. Sanderson, Z. Dai, M.A. Reid, D.E. Cooper, M. Lu, J.P. Richie Jr., A. Ciccarella, A. Calcagnotto, P.G. Mikhael, et al., Dietary methionine influences therapy in mouse cancer models and alters human metabolism, Nature 572 (7769) (2019) 397–401.

[76] X. Durando, M.C. Farges, E. Buc, C. Abrial, C. Petorin-Lesens, B. Gillet, M.P. Vasson, D. Pezet, P. Chollet, E. Thivat, Dietary methionine restriction with FOLFOX regimen as first line therapy of metastatic colorectal cancer: a feasibility study, Oncology 78 (3–4) (2010) 205–209.

[77] G. Deblois, S.A.M. Tonekaboni, G. Grillo, C. Martinez, Y.I. Kao, F. Tai, I. Ettayebi, A.M. Fortier, P. Savage, A.N. Fedor, et al., Epigenetic switch-induced viral mimicry evasion in chemotherapy-resistant breast cancer, Cancer Discov. 10 (9) (2020) 1312–1329.

[78] H. Jeon, J.H. Kim, E. Lee, Y.J. Jang, J.E. Son, J.Y. Kwon, T.G. Lim, S. Kim, J.H.Y. Park, J.E. Kim, K.W. Lee, Methionine deprivation suppresses triple-negative breast cancer metastasis in vitro and in vivo, Oncotarget 7 (41) (2016) 67223.

[79] A. Barve, A. Vega, P.P. Shah, S. Ghare, L. Casson, M. Wunderlich, L.J. Siskind, L.J. Beverly, Perturbation of methionine/S-adenosylmethionine metabolism as a novel vulnerability in MLL rearranged leukemia, Cells 8 (11) (2019) 1322.

[80] S.J. Mentch, M. Mehrmohamadi, L. Huang, X.J. Liu, D. Gupta, D. Mattocks, P.G. Padilla, G. Ables, M.M. Bamman, A.E. Thalacker-Mercer, et al., Histone methylation dynamics and gene regulation occur through the sensing of one-carbon metabolism, Cell Metab. 22 (5) (2015) 861–873.

[81] B. Kelly, E.L. Pearce, Amino assets: how amino acids support immunity, Cell Metab. 32 (2) (2020) 154–175.

[82] L. Fang, et al., Methionine restriction promotes cGAS activation and chromatin untethering through demethylation to enhance antitumor immunity, Cancer Cell 41 (6) (2023) 1118–1133.

[83] N. Shiraki, Y. Shiraki, T. Tsuyama, F. Obata, M. Miura, G. Nagae, H. Aburatani, K. Kume, F. Endo, S. Kume, Methionine metabolism regulates maintenance and differentiation of human pluripotent stem cells, Cell Metab. 19 (5) (2014) 780–794.

[84] E. Strekalova, D. Malin, E.M.M. Weisenhorn, J.D. Russell, D. Hoelper, A. Jain, J.J. Coon, P.W. Lewis, V.L. Cryns, S-adenosylmethionine biosynthesis is a targetable metabolic vulnerability of cancer stem cells, Breast Cancer Res. Treat. 175 (2019) 39–50.

[85] E. Strekalova, D. Malin, D.M. Good, V.L. Cryns, Methionine deprivation induces a targetable vulnerability in triple-negative breast cancer cells by enhancing TRAIL receptor-2 expression, Clin. Cancer Res. 21 (12) (2015) 2780–2791.

[86] D.E. Epner, S. Morrow, M. Wilcox, J.L. Houghton, Nutrient intake and nutritional indexes in adults with metastatic cancer on a phase I clinical trial of dietary methionine restriction, Nutr Cancer 42 (2) (2002) 158–166.

[87] J.L. Davis, H.J. Fallon, H.P. Morris, Two enzymes of serine metabolism in rat liver and hepatomas, Cancer Res. 30 (12) (1970) 2917.

[88] A. Luengo, D.Y. Gui, M.G. Vander Heiden, Targeting metabolism for cancer therapy, Cell Chem. Biol. 24 (9) (2017) 1161–1180.

[89] J.W. Locasale, A.R. Grassian, T. Melman, C.A. Lyssiotis, K.R. Mattaini, A.J. Bass, G. Heffron, C.M. Metallo, T. Muranen, H. Sharfi, A.T. Sasaki, Phosphoglycerate dehydrogenase diverts glycolytic flux and contributes to oncogenesis, Nat. Genet. 43 (9) (2011) 869–874.

[90] E. Cerami, J. Gao, U. Dogrusoz, B.E. Gross, S.O. Sumer, B.A. Aksoy, A. Jacobsen, C.J. Byrne, M.L. Heuer, E. Larsson, Y. Antipin, The cBio cancer genomics portal: an open platform for exploring multidimensional cancer genomics data, Cancer Discov. 2 (5) (2012) 401–404.

[91] X. Zhao, J. Fu, J. Du, W. Xu, The role of D-3-phosphoglycerate dehydrogenase in cancer, Int. J. Biol. Sci. 16 (9) (2020) 1495–1506.

[92] S. Ravez, C. Corbet, Q. Spillier, A. Dutu, A.D. Robin, E. Mullarky, L.C. Cantley, O. Feron, R. Frédérick, α-Ketothioamide derivatives: a promising tool to interrogate phosphoglycerate dehydrogenase (PHGDH), J. Med. Chem. 60 (4) (2017) 1591–1597.

[93] H. Weinstabl, M. Treu, J. Rinnenthal, S.K. Zahn, P. Ettmayer, G. Bader, G. Dahmann, D. Kessler, K. Rumpel, N. Mischerikow, F. Savarese, Intracellular trapping of the selective phosphoglycerate dehydrogenase (PHGDH) inhibitor BI-4924 disrupts serine biosynthesis, J. Med. Chem. 62 (17) (2019) 7976–7997.

[94] E. Mullarky, J. Xu, A.D. Robin, D.J. Huggins, A. Jennings, N. Noguchi, A. Olland, D. Lakshminarasimhan, M. Miller, D. Tomita, M. Michino, Inhibition of 3-phosphoglycerate dehydrogenase (PHGDH) by indole amides abrogates *de novo* serine synthesis in cancer cells, Bioorg. Med. Chem. Lett. 29 (17) (2019) 2503–2510.

[95] J.M. Rohde, K.R. Brimacombe, L. Liu, M.E. Pacold, A. Yasgar, D.M. Cheff, T.D. Lee, G. Rai, B. Baljinnyam, Z. Li, A. Simeonov, Discovery and optimization of piperazine-1-thiourea-based human phosphoglycerate dehydrogenase inhibitors, Bioorg. Med. Chem. 26 (8) (2018) 1727–1739.

[96] Q. Wang, M.V. Liberti, P. Liu, X. Deng, Y. Liu, J.W. Locasale, L. Lai, Rational design of selective allosteric inhibitors of PHGDH and serine synthesis with anti-tumor activity, Cell Chem. Biol. 24 (1) (2017) 55–65.

[97] M.E. Pacold, K.R. Brimacombe, S.H. Chan, J.M. Rohde, C.A. Lewis, L.J. Swier, R. Possemato, W.W. Chen, L.B. Sullivan, B.P. Fiske, S. Cho, A PHGDH inhibitor reveals coordination of serine synthesis and one-carbon unit fate, Nat. Chem. Biol. 12 (6) (2016) 452–458.

[98] B. Ngo, E. Kim, V. Osorio-Vasquez, S. Doll, S. Bustraan, R.J. Liang, A. Luengo, S.M. Davidson, A. Ali, G.B. Ferraro, G.M. Fischer, Limited environmental serine and glycine confer brain metastasis sensitivity to PHGDH inhibition, Cancer Discov. 10 (9) (2020) 1352–1373.

[99] Z.E. Stine, Z.T. Schug, J.M. Salvino, C.V. Dang, Targeting cancer metabolism in the era of precision oncology, Nat. Rev. Drug Discov. 21 (2) (2022) 141–162.

[100] A.S. Dekhne, C. Ning, M.J. Nayeen, K. Shah, H. Kalpage, J. Frühauf, A. Wallace-Povirk, C. O'Connor, Z. Hou, S. Kim, M. Hüttemann, Cellular pharmacodynamics of a novel pyrrolo [3, 2-d] pyrimidine inhibitor targeting mitochondrial and cytosolic one-carbon metabolism, Mol. Pharmacol. 97 (1) (2020) 9–22.

[101] A.S. Dekhne, K. Shah, G.S. Ducker, J.M. Katinas, J. Wong-Roushar, M.J. Nayeen, A. Doshi, C. Ning, X. Bao, J. Frühauf, J. Liu, Novel pyrrolo [3, 2-d] pyrimidine compounds

target mitochondrial and cytosolic one-carbon metabolism with broad-spectrum antitumor efficacy, Mol. Cancer Ther. 18 (10) (2019) 1787–1799.

[102] G. Schwertz, M.S. Frei, M.C. Witschel, M. Rottmann, U. Leartsakulpanich, P. Chitnumsub, A. Jaruwat, W. Ittarat, A. Schäfer, R.A. Aponte, N. Trapp, Conformational aspects in the design of inhibitors for serine hydroxymethyltransferase (SHMT): biphenyl, aryl sulfonamide, and aryl sulfone motifs, Chem. Eur. J 23 (57) (2017) 14345–14357.

[103] G.S. Ducker, J.M. Ghergurovich, N. Mainolfi, V. Suri, S.K. Jeong, S. Hsin-Jung Li, A. Friedman, M.G. Manfredi, Z. Gitai, H. Kim, J.D. Rabinowitz, Human SHMT inhibitors reveal defective glycine import as a targetable metabolic vulnerability of diffuse large B-cell lymphoma, Proc. Natl. Acad. Sci. 114 (43) (2017) 11404–11409.

[104] J.C. García-Cañaveras, O. Lancho, G.S. Ducker, J.M. Ghergurovich, X. Xu, V. da Silva-Diz, S. Minuzzo, S. Indraccolo, H. Kim, D. Herranz, J.D. Rabinowitz, SHMT inhibition is effective and synergizes with methotrexate in T-cell acute lymphoblastic leukemia, Leukemia 35 (2) (2021) 377–388.

[105] S.L. Geeraerts, K.R. Kampen, G. Rinaldi, P. Gupta, M. Planque, N. Louros, E. Heylen, K. De Cremer, K. De Brucker, S. Vereecke, B. Verbelen, Repurposing the antidepressant sertraline as SHMT inhibitor to suppress serine/glycine synthesis–addicted breast tumor growth, Mol. Cancer Ther. 20 (1) (2021) 50–63.

[106] O.D. Maddocks, C.R. Berkers, S.M. Mason, L. Zheng, K. Blyth, E. Gottlieb, K.H. Vousden, Serine starvation induces stress and p53-dependent metabolic remodelling in cancer cells, Nature 493 (7433) (2013) 542–546.

[107] O.D. Maddocks, D. Athineos, E.C. Cheung, P. Lee, T. Zhang, N.J. Van Den Broek, G.M. Mackay, C.F. Labuschagne, D. Gay, F. Kruiswijk, J. Blagih, Modulating the therapeutic response of tumours to dietary serine and glycine starvation, Nature 544 (7650) (2017) 372–376.

[108] G. Bergers, S.M. Fendt, The metabolism of cancer cells during metastasis, Nat. Rev. Cancer 21 (3) (2021) 162–180.

[109] M. Tajan, M. Hennequart, E.C. Cheung, F. Zani, A.K. Hock, N. Legrave, O.D. Maddocks, R.A. Ridgway, D. Athineos, A. Suárez-Bonnet, R.L. Ludwig, Serine synthesis pathway inhibition cooperates with dietary serine and glycine limitation for cancer therapy, Nat. Commun. 12 (1) (2021) 366.

Environmental causes of cancer

Priya Wadgaonkar

Department of Pharmaceutical Sciences, Eugene Applebaum College of Pharmacy and Health Sciences, Wayne State University, Detroit, MI, United States

Introduction

Cancer can be defined as a group of diseases characterized by abnormal cell transformation leading to uncontrolled cell growth. These cells have an enhanced ability to invade and metastasize the surrounding and distant tissues and organs. Cancer remains the leading cause of death globally, with an estimated 19.3 million new cancer cases and almost 10 million cancer deaths occurring in 2020, according to the GLOBOCAN 2020 estimates. The most common cancers are breast, lung, colon, rectum, and prostate [1]. There is a tremendous burden of cancer in terms of public health, societal, and economic point of view, and there are ongoing efforts to improve cancer-related mortality rates [2]. Significant progress has been made in cancer diagnosis and personalized medicine that has improved overall cancer survival rates, such as in the case of breast, lung, colorectal, and kidney cancers. However, pancreatic, liver, and esophageal cancers still have a poor survival rate. Identifying early biomarkers in cancers and developing new targeted therapies will improve cancer-related morbidity and mortality.

There are different causative factors for cancer development, including genetic abnormalities, environmental exposures to carcinogens, and lifestyle factors such as poor diet, smoking, and alcohol consumption [3]. An amalgamation of these causative factors significantly increases the risk of cancer development. Prevention of environmental carcinogenic exposures and avoidance of unhealthy lifestyle habits can markedly assist in reducing the risk of cancers. Four groups of genes are commonly mutated in human cancers: oncogenes, tumor suppressors, DNA repair, and apoptotic genes. Some studies suggest that 93% of human cancers are caused by the interaction of genes with environmental factors, and only 7% of cancers are caused by hereditary factors. Besides these causative factors for cancer, epigenetics dysregulation is now considered equally important in causing cancer. Epigenetics can be defined as the changes in gene expression without hereditary changes in DNA sequence. DNA methylation, histone modifications, and regulation of gene

69

Cancer Epigenetics and Nanomedicine. https://doi.org/10.1016/B978-0-443-13209-4.00017-9
Copyright © 2024 Elsevier Inc. All rights reserved, including those for text and data mining, AI training, and similar technologies.

expression by microRNAs are some of the common epigenetic modifications implicated in cancers. These epigenetic alterations promote the expression of oncogenes
such as *KRAS*, *BRAF*, and *c-MYC* and inhibit tumor suppressor activity, contributing
to cancer development. Environmental exposure to carcinogens such as arsenic has
been demonstrated to cause epigenetic dysregulation that plays a role in carcinogenesis [4,5]. This highlights the critical role of environmental factors in developing
human cancers. Lifestyle factors are also considered environmental causes of cancer
by some researchers and will be discussed in this section.

Environmental factors that cause cancer can be physical, chemical, or other pollutants released from industrial emissions, household smoke, and second-hand
smoke. Physical environmental factors include ionizing and nonionizing radiation
(X, gamma, radon, or UV radiation exposures). Chemical agents include carcinogens
such as asbestos, arsenic, nickel, cobalt, and chromium [6]. The Report on Carcinogens, 15th edition, by the US National Toxicology Program lists 62 human carcinogens, predominantly environmental carcinogens. Besides environmental exposures,
occupational exposure to human carcinogens remains a major risk factor in cancer
development. According to a study published in the *Lancet*, 2.43 million deaths out
of the total 7 million deaths in 2001 were attributed to 9 potentially modifiable risk
factors. In high-income countries, obesity, alcohol use, and smoking are the main
causes of cancer. In low and middle-income countries, alcohol use, smoking, and
poor diet were the important causes of cancer. Infection-related cancers are also
prominent in low-income countries. For example, the human papillomavirus
(HPV) is a leading risk factor causing cervical cancer in women in low- and
middle-income countries. Early diagnosis of cancer, timely vaccinations, awareness
programs, and government policies to moderate the costs of cancer therapeutics will
go a long way in improving the public health and economic burden of cancer in the
world [7]. The following environmental causes of cancer are discussed here that significantly increase the risk of human cancers.

Smoking and tobacco use

Smoking and tobacco use are among the most significant contributors and prevent-
able causes of cancer-related deaths worldwide [4]. According to the World Health
Organization (WHO), tobacco use causes 25% of all cancer deaths globally. It is the
main culprit behind lung cancer. Globally, lung cancer is the leading cause of cancer-
related mortality and morbidity, and 80% of lung cancers are caused due to smoking.
Other causes of lung cancer include passive smoking, outdoor air pollution, smoke
from solid fuels especially used in cooking and heating in developing countries, and
other second-hand smoke [6]. Besides lung cancers, smoking and tobacco use also
cause cancers of the larynx, pharynx, esophagus, oral cavity, pancreas, bladder,
stomach, cervix, colorectal, liver cancers, and acute myeloid leukemia. Cigarette
smoking leads to inhaling a mixture of thousands of chemicals, including up to
60 carcinogens [8]. According to the latest research by the International Agency
for Research on Cancer (IARC), the total number of carcinogens in tobacco and

tobacco smoke has increased to 83 [9]. The carcinogens in cigarette smoke can be categorized into chemical classes such as *N*-nitrosamines, polycyclic aromatic hydrocarbons (PAHs), aldehydes, aromatic amines, volatile organic hydrocarbons, and metals/metalloids. Other less investigated chemicals in smoke that may have a possible role in causing cancers include oxidants, free radicals, alkylated PAHs, and ethylating agents.

The carcinogens in tobacco smoke cause cancers via different molecular mechanisms. Most of these carcinogens undergo metabolic activation by cytochrome CYP450 enzymes that convert them to configurations that covalently bind to DNA and form adducts. Formation of these DNA adducts increases the risk of forming genetic mutations, such as in oncogenes and tumor suppressor genes, leading to uncontrolled cell proliferation. Examples of such gene mutations induced by cigarette smoking include *KRAS* oncogene in lung cancer and the *TP53* gene in other cancers. Cigarette smoking leads to the uptake of various carcinogens that undergo metabolic activation as well as metabolic detoxification, leading to their excretion. Individuals who smoke and have a higher metabolic activation and lower metabolic detoxification capacity are at increased risk of developing cancers. Besides genetic mutations, carcinogens in cigarette smoke and tobacco also cause cancers via other pathways. For example, nicotine and tobacco-specific nitrosamines bind to specific receptors (e.g., nicotine receptors) that activate protein kinase B, protein kinase A, and other signaling pathways that promote the loss of normal growth control mechanisms. Tobacco and smoke also contain carcinogens, cocarcinogens, and tumor promoter chemicals that cause epigenetic modifications such as gene promoter hypermethylation which, especially if it occurs in the tumor suppressor genes, leads to uncontrolled cell growth. Measurements of carcinogens and their metabolites associated with tobacco use and smoking can be detected in urine, blood, and breath [8].

Radiation

Radiation is a form of energy that travels in the form of waves or particles through a material medium or space. There are two types of radiation, namely ionizing and nonionizing, based on the energy of the radiated particles. There are two main mechanisms by which radiation, especially ionizing radiation, causes cancers, namely the direct and indirect action of radiation on DNA molecules. Nonionizing radiation has energy only to vibrate the atoms or move them in a molecule. On the other hand, ionizing radiation has high energy (more than 10 eV), enough to ionize atoms and molecules into positive and negative ions and break chemical bonds. Hence, ionizing radiation is more toxic, and its exposure increases the risk of the development of cancers compared to nonionizing radiation. Examples of ionizing radiation include ultraviolet (UV) radiation (10–125 nm), X-rays, gamma radiation, alpha radiation, beta radiation, and cosmic and neutron radiation. Ultraviolet light/soft UV, visible light, infrared, microwave, and radio waves are examples of nonionizing radiation.

In direct action, the DNA molecule is directly hit by the high energy radiation disrupting its molecular structure. This leads to gene mutations, cell damage (DNA strand breaks), or cell death. In the indirect action, the high energy radiation molecules hit the water molecules and other organic molecules, leading to the formation of free radicals such as alkoxy ($RO2\bullet$) and hydroxyl ($HO\bullet$) radicals. Free radicals are atoms, ions, or molecules with at least one unpaired electron in their valence shell, making them unstable and highly reactive. Therefore, these highly unstable radicals react with the nearby DNA molecules, causing structural damage. These structural DNA damages may result in gene mutations, cell damage, or apoptosis. Most of the radiation-induced DNA damage occurs due to the indirect action of radiation due to the high water content of the cells. Besides the damages caused by water radiolysis products (indirect action of radiation), reactive nitrogen species (RNS) and other species formed due to the ionization of atoms can also cause cell damage [10].

Exposure to UV radiation is the main cause of skin cancers [11]. Humans are exposed to UV radiation from the sun, tanning booths, and sunlamps [4]. UV radiation comprises three types: ultraviolet A (UVA, 320–400 nm), ultraviolet B (UVB, 290–320 nm), and ultraviolet C (UVC, 200–290 nm). UVC has limited penetration in the deeper layers of the skin compared to UVA and UVB and is the least toxic. UVA has the highest skin penetration compared to UVB and UVC but does not cause much damage to the epidermis. UVB, on the other hand, has intermediate penetration compared to UVA and UVC. However, UVB causes the most damage to the epidermis and is the most significant contributor to the development of skin cancers. Basal cell carcinoma, squamous carcinoma, and melanoma are the three types of skin cancers. Of these three types of skin cancers, nonmelanoma cancers (basal cell carcinoma, squamous carcinoma) represent 98% of all skin cancer cases in the United States. Even though melanoma has the least number of skin cancer cases in the United States, its high metastatic potential and resistance to chemotherapy and radiation lead to most skin cancer-related deaths [11]. Two main pathways are involved in causing skin cancer due to UV light exposure. The first pathway requires UV light's direct action on keratinocytes, resulting in their neoplastic transformation. This involves UV-induced DNA damage that causes genetic mutations such as in tumor suppressor genes (p53) and proto-oncogene activation (*HRAS, KRAS*). The second pathway involves producing immunosuppressive cytokines and other responses that promote abnormal cell proliferation, leading to tumorigenesis [12]. The review article here describes a more detailed molecular mechanism of melanoma genesis [11]. To protect from UV radiation-associated skin cancers and other skin problems like hyperpigmentation and sunburns, a high sun protection factor (SPF) sunscreen should be applied to the skin before going out in the sun. Wearing long pants, long sleeves, a hat, and sunglasses and avoiding afternoon exposure to the sun are other remedies to prevent high penetrating UV light. One should also avoid sunlamps and tanning booths.

Besides, UV light exposure to radiation such as radon, X-rays, gamma rays, alpha particles, beta particles, and neutrons can also damage DNA and cause cancer. The exposure to such ionizing radiations can be due to biological activities (cosmic rays, radionuclides) or artificial events (X-ray machines, nuclear accidents, nuclear reactors, accelerators) [13]. According to the US Environmental Protection Agency (US EPA), 37% of radiation exposure comes from radon and thoron, naturally occurring radionuclides. Radon is a naturally found radioactive gas formed when the radioactive element radium undergoes degradation. Radium is formed when radioactive elements thorium and uranium break down. The decay of radon emits mainly alpha radiation. Radon exposure significantly increases the risk of lung cancer. Hence, it has been classified as a group I human carcinogen by the IARC [13]. Besides radon and thoron, other major sources of radiation exposures, according to the US EPA, include medical X-rays, computed tomography (24%), nuclear medicine (12%), radiography/fluoroscopy (5%–7%), cosmic rays/space (5%), and miscellaneous (10%).

Alcohol consumption

Alcohol has been classified as a group 1 (highest level of risk) human carcinogen by the IARC since 1988. Globally, alcohol consumption accounts for 4.65% of the burden of injury and disease. Various epidemiological studies have provided evidence that alcohol increases the risk of several types of cancers, such as head and neck, mouth, throat, larynx, esophagus, colorectal breast, and liver [14]. Mutagenic agents commonly cause cancer. However, alcohol is not a mutagen by itself. The formation of acetaldehyde after the metabolism of the ingested alcohol in the liver is responsible for the carcinogenicity of alcohol. Acetaldehyde is a toxic chemical and a carcinogen that can damage DNA and proteins. Strong evidence suggests its role in developing head and neck, esophagus, and liver cancers. Alcoholic beverages are also known to increase the blood levels of estrogen, leading to an increased risk of breast cancer, especially in women. Other mechanisms by which alcohol consumption causes cancer include the generation of reactive oxygen and nitrogen species, dysregulated DNA damage repair systems, changes in folate metabolism, impairment of the body's ability to absorb nutrients (vitamins), and reduced immune surveillance [15,16]. Individuals who consume both alcohol and tobacco have a 35% higher risk of the development of cancer such as in the liver [4].

Diet and obesity

An unhealthy diet and obesity are important risk factors for cancer development. Globally, the burden of obesity as a causative factor for cancer is 13.1% in women and 11.9% in men, expressed as a population-attributable fraction [17]. The strongest evidence of the association of obesity with cancer exists for endometrial, colorectal, esophageal adenocarcinoma, breast, renal, and prostate cancers based on reports from the IARC and the World Cancer Research Fund (WCRF). The less correlated malignancies with obesity are melanomas, myeloma, leukemia, non-Hodgkin's lymphoma, and thyroid cancers [18]. Besides, cancer obesity has also been associated with diabetes, hypertension, cardiovascular disease, metabolic syndromes, and other diseases. Obesity is measured in terms of body mass index (BMI), an individual's weight in kilograms or pounds divided by the square of height in meters or feet. A BMI higher than or equal to $25 \, kg/m^2$ is overweight, whereas a BMI higher than or equal to $30 \, kg/m^2$ is considered obese [19].

Various biological mechanisms of action have been proposed to explain the relationship between obesity and cancer. The main basis for the link between being overweight or obese and cancer is that excess fat cells increase inflammation and the production of growth factors and hormones. This results in the upregulation of growth-associated signaling pathways such as PI3K/Akt/mTOR, leading to uncontrolled cell proliferation. Three proteins are mostly studied and implicated as causative factors in obesity-linked cancer: insulin and insulin-like growth factors (IGFs), adipokines, and sex hormones. Researchers have proposed that insulin and IGFs are increased in obese individuals working to promote cell proliferation and inhibit apoptosis. An escalated level of IGF-1 has been associated with an increased risk of prostate and breast cancers. Increased levels of steroid hormones such as progesterone, estrogen, androgens, and adrenal steroids relate to obesity-related progression of male and female cancers such as breast, ovarian, and prostate cancers [20,21]. Obesity is also associated with inflammation, an important contributor to cancer promotion [22]. Detailed molecular mechanisms for obesity-induced inflammation and its connection to breast, liver, and colorectum cancers are described here [23].

Air pollution

Air pollution is one of the greatest environmental risk factors and is associated with a range of health issues such as stroke, cancer, heart, and respiratory diseases. According to the WHO records, outdoor air pollution caused 4.2 million premature deaths in 2019. About 11% of these deaths were associated with respiratory tract cancers. One of the reasons for high mortality linked to air pollution is that most of the world's population resides in areas where air pollution levels are high due to emissions from industry, transportation, power generation, and fossil fuel burning. Besides the outdoor sources of air pollution, indoor pollution also plays an important role in affecting human health. Indoor sources of air pollution include tobacco smoking, unvented gas heaters, mold spores, dust, fungicides, fuel, and paint vapors. Air pollutants can further be categorized into primary and secondary air pollutants. Primary air pollutants include gaseous pollutants such as carbon monoxide, sulfur dioxide, nitrogen dioxide, volatile organic compounds (VOCs), particulate matter (PM), and carbon-based aerosol particles. The main culprit behind the release of these primary air pollutants in the environment is the combustion of biomass and fossil fuels. The primary air pollutants also produce secondary air pollutants in the atmosphere, such as particulate sulfate, nitrate, and gaseous ozone [24].

One of the major components of air pollution is PM. PM can be classified into three categories based on the diameter of the particles. PM10 includes particles with aerodynamic diameters equal to or greater than $10 \, \mu m$. These are the largest inhalable particles not inhaled beyond the trachea and not deposited in the lungs. PM2.5-10 has a diameter between 2.5 and $10 \, \mu m$. These are also known as coarse fraction particles.

PM2.5 is fine PM with the highest penetration in the lungs, including the alveoli sacs where oxygen exchange occurs, and has an aerodynamic diameter less than or equal to 2.5 μm. PM2.5 also contains nanoparticles or ultrafine particles with an aerodynamic diameter less than or equal to 0.1 μm. Inhalation of PM2.5 particles primarily affects the respiratory system and causes various pathological conditions such as asthma, chronic obstructive pulmonary disease, and lung cancers. PM2.5 comprises organic, inorganic, and biological compounds such as endotoxins, fungi, and PAHs. PAHs form a majority of PM2.5 and are derived from the combustion of fossil fuels. Inhalation of PAHs is known to increase the risk of lung cancer. Studies by Tong-Hong Wang and others demonstrated that Pm2.5 promotes lung cancer by activating the AhR-TMPRSS2-IL18 and EGFR pathways in lung cancer cells and in vivo models [24,25]. PM2.5 has also been suggested to participate in lung cancer pathogenesis via epigenetic modifications. Common epigenetic changes include DNA methylations that lead to p53 tumor suppressor inactivation and microRNA activation that promotes oncogenes expression. PM2.5 may also support tumor growth and metastasis by stimulating inflammation, angiogenesis, and alteration of the tumor microenvironment [26]. PM2.5 also exerts its carcinogenic effect by generating reactive oxygen species (ROS) that cause oxidative stress in cells. The oxidative stress induced by chronic exposure to PM2.5 activates various signaling pathways such as PI3K/Akt, mitogen-activated protein kinase (MAPKs), and NFκβ, AP-1 that regulate cellular differentiation, proliferation, apoptosis, and metastasis. Excessive oxidative stress induced by chronic PM2.5 exposure can also cause oxidative DNA damage, leading to genetic mutations [27]. Exposure to PM2.5 has also been associated with breast, cervical, esophageal, bladder, and cervical cancers. To overcome the health risks associated with air pollution, such as cancers, preventive measures such as proper garbage disposal and using sustainable clean energy sources wherever possible should be implemented at the local, national, and international levels. Such interventions to reduce air pollution have improved outdoor air quality in some middle and high-income countries. However, further research is needed, especially in low income and some middle-income countries as the air quality in those countries continues to worsen [24,28,29].

Water pollution

Water is an essential commodity needed to support life on the earth. Therefore, the water for consumption should be easily accessible, safe, and free from contaminants. Several pollutants are found in water bodies, including organic impurities, inorganic pollutants, radioactive substances, thermal pollutants, etc. [30]. Sources of these pollutants in water are due to agricultural activities, natural factors, industrialization, and untreated sewage discharge into water bodies. The presence of pollutants in water poses a serious threat to human health. The major water contaminants associated with increased cancer risk include arsenic, chromium, heavy metals, nitrate, disinfection/chlorination byproducts, and per- and polyfluoroalkyl substances (PFASs).

Arsenic contamination of drinking water is a global health issue, as about 94 to 220 million people worldwide are exposed to high levels of arsenic. Various epidemiological and case-control studies have demonstrated that acute and chronic exposures to arsenic in drinking water increase the risk of skin, lung, bladder, kidney, and liver cancers. Arsenic has been categorized as a group I human carcinogen by the IARC based on experimental and population-based evidence for carcinogenicity [30]. The WHO and US EPA limit arsenic in drinking water as not more than 10 μg/L or 10 ppb. However, high levels of arsenic are found in water (2–5000 μg/L) in Bangladesh, India, China, Mexico, Argentina, Taiwan, Thailand, the United States (Arizona, Nevada, California), and Vietnam. The most serious arsenic exposures occur in the Gulf of Bengal, Taiwan, and South America in terms of population and levels. Intermediate levels (<200 μg/L) are found in European countries of Spain, Greece, Germany, Romania, and Hungary [31].

The molecular mechanisms of arsenic carcinogenicity are not completely understood yet. However, multiple cellular processes are implicated in arsenic-induced tumorigenesis. The mechanisms of arsenic-induced carcinogenesis include oxidative stress-induced damage, epigenetic alterations, activation of stress signaling pathways, mitochondrial dysfunction, impairment of immune systems, and DNA repair. Arsenic is not directly genotoxic, but its ability to induce excessive reactive oxygen species causes DNA lesions. It also inhibits the *PARP-1* activity, an important oxidative DNA damage repair enzyme [32,33]. Besides genetic damage by indirect action, arsenic also alters gene expression via epigenetic alterations. During the biotransformation of arsenic, it undergoes multiple methylation reactions, which require *S*-adenosylmethionine (SAM) as a methyl donor. This results in changes in global methylation patterns [34]. Administration of sodium arsenite in drinking water increased DNA hypomethylation, especially in the Ha-Ras gene promoter in methyl-deficient C57BL/6J mice. *Ha-Ras* gene is a known oncogene upregulated in many cancers [35]. Arsenic also upregulates proliferative signaling pathways such as ERK1/2, JNK, and p-Raf1 [33]. Arsenic exposure has also been shown to induce malignant transformation of human bronchial epithelial BEAS-2B cells. Some of these cells showed cancer stem cell features (CSCs). These arsenic-induced CSCs formed tumors in vivo [36]. CSCs represent a subpopulation of the tumor responsible for cancer metastasis, chemoresistance, and cancer relapse. Besides cancer, arsenic contamination in drinking water causes cardiovascular disorders, diabetes, neurological impairments, and other diseases.

Nitrate contamination of drinking water is a growing problem affecting human health and natural ecosystems. The use of nitrogen-based fertilizers in agricultural activities, especially in South Asia, has increased substantially over recent years. Although using these fertilizers has assisted in feeding the global population, it has also negatively impacted the ecosystem and human health. Nitrogen fertilizers are the main source of nitrate and nitrite compounds in the soil that can be carried via surface runoff to enter the rivers, groundwater, and other drinking water sources. Human, animal, and industrial wastes infiltrating drinking water systems are other sources of nitrate contamination. Ingested nitrate and nitrite can lead to the formation of *N*-nitroso compounds inside the human body which are potential carcinogens. According to the IARC, ingested nitrate and nitrite compounds are classified in group 2A (probably carcinogenic to humans) [37]. To protect human health, the WHO has set a limit of 50 mg/L as NO_3 or 11.3 mg/L as NO_3-N. Besides cancer, nitrate and nitrite-based compounds cause congenital disabilities, thyroid diseases, and other adverse effects, especially in pregnant women [38]. In a population-based cohort study in Denmark, an increased risk of colorectal cancer was observed in individuals exposed to nitrate levels even below the current drinking standard of 50 mg/L [39]. This suggests the need to put more research effort into studying the safe standard limit for nitrate contamination in drinking water.

Using chlorine in water supply systems is a common practice in many countries to disinfect water and prevent the spread of waterborne diseases. However, due to the addition of chlorine in the water bodies, reactions occur between chlorine and the natural organic matter, producing different types of disinfection byproducts (DBPs). Some examples of DBPs include trihalomethanes (THMs), haloacetonitriles (HANs), halo acetic acids (HAAs), iodo-THMs, halo ketones (HKs), *N*-nitroso dimethylamine (NDMA) and other compounds. Exposure to DBPs may occur through drinking water and dermal contact during activities such as bathing, showering, swimming, and inhalation. The DBPs are a public health issue because their exposure has been associated with an increased risk of cancers, stillbirth, preterm delivery, and cardiac anomalies [40]. Major DBPs formed by the reaction between chlorine and organic/inorganic matter are THMs. THM species include bromodichloromethane (BDCM), chloroform, dibromochloromethane (DBCM), and bromoform. These THMs are potential carcinogens; hence, the US EPA has set a limit of not more than 80 μg/L in water systems. In a prospective cohort study of a representative US population, the presence of brominated THMs in the blood was associated with a high risk of cancer mortality [41]. Various studies have demonstrated the link between exposure to disinfection by-products and bladder, pancreatic, kidney, and endometrial cancers [42–45]. A comprehensive overview of the occurrence, genotoxicity, and carcinogenicity of disinfection by-products in drinking water is explained in this review paper [46].

PFASs are synthetic organofluorine chemical compounds with water-resistant properties leading to their use in aqueous film-forming foam (AFFF), Teflon, and other industries. Humans are exposed to PFASs via contaminated drinking water, air, and seafood, occupational exposures (e.g., firefighters), and contact with contaminated media [47]. The WHO, US EPA, and IARC have classified perfluorooctanoic acid (PFOA), the most studied PFAS, as possibly carcinogenic (Group 2B) to humans based on limited epidemiological data. Chemically, PFASs are fluorinated aliphatic compounds with one or more carbon atoms that have hydrogen atoms substituted by fluorine atoms in such a way that they contain the perfluoroalkyl moiety $C_nF_{2n+1}-$. In per-fluoroalkyl substances, all hydrogen atoms attached to carbon atoms are replaced by fluorine atoms. Meanwhile, in the case of polyfluoroalkyl substances, multiple sites have fluorine substitutions. The presence of fluorine in the PFASs bestows them with distinctive physical and chemical properties such as heat stability, water and oil repellency, and surfactant properties. These properties are used in many industries, such as adhesives, plastics, carpets, clothing, paints, and coatings. The PFASs are thermally and chemically stable because of the strong carbon-fluorine bonds. Besides being long-lasting, the hydrophobic and lipophobic nature of the PFASs can result in longer degradation times. Some PFASs can take over 1000 years to degrade completely in a typical soil environment, suggesting their bio-accumulative nature [48]. The molecular mechanisms of PFAS carcinogenesis are not completely understood. However, studies have provided strong evidence that multiple PFASs induce oxidative stress, cause epigenetic alterations, are immuno-suppressive, modulate receptor-mediated effects, and influence cell proliferation. Experimental data demonstrated that PFASs are not directly genotoxic or undergo metabolic activation. Future studies are warranted to better understand the carcinogenic mechanisms of PFASs [49].

Soil pollution

Soil is the foundation of human health. Healthy soil is essential to yield good quality crops, provide food, support ecosystems, and store water. Soil also catches large quantities of carbon and decelerates the pace of climate change. However, there is an increased threat to soil quality and global health due to soil pollution. According to the Lancet Commission on Pollution and Health, pollution is the world's largest environmental cause of disease and premature death. Soil pollution can be defined as soil contamination by chemicals or other waste materials predominantly of human origin that are present at higher-than-normal levels in the soil. Soil pollutants include agricultural herbicides, pesticides and other waste, industrial waste, heavy metals, plastic, and biological pathogens [50]. Soil pollutants can be chemically classified as inorganic and organic pollutants. Inorganic soil pollutants include heavy metals, nonmetals, and metalloids. Organic soil pollutants can be categorized as halogenated and nonhalogenated, which can be further classified as aliphatic and aromatic based on their chemical structures. Humans are exposed to these soil contaminants via ingestion, respiration, or dermal penetration. In this section, important soil pollutants and the risk of cancer due to their exposure are discussed [51].

Lead

Lead is one of the most omnipresent metals in the environment to which we are exposed due to natural and anthropogenic activities. It is probably one of the largest soil contaminants worldwide. Lead is used in lead-based batteries, pigments, munitions, cable sheathing, and rolled extrusions [51]. Humans are exposed to lead from air and food. Mines, smelters, welding of lead-painted metals, glass industries, and battery plants are important sources of occupational exposure to inorganic lead. Lead in the air can be deposited in water and soil, reaching humans via the food chain [52]. The IARC has classified inorganic lead as possibly carcinogenic to humans (Group IIB) and organic lead as probably carcinogenic (Group IIA). Epidemiological studies have indicated a weak association between inorganic lead exposure and lung, kidney, stomach, and brain cancer development [53]. A hospital-based case-control study conducted in the Chaoshan population in the Guangdong Province of China observed that blood cadmium and lead levels were significantly higher in gastrointestinal cancer patients than in noncancer patients. The rivers in the Chasoshan region have been known to be heavily polluted by heavy metals such as lead and cadmium. Thus, the study suggests that exposure to lead and cadmium may be potential risk factors for gastrointestinal cancers [54]. Research also indicates that lead exposure increases the risk of meningioma and brain cancer [55]. Occupational exposure to lead in workers in Finland showed that lead increased the risk of lung cancers [56]. Lungs absorb about 50% of inhaled lead. Human adults take up 10%–15% of lead in food. Conversely, children may absorb 50% lead via the GI tract. Inhaled or ingested lead in blood is bound to the red blood cells. Elimination of lead in the human body is slow and primarily occurs via the urine. Lead is also known to accumulate in the human skeleton. The half-life of lead in the skeleton is 20–30 years, whereas it is 1 month in the blood. Children are more susceptible to the toxic effects of lead due to high gastrointestinal uptake and higher permeability of lead in the blood-brain barrier. In adults, organic lead compounds may cross the blood-brain barrier more easily than inorganic lead. Hence, adults may endure lead encephalopathy and acute lead poisoning from organic lead compounds. Toxic health effects of lead are kidney damage, high blood pressure, digestive and reproductive problems, reduced growth, anemia, speech, language, and behavior problems, brain and nerve damage, hearing problems, and decreased mental abilities and learning difficulties [52]. Exposure to lead has also been linked to increased risk of various cancers.

The carcinogenic mechanisms of lead are still under investigation. However, plausible mechanisms of lead carcinogenesis suggested are induction of oxidative stress, direct DNA damage, inhibition of DNA repair, and deregulation of cellular proliferation. The two mechanisms of genotoxic effects of lead at concentrations possible for human exposure are disruption of the pro-oxidant and antioxidant balance and interference with the DNA repair systems. The suggested mechanisms of lead-induced oxidative stress include Fenton-type reactions, lipid peroxidation, and inhibition of antioxidant defense systems. Lead is also known to interact with two DNA repair systems, namely the base excision repair (BER) and nucleotide excision repair (NER) [57,58]. Most in vitro and epidemiological studies suggest that exposure to lead downregulates the expression of DNA repair genes. These DNA repair genes are part of the BER, NER, and DNA double-strand break pathways. The DNA repair genes *APE1*, *OGG1*, and *XRCC1*, part of the BER pathway, were downregulated by lead toxicity. BER repair pathway is known to amend oxidized base damage. The expression of DNA repair genes *POLD*1 and *XPD* involved in the NER pathway was reported to be downregulated by lead. NER plays a crucial role in removing bulky DNA lesions. DNA repair gene *BRCA1*, involved in the homologous recombinant double-strand break repair pathway, was downregulated with lead exposure. The molecular mechanisms involved in the lead-associated toxicity of DNA repair systems are unclear; however, some studies suggest the role of epigenetic mechanisms [59]. Other biochemical processes involved in lead toxicity include the ability of lead to react with proteins and inhibit calcium actions. Once ingested inside the body, lead is integrated into minerals instead of calcium. The ingested lead then interacts with biological molecules, interfering with their normal activity. Lead also impairs the activity of enzymes by generating changes in the structures, such as that of amide and sulfhydryl enzymes. Lead also inhibits enzyme activity by competing with cations for binding sites [60].

Cadmium

Cadmium is a toxic transition metal and nonessential trace element dispersed in the environment. It is generally rare in the natural environment. Some studies suggest that humans are mostly exposed to cadmium from industrial and agricultural wastes [61]. However, various natural as well as anthropogenic activities can raise the levels of cadmium in soil and groundwater. Volcanic activity, sea spray, weathering of cadmium-bearing rocks, and mobilization of cadmium deposited in soils are some of the natural sources of cadmium. Combustion of fossil fuels, waste incineration, release from tailings piles or municipal wastes, mining, and smelting are some of the anthropogenic activities that elevate cadmium levels in the environment. Occupational exposure is also a significant source of cadmium exposure. The major route of exposure in occupational settings is through the respiratory tract. There may also be cadmium exposure by ingesting dust from contaminated food and hands. Extensive use of phosphate fertilizers is also a significant source of cadmium exposure. When sewage sludge and phosphate fertilizers are used on crops, crops take in cadmium, which humans finally eat [60,62,63].

The first accepted epidemiological study conducted in 1976 by Lemen et al. demonstrated the development of lung and prostate cancers in human workers exposed to cadmium. Further, a report by Takenaka et al. showed that rats exposed to cadmium chloride aerosol developed lung cancers. Based on various epidemiological and in vitro/in vivo studies, the IARC classified cadmium as a class I human carcinogen [61,62]. The toxic effects of cadmium were first identified globally after an outbreak of "itai-itai" disease in Toyama Prefecture, Japan, in 1950. It was the first cadmium poisoning in the world. This poisoning was caused due to consumption of water containing cadmium liberated from mining activities. Exposure to cadmium is known to cause a variety of health issues, one of which is the "itai-itai" disease. Inhalational short-term exposures of cadmium primarily affect the lungs, causing pulmonary irritation. Prolonged cadmium exposure leads to kidney disease, bronchiolitis, emphysema, proteinuria, and cancer. Other organ systems affected by long-term exposure to cadmium include the liver, immune system, blood, bone, and nervous system. Cadmium uptake occurs via inhalation or ingestion, which is absorbed from the entry site and transported in the blood to other tissues. In blood, cadmium is bound to blood proteins such as albumin. Cadmium that is attached to albumin is transferred to the liver. Cadmium is also bound to a protein called metallothionein (MT), which is rich in sulfhydryl groups. The binding of cadmium to MT leads to its reabsorption from the kidneys and subsequent accumulation of cadmium in kidney tubules. Cadmium, not attached to proteins, forms complexes with nonprotein sulfhydryls, such as cysteine and glutathione. The excretion of accumulated cadmium occurs via urine and feces. The excretion rate of cadmium is generally very low [62,63]. Cadmium is known to mimic zinc (Zn) and also calcium to a lesser extent [64]. This results in the displacement of zinc ions from proteins with Zn-finger structures. Proteins with Zn-finger structures are found in DNA repair proteins and transcription factors that regulate many biochemical processes and protein interactions. The alteration of protein conformation and activity, especially of zinc-containing proteins by cadmium, is assumed to be a major cause of lead-induced carcinogenicity. Studies have demonstrated an association between cadmium exposure and the risk of human cancers such as kidney, liver, lung, prostate, stomach, and bladder cancers. Cadmium is not a direct mutagen, but it causes DNA damage by impairment of DNA repair and generation of oxidative stress. Cadmium also affects the antioxidant response by depleting glutathione and inhibiting antioxidant enzymes such as GSH peroxidase and superoxide dismutase. Cadmium is a metalloestrogen linked to breast cancer development in humans. Metalloestrogens are metalloids or small ionic metals that can activate estrogen receptors in the absence of estradiol. In vitro and in vivo studies have reported that cadmium activates estrogen receptors and activates the proliferation of estrogen-dependent breast cancer cells. Cadmium is also known to be involved in carcinogenesis via epigenetic mechanisms. Cadmium can alter DNA methylation patterns, leading to gene-specific changes such as promoter hypermethylation at *XRCC1*, *ERCC1* (DNA repair genes), and p16 promoter. Lysine demethylase 5A and lysine demethylase 3A are zinc finger-containing demethylase proteins in which cadmium substitution results in the impairment of histone demethylase activity and higher global methylation [65].

Polycyclic aromatic hydrocarbons

PAHs are substances generated by the incomplete combustion of organic substances such as petrol, coal, oil, and wood. PAHs consist of a diverse group of cyclic organic compounds. The general chemical structure of PAH consists of two or more aromatic rings laid out in different structural configurations. One of the typical examples of a PAH is naphthalene having two fused aromatic rings [66]. The presence of fused rings imparts mutagenic and carcinogenic properties to the PAHs. Various anthropogenic and natural activities disperse the PAHs in water, air, soil, and sediment. However, due to the lipophilicity and hydrophobicity of PAHs, the soil is the most important sink for PAHs. Some studies report that soil can reserve up to 90% of PAHs. Anthropogenic activities such as motor vehicle exhaust, fossil fuel combustion, cigarette or wood smoke, runoff from industrial areas, oil tank spills, pyrolysis, excessive use of synthetic fertilizers, and reuse of sewage sludge are the primary sources of elevating the levels of PAHs in the soil environment. The adsorption of PAHs on the organic components in the soil and sediment is fast because of their hydrophobicity and chemical structure [67]. Natural sources of PAHs include volcanic activity and forest fires. Smoking, charring, or grilling food over a fire increases the PAHs in the food. Certain cosmetics also contain PAHs [68].

Inhalation, ingestion, and skin absorption are the three common routes by which PAHs enter the human body. PAHs are highly lipophilic and easily absorbed from the gastrointestinal tract after ingestion. They are quickly distributed across the mammalian body, with a higher likelihood of absorption in fatty tissues due to their lipid-soluble nature. Cytochrome P450 mixed function oxidase system in the liver is responsible for the metabolism of PAHs where hydroxylation or oxidations is the first step of biotransformation [69]. In addition to the liver, kidneys, testes, thyroid, adrenal glands, lungs, sebaceous glands, small intestines, and skin can also metabolize PAHs. PAHs are metabolized to epoxides and further to phenols and dihydrodiol derivatives. Sulfate and glucuronide conjugates of these metabolites are excreted in the urine and bile. Glutathione conjugates formed from PAH metabolites are bio-transformed to mercapturic acids in the kidney before being eliminated in the urine [70].

Exposure to PAHs has been associated with the development of human cancers such as lung, breast, and childhood cancers. PAHs are considered procarcinogens because they are not directly carcinogenic. Metabolism of PAHs results in carcinogenic metabolites that form DNA adducts. For example, PAH benzopyrene (BP) is metabolized to 7,8-epoxide by the CYP1A1/1B1 enzymes. The 7,8-epoxide is hydrolyzed by epoxide-hydrolase to form 7,8-diol and further metabolized by CYP1A1/1B1 to form benzopyrene 7,8-diol-9,10-epoxide (BPDE). BPDE interacts with N2 of guanosine to create a DNA adduct. The formation of DNA adducts is a significant event in generating mutations in specific genes, such as tumor suppressors and oncogenes, that lead to cancer development. For instance, Denissenko et al. showed benzopyrene adducts formed at tumor suppressor p53 guanine positions in codons 157, 248, and 273 in BPDE-treated bronchial epithelial and HeLa cells. The mutations of these codons had a connection with human lung cancer. Another molecular mechanism by which PAHs promote carcinogenesis is producing reactive oxygen species (ROS). PAH metabolism produces excessive ROS, leading to increased oxidative stress. The PAHs-induced oxidative stress causes the oxidation of lipids. DNA, RNA, and proteins that alter the function/activities of key macromolecules, leading to cancer development [71,72]. Exposure to PAHs has also been demonstrated to cause neurotoxicity and immunotoxicity and disrupt endocrine and reproductive physiological functioning [73]. Human and environmental health must be protected from PAHs' toxic effects. Soil remediation is a crucial strategy to eliminate PAHs from contaminated soils effectively. Some commonly used remediation technologies for PAH-contaminated soils include supercritical fluid extraction, composting, land farming, solvent extraction, subcritical extraction, chemical oxidation, phytoremediation, photocatalytic degradation, etc. [74].

Asbestos

Asbestos is a name given to a group of six minerals naturally occurring as bundles of fibrous silicate minerals. The chemical structure of asbestos consists of silicon and oxygen atoms in their molecular structure. Asbestos has been broadly used in thermal insulators, vehicle brakes, building materials, and other industrial applications due to its physical properties, such as resistance to heat, chemicals, fire, and insulation properties. Asbestos can be categorized based on its chemical composition, structure, and thermal resistance. Two main groups of asbestos include serpentine asbestos and amphibole asbestos. Serpentine asbestos, including chrysotile mineral or white asbestos, is currently used where asbestos use is permitted. Minerals tremolite, crocidolite, amosite, anthophyllite, and actinolite belong to the amphibole asbestos group. Crocidolite and amosite are stronger in strength, durability, and heat resistance than chrysotile. However, amphibole asbestos is more brittle and is more limited in its ability to be assembled [75].

Dr. Montague Murray first identified the adverse health effects of asbestos in 1899. However, the use of asbestos increased significantly from 1899 until 1971, when legislation was enacted that limited the use of asbestos in North America. Globally, 66 countries worldwide have prohibited the use of asbestos with some exemptions [76]. People are exposed to asbestos in their homes, workplaces, or communities. Humans can be exposed to asbestos from natural and anthropogenic activities, contaminating the air, water, and soil. Weathering and erosion of asbestos-bearing rocks is the primary natural source of asbestos release in the environment. Open-pit mining, crushing and milling ore, manufacture, transport, use of asbestos-containing materials, and demolition of buildings constructed with asbestos are some anthropogenic activities that release asbestos into the atmospheric environment. Untreated industrial wastewater runoff and erosion of asbestos cement pipes liberate asbestos in the water. When asbestos-containing waste is disposed of in landfills, it releases asbestos into the soil. However, compared to the 1900s, with strict regulations, disposal of asbestos in landfills is restricted [77]. The most common route of asbestos entry into the human body is via inhalation of air contaminated with asbestos fibers. Other routes include dermal exposure and ingestion. Asbestos exposure has been known to cause lung cancer, malignant mesothelioma, laryngeal cancer, ovarian cancer, asbestosis, and pleural disease. Globally, 125 million people are exposed to asbestos in the occupational settings. At least 107,000 people die each year from asbestos-related malignancies. Hence, the IARC has classified asbestos as a group I human carcinogen [78,79].

Exposure to asbestos causes both cellular and genomic damage, which promotes tumorigenesis. The damage generated by asbestos depends on its duration of exposure, concentration, and type of fiber. Chrysotile is the most toxic asbestos fiber, followed by crocidolite. Oxidative stress is the major molecular mechanism of asbestos-associated carcinogenesis. The presence of asbestos fibers on the pleural surface and interaction with the mesothelial cell layer leads to the formation of ROS and RNS. The ROS and RNS generation is due to the chronic inflammation produced by the prolonged phagocytic activity of macrophages that function to remove the accumulated asbestos fibers. Another source of ROS is due to the catalytic iron associated with asbestos fibers. It has been proposed that the production of free radicals, RNS, ROS, growth factors, and inflammatory cytokines result in DNA damage, increased susceptibility to mutations, induces cell proliferation, and activation of proto-oncogenes. Besides causing DNA damage and mutations, oxidative stress and chronic inflammation generated by asbestos also activate many cellular signaling pathways. MAPK is activated by asbestos, which further activates downstream transcription factors JUN and FOS (AP-1) associated with cell proliferation and tumor promotion. Similarly, asbestos activates the NF-κβ and EGFR signaling pathways that regulate cell growth and apoptosis [79]. A more detailed investigation into the carcinogenic mechanisms of asbestos is essential to mitigate its toxic effects on human health.

Pathogenic microbes

Infectious agents such as bacteria, viruses, fungi, and parasites are known to be involved in approximately 20% of cancer cases worldwide. About one in five cancers are associated with an infectious agent globally. There are three oncogenic parasites (*Opisthorchis viverrine*, *Schistosoma haematobium*, and *Clonorchis sinensis*), seven oncogenic viruses (HPV, hepatitis virus B and C, Epstein Barr virus (EBV), human T-cell lymphoma virus 1, Kaposi's sarcoma virus and Merkel cell polyomavirus) and two oncogenic bacteria (*Helicobacter Pylori*, *Fusobacterium nucleatum*) that have been linked with the development of cancer [80]. *Aspergillus* spp., fungi, is known to be an etiological factor in the formation of liver cancer. The IARC has classified most pathogens, including viruses, bacteria, fungi, and parasites, as Group I human carcinogens. These infectious agents engender carcinogenesis by three main mechanisms. The first mechanism is persistent inflammation that causes DNA damage and mutagenesis. Secondly, initiation of oncogene expression or inhibition of tumor suppressor activity, and thirdly, evading the immune action of the host. *Helicobacter pylori* (HP) and EBV are known to cause gastric cancers, HPV is known to cause cervical cancer, Kaposi's sarcoma herpesvirus (KSHV) causes Kaposi's sarcoma, Hepatitis virus, and *Aspergillus* spp. induces liver cancer, *Fusobacterium nucleatum* engenders colon cancer, *Schistosoma haematobium* is associated with bladder cancer, and *Clonorchis sinensis* and *Opisthorchis viverrine* cause bile duct cancer [81]. These review papers have discussed the carcinogenic mechanisms of these microbes and parasites in more detail [80–82].

Environmental carcinogens

Environmental and occupational exposure to hazardous substances such as aflatoxins, arsenic, asbestos, benzene, beryllium, cadmium, coal tar, coke-oven emissions, formaldehyde, chromium, nickel, radon, tobacco smoke, soot, thorium, vinyl chloride, and wood dust can induce malignant tumors in humans. The US National Toxicology Program (NTP) has listed 256 substances, including chemical, biological, and physical agents associated with human cancer development. Some of the important environmental carcinogens will be discussed in this section.

Aflatoxins

Aflatoxins are mycotoxins primarily produced by the mold species *Aspergillus flavus* and *Aspergillus parasiticus*. Aflatoxins are widely spread in the environment and are found in foods such as rice, corn, dried fruits, peanuts, and oil seeds. They are also found in the meat, eggs, and milk of farm animals that eat the aflatoxin-contaminated fodder. Even though hot and humid weather promotes the diffusion of aflatoxin-producing molds, being a greater hazard in tropical regions, other sources cause aflatoxin contamination, such as improper agricultural practices, meteorological conditions, and various environmental factors. The negative health effects of aflatoxins were first observed when an acute feed-related mycotoxicosis outbreak occurred in England around the 1960s. Since then, the carcinogenic, mutagenic, immunosuppressive, and teratogenic effects of aflatoxins have been studied in various animal and human models. The IARC has categorized Aflatoxin B1 (AFB1) as group I and Aflatoxin M1 (AFM1) as group II B human carcinogens. AFB1 is a major causative agent of liver cancer [83,84].

Aflatoxins are highly lipophilic substances and are easily absorbed from the exposure site. After uptake into the body, aflatoxins are distributed to different tissues, primarily the liver, where it undergoes metabolism. Aflatoxins are metabolized to a reactive epoxide intermediate aflatoxin-8,9-epoxide or hydroxylated to less harmful aflatoxin M1. The formation of reactive oxygen species aflatoxin-8,9-epoxide results in its binding to albumin in the blood serum or DNA forming adducts that induce DNA damage. The formation of DNA adducts leading to DNA mutagenesis is the major molecular mechanism of aflatoxin-induced liver cancer [85]. The epoxide intermediate generated can also form a conjugate with glutathione (GSH) and get excreted from the body as AFB-marcapturate. The utilization of GSH during aflatoxin biotransformation can also cause an imbalance of antioxidant responses in the body, leading to oxidative stress. The binding of aflatoxin-8,9-epoxide metabolite to macromolecules such as RNA, DNA, and proteins can impair its function and activity, promoting tumorigenesis. Besides liver cancer, epidemiological and animal studies have demonstrated that aflatoxins also induce lung cancer. Mutations in oncogene *KRAS* and tumor suppressor *p53* were observed in the lung cells of rabbits and mice treated with aflatoxin. Epigenetic alterations were also implicated in aflatoxin-induced cancers, which require further investigations [84]. Health regulations should be implemented to minimize health risks associated with aflatoxin-associated toxicity. Consumers must be alert when buying foodstuffs and discard moldy, shriveled, or discolored foods.

Benzene

Benzene (C_6H_6) is an organic chemical compound found naturally in petroleum, crude oil, and cigarette smoke. Other natural sources that release benzene into the environment include forest fires and volcanic activity. Benzene is widely used as an industrial solvent and additive in various chemical processes. Chemical uses of benzene include plastic and rubber products, detergents, fabrics such as nylon, resins, and polyester resins, and intermediates for dyes, drugs, and pesticides. Humans are exposed to benzene through inhalation via vapors in occupational settings, environment, and intake of processed foodstuffs such as canned and smoked fish. Benzene is now globally acknowledged as a human carcinogen and hematotoxin because it can cause myelotoxicity and leukemogenicity in humans and animals. The IARC agency has categorized benzene as a group I human carcinogen. Exposure to benzene primarily increases the risk of leukemia and other blood disorders [86,87].

The metabolism of benzene plays a crucial role in the development of blood malignancies. Benzene is primarily metabolized in the liver, where it initially undergoes epoxidation by cytochrome enzyme P450, generating benzene oxide and oxepine. Benzene oxide is further oxidized into phenol and subsequently metabolized to catechol or hydroquinone by CYP 2E1. These metabolites are transferred to the bone marrow, where they additionally undergo secondary metabolism. Oxidation of hydroquinone to a more toxic metabolite, p-benzoquinone, is proposed to be involved in benzene-mediated carcinogenicity. Besides p-benzoquinone, catechol, phenol, and hydroquinone, the other three liver-associated benzene metabolites have been observed to produce hematotoxicity and myelotoxicity. These metabolites especially target cells in bone marrow, including the hematopoietic stem cells (HSCs) [88]. The carcinogenic mechanisms of benzene are not completely understood as the toxic effects of benzene depend upon several factors such as duration of exposure and concentration of benzene, genetic makeup, and metabolizing capacity of an individual. However, some of the proposed molecular mechanisms of benzene carcinogenesis are the formation of toxic metabolites (phenol, catechol, 1,4-benzoquinone) that cause oxidative stress, DNA damage and mutations, chromosomal damage, oncogene activation, transcription factor overexpression, hyperproliferative cellular responses and downregulation of immune tumor surveillance mechanisms. Currently, no treatment options exist for benzene poisoning or long-term benzene exposure. The chemotherapeutic agents used for hematopoietic malignancies are used in benzene-associated blood cancers such as leukemias and lymphomas. Future attractive therapeutic options for benzene-associated cancers can target metabolizing enzymes such as CYP450E1 inhibition or genes involved in DNA repair [86].

Hexavalent chromium compounds

Chromium (Cr) is a chemical element in the class of heavy metals. It is found in various oxidation states from −2 to +6. Chromium's most stable oxidation states are trivalent chromium (CrIII) and hexavalent chromium (CrVI). Traces of chromium, especially CrIII, are essential for animal and human nutrition. However, exposure to hexavalent chromium compounds (CrVI) has been strongly linked with cancers of the respiratory and gastrointestinal tracts. CrVI is highly toxic and is classified as a group I human carcinogen by the IARC. CrVI is 100 times more toxic than CrIII. CrVI compounds possess physical properties such as hardness and resistance to corrosion and confer a bright appearance to other metals. Hence, CrVI has been used in various commercial applications such as pigments, cement, electroplating, leather, metallurgic, chromates, welding, and agricultural fertilizers. Humans are primarily exposed to hexavalent chromium from inhaling chromium-containing dust and fumes or through skin and eye contact. Humans working in welding, electroplating, and chromate painting industries are exposed to the highest concentration of airborne hexavalent chromium compounds [58,89].

Hexavalent chromium compounds have been demonstrated to induce genotoxicity both in vitro and in vivo. For example, lymphocytes of workers exposed to CrVI dust showed increased frequencies of DNA strand breaks, sister chromatid exchanges, and micronuclei. Similar genotoxic effects were observed in rats and mice injected with CrVI. Further, in vitro, mutagenic tests involving bacterial and mammalian test systems showed positive outcomes for mutagenicity. Besides genotoxic effects that lead to cancer-causing mutations, CrVI exposure generates toxic oxygen and sulfur free radicals. The possible role of chromium-induced oxidative stress in the formation of DNA adducts is still under investigation. CrVI is also known to activate various stress signaling pathways, such as the MAPKs, via the generation of reactive oxygen species. Besides activating MAPKs, CrVI is known to stimulate mitogenic transcription factors such as NF-κβ (human lymphocyte culture) and activate transcription factor 2 and oncogenic transcription factor c-Jun in human bronchial epithelial cells. These stress kinases and transcription factors are implicated in tumor growth and inflammation, contributing to CrVI-induced carcinogenesis. The activation of these factors and protein kinases constitutes a nongenotoxic CrVI carcinogenic mechanism of action in addition to direct mutagenesis [58,90].

Perspectives

Cancer is a leading cause of morbidity and mortality worldwide. It is a complex multifactorial disease where environmental and lifestyle factors contribute to approximately 93% of cancers. Studies indicate that 7% of all human cancers are hereditary. Environmental causes of cancers include lifestyle factors such as smoking, tobacco and alcohol consumption, diet, lack of physical activity, obesity, sunlight/UV exposure, hormone therapy, pathogenic microbes/infections, and others. Occupational and household exposure to chemical carcinogens such as aflatoxins, arsenic, asbestos, benzene, beryllium, cadmium, chromium, coke oven fumes, ethylene oxide, formaldehyde, lead, PAHs, vinyl chloride, and others also constitute the environmental causes of cancers. The National Toxicology Program has enlisted 256 substances, including physical, chemical, and biological compounds known to induce human cancers. Some of the important environmental cancer-causing agents have been discussed here. Humans are exposed to environmental carcinogens via contaminated air, water, and soil. Occupational exposure is a very significant source of environmental carcinogens. Lifestyle factors considered by some studies as environmental causes of cancers are modifiable habits of humans that can also markedly increase the risk of cancer development [4].

The carcinogenic mechanisms of the various environmental factors range from direct DNA damage, as in the case of ionizing radiation, to indirect DNA damage, such as arsenic. Common molecular mechanisms of environmental causes of cancer are DNA adduct formation and mutagenesis, macromolecule damage, oncogene activation, tumor suppressor inactivation, hyperproliferation, malignant transformation and induction of cancer stem cells, metabolic alterations, oxidative stress, epigenetic alterations, activation of stress signaling pathways and oncogenic transcription factors, inhibition of DNA repair systems, inflammation, and immune surveillance dysregulation. The duration of exposure, the concentration of the carcinogen, genetic makeup, and the medical history of an individual significantly affect the ability of environmental carcinogens in causing cancer. Also, as in the case of heavy metals carcinogens such as lead, arsenic, and chromium, the molecular mechanisms of carcinogens are not completely understood. Further investigations and epidemiological studies are warranted to decipher the environmental causes of cancer to develop effective cancer therapeutic agents.

References

[1] H. Sung, et al., Global cancer statistics 2020: GLOBOCAN estimates of incidence and mortality worldwide for 36 cancers in 185 countries, CA Cancer J. Clin. 71 (3) (2021) 209–249.

[2] P. Brennan, G. Davey-Smith, Identifying novel causes of cancers to enhance cancer prevention: new strategies are needed, J. Natl. Cancer Inst. 114 (3) (2022) 353–360.

[3] A. Sahar, et al., Lifestyle and habits as a risk factor of breast-cancer; a questionnaire-based study from Al-Resafa breast tumours hospitals and centres, New Iraqi J. Med. 7 (2021) 103–112.

[4] N. Parsa, Environmental factors inducing human cancers, Iran. J. Public Health 41 (11) (2012) 1–9.

[5] C. Thakur, et al., Deletion of mdig enhances H3K36me3 and metastatic potential of the triple negative breast cancer cells, iScience 25 (10) (2022) 105057.

[6] A. Shankar, et al., Environmental and occupational determinants of lung cancer, Transl. Lung Cancer Res. 8 (Suppl. 1) (2019) S31–s49.

[7] G. Danaei, et al., Causes of cancer in the world: comparative risk assessment of nine behavioural and environmental risk factors, Lancet 366 (9499) (2005) 1784–1793.

[8] Centers for Disease Control and Prevention (US), et al., How Tobacco Smoke Causes Disease: The Biology and Behavioral Basis for Smoking-Attributable Disease: A Report of the Surgeon General, Centers for Disease Control and Prevention (US), Atlanta, GA, 2010. Publications and Reports of the Surgeon General.

[9] P. Hikisz, D. Jacenik, The tobacco smoke component, acrolein, as a major culprit in lung diseases and respiratory cancers: molecular mechanisms of acrolein cytotoxic activity, Cells 12 (6) (2023) 879–907.

[10] O. Desouky, N. Ding, G. Zhou, Targeted and non-targeted effects of ionizing radiation, J. Radiat. Res. Appl. Sci. 8 (2) (2015) 247–254.

[11] X. Sun, et al., Ultraviolet radiation and melanomagenesis: from mechanism to immunotherapy, Front. Oncol. 10 (2020) 951.

[12] H. Soehnge, A. Ouhtit, H.N. Ananthaswamy, Mechanisms of induction of skin cancer by UV radiation, FBL 2 (4) (1997) 538–551.

[13] M.M. Dobrzyńska, A. Gajowik, K. Wieprzowski, Radon—occurrence and impact on the health, Rocz. Panstw. Zakl. Hig. 74 (1) (2023) 5–14.

[14] J.K. Scheideler, W.M.P. Klein, Awareness of the link between alcohol consumption and cancer across the world: a review, Cancer Epidemiol. Biomarkers Prev. 27 (4) (2018) 429–437.

[15] M. López-Lázaro, A local mechanism by which alcohol consumption causes cancer, Oral Oncol. 62 (2016) 149–152.

[16] P. Boffetta, M. Hashibe, Alcohol and cancer, Lancet Oncol. 7 (2) (2006) 149–156.

[17] K.I. Avgerinos, et al., Obesity and cancer risk: emerging biological mechanisms and perspectives, Metabolism 92 (2019) 121–135.

[18] G. De Pergola, F. Silvestris, Obesity as a major risk factor for cancer, J. Obes. 2013 (2013) 291546.

[19] I. Vucenik, J.P. Stains, Obesity and cancer risk: evidence, mechanisms, and recommendations, Ann. N. Y. Acad. Sci. 1271 (1) (2012) 37–43.

[20] K. Basen-Engquist, M. Chang, Obesity and cancer risk: recent review and evidence, Curr. Oncol. Rep. 13 (1) (2011) 71–76.

[21] E.E. Calle, R. Kaaks, Overweight, obesity and cancer: epidemiological evidence and proposed mechanisms, Nat. Rev. Cancer 4 (8) (2004) 579–591.

[22] L.M. Coussens, Z. Werb, Inflammation and cancer, Nature 420 (6917) (2002) 860–867.

[23] R. Kolb, F.S. Sutterwala, W. Zhang, Obesity and cancer: inflammation bridges the two, Curr. Opin. Pharmacol. 29 (2016) 77–89.

[24] M.C. Turner, et al., Outdoor air pollution and cancer: an overview of the current evidence and public health recommendations, CA Cancer J. Clin. 70 (6) (2020) 460–479.

[25] T.H. Wang, et al., PM2.5 promotes lung cancer progression through activation of the AhR-TMPRSS2-IL18 pathway, EMBO Mol. Med. 15 (6) (2023) e17014.

[26] R. Li, R. Zhou, J. Zhang, Function of PM2.5 in the pathogenesis of lung cancer and chronic airway inflammatory diseases, Oncol. Lett. 15 (5) (2018) 7506–7514.

[27] C.-W. Lee, et al., The inducible role of ambient particulate matter in cancer progression via oxidative stress-mediated reactive oxygen species pathways: a recent perception, Cancers 12 (2020), https://doi.org/10.3390/cancers12092505.

[28] G. Liu, et al., PM(2.5) exposure and cervical cancer survival in Liaoning Province, northeastern China, Environ. Sci. Pollut. Res. Int. 29 (49) (2022) 74669–74676.

[29] P.V. Parikh, Y. Wei, PAHs and PM2.5 emissions and female breast cancer incidence in metro Atlanta and rural Georgia, Int. J. Environ. Health Res. 26 (4) (2016) 458–466.

[30] P. Wadgaonkar, F. Chen, Connections between endoplasmic reticulum stress-associated unfolded protein response, mitochondria, and autophagy in arsenic-induced carcinogenesis, Semin. Cancer Biol. 76 (2021) 258–266.

[31] P. Boffetta, F. Nyberg, Contribution of environmental factors to cancer risk, Br. Med. Bull. 68 (1) (2003) 71–94.

[32] L. Li, F. Chen, Oxidative stress, epigenetics, and cancer stem cells in arsenic carcinogenesis and prevention, Curr. Pharmacol. Rep. 2 (2) (2016) 57–63.

[33] I. Palma-Lara, et al., Arsenic exposure: a public health problem leading to several cancers, Regul. Toxicol. Pharmacol. 110 (2020) 104539.

[34] J.F. Reichard, A. Puga, Effects of arsenic exposure on DNA methylation and epigenetic gene regulation, Epigenomics 2 (1) (2010) 87–104.

[35] R.S. Okoji, et al., Sodium arsenite administration via drinking water increases genome-wide and Ha-ras DNA hypomethylation in methyl-deficient C57BL/6J mice, Carcinogenesis 23 (5) (2002) 777–785.

[36] Q. Chang, et al., Arsenic-induced sub-lethal stress reprograms human bronchial epithelial cells to CD6I cancer stem cells, Oncotarget 5 (5) (2014) 1290–1303.

[37] R. Picetti, et al., Nitrate and nitrite contamination in drinking water and cancer risk: a systematic review with meta-analysis, Environ. Res. 210 (2022) 112988.

[38] M.H. Ward, et al., Drinking water nitrate and human health: an updated review, Int. J. Environ. Res. Public Health 15 (7) (2018) 1557–1588.

[39] J. Schullehner, et al., Nitrate in drinking water and colorectal cancer risk: a nationwide population-based cohort study, Int. J. Cancer 143 (1) (2018) 73–79.

[40] S. Chowdhury, M.J. Rodriguez, R. Sadiq, Disinfection byproducts in Canadian provinces: associated cancer risks and medical expenses, J. Hazard. Mater. 187 (1–3) (2011) 574–584.

[41] J.Y. Min, K.B. Min, Blood trihalomethane levels and the risk of total cancer mortality in US adults, Environ. Pollut. 212 (2016) 90–96.

[42] M. Diana, M. Felipe-Sotelo, T. Bond, Disinfection byproducts potentially responsible for the association between chlorinated drinking water and bladder cancer: a review, Water Res. 162 (2019) 492–504.

[43] R.R. Jones, et al., Ingested nitrate, disinfection by-products, and kidney cancer risk in older women, Epidemiology 28 (5) (2017) 703–711.

[44] A.J.L. Quist, et al., Ingested nitrate and nitrite, disinfection by-products, and pancreatic cancer risk in postmenopausal women, Int. J. Cancer 142 (2) (2018) 251–261.

[45] D.N. Medgyesi, et al., Drinking water disinfection byproducts, ingested nitrate, and risk of endometrial cancer in postmenopausal women, Environ. Health Perspect. 130 (5) (2022) 57012.

[46] S.D. Richardson, et al., Occurrence, genotoxicity, and carcinogenicity of regulated and emerging disinfection by-products in drinking water: a review and roadmap for research, Mut. Res. Rev. Mut. Res. 636 (1) (2007) 178–242.

[47] E.M. Sunderland, et al., A review of the pathways of human exposure to poly- and perfluoroalkyl substances (PFASs) and present understanding of health effects, J. Expo. Sci. Environ. Epidemiol. 29 (2) (2019) 131–147.

[48] P.E. Rosenfeld, et al., Perfluoroalkyl substances exposure in firefighters: sources and implications, Environ. Res. 220 (2023) 115164.

[49] A.M. Temkin, et al., Application of the key characteristics of carcinogens to per and Polyfluoroalkyl substances, Int. J. Environ. Res. Public Health 17 (5) (2020).

[50] T. Münzel, et al., Soil and water pollution and human health: what should cardiologists worry about? Cardiovasc. Res. 119 (2) (2022) 440–449.

[51] J.J. Steffan, et al., The effect of soil on human health: an overview, Eur. J. Soil Sci. 69 (1) (2018) 159–171.

[52] L. Järup, Hazards of heavy metal contamination, Br. Med. Bull. 68 (2003) 167–182.

[53] M.-C. Rousseau, et al., Occupational exposure to Lead compounds and risk of cancer among men: a population-based case-control study, Am. J. Epidemiol. 166 (9) (2007) 1005–1014.

[54] X. Lin, et al., Connecting gastrointestinal cancer risk to cadmium and lead exposure in the Chaoshan population of Southeast China, Environ. Sci. Pollut. Res. 25 (18) (2018) 17611–17619.

[55] Y. Meng, et al., Exposure to lead increases the risk of meningioma and brain cancer: a meta-analysis, J. Trace Elem. Med. Biol. 60 (2020) 126474.

[56] A. Anttila, et al., Lung cancer incidence among workers biologically monitored for occupational exposure to lead: a cohort study, Scand. J. Work Environ. Health 48 (7) (2022) 540–548.

[57] E.K. Silbergeld, M. Waalkes, J.M. Rice, Lead as a carcinogen: experimental evidence and mechanisms of action, Am. J. Ind. Med. 38 (3) (2000) 316–323.

[58] D. Beyersmann, A. Hartwig, Carcinogenic metal compounds: recent insight into molecular and cellular mechanisms, Arch. Toxicol. 82 (8) (2008) 493–512.

[59] S. Hemmaphan, N.K. Bordeerat, Genotoxic effects of lead and their impact on the expression of DNA repair genes, Int. J. Environ. Res. Public Health 19 (7) (2022) 4307–4315.

[60] K. Rehman, et al., Prevalence of exposure of heavy metals and their impact on health consequences, J. Cell. Biochem. 119 (1) (2018) 157–184.

[61] H.S. Kim, Y.J. Kim, Y.R. Seo, An overview of carcinogenic heavy metal: molecular toxicity mechanism and prevention, J. Cancer Prev. 20 (4) (2015) 232–240.

[62] J. Huff, et al., Cadmium-induced cancers in animals and in humans, Int. J. Occup. Environ. Health 13 (2) (2007) 202–212.

[63] G.F. Nordberg, et al., Risk assessment of effects of cadmium on human health (IUPAC Technical Report), Pure Appl. Chem. 90 (4) (2018) 755–808.

[64] M.P. Waalkes, Cadmium carcinogenesis, Mutat. Res. Fundam. Mol. Mech. Mutagen. 533 (1) (2003) 107–120.

[65] Y. Zhu, M. Costa, Metals and molecular carcinogenesis, Carcinogenesis 41 (9) (2020) 1161–1172.

[66] Y.B. Man, et al., Cancer risk assessments of Hong Kong soils contaminated by polycyclic aromatic hydrocarbons, J. Hazard. Mater. 261 (2013) 770–776.

[67] D. Wang, et al., Concentration and potential ecological risk of PAHs in different layers of soil in the petroleum-contaminated areas of the loess plateau, China, Int. J. Environ. Res. Public Health 15 (8) (2018) 1785–1800.

[68] D. Roy, et al., Cancer risk levels for sediment- and soil-bound polycyclic aromatic hydrocarbons in coastal areas of South Korea, Front. Environ. Sci. 9 (2021) 719243–719254.

[69] H.I. Abdel-Shafy, M.S.M. Mansour, A review on polycyclic aromatic hydrocarbons: source, environmental impact, effect on human health and remediation, Egypt. J. Pet. 25 (1) (2016) 107–123.

[70] G. Becher, A. Bjørseth, Determination of exposure to polycyclic aromatic hydrocarbons by analysis of human urine, Cancer Lett. 17 (3) (1983) 301–311.

[71] R. Stading, et al., Molecular mechanisms of pulmonary carcinogenesis by polycyclic aromatic hydrocarbons (PAHs): implications for human lung cancer, Semin. Cancer Biol. 76 (2021) 3–16.

[72] B. Moorthy, C. Chu, D.J. Carlin, Polycyclic aromatic hydrocarbons: from metabolism to lung cancer, Toxicol. Sci. 145 (1) (2015) 5–15.

[73] K. Sun, et al., A review of human and animals exposure to polycyclic aromatic hydrocarbons: health risk and adverse effects, photo-induced toxicity and regulating effect of microplastics, Sci. Total Environ. 773 (2021) 145403.

[74] S. Shukla, et al., Concentration, source apportionment and potential carcinogenic risks of polycyclic aromatic hydrocarbons (PAHs) in roadside soils, Chemosphere 292 (2022) 133413.

[75] Y. Ngamwong, et al., Additive synergism between asbestos and smoking in lung cancer risk: a systematic review and meta-analysis, PLoS One 10 (8) (2015) e0135798.

[76] K. Luus, Asbestos: mining exposure, health effects and policy implications, Mcgill J. Med. 10 (2) (2007) 121–126.

[77] W. IARC, Asbestos (chrysotile, amosite, crocidolite, tremolite, actinolite, and anthophyllite), IARC Monographs on the Evaluation of Carcinogenic Risks to Humans. A Review of Human Carcinogens; Part C: Arsenic, Metals, Fibres, and Dusts, 2012, p. 219.

[78] M. Peña-Castro, M. Montero-Acosta, M. Saba, A critical review of asbestos concentrations in water and air, according to exposure sources, Heliyon 9 (5) (2023) e15730.

[79] D. Ospina, et al., Analyzing biological and molecular characteristics and genomic damage induced by exposure to asbestos, Cancer Manag. Res. 11 (2019) 4997–5012.

[80] N. Vandeven, P. Nghiem, Pathogen-driven cancers and emerging immune therapeutic strategies, Cancer Immunol. Res. 2 (1) (2014) 9–14.

[81] M.N.A. Hatta, et al., Pathogens and carcinogenesis: a review, Biology (Basel) 10 (2021) 6.

[82] D. Zella, R.C. Gallo, Viruses and bacteria associated with cancer: an overview, Viruses 13 (6) (2021) 1039.

[83] A.S. Hamid, et al., Aflatoxin B1-induced hepatocellular carcinoma in developing countries: geographical distribution, mechanism of action and prevention, Oncol. Lett. 5 (4) (2013) 1087–1092.

[84] S. Marchese, et al., Aflatoxin B1 and M1: biological properties and their involvement in cancer development, Toxins 10 (6) (2018) 214.

[85] G.S. Bbosa, et al., Review of the biological and health effects of aflatoxins on body organs and body systems, in: Aflatoxins—Recent Advances and Future Prospects, 12, 2013, pp. 239–265.

[86] T.J. Atkinson, A review of the role of benzene metabolites and mechanisms in malignant transformation: summative evidence for a lack of research in nonmyelogenous cancer types, Int. J. Hyg. Environ. Health 212 (1) (2009) 1–10.

[87] H. Bahadar, S. Mostafalou, M. Abdollahi, Current understandings and perspectives on non-cancer health effects of benzene: a global concern, Toxicol. Appl. Pharmacol. 276 (2) (2014) 83–94.

[88] R. Dewi, et al., Genetic, epigenetic, and lineage-directed mechanisms in benzene-induced malignancies and hematotoxicity targeting hematopoietic stem cells niche, Hum. Exp. Toxicol. 39 (5) (2020) 577–595.

[89] C.C. Alvarez, M.E. Bravo Gómez, A. Hernández Zavala, Hexavalent chromium: regulation and health effects, J. Trace Elem. Med. Biol. 65 (2021) 126729.

[90] T. Pavesi, J.C. Moreira, Mechanisms and individuality in chromium toxicity in humans, J. Appl. Toxicol. 40 (9) (2020) 1183–1197.

Cancer stem cells—Challenges for cancer therapies

Rashi Arora[a], Apoorva Uboveja[b], and Rama Kadamb[c]

[a]*University Flow Cytometry Resource, University of Minnesota, Minneapolis, MN, United States,* [b]*UPMC Hillman Cancer Center, University of Pittsburgh School of Medicine, Pittsburgh, PA, United States,* [c]*Department of Cell Biology, Cancer Dormancy and Tumor Microenvironment Institute, Gruss-Lipper Biophotonics Center, Albert Einstein Cancer Center, Albert Einstein College of Medicine, Bronx, NY, United States*

Introduction

The process of development of a multicellular organism, including humans, begins from a single fertilized egg called zygote. The zygote develops into a totipotent ball of cells that further differentiates into the three germ layers: endoderm, ectoderm, and mesoderm [1]. These three primitive cell types eventually develop into all tissues in the adult body. During the development process the single cell undergoes multiple proliferation, specialization, interaction, and rearrangement in a predetermined way to produce the spectacularly complex multicellular organism. The unspecialized cells that have the ability of self-renewal and can differentiate into various cells of an organism are stem cells. The process of attaining specialization involves multiple steps, and the developmental potency is reduced with each step. Therefore, totipotent stem cells, e.g., zygotes, are able to divide and differentiate into cells of the whole organism, but the spectrum of differentiation narrows down from pluripotent to multi-, oligo- or unipotent cells [2].

The stem cells exist both in embryos, called embryonic stem cells (ESCs), and in adults, called adult stem cells or somatic stem cells (SSCs). ESCs are pluripotent stem cells that form cells of all germ layers, that are capable of differentiating into all tissues during embryonic development [3] and characteristically similar to ESCs are induced pluripotent stem cells (iPSCs), that researchers have developed by successfully reprogramming somatic cells into stem-like cells [4]. Many adult tissues, such as the blood or the epithelial tissues lining surrounding most organs, have a tightly regulated process of renovation owing to the activity of a dedicated population of tissue-specific SSCs [5]. While the bulk of the cells constituting these heterogeneous tissues in adults are specialized, short-lived, and perform tissue-specific functions, the tissues maintain their mass and architecture over time. The relatively

93

Copyright © 2024 Elsevier Inc. All rights reserved, including those for text and data mining, AI training, and similar technologies.

sparse population of SSCs here plays the important role of generating cellular progeny that differ in their apparent state of differentiation, replenishing and repairing the adult tissues [6]. These tissues, which are organized as a cellular hierarchy with a small population of tissue-specific SSCs, are the hub for malignancies.

As a matter of fact, cancerous cells that eventually form tumors are the results of the multiple genetic mutations that accumulate in a single target cell, sometimes over a period of many years [7]. The long-lived SSCs with extraordinary expansion potential are under characteristic homeostatic control by environmental stimuli and genetic constraints that enable them to modulate and balance differentiation and self-renewal. At the same time, due to their longevity and replicability, these are the obvious natural candidates in which early transforming mutations may accumulate. Tumors, identical to their normal tissue counterparts, are composed of heterogeneous populations of cells that differ in their apparent state of differentiation. In fact, the differentiation features of a tumor are routinely used clinically by pathologists to define primary anatomical origin along with its morphological and architecture of the tumor. Furthermore, it has been postulated that akin to healthy tissue, the growth of tumors is sustained by a small number of stem-like cells hidden within the tumors.

Cancer stem cells (CSCs) are the small subset of cells within tumor cell population that display stemness characteristics, including the ability to proliferate and the differentiation capacities along with tumorigenicity, that is, potential to initiate tumor when transplanted into an animal host [8]. They are believed to be responsible for the biological characteristics of cancer including rapid growth, invasion, and metastasis, and clinical observations such as the almost inevitable recurrence of tumors after initially successful chemotherapy and/or radiation therapy and the phenomenon of tumor dormancy [9]. It is the ability of these CSCs to self-renew and to create the heterogeneous milieu of nontumorigenic cells that make up the bulk of a tumor. CSCs' existence in tumor cells is the main cause for relapse, metastasis, and also a major player in making these tumor cells resistant to drugs and radiation therapy. Beginning this century, the research in the cancer and stem cell research sector has been dominated by the CSCs. The marriage of stem cell biology and oncology ensued a wave of reports on the identification of CSCs in several common cancer types, including leukemia [10–12], breast cancer [13], colorectal cancer [14–16], and brain cancer [17]. Several groups have proposed that CSC stemness may help identify the cancer cell of origin and account for the molecular and phenotypic differences within and between these diverse types of cancer. Thereafter, the CSC theory has shifted the paradigm of designing innovative treatment strategies for various cancers toward targeting CSCs, the real culprit for tumor's longevity, and not merely aiming at shrinking tumor bulk.

The identification of the CSCs

The existence of the concept of "stem cells" can be traced back to the 19th century [18]. Early 20th century witnessed studies that reported tumor initiation by single cells derived from mouse tumors [19], and later studies reported their minority in the tumor [20–22]. Based on clinical observations in myeloproliferative disorders, William Dameshek, in the mid-20th century, made remarkable and insightful speculation of the common origin of these diseases from a multipotent hematopoietic stem cell. However, reports providing evidence for the existence of stem cells in human tissue came a few years later when Pierce et al. studied germ cell tumors, teratocarcinoma, in humans and established their heterogeneity by finding both differentiated and undifferentiated cells [23]. Their study pioneered in indicating the existence of multipotent stem cells. In another study they further found higher mitotic activity in the undifferentiated multipotent cells in teratocarcinomas [23]. At the same time, Becker et al. provided the genetic evidence of hematopoietic stem cells [24]. Herein genetically marked cells, generated by sublethal irradiation of the donor bone marrow, were demonstrated to self-renew and differentiate in spleens of conditioned transplanted host mice. The Pierce group, further in 1971, showed the appearance of early labeled DNA from the undifferentiated areas at later time points in the well-differentiated areas of a mouse squamous cell carcinoma. The cells from these well-differentiated areas, shown to be derived from undifferentiated cells, were incapable of initiating tumors when transplanted into compatible hosts, which were thus shown to derive from undifferentiated cells [25]. A series of such reports on proliferative heterogeneity and hierarchical organization [26–28] led to early definitions of the CSC concept. "Carcinomas are caricatures of tissue renewal, in that they are composed of a mixture of malignant stem cells, which have a marked capacity for proliferation and a limited capacity for differentiation under normal homeostatic conditions, and of the differentiated, possibly benign, progeny of these malignant cells" [29].

By the end of the 20th century, there was limited in vivo experimental evidence on the CSC concept due to a lack of models to investigate the biological properties of malignant cells with transplantable tumorigenic ability. In 1963, the first in vivo colony assay was developed by Bruce and Van Der Gaag for a mouse lymphoma-initiating cell [22]. The early 90s marked the generation of a series of immunodeficient genetically modified mice that could be just the perfect xenograft models, making detection and quantification of tumorigenic cells from many primary human tumors [30]. The severe combined immunodeficiency disease (SCID) mice, along with significant research advances on hematopoietic stem cells and advent of FACS by then combined with large sets of well-validated cell surface markers, had proved to be instrumental in bringing up multiple evidence reports on the percentage of tumorigenic cells within the transplanted tumor cells. One of the first such studies was by Bonnet and Dick, where they successfully generated most subtypes of human acute myeloid leukemia (AML) in SCID mice. They found that only CD34+CD38-fractions were able to initiate leukemias and thus, a CSC was first identified in AML. Using the xenograft assay, the occurrence of initiating tumorigenic cells was reported by them to be on the order of one per million tumor cells [12]. Clarke et al. pioneered in following this concept and experimental approach to a solid breast cancer tumor [13], and then several studies followed suit on other solid tumors including brain tumors, colon cancer, etc. [14–17]. While cluster of differentiation (CD) biomarkers were the first few ones to be identified, lately, other properties like sphere forming capacity in serum-free medium or soft agar and overexpression of drug-efflux pumps ATP-binding cassette (ABC) transporter and the resulting dye exclusion ability, functional markers like enzymatic activity like aldehyde dehydrogenase1 (ALDH1), epithelial-specific antigen (ESA), components of some key signaling pathways, kinetics measurement markers and miRNAs have been used to characterize the CSCs [15,31,32]. The CSC markers vary with the type of tumor, and after tremendous efforts, an overwhelming and progressive list of these markers is available that can be used for the detection of CSCs (see Table 1).

Table 1 Several biomarkers for CSC in some solid tumors.

Marker	Role	Cancer
CD133	Glycoprotein that maintains lipid composition in cell membranes	B, BN, G, C, L, LV, M, O, P, PT, S
CD44	Glycoprotein involved in cell-cell interactions, cell adhesion, and migration	B, BN, C, L, LV, O, P, PT, S, HN
CD24	Signal transducer	B, C, O, P, S, LV
CD90	Adhesion and signal transduction	B, BN, G, L, LV, S
CD117	A type of receptor tyrosine kinase also called c-kit	L, O, PT
CD166	Activated leukocyte cell adhesion molecule	C, L, PT, HN
CD49f	Also known as integrin α6, has a role in cell surface adhesion and signaling	B, BN, S, C
CD200	Regulation of immunosuppression	C
CD206	A mannose receptor with a role in endocytosis, phagocytosis, and immune homeostasis	LI, C
CD271	Nerve growth factor receptor	M
ALDH1	Enzyme from cellular metabolic pathway	B, C, L, M, P, PT, S, O, HN
ABCB5	ABC transporter with a role in drug efflux	C, M
ABCG2	ABC transporter with a role in drug efflux	L, P
EpCAM	Homotypic calcium-independent cell adhesion molecule	C, LI, P, PT, S, O
CXCR4	Chemokine	P, PT
α2β1-integrin	Cell adhesion and recognition	PT
α6-integrin	Cell adhesion	B, G, PT
L1CAM	Cell adhesion molecules involved in neuronal migration and differentiation	BN

B, *breast cancer;* BN, *brain tumor;* C, *colorectal cancer;* G, *glioma;* HN, *head and neck cancer;* L, *lung cancer;* LV, *liver cancer;* M, *melanoma;* O, *ovarian cancer;* P, *pancreatic cancer;* PT, *prostate cancer;* S, *stomach cancer. Refs. [41, 67].*

CSCs in tumorigenesis models

Inconsistent with the traditional belief that most cancer cells can proliferate extensively and metastasize, the CSC theory proposes that similar to normal tissue, cancer is hierarchically organized, and its growth and progression are driven by a very small fraction of cells, the CSCs. Much like the SSCs, the CSCs differentiate into phenotypically diverse progeny with limited proliferative potential that compose the bulk of cells in a tumor and contribute only in a limited capacity to disease progression. This has been called the hierarchical model as well.

The discovery of the Philadelphia (Ph) chromosome and its unique association with chronic myeloid leukemia (CML) brought a breakthrough in cancer research [33]. It was the primary genetic evidence that cancers are usually individual clones of cells associated with specific genetic aberrations. This shifted the cancer research spotlight toward mutations in oncogenes and tumor suppressor genes. The clonal evolution (CE) theory was hence developed, which postulates cancer development to be an evolutionary process that is driven by the stepwise acquisition of random somatic-cell mutations within oncogenes and the associated sequential clonal selection [7,34]. The concept laid the foundation for the stochastic model wherein every cell of a tumor has equal potential to generate the tumor.

As per the CSC theory, the actual tumorigenic cells are sparsely populated in whole cancer, which implies that epigenetic differences could distinguish them from the bulk nontumorigenic cells. Although there is no direct evidence that tumorigenic cells differ from nontumorigenic cells because of epigenetic rather than genetic differences, it's inconvincible that only rare cancer cells have a genotype permissive for extensive proliferation. In contrast, the CE model indicates the cancer cells acquire both genetic and epigenetic changes that confer them selective proliferative advantage, and these then abundantly populate the cancer tissue. While being phenotypically heterogeneous and hierarchically organized are characteristics of tumor models based on CS theory, the tumors that develop with CE could be homogeneous or heterogeneous and may or may not have a hierarchical pattern [35]. A major contrasting factor among the two, guiding the rationale for therapy, is determining the culprit. If the bulk of cancer has aggressively proliferating clones, then virtually all cells must be eliminated to treat the disease, which is the case with the CE model. However, the CSC theory directs targeting the small subpopulations of tumorigenic cells that drive tumor growth and progression.

It's noteworthy that genomic instability is the driving force in either model. Further, the two model systems are not mutually exclusive, and both pathways can occur in a tumor [35]. The CSC concept can attain full worth only with insights derived from CE [36]. The recent exploration of the concept of plasticity, that is, the potential of a stem cell to switch between a proliferating stem-like state and a differentiated state, particularly in the epithelial tissues, has, in fact, unified the two concepts into one model [37,38]. This novel model spells out a more likely process of multistep tumor progression wherein both genetic and microenvironmental signaling guides the dedifferentiation of mitotically more active progenitor progeny back to the CSC. The amplifying transit progeny cells may accumulate genetic alteration (stochastic model) and feed those into the CSC pool (hierarchical model) via the process of dedifferentiation.

Biology of CSCs

Stemness of a cell is defined by its virtue of self-renewal and ability to generate progeny committed to differentiate. Stem cells achieve this by regulating the switch between two modes of division—asymmetric and symmetric. A stem cell undergoing asymmetric cell division generates one daughter cell with the stemness and the other daughter cell with differentiation potential. In contrast, symmetric division in a stem cell results in identical progeny, thereby enabling it to maintain the pool of either type of cell depending upon the immediate requirement [39]. The homeostatic state of stem cells is achieved by tight regulation of several highly regulated molecular pathways that are reportedly aberrant in CSCs [40]. The list of dysfunctional signaling pathways contributing to the characteristic unregulated self-renewal and differentiation in CSC includes but is not limited to the Wnt, Notch, JAK/STAT, Hedgehog, phosphatidylinositol 3-kinase/phosphatase and tensin homolog (PI3K/PTEN), and nuclear factor-κB (NF-κB) pathway. Genetic and/or epigenetic factors are also being found associated with the aberrations observed in the signaling pathways thereby identifying oncogenes like AKT1, a serine-threonine protein kinase, ABL1, a tyrosine kinase, etc. Promoting symmetrical cell divisions (like planar cell polarity pathway), inducing cell cycle proliferating target genes (like cyclin D1), growth factor receptors (like EGFR), and antiapoptotic proteins (like BCL-2), coordinating interactions between growth factor receptor signaling and cell cycle progression are some of the ways in which the above mentioned pathways drive tumorigenic potential of CSCs [31,41]. For example, aberrant PI3K/AKT signaling reported in several forms of leukemia promotes tumorigenesis through enhanced activation of AKT1 that stimulates the expression of antiapoptotic Bcl-2 and inhibits pro-apoptotic protein BAD by phosphorylation [42]. Similarly, NF-κB pathway regulates the cell cycle regulatory components and apoptosis-related proteins. Its aberrant activation reported in tumor cells results in increased levels of Bcl-xL, Bcl-2, cIAPs (cellular inhibitors of apoptosis), CyclinD1, IL-6, survivin, TRAF (TNF receptor-associated factor), etc. [43]. Likewise, to date a plethora of studies in almost all cancer types have established the role and the mechanism of these pathways in promoting cell renewal, survival and metastasis and inhibiting apoptosis, differentiation [31,40,41]. Many transcription factors associated with one or the other pathways have also been reported to be overexpressed in CSCs like Oct4, Sox2, Nanog, KLF4, MYC, etc. [41].

Other than the intrinsic dysregulated pathways, the CSCs' interaction with other cells and their surrounding environment, called tumor microenvironment (TME), plays a vital role in their survival and functioning. CSCs, in fact, have the right to influence and modify their microenvironment by regulating surrounding cells to suit themselves and create their own CSC niche [44]. The CSC niche is complex in terms of secretory factors and cellular interaction. Although the precise composition varies depending upon organism, tissue type, and functionality, the niche usually includes the CSC, surrounding non-CSCs, cancer associated fibroblast (CAFs), immune cells, vascular endothelial cells (ECs), neighboring connective tissue cells such as mesenchymal stem cells (MSCs), extracellular matrix (ECM), network of signaling molecules, growth factors, blood vessels and other cellular and acellular components. The complexity of the niche is indicative of its critical importance in facilitating primary tumor growth and their metastatic potential [45]. CAFs are irreversibly activated and influence cell cycle processes, such as differentiation, proliferation, cell survival, adult-tissue homeostasis, and tumorigenesis, by secreting a number of proteins, including growth factors and cytokines, which bind to altered fibroblast growth factor receptors (FGFR) family: FGFR1/2/3/4 on cancer cell surface [46]. CAFs like myofibroblasts, particularly found in stroma of invasive tumors, have been reported to play a role in maintaining stemness of CSCs, remodeling and reprogramming the ECM by secreting cytokines, growth factors, chemokines, hormones, inflammatory mediators, adhesion and ECM proteins that promotes cancer cells proliferation, migration and invasion [47,48]. Likewise, there have been several reports on other components of TEM like MSCs, ECs, tumor-associated macrophages (TAMs), etc., underlining the role in subordinating CSCs in tumor progression, immune evasion, and metastasis through secretory proteins (like IL-6, CXCL8, CXCL10, EGF, etc.) and regulatory pathways such as STAT3, Akt and ERK [49–51]. TME signaling has also been reported to influence immune cell activity, such as the phenotypic switching of cytotoxic M1 macrophages to antiinflammatory M2 type, which promotes cancer progression [52,53]. The increasing reports and evidence on the complexity of CSCs and their niche have been instrumental in understanding the process of tumor malignancy, metastasis, and therapy resistance.

Challenges posed by CSCs in cancer therapies

As the concept of tumorigenesis evolves, so does the therapeutic regimen. The current belief indicates that CSCs are the key components within the tumor and are the primary targets of novel therapies. At the same time, CSCs are also the major contributor to metastasis, tumor recurrence, and therapy resistance, which is a crucial challenge in cancer treatment. Cancer cells initially respond to the treatment, but sustained administration is not effective as cancer cells develop resistance mechanisms leading to a more aggressive phenotype accompanied with a poor prognosis. The mechanisms of therapy resistance are multifactorial and can be broadly divided into two categories: intrinsic and acquired. Intrinsic resistance arises due to preexisting factors in the cancer cells prior to any treatment, which renders chemotherapeutic treatments useless, and acquired resistance arises during chemotherapeutic treatments. Lately, acquired drug resistance has gained more attention and is being recognized as the major cause of treatment failure in cancer patients, especially in relapse cases [54]. CSCs evade the conventional chemotherapeutic approaches, based on targeting its removal and, thereby, tumor elimination with no relapse, in a number of ways, which are discussed in this section. Accumulating evidence suggests that the resistant CSC, which arises either due to intrinsic or extrinsic factors, is the driver for tumor relapse and metastasis.

Ambiguity of the CSC markers

The CSCs have been increasingly identified and distinguished from other cells using specific markers, some of which are listed in Table 1. As the paradigm of cancer therapy shifted toward CSCs targeted therapy, CSC surface markers emerged to be an obvious lucrative molecular target. Several immunotoxins and antibodies have been developed against the surface markers for selective eradication of CSCs [55,56]. Monoclonal antibodies (MABs) H90 against CD44, 7G3 against CD47, and B6H12 against CD125 were effective in eliminating AML CSCs in the preclinical model [57]. For solid cancers, CD133, a 5-transmembrane glycoprotein, also called Prominin 1, has been considered a promiscuous target. Several preclinical in vivo evidence on therapeutic efficacy of targeted antibodies and FDA-approved compound Oxytetracycline against CD133 have lined up [58–60]. Furthermore, rituximab (anti-CD20), cetuximab (anti-EGFR), Campath-1H/alemtuzumab (anti-CD52), trastuzumab (anti-HER2), bevacizumab (anti-VEGF-A), pembrolizumab (anti-PD-1) are some other FDA approved immunotherapy against tumor cells [61].

While increasing evidence on the efficacy of targeted immunotherapy is being presented [62], none of them is highly specific to the CSCs. The markers displayed on the CSCs might also be displayed on normal stem cells or rarely other somatic cells, thus limiting their potential in exclusive targeting and compromising the targeted therapeutic regimen based on them [63]. The resultant toxicity due to nonexclusivity is very well reported, like skin eruption caused by cetuximab therapy directed against EGFR or cardiac toxicity caused in breast cancer therapy due to the use of anti-HER2/*neu* antibody, trastuzumab [64,65]. Furthermore, the CSCs tend to be a heterogeneous population, and there has not yet been a universal CSC marker identified that could clearly differentiate all types of CSCs. In fact, tumor subtypes have been found without the identifying CSC marker, such as CD133-type glioblastoma [66]. Due to continuous CE and epigenetic regulation, CSC marker expression may get lost at any stage in a given tumor [67]. Thus, the reliability on the surface markers for eliminating every single CSC in order to prevent relapse is highly questionable. Probably identification of more specific markers, which itself is a hurricane task due to the rarity of CSCs, use of a combination of markers, exploring the possibility of the existence of different splice variants of these markers in normal cells vs CSCs and thereby identifying CSC specific epitopes are some of the approaches that could potentially improve the outcome of therapeutic targeting of CSCs based on surface markers.

Crosstalk among the regulatory pathways

As mentioned previously, dysregulated signaling pathways lay the foundation of biology of the CSCs, enabling them to retain stemness and generate tumors. These pathways have remained to be the hotspots for researchers exploring therapeutic targets for various tumors. Correspondingly, numerous compounds that inhibit the aberrated pathways have used as anticancer drugs like imatinib (receptor tyrosine kinase inhibitor targeting P13/AKT pathway), thalidomide (TNF-α inhibitor targeting NF-kB pathway), bortezomib (targeting NF-kB pathway), vismodegib (transmembrane protein smooth ened inhibitor targeting hedgehog pathway) and even more are still being developed like DAPT/GSI-IX and quinomycin A (notch ligand inhibitors), Wnt 974 and niclosamide (Wnt/β-catenin pathway inhibitor), etc. [68–70]. Although these have significantly improved 5-year survival rates in cancer patients, loss of efficacy and nonspecific toxicity remain associated with the use of pathway inhibitory drugs. Other than being involved in the maintenance of the CSCs and their tumorigenic potential, these pathways have obligatory roles in other cells as well, which explains the off-target toxicity of the compounds targeting the pathways. Their approval for use as anticancer drugs is based on accessing their variable degree of toxicities in other tissues, including cardiac toxicity, neural toxicity, skin toxicity, etc., and striking a balance between the anticancer effects and side effects.

Further, the CSC regulatory pathways demonstrate a high degree of crosstalk to maintain the tumor phenotype of CSCs. Like the regulation of NF-κB signaling by Wnt/β-catenin mediated through a TNF superfamily receptor, TNFRSF19 [71] and inhibition of Wnt and Notch signaling by TGF-β1 silencing through decreases the expression of Smad2/3, β-catenin [72]. Thus, it will be mindful to say that signaling pathways create an intricate network of signaling molecules that promote tumorigenesis. Evidently, the crosstalks render a certain degree of resistance to the CSCs against drugs specifically targeting one pathway of cancer cells. The loss of efficacy of P13K inhibitors in breast cancer cells can be explained by increased expression of Notch1 in the resistant cells [73]. Similar cooperation has been reported amongst Wnt, Notch and Hedgehog pathway and also between P13K and hedgehog pathway. These reports provide a plausible explanation for resistant phenotypes in CSCs and the limitation of single-agent therapy in targeting CSCs [74,75]. Perhaps combination approaches might overcome the crosstalk among different pathways and provide efficient means for the targeting of CSCs.

CSC-mediated tumor dormancy

Cancer dormancy, a clinically obscure state of cancer, poses a major problem to the prolonged efficacy of chemotherapeutic treatments. It is a major contributing factor to multidrug resistance (MDR), cancer relapse, and metastasis. Tendency to alternate between an actively proliferating state and a quiescence state is another classic attribute of the stem cells reported in CSCs that facilitates tumor dormancy. Dormant cancer cells stay in the G0 phase of the cell cycle but can reenter cell division upon mitotic stimulus [76,77]. The dormant state allows the CSCs to pose long-term tumorigenic potential by evading the conventional cancer treatments that, however, combat their progeny.

CSCs isolated from leukemias showed increased resistance to drugs targeting actively proliferating cells mediated by increased G0/G1 arrest in their cell cycle [78,79]. Human AML xenograft mice model evaded the treatment with cytosine arabinoside (Ara-C) by forming a dormancy supportive niche that promotes *p21Cip1/Waf1*-dependent reversible cell cycle arrest [80]. Similar mechanistic studies have revealed a few ways and pathways that facilitate CSCs to switch between active and quiescent states depending upon the microenvironment cues [81,82]. This includes downregulation of the cell cycle regulators cyclin A2 and E2 and mitotic regulators like survivin.

Much research is needed beyond the scope of conventional antiproliferative agents to target the quiescent CSCs. Possible approaches can be driving quiescent cells to reenter a proliferative phase and then targeting, irreversibly arresting the CSCs in the G0 state, or lastly, targeting CSCs while they are still in the quiescent state [83]. However, it is still unknown if the activation of the quiescent cells for them to be eradicated using antiproliferative drugs is even controlled or that might just increase their proliferative potential altogether. Further, a deeper insight into the quiescence-associated pathways is needed to be able to prevent the reversion to active state or eradicating the quiescent cell itself.

Enhanced drug efflux activity of CSCs

One of the crucial properties of CSCs that makes them chemo resistant is the expression of drug efflux transporters on their cell surface, thus aiding them to exhibit a MDR phenotype. These transporters are unidirectional cellular pumps that are ATP-driven and known as ABC transporters. High expression of these ABC transporters increases the efflux of chemotherapeutic agents within the cell, thus maintaining cell viability of stemness of CSCs [84]. Several chemotherapeutic drugs are prone to ABC transporter-mediated efflux such as topoisomerase inhibitors (etoposide and topotecan) [85], tyrosine kinase inhibitors (gefitinib) [86], and microtubule targeting compounds (paclitaxel) [87]. Multiple ABC transporters, such as ABC subfamily B member 1 (ABCB1) and ABC subfamily G member 2 (ABCG2), have been identified as markers on CSCs [88], and they portray a crucial role in the drug resistance of CSCs to chemotherapeutic agents. Another type of ABC transporter commonly upregulated in CSCs is P-glycoprotein (P-gp) [89,90]. Hence, effective targeting of ABC efflux transporters is very crucial to make CSCs resistant to chemotherapeutic agents.

The importance of expression levels of ABC transporters on CSCs as a prognostic marker has been evaluated in many studies in colorectal cancer [91,92]. It has been reported that inhibition of ABC subfamily C member 3 (ABCC3) increases the sensitivity of HT29 and SW480 cells to 5-florouracil [93]. Additionally, metastatic colorectal cancer patients have demonstrated overexpression of ABCG2 transporter, which resulted in resistance to 5-fluoruracil-based treatment, and anomalistic protein expression of ABCC3 transporter is often associated with chemoresistance in rectal cancer patients [94]. Many ongoing research studies that are developing strategies to target ABC transporters mainly focus on three approaches: (1) modulating the activity of ABC transporters via the use of competitive or allosteric inhibitors, (2) regulating gene expression levels (transcriptional and translational) of ABC transporters, and (3) using chemotherapeutic drugs that bind poorly to P-gp (most commonly upregulated ABC transporter in CSCs), such as ixabepilone [95]. However, developing drugs that can inhibit P-gp as a therapeutic strategy to target CSCs has been challenging as P-gp is also expressed in hematopoietic stem cells and MSCs, which require P-gp to protect themselves from cytotoxic agents. Hence, targeting ABC transporters can cause serious hematopoietic disorders because of bone marrow dysfunction.

Increased DNA repair in CSC's

Normally, cancer cells portray a decrease in DNA repair efficiency due to mutations or alterations in key DNA repair proteins, leading to genomic instability and apoptosis after multiple rounds of chemotherapy [96]. However, CSCs portray a highly efficient DNA repair machinery resulting in effective DNA protection, which is considered a crucial contributor to their resistance to DNA damaging drugs [97]. Hence, targeting the efficient DNA repair machinery in CSCs is a major therapeutic approach for the eradication of CSC populations in cancer treatment.

The two major players in DNA damage response are ataxia telangiectasia mutated (ATM) and ataxia telangiectasia mutated-RAD3-related (ATR) protein kinase [98]. Upon receiving DNA damage stimuli, ATM and ATR kinases get activated and form complexes with poly ADP-ribose polymerase (PARP-1) and breast cancer 1 (BRCA1), respectively, which further phosphorylates checkpoint kinases Chk1 and Chk2 [98]. Chk1 and Chk2 further drive the activation of DNA repair target genes [98]. Several studies have published that Chk1/Chk2-mediated phosphorylation is one of the major contributors to therapy resistance in CSCs. A clinical study published that Chk1 phosphorylation at serine 345 serves as a prognostic marker for radioresistance in breast cancer [99]. Another interesting study pointed out that c-MYC also regulates the Chk1/Chk2 axis which modulates the DNA damage response mechanisms leading to radiotherapy resistance [100]. In contrast, pharmacological inhibition of Chk1 and Chk2 can sensitize CSs to radiotherapy [101]. Additionally, CSC's mediated dormancy also contributes to the enhanced DNA repair response, as when the DNA damage repair is efficiently carried out, CSCs escape from the G0 phase of the cell cycle, resume tumorigenesis, and evade apoptosis [102]. A study reported that CD133+ Glioma stem cells (GSCs) lead to radioresistance and tumor metastasis by increasing cell cycle checkpoint response and DNA damage repair in glioma cancer cells [101]. This study was further corroborated by the observation that a specific inhibitor of Chk1 and Chk2 checkpoint kinases can sensitize the CD133+ GSCs to radioresistance [103]. Additionally, it was reported that upon DNA damage, GSCs express L1CAM (CD171) on its surface, which is responsible for the activation of Chk1 and chk2 kinases, leading to radiotherapy resistance in GSCs [104].

Increased DNA repair response has also been reported in other CSCs. For example, CD133+ CSCs isolated from A549 human lung carcinoma cell lines also portray upregulated expression of DNA repair genes and enhanced double-stranded DNA repair [105]. Additionally, enhanced expression of DNA damage repair genes and increased DNA repair was also observed in LinCD29HCD24H tumor-initiating cells isolated from mouse mammary gland tumors [106]. Pancreatic CSCs have also been reported to portray increased expression of BRCA1 and RAD51 DNA repair genes [107]. In fact, pancreatic CSCs were found to repair DNA double-strand breaks more efficiently than the bulk cancer cells after exposure to gemcitabine treatment [107]. Additionally, studies have reported that patient-derived nonsmall cell lung cancer (NSCLC) stem cells portray an enhanced activation of Chk1 postexposure to several DNA damaging drugs and pharmacological inhibition of Chk1 reduced the NSCLC stem cell population in vitro by inducing cell cycle progression and promoting a mitotic catastrophe [108].

Enhanced autophagy and mitophagy in CSC's

Autophagy is an evolutionarily conserved self-digestion process in which cytoplasmic contents, damaged organelles, and proteins are sequestered into vesicles for degradation and recycling of nutrients to support cell survival and cell homeostasis during stressful conditions such as hypoxia or nutrient deprivation [109,110]. It is also a fundamental process in cancer cells to survive and adapt to the TME. Recent studies have demonstrated that autophagy plays a major role in CSC survival and resistance. A study reported that in ovarian CSCs, autophagy was upregulated in CD133+ cells, which promoted resistance to photodynamic therapy (PDT) [111]. Additionally, CD44+CD17+ ovarian CSCs expressed higher autophagy levels than the nonstem cell populations [112]. Similarly, it was reported that autophagic homeostasis is a crucial feature for maintaining pluripotency in breast CSCs [113]. Both Beclin1 and ATG4, two important autophagy proteins, were upregulated in mammospheres as compared to the adherent cells [114]. Furthermore, it has been shown that ATG7 or ATG12 knockdown could decrease the pluripotency and promote the differentiation senescence of CSCs [113]. A study revealed that inhibition of autophagy in CD118+CD44+ ovarian CSCs by ATG5 KO or CQ treatment impaired their cell viability, inhibited spheroid formation, decreased the expression of stem cell markers (Nanog, OCT4, SOX2) and tumorigenesis, indicating that increased autophagy is crucial for maintaining ovarian CSCs stemness [115]. Additionally, another study reported that suppression of autophagy via ATG3 KD, ATG7 KD, or CQ treatment decreased the population of hepatic Axin2+CD90+ CSCs [116]. Interestingly, suppression of autophagy downregulates the expression of hepatocyte growth factor (HGF), which is known to upregulate the JAK/STAT signaling pathway which supports CSC tumorigenesis, further confirming the fact that autophagy plays a crucial role in the maintenance of CSC stemness [117]. In vivo studies have revealed that synergistic combination treatment with chemotherapeutic agent Irinotecan and autophagy inhibitor CQ significantly reduced tumor size compared to alone treatments [118]. Similarly, combination treatment with chemotherapeutic agent Taxol and Beclin1 inhibitor/ATG5 KD resulted in increased apoptosis in radioresistance bladder CSCs [119]. These studies validate the need for therapeutic strategies targeting inhibition of autophagy and combination treatments with autophagy inhibitors for efficient eradication of CSC populations.

Mitophagy is a subset of autophagy and removes damaged or dysfunctional mitochondria from the CSCs by activating the formation of autophagy machinery around the mitochondria to form mitophagosomes, which initiates lysosomal degradation [120]. CSCs have an elevated mitophagy mechanism to selectively eliminate damaged mitochondria and balance reactive oxygen species (ROS) levels, which limits apoptotic cell death and maintains homeostasis of the stem cell pool [121]. A study reported that in esophageal squamous cell carcinoma, mitophagy sustained the growth of CD44+ cells by regulating oxidative stress, whereas inhibition of mitophagy led to a loss of CD44+ population leading to cell death [122]. Mitophagy is also known to regulate the stem cell population in the hypoxic region of glioblastoma [123]. Additionally, NIX-mediated mitophagy regulates the GSC population by modulating the mTOR/AKT/HIF axis [123]. Another study observed that mitophagy regulates hepatic CSC stemness by suppressing the p53 tumor suppressor [124]. Enhanced mitophagy removes phosphorylated p53 bound to the mitochondrial membrane along with the damaged mitochondria, which causes an upregulation in the transcriptional activation of NANOG (essential for self-renewal capacity of CSCs), which is inhibited by p53 [124]. However, inhibition of autophagy leads to an increase in the levels of phosphorylated p53 bound to the mitochondrial membrane, which inhibits the transcriptional activation of NANOG, resulting in the eradication of hepatic CSCs [124]. In pancreatic cancer stem cells (PaCSCs) ubiquitin-like protein ISG15 ISGylates Parkin, which promotes mitophagy to sustain CSCs self-renewal capability [125]. ISG15 suppression results in Parkin inhibition and impaired mitophagy, which leads to PaCSC tumorigenic potential [125]. Furthermore, mitophagy is also known to contribute to CSC-mediated drug resistance. For example, Caveolin-1/Parkin-mediated mitophagy contributes to cisplatin resistance in nonsmall cell lung CSCs [126]. Hence, exploring the mechanism of mitophagy in CSCs can serve as a promising therapeutic strategy for the eradication of CSCs.

Suppressed ferroptosis in CSCs

Ferroptosis is an iron-dependent programmed cell death mechanism that is distinct from other types of cell death mechanisms such as apoptosis, necrosis, etc. Iron is an important nutrient required by cells for the maintenance of various biological processes such as hemoglobin synthesis, oxygen transport, mitochondrial respiration, and energy metabolism [127]. However, excess free iron in cells leads to the formation and accumulation of free radicals, leading to lipid peroxidation, ROS formation, and oxidative stress [128]. CSCs are, however, characterized by a high intracellular iron demand and reduced ferroptosis. Transferrin binds to iron in Fe^{3+} form, which is recognized by its transferrin receptor 1 (TFR1/TRFC) at the cell surface and is subsequently endocytosed. Within the endosomes, they are converted to ferrous (Fe^{2+}) form and released into the cytosol as free iron. A study reported increased expression of transferrin and TFR1 in glioblastoma stem cells (GSCs) through iron tracing experiments, which is crucial for their maintenance [129]. Breast cancer stem cells (BCSCs) also portrayed a higher uptake of cellular iron and transferrin, supporting the evidence that CSCs portray increased iron trafficking than their non-CSC counterparts [130]. Hence, targeting iron addiction in CSCs can serve as a promising therapeutic strategy. It was observed that a forced suppression in intracellular iron concentration in ovarian CSCs reduced their proliferation. Additionally, the expression of CD44 marker suppressed ferroptosis in ovarian CSCs [131], establishing a link between CSC and ferroptosis. Hence, inducing ferroptosis could sensitize ovarian CSCs to chemotherapy. Additionally, salinomycin, a selective agent against CSCs, was found to initiate ferritin degradation and trigger ROS-mediated ferroptosis in CSCs, which could potentially reverse radioresistance in CSCs [132].

Metastatic potential of CSC's

Metastasis is a multistep process that involves (a) the formation of mobile tumor cells from benign tumors, (b) transendothelial migration of cancer cells into blood vessels known as intravasation, (c) survival in the circulatory system, (d) attachment to ECs and extravasation, and (e) colonization and proliferation in the host organ. It is proposed that CSC's most likely facilitate the very first step of the metastasis cascade, i.e., the formation of mobile tumor cells from benign tumors. Epithelial-mesenchymal transition (EMT) is an important event during which the epithelial cells gain a mesenchymal phenotype with migratory and invasive characteristics. It has been proposed that CSCs might also initiate their migration through the process of EMT and acquire a migratory and invasive phenotype. To further corroborate this observation that CSCs act as metastatic precursors, certain metastatic genetic signatures were identified to be present in CSCs. For example, the expression of CD133 CSC markers in glioblastoma and lung adenocarcinoma positively correlates with the proliferation marker Ki67, resulting in bad clinical outcomes [133]. It has been studied that experimental induction of EMT by Twist1 overexpression or TGF-ß treatment in epithelial carcinoma cells bestows on them many characteristics of CSCs, such as enhanced expression of CSC-specific cell surface marker CD44, an increased potential to seed tumors in mice and an enhanced ability to form spheres in a suspension culture [134]. Additionally, it has been studied that untransformed immortalized human mammary epithelial cells can undergo EMT by increasing the expression of CSC markers such as FoxC2, Zeb factors, and N-cadherin. Similarly, overexpressing Ras or Her2/neu leads to the formation of a subpopulation of CD44high and CD24low cells, which possess an enhanced EMT phenotype [135].

This close link between EMT and CSC states highlights the idea that activation of EMT in non-CSC populations can convert them into CSCs. In contrast, CSCs should also have the ability to transition back into a non-CSC state triggered by the activation of mesenchymal-to-epithelial transition (MET). These assumptions suggest the presence of phenotypic plasticity (introduced earlier in "CSCs in tumorigenesis models" section) due to which these cells can switch between CSC and non-CSC states. The plasticity further enables them to switch phenotypes in response to chemotherapy, renovate their niche by changing gene expression, thus evading the therapies, and gaining drug resistance. Keeping the above-discussed studies in mind, the development of drugs targeting EMT activation can have a profound impact on the CSC therapy area. However, this approach faces a lot of challenges as the mechanism that modulates the activation or retention of EMT in CSCs is still understudied.

Hypoxic adaptation

CSCs have the inherent capacity to survive in an environment with as low as 1% oxygen, called a hypoxic environment. The hypoxic state of CSC is now well known to drive stemness, malignancy, and therapy resistance of CSCs in various ways [136]. The ROS-activated stress response pathways get activated under hypoxic conditions that promote CSC survival and metastasis [137]. It prevents oxidative stress in the CSCs by reducing ROS levels that can otherwise cause DNA damage. It decreases immunosurveillance by inhibiting CD8+ T cell proliferation and activation [137]. Tumor progression under hypoxic conditions is coordinated by enhanced expression of hypoxia-inducible factors (HIF), made of two subtypes—HIFα (regulated by the von Hippel-Lindau protein, VHL) and HIFβ (constitutively expressed), that binds together to regulate expression of several genes for mechanisms required for the survival of cells under hypoxic conditions like oxygen homeostasis, glucose and iron metabolism, as well as, activation of several signaling pathways driving stemness [136,138]. For example, HIF-1α regulates genes such as vascular endothelial growth factor (VEGF) and Glucose transporter 1 (GLUT-1) that are responsible for angiogenesis, as well as regulates the Notch and Oct4 pathways [139]. Notch activation under hypoxic conditions has also been related to the suppression of E-cadherin (an epithelial marker), thus promoting EMT [140]. Some reports have also reported HIFs' influence on the ABC drug transporter localization as well as quiescence pathways of CSCs, such as cell cycle control via cyclin-dependent kinase and antiapoptosis via BCL-XL [136]. The increased HIF-1 activity in cancer patients within 24 to 48h following radiation exposure indicates its major role in protecting CSCs from therapeutic targeting.

CSCs generate a tumor supporting niche

The CSC exists in a symbiotic relationship with its microenvironment, whereby it creates its own safe niche that nurses and protects it. CSCs tend to specifically recruit and activate specific nontumor cell types that maintain cell-cell interactions and

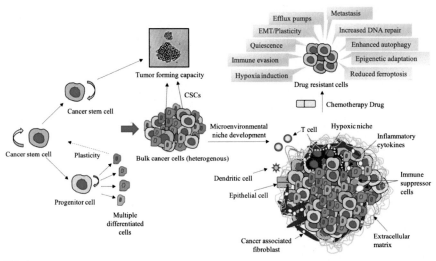

FIG. 1

Hallmarks of cancer stem cells providing resistance to therapies. Cancer stem cells have both self-renewal ability and differentiation potential that leads to heterogeneity within a tumor. They also have the ability to generate tumors in vitro. Cancer stem cells inherently resist the therapies through a combination of factors like hypoxic adaptation, immune evasion, quiescence, etc.

constitutively generate signals to contribute to the tumorigenic secretome of the CSC niche. The non-CSCs subordinate CSCs by promoting cell proliferation signaling, generating heterogeneity as well as assisting them in adapting better through processes such as hypoxia, immune evasion, promoting EMT, etc. (Fig. 1) that indeed make them resistant to therapy. The physical attributes of the niche, as well as the extensive crosstalking of CSCs with surrounding cells and the stroma within this niche, is a major contributor to CSCs' resistance to chemotherapy.

To begin with, it has been reported that the ECM in the CSE niche is denser and stiffer compared to surrounding tissue, which impedes the diffusion of biomolecules through them [141]. Further, there is also significant tumor mass expansion and increased vascular supply (tumor angiogenesis) but poor quality of vascularization that impacts blood perfusion and diffusion of substances it carries. Altogether, the CSC niche is able to provide a physical barrier to the chemotherapeutic and radio-therapeutic agents and decreased oxygen supply, generating a hypoxic environment, both of which are factors contributing to poor response to treatment [141,142]. Tumor angiogenesis is facilitated by stromal cells ECs that produce angiogenesis factor VEGF together with CSCs. HIF-1α activation in CSCs also promotes the release of VEGF-A and another factor, CXCL12, which protects ECs and favors vas-cularization [143]. While reports in glioblastoma have shown the efficacy of strat-egies targeting VEGF using drugs like bevacizumab that disrupts the CSC niche [144], but in breast cancer, increased hypoxia was reported upon inhibition of VEGFR that conferred resistance [145].

CSCs also transform fibroblasts into CAFs by producing factor TGF-β [139]. CAFs secrete several essential factors like CXCL12, VEGF, PDGF, HGF, and matrix metalloproteinases (MMPs)-MMP2, 3, and 9 [146]. Increased MMPs degrade ECM and release biomolecules from them that drive CSCs in several ways like activating canonical WNT signaling to promote stemness, causing genomic instability, and, most importantly, facilitating ECM remodeling to promote EMT and thus metastasis [147–149]. Lately CAFs have become an attractive target for cancer therapy, and agents such as sibrotuzumab, 5C3, and ADC specific to CAF surface proteins FAP, S1004A, and TEM8 are being tested in several cancers for targeted drug delivery [150].

It is now considered that all the signals and conditions required for EMT come from the TME, and the cells having undergone EMT are associated with more invasive and resistant to apoptosis [151]. The MSCs recruited by CSCs at primary tumor site by secreting IL-6, thereby secreting CXCR7 that interacts with CXCR2 to promote tumor growth, invasiveness, and metastasis in murine models by inducing EMT [152,153]. MSCs are also associated with increased SDF-1 production, which is linked to metastasis in solid tumors [154]. Another key factor, TGF-ß, has been reported to promote metastasis by inducing EMT and is secreted by CSCs as well as other cells like TAMs and CAFs [155]. The niche components also regulate transcription factors such as Snail, Twist, Six1, etc., that activate EMT by downregulating important molecules such as E-cadherin and catenins [156]. Further, several proinflammatory mediators like TNF and IL-6 also drive EMT or plasticity in niche by stimulating mesenchymal markers [157].

Another important role of the CSC niche is modulating the level of tumor immunity. Immune infiltration is a hallmark of tumors, and the immune system can exhibit antitumor activity, but the CSC niche evades immune surveillance by suppressing the infiltration and cytotoxicity of natural killer cells (NKs) and CD8+ T cells [158]. The cytokines and chemokines secreted within the niche attract immune cells like macrophages, but CSCs activate them to TAM by secreting IL4, TGF-ß, and macrophage inhibitory cytokine 1 (MIC-1) that potentiates immunosuppression. M2 type TAMs have been specifically associated with immunosuppression and promoting EMT by secreting IL-8 and CCL18, which activate STAT in mesenchymal-like cells in breast cancer [159]. Further, TGF-ß secreted by CSCs stimulates the synthesis of FOXP3 in CD4+T lymphocytes, differentiating them from regulatory T lymphocytes (Tregs) that have an immunosuppressive effect on the tumor [160]. Tregs further release other immunosuppressive factors such as TGF-ß and IL-10.

In summary, the CSC niche confers protection, stimulates tumor growth and metastasis by increasing EMT induction, tumor invasiveness, angiogenesis, and CSC self-renewal, and makes it an indispensable target to be explored for achieving success in therapeutics.

Epigenetic regulation

As previously mentioned, the origin of CSCs has been postulated in different ways in different theories, from a normal stem cell or progenitor cell that acquires oncogenic mutations or from cancer cells or somatic cells or differentiated cells that undergo genetic and/or epigenetic changes [37]. Moreover, the CSCs are bound to dynamically alter their gene expression profile for maintaining its stemness and tumorigenic potential, which is facilitated not only by the network of regulatory transcription factors but also by epigenetic regulation. In recent times, epigenetic mechanisms have gained more attention due to their potential to modulate treatment responses [161,162]. Several epigenetic regulation mechanisms, such as DNA methylation, chromatin remodeling, changes in noncoding RNAs, miRNAs, etc., enable CSCs to regulate the cell fate without bringing a change to the DNA sequences. For example, a study reported the role of increased H3K79 histone methylation mediated by DOT1L in increased invasiveness and therapy resistance of CSCs in head and neck squamous cell carcinoma by promoting survival proteins and Rho GTPases. A reversal of the same using DOT1L specific small interfering RNAs (siRNAs) rendered the CSCs less invasive and chemosensitive [163]. Similarly, activation of DNA methylases (DNMT) has been reported to mediate silencing of tumor suppressor genes, thereby maintaining CSC properties in leukemias, lung, colon, and other cancers [164–166]. Noncoding RNAs (ncRNAs) are another class of epigenetic modulators including small chain noncoding RNAs (siRNAs, miRNAs, and piRNAs) and long noncoding RNAs (lncRNAs) that are reportedly aberrantly expressed in the CSCs playing a vital role in regulating signaling pathways associated with tumor initiation, progression metastasis and therapy resistance [167]. For example, several upregulated oncogenic miRNAs like miR-21, miR-30, etc. and downregulated tumor suppressor miRNA like miRNA-34a have been reported in CSCs such as pancreatic and gastric to exert their effect on pathways such as PI3K/AKT, Notch, etc. and regulating genes like CD133-a mesenchymal markers, CD44, Bcl-2, HMGA2, Nanog, Oct4, SOX-2 and YY1, etc. and conferring them resistance by various ways previously described [168–170].

Owing to the numerous studies reporting abnormalities in epigenetic regulators driving tumorigenic potential and resistance in CSCs, these have been attractive therapeutic targets. Indeed, a variety of inhibitors of epigenetic modulatory enzymes, such as histone deacetylases (HDACs), DNMTs, etc., have been successfully investigated for their cancer therapeutic potential [161]. Recent advances have also been made in exploring the therapeutic potential of ncRNAs by using nanoparticles as efficient delivery systems [171].

Perspective

The evidence presented in this chapter sufficiently demonstrates the inherent capacity of the CSC to evade therapeutic interventions one way or the other. It is of utmost necessity to identify CSC-specific targets, develop a greater understanding of the crosstalking pathways involved in tumorigenesis, and, most importantly, develop better insight into the CSC niche involvement in survival, tumorigenicity, and plasticity to pave the way for the development of new antitumor therapies. While intratumoral heterogeneity is very well recognized in all tumor forms, the origin of the same and the complex process responsible for it is still debatable. The concept of bidirectional processes, EMT and MET, gave a new complex angle of plasticity to the previous hierarchical and stochastic model. However, the existence of this phenomenon in human patient tumors is still questionable and is a major roadblock in deciding independent therapeutic approaches for multiple clones if that generates realistically.

Furthermore, to achieve complete remission and prevent relapse, these therapies necessarily need to be based on combined approaches. Development of immune-modulating therapies preventing immune evasion, targeting CSCs in their dynamic state, or the dormant state, targeting indispensable components of the niche to starve CSC, and ultimately rationally combining the different therapeutic approaches could envisage better outcomes for cancer patients. Although it is highly speculated that due to heterogeneity between patients, no single treatment line can be universally beneficial to all patients and can be ineffective or even harmful for some. Personalized antitumor approaches based on individual patient's molecular and genetic profiling could be the ultimate resort.

References

[1] E.S. Bardot, A.K. Hadjantonakis, Mouse gastrulation: coordination of tissue patterning, specification and diversification of cell fate, Mech. Dev. 163 (2020) 103617.
[2] W. Zakrzewski, M. Dobrzyński, M. Szymonowicz, Z. Rybak, Stem cells: past, present, and future, Stem Cell Res Ther 10 (1) (2019) 68.
[3] M.A. Sukoyan, S.Y. Vatolin, A.N. Golubitsa, A.I. Zhelezova, L.A. Semenova, O.L. Serov, Embryonic stem cells derived from morulae, inner cell mass, and blastocysts of mink: comparisons of their pluripotencies, Mol. Reprod. Dev. 36 (2) (1993) 148–158.
[4] K. Takahashi, S. Yamanaka, Induction of pluripotent stem cells from mouse embryonic and adult fibroblast cultures by defined factors, Cell 126 (4) (2006) 663–676.
[5] S. Doulatov, F. Notta, E. Laurenti, J.E. Dick, Hematopoiesis: a human perspective, Cell Stem Cell 10 (2) (2012) 120–136.
[6] P. Dalerba, R.W. Cho, M.F. Clarke, Cancer stem cells: models and concepts, Annu. Rev. Med. 58 (2007) 267–284.
[7] E.R. Fearon, B. Vogelstein, A genetic model for colorectal tumorigenesis, Cell 61 (5) (1990) 759–767.
[8] T. Reya, S.J. Morrison, M.F. Clarke, I.L. Weissman, Stem cells, cancer, and cancer stem cells, Nature 414 (6859) (2001) 105–111.
[9] K.E. Allen, G.J. Weiss, Resistance may not be futile: microRNA biomarkers for chemoresistance and potential therapeutics, Mol. Cancer Ther. 9 (12) (2010) 3126–3136.
[10] F.M. Uckun, H. Sather, G. Reaman, J. Shuster, V. Land, M. Trigg, et al., Leukemic cell growth in SCID mice as a predictor of relapse in high-risk B-lineage acute lymphoblastic leukemia, Blood 85 (4) (1995) 873–878.
[11] T. Lapidot, C. Sirard, J. Vormoor, B. Murdoch, T. Hoang, J. Caceres-Cortes, et al., A cell initiating human acute myeloid leukaemia after transplantation into SCID mice, Nature 367 (6464) (1994) 645–648.
[12] D. Bonnet, J.E. Dick, Human acute myeloid leukemia is organized as a hierarchy that originates from a primitive hematopoietic cell, Nat. Med. 3 (7) (1997) 730–737.

[13] M. Al-Hajj, M.S. Wicha, A. Benito-Hernandez, S.J. Morrison, M.F. Clarke, Prospective identification of tumorigenic breast cancer cells, Proc. Natl. Acad. Sci. USA 100 (7) (2003) 3983–3988.

[14] C.A. O'Brien, A. Pollett, S. Gallinger, J.E. Dick, A human colon cancer cell capable of initiating tumour growth in immunodeficient mice, Nature 445 (7123) (2007) 106–110.

[15] L. Ricci-Vitiani, D.G. Lombardi, E. Pilozzi, M. Biffoni, M. Todaro, C. Peschle, et al., Identification and expansion of human colon-cancer-initiating cells, Nature 445 (7123) (2007) 111–115.

[16] P. Dalerba, S.J. Dylla, I.K. Park, R. Liu, X. Wang, R.W. Cho, et al., Phenotypic characterization of human colorectal cancer stem cells, Proc. Natl. Acad. Sci. USA 104 (24) (2007) 10158–10163.

[17] S.K. Singh, C. Hawkins, I.D. Clarke, J.A. Squire, J. Bayani, T. Hide, et al., Identification of human brain tumour initiating cells, Nature 432 (7015) (2004) 396–401.

[18] M. Ramalho-Santos, H. Willenbring, On the origin of the term "stem cell", Cell Stem Cell 1 (1) (2007) 35–38.

[19] J. Furth, Transmission of myeloid leukemia of mice: its relation to myeloma, J. Exp. Med. 61 (3) (1935) 423–446.

[20] S. Makino, Further evidence favoring the concept of the stem cell in ascites tumors of rats, Ann. N. Y. Acad. Sci. 63 (5) (1956) 818–830.

[21] H.B. Hewitt, Studies of the dissemination and quantitative transplantation of a lymphocytic leukaemia of CBA mice, Br. J. Cancer 12 (3) (1958) 378–401.

[22] W.R. Bruce, H. Van Der Gaag, A quantitative assay for the number of murine lymphoma cells capable of proliferation in vivo, Nature 199 (1963) 79–80.

[23] G.B. Pierce Jr., F.J. Dixon Jr., E.L. Verney, Teratocarcinogenic and tissue-forming potentials of the cell types comprising neoplastic embryoid bodies, Lab. Investig. 9 (1960) 583–602.

[24] A.J. Becker, C.E. Mc, J.E. Till, Cytological demonstration of the clonal nature of spleen colonies derived from transplanted mouse marrow cells, Nature 197 (1963) 452–454.

[25] G.B. Pierce, C. Wallace, Differentiation of malignant to benign cells, Cancer Res. 31 (2) (1971) 127–134.

[26] L.J. Kleinsmith, G.B. Pierce Jr., Multipotentiality of single embryonal carcinoma cells, Cancer Res. 24 (1964) 1544–1551.

[27] S.A. Killmann, E.P. Cronkite, J.S. Robertson, T.M. Fliedner, V.P. Bond, Estimation of phases of the life cycle of leukemic cells from labeling in human beings in vivo with tritiated thymidine, Lab. Investig. 12 (1963) 671–684.

[28] R.G. Worton, E.A. McCulloch, J.E. Till, Physical separation of hemopoietic stem cells from cells forming colonies in culture, J. Cell. Physiol. 74 (2) (1969) 171–182.

[29] G.B. Pierce, W.C. Speers, Tumors as caricatures of the process of tissue renewal: prospects for therapy by directing differentiation, Cancer Res. 48 (8) (1988) 1996–2004.

[30] L.D. Shultz, C.L. Sidman, Genetically determined murine models of immunodeficiency, Annu. Rev. Immunol. 5 (1987) 367–403.

[31] Z. Yu, T.G. Pestell, M.P. Lisanti, R.G. Pestell, Cancer stem cells, Int. J. Biochem. Cell Biol. 44 (12) (2012) 2144–2151.

[32] E. Dogan, A. Kisim, G. Bati-Ayaz, G.J. Kubicek, D. Pesen-Okvur, A.K. Miri, Cancer stem cells in tumor modeling: challenges and future directions, Adv. Nanobiomed. Res. 1 (11) (2021). https://onlinelibrary.wiley.com/doi/epdf/10.1002/anbr.202100017.

[33] P.C. Nowell, The minute chromosome (Phl) in chronic granulocytic leukemia, Blut 8 (1962) 65–66.

[34] P.C. Nowell, The clonal evolution of tumor cell populations, Science 194 (4260) (1976) 23–28.

[35] M. Shackleton, E. Quintana, E.R. Fearon, S.J. Morrison, Heterogeneity in cancer: cancer stem cells versus clonal evolution, Cell 138 (5) (2009) 822–829.

[36] H. Clevers, The cancer stem cell: premises, promises and challenges, Nat. Med. 17 (3) (2011) 313–319.

[37] C.L. Chaffer, R.A. Weinberg, How does multistep tumorigenesis really proceed? Cancer Discov. 5 (1) (2015) 22–24.

[38] V. Plaks, N. Kong, Z. Werb, The cancer stem cell niche: how essential is the niche in regulating stemness of tumor cells? Cell Stem Cell 16 (3) (2015) 225–238.

[39] S.J. Morrison, J. Kimble, Asymmetric and symmetric stem-cell divisions in development and cancer, Nature 441 (7097) (2006) 1068–1074.

[40] W.H. Matsui, Cancer stem cell signaling pathways, Medicine (Baltimore) 95 (1 Suppl. 1) (2016) S8–S19.

[41] L. Yang, P. Shi, G. Zhao, J. Xu, W. Peng, J. Zhang, et al., Targeting cancer stem cell pathways for cancer therapy, Signal Transduct. Target. Ther. 5 (1) (2020) 8.

[42] R. Liu, Y. Chen, G. Liu, C. Li, Y. Song, Z. Cao, et al., PI3K/AKT pathway as a key link modulates the multidrug resistance of cancers, Cell Death Dis. 11 (9) (2020) 797.

[43] V. Baud, M. Karin, Is NF-kappaB a good target for cancer therapy? Hopes and pitfalls, Nat. Rev. Drug Discov. 8 (1) (2009) 33–40.

[44] J. López de Andrés, C. Griñán-Lisón, G. Jiménez, J.A. Marchal, Cancer stem cell secretome in the tumor microenvironment: a key point for an effective personalized cancer treatment, J. Hematol. Oncol. 13 (1) (2020) 136.

[45] T. Kolenda, W. Przybyła, M. Kapałczyńska, A. Teresiak, M. Zajączkowska, R. Bliźniak, et al., Tumor microenvironment—unknown niche with powerful therapeutic potential, Rep. Pract. Oncol. Radiother. 23 (3) (2018) 143–153.

[46] A. Schröck, F. Göke, P. Wagner, M. Bode, A. Franzen, S. Huss, et al., Fibroblast growth factor receptor-1 as a potential therapeutic target in sinonasal cancer, Head Neck 36 (9) (2014) 1253–1257.

[47] H.K. Sekhon, K. Sircar, G. Kaur, M. Marwah, Evaluation of role of myofibroblasts in oral cancer: a systematic review, Int. J. Clin. Pediatr. Dent. 9 (3) (2016) 233–239.

[48] J.A. Eble, S. Niland, The extracellular matrix in tumor progression and metastasis, Clin. Exp. Metastasis 36 (3) (2019) 171–198.

[49] F. Liotta, V. Querci, G. Mannelli, V. Santarlasci, L. Maggi, M. Capone, et al., Mesenchymal stem cells are enriched in head neck squamous cell carcinoma, correlates with tumour size and inhibit T-cell proliferation, Br. J. Cancer 112 (4) (2015) 745–754.

[50] K.G. Neiva, Z. Zhang, M. Miyazawa, K.A. Warner, E. Karl, J.E. Nör, Cross talk initiated by endothelial cells enhances migration and inhibits anoikis of squamous cell carcinoma cells through STAT3/Akt/ERK signaling, Neoplasia 11 (6) (2009) 583–593.

[51] A. Scherzad, M. Steber, T. Gehrke, K. Rak, K. Froelich, P. Schendzielorz, et al., Human mesenchymal stem cells enhance cancer cell proliferation via IL-6 secretion and activation of ERK1/2, Int. J. Oncol. 47 (1) (2015) 391–397.

[52] A. Wu, J. Wei, L.Y. Kong, Y. Wang, W. Priebe, W. Qiao, et al., Glioma cancer stem cells induce immunosuppressive macrophages/microglia, Neuro-Oncology 12 (11) (2010) 1113–1125.

[53] S.K. Biswas, A. Mantovani, Macrophage plasticity and interaction with lymphocyte subsets: cancer as a paradigm, Nat. Immunol. 11 (10) (2010) 889–896.

[54] Y. Garcia-Mayea, C. Mir, F. Masson, R. Paciucci, ME LL., Insights into new mechanisms and models of cancer stem cell multidrug resistance, Semin. Cancer Biol. 60 (2020) 166–180.

[55] H.R. Sun, S. Wang, S.C. Yan, Y. Zhang, P.J. Nelson, H.L. Jia, et al., Therapeutic strategies targeting cancer stem cells and their microenvironment, Front. Oncol. 9 (2019) 1104.

[56] D.L. Dragu, L.G. Necula, C. Bleotu, C.C. Diaconu, M. Chivu-Economescu, Therapies targeting cancer stem cells: current trends and future challenges, World J. Stem Cells 7 (9) (2015) 1185–1201.

[57] R. Majeti, Monoclonal antibody therapy directed against human acute myeloid leukemia stem cells, Oncogene 30 (9) (2011) 1009–1019.

[58] S.K. Swaminathan, E. Roger, U. Toti, L. Niu, J.R. Ohlfest, J. Panyam, CD133-targeted paclitaxel delivery inhibits local tumor recurrence in a mouse model of breast cancer, J. Control. Release 171 (3) (2013) 280–287.

[59] A.P. Skubitz, E.P. Taras, K.L. Boylan, N.N. Waldron, S. Oh, A. Panoskaltsis-Mortari, et al., Targeting CD133 in an in vivo ovarian cancer model reduces ovarian cancer progression, Gynecol. Oncol. 130 (3) (2013) 579–587.

[60] Y. Song, I.K. Kim, I. Choi, S.H. Kim, H.R. Seo, Oxytetracycline have the therapeutic efficiency in CD133(+) HCC population through suppression CD133 expression by decreasing of protein stability of CD133, Sci. Rep. 8 (1) (2018) 16100.

[61] G.P. Adams, L.M. Weiner, Monoclonal antibody therapy of cancer, Nat. Biotechnol. 23 (9) (2005) 1147–1157.

[62] T. Schatton, N.Y. Frank, M.H. Frank, Identification and targeting of cancer stem cells, BioEssays 31 (10) (2009) 1038–1049.

[63] W.T. Kim, C.J. Ryu, Cancer stem cell surface markers on normal stem cells, BMB Rep. 50 (6) (2017) 285–298.

[64] R.S. Herbst, C.J. Langer, Epidermal growth factor receptors as a target for cancer treatment: the emerging role of IMC-C225 in the treatment of lung and head and neck cancers, Semin. Oncol. 29 (1 Suppl. 4) (2002) 27–36.

[65] D.J. Slamon, B. Leyland-Jones, S. Shak, H. Fuchs, V. Paton, A. Bajamonde, et al., Use of chemotherapy plus a monoclonal antibody against HER2 for metastatic breast cancer that overexpresses HER2, N. Engl. J. Med. 344 (11) (2001) 783–792.

[66] D. Beier, P. Hau, M. Proescholdt, A. Lohmeier, J. Wischhusen, P.J. Oefner, et al., CD133(+) and CD133(−) glioblastoma-derived cancer stem cells show differential growth characteristics and molecular profiles, Cancer Res. 67 (9) (2007) 4010–4015.

[67] J.P. Medema, Cancer stem cells: the challenges ahead, Nat. Cell Biol. 15 (4) (2013) 338–344.

[68] H.Y.K. Yip, A. Papa, Signaling pathways in cancer: therapeutic targets, combinatorial treatments, and new developments, Cells 10 (3) (2021) 659, https://doi.org/10.3390/cells10030659 [PMID: 33809714; PMCID: PMC8002322].

[69] A. Espinosa-Sánchez, E. Suárez-Martínez, L. Sánchez-Díaz, A. Carnero, Therapeutic targeting of signaling pathways related to cancer stemness, Front. Oncol. 10 (2020) 1533.

[70] Y. Yang, X. Li, T. Wang, Q. Guo, T. Xi, L. Zheng, Emerging agents that target signaling pathways in cancer stem cells, J. Hematol. Oncol. 13 (1) (2020) 60.

[71] S. Schön, I. Flierman, A. Ofner, A. Stahringer, L.M. Holdt, F.T. Kolligs, et al., β-Catenin regulates NF-κB activity via TNFRSF19 in colorectal cancer cells, Int. J. Cancer 135 (8) (2014) 1800–1811.

[72] W. Xia, C.M. Lo, R.Y.C. Poon, T.T. Cheung, A.C.Y. Chan, L. Chen, et al., Smad inhibitor induces CSC differentiation for effective chemosensitization in cyclin D1- and TGF-β/Smad-regulated liver cancer stem cell-like cells, Oncotarget 8 (24) (2017) 38811–38824.

[73] N.E. Bhola, V.M. Jansen, J.P. Koch, H. Li, L. Formisano, J.A. Williams, et al., Treatment of triple-negative breast cancer with TORC1/2 inhibitors sustains a drug-resistant and notch-dependent cancer stem cell population, Cancer Res. 76 (2) (2016) 440–452.

[74] N. Sharma, R. Nanta, J. Sharma, S. Gunewardena, K.P. Singh, S. Shankar, et al., PI3K/AKT/mTOR and sonic hedgehog pathways cooperate together to inhibit human pancreatic cancer stem cell characteristics and tumor growth, Oncotarget 6 (31) (2015) 32039–32060.

[75] N. Takebe, L. Miele, P.J. Harris, W. Jeong, H. Bando, M. Kahn, et al., Targeting notch, hedgehog, and Wnt pathways in cancer stem cells: clinical update, Nat. Rev. Clin. Oncol. 12 (8) (2015) 445–464.

[76] N. Moore, S. Lyle, Quiescent, slow-cycling stem cell populations in cancer: a review of the evidence and discussion of significance, J. Oncol. 2011 (2011) 396076, https://doi.org/10.1155/2011/396076 [Epub 2010 Sep 29. PMID: 20936110; PMCID: PMC2948913].

[77] A. Recasens, L. Munoz, Targeting cancer cell dormancy, Trends Pharmacol. Sci. 40 (2) (2019) 128–141.

[78] Y. Guan, B. Gerhard, D.E. Hogge, Detection, isolation, and stimulation of quiescent primitive leukemic progenitor cells from patients with acute myeloid leukemia (AML), Blood 101 (8) (2003) 3142–3149.

[79] F. Ishikawa, S. Yoshida, Y. Saito, A. Hijikata, H. Kitamura, S. Tanaka, et al., Chemotherapy-resistant human AML stem cells home to and engraft within the bone-marrow endosteal region, Nat. Biotechnol. 25 (11) (2007) 1315–1321.

[80] A. Viale, F. De Franco, A. Orleth, V. Cambiaghi, V. Giuliani, D. Bossi, et al., Cell-cycle restriction limits DNA damage and maintains self-renewal of leukaemia stem cells, Nature 457 (7225) (2009) 51–56.

[81] K. Ito, R. Bernardi, A. Morotti, S. Matsuoka, G. Saglio, Y. Ikeda, et al., PML targeting eradicates quiescent leukaemia-initiating cells, Nature 453 (7198) (2008) 1072–1078.

[82] T.H. Cheung, T.A. Rando, Molecular regulation of stem cell quiescence, Nat. Rev. Mol. Cell Biol. 14 (6) (2013) 329–340.

[83] W. Chen, J. Dong, J. Haiech, M.C. Kilhoffer, M. Zeniou, Cancer stem cell quiescence and plasticity as major challenges in cancer therapy, Stem Cells Int. 2016 (2016) 1740936.

[84] N.A. Colabufo, F. Berardi, M. Cantore, M. Contino, C. Inglese, M. Niso, et al., Perspectives of P-glycoprotein modulating agents in oncology and neurodegenerative diseases: pharmaceutical, biological, and diagnostic potentials, J. Med. Chem. 53 (5) (2010) 1883–1897.

[85] M. Omori, R. Noro, M. Seike, K. Matsuda, M. Hirao, A. Fukuizumi, et al., Inhibitors of ABCB1 and ABCG2 overcame resistance to topoisomerase inhibitors in small cell lung cancer, Thorac Cancer 13 (15) (2022) 2142–2151.

[86] M. Galetti, P.G. Petronini, C. Fumarola, D. Cretella, S. La Monica, M. Bonelli, et al., Effect of ABCG2/BCRP expression on efflux and uptake of gefitinib in NSCLC cell lines, PLoS One 10 (11) (2015) e0141795.

[87] B. Gao, A. Russell, J. Beesley, X.Q. Chen, S. Healey, M. Henderson, et al., Paclitaxel sensitivity in relation to ABCB1 expression, efflux and single nucleotide polymorphisms in ovarian cancer, Sci. Rep. 4 (2014) 4669.

[88] W. Yin, D. Xiang, T. Wang, Y. Zhang, C.V. Pham, S. Zhou, et al., The inhibition of ABCB1/MDR1 or ABCG2/BCRP enables doxorubicin to eliminate liver cancer stem cells, Sci. Rep. 11 (1) (2021) 10791.

[89] E.A. Roundhill, S. Jabri, S.A. Burchill, ABCG1 and Pgp identify drug resistant, self-renewing osteosarcoma cells, Cancer Lett. 453 (2019) 142–157.

[90] C. Riganti, I.C. Salaroglio, V. Caldera, I. Campia, J. Kopecka, M. Mellai, et al., Temozolomide downregulates P-glycoprotein expression in glioblastoma stem cells by interfering with the Wnt3a/glycogen synthase-3 kinase/β-catenin pathway, Neuro-Oncology 15 (11) (2013) 1502–1517.

[91] R. Artells, I. Moreno, T. Díaz, F. Martínez, B. Gel, A. Navarro, et al., Tumour CD133 mRNA expression and clinical outcome in surgically resected colorectal cancer patients, Eur. J. Cancer 46 (3) (2010) 642–649.

[92] X. Wang, B. Xia, Y. Liang, L. Peng, Z. Wang, J. Zhuo, et al., Membranous ABCG2 expression in colorectal cancer independently correlates with shortened patient survival, Cancer Biomark. 13 (2) (2013) 81–88.

[93] M. Kobayashi, R. Funayama, S. Ohnuma, M. Unno, K. Nakayama, Wnt-β-catenin signaling regulates ABCC3 (MRP3) transporter expression in colorectal cancer, Cancer Sci. 107 (12) (2016) 1776–1784.

[94] S.H. Han, J.W. Kim, M. Kim, J.H. Kim, K.W. Lee, B.H. Kim, et al., Prognostic implication of ABC transporters and cancer stem cell markers in patients with stage III colon cancer receiving adjuvant FOLFOX-4 chemotherapy, Oncol. Lett. 17 (6) (2019) 5572–5580.

[95] H. Shen, F.Y. Lee, J. Gan, Ixabepilone, a novel microtubule-targeting agent for breast cancer, is a substrate for P-glycoprotein (P-gp/MDR1/ABCB1) but not breast cancer resistance protein (BCRP/ABCG2), J. Pharmacol. Exp. Ther. 337 (2) (2011) 423–432.

[96] K. Kiwerska, K. Szyfter, DNA repair in cancer initiation, progression, and therapy-a double-edged sword, J. Appl. Genet. 60 (3–4) (2019) 329–334.

[97] E. Abad, D. Graifer, A. Lyakhovich, DNA damage response and resistance of cancer stem cells, Cancer Lett. 474 (2020) 106–117.

[98] A. Maréchal, L. Zou, DNA damage sensing by the ATM and ATR kinases, Cold Spring Harb. Perspect. Biol. 5 (9) (2013) a012716, https://doi.org/10.1101/cshperspect. a012716 [PMID: 24003211; PMCID: PMC3753707].

[99] N. Alsubhi, F. Middleton, T.M. Abdel-Fatah, P. Stephens, R. Doherty, A. Arora, et al., Chk1 phosphorylated at serine345 is a predictor of early local recurrence and radioresistance in breast cancer, Mol. Oncol. 10 (2) (2016) 213–223.

[100] W.J. Wang, S.P. Wu, J.B. Liu, Y.S. Shi, X. Huang, Q.B. Zhang, et al., MYC regulation of CHK1 and CHK2 promotes radioresistance in a stem cell-like population of nasopharyngeal carcinoma cells, Cancer Res. 73 (3) (2013) 1219–1231.

[101] S. Bao, Q. Wu, R.E. McLendon, Y. Hao, Q. Shi, A.B. Hjelmeland, et al., Glioma stem cells promote radioresistance by preferential activation of the DNA damage response, Nature 444 (7120) (2006) 756–760.

[102] P. Patel, E.I. Chen, Cancer stem cells, tumor dormancy, and metastasis, Front. Endocrinol. (Lausanne) 3 (2012) 125.

[103] C. Ronco, A.R. Martin, L. Demange, R. Benhida, ATM, ATR, CHK1, CHK2 and WEE1 inhibitors in cancer and cancer stem cells, Medchemcomm. 8 (2) (2017) 295–319.

[104] L. Cheng, Q. Wu, Z. Huang, O.A. Guryanova, Q. Huang, W. Shou, et al., L1CAM regulates DNA damage checkpoint response of glioblastoma stem cells through NBS1, EMBO J. 30 (5) (2011) 800–813.

[105] A. Desai, B. Webb, S.L. Gerson, CD133+ cells contribute to radioresistance via altered regulation of DNA repair genes in human lung cancer cells, Radiother. Oncol. 110 (3) (2014) 538–545.

[106] C.H. Chang, M. Zhang, K. Rajapakshe, C. Coarfa, D. Edwards, S. Huang, et al., Mammary stem cells and tumor-initiating cells are more resistant to apoptosis and exhibit increased DNA repair activity in response to DNA damage, Stem Cell Reports 5 (3) (2015) 378–391.

[107] L.A. Mathews, S.M. Cabarcas, E.M. Hurt, X. Zhang, E.M. Jaffee, W.L. Farrar, Increased expression of DNA repair genes in invasive human pancreatic cancer cells, Pancreas 40 (5) (2011) 730–739.

[108] M. Bartucci, S. Svensson, P. Romania, R. Dattilo, M. Patrizii, M. Signore, et al., Therapeutic targeting of Chk1 in NSCLC stem cells during chemotherapy, Cell Death Differ. 19 (5) (2012) 768–778.

[109] N. Mizushima, M. Komatsu, Autophagy: renovation of cells and tissues, Cell 147 (4) (2011) 728–741.

[110] G. Kroemer, G. Mariño, B. Levine, Autophagy and the integrated stress response, Mol. Cell 40 (2) (2010) 280–293.

[111] M.F. Wei, M.W. Chen, K.C. Chen, P.J. Lou, S.Y. Lin, S.C. Hung, et al., Autophagy promotes resistance to photodynamic therapy-induced apoptosis selectively in colorectal cancer stem-like cells, Autophagy 10 (7) (2014) 1179–1192.

[112] Y. Chen, H. Zhao, W. Liang, E. Jiang, X. Zhou, Z. Shao, et al., Autophagy regulates the cancer stem cell phenotype of head and neck squamous cell carcinoma through the non-canonical FOXO3/SOX2 axis, Oncogene 41 (5) (2022) 634–646.

[113] T. Sharif, E. Martell, C. Dai, B.E. Kennedy, P. Murphy, D.R. Clements, et al., Autophagic homeostasis is required for the pluripotency of cancer stem cells, Autophagy 13 (2) (2017) 264–284.

[114] C.W. Yun, J. Jeon, G. Go, J.H. Lee, S.H. Lee, The dual role of autophagy in cancer development and a therapeutic strategy for cancer by targeting autophagy, Int. J. Mol. Sci. 22 (1) (2020).

[115] X. Wang, J. Lee, C. Xie, Autophagy regulation on cancer stem cell maintenance, metastasis, and therapy resistance, Cancers (Basel) 14 (2) (2022) 381, https://doi.org/10.3390/cancers14020381 [PMID: 35053542; PMCID: PMC8774167].

[116] J. Li, S.B. Hu, L.Y. Wang, X. Zhang, X. Zhou, B. Yang, et al., Autophagy-dependent generation of Axin2+ cancer stem-like cells promotes hepatocarcinogenesis in liver cirrhosis, Oncogene 36 (48) (2017) 6725–6737.

[117] C. Kitanaka, A. Sato, M. Okada, JNK signaling in the control of the tumor-initiating capacity associated with cancer stem cells, Genes Cancer 4 (9–10) (2013) 388–396.

[118] Y. Zhu, S. Huang, S. Chen, J. Chen, Z. Wang, Y. Wang, et al., SOX2 promotes chemoresistance, cancer stem cells properties, and epithelial-mesenchymal transition by β-catenin and Beclin1/autophagy signaling in colorectal cancer, Cell Death Dis. 12 (5) (2021) 449.

[119] X. Ma, G. Mao, R. Chang, F. Wang, X. Zhang, Z. Kong, Down-regulation of autophagy-associated protein increased acquired radio-resistance bladder cancer cells sensitivity to taxol, Int. J. Radiat. Biol. 97 (4) (2021) 507–516.

[120] A.P. Trotta, J.E. Chipuk, Mitochondrial dynamics as regulators of cancer biology, Cell. Mol. Life Sci. 74 (11) (2017) 1999–2017.

[121] S.E. Koschade, C.H. Brandts, Selective autophagy in normal and malignant hematopoiesis, J. Mol. Biol. 432 (1) (2020) 261–282.

[122] K.A. Whelan, P.M. Chandramouleeswaran, K. Tanaka, M. Natsuizaka, M. Guha, S. Srinivasan, et al., Autophagy supports generation of cells with high CD44 expression via modulation of oxidative stress and Parkin-mediated mitochondrial clearance, Oncogene 36 (34) (2017) 4843–4858.

[123] J. Jung, Y. Zhang, O. Celiku, W. Zhang, H. Song, B.J. Williams, et al., Mitochondrial NIX promotes tumor survival in the hypoxic niche of glioblastoma, Cancer Res. 79 (20) (2019) 5218–5232.

[124] K. Liu, J. Lee, J.Y. Kim, L. Wang, Y. Tian, S.T. Chan, et al., Mitophagy controls the activities of tumor suppressor p53 to regulate hepatic cancer stem cells, Mol. Cell 68 (2) (2017) 281–292.e5.

[125] S. Alcalá, P. Sancho, P. Martinelli, D. Navarro, C. Pedrero, L. Martín-Hijano, et al., ISG15 and ISGylation is required for pancreatic cancer stem cell mitophagy and metabolic plasticity, Nat. Commun. 11 (1) (2020) 2682.

[126] Y. Liu, Y. Fu, X. Hu, S. Chen, J. Miao, Y. Wang, et al., Caveolin-1 knockdown increases the therapeutic sensitivity of lung cancer to cisplatin-induced apoptosis by repressing Parkin-related mitophagy and activating the ROCK1 pathway, J. Cell. Physiol. 235 (2) (2020) 1197–1208.

[127] K. Pantopoulos, S.K. Porwal, A. Tartakoff, L. Devireddy, Mechanisms of mammalian iron homeostasis, Biochemistry 51 (29) (2012) 5705–5724.

[128] D.H. Manz, N.L. Blanchette, B.T. Paul, F.M. Torti, S.V. Torti, Iron and cancer: recent insights, Ann. N. Y. Acad. Sci. 1368 (1) (2016) 149–161.

[129] C. Xiao, X. Fu, Y. Wang, H. Liu, Y. Jiang, Z. Zhao, et al., Transferrin receptor regulates malignancies and the stemness of hepatocellular carcinoma-derived cancer stem-like cells by affecting iron accumulation, PLoS One 15 (12) (2020) e0243812.

[130] A. Hamaï, T. Cañeque, S. Müller, T.T. Mai, A. Hienzsch, C. Ginestier, et al., An iron hand over cancer stem cells, Autophagy 13 (8) (2017) 1465–1466.

[131] T. Ishimoto, O. Nagano, T. Yae, M. Tamada, T. Motohara, H. Oshima, et al., CD44 variant regulates redox status in cancer cells by stabilizing the xCT subunit of system xc(−) and thereby promotes tumor growth, Cancer Cell 19 (3) (2011) 387–400.

[132] T.T. Mai, A. Hamaï, A. Hienzsch, T. Cañeque, S. Müller, J. Wicinski, et al., Salinomycin kills cancer stem cells by sequestering iron in lysosomes, Nat. Chem. 9 (10) (2017) 1025–1033.

[133] P. Zhao, Y. Li, Y. Lu, Aberrant expression of CD133 protein correlates with Ki-67 expression and is a prognostic marker in gastric adenocarcinoma, BMC Cancer 10 (2010) 218.

[134] S.A. Khales, S. Mozaffari-Jovin, D. Geerts, M.R. Abbaszadegan, TWIST1 activates cancer stem cell marker genes to promote epithelial-mesenchymal transition and tumorigenesis in esophageal squamous cell carcinoma, BMC Cancer 22 (1) (2022) 1272.

[135] C. Moyret-Lalle, E. Ruiz, A. Puisieux, Epithelial-mesenchymal transition transcription factors and miRNAs: "plastic surgeons" of breast cancer, World J. Clin. Oncol. 5 (3) (2014) 311–322.

[136] J.P. Schöning, M. Monteiro, W. Gu, Drug resistance and cancer stem cells: the shared but distinct roles of hypoxia-inducible factors HIF1α and HIF2α, Clin. Exp. Pharmacol. Physiol. 44 (2) (2017) 153–161.

[137] L. Liu, D.R. Wise, J.A. Diehl, M.C. Simon, Hypoxic reactive oxygen species regulate the integrated stress response and cell survival, J. Biol. Chem. 283 (45) (2008) 31153–31162.

[138] H. Choudhry, A.L. Harris, Advances in hypoxia-inducible factor biology, Cell Metab. 27 (2) (2018) 281–298.

[139] S.M. Cabarcas, L.A. Mathews, W.L. Farrar, The cancer stem cell niche—there goes the neighborhood? Int. J. Cancer 129 (10) (2011) 2315–2327.

[140] A. Dhawan, S.A. Madani Tonekaboni, J.H. Taube, S. Hu, N. Sphyris, S.A. Mani, et al., Mathematical modelling of phenotypic plasticity and conversion to a stem-cell state under hypoxia, Sci. Rep. 6 (2016) 18074.

[141] E. Henke, R. Nandigama, S. Ergün, Extracellular matrix in the tumor microenvironment and its impact on cancer therapy, Front. Mol. Biosci. 6 (2019) 160.

[142] X. Jing, F. Yang, C. Shao, K. Wei, M. Xie, H. Shen, et al., Role of hypoxia in cancer therapy by regulating the tumor microenvironment, Mol. Cancer 18 (1) (2019) 157.

[143] L. Ricci-Vitiani, R. Pallini, M. Biffoni, M. Todaro, G. Invernici, T. Cenci, et al., Tumour vascularization via endothelial differentiation of glioblastoma stem-like cells, Nature 468 (7325) (2010) 824–828.

[144] J.K. Burkhardt, C.P. Hofstetter, A. Santillan, B.J. Shin, C.P. Foley, D.J. Ballon, et al., Orthotopic glioblastoma stem-like cell xenograft model in mice to evaluate intra-arterial delivery of bevacizumab: from bedside to bench, J. Clin. Neurosci. 19 (11) (2012) 1568–1572.

[145] S.J. Conley, E. Gheordunescu, P. Kakarala, B. Newman, H. Korkaya, A.N. Heath, et al., Antiangiogenic agents increase breast cancer stem cells via the generation of tumor hypoxia, Proc. Natl. Acad. Sci. USA 109 (8) (2012) 2784–2789.

[146] K. Kessenbrock, G.J. Dijkgraaf, D.A. Lawson, L.E. Littlepage, P. Shahi, U. Pieper, et al., A role for matrix metalloproteinases in regulating mammary stem cell function via the Wnt signaling pathway, Cell Stem Cell 13 (3) (2013) 300–313.

[147] A. Noël, A. Gutiérrez-Fernández, N.E. Sounni, N. Behrendt, E. Maquoi, I.K. Lund, et al., New and paradoxical roles of matrix metalloproteinases in the tumor microenvironment, Front. Pharmacol. 3 (2012) 140.

[148] S.A. Siefert, R. Sarkar, Matrix metalloproteinases in vascular physiology and disease, Vascular 20 (4) (2012) 210–216.

[149] K. Kessenbrock, V. Plaks, Z. Werb, Matrix metalloproteinases: regulators of the tumor microenvironment, Cell 141 (1) (2010) 52–67.

[150] Z. Zhen, W. Tang, M. Wang, S. Zhou, H. Wang, Z. Wu, et al., Protein nanocage mediated fibroblast-activation protein targeted photoimmunotherapy to enhance cytotoxic T cell infiltration and tumor control, Nano Lett. 17 (2) (2017) 862–869.

[151] S.Y. Yi, Y.B. Hao, K.J. Nan, T.L. Fan, Cancer stem cells niche: a target for novel cancer therapeutics, Cancer Treat. Rev. 39 (3) (2013) 290–296.

[152] Z. Tang, M. Yu, F. Miller, R.S. Berk, G. Tromp, M.A. Kosir, Increased invasion through basement membrane by CXCL7-transfected breast cells, Am. J. Surg. 196 (5) (2008) 690–696.

[153] T. Desurmont, N. Skrypek, A. Duhamel, N. Jonckheere, G. Millet, E. Leteurtre, et al., Overexpression of chemokine receptor CXCR2 and ligand CXCL7 in liver metastases from colon cancer is correlated to shorter disease-free and overall survival, Cancer Sci. 106 (3) (2015) 262–269.

[154] P. Dillenburg-Pilla, V. Patel, C.M. Mikelis, C.R. Zárate-Bladés, C.L. Doçi, P. Amornphimoltham, et al., SDF-1/CXCL12 induces directional cell migration and

spontaneous metastasis via a CXCR4/Gαi/mTORC1 axis, FASEB J. 29 (3) (2015) 1056–1068.

[155] X.Z. Ye, S.L. Xu, Y.H. Xin, S.C. Yu, Y.F. Ping, L. Chen, et al., Tumor-associated microglia/macrophages enhance the invasion of glioma stem-like cells via TGF-β1 signaling pathway, J. Immunol. 189 (1) (2012) 444–453.

[156] S. Shigdar, Y. Li, S. Bhattacharya, M. O'Connor, C. Pu, J. Lin, et al., Inflammation and cancer stem cells, Cancer Lett. 345 (2) (2014) 271–278.

[157] M. Santisteban, J.M. Reiman, M.K. Asiedu, M.D. Behrens, A. Nassar, K.R. Kalli, et al., Immune-induced epithelial to mesenchymal transition in vivo generates breast cancer stem cells, Cancer Res. 69 (7) (2009) 2887–2895.

[158] T. Kitamura, B.Z. Qian, J.W. Pollard, Immune cell promotion of metastasis, Nat. Rev. Immunol. 15 (2) (2015) 73–86.

[159] S. Su, Q. Liu, J. Chen, J. Chen, F. Chen, C. He, et al., A positive feedback loop between mesenchymal-like cancer cells and macrophages is essential to breast cancer metastasis, Cancer Cell 25 (5) (2014) 605–620.

[160] V.C. Liu, L.Y. Wong, T. Jang, A.H. Shah, I. Park, X. Yang, et al., Tumor evasion of the immune system by converting CD4+CD25- T cells into CD4+CD25+ T regulatory cells: role of tumor-derived TGF-beta, J. Immunol. 178 (5) (2007) 2883–2892.

[161] T.B. Toh, J.J. Lim, E.K. Chow, Epigenetics in cancer stem cells, Mol. Cancer 16 (1) (2017) 29.

[162] S. Keyvani-Ghamsari, K. Khorsandi, A. Rasul, M.K. Zaman, Current understanding of epigenetics mechanism as a novel target in reducing cancer stem cells resistance, Clin. Epigenetics 13 (1) (2021) 120.

[163] L.Y. Bourguignon, G. Wong, M. Shiina, Up-regulation of histone methyltransferase, DOT1L, by matrix hyaluronan promotes microRNA-10 expression leading to tumor cell invasion and chemoresistance in cancer stem cells from head and neck squamous cell carcinoma, J. Biol. Chem. 291 (20) (2016) 10571–10585.

[164] A.M. Bröske, L. Vockentanz, S. Kharazi, M.R. Huska, E. Mancini, M. Scheller, et al., DNA methylation protects hematopoietic stem cell multipotency from myeloerythroid restriction, Nat. Genet. 41 (11) (2009) 1207–1215.

[165] C.C. Liu, J.H. Lin, T.W. Hsu, K. Su, A.F. Li, H.S. Hsu, et al., IL-6 enriched lung cancer stem-like cell population by inhibition of cell cycle regulators via DNMT1 upregulation, Int. J. Cancer 136 (3) (2015) 547–559.

[166] R. Morita, Y. Hirohashi, H. Suzuki, A. Takahashi, Y. Tamura, T. Kanaseki, et al., DNA methyltransferase 1 is essential for initiation of the colon cancers, Exp. Mol. Pathol. 94 (2) (2013) 322–329.

[167] X. Yang, M. Liu, M. Li, S. Zhang, H. Hiju, J. Sun, et al., Epigenetic modulations of noncoding RNA: a novel dimension of cancer biology, Mol. Cancer 19 (1) (2020) 64.

[168] S. Bimonte, A. Barbieri, M. Leongito, G. Palma, V. Del Vecchio, M. Falco, et al., The role of miRNAs in the regulation of pancreatic cancer stem cells, Stem Cells Int. 2016 (2016) 8352684.

[169] M. Agostini, R.A. Knight, miR-34: from bench to bedside, Oncotarget 5 (4) (2014) 872–881.

[170] S. Xiong, M. Hu, C. Li, X. Zhou, H. Chen, Role of miR-34 in gastric cancer: from bench to bedside (review), Oncol. Rep. 42 (5) (2019) 1635–1646.

[171] W.T. Wang, C. Han, Y.M. Sun, T.Q. Chen, Y.Q. Chen, Noncoding RNAs in cancer therapy resistance and targeted drug development, J. Hematol. Oncol. 12 (1) (2019) 55.

Carving a therapeutic niche for metastatic cancer: Opportunities and challenges

Sireesha V. Garimella[a],*, Rahul Roy[b],*, Siri Chandana Gampa[a], and Santhi Latha Pandrangi[c]

[a]*Department of Biotechnology, GITAM School of Science, GITAM Deemed to be University, Visakhapatnam, India,* [b]*Centre for Biomedical Engineering, Indian Institute of Technology, New Delhi, Delhi, India,* [c]*Onco-Stem Cell Research Laboratory, Department of Biochemistry and Bioinformatics, GITAM School of Science, GITAM Deemed to be University, Visakhapatnam, India*

Introduction

Cancer is a significant global public health issue and is one of the greatest causes of mortality, causing nearly one in six deaths in 2020. The term "cancer" refers to a broad range of diseases that can manifest as 200 different disease entities, each reflecting variations in the normal cells that gave rise to the disease, acquired somatic mutations, variable transcriptional network alterations, and the effects of local tissue microenvironments [1]. World Health Organization defines cancer as a large category of disorders that has the potential to start its growth in every possible organ or tissue of the body when specific cells grow out of control, transcend normal boundaries to invade surrounding body parts, and/or spread to other organs. According to the US Centers for Disease Control and Prevention (CDC), cancers of the lungs, colon/rectum, and prostate are the primary causes of death in males. The Global Burden of Cancer in Women states that in females, breast, colorectal, and lung cancer deaths are observed to be customary. The International Agency for Research on Cancer (IARC) predicts an increase in the global prevalence of cancer from 19.3 million cases in 2020 to 28.4 million cases, with a 47% increase by 2040, and a significant burden will occur in countries having low (a 95% rise) or medium (a 64% rise) Human Development Index (HDI).

---

*Both authors contributed equally.

Cancer Epigenetics and Nanomedicine. https://doi.org/10.1016/B978-0-443-13209-4.00023-4
Copyright © 2024 Elsevier Inc. All rights reserved, including those for text and data mining, AI training, and similar technologies.

Table 1 Grading of cancer.

Grade	Definition
Grade X	Grade cannot be assessed (undetermined grade)
Grade 1	Well differentiated (low grade)
Grade 2	Moderately differentiated (intermediate grade)
Grade 3	Poorly differentiated (high grade)
Grade 4	Undifferentiated (high grade)

Cancer can affect almost all cell types and arises from the malignant transformation of normal cells into tumor cells in a multistage process, leading to uncontrolled cellular growth that results in aberrant cell proliferation. The development of cancerous cells originates from a variety of causes. Oncogene activation and/or tumor suppressor gene inactivation frequently results in unchecked cell cycle progression and inactivation of apoptotic mechanisms. Mutations, chromosomal translocations or deletions, and dysregulated expression or activity of signaling pathways also activate genes that promote dysregulated cell cycling and/or inactivate apoptotic pathways, leading to the development of cancerous cells. Epigenetic alteration is another characteristic of cancer due to its role in developing cancer progenitor cells and subsequent induction of carcinogenesis that affects histones or DNA residues [2].

Cancerous cells become more dangerous by gradual modifications over the course of several stages in the development of the disease, established within a tissue, compete with wild-type cells, and form tumors [3]. These alterations categorize the tumors into distinct classes and aid in determining their severity. One such modification is the morphology of the cells; low-grade tumors are well differentiated and look similar to normal tissues, i.e., the cancer is small and hasn't spread anywhere else (grade 1), and some cells are moderately differentiated, i.e., cancer has grown but hasn't spread (grade 2), whereas high-grade tumors are poorly differentiated, i.e., the cancer is more prominent and may have spread to the surrounding tissues and/or the lymph nodes (grade 3) or remain undifferentiated, i.e., cancer has spread from where it started to at least one body organ also known as secondary or metastatic cancer (grade 4), and the grade X: the cancer is where it started (in situ) and hasn't spread [4–6] (Table 1).

Hallmarks of cancer

This complex disease has been attempted to be reduced to a single set of organizing principles known as "Hallmarks of Cancer." This concept refers to a set of functional abilities that human cells acquire as a transition of growth stages from normalcy to neoplasm, especially abilities that are essential for the development of malignant tumors [7]. These features serve as an organizational element for rationalizing the intricacies of neoplastic disease and offer a robust framework for understanding

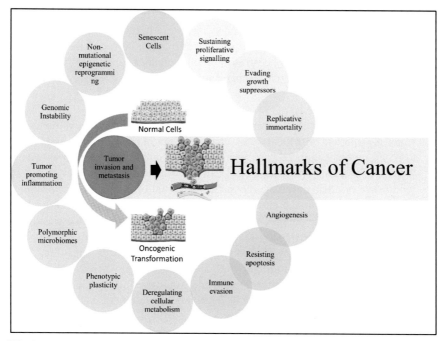

FIG. 1

The hallmarks of cancer.

the biology of cancer [8]. Hitherto, 14 hallmarks of cancer have been identified (Fig. 1), which are outlined below.

(1) Sustained signaling for proliferation

The growth and spread of cancer depend primarily on proliferation. The cancer cell possesses qualities that allow it to live longer than it should and to multiply abnormally. Upon receiving a growth factor signal from nearby cells, a receptor on the surface of each cell starts an intracellular signaling cascade that promotes cell growth and division. Typically, cells rely on feedback from neighboring cells to choose when to divide, ensuring that proliferation occurs in an orderly fashion. Due to their ability to divide, even in the absence of these signals, cancer cells can proliferate out of control. A growth signaling cascade is actively maintained even in the absence of a signal due to overexpression of the receptor or mutation in the receptor gene [9].

(2) Evasion of growth suppressors

Avoiding growth inhibition is a crucial characteristic skill for maintaining proliferative signals in cancer cells. Many tumors' suppressive protein-coding genes, such as TP53, PTEN, or RB, have been identified. These genes function in various ways to prevent cell growth and proliferation. One way cancer cells respond to this is by completely losing the tumor suppressor gene or by amassing mutations that make this gene inactive. Alternately, tumor suppressor genes could bind to other proteins produced in tumor cells and thereafter become inactive or quickly destroyed. With the aid of long ncRNAs, cancer cells have created additional mechanisms to disrupt tumor suppressor functions [10].

(3) Replicative immortality

The third characteristic hallmark of cancer is infinite replicative potential, which is consistent with the first two characteristics of cancer that strongly relate to proliferation. Tumor cells replicate almost infinitely, unlike normal cells, which go through a finite number of cell division cycles. The onset of senescence or crisis limits the replicating potential of normal cells. For this replication restriction, the chromosomal ends, or telomeres, are essential. The ability to preserve telomeres, which are protective structures at the ends of chromosomes and function as a kind of cellular clock, is thought to be connected to the process of replicative immortality. Cancer cells lack this restraint mechanism, which is controlled by telomere shortening, whereas normal cells have a limited capacity for proliferation and would eventually stop proliferating if cultivated in vitro. Malignant cells depend on the telomerase enzyme to keep the length of their telomeres over a crucial cutoff that permits them to continue dividing to become immortal [11].

(4) Inducing or accessing the vasculature

The term "angiogenic" refers to the process by which new blood and lymphatic vessels develop from an already existing vasculature. This gives tumor cells the ability to take in nutrition in the form of nutrients and oxygen as well as the ability to expel metabolic waste. A shift to angiogenesis in cancer appears to be caused by an imbalance between stimulatory and inhibitory factors, which results in a proangiogenic state. This happens when hyperplasia with relatively low blood supply transforms into an unregulated new vessel development, ultimately leading to the growth of malignant tumors. Many angiogenic substances, such as vascular endothelial growth factor A (VEGF-A), vascular endothelial growth factor C (VEGF-C), etc., bind to the appropriate receptors, causing angiogenesis and the proliferation of lymphatic capillaries. In addition, tumor-associated macrophages (TAMs), which are renowned for their protumor actions, release VEGF in hypoxic tumors. Other angiogenesis promoters include platelet-derived growth factor (PDGF)-B and -C and fibroblast growth factor (FGF)-1 and -2, as well as a large variety of polypeptides, metabolites, and hormones that aid in the development of new blood vessels in both a healthy and diseased state [12].

(5) Resistance to cell death

In order to eliminate unneeded or diseased cells during growth or in response to cellular stress, organisms have developed a process called apoptosis. Several cellular steps are involved, and the culmination of these processes is activating the caspase family of cysteine proteases. One of the characteristics of cancer is the evasion of cell death. Cancer cells experience ongoing stress, such as oncogenic stress, genomic instability, and cellular hypoxia, in contrast to normal cells. The intrinsic route of apoptosis would ordinarily be initiated in response to such internal apoptotic stimuli. Nevertheless, by blocking the apoptotic pathways, cancer cells frequently manage to prevent this biological reaction. Numerous malignancies have been found to have increased levels of the antiapoptotic BCL-2 proteins and decreased levels of proapoptotic BH3 proteins [13].

(6) Escape from immune destruction

A cancer cell acquires genetic alterations that can dodge or endure the immune system's regular killing procedures. This cancer cell's offspring will carry on this inherited survival trait because of the mutated DNA in its parent cell. It has been acknowledged that a prevalent feature in cancer is the capacity to instruct the immune system to sluggish immune responses or halt them entirely. Cancer cells elude immune attack through the production of tumor mutations and immune system inhibition [14].

(7) Deregulated cellular metabolism

Altered patterns of metabolic pathways result in the exacerbated synthesis of macromolecules, increased proliferation, and resistance to treatment via alteration of drug processing. This deregulation involves metabolic reprogramming that leads to high production of lactate. Lactate efflux, besides contributing to the glycolytic flux, also acts in the extracellular matrix, contributing to cancer malignancy by, among other effects, induction of angiogenesis [15].

(8) Phenotypic plasticity

The most significant characteristic of a cancer cell is its ability to change its morphological and functional characteristics momentarily when it travels to the location of metastatic niche. As the disease progresses and chemotherapeutic treatments are avoided, cancer cells activate phenotypic plasticity pathways through several ways: neoplastic cells derived from undifferentiated progenitor cells could halt differentiation and remain in that partially differentiated, progenitor-like state or cells that were committed to a particular differentiation phenotype can switch developmental programs, or transdifferentiate, and acquire traits that are not associated with their cell type of origin [16].

(9) Senescence

Senescent fibroblasts and macrophages in cancer tissue have been found to secrete senescence-associated secretory phenotypes (SASP), which have been shown to boost the malignant potency of cancer cells. Senescent cell removal from the murine skin wound healing model decreased the amount of angiogenesis that occurred within the healing wound. Recent research has shown that cancer tissue, especially in metastatic areas, has a sizable number of senescent tumor cells (STC). STCs actually play a significant role in the spread of cancer by encouraging collective invasion and creating a cytokine barrier to shield nonsenescent tumor cells from immune response [17].

(10) Genomic instability

Genomic instability is an increased propensity for genomic modification during cell cycle. For cells to remain intact, genomic stability must be maintained in order to guard against exogenous carcinogen assaults, mistakes resulting from DNA replication, and endogenous genotoxic stress, such as reactive oxygen species (ROS) from cellular metabolism. A genomic instability that predisposes the cell to malignant transformation frequently occurs from a problem with the control of any of these processes (a number of surveillance mechanisms, DNA damage checkpoint, DNA repair machinery, and mitotic checkpoint). The causes of genomic instability include microsatellite instability (MSI) and increased frequencies of base pair mutation, as well as chromosome instability (CIN), the variation in chromosome number, or structure changes [18].

(11) Polymorphic microbiomes

The addition of polymorphic microbes is a reflection of the growing understanding that the complex microbial ecosystems, or "microbiome," which include bacteria, fungi, and viruses that symbiotically associate with the human body, have a significant influence on cancer etiology [19].

(12) Tumor promoting inflammation

There is ongoing debate on how inflammation contributes to the development of cancer. In healthy tissue, inflammation assists with recovery and repair, but in cancer, it encourages cell proliferation, boosts growth signaling, and energizes cells that are linked to tumors. Antiinflammatory medications have also been demonstrated to lower mortality rates in a number of malignancies, indicating that inflammation in the tumor microenvironment is a critical factor in the development of cancer [20].

(13) Nonmutational epigenetic reprogramming

Insights into the functions of transcription factors and chromatin regulators in mediating cell state transitions have been remarkably revealed as a result of the demonstration of induced pluripotency and direct lineage conversion. It is acknowledged that many malignancies share global changes in the epigenetic landscape. Cancer cells can reprogram a wide number of gene-regulation networks to alter gene expression and encourage the acquisition of signature skills, mimicking what occurs during normal embryogenesis and development [21].

(14) Tumor invasion and metastasis

Cancer metastasis, one of the hallmarks of cancer, is a process in which cancer cells spread out from the primary tumor, settle, and develop at a location other than the original tumor site [22,23]. Cancer metastasis, not the initial tumor, is what typically results in cancer mortality. The majority of cancer deaths—about 90%—are caused by metastasis, which is the main cause of morbidity and mortality [24]. This significant feature of cancer is discussed in detail in this chapter.

History of metastasis

Metastasis is the major cause of treatment failure in cancer patients and of cancer-related deaths. In 1829, French gynecologist Joseph Recamier (1774–1852) first used the term "metastasis" to describe the process by which cancer invades blood vessels [25]. A German physician named Rudolf Virchow further defined tumor dispersion in 1858, asserting that the majority of cancer patients will develop a metastatic lesion and that all solid tumors have the potential to metastasize [26]. In landmark research published in 1889, Stephen Paget examined the patterns of breast cancer metastases and found that the bone is disproportionately affected [27]. In his study, he discussed the location of metastases after analyzing roughly 735 fatal breast cancer cases. Additionally, he understood that metastatic patterns do not correspond to blood flow. Paget also presented the "seed and soil" idea, in which he refers to cancer cells as seeds and the spread of these cells throughout the body as the secondary organs' soil. As some inquiries went unanswered, he omitted explaining the nutritional information [28,29]. In 1915, Makoto Takahashi developed the first murine model of metastasis [30]. James Ewing later asserted in 1928 that the anatomy of arterial and lymphatic channels governs the seed and soil concept in metastasis [31]. Growth occurs as the initial tumor spreads to an additional organ in the body. When cancer cells spread from one organ to another, metastasis happens in significant steps, according to Josh Fiddler, a pioneer in cancer metastasis. Various seeds will depart from the parent tumor and land in hospitable terrain. His work has significantly contributed to a better understanding of metastasis [32]. Important observations made in this domain of cancer metastasis have been tabulated chronologically in Table 2.

Table 2 Timeline of cancer metastasis studies.

Year	Contribution	References
1944	Identification of the role of cellular adhesiveness to metastasis and the distribution of embolic tumor cells by Dale Rex Coman	[33]
1952	Demonstration of the transpulmonary passage of tumor cell emboli resulting in metastases on the arterial side by Irving Zeidman A study on the organ specificity of tumor growth following intravenous injection of tumor cells and comparing growth in the liver and lung by Balduin Lucke	[34,35]
1955	Cells adapted to ascites growth preexist within the parent tumor and have an increased malignant phenotype by Eva Kline	[36]
1962	Enzymatic manipulation of cell surfaces can affect metastatic potential by Gabriel and Tatiana Gasic	[37]
1965	Application of ^{51}chromium-labeled tumor cells in quantitative dissemination studies by Bernard and Edwin Fisher	[38]
1966	Differentiation of lymphatic from hematogenous metastasis by Bernard and Edwin Fisher	[39]

Continued

Table 2 Timeline of cancer metastasis studies—cont'd

Year	Contribution	References
1970	Metastasis can result from the survival of only a few tumor cells using IUdR-labeled tumor cells by Isaiah Fidler	[40]
1973	The in vivo selection of tumor cells for enhanced metastatic potential by Isaiah Fidler Human tumors can metastasize in thymic-deficient nude mice by Beppino Giovanella and coworkers	[41,42]
1975	A proposal on metastatic cascade to define a number of sequential events needed for disseminated cancer by Irwin Bross The organ specificity of metastasis is determined by cell adhesion by Garth Nicolson	[43,44]
1976	A proposal on the clonal evolution of tumor-cell population by Peter Nowell Linkage of invasion and metastasis to the production of proteolytic enzymes by metastatic cells by Lance Liotta and Jerome Kleinerman	[45,46]
1977	The metastatic heterogeneity of neoplasms by Isaiah Fidler and Margaret Kripke	[47]
1980	Metastatic potential is correlated with enzymatic degradation of basement membrane collagen by Lance Liotta The organ specificity of metastasis using ectopic organs by Ian Hart and Isaiah Fidler The regulatory role of NK cells in tumor metastasis by James Talmadge and collaborators	[48–50]
1981	Interactions between clonal subpopulations could stabilize their metastatic properties, whereas a clonal subpopulation is unstable that following a short coculture results in the emergence of metastatic variants by George Poste and Isaiah Fidler	[51]
1982	First antimetastasis drug clinical trial (Razoxane) design by Karl Hellman Cancer metastases are clonal, and metastases originate from a single surviving cell by James Talmadge and Sandra Wolman The metastatic process was selective, as demonstrated using spontaneous metastases from multiple metastatic variants by James Talmadge and Isaiah Fidler The rapid development of metastatic heterogeneity by clonal origin metastases by George Poste and Irving Zeidman Metastasis is not due to adaption to a new organ environment but rather was a selective process by Garth Nicolson and Susan Custead	[52–56]
1984	The evidence of organ-specific metastasis in ovarian carcinoma patients who were treated with peritoneovenous shunts by David Tarin and colleagues Metastatic heterogeneity of human tumors using immune incompetent mice by James Kozlowski and coworkers Tumor heterogeneity for motility and adhesive properties and their association with metastasis by Avraham Raz and coworkers	[57–59]

Table 2 Timeline of cancer metastasis studies—cont'd

Year	Contribution	References
1985	The critical role of macrophages in the process of metastasis by Isaiah Fidler and coworkers	[60]
1986	The concept of metastatic inefficiency by Leonard Weiss and coworkers	[61]
1988	The first metastasis suppressor gene identification by Patricia Steeg and collaborators	[62]
1990	The ability of FDG to detect LN metastases with PET scans by Richard Wahl and coworkers The utility of bacterial LacZ as a marker to detect micrometastases during tumor progression by Lloyd Culp and collaborators	[63,64]
1991	A relationship between metastasis and angiogenesis in patients with breast cancer by Judah Folkman and coworkers	[65]
1992	The role of chemokines in tumor-associated macrophage facilitation of metastasis by Jo Van Damme	[66]
1994	The removal of a malignant primary tumor in mice spurs the growth of remote tumors, or metastases by Judah Folkman	[67]
1997	The visualization of tumor cell invasion and metastasis using GFP expression by Robert Hoffman	[68]
2000	Diversity in the gene expression patterns by breast cancer tissues by David Botstein	[69]
2001	The role of cancer stem cells in metastasis by Irving Weissman and coworkers	[70]
2002	Metastatic potential is determined early in tumorigenesis, explaining the apparent metastatic molecular signature by most cells in a primary tumor by Rene Bernards and Robert Weinberg EMT could explain metastatic progression by Jean Paul Thiery and Robert Weinberg The genetic heterogeneity of single disseminated tumor cells in minimal residual cancer by Christopher Klein and collaborators A specific gene expression profile of primary breast cancers was associated with the development of metastasis and a poor clinical outcome by Laura van 't Veer and co-workers in 2002	[71–74]
2003	A molecular signature associated with metastasis of breast tumors to bone by Yibin Kang and colleagues The ability of breast cancer tumors to metastasize resides in just a few "breast cancer stem cells" that are highly resistant to chemotherapy by Michael Clarke and Max Wicha	[75,76]
2006	The role of genetic susceptibility for metastatic by Kent Hunter	[77]
2007	The first metastasis-promoting micro-RNA by Li Ma and Robert Weinberg	[78]
2008	Micro-RNA expression patterns could predict metastatic risk by William Harbour and coworkers Micro-RNAs can suppress metastases by Joan Massagué and coworkers	[79,80]

Mechanism of metastasis

The intricate process of metastasis includes numerous sequential and connected steps and multiple molecular reactions involving the spread of tumor cells from a primary tumor mass to an additional place via blood and lymphatic arteries. The "invasion-metastasis cascade" is a complicated sequence of cell-biological occurrences. The cascade includes angiogenesis (the growth of new blood vessels), detachment and migration of metastatic cells from the primary tumor, invasion through the basement membrane (BM) and extracellular matrix (ECM) surrounding the tumor, invasion of the BM supporting the endothelium of nearby blood and lymphatic vessels, intravasation of the metastatic cells into the blood and/or lymphatic vessels, and adhesion of the circulating metastatic cells to the endothelium of capillaries of the body, the extravasation of the circulating metastatic cells via the endothelial cell layer and the surrounding BM, and finally the establishment and development of secondary malignancies at the target organ site (colonization). The different steps involved in metastasis are represented in Fig. 2 and described below.

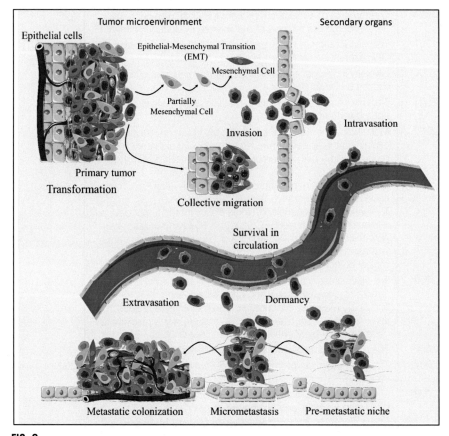

FIG. 2

The mechanism of cancer metastasis.

Detachment: The first stage of metastatic cascade is cell detachment. Mechanical and protease-mediated cleavage forces are both involved in cell separation. The dissociation of substrate adhesions at both the cytosolic site and the extracellular site is thought to be facilitated by mechanical stresses produced by actomyosin-driven contraction. Additionally, cytosolic adapter proteins can be phosphorylated or dephosphorylated, integrins or adapter proteins can undergo posttranslational modification, and calpain cysteine proteases can phosphorylate or dephosphorylate cytosolic adapter proteins. Extracellular separation of cell-substrate adhesions can be accomplished by proteolytic cleavage of matrix materials mediated by matrix proteases or by shedding of matrix receptors such as integrins by certain sheddases, leaving sections of the receptors on the substrate [24].

Invasion: Two distinct mechanisms—mesenchymal (fibroblastic) cell migration and amoeboid cell migration—allow metastatic cells to penetrate the ECM. While amoeboid cell migration is a protease-independent process where cells use mechanical forces to clear a way in the ECM rather than degrading them, mesenchymal cell migration requires protease activity (protease-dependent) to breakdown the ECM for cell passage, such as MMPs. Extracellular proteolytic enzymes such as matrix metalloproteinases (MMPs) and serine proteases play a significant role in the invasion and metastasis of cancer. In some cases, the malignant cell undergoes epithelial-mesenchymal transitions at specific times. The process of epithelial cells losing their cell polarity and cell-cell adhesion and acquiring migratory and invasive properties to become mesenchymal stem cells is known as the epithelial-mesenchymal transition. Epithelial-mesenchymal transition is characterized by the disintegration of the intercellular network and the enhancement of cell motility, leading to the release of cells from the parent epithelial tissue. The mesenchyme-like phenotype promotes cell invasion and migration as a result, which leads to the spread of tumor cells and the ability to metastasize. Proteases are known to be crucial in the breakdown of extracellular matrix, the basement membrane, and tissue remodeling. Proteases have a significant role in the initiation and progression of cancer, including tumor growth, survival, invasion, migration, vascularization, and metastasis. This is due to their direct proteolytic activity as well as their ability to regulate cellular processes and activities [24].

Intravasation: Intravasation, the process of entering the bloodstream, is a crucial stage in the growth of distant metastases. Other cells in the tumor microenvironment, proteases, signaling molecules, environmental variables at the tumor, and surrounding vasculature are a few of the elements that affect the intravasation of cancer cells. These tissues and chemicals are crucial in enabling tumor cells to penetrate the basement membrane, attach, and cross endothelial cell junctions in order to enter the bloodstream. Tumor cell invasion into blood vessels or lymphatic vessels can happen, with the majority of invasion taking place through hematogenous (blood vessel) routes and depending on various variables [81]. There is strong evidence that the urokinase-type plasminogen activator (uPA) and its receptor (uPAR) play a function in proliferation of some tumor cells and migration of tumor and endothelial cells. The extracellular matrix components are broken down due to the interaction of uPA with uPAR, triggering a series of proteolytic cascades that cause tumor cells to migrate from their primary site of origin to a distant secondary organ. MMPs, EGF receptor family members, and TGFB signaling molecules also participate in intravasation. Other receptors that can contribute to intravasation include platelets, neutrophils, cancer-associated fibroblasts (CAFs), fibroblasts, macrophages, and fibroblasts can all help tumor cells overcome the endothelium barrier. G protein-coupled receptors are another class of receptors that can aid in intravasation [82,83].

Circulation: Cancer cells are classified as circulating tumor cells (CTCs) when they have successfully invaded blood arteries and move through the venous and arterial circulation. Cancer cells can enter the circulatory system as single cells, clusters, or microemboli. Due to their ability to prolong cell life and lower apoptosis rates, these clusters have a higher metastatic potential than single cells. In addition, CTC clustering causes particular methylation alterations in DNA that support metastatic formation and stemness characteristics. Additionally, CTC clustering with neutrophils promotes cell-cycle progression and survival, encouraging metastatic advances. TEPs encourage CTC survival, evasion of immunological vigilance, contact between the tumor and the endothelium, and diffusion. By interacting with platelets, which may surround CTCs in the form of a kind of coat, CTCs can also obtain physical and immune protection. CTCs are protected and are more likely to survive in the bloodstream when they form microemboli or clusters. Tumor CD44 interacts with platelet P-selectin and the fibrinogen receptor GPIIb-IIIa, which are involved in the platelet coating of CTCs, to cause this. EMT is facilitated by platelets, which increase tissue factor and P2Y12 receptor activity. Additionally, the critical molecular pathways associated with the production of EMT, the TGF/SMAD and NF-B pathways, can be activated by platelet-mediated TGF-secretion, enhancing the potential for metastatic spread of CTC. Heat shock protein 47 (HSP47), a chaperone involved in collagen secretion and deposition, is expressed by EMT in CTCs, increasing their contact with platelets as a result. This could facilitate the development of CTC clusters linked with platelets. Finally, there is evidence that HSP47 amplification in CTCs is linked to a higher metastatic rate [84].

Extravasation: Tumor cells extravasate into the parenchyma of distant tissues after surviving in the abrasive bloodstream and become arrested in a secondary location. Adhesion of tumor cells to endothelial cells and transmigration through the endothelium wall are necessary for extravasation, which calls for a tumor cell transendothelial migration. This is accomplished through pairing of many cell ligands and receptors, such as selectins, cadherins, integrins, and immunoglobulins, and several mechanical elements necessary for tumor cell-endothelial cell adhesion. E- and P-selectin make it easier for cancer cells to stick to the endothelium. Sialyl Lewisx/a (sLex/sLea), a tetrasaccharide structure found on the glycoproteins and glycolipids of selectin ligands, promotes CTC-endothelium contact and is frequently overexpressed in clinical diagnoses. In addition, the binding of selectin ligands on cancer cells and P-selectins expressed by platelets can connect cancer cells and platelets, allowing for indirect adherence of cancer cells to endothelial cells. The integrins are a different group of molecules that are crucial for adhesion between cancer cells and the EC and cell-cell and cell-ECM interactions. Cancer cells can firmly adhere to the endothelium by using the α4β1 integrins that they express as an alternative ligand for VCAM-1 (vascular cell adhesion molecule 1, CD106). Tumor cell-EC adhesion may also be influenced by interactions between L1-CAM (neuronal cell adhesion molecule) and the V1 or V3 integrins. Once a stable attachment has been established, cancer cells will gradually cross the vascular endothelial barrier to avoid the ECM surrounding the vasculature. The extravasated cancer cells will then either form secondary tumors or remain dormant in the tissue. This process is known as transendothelial migration. Invadopodia are protrusions made of structural proteins like cortactin, N-WASP, Tks4, and Tks5, as well as pericellular proteases such as MT1-MMP, MMP9, and MMP2, resulting in the degradation of ECM favoring the invasion and TEM of cancer cells [85].

Micrometastasis formation: Tumor cells risk succumbing to apoptosis after extravasation and the loss of their protective coating in a process known as anoikis (detachment-induced apoptosis). Isolated cancer cells are vulnerable to this fate due to the absence of a protective environment unless they can find a new home at the site of their metastasis. The term "micrometastatic niche" refers to this new location for the rogue tumor cells, and platelets once more serve as the primary catalyst for its development. CTCs must travel to locations far from the main site for the micrometastatic niche to emerge. Platelets have a particular role in forming the "early metastatic niche" based on the hypothesis that platelet-derived signals, in addition to signals derived from the tumor itself, are responsible for the recruitment of granulocytes in the early metastatic sites, where cancer cells begin to accumulate. The recruitment of a variety of host-derived cells, which will eventually form the tumor stroma, is mediated by the chemokines CXCL5 and CXCL7, which are secreted by the platelets that become activated after interacting with the tumor cells [86].

Colonization: The spread of cancer cells to distant tissues is the last stage of metastasis. Cancer stem cells (CSCs) or metastatic initiating cells (MIC) are crucial in this process because they have the metabolic adaptability to the microenvironment and the capacity to self-renew and sustain carcinogenesis that non-CSCs lack. Different metabolic processes that are important in the maintenance of stemness features have been seen in CSCs. The mesenchymal-epithelial transition, which is analogous to EMT, is the process by which a metastatic colony expands and involves the conversion of cells to an epithelial phenotype.

Dissemination: Dissemination is the movement of tumor cells from their primary site to a secondary site, where they settle in the capillaries of other organs and then leave those organs, where they develop and form new metastases. Two distinct models of dissemination have been presented, depending on the timing of the dissemination of tumor cells. Based on the naturally occurring stepwise progression of cancer and the previously mentioned relationship between the size of the primary tumor and the risk of relapse, the linear model hypothesizes that only advanced neoplasms contain sufficient molecular aberrations to facilitate all of the necessary steps of the metastatic cascade. Accordingly, only cancer cells that are fully malignant (also known as "late" disseminating tumor cells or DTCs) can separate from the primary source and give rise to lethal metastases. The parallel model, in contrast, contends that metastasis can occur prematurely during carcinogenesis and that developing tumor cells, referred to as "early DTCs," might transform into lethal metastases concurrently with the primary tumor. In light of this, early DTCs would simultaneously yet independently acquire genetic and epigenetic changes in comparison to their tumor of origin, maybe as a result of the particular niche-related microenvironments they lodge. CTCs, also known as disseminated tumor cells (DTCs), can remain dormant after surviving in the bloodstream and extravasating to a different place.

Challenges for therapy of metastasis

Cancer's tendency to spread across the body is one of the key causes of the challenges involved in treating it. Certain cancers can spread from their primary site of growth to other sections of the body without the need for medical intervention since they are asymptomatic and cannot be diagnosed. Metastases have variable cellular compositions, both across and within individual metastases (interlesional heterogeneity) [87] as well as within a single metastasis (intralesional heterogeneity) [88]. Metastases can arise from a single surviving cell and are clonal in origin, according to karyotypic investigations [89] and single-cell sequencing [90]. Their heightened genetic instability, however, is what makes them the most dangerous [91]. This attribute allows for the rapid formation of novel variants; those that are resistant to treatment gain a selective advantage and eventually outgrow the sensitive cells, resulting in the recurrence of metastatic illness [92]. Additionally, some cancer metastasis occurrences are too minute to be noticed in clinical diagnostic scans but still exist as prospective sites for eventual metastatic relapse. These are referred to as micrometastases events, which are multicellular secondary tumor cell clusters or disseminated solitary tumor cells (DTCs) [93]. Although the precise characteristics of these niches seem to be tumor- and organ-dependent, the premetastatic niche is characterized by vascular leakiness, increased inflammation (e.g., TLR4 activation), alteration of the extracellular matrix (ECM), recruitment of immunosuppressive cells (including macrophages, bone marrow-derived cells (BMDCs), and regulatory T cells), as well as activation and metabolic reprogramming of local stromal cells. By improving nutrition availability, vascular permeability, inflammation, and cancer cell migration, survival, and adherence to ECM components at these remote locales, these modifications collectively alter the premetastatic niche to be more amenable to the tumor cell. Emerging imaging agents targeted against specific features of the premetastatic niche, such as overexpression of the $\alpha4\beta1$ integrin receptor or the presence of specific fibronectin isoforms in the ECM, are also showing promise in the detection of these premetastatic niches. These features include altered textural features in radiological scans of axillary lymph nodes and metastatic sites that reflect increased matrix deposition or tissue density, for example.

Metastasis may result from dormant, dispersed cancer cells that are present at the time of surgery and manage to elude immune system destruction. Even after the primary tumor has been removed, it's possible for dispersed cancer cells to continue to exist and retain their ability to invade. Dormant disseminated cancer cells do not express a cell surface protein that triggers T-cell-mediated assaults, according to research on mice models and tissue samples from people who have pancreatic ductal adenocarcinoma. They are unable to alleviate endoplasmic reticulum stress, which accounts for this phenotype. When this stress is relieved, dispersed cells begin to proliferate and invade to become metastases [94].

Accurate information about the occurrence of metastatic spread and how this process affects an individual's risk profile at diagnosis and throughout therapy is crucial for optimizing the management of metastatic illness. The basis of metastatic disease staging in surgically resected malignancies has instead been lymph node assessment, including sentinel node mapping with pathological assessment and ultra staging (e.g., cytokeratin staining) as a surrogate for metastatic dissemination. However, the sensitivity and repeatability of pathological metastasis staging are being improved by the recent integration of deep learning image analysis algorithms into clinically established pipelines, which use various tissue features to determine the presence of cancer cells. Despite these advancements, metastatic lymph node assessment is still limited by its nature to capturing only lymphatic system-based cancer cells and misses cancer cells that have already spread to distant organs. As a result, there is a clear need to increase the sensitivity and specificity of existing diagnostic scans and create label-free technologies that, when combined, can give a complete picture of the burden of micrometastatic disease and thus help determine prognosis [95].

Antimetastatic medications block tumor angiogenesis, suppress tumor cell growth, or improve immune response. Limited survival gains have, however, so far been attained for the majority of patients with solid cancer. The main issue is that only a few of these medications prevent cancer metastasis, which kills the majority of patients as a result of metastasis. The development of antimetastatic medications is hampered by numerous issues. The first problem is that pharmaceutical companies lack many efficient high-throughput tools for screening their compound library for possible antimetastatic drugs. Second, while relevant animal models for preclinical antimetastatic evaluation are well established in university laboratories, the majority of pharmaceutical corporations have not created standard methodologies for using them. Third, it may be necessary to change clinical trial designs to make metastasis-free survival the main goal in order to better facilitate the discovery of antimetastatic medications [96].

Conclusion

Cancer is a complex disease and a major cause of death worldwide. Although the cancer survival rate has been significantly improved over the years, the improvement is primarily due to early diagnosis and cancer growth inhibition. Limited progress has been made in the treatment of cancer metastasis due to various factors. The biochemical events and parameters involved in the metastatic process and tumor microenvironment have been targeted or can be potential targets for metastasis prevention and inhibition. The treatment opportunities of metastatic cancers are limited by the challenges posed by metastasis, including the absence of specific biomarkers that can identify the progression of metastasis, lack of treatment access at metastatic sites, altered phenotype and metabolism of the metastasized cells compared to the cells in the parent tumor. Future studies should be focused on understanding these challenges in therapy of metastatic cancer.

References

[1] K. Stoletov, P.H. Beatty, J.D. Lewis, Novel therapeutic targets for cancer metastasis, Expert. Rev. Anticancer. Ther. 20 (2) (2020) 97–109, https://doi.org/10.1080/14737140.2020.1718496. Epub 2020 Jan. 30. PMID: 31997674.

[2] S. Sarkar, G. Horn, K. Moulton, A. Oza, S. Byler, S. Kokolus, M. Longacre, Cancer development, progression, and therapy: an epigenetic overview, Int. J. Mol. Sci. 14 (10) (2013) 21087–21113, https://doi.org/10.3390/ijms141021087. PMID: 24152442. PMCID: PMC3821660.

[3] T. Buder, A. Deutsch, B. Klink, A. Voss-Böhme, Patterns of tumor progression predict small and tissue-specific tumor-originating niches, Front. Oncol. 8 (2019) 668, https://doi.org/10.3389/fonc.2018.00668. PMID: 30687642. PMCID: PMC6335293.

[4] https://www.urmc.rochester.edu/encyclopedia/content.aspx?contenttypeid=85&contentid=p00554.

[5] https://www.cancer.gov/about-cancer/diagnosis-staging/diagnosis/tumor-grade.

[6] https://www.nhs.uk/common-health-questions/operations-tests-and-procedures/what-do-cancer-stages-and-gradesmean/#:~:text=Cancer%20grades&text=grade%201%20%E2%80%93%20cancer%20cells%20that,grow%20or%20spread%20more%20aggressively.

[7] D. Hanahan, Hallmarks of cancer: new dimensions, Cancer Discov. 12 (1) (2022) 31–46, https://doi.org/10.1158/2159-8290.CD-21-1059. PMID: 35022204.

[8] D. Hanahan, R.A. Weinberg, Hallmarks of cancer: the next generation, Cell 144 (5) (2011) 646–674, https://doi.org/10.1016/j.cell.2011.02.013. PMID: 21376230.

[9] M.A. Feitelson, A. Arzumanyan, R.J. Kulathinal, S.W. Blain, R.F. Holcombe, J. Mahajna, M. Marino, M.L. Martinez-Chantar, R. Nawroth, I. Sanchez-Garcia, D. Sharma, N.K. Saxena, N. Singh, P.J. Vlachostergios, S. Guo, K. Honoki, H. Fujii, A.G. Georgakilas, A. Bilsland, A. Amedei, E. Niccolai, A. Amin, S.S. Ashraf, C.S. Boosani, G. Guha, M.R. Ciriolo, K. Aquilano, S. Chen, S.I. Mohammed, A.S. Azmi, D. Bhakta, D. Halicka, W.N. Keith, S. Nowsheen, Sustained proliferation in cancer: mechanisms and novel therapeutic targets, Semin. Cancer Biol. 35 (Suppl) (2015) S25–S54, https://doi.org/10.1016/j.semcancer.2015.02.006. Epub 2015 Apr. 17. PMID: 25892662. PMCID: PMC4898971.

[10] T. Gutschner, S. Diederichs, The hallmarks of cancer: a long non-coding RNA point of view, RNA Biol. 9 (6) (2012) 703–719, https://doi.org/10.4161/rna.20481. Epub 2012 Jun. 1. PMID: 22664915. PMCID: PMC3495743.

[11] P. Yaswen, K.L. MacKenzie, W.N. Keith, P. Hentosh, F. Rodier, J. Zhu, G.L. Firestone, A. Matheu, A. Carnero, A. Bilsland, T. Sundin, K. Honoki, H. Fujii, A.G. Georgakilas, A. Amedei, A. Amin, B. Helferich, C.S. Boosani, G. Guha, M.R. Ciriolo, S. Chen, S.I.

Mohammed, A.S. Azmi, D. Bhakta, D. Halicka, E. Niccolai, K. Aquilano, S.S. Ashraf, S. Nowsheen, X. Yang, Therapeutic targeting of replicative immortality, Semin. Cancer Biol. 35 (Suppl) (2015) S104–S128, https://doi.org/10.1016/j.semcancer.2015.03.007. Epub 2015 Apr. 11. PMID: 25869441. PMCID: PMC4600408.

[12] H. Saman, S.S. Raza, S. Uddin, K. Rasul, Inducing angiogenesis, a key step in cancer vascularization, and treatment approaches, Cancers (Basel) 12 (5) (2020) 1172, https://doi.org/10.3390/cancers12051172. PMID: 32384792. PMCID: PMC7281705.

[13] A. Sharma, L.H. Boise, M. Shanmugam, Cancer metabolism and the evasion of apoptotic cell death, Cancers (Basel) 11 (8) (2019) 1144, https://doi.org/10.3390/cancers11081144. PMID: 31405035. PMCID: PMC6721599.

[14] J.L. Messerschmidt, G.C. Prendergast, G.L. Messerschmidt, How cancers escape immune destruction and mechanisms of action for the new significantly active immune therapies: helping nonimmunologists decipher recent advances, Oncologist 21 (2) (2016) 233–243, https://doi.org/10.1634/theoncologist.2015-0282. Epub 2016 Feb. 1. PMID: 26834161. PMCID: PMC4746082.

[15] C. Pinheiro, E.A. Garcia, F. Morais-Santos, M.A. Moreira, F.M. Almeida, L.F. Jubé, G.S. Queiroz, É.C. Paula, M.A. Andreoli, L.L. Villa, A. Longatto-Filho, F. Baltazar, Reprogramming energy metabolism and inducing angiogenesis: co-expression of monocarboxylate transporters with VEGF family members in cervical adenocarcinomas, BMC Cancer 15 (2015) 835, https://doi.org/10.1186/s12885-015-1842-4. PMID: 26525902. PMCID: PMC4630851.

[16] S. Qin, J. Jiang, Y. Lu, E.C. Nice, C. Huang, J. Zhang, W. He, Emerging role of tumor cell plasticity in modifying therapeutic response, Signal. Transduct. Target Ther. 5 (1) (2020) 228, https://doi.org/10.1038/s41392-020-00313-5. PMID: 33028808. PMCID: PMC7541492.

[17] S.S. Park, Y.W. Choi, J.H. Kim, H.S. Kim, T.J. Park, Senescent tumor cells: an overlooked adversary in the battle against cancer, Exp. Mol. Med. 53 (12) (2021) 1834–1841, https://doi.org/10.1038/s12276-021-00717-5. Epub 2021 Dec. 16. PMID: 34916607. PMCID: PMC8741813.

[18] Y. Yao, W. Dai, Genomic instability and cancer, J. Carcinog. Mutagen. 5 (2014) 1000165, https://doi.org/10.4172/2157-2518.1000165. PMID: 25541596. PMCID: PMC4274643.

[19] M.P. Lythgoe, B.H. Mullish, A.E. Frampton, J. Krell, Polymorphic microbes: a new emerging hallmark of cancer, Trends Microbiol. (2022), https://doi.org/10.1016/j.tim.2022.08.004. S0966-842X(22)00216-5. Epub ahead of print. PMID: 36058787.

[20] G. Khusnurrokhman, F.F. Wati, Tumor-promoting inflammation in lung cancer: a literature review, Ann. Med. Surg. (Lond.) 79 (2022) 104022, https://doi.org/10.1016/j.amsu.2022.104022. PMID: 35860063. PMCID: PMC9289429.

[21] M.L. Suvà, N. Riggi, B.E. Bernstein, Epigenetic reprogramming in cancer, Science 339 (6127) (2013) 1567–1570, https://doi.org/10.1126/science.1230184. PMID: 23539597. PMCID: PMC3821556.

[22] C. Wittekind, M. Neid, Cancer invasion and metastasis, Oncology 69 (Suppl. 1) (2005) 14–16, https://doi.org/10.1159/000086626. Epub 2005 Sep. 19. PMID: 16210871.

[23] M. Liu, J. Yang, B. Xu, X. Zhang, Tumor metastasis: mechanistic insights and therapeutic interventions, MedComm 2 (4) (2020) 587–617, https://doi.org/10.1002/mco2.100. PMID: 34977870. PMCID: PMC8706758.

[24] X. Guan, Cancer metastases: challenges and opportunities, Acta Pharm. Sin. B 5 (5) (2015) 402–418, https://doi.org/10.1016/j.apsb.2015.07.005. Epub 2015 Sep. 8. PMID: 26579471. PMCID: PMC4629446.

[25] S.I. Hajdu, A note from history: landmarks in history of cancer, part 3, Cancer 118 (4) (2012) 1155–1168, https://doi.org/10.1002/cncr.26320. Epub 2011 Jul. 12. PMID: 21751192.

[26] https://www.ijeast.com/papers/355-359,Tesma504,IJEAST.pdf.

[27] S. Paget, The distribution of secondary growths in cancer of the breast, Cancer Metastasis Rev. 8 (2) (1989) 98–101. PMID: 2673568.

[28] D.R. Welch, D.R. Hurst, Defining the hallmarks of metastasis, Cancer Res. 79 (12) (2019) 3011–3027, https://doi.org/10.1158/0008-5472.CAN-19-0458. Epub 2019 May 3. PMID: 31053634. PMCID: PMC6571042.

[29] G.L. Nicolson, Organ specificity of tumor metastasis: role of preferential adhesion, invasion and growth of malignant cells at specific secondary sites, Cancer Metastasis Rev. 7 (2) (1988) 143–188, https://doi.org/10.1007/BF00046483. PMID: 3293836.

[30] M. Takahashi, An experimental study of metastasis, J. Pathol. Bacteriol. 20 (1915) 1–13.

[31] J. Ewing, Neoplastic Diseases: A Treatise on Tumors, third ed., WB Saunders, Philadelphia, 1928.

[32] J.E. Talmadge, I.J. Fidler, AACR centennial series: the biology of cancer metastasis: historical perspective, Cancer Res. 70 (14) (2010) 5649–5669, https://doi.org/10.1158/0008-5472.CAN-10-1040. Epub 2010 Jul. 7. PMID: 20610625. PMCID: PMC4037932.

[33] D.R. Coman, Decreased mutual adhesiveness, a property of cells from squamous cell carcinomas, Cancer Res. 4 (1944) 625–629.

[34] I. Zeidman, BUSS JM., Transpulmonary passage of tumor cell emboli, Cancer Res. 12 (1952) 731–733.

[35] B. Lucke, C. Breedis, Z.P. Woo, L. Berwick, P. Nowell, Differential growth of metastatic tumors in liver and lung: experiments with rabbit V2 carcinoma, Cancer Res. 12 (1952) 734–738.

[36] E. Klein, Immediate transformation of solid into ascites tumors; studies on a mammary carcinoma of an inbred mouse strain, Exp. Cell Res. 8 (1955) 213–225.

[37] G. Gasic, T. Gasic, Removal of sialic acid from the cell coat in tumor cells and vascular endothelium, and its effects on metastasis, Proc. Natl. Acad. Sci. USA 48 (1962) 1172–1177.

[38] B. Fisher, E.R. Fisher, The organ distribution of disseminated ^{51}Cr-labeled tumor cells, Cancer Res. 27 (1967) 412–420.

[39] B. Fisher, E.R. Fisher, The interrelationship of hematogenous and lymphatic tumor cell dissemination, Surg. Gynecol. Obstet. 122 (1966) 791–798.

[40] I.J. Fidler, Metastasis: guantitative analysis of distribution and fate of tumor embolilabeled with ^{125}I-5-iodo-2′-deoxyuridine, J. Natl. Cancer Inst. 45 (1970) 773–782.

[41] I.J. Fidler, Selection of successive tumour lines for metastasis, Nat. New Biol. 242 (1973) 148–149.

[42] B.C. Giovanella, S.O. Yim, A.C. Morgan, J.S. Stehlin, L.J. Williams Jr., Brief communication: metastases of human melanomas transplanted in "nude" mice, J. Natl. Cancer Inst. 50 (1973) 1051–1053.

[43] I.D. Bross, E. Viadana, J.W. Pickren, The metastatic spread of myeloma and leukemias in men, Virchows Arch. A Pathol. Anat. Histol. 365 (1975) 91–101.

[44] G.L. Nicolson, J.L. Winkelhake, Organ specificity of blood-borne tumour metastasis determined by cell adhesion? Nature 255 (1975) 230–232.

[45] P.C. Nowell, The clonal evolution of tumor cell populations, Science 194 (1976) 23–28.

[46] L.A. Liotta, J. Kleinerman, P. Catanzaro, D. Rynbrandt, Degradation of basement membrane by murine tumor cells, J. Natl. Cancer Inst. 58 (1977) 1427–1431.

[47] I.J. Fidler, M.L. Kripke, Metastasis results from preexisting variant cells within a malignant tumor, Science 197 (1977) 893–895.

[48] L.A. Liotta, K. Tryggvason, S. Garbisa, et al., Metastatic potential correlates with enzymatic degradation of basement membrane collagen, Nature 284 (1980) 67–68.

[49] I.R. Hart, I.J. Fidler, Role of organ selectivity in the determination of metastatic patterns of B16 melanoma, Cancer Res. 40 (1980) 2281–2287.

[50] J.E. Talmadge, K.M. Meyers, D.J. Prieur, J.R. Starkey, Role of NK cells in tumour growth and metastasis in beige mice, Nature 284 (1980) 622–624.

[51] G. Poste, J. Doll, I.J. Fidler, Interactions among clonal subpopulations affect stability of the metastatic phenotype in polyclonal populations of B16 melanoma cells, Proc. Natl. Acad. Sci. USA 78 (1981) 6226–6230.

[52] E.H. Herman, D.T. Witiak, K. Hellmann, V.S. Waravdekar, Biological properties of ICRF-159 and related bis(dioxopiperazine) compounds, Adv. Pharmacol. Chemother. 19 (1982) 249–290.

[53] J.E. Talmadge, S.R. Wolman, I.J. Fidler, Evidence for the clonal origin of spontaneous metastases, Science 217 (1982) 361–363.

[54] J.E. Talmadge, I.J. Fidler, Enhanced metastatic potential of tumor cells harvested from spontaneous metastases of heterogeneous murine tumors, J. Natl. Cancer Inst. 69 (1982) 975–980.

[55] G. Poste, J. Tzeng, J. Doll, et al., Evolution of tumor cell heterogeneity during progressive growth of individual lung metastases, Proc. Natl. Acad. Sci. USA 79 (1982) 6574–6578.

[56] G.L. Nicolson, S.E. Custead, Tumor metastasis is not due to adaptation of cells to a new organ environment, Science 215 (1982) 176–178.

[57] D. Tarin, J.E. Price, M.G. Kettlewell, et al., Mechanisms of human tumor metastasis studied in patients with peritoneovenous shunts, Cancer Res. 44 (1984) 3584–3592.

[58] J.M. Kozlowski, I.R. Hart, I.J. Fidler, N. Hanna, A human melanoma line heterogeneous with respect to metastatic capacity in athymic nude mice, J. Natl. Cancer Inst. 72 (1984) 913–917.

[59] T. Volk, B. Geiger, A. Raz, Motility and adhesive properties of high- and low-metastatic murine neoplastic cells, Cancer Res. 44 (1984) 811–824.

[60] I.J. Fidler, Macrophages and metastasis—a biological approach to cancer therapy, Cancer Res. 45 (1985) 4714–4726.

[61] L. Weiss, E. Mayhew, D.G. Rapp, J.C. Holmes, Metastatic inefficiency in mice bearing B16 melanomas, Br. J. Cancer 45 (1982) 44–53.

[62] P.S. Steeg, G. Bevilacqua, L. Kopper, et al., Evidence for a novel gene associated with low tumor metastatic potential, J. Natl. Cancer Inst. 80 (1988) 200–204.

[63] R.L. Wahl, M.S. Kaminski, S.P. Ethier, G.D. Hutchins, The potential of 2-deoxy-2[18F] fluoro-D-glucose (FDG) for the detection of tumor involvement in lymph nodes, J. Nucl. Med. 31 (1990) 1831–1835.

[64] W.C. Lin, T.P. Pretlow, T.G. Pretlow, L.A. Culp, Bacterial lacZ gene as a highly sensitive marker to detect micrometastasis formation during tumor progression, Cancer Res. 50 (1990) 2808–2817.

[65] N. Weidner, J.P. Semple, W.R. Welch, J. Folkman, Tumor angiogenesis and metastasis—correlation in invasive breast carcinoma, N. Engl. J. Med. 324 (1991) 1–8.

[66] G. Opdenakker, D.J. Van, Chemotactic factors, passive invasion and metastasis of cancer cells, Immunol. Today 13 (1992) 463–464.

[67] M.S. O'Reilly, L. Holmgren, Y. Shing, et al., Angiostatin: a novel angiogenesis inhibitor that mediates the suppression of metastases by a Lewis lung carcinoma, Cell 79 (1994) 315–328.

[68] T. Chishima, Y. Miyagi, X. Wang, et al., Cancer invasion and micrometastasis visualized in live tissue by green fluorescent protein expression, Cancer Res. 57 (1997) 2042–2047.

[69] C.M. Perou, T. Sorlie, M.B. Eisen, et al., Molecular portraits of human breast tumours, Nature 406 (2000) 747–752.

[70] T. Reya, S.J. Morrison, M.F. Clarke, I.L. Weissman, Stem cells, cancer, and cancer stem cells, Nature 414 (2001) 105–111.

[71] R. Bernards, R.A. Weinberg, A progression puzzle, Nature 418 (2002) 823.

[72] J.P. Thiery, Epithelial-mesenchymal transitions in tumour progression, Nat. Rev. Cancer 2 (2002) 442–454.

[73] C.A. Klein, T.J. Blankenstein, O. Schmidt-Kittler, et al., Genetic heterogeneity of single disseminated tumour cells in minimal residual cancer, Lancet 360 (2002) 683–689.

[74] L.N. van 't Veer, H. Dai, M.J. van de Vijver, et al., Gene expression profiling predicts clinical outcome of breast cancer, Nature 415 (2002) 530–536.

[75] Y. Kang, P.M. Siegel, W. Shu, et al., A multigenic program mediating breast cancer metastasis to bone, Cancer Cell 3 (2003) 537–549.

[76] G. Dontu, M. Al-Hajj, W.M. Abdallah, M.F. Clarke, M.S. Wicha, Stem cells in normal breast development and breast cancer, Cell Prolif. 36 (Suppl. 1) (2003) 59–72.

[77] K. Hunter, Host genetics influence tumour metastasis, Nat. Rev. Cancer 6 (2006) 141–146.

[78] L. Ma, J. Teruya-Feldstein, R.A. Weinberg, Tumour invasion and metastasis initiated by microRNA-10b in breast cancer, Nature 449 (2007) 682–688.

[79] L.A. Worley, M.D. Long, M.D. Onken, J.W. Harbour, Micro-RNAs associated with metastasis in uveal melanoma identified by multiplexed microarray profiling, Melanoma Res. 18 (2008) 184–190.

[80] S.F. Tavazoie, C. Alarcon, T. Oskarsson, et al., Endogenous human microRNAs that suppress breast cancer metastasis, Nature 451 (2008) 147–152.

[81] S.P. Chiang, R.M. Cabrera, J.E. Segall, Tumor cell intravasation, Am. J. Physiol. Cell Physiol. 311 (1) (2016) C1–C14, https://doi.org/10.1152/ajpcell.00238.2015. Epub 2016 Apr. 13. PMID: 27076614. PMCID: PMC4967137.

[82] U. Reuning, S. Sperl, C. Kopitz, H. Kessler, A. Krüger, M. Schmitt, V. Magdolen, Urokinase-type plasminogen activator (uPA) and its receptor (uPAR): development of antagonists of uPA/uPAR interaction and their effects in vitro and in vivo, Curr. Pharm. Des. 9 (19) (2003) 1529–1543, https://doi.org/10.2174/1381612033454612. PMID: 12871066.

[83] N. Mahmood, C. Mihalcioiu, S.A. Rabbani, Multifaceted role of the urokinase-type plasminogen activator (uPA) and its receptor (uPAR): diagnostic, prognostic, and therapeutic applications, Front. Oncol. 8 (2018) 24, https://doi.org/10.3389/fonc.2018.00024. PMID: 29484286. PMCID: PMC5816037.

[84] Z. Eslami-S, L.E. Cortés-Hernández, C. Alix-Panabières, The metastatic cascade as the basis for liquid biopsy development, Front. Oncol. 10 (2020) 1055, https://doi.org/10.3389/fonc.2020.01055. PMID: 32850309. PMCID: PMC7396546.

[85] X. Cheng, K. Cheng, Visualizing cancer extravasation: from mechanistic studies to drug development, Cancer Metastasis Rev. 40 (1) (2021) 71–88, https://doi.org/10.1007/s10555-020-09942-2. Epub 2020 Nov. 6. PMID: 33156478. PMCID: PMC7897269.

[86] S. Gkolfinopoulos, R.L. Jones, A. Constantinidou, The emerging role of platelets in the formation of the micrometastatic niche: current evidence and future perspectives, Front. Oncol. 10 (2020) 374, https://doi.org/10.3389/fonc.2020.00374. PMID: 32257952. PMCID: PMC7093714.

[87] T. Kuwai, T. Nakamura, S.J. Kim, T. Sasaki, Y. Kitadai, R.R. Langley, D. Fan, S.R. Hamilton, I.J. Fidler, Intratumoral heterogeneity for expression of tyrosine kinase growth

factor receptors in human colon cancer surgical specimens and orthotopic tumors, Am. J. Pathol. 172 (2) (2008) 358–366, https://doi.org/10.2353/ajpath.2008.070625. Epub 2008 Jan. 17. PMID: 18202197. PMCID: PMC2312354.

[88] G.R. Bignell, C.D. Greenman, H. Davies, A.P. Butler, S. Edkins, J.M. Andrews, G. Buck, L. Chen, D. Beare, C. Latimer, S. Widaa, J. Hinton, C. Fahey, B. Fu, S. Swamy, G.L. Dalgliesh, B.T. Teh, P. Deloukas, F. Yang, P.J. Campbell, P.A. Futreal, M.R. Stratton, Signatures of mutation and selection in the cancer genome, Nature 463 (7283) (2010) 893–898, https://doi.org/10.1038/nature08768. PMID: 20164919. PMCID: PMC3145113.

[89] K. Harbst, J. Staaf, A. Måsbäck, H. Olsson, C. Ingvar, J. Vallon-Christersson, M. Ringnér, A. Borg, G. Jönsson, Multiple metastases from cutaneous malignant melanoma patients may display heterogeneous genomic and epigenomic patterns, Melanoma Res. 20 (5) (2010) 381–391. PMID: 20848731.

[90] N. Navin, J. Kendall, J. Troge, P. Andrews, L. Rodgers, J. McIndoo, K. Cook, A. Stepansky, D. Levy, D. Esposito, L. Muthuswamy, A. Krasnitz, W.R. McCombie, J. Hicks, M. Wigler, Tumour evolution inferred by single-cell sequencing, Nature 472 (7341) (2011) 90–94, https://doi.org/10.1038/nature09807. Epub 2011 Mar. 13. PMID: 21399628. PMCID: PMC4504184.

[91] M.A. Cifone, I.J. Fidler, Increasing metastatic potential is associated with increasing genetic instability of clones isolated from murine neoplasms, Proc. Natl. Acad. Sci. USA 78 (11) (1981) 6949–6952, https://doi.org/10.1073/pnas.78.11.6949. PMID: 6947269. PMCID: PMC349170.

[92] I.J. Fidler, M.L. Kripke, The challenge of targeting metastasis, Cancer Metastasis Rev. 34 (4) (2015) 635–641, https://doi.org/10.1007/s10555-015-9586-9. PMID: 26328524. PMCID: PMC4661188.

[93] S. Chakraborty, T. Rahman, The difficulties in cancer treatment, Ecancermedicalscience 6 (2012) ed16, https://doi.org/10.3332/ecancer.2012.ed16. PMID: 24883085. PMCID: PMC4024849.

[94] J. Fares, M.Y. Fares, H.H. Khachfe, H.A. Salhab, Y. Fares, Molecular principles of metastasis: a hallmark of cancer revisited, Signal. Transduct. Target Ther. 5 (1) (2020) 28, https://doi.org/10.1038/s41392-020-0134-x. PMID: 32296047. PMCID: PMC7067809.

[95] A.L. Parker, M. Benguigui, J. Fornetti, E. Goddard, S. Lucotti, J. Insua-Rodríguez, A.P. Wiegmans, Early Career Leadership Council of the Metastasis Research Society, Current challenges in metastasis research and future innovation for clinical translation, Clin. Exp. Metastasis 39 (2) (2022) 263–277, https://doi.org/10.1007/s10585-021-10144-5. Epub 2022 Jan. 24. PMID: 35072851. PMCID: PMC8971179.

[96] C.N. Qian, Y. Mei, J. Zhang, Cancer metastasis: issues and challenges, Chin. J. Cancer 36 (1) (2017) 38, https://doi.org/10.1186/s40880-017-0206-7. PMID: 28372569. PMCID: PMC5379757.

Epigenetics and its importance in cancer therapies

An overview of epigenetics and cancer

Rajendra P. Pangeni[a,b]

[a]*Institute of Neuro-Immune Medicine, Dr. Kiran Patel College of Osteopathic Medicine, Nova Southeastern University, Fort Lauderdale, FL, United States, *[b]*Department of Natural and Applied Sciences, Nexus Institute of Research and Innovation, Lalitpur, Nepal*

Role of epigenetics in normal and cancer cells

Epigenetics, first used by Conrad Waddington, explains the interactions between the genes and their environment, which further refers to the heritable changes in the pattern of gene expression not directly mediated by alterations in the primary nucleotide sequence [1,2]. Epigenetics has remained one of the most promising fields of biomedical research since 1940 and is associated with human diseases including various cancers [3]. In normal cells, epigenetic regulation is tightly controlled and plays a crucial role in maintaining cellular identity and functions [4,5]. During development, epigenetic changes are responsible for directing cells to differentiate into multiple cell types with specialized functions, such as neurons, muscle cells, or skin cells [6]. Further, epigenetic modifications help to maintain the specific gene expression patterns and their response to environmental cues, such as changes in nutrition, stress, or exposure to toxins [7]. Therefore, an epigenetic dysregulation in cellular progenitor genes in normally functioning healthy cell is one of the bases of cancer that contribute to tumor tumorigenicity, and tumor heterogeneity that drive tumor progression [8]. Dysregulation in epigenetics processes such as DNA methylation, histone modifications, and chromatin architecture lead to aberration in gene expression that provide cells a selective growth advantage contributing to cancer development [9].

Cancer begins from uncontrolled proliferations of the cells followed by metastasis to the different organs. The origin of cancer or tumorigenesis is a result of a series of genetic and epigenetic changes that lead to defects in cellular growth, proliferation, and differentiation [10]. In the late 19th century, unusual chromosomal abnormalities were observed in dividing cancer cells under the microscope, which suggested an involvement of gene aberrations in cancer [11]. The acquired epigenetic dysregulation results in aberration in chromatin structure and gene expression patterns either through methylation status of cytosine residues in the DNA (DNA

Cancer Epigenetics and Nanomedicine. https://doi.org/10.1016/B978-0-443-13209-4.00011-8
Copyright © 2024 Elsevier Inc. All rights are reserved, including those for text and data mining, AI training, and similar technologies.

145

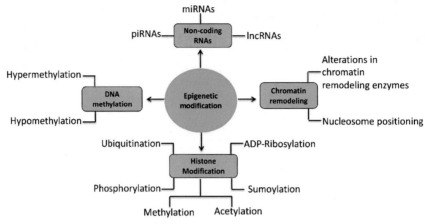

FIG. 1

Overview of epigenetic mechanisms. DNA methylation, histone modification, chromatin remodeling, and the roles played by noncoding RNAs together form epigenetic machinery or epigenetic mechanisms. Chromatin remodeling involves either nucleosome positioning or the alterations of chromatin remodeling enzymes. Epigenetic modification by noncoding RNAs includes microRNAs (miRNAs), long noncoding RNAs (lncRNAs), and piwi-interacting RNAs (piRNAs).

methylation) or modifications of some amino acid residues in histone proteins (histone modifications) or chromatin remodeling or through the dysregulation of non-coding RNAs [11] (Fig. 1). Dysregulation of DNA methylation leads to gene silencing of tumor suppressor genes or in activation of already silenced oncogenes expression, resulting in the dysregulation of cell growth and development of cancer [12]. Histone modifications involve alterations of histone proteins, which help package DNA into a compact structure called chromatin, resulting in changes in the accessibility of genes for transcription and leading to gene activation or repression [12]. Epigenetic dysregulation of noncoding RNA molecules, such as microRNAs and long noncoding RNAs, involves alterations of their capacity to bind with protein-coding genes resulting in their dysregulation [13].

Epigenetics mechanism and their regulation on cancer
DNA methylation in cancer

DNA methylation is the addition of a methyl group to the cytosine base of DNA that typically occurs at CpG dinucleotides. The methyl groups are added to the carbon 5 position of the cytosine ring, leading to the repression of gene expression by preventing the binding of transcription factors and other proteins to the DNA [14]. The binding of transcription factors and other proteins to the DNA inhibits the recruitment of transcriptional machinery and creates a condensed chromatin structure that is inaccessible to transcriptional machinery [15].

In cancers, regulation of DNA methylation occurs either by an increase in DNA methylation in cells, which we refer to as DNA hypermethylation leading to gene silencing, or by a decrease in DNA methylation (DNA hypomethylation), leading to gene activation. In cancer, hypermethylation in cancer often occurs in CpG islands, which are regions of the genome that are rich in CpG dinucleotides and are usually located near gene promoters [16]. Promoter hypermethylation can lead to the silencing of tumor suppressor genes, resulting in the loss of their regulatory function, allowing cells to grow and divide uncontrollably, and contributing to tumorigenesis (Fig. 2), as well as to invasion and metastases to secondary organs from the primary site of tumor origin [17].

Downregulation of calcitonin gene due to promoter hypermethylation in lung cancer and lymphomas was identified in 1996 [18]. Later, silencing or downregulation of common tumor suppressor genes due to promoter hypermethylation was observed in many cancers such as RB1 in retinoblastoma [19,20], *VHL* in renal cell carcinoma [21], and *CDKN2A* (cyclin-dependent kinase inhibitor 2A) in multiple tumor types [22]. Earlier, silencing or downregulation of tumor suppressor genes was identified in various cancers such as *RASSF1A* inactivation in lung, breast, glioma, and colorectal cancer and RCC [23–27], *HIC1* inactivation in leukemia and breast cancer [28–30], and *CHD1* in various cancers [31]. At present, we have DNA methylation landscapes of a large number of genes dysregulated due to aberrant DNA methylation in human cancers. These large number of genes have provided us with the DNA methylation landscape of genes dysregulated due to aberrant DNA methylation resulting in tumorigenicity, which could either be a driver, passenger, or just a byproduct of genome deregulation due to epigenetic dysregulation [32].

In contrast, DNA hypomethylation in cancer leads to an activation of the repeat sequences, resulting in chromosomal rearrangement and genomic instability, which otherwise remain silenced in the genome. This can lead to the activation of normally silent genes, including oncogenes, which promote cell growth and division [32]. Previous studies have shown that the global hypomethylation in repeat elements such as Alu and long interspersed nuclear elements (LINES) has resulted in genomic rearrangement and activation of these transposable genetic elements [33]. In addition, analysis of chromosome 11 in mice that contains Dnmt1 allele, an allele with a partial loss of Dnmt1 function (Dnmt+/−), and a single copy of *TP53* and *NF1* has shown the genomic instability due to hypomethylation [34]. In addition to the primary tumors, DNA hypomethylation occurs in protein-coding oncogenes, pseudogenes, and noncoding RNA, resulting in invasion and metastases of tumor cells to distant organs [13].

Abnormal DNA methylation patterns in cancer can be influenced by various factors, such as genetic mutations, environmental exposures, and lifestyle choices [35]. DNA methylation changes may occur early in cancer development and may remain stable throughout tumor progression, making them promising targets for cancer diagnosis, prognosis, and treatment [36].

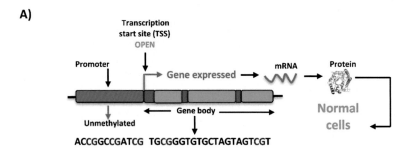

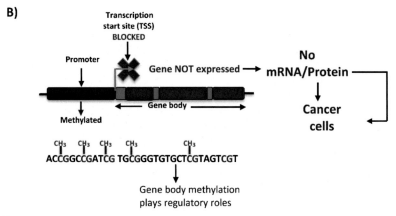

FIG. 2

Mechanism of DNA methylation in genes that contributes to genes switch-off or switch-on (expression or repression of genes) regulating the state of normal cells or cancers. (A) In healthy cells, promoters of the genes are unmethylated, and the transcription start site is accessible (open) to RNA polymerase enzyme to transcribe genes (gene expression). (B) In the disease state, the promoter is methylated, and it blocks access of transcription start site (TSS) to RNA polymerase enzyme, resulting in no mRNA or protein produced (repression of genes) that leads to a diseased state.

Role of histone modifications in cancer

Histone modification is a crucial epigenetic modification that plays a significant role in cancer initiation, development, and progression. Histones are proteins that package DNA into a compact structure called chromatin. Histone modification refers to the posttranslational modifications (PTMs) of histones that involve the addition or removal of various chemical groups, such as acetyl, methyl, phosphate groups, etc., to the histones which affect the accessibility of the DNA, either activating or inhibiting gene expression. In a normal cell, one or more types of histone modifications maintain the chromatin either in euchromatin (less condensed and accessible) or in heterochromatin (more condensed and less accessible) to transcriptional machinery to promote or inhibit expression of genes, respectively [37]. Based on the addition of modifying groups, the histone modification either serves as active marks (if they activate gene expression) or repressor marks (if they inhibit gene expression), which, however, depends on various factors such as the level of histone modification (such as methylation), the specific site of modification within the histone (e.g., lysine or arginine, etc.), and the location of the target nucleosome within transcriptionally active or silent regions of the genome [38].

One of the key mechanisms that contributes to tumorigenesis and tumor progression is significant alterations in gene expression as a result of restructuring of chromatin to facilitate access to transcription factors [39]. Chromatin is a highly dense structure consisting of nucleosomes containing histones in which the DNA is wrapped (for detail, refer to "Chromatin remodeling in cancer" section). Nucleosome is comprised of two copies of each of four histones (H2A, H2B, H3, and H4) [40]. Chromatin exhibits either "open" configuration that is accessible to transcription machinery or "closed" configuration that is not accessible to transcription machinery, thus affecting gene expression. The transition between open and closed chromatin is governed by PTMs of histones. PTMs, thus, is a reversible process that occurs most frequently in histone H3 as the targets for histone modifications. PTMs include acetylation, methylation, phosphorylation, ubiquitination, sumoylation, ADP-ribosylation, deimination, proline isomerism, and propionylation that may occur either in the surface of the histone N-terminal histone tails or in the main globular domains [41,42]. However, histone acetylation and methylation are more common in cancer (Fig. 3).

Histone acetylation removes positive charge at lysine residues on histone tail to make chromatin confirmation accessible to DNA as removing positive charge at lysine weakens the DNA-histone or nucleosome-nucleosome interactions [43]. Histone acetylation is governed by two enzymes: histone acetyltransferases (HATs), which make chromosomes accessible, and histone deacetylases (HDACs), which make chromatin less accessible to the DNA. In addition to the role of histone acetylation in multiple cancer types, mutation in HATs and HDACs is reported in multiple cancers, showing that acetylation is a key regulatory mechanism in tumorigenesis and in other stages of cancer progression [44].

Histone methylation is regulated by histone methyltransferases (HMTs) that occur either at positively charged lysine residues, which could be either mono-, di-, or trimethylated or less commonly at arginine residues which is trimethylated or based on the number of methyl group attached, and the demethylation (removal of methyl group) is regulated by histone lysine demethylases (KDMs) [41]. Dysregulation of histone demethylases is associated with multiple cancers; for example, LSD1 (lysine (K)-specific demethylase 1A) is upregulated in bladder and breast cancers, and neuroblastoma [45–47].

Lysine 9 residues in H3 protein (H3K9) undergo mono-, di-, and trimethylation, contributing to repressive marks. Mono- and dimethylation in H3K9 (H3K9me1 and

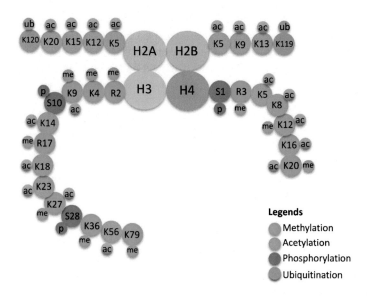

FIG. 3

Histone modification. The histone modifications involve the modification of specific amino acid residues in polypeptide chain of the protein. In H2A and H2B, histone modification involves acetylation of multiple lysine residues and ubiquitination of lysine 120 (in H2A) and lysine 119 (in H2B). Histone H3 and H4 undergo methylation (in lysine and arginine residues), phosphorylation (in serine residues), and acetylation (in lysine residues). Some of the amino acid residues, such as K9 and K27 in H3 and K12 and K20 in H4, are targets for both acetylation and methylation.

H3K9me2 respectively) are governed by H3K9 dimethyl transferases, i.e., euchromatic histone-lysine *N*-methyltransferase 1 and 2 (EHMT1 and EHMT2/G9A) [14]. One of the interesting factors is that the mono- and demethylation in H3K9 is associated with DNA methylation marks at the CpG islands, further aiding the DNA hypermethylation and subsequent gene silencing [48]. Similarly, H3K9me3 modifications are catalyzed by histone methyltransferases SUV39H1, SUV39H2, and SETDB1 [49].

Lysine 36 residues of H3 protein (H3K36) undergoes mono-, di-, and trimethylation (H3K36me1, H3K36me2, and H3K36me3). H3K36me1 is widely distributed throughout the genome and is generally an intermediate state without having a functional role in transcriptional regulation [50]. In contrast, H3K36me2 marks are concentrated in intergenic and regulatory regions, and H3K36me3 marks are more prevalent in gene body (protein-coding sequences) regions [51]. Therefore, H3K36me2 and H3K36me3 are associated with specific genomic regions that undergo active transcription. This shows that regulation of methylation of histone H3K36 is crucial in maintaining chromatin integrity and controlling gene expression.

The addition and removal of H3K36me2 and H3K36me3 across the genome is regulated by histone lysine methyltransferases (KMTs) and lysine demethylases (KDMs), respectively. Among the various groups of KMTs are the NSD1, NSD2, and NSD3; ASH1L, SMYD2, and SETMAR; and SETD3 mediate mono- and dimethylation of H3K36, whereas the trimethylation of H3K36 is mediated by a single enzyme, SETD2 [50]. Similarly, demethylation (removal of methyl groups) is mediated by histone demethylases KDM2A, KDM2AB, JHDM1, and JHDM2 that target H3K36me1 and H3K36me2, whereas JHDM3 (JMJD2/KDM4A-D) demethylates H3K36me2 and H3K36me3 and H3K9Me3.

Chromatin remodeling in cancer

Chromatin remodeling is one of the mechanisms that alters the organization of chromosomes. It refers to the dynamic changes in the structure and organization of chromatin that play a crucial role in the regulation of gene expression. Significant progress in mass spectrometry and high-throughput sequencing has led to the discovery and detailed characterization of several ATP-dependent chromatin-remodeling complexes in mammals. These complexes play a crucial role in establishing cell identity by enabling transcription for a specific group required for that cell type while simultaneously preventing the unsuitable expression of other genes [52]. Chromatin remodeling is mediated by chromatin remodeler proteins by either facilitating or hindering the access of transcriptional machinery to DNA, thus controlling the activation or repression of genes [53]. Nucleosomes are nucleoprotein complexes that serve as the building blocks of chromatin, consisting of DNA molecules wrapped in histones. Each nucleosome is comprised of 146 base pairs of DNA wrapped in a histone octamer containing two units of each of the four types of histones, H2A, H2B, H3, and H4, joined by a linker DNA. Nucleosomes are linked by a linker histone H1 and nonhistone proteins to form the chromatin structure [54].

Dysregulation in chromatin remodeling contributes to cancer initiation and progression through the following mechanisms.

Alterations in chromatin remodeling enzymes

The role of the chromatin remodeler protein is to either loosen or tighten the chromatin structure to regulate the access of transcriptional machinery, which further influences gene expression. Based on the sequence homology of ATPase and their subunits, four remodeler families have been identified and well characterized, which include (1) switch/sucrose nonfermentable (SWI/SNF), (2) chromodomain-helicase DNA-binding protein (CHD)/nucleosome remodeling/deacetylase (NuRD)/Mi-2, (3) inositol-requiring mutant 80 (INO80), and (4) imitation switch (ISWI) [52]. The main functions of these four remodeler proteins shared between among them are: the capacity to engage with the nucleosome core, their affinity for binding with post-translationally modified nucleosomal histone-tail residues, core ATPase activity, utilizing ATP hydrolysis to power their remodeling functions, regulatory domains susceptible to diverse biochemical and epigenetic modifications, and specific motifs and protein domains facilitating their interactions with other proteins [54]. In addition, these remodeling proteins have evolved mechanistically to perform their specialized functions, regulating distinct transcriptional programs in response to cellular cues. For instance, SWI/SNF complexes are involved in ATP-dependent chromatin remodeling, altering the nucleosome position and structure to regulate gene expression. ISWI complexes utilize ATP to slide nucleosomes along the DNA, leading to changes in chromatin structure and accessibility through epigenetic mechanisms [55]. Similarly, CHD enzymes possess helicase and ATPase activities, enabling them to remodel chromatin by altering nucleosome positioning and histone-DNA contacts. Mi-2/NuRD is associated with methylated DNA. The NuRD/Mi-2 are the heterogeneous complexes possessing both nucleosome sliding and HDAC activities that contribute to chromatin compaction and are associated with methylated DNA playing a role in gene silencing and transcriptional regulation through epigenetic mechanisms [56].

The INO80 complex is involved in ATP-dependent nucleosome sliding and exchange, impacting chromatin accessibility and gene regulation.

Some of the mechanisms that contribute to dysregulation in chromatin remodeling in cancer are mutations, aberrant expression, or functional alterations in these chromatin remodeling proteins [57,58]. Mutations in genes encoding proteins such as SWI/SNF (switch/sucrose nonfermentable) complex components, which are involved in ATP-dependent nucleosome remodeling, have been implicated in multiple cancer types [59,60]. Dysregulation of other chromatin remodeling complexes, such as the Polycomb repressive complex (PRC) and the NuRD (nucleosome remodeling and deacetylase) complex, has also been reported in cancers [61,62].

Aberrations in nucleosome positioning

Proper positioning of nucleosomes along the DNA sequence is critical for gene regulation. Alterations in nucleosome positioning affect the accessibility of transcription factors and other regulatory proteins to DNA, resulting in abnormal gene expression [63]. Nucleosome positioning refers to the precise location of a given nucleosome, and in addition to this, nucleosome occupancy (the fraction of molecules carrying a nucleosome at a particular location at any given instant) plays an important role in gene regulation [64]. DNA binding proteins and other transcription factors are attached to the nucleosome at gene promoter regions, and there is evidence that nucleosomes are depleted during the active transcription, and they rapidly reform when the process of transcription is completed or during the gene silencing [65]. Further, the alterations in nucleosome positioning and occupancy at specific gene loci are associated with carcinogenesis and other related processes, such as cell cycle regulation, DNA repair, and regulation of tumor suppressor genes [65].

DNA methylation and histone methylation cross-talks

There have been dynamic interactions between the two epigenetics mechanisms, namely DNA methylation and histone methylation, in the regulation of gene expression that further add up another layer of intricacy in regulation of gene expression

[63]. These complex interactions between histone methylation and DNA methylation contribute to cancer development and progression, and their understanding may help in the development of novel epigenetic therapies for cancer treatment. However, the interplay between these two epigenetic mechanisms is extremely dynamic and dependent on cellular context to determine the status of the gene expression, chromatin organizations, and cellular identity expression [63]. The cross-talk between DNA methylation and histone methylation thus works in coordination to reprogram epigenetic state of the cells, contributing to either active or repressive marks and further contributing to diseases including cancer. Some of the examples of such cross-talks are as follows.

DNA methylation recruits HMTs, leading to gene expression changes. This generally happens at CpG islands, which recruit the methyltransferase EZH2, a component of the Polycomb repressive complex 2 (PRC2), to methylate histone H3 at lysine 27 (H3K27), resulting in gene silencing. In addition, DNMTs recruit HDACs and methyl-binding proteins (MBDs) to establish chromatin condensation, resulting in gene silencing. Further, DNA methylation directs H3K9 methylation through effector proteins, such as MeCP2, to establish a repressive mark. Conversely, histone H3K27 methylation can recruit DNA methyltransferases, leading to DNA methylation and further reinforcing gene silencing (Fig. 4). Similarly, histone H3 lysine 9 (H3K9) methylation that is associated with transcriptional repression recruits DNA methyltransferases, DNMT3A and DNMT3B, to the chromatin, resulting in DNA methylation and gene silencing [66]. Some of the HMTs that recruit DNMTs include direct DNA methylation in specific genomic targets including G9a,

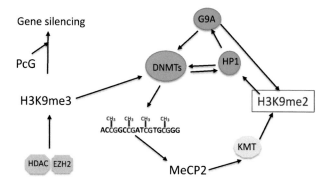

FIG. 4

DNA methylation cross-talk. DNA methyltransferases mediate methylation to CpGs sites in the genome, which recruits MeCP2 proteins. MeCP2 protein recruits lysine methyltransferases that mediate H3K9me2. Methylation of H3K9 causes recruitment of transcription factor Hp1 that further recruits DNMTs in gene promoters. HP1 also recruits G9A that mediates H3K9me2, and G9A further recruits DNMTs in gene promoters. In addition, DNMTs also recruit HP1, which recruits G9A. Moreover, HDAC, along with EZH2, mediates H3K927 me3, which further promotes DNA methylation through DNMTs and gene silencing by further recruiting polycomb complex group (PcG), which is specific to stem cells.

SUV39H1, and PRMT5, to enhance stable epigenetic marks. In addition, HMTs and demethylases also influence DNA methylation levels by regulating the stability of DNMT and their direct recruitment. In non-small cell lung cancer (NSCLC), knock-down of *G9A* as well as treatment of cells with G9a inhibitor resulted in hypomethylation of *APC2* gene promoter, leading to reactivation of its expression showing the role of G9a in DNA methylation [14]. Similarly, knocking down *G9A* in tumor initiating cells TICs enriched in stem cell markers CD44 in NSCLC resulted in genome-wide DNA methylation and expression changes in a large number of genes. These data further demonstrate that the HMTs play a role in programming DNA methylation in genome-wide level including stem-like cell populations [48]. These data suggested that UNC0638 may restore these silenced genes' expression through promoter demethylation in NSCLC cells. This cross-talk between histone methylation and DNA methylation mutually establishes a repressive chromatin state to reinforce gene silencing and contribute to the stable maintenance of epigenetic marks and in epigenetic silencing of tumor suppressor genes in cancer cells.

Further, interplay between histone and DNA methylation activates gene expression. The promoters of transcriptionally active genes are often marked by histone H3 lysine 4 (H3K4) methylation, which recruits DNA demethylases. DNA demethylases, in turn, remove DNA methylation marks in promoters, resulting in stable gene activation.

Previous studies have shown that dynamic cross-talk between DNA methylation and histone modification plays important roles during different stages of cancer progression. In the early stages of cancer, global hypomethylation of DNA leads to the loss of repressive histone marks, which further stably activates normally silenced oncogenes. In contrast, in advanced stages of cancer, DNA hypermethylation and increased histone methylation together lead to widespread gene silencing, including tumor suppressor genes, contributing to tumor progression.

Role of epigenetic dysregulation of noncoding RNAs in cancer

Noncoding RNA (ncRNA) do not code for proteins; however, they have regulatory functions within the cell through several mechanisms. There are several classes of ncRNAs that include small nuclear RNAs (snRNAs), small nucleolar RNAs (snoRNAs), ribosomal RNAs (rRNAs), transfer RNAs (tRNAs), microRNAs, piwi-interacting RNAs (piRNAs), and long noncoding RNAs (lncRNAs) [67]. MicroRNAs are small RNA molecules that bind to messenger RNAs (mRNAs) and prevent their translation into proteins or induce their degradation. This can result in the inhibition of gene expression. Similarly, long noncoding RNAs (lncRNAs) interact with DNA, RNA, and proteins to influence gene expression in multiple ways such as by acting as molecular scaffolds, guides, or decoys. Noncoding RNA plays a significant role in modulating gene expression by interacting with epigenetic modifiers, exhibiting their strong association with epigenetic alterations in cancer [68]. Similar to the protein-coding genes, ncRNAs act either as oncogenic ncRNAs or as tumor suppressor ncRNAs. Aberrant DNA methylation or histone modifications in the promoter regions of these RNAs lead to either their silencing or their overexpression, promoting cancer cell growth, survival, and metastasis based on the protein-coding genes that they interact with. Oncogenic ncRNAs inhibit the expression of protein-coding TSGs, and their overexpression is associated with poor clinical prognosis of cancer patients. Gene expression profiling of lncRNAs in NSCLC showed that their differential expression in tumors differs from the normal patients, including their differing methylation levels in tumors compared to normal lung tissues [69].

Similarly, tumor suppressor ncRNAs function as tumor suppressors by inhibiting protein-coding oncogenes, thereby inhibiting proliferation of cancer cells or by promoting tumor cell apoptosis. Zhao et al. have reported landscape of over 1900 lncRNAs, which were associated with DNA methylation and histone methylation alterations at regulatory elements specific to three breast cancer subtypes [70]. Further, they were involved with multiple biological functions, molecular pathways, and immune cell regulation. This demonstrates that epigenetic silencing of tumor suppressor ncRNAs through DNA methylation, histone modifications, or chromatin remodeling can lead to their downregulation or loss of function, contributing to cancer development.

Among the ncRNAs in cancer, microRNAs are extensively studied. MicroRNA profiling in multiple cancer types has shown that all miRNAs in multiple cancers exhibit distinct gene expression profiling correlating their potential roles in diagnostics and therapeutic intervention [71]. A large number of epigenetically driven miRNA genes have been identified that lead to the silencing of tumor suppressor genes by upregulation of DNA methyltransferases, showing that miRNA plays critical roles in epigenetic regulation in human cancers [72]. Further, some of the microRNAs are dysregulated in multiple human tumors which suggests that these commonly dysregulated miRNAs may be the common downstream targets of pathways in human cancer, and these miRNAs may serve as the targets for anticancer treatment. One such example is *miRNA-34a*, which acts as a tumor suppressor and is frequently downregulated in various cancers due to hypermethylation of its promoter region [73].

Further, epigenetic modifications of miRNAs using miRNA gene expression were reported to a panel of biomarkers for therapeutic response in breast cancer models [74]. miRNAs can also directly regulate the expression of other ncRNAs by targeting their own promoters or enhancer regions. For instance, a class of ncRNAs transcribed referred to as enhancer RNAs (eRNAs) that are transcribed from the enhancer regions are largely driven by tissue-specific transcriptional factors (TFs) which regulate cancer signaling pathways, clinically actionable target genes, and immune checkpoints [75]. Dysregulation of eRNAs and their aberrant expression through epigenetic modifications could serve as potential therapeutic targets or biomarkers in various cancers [76].

Epigenetic dysregulation in cancer stem cells, a promise for therapeutic intervention

Epigenetic dysregulation is a hallmark of cancer stem cells (CSCs), which are a subset of cells within a tumor with some unique characteristics, including self-renewal ability, multilineage differentiation potential, and resistance to therapy [77]. With their ability to self-renew and differentiate into multiple cell types within the tumor, CSCs play a crucial role in tumor initiation, progression, recurrence, and metastasis, providing a driving force of tumorigenesis and posing challenge to treat cancer [78]. Aberrant epigenetic dysregulation provides these cells selective advantages to drive cellular features to disrupt normal epigenetic landscape and to contribute to stem cell properties. Previous studies have helped to establish markers to identify these populations of cells (CSCs) in tumors or tissues, such as CD13, CD24, CD44, CD90, CD133, and ALDH1A, and these markers have been utilized to characterize CSCs in bulk of the tissues or in tumors [79].

In CSCs, DNA methylation patterns are often altered, leading to aberrant gene expression. Many oncogenes that are normally silenced by DNA methylation may be hypomethylated and activated, and on the other hand, tumor suppressor genes that are normally activated in normal stem cells may be hypermethylated and silenced in CSCs, increasing the differentiation potential. For example, a previous study shows that the DNA hypermethylation and silencing of the two important tumor suppressor genes P53 and P21 enhanced cancer initiation and proliferation of lung CSCs, and DNMTs inhibition led to the loss of spheroid forming capacity of tumor-initiating cells in lung cancer [80]. It has been observed that the constitutive levels of DNA methylation are necessary for self-renewal of hematopoietic stem cells (HSCs) as well as in governing stem cell functions during tissue homeostasis and in the context of cancer [81]. In glioblastoma (GBM), one of the most aggressive forms of brain tumors, glioma stem cells (GSCs) derived from GBM tumors showed distinct DNA hypermethylation and hypomethylation patterns based on genome-wide DNA methylation array, showing that correlated to gene expression which demonstrated that the aberrant DNA methylation contributes to CSCs [82]. In addition, The two GSC phenotypes exhibited differing DNA methylation patterns, which showed that the aberrant DNA methylation contributes to specific CSC phenotypes [82]. Further, treating proneural phenotypes of GSCs, which are less aggressive and are hypermethylated for *MST4* gene by irradiation converted them to more aggressive mesenchymal GSCs due to the changes in DNA methylation patterns resulting in hypomethylation at its gene promoter [83]. This showed that DNA methylation contributes to clinical outcomes of patients treated with irradiation by altering the DNA methylation profiling of CSC population in tumors. These data highlight the role of DNA methylation as a fundamental epigenetic mechanism, safeguarding stem cells against premature activation of predominant differentiation pathways. Thus, in addition to the role of DNA methylation in maintaining self-renewal and multipotency of stem cells, retention or reestablishment of stem cell-specific methylation patterns is an important step in the development and function of CSCs.

Similarly, histone modifications: Histone modifications, such as methylation, acetylation, and phosphorylation, play a crucial role in regulating gene expression by modulating chromatin structure and initiating stem cell behavior in cells. In CSCs, aberrant histone modifications, such as H3K4me3 and H3K27me3, are associated with transcriptional activation and repression, respectively, leading to disruption of the normal epigenetic landscape to contribute to the maintenance of stemness properties. In mixed lineage leukemia (MLL)-associated leukemia such as acute myeloid leukemia (AML) and acute lymphoblastic leukemia (ALL), chromosomal rearrangements involving the *KMT2A/MLL* gene that encode a HMT induce leukemia stem cells (LSC) formation, contributing to epigenetic plasticity that allows CSCs to adapt and survive under changing cellular environments and to contribute to tumor heterogeneity, therapy resistance, and tumor recurrence [84]. Similarly, monoubiquitination of histone 2B (H2Bub1), one of the histone modifications by USP22 enzymes, is implicated in treatment resistance, angiogenesis, and metastases of lung adenocarcinoma [85]. The treatment resistance is exhibited by cancer-initiating cells (CICs) with stem-like cell properties in lung adenocarcinoma, and knocking down USP22 resulted in downregulation of stem cell markers and better treatment response by cisplatin in those CICs [86].

Epigenetics in the clinics: Prognostics, diagnostics, and therapeutic intervention for cancers

Harnessing epigenetics mechanism in prognosis and diagnosis of cancer

Epigenetic changes hold great potential as prognostic and diagnostic markers, offering valuable insights into the likely outcomes of diseases, particularly cancer. One of the advantages of epigenetic biomarkers is that the epigenetic alterations are relatively stable and are reversible in nature, which provide the potential for assay development for diagnosis and prognosis [87]. Epigenetic biomarkers include detecting aberrations in DNA methylation, histone modifications, chromatin remodeling, and these changes in noncoding RNAs as prognostic indicators in cancer, enabling the prediction of tumor aggressiveness, metastatic potential, and patients' clinical prognosis [88,89]. Specific DNA methylation signatures in cancer cells have been linked to favorable or unfavorable prognoses in various cancer types, facilitating the classification of patients into distinct risk groups for personalized treatment strategies. A well-established routinely used example is an epigenetic silencing of the *MGMT* (O6-methylguanine-DNA methyltransferase) in GBM, and the patients with *MGMT* methylation benefit from the temozolomide treatment [90]. Similarly, early detection of dysregulation in DNA methylation pattern has been reported as noninvasive test for various cancer types as a prognostic test [91].

Further, a previous study has reported a possibility of minimally invasive DNA methylation-based test for early detection of lung, pancreatic, and colorectal cancers as a panel of prognostic indicators using liquid biopsies [92]. Similarly, the detection of DNA methylation in liquid biopsies using cell-free DNA has been utilized in multiple cancer types [93–97]; in addition to the blood/serum as liquid biopsies, epigenetic markers can be detected in several other forms of clinical samples that include tissue, and body fluids such as urine and recently in fecal samples from cancer patients which provide critical information about the tumor grade, subtype and the disease pathology [98,99]. Thus, DNA methylation status detected in patients' serum could be utilized for early cancer detection and monitoring of treatment response.

Furthermore, abnormal histone modifications, such as histone acetylation and methylation, can be valuable diagnostic and prognostic markers in cancer. Specific histone marks, like trimethylation of histone H3 at lysine 4 (H3K4me3) and lysine 27 (H3K27me3), have been associated with gene activation and repression, respectively, and their levels in tumor tissue can serve as prognostic indicators in various cancers.

Epigenetic therapy: A targeted approach to cancer treatment

Epigenetic therapy has emerged as a promising approach for therapeutic interventions in the treatment of various cancers. Epigenetic modifications are reversible in nature, and they have opened doors for developing targeted therapies to reverse abnormal epigenetic patterns in cancer cells to normal state. Epigenetic therapies encompass a range of interventions that include DNA demethylating agents, HDAC inhibitors, HMT inhibitors, and other epigenetic modulators, which are either FDA approved or are under clinical trials.

The primary goal of epigenetic therapy is to restore normal epigenetic patterns within cells, with a focus on reactivating tumor suppressor genes while silencing oncogenes in order to effectively reprogram cancer cells, potentially converting them back to a more normal state.

DNA methyltransferase inhibitors are drugs designed to block the action of DNA methyltransferases to reverse abnormal DNA methylation patterns in cancer cells [100]. This will consequently regain the expression of tumor suppressor genes, and resulting in the suppression of cancer cell growth. The most widely used DNA methylation inhibitors are 5-azacytidine (azacytidine) and 2′-deoxy-5-azacytidine (decitabine), which are FDA-approved drugs used in treating myelodysplastic syndrome (MDS), a group of myeloid cancers [101,102]. In addition, azacytidine and decitabine have been shown to inhibit the growth of cancer cells in other multiple cancer types. Further, combinations of epigenetics therapies have shown better responses in various cancers by overcoming the limited biological activities of DNA methylation inhibitors. In hepatocellular carcinoma, combinational therapies using decitabine and EZH2 (a component of polycomb repressor complex) inhibitor produced prolonged antitumor proliferation response by reactivating genes that were still silenced when treated with decitabine alone [103]. Similarly, other DNMT inhibitors, 5-fluoro-2′-deoxycytidine (Fdcyd), produced a therapeutic response in *PBRM1* (a tumor suppressor gene)-deficient tumor growth in RCC showing the therapeutic utility of the drug in a selected cell population. Further, treatment of Murine Embryonic Stem cells (ESCs) with a DNMT inhibitor GSK-3484862 has shown global methylation loss of genes silenced by DNA methylation, exhibiting its therapeutic response [104]. Likewise, a combinational treatment of HMT, G9A inhibitor, and decitabine has resulted in reduced cell proliferation with a synergistic effect when used with cisplatin and the ERBB-targeted inhibitor, Lapatinib in Cholangiocarcinoma (CCA) showing a promise of epigenetic therapies in treating cancer. Similarly, a DNMT inhibitor, zebularine, was able to decrease the growth of breast cancer cells and reactivate various genes with its ability to be an effective therapeutic agent [105].

Furthermore, inhibitors of histone lysine methyltransferase have been used in treating several cancer types. The first FDA-approved histone lysine methylation inhibitor, Tazemetostat, has been used to treat epithelioid sarcomas, which blocks lysine methyltransferase activity of EZH2 [106]. There are other EZH2 inhibitors in clinical trials, and in addition, other histone methyltransferases inhibitors such as inhibitors of DOTL, SET7, and SET8 (lysine methyltransferases), PMRT1, CARM1/PRMT4, and PRMT5 (arginine methyltransferases) are under the clinical trials for the treatment of many cancers including metastatic solid tumors [107]. Similarly, KDM5A is a potential therapeutic target showing histone demethylase inhibitors as promising epigenetic therapy for cancers [108].

In addition to the FDA-approved epigenetic drugs, the other drugs that are under development and in clinical trials hold great promise for precision medicine and personalized therapeutics, as they have the potential to target specific epigenetic alterations which are unique to individual patients. However, due to the complexity of epigenetic regulation, it's important to fully understand the mechanisms, efficacy, and safety of these interventions in patients. It is possible that epigenetic therapies play a crucial role in shaping the future of cancer therapeutics, bringing us closer to more effective and personalized approaches for combating this challenging disease.

Advancements and innovation in epigenetic technologies in investigating mechanisms in cancer cells

Epigenetic technologies have significantly advanced our understanding of the mechanisms underlying cancer development and progression. These innovative tools have provided us with powerful methods to study epigenetic alterations in cancer cells, and to understand how these alterations lead to changes in gene expression patterns and contribute to the disease. Here are some key innovations and advancements in epigenetic technologies that have revolutionized cancer research from the past to the present.

Epigenetic profiling

Epigenetic technologies, such as DNA methylation arrays, next-generation sequencing-based methods such as whole genome bisulfite sequencing (WGBS) and reduced representation bisulfite sequencing (RRBS), and chromatin immunoprecipitation (ChIP) followed by sequencing (ChIP-seq), enable comprehensive profiling of epigenctic modifications in cancer cells. The latest version of DNA methylation array, i.e., HumanMethylationEPIC version 2.0 (900K EPIC v2), covers over 900,000 CpG sites in the entire human epigenome that include enhancers, super-enhancers, and CTCF binding regions [109]. This version was an improved version of its previous 850K EPIC arrays. These arrays have been developed from its very first array, 27K, which covered 27K CpG sites, followed by 450K array, covering over 450K CpG sites and spanning the entire human epigenome [110]. Therefore, there has been a continuous development of methylation arrays in terms of size and coverage of the genomic regions. Similarly, WGBS covers the entire 28 million CpGs helping us to identify DNA methylation status at single CpG level in entire human epigenome. RBPS covers 5%–10% of all CpG sites in the mammalian genome, which is a cost-effective method for DNA methylation patterns mainly to detect methylation at gene promoters and CpG islands [111]. ChIP is another powerful method that can be used to analyze the interaction between the regulatory proteins (such as transcription factors) and the gene promoters in a native chromatin environment [112]. In addition, ChIP assay enables us to look at this chromatin-protein interaction at a genome-wide level. Thus, these approaches allow us to identify DNA methylation status in specific CpG regions, histone modifications, and changes in chromatin accessibility that will further help us to pinpoint critical regulatory regions and identify potential oncogenes or tumor suppressor genes in cancers.

Epigenome editing

CRISPR-Cas9-based epigenome editing technologies allow us to modify or mimic the activity of the genes through the targeted DNA methylation machinery [113]. Further, CRISPR-based screening can be utilized to investigate the functionality of epigenetic modifiers by creating a comprehensive guide RNA (gRNA) library that precisely focuses on dCas-fused modifiers in order to observe changes in their transcription [114]. Further, CRISPR epigenome editing has been used to analyze m6A (N^6-Methyladenosine) modification sites mainly associated with embryonic mRNA in telomerase to understand the regulation of telomerase activity in CSCs, antiaging, and tumor-related diseases [115]. Thus, epigenome editing has been crucial in elucidating the relationships between specific epigenetic alterations in cancer and its phenotypes.

Single-cell epigenomics

Recent advancements in single-cell epigenomic technologies have revolutionized our understanding of cellular heterogeneity within tumors. By analyzing epigenetic patterns at the single-cell level, researchers can identify distinct cell subpopulations and study their epigenetic differences. This knowledge is critical for understanding tumor evolution, resistance to therapy, and the identification of rare subpopulations that may drive cancer progression and metastasis. One of the latest advancements in single-cell DNA epigenomics is the single-cell DNA methylation (scDNAm) technology that has paved the way for novel approaches to dissecting and deciphering bulk DNA methylation data [116]. However, this technology is still in development, and it is challenging to utilize it due to insufficient coverage [117]. Other new technologies, such as droplet-based Bisulfite sequencing, could possibly provide a solution for single-cell methylome studies, especially for the large cell population [118]. Further, in order to co-relate DNA methylome profilings with transcriptomics, epigenome-transcriptome comapping technology has been developed that helps us to understand how DNA methylome has a role in cell dynamics and transcriptional phenotypes at genome-wide levels [119]. Therefore, single-cell epigenomics has opened new avenues in our understanding of fundamental biological processes, tumor heterogeneity and disease mechanisms, which we could utilize for personalized therapeutic interventions.

References

[1] R.S. Dwivedi, et al., Beyond genetics: epigenetic code in chronic kidney disease, Kidney Int. 79 (1) (2011) 23–32.

[2] P.A. Jones, S.B. Baylin, The epigenomics of cancer, Cell 128 (4) (2007) 683–692.

[3] M. Rodriguez-Paredes, M. Esteller, Cancer epigenetics reaches mainstream oncology, Nat. Med. 17 (3) (2011) 330–339.

[4] N. Loyfer, et al., A DNA methylation atlas of normal human cell types, Nature 613 (7943) (2023) 355–364.

[5] R. Roy, et al., DNA methylation signatures reveal that distinct combinations of transcription factors specify human immune cell epigenetic identity, Immunity 54 (11) (2021) 2465–2480 e5.

[6] M.J. Boland, K.L. Nazor, J.F. Loring, Epigenetic regulation of pluripotency and differentiation, Circ. Res. 115 (2) (2014) 311–324.

[7] Z. Herceg, Epigenetic mechanisms as an interface between the environment and genome, Adv. Exp. Med. Biol. 903 (2016) 3–15.

[8] A.P. Feinberg, R. Ohlsson, S. Henikoff, The epigenetic progenitor origin of human cancer, Nat. Rev. Genet. 7 (1) (2006) 21–33.

[9] H.C. Tsai, S.B. Baylin, Cancer epigenetics: linking basic biology to clinical medicine, Cell Res. 21 (3) (2011) 502–517.

[10] A.C. Schinzel, W. Hahn, Oncogenic transformation and experimental models of human cancer, Front. Biosci. 13 (2008) 71–84.

[11] M.R. Stratton, P.J. Campbell, P.A. Futreal, The cancer genome, Nature 458 (7239) (2009) 719–724.

[12] S.B. Baylin, et al., Aberrant patterns of DNA methylation, chromatin formation and gene expression in cancer, Hum. Mol. Genet. 10 (7) (2001) 687–692.

[13] R.P. Pangeni, et al., Genome-wide methylation analyses identifies non-coding RNA genes dysregulated in breast tumours that metastasise to the brain, Sci. Rep. 12 (1) (2022) 1102.

[14] K. Zhang, et al., Targeting histone methyltransferase G9a inhibits growth and Wnt signaling pathway by epigenetically regulating HP1alpha and APC2 gene expression in non-small cell lung cancer, Mol. Cancer 17 (1) (2018) 153.

[15] Y. Okada, Sperm chromatin condensation: epigenetic mechanisms to compact the genome and spatiotemporal regulation from inside and outside the nucleus, Genes Genet. Syst. 97 (1) (2022) 41–53.

[16] M.R. Morris, et al., Multigene methylation analysis of Wilms' tumour and adult renal cell carcinoma, Oncogene 22 (43) (2003) 6794–6801.

[17] R.P. Pangeni, et al., The GALNT9, BNC1 and CCDC8 genes are frequently epigenetically dysregulated in breast tumours that metastasise to the brain, Clin. Epigenetics 7 (1) (2015) 57.

[18] S.B. Baylin, et al., DNA methylation patterns of the calcitonin gene in human lung cancers and lymphomas, Cancer Res. 46 (6) (1986) 2917–2922.

[19] V. Greger, E. Passarge, W. Höpping, E. Messmer, B. Horsthemke, Epigenetic changes may contribute to the formation and spontaneous regression of retinoblastoma, Hum. Genet. 83 (2) (1989) 155–158.

[20] T. Sakai, J. Toguchida, N. Ohtani, D.W. Yandell, J.M. Rapaport, T.P. Dryja, Allele-specific hypermethylation of the retinoblastoma tumor-suppressor gene, Am. J. Hum. Genet. 48 (5) (1991) 880–888.

[21] J.G. Herman, F. Latif, Y. Weng, M.I. Lerman, B. Zbar, S. Liu, D. Samid, D.S. Duan, J. R. Gnarra, W.M. Linehan, et al., Silencing of the VHL tumor-suppressor gene by DNA methylation in renal carcinoma, Proc. Natl. Acad. Sci. 91 (21) (1994) 9700–9704.

[22] J.G. Herman, A. Merlo, L. Mao, R.G. Lapidus, J.P. Issa, N.E. Davidson, D. Sidransky, S.B. Baylin, Inactivation of the CDKN2/p16/MTS1 gene is frequently associated with aberrant DNA methylation in all common human cancers, Cancer Res. 55 (20) (1995) 4525–4530.

[23] R. Dammann, C. Li, J.H. Yoon, P.L. Chin, S. Bates, G.P. Pfeifer, Epigenetic inactivation of a RAS association domain family protein from the lung tumour suppressor locus 3p21.3, Nat. Genet. 25 (3) (2000) 315–319.

[24] R. Dammann, G. Yang, G.P. Pfeifer, Hypermethylation of the cpG island of Ras association domain family 1A (RASSF1A), a putative tumor suppressor gene from the 3p21.3 locus, occurs in a large percentage of human breast cancers, Cancer Res. 61 (7) (2001) 3105–3109.

[25] L. Hesson, I. Bièche, D. Krex, E. Criniere, K. Hoang-Xuan, E.R. Maher, F. Latif, Frequent epigenetic inactivation of RASSF1A and BLU genes located within the critical 3p21.3 region in gliomas, Oncogene 23 (13) (2004) 2408–2419.

[26] M. van Engeland, G. Roemen, M. Brink, M.M. Pachen, M.P. Weijenberg, A.P. de Bruïne, J.W. Arends, P. van den Brandt, A.F. de Goeij, J.G. Herman, K-ras mutations and RASSF1A promoter methylation in colorectal cancer, Oncogene 21 (23) (2002) 3792–3795.

[27] C. Morrissey, A. Martinez, M. Zatyka, A. Agathanggelou, S. Honorio, D. Astuti, N.V. Morgan, H. Moch, F.M. Richards, T. Kishida, M. Yao, P. Schraml, F. Latif, E.R. Maher, Epigenetic inactivation of the RASSF1A 3p21.3 tumor suppressor gene in both clear cell and papillary renal cell carcinoma, Cancer Res. 61 (19) (2001) 7277–7281.

[28] J.P. Issa, B. Zehnbaue, S.H. Kaufmann, M.A. Biel, S.B. Baylin, HIC1 hypermethylation is a late event in hematopoietic neoplasms, Cancer Res. 57 (9) (1997) 1678–1681.

[29] H. Fujii, M. Biel, W. Zhou, S.A. Weitzman, S.B. Baylin, E. Gabrielson, Methylation of the HIC-1 candidate tumor suppressor gene in human breast cancer, Oncogene 16 (16) (1998) 2159–2164.

[30] J.R. Melki, P. Vincent, S.J. Clark, Cancer-specific region of hypermethylation identified within the HIC1 putative tumour suppressor gene in acute myeloid leukaemia, Leukemia 13 (6) (1999) 877–883.

[31] W.M. Grady, J. Willis, P.J. Guilford, A.K. Dunbier, T.T. Toro, H. Lynch, G. Wiesner, C. Eng, K. Ferguson, J.G. Park, S.J. Kim, S. Markowitz, Methylation of the CDH1 promoter as the second genetic hit in hereditary diffuse gastric cancer, Nat. Genet. 26 (1) (2000) 16–17.

[32] S. Saghafinia, et al., Pan-cancer landscape of aberrant DNA methylation across human tumors, Cell Rep. 25 (4) (2018) 1066–1080 e8.

[33] M. Ehrlich, DNA hypomethylation in cancer cells, Epigenomics 1 (2) (2009) 239–259.

[34] A. Eden, F. Gaudet, A. Waghmare, R. Jaenisch, Chromosomal instability and tumors promoted by DNA hypomethylation, Science 300 (5618) (2003) 455.

[35] H.S. Lee, T. Park, The influences of DNA methylation and epigenetic clocks, on metabolic disease, in middle-aged Koreans, Clin. Epigenetics 12 (1) (2020) 148.

[36] Y. Pan, et al., DNA methylation profiles in cancer diagnosis and therapeutics, Clin. Exp. Med. 18 (1) (2018) 1–14.

[37] A.S. Quina, M. Buschbeck, L. Di Croce, Chromatin structure and epigenetics, Biochem. Pharmacol. 72 (11) (2006) 1563–1569.

[38] J.C. Black, C. Van Rechem, J.R. Whetstine, Histone lysine methylation dynamics: establishment, regulation, and biological impact, Mol. Cell 48 (4) (2012) 491–507.

[39] O. Elemento, M.A. Rubin, D.S. Rickman, Oncogenic transcription factors as master regulators of chromatin topology: a new role for ERG in prostate cancer, Cell Cycle 11 (18) (2012) 3380–3383.

[40] M.E. Neganova, et al., Histone modifications in epigenetic regulation of cancer: perspectives and achieved progress, Semin. Cancer Biol. 83 (2022) 452–471.

[41] C. Sawan, H. Zdenko, Histone modifications and cancer, Adv. Genet. 70 (2010) 57–85.

[42] C.L. Peterson, M.A. Laniel, Histones and histone modifications, Curr. Biol. 14 (14) (2004) R546–R551.

[43] J.E. Audia, R.M. Campbell, Histone modifications and cancer, Cold Spring Harb. Perspect. Biol. 8 (4) (2016) a019521.

[44] L.M. Lasko, et al., Discovery of a selective catalytic p300/CBP inhibitor that targets lineage-specific tumours, Nature 550 (7674) (2017) 128–132.

[45] S. Hayami, J. Kelly, H.S. Cho, M. Yoshimatsu, M. Unoki, T. Tsunoda, H.I. Field, D.E. Neal, H. Yamaue, B.A. Ponder, Y. Nakamura, R. Hamamoto, Overexpression of LSD1 contributes to human carcinogenesis through chromatin regulation in various cancers, Int. J. Cancer 128 (3) (2011) 574–586.

[46] S. Lim, A. Janzer, A. Becker, A. Zimmer, R. Schüle, R. Buettner, J. Kirfel, Lysine-specific demethylase 1 (LSD1) is highly expressed in ER-negative breast cancers and a biomarker predicting aggressive biology, Carcinogenesis 31 (3) (2010) 512–520.

[47] J.H. Schulte, S. Lim, A. Schramm, N. Friedrichs, J. Koster, R. Versteeg, I. Ora, K. Pajtler, L. Klein-Hitpass, S. Kuhfittig-Kulle, E. Metzger, R. Schüle, A. Eggert, R. Buettner, J. Kirfel, Lysine-specific demethylase 1 is strongly expressed in poorly differentiated neuroblastoma: implications for therapy, Cancer Res. 69 (5) (2009) 2065.

[48] R.P. Pangeni, et al., G9a regulates tumorigenicity and stemness through genome-wide DNA methylation reprogramming in non-small cell lung cancer, Clin. Epigenetics 12 (1) (2020) 88.

[49] D. Nicetto, K.S. Zaret, Role of H3K9me3 heterochromatin in cell identity establishment and maintenance, Curr. Opin. Genet. Dev. 55 (2019) 1–10.

[50] I. Topchu, et al., The role of NSD1, NSD2, and NSD3 histone methyltransferases in solid tumors, Cell. Mol. Life Sci. 79 (6) (2022) 285.

[51] A.J. Bannister, et al., Spatial distribution of di- and tri-methyl lysine 36 of histone H3 at active genes, J. Biol. Chem. 280 (18) (2005) 17732–17736.

[52] S.K. Hota, B.G. Bruneau, ATP-dependent chromatin remodeling during mammalian development, Development 143 (16) (2016) 2882–2897.

[53] B. Li, M. Carey, J.L. Workman, The role of chromatin during transcription, Cell 128 (4) (2007) 707–719.

[54] S.S. Nair, R. Kumar, Chromatin remodeling in cancer: a gateway to regulate gene transcription, Mol. Oncol. 6 (6) (2012) 611–619.

[55] Y. Li, et al., The emerging role of ISWI chromatin remodeling complexes in cancer, J. Exp. Clin. Cancer Res. 40 (1) (2021) 346.

[56] H. Gao, et al., Opposing effects of SWI/SNF and Mi-2/NuRD chromatin remodeling complexes on epigenetic reprogramming by EBF and Pax5, Proc. Natl. Acad. Sci. USA 106 (27) (2009) 11258–11263.

[57] J. Schwartzentruber, et al., Driver mutations in histone H3.3 and chromatin remodelling genes in paediatric glioblastoma, Nature 482 (7384) (2012) 226–231.

[58] K.A. Skulte, et al., Chromatin remodeler mutations in human cancers: epigenetic implications, Epigenomics 6 (4) (2014) 397–414.

[59] A.H. Shain, J.R. Pollack, The spectrum of SWI/SNF mutations, ubiquitous in human cancers, PLoS One 8 (1) (2013) e55119.

[60] P. Bailey, et al., Genomic analyses identify molecular subtypes of pancreatic cancer, Nature 531 (7592) (2016) 47–52.

[61] M.P. Torchy, A. Hamiche, B.P. Klaholz, Structure and function insights into the NuRD chromatin remodeling complex, Cell. Mol. Life Sci. 72 (13) (2015) 2491–2507.

[62] R. Margueron, D. Reinberg, The polycomb complex PRC2 and its mark in life, Nature 469 (7330) (2011) 343–349.

[63] S. Sharma, T.K. Kelly, P.A. Jones, Epigenetics in cancer, Carcinogenesis 31 (1) (2010) 27–36.

[64] L.B. Hesson, et al., Altered promoter nucleosome positioning is an early event in gene silencing, Epigenetics 9 (10) (2014) 1422–1430.

[65] J.C. Lin, et al., Role of nucleosomal occupancy in the epigenetic silencing of the MLH1 CpG island, Cancer Cell 12 (5) (2007) 432–444.

[66] J. Du, et al., DNA methylation pathways and their crosstalk with histone methylation, Nat. Rev. Mol. Cell Biol. 16 (9) (2015) 519–532.

[67] S. Kumar, et al., Non-coding RNAs as mediators of epigenetic changes in malignancies, Cancers (Basel) 12 (12) (2020) 3657–3689.

[68] F.J. Slack, A.M. Chinnaiyan, The role of non-coding RNAs in oncology, Cell 179 (5) (2019) 1033–1055.

[69] A. Acha-Sagredo, et al., Long non-coding RNA dysregulation is a frequent event in non-small cell lung carcinoma pathogenesis, Br. J. Cancer 122 (7) (2020) 1050–1058.

[70] H. Zhao, et al., Comprehensive landscape of epigenetic-dysregulated lncRNAs reveals a profound role of enhancers in carcinogenesis in BC subtypes, Mol. Ther. Nucleic Acids 23 (2021) 667–681.

[71] J. Lu, et al., MicroRNA expression profiles classify human cancers, Nature 435 (7043) (2005) 834–838.

[72] C.M. Croce, Causes and consequences of microRNA dysregulation in cancer, Nat. Rev. Genet. 10 (10) (2009) 704–714.

[73] S. Li, et al., The comprehensive landscape of miR-34a in cancer research, Cancer Metastasis Rev. 40 (3) (2021) 925–948.

[74] H. Li, et al., A serum microRNA signature predicts trastuzumab benefit in HER2-positive metastatic breast cancer patients, Nat. Commun. 9 (1) (2018) 1614.

[75] Z. Zhang, et al., Transcriptional landscape and clinical utility of enhancer RNAs for eRNA-targeted therapy in cancer, Nat. Commun. 10 (1) (2019) 4562.

[76] S. Adhikary, et al., Implications of enhancer transcription and eRNAs in cancer, Cancer Res. 81 (16) (2021) 4174–4182.

[77] L. Barbato, et al., Cancer stem cells and targeting strategies, Cells 8 (8) (2019) 926–945.

[78] T.B. Toh, J.J. Lim, E.K. Chow, Epigenetics in cancer stem cells, Mol. Cancer 16 (1) (2017) 29.

[79] P.R. Prasetyanti, J.P. Medema, Intra-tumor heterogeneity from a cancer stem cell perspective, Mol. Cancer 16 (1) (2017) 41.

[80] C.C. Liu, et al., IL-6 enriched lung cancer stem-like cell population by inhibition of cell cycle regulators via DNMT1 upregulation, Int. J. Cancer 136 (3) (2015) 547–559.

[81] A.M. Broske, et al., DNA methylation protects hematopoietic stem cell multipotency from myeloerythroid restriction, Nat. Genet. 41 (11) (2009) 1207–1215.

[82] R.P. Pangeni, et al., Genome-wide methylomic and transcriptomic analyses identify subtype-specific epigenetic signatures commonly dysregulated in glioma stem cells and glioblastoma, Epigenetics 13 (4) (2018) 432–448.

[83] T. Huang, et al., MST4 phosphorylation of ATG4B regulates autophagic activity, tumorigenicity, and radioresistance in glioblastoma, Cancer Cell 32 (6) (2017) 840–855 e8.

[84] E.N. Wainwright, P. Scaffidi, Epigenetics and cancer stem cells: unleashing, hijacking, and restricting cellular plasticity, Trends Cancer 3 (5) (2017) 372–386.

[85] K. Zhang, et al., Ubiquitin-specific protease 22 is critical to in vivo angiogenesis, growth and metastasis of non-small cell lung cancer, Cell Commun. Signal. 17 (1) (2019) 167.

[86] X. Yun, et al., Targeting USP22 suppresses tumorigenicity and enhances cisplatin sensitivity through ALDH1A3 downregulation in cancer-initiating cells from lung adenocarcinoma, Mol. Cancer Res. 16 (7) (2018) 1161–1171.

[87] P. Costa-Pinheiro, et al., Diagnostic and prognostic epigenetic biomarkers in cancer, Epigenomics 7 (6) (2015) 1003–1015.

[88] D. Deng, Z. Liu, Y. Du, Epigenetic alterations as cancer diagnostic, prognostic, and predictive biomarkers, Adv. Genet. 71 (2010) 125–176.

[89] M. Herranz, M. Esteller, DNA methylation and histone modifications in patients with cancer: potential prognostic and therapeutic targets, Methods Mol. Biol. 361 (2007) 25–62.

[90] M.E. Hegi, et al., MGMT gene silencing and benefit from temozolomide in glioblastoma, N. Engl. J. Med. 352 (10) (2005) 997–1003.

[91] X. Chen, et al., Non-invasive early detection of cancer four years before conventional diagnosis using a blood test, Nat. Commun. 11 (1) (2020) 3475.

[92] V. Constancio, et al., Early detection of the major male cancer types in blood-based liquid biopsies using a DNA methylation panel, Clin. Epigenetics 11 (1) (2019) 175.

[93] S.O. Jensen, et al., Novel DNA methylation biomarkers show high sensitivity and specificity for blood-based detection of colorectal cancer-a clinical biomarker discovery and validation study, Clin. Epigenetics 11 (1) (2019) 158.

[94] C. Moreira-Barbosa, et al., Comparing diagnostic and prognostic performance of two-gene promoter methylation panels in tissue biopsies and urines of prostate cancer patients, Clin. Epigenetics 10 (1) (2018) 132.

[95] F. Zhao, et al., A urine-based DNA methylation assay, ProCUrE, to identify clinically significant prostate cancer, Clin. Epigenetics 10 (1) (2018) 147.

[96] M.R. Peter, et al., Investigating urinary circular RNA biomarkers for improved detection of renal cell carcinoma, Front. Oncol. 11 (2021) 814228.

[97] W. Li, et al., 5-Hydroxymethylcytosine signatures in circulating cell-free DNA as diagnostic biomarkers for human cancers, Cell Res. 27 (10) (2017) 1243–1257.

[98] M.A.L. Eissa, et al., Promoter methylation of ADAMTS1 and BNC1 as potential biomarkers for early detection of pancreatic cancer in blood, Clin. Epigenetics 11 (1) (2019) 59.

[99] Q. Zhang, et al., Novel GIRlncRNA signature for predicting the clinical outcome and therapeutic response in NSCLC, Front. Pharmacol. 13 (2022) 937531.

[100] C. Stresemann, F. Lyko, Modes of action of the DNA methyltransferase inhibitors azacytidine and decitabine, Int. J. Cancer 123 (1) (2008) 8–13.

[101] L.R. Silverman, et al., Randomized controlled trial of azacitidine in patients with the myelodysplastic syndrome: a study of the cancer and leukemia group B, J. Clin. Oncol. 20 (10) (2002) 2429–2440.

[102] C. Mund, et al., Characterization of DNA demethylation effects induced by 5-Aza-2′-deoxycytidine in patients with myelodysplastic syndrome, Cancer Res. 65 (16) (2005) 7086–7090.

[103] L. Zhang, et al., DNMT and EZH2 inhibitors synergize to activate therapeutic targets in hepatocellular carcinoma, Cancer Lett. 548 (2022) 215899.

[104] N. Azevedo Portilho, et al., The DNMT1 inhibitor GSK-3484862 mediates global demethylation in murine embryonic stem cells, Epigenetics Chromatin 14 (1) (2021) 56.

[105] M. Billam, M.D. Sobolewski, N.E. Davidson, Effects of a novel DNA methyltransferase inhibitor zebularine on human breast cancer cells, Breast Cancer Res. Treat. 120 (3) (2010) 581–592.

[106] S.B. Rothbart, S.B. Baylin, Epigenetic therapy for epithelioid sarcoma, Cell 181 (2) (2020) 211.

[107] H.S. Rugo, et al., The promise for histone methyltransferase inhibitors for epigenetic therapy in clinical oncology: a narrative review, Adv. Ther. 37 (7) (2020) 3059–3082.

[108] G.J. Yang, et al., The emerging role of KDM5A in human cancer, J. Hematol. Oncol. 14 (1) (2021) 30.

[109] A. Noguera-Castells, et al., Validation of the new EPIC DNA methylation microarray (900K EPIC v2) for high-throughput profiling of the human DNA methylome, Epigenetics 18 (1) (2023) 2185742.

[110] F. Marabita, et al., An evaluation of analysis pipelines for DNA methylation profiling using the Illumina HumanMethylation450 BeadChip platform, Epigenetics 8 (3) (2013) 333–346.

[111] K. Nakabayashi, et al., Reduced representation bisulfite sequencing (RRBS), Methods Mol. Biol. 2577 (2023) 39–51.

[112] P. Dasgupta, S.P. Chellappan, Chromatin immunoprecipitation assays: molecular analysis of chromatin modification and gene regulation, Methods Mol. Biol. 383 (2007) 135–152.

[113] T.S. Klann, et al., CRISPR-Cas9 epigenome editing enables high-throughput screening for functional regulatory elements in the human genome, Nat. Biotechnol. 35 (6) (2017) 561–568.

[114] M. Nakamura, et al., CRISPR technologies for precise epigenome editing, Nat. Cell Biol. 23 (1) (2021) 11–22.

[115] M. Yi, et al., CRISPR-based m(6)A modification and its potential applications in telomerase regulation, Front. Cell Dev. Biol. 11 (2023) 1200734.

[116] M. Cai, et al., scMD facilitates cell type deconvolution using single-cell DNA methylation references, Commun. Biol. 7 (1) (2024) 1–11.

[117] S. Park, et al., iCpG-Pos: an accurate computational approach for identification of CpG sites using positional features on single-cell whole genome sequence data, Bioinformatics 39 (8) (2023) 1–9.

[118] Q. Zhang, et al., Droplet-based bisulfite sequencing for high-throughput profiling of single-cell DNA methylomes, Nat. Commun. 14 (1) (2023) 4672.

[119] M. Farlik, et al., Single-cell DNA methylome sequencing and bioinformatic inference of epigenomic cell-state dynamics, Cell Rep. 10 (8) (2015) 1386–1397.

Metabolic adaptation and epigenetic modulations: Unraveling tumor plasticity under variable tumor microenvironment

Jowana Obeid[a,b] and Mehdi Damaghi[a,b,c,d]

[a]*Stony Brook Cancer Center, Stony Brook University, Stony Brook, NY, United States,* [b]*Department of Biochemistry and Cell Biology, Stony Brook University, Stony Brook, NY, United States,* [c]*Department of Pathology, Renaissance School of Medicine, Stony Brook University, Stony Brook, NY, United States,* [d]*Department of Mathematics and Statistics, Stony Brook University, Stony Brook, NY, United States*

Introduction

When Hanahan and Weinberg first released the hallmarks of cancer, they only included six hallmarks as drivers of cancer initiation and progression [1]. Back then, there was a reductionist view on how cancer emerges, focusing on the seed (cancer cell) and not enough on the soil (the microenvironmental niche in which cancer cells live) [2]. Recently, Hanahan updated these hallmarks to include new features due to increasing evidence on the role of tumor microenvironment (TME) in driving tumor evolution [3]. Though the TME was not specifically stated in the hallmarks, it was implied by different hallmarks added, like deregulating cellular metabolism and inducing or accessing vasculature, as well as nonmutational epigenetic reprogramming and unlocking phenotypic plasticity as emerging and enabling characteristics respectively.

TME is part of the dynamic cancer ecosystem consisting of immune cells, surrounding stroma, vasculature, signaling networks, structural components, and metabolic factors such as lactate, protons, nutrients molecules, and oxygen [4]. The TME is dynamic and ever-changing, shaped by the interactions between tumor cells and the other components of tumor ecosystem. Tumor cells respond to the signals from TME by undergoing epigenetic changes due to metabolite-induced modifications, which sets off a series of interconnected events [5,6].

Metabolites present in the TME can induce epigenetic changes with influence on subsequent epigenetic modifications [5]. These small molecules, generated as

Cancer Epigenetics and Nanomedicine. https://doi.org/10.1016/B978-0-443-13209-4.00012-X
Copyright © 2024 Elsevier Inc. All rights reserved, including those for text and data mining, AI training, and similar technologies.

byproducts of various cellular processes, possess a remarkable capacity to initiate epigenetic alterations. These changes can affect the regulation of gene expression, chromatin structure, and other essential cellular functions [5]. The dynamic reciprocal interaction between the TME and tumor cells creates a complex cascade of events with far-reaching consequences. This intricate interplay doesn't just influence the cellular phenotype; it goes further, leading to significant changes within the TME itself [7]. These events can lead to shifts in the cellular phenotype of both tumor and nontumor cells within the TME. These phenotypic changes can involve alterations in cell survival, migration, invasion, and communication. Moreover, the changes initiated by these interactions can transform the TME itself, influencing its composition, structure, and functionality [8]. In tumor ecosystems, the microenvironment conditions fluctuate very quickly, such as changes in nutrient availability, oxygen levels, or the presence of immune cells; cancer cells must display adaptive metabolic responses to maintain their survival and aggressive behavior [9]. This remarkable capability of cancer cells to adjust and modify their metabolic processes in response to the specific conditions within the TME is referred to as metabolic plasticity [10]. This adaptive behavior allows cancer cells to survive and thrive in challenging and ever-changing TME conditions, contributing to their resilience and ability to evade therapeutic interventions. Metabolic plasticity can change the evolutionary trajectories of cancer cells [11]. When cancer cells face challenging conditions within the TME, such as limited nutrients, hypoxia, or immune system attacks, those with enhanced metabolic plasticity gain a significant advantage [11]. They can adjust their metabolic pathways to sustain energy production and biosynthesis, enabling them to survive and proliferate in these adverse environments [12]. This adaptability often leads to the selection and propagation of cancer cell subpopulations that possess more flexible metabolic phenotypes. Over time, this can result in the dominance of cancer cell clones with heightened metabolic plasticity, leading to a shift in the tumor's overall metabolic profile [12]. The regulation of metabolic plasticity in cancer and normal cells is not very well known particularly in the scope of cancer evolution in the tumor ecosystem. With the current state of research on how variable TME induced deregulated metabolism correlates with epigenetic reprogramming leading to a major effect on tumor evolution and response to therapy, we can foresee that TME will be added as a major hallmark in the next decade or so as we are starting to shift from the seed to the soil in tumor evolutionary research.

Metabolic adaptation to TME

Major metabolic reprogramming occurs in every solid tumor mainly due to adaptation to the novel TME conditions. This reprogramming arises from the convergence of various factors operating at multiple levels of cellular regulation, including metabolic, genomic, epigenomic, and proteomic factors [5,13]. These metabolic adaptations not only enable cancer cells to survive in the novel, extremely harsh, and variable TME but also give evolutionary advantages to plastic cancer cells who can adapt faster. A plastic phenotype can be acquired through several mechanisms that further promote tumor progression and aggressiveness [7,9,11]. We will expand on these conditions in the following sections.

Metabolic microenvironment in solid tumors

Reprogramming cellular metabolism has been recently considered a major hallmark of cancer in solid tumors [3]. With the transition from hyperplasia to a full-blown tumor, the tumor mass results in the emergence of several new microenvironmental conditions due to the fast proliferation of cancer cells in a limited space and vasculature leading to hypoxia, acidosis, and nutrient deprivation (Fig. 1) [14]. These emerging microenvironments themselves lead to metabolic rewiring and selection

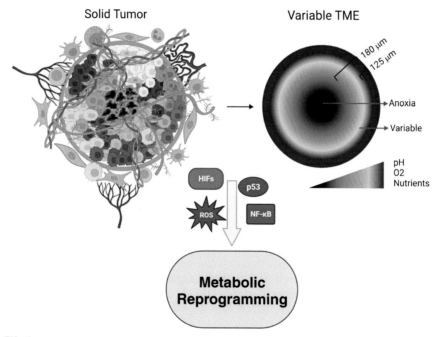

FIG. 1

Variable tumor microenvironment in solid tumors. Physical and chemical TME of solid tumors is heterogenous with a necrotic, anoxic, and nutrient deprived niche, followed by a fairly stable hypoxic zone. Next to the hypoxic zone and before the oxygenated niche, closest to the basal membrane, comes the most variable TME with fluctuating oxygen, acid, and nutrients. Outside the early tumor that can also be affected by the metabolites released by tumor cells consists of stromal cells, immune cells, extracellular matrix components, and various secreted factors, including metabolites. Different metabolic conditions arise like decrease in O_2, pH, and nutrient availability due to the altered vasculature that leads to metabolic reprogramming and adaptation partly through major transcription factors and ROS-induced signaling.

Created with BioRender.com.

of the fittest cancer clones that can survive in this novel and variable ecosystem [12]. The abnormal tumor microcirculation is mainly caused by limited vasculature designed for physiological conditions of cells, defective new angiogenesis, cooption of existing vessels, vasculogenesis, and formation of pseudovascular channels [15]. These pathogenic mechanisms result in hostile conditions including oxygen depletion, extracellular acidosis, high lactate levels, varied nutrient availability, and nutrient deprivation in extreme conditions [15–18].

In solid tumors, mainly at the early stages when the cancer is still an avascular disease, hypoxia induces the expression of the transcription factor hypoxia-induced factor 1 (HIF1) as probably one of the first regulators of metabolic reprogramming [19]. The direct oxygen tension sensors that can control hypoxia-mediated HIF action are prolyl hydroxylase domain that hydroxylates conserved proline residues on HIF1α for targeted degradation and asparaginyl hydroxylase that hydroxylates arginine residues for HIF1α inactivation [20]. HIF1 orchestrates metabolic reprogramming through multiple pathways and different factors. For example, the mitochondrial protease OMA1 increases reactive oxygen species (ROS) to stabilize HIF1α and shifts glucose metabolism to glycolysis from oxidative phosphorylation in colorectal cancer [21]. HIF1α can also modulate the expression of several proteins and enzymes in the glycolysis pathway such as GLUT1 and GLUT3 (glucose transporters), hexokinase II, hexose phosphate isomerase, phosphofructokinase-L, aldolase-A, triosephosphate isomerase, glyceraldehyde-3-phosphate dehydrogenase, phosphoglycerate mutase-B, enolase-α, and pyruvate kinase-M2. HIF1α regulates pyruvate dehydrogenase kinase, which deactivates pyruvate dehydrogenase through phosphorylation, thus inhibiting the entrance of pyruvate in the tricarboxylic acid (TCA) cycle and its transformation into acetyl-CoA, the main precursor in fatty acid synthesis and protein acetylation [22]. HIF1α as a hypoxic master regulator also induces lactate dehydrogenase-A (LDHA) enzyme, which converts pyruvate into lactate and increases the acidity of the surrounding environment [22]. HIF1α hyperactivation through mTOR and AMPK signaling can shift metabolism to aerobic glycolysis, a.k.a. Warburg phenotype, and play roles in resistance to anticancer drugs such as tamoxifen possibly by providing the energy needed [23]. Hypoxia also partakes in cisplatin resistance, and one possible mechanism is through inducing the expression of exosomal PKM2 [24]. Consequently, transfer to tumor cells is facilitated and a metabolic shift to glycolysis occurs in NSCLC [24]. One mechanism of HIF1α activated metabolic reprogramming in hypoxia is through lncRNA AC020978. lncRNA AC020978 can promote metabolic reprogramming through direct interaction with PKM2 that enhances its stability and promotes its nuclear translocation in NSCLC [25]. Furthermore, HIF1 upregulation due to hypoxia increases PDK1 expression, which decreases mitochondrial oxygen consumption [26].

Nutrient deprivation is another microenvironmental condition in solid tumors due to the altered blood perfusion and increased proliferation rate of cancer cells [12]. mTOR signaling complexes act as nutrient sensors to promote the survival of cancer cells in response to such harsh conditions [27,28]. It was shown that serum deprivation in prostate cancer leads to a quiescent state to prevent apoptosis and promote cancer cell survival in response to the resulting oxidative stress [29]. Furthermore, alterations in the levels of AMPK are correlated to cellular energy status and have been shown to sense nutrient deprivation. This process is highly context dependent, leading to changes in several catabolic processes' activation [30]. Its activation can either promote oxidative phosphorylation in glucose-deprived conditions or glycolysis when ATP levels are low; the energy demands of cancer cells dictate how it shifts metabolic processes [30].

The metabolic alterations resulting from hypoxia and nutrient deprivation conditions in solid tumors create an acidic microenvironment, primarily due to elevated levels of the glycolytic byproduct lactate [12]. When lactate is produced, it's shuttled out of cancer cells along with a proton, mainly through monocarboxylate transporters (MCTs) to neutralize intracellular acidification. Overactivity of proton pumps can lead to an alkaline intracellular pH (pHi) and an acidic extracellular pH (pHe) [14,16,31]. The acidic pHe can modify enzymatic activity that functions in metabolic pathways. Alkaline pHi can sustain the Warburg effect (WE) and promote tumor growth in such conditions [31]. Extracellular acidosis can also alter glucose metabolism by increasing TCA cycle metabolism and decreasing glycolysis to shift the metabolic phenotype to a more oxidative one, depending on glucose availability [32–37]. Autophagy, the catabolic pathway characterized by lysosomal degradation and recycling of proteins and organelles, has been identified as another survival mechanism that melanoma and breast cancer cells utilize to survive acute acidic stress and it was shown to be sustained in chronic acidosis [38,39].

TME altered metabolic pathways

Glucose metabolism

Under physiologic conditions, glucose is metabolized by fermentation or oxidation depending on oxygen availability. If oxygen is available, glucose undergoes oxidative phosphorylation, where it is converted to pyruvate and further oxidized to CO_2, yielding 36 molecules of ATP [40]. Under hypoxic conditions, cells shift to anaerobic glycolysis, an energy-inefficient process, where glucose is fermented into lactate to produce two molecules of ATP. However, Otto Warburg noted that cancer cells keep their glycolysis high even in the presence of oxygen (normoxic conditions) with increased uptake and fermentation of glucose at a significantly high rate [40]. This phenomenon was termed the Warburg Effect (WE) or aerobic glycolysis after the scientist who discovered it. It is still not fully understood why cancer cells would shift to an ineffective low-energy-producing pathway while they can produce more ATP from oxidative phosphorylation. Several theories have been suggested to explain the survival advantage that the WE provides to cancer cells. Initially, it was proposed that dysfunctional mitochondria might be promoting this phenotype [40]. Another suggestion is that cancer cells with aggressive and invasive traits become highly glycolytic due to the dynamic shifts in energy requirements. This hypothesis argues that despite being less efficient in energy production, glycolysis has a rapid response to energy needs at the location it is needed, such as next to the membrane at invadopodia sites, which can enhance cancer cell migration and invasion [41]. Furthermore, the intermediates from the metabolic shift to glycolysis can provide precursors to other metabolic pathways that generate the necessary nutrients aiding in cancer cell survival and proliferation [42]. As discussed above, extracellular acidosis can also decrease glycolysis in cancer cells, and this acidosis-induced reduction can shift the metabolism of cancer cells to the pentose phosphate pathway (PPP), as it has been shown in different cancers [32,43].

One note that needs to be discussed here is the heterogeneous genetic background of cancer cells and their phenotypic plasticity, which is usually overlooked in many studies discussed above. We can tell with high certainty that different cells inside a tumor can use any of those mentioned mechanisms alone or in combination depending on their genetic background, epigenetic state, and phenotypic state. Furthermore, the tumor ecological context and microenvironment each cancer cell is inhabiting can also fine-tune the response.

Amino acid metabolism

In cancer, amino acid metabolism is altered to meet the biosynthetic and bioenergetic needs of the increasingly proliferating cancer cells [44]. mTORC1 signaling plays an important role in amino acid sensing, mainly in response to glucose starvation [45]. This process is employed by normal cells and can be exploited by cancer cells as a survival mechanism [27]. Under hypoxic conditions, cancer cells show an increased dependency on glutamine, and consequently, reductive glutamine metabolism is activated to provide precursors for alternative biosynthetic pathways where glucose might be scarce [46,47]. Recently, it was also shown that chronic hypoxia in prostate tumors shifts cancer cells to an androgen-independent state. This transition involves metabolic changes similar to castration-resistant prostate cancer, including heightened expression of methionine cycle transporters and glycolysis-related enzymes [48].

Although acidic microenvironments are known to trigger a shift toward glutamine dependency, it's important to note that they don't necessarily lead to a reduction in glutamine levels [32,49]. However, extracellular acidosis does exert a significant influence on glutamine metabolism [50]. This alteration is characterized by an increase in both the transport of glutamine into the cells and its subsequent utilization within the TCA cycle that is possibly caused by shutting down the glycolysis pathways to reduce the proton efflux [31]. Furthermore, the phenomenon of glutaminolysis, which involves the breakdown of glutamine, is enhanced under conditions of extracellular acidosis. These metabolic changes primarily serve bioenergetic purposes, aiming to sustain the energy needs of the cells within the challenging acidic microenvironment [32,49].

Lipid metabolism

In hypoxic microenvironments, de novo lipogenesis is activated by regulation and utilization of glutamine metabolism [46,47]. The coordination between glutamine metabolism and de novo lipogenesis in hypoxic conditions underscores the intricate adaptability of cells when faced with challenging environments. This phenomenon also highlights the dynamic interplay between different metabolic pathways, each playing a distinct role in cancer cell survival and functionality. Through the action of the cytosolic isocitrate dehydrogenase 1, glucose-independent acetyl-CoA generation is facilitated by the reductive metabolism of alpha-ketoglutarate derived from glutamine to activate lipid synthesis [46,47]. Extracellular acidosis increases fatty acid β-oxidation to satisfy the need for TCA metabolites [32] and enhances lipid peroxidation through ROS generation [51–53]. The interplay between extracellular acidosis, ROS generation, and lipid peroxidation underscores the intricate mechanisms through which cells respond to changes in their microenvironment. While ROS can serve as signaling molecules under physiological conditions, their excess production, as seen in the context of extracellular acidosis, can have detrimental effects on cellular health.

Metabolic reprogramming via transcription factors in the TME
p53
Aside from its role in regulating cell cycle, apoptosis, and DNA repair, p53 has been shown to reprogram metabolism by regulating the shift between oxidative phosphorylation and glycolysis through the activation of different targets based on the cellular context [54]. When cancer cells are confronted with oxidative stress as an outcome of the disproportion between ROS production and the cellular antioxidant defense mechanisms, p53 can regulate the expression of genes linked to both ROS generation and neutralization. Additionally, p53 influences genes associated with metabolic pathways. This orchestrated regulation contributes to upholding cellular redox equilibrium and curbing the undue harm induced by ROS [32,55–57]. The p53-dependent metabolic reprogramming is activated by different microenvironmental stressors such as hypoxia, acidosis, and nutrient deprivation [28,32]. It contributes to metabolic adaptation in response to extracellular acidosis by modifying glutamine metabolism, reorienting the ATP production pathway, and triggering the oxidative segment of the pentose phosphate pathway [32]. Moreover, it has been shown to be activated or stabilized in response to hypoxia and nutrient deprivation to regulate different metabolic pathways and promote cell survival [28]. In addition to its role in regulating glucose metabolism, p53 can also regulate lipid, amino acid, and iron metabolism in response to metabolic stress [58]. Consequently, mutations in p53 can play a major role in metabolic reprogramming of cancer cells to facilitate tumor progression [59,60]. Most p53 mutations in cancers occur in the DNA binding domain, resulting in the loss of the tumor suppressor function in addition to gain of oncogenic ones [60]. One way the mutant p53-driven metabolic alteration occurs is through promoting lipid anabolism by activation of the mevalonate and fatty acid synthesis pathways for tumor progression. This promotes mutant p53 stability, leading to inhibition of AMPK activation, glycolysis induction through increased glucose uptake by GLUT1 translocation, and nucleotide biosynthesis promotion [59,60].

HIFs

The heterodimeric family of transcription factors, hypoxia-inducible factors (HIFs), are the master regulators of oxygen homeostasis [20]. HIFs consist of a stable B subunit and oxygen-regulated α subunit. HIF1α has ubiquitous expression, whereas HIF2α expression is more limited to specific cell types like hepatocytes and endothelial cells [61]. HIF1α and HIF2α are the main controllers of the cellular response to hypoxic environments, while HIF3α mainly acts as an antagonist to the transcriptional activation directed by the other HIF members under hypoxia [62]. The first step in hypoxia-mediated adaptation response is the stabilization of HIF1α/HIF2α by proline hydroxylation inhibition and degradation prevention, which results in gene expression activation leading to metabolic reprogramming, cell cycle regulation, and tumorigenesis [62,63]. After stabilization, HIF1α dimerizes with HIF1β, enabling transcription activation by binding to hypoxia response elements in target genes [63].

In many cancers, the hypoxia-driven activation of HIF1 has been well established to alter glucose metabolism, shifting to glycolysis by regulating glucose transporters and glycolytic enzymes as discussed previously [63]. This switch was previously thought to be mainly for ATP level maintenance; however, it was suggested to be for the control of ROS levels produced [63]. HIF1 also decreases mitochondrial respiration by impairing ETC I assembly through miR-210 expression [63]. HIF1 is regulated by the interplay between redox and oxygen sensing; in normoxic conditions, SIRT1 inhibits HIF1 signaling by deacetylation, and this repression is reverted by SIRT1 inhibition due to NAD+ depletion [64]. HIF1α can also alter lipid metabolism by regulating de novo FA biosynthesis [65].

HIF2α shifts glucose metabolism to reductive glutamine metabolism to promote lipogenesis [46]. This could be occurring due to c-Myc activity enhancement by HIF2α, which was shown to upregulate mitochondrial glutaminase, leading to glutamine catabolism upregulation [66,67]. Under chronic acidic conditions, HIF1α and HIF2α transcriptional activity is regulated through deacetylation driven by the deacetylase SIRT1, in which only HIF2α is activated to drive the shift from glucose metabolism to that of glutamine [50]. This activation was also reported in hypoxic environments [68].

NF-κB

The nuclear factor kappa light chain-enhancer of activated B cells (NF-κB) is a transcription factor that plays an important role in oxidative stress cellular response and is involved in regulating several cellular processes associated with cancer progression [69]. NF-κB comprises five different subunits (p50, p52, RelA, RelB, and c-Rel). Hypoxia activates NF-κB through the induction of the inhibitor of nuclear factor-κB (IκB) kinases (IKK) that regulate it [69]. For transcriptional activation, NF-κB only requires homo/heterodimerization of two subunits only [69]. It plays a role in regulating glycolysis, leading to GLUT3 upregulation [70], and blocks mitochondrial oxidative phosphorylation in p53-deficient settings [71]. In metabolic adaptations to nutrient deprivation, NF-κB can alter glycolysis, glutaminolysis, oxidative phosphorylation, and other metabolic pathways [72]. Glucose-depleted conditions in glioblastoma result in glutamate conversion to α-ketoglutarate by glutamate dehydrogenase 1 from the glutaminolysis pathway [73]. α-KG can then activate IKKβ and NF-κB signaling to upregulate GLUT1 and promote glucose uptake, which further supports gliomagenesis [73]. In colorectal cancer, NF-κB enhances triacylglycerol catabolism in response to nutrient deprivation; it activates this pathway by regulating the lipase carboxylesterase1, resulting in endogenous free fatty acids mobilization from lipid droplets and fueling fatty acid oxidation and oxidative phosphorylation for energy production [72]. Starvation-induced oxidative stress also activates NF-κB, which induces a quiescence program in prostate cancer as a protective measure [29]. ROS can modulate NF-κB activity by targeting upstream kinases like IKK and Akt that dictate the dissociation from its negative regulator and its consequent nuclear translocation [74].

ROS and redox signaling in a harsh TME

ROS are byproducts of normal physiological processes [75]. They are a collection of oxygen derivatives that are highly reactive and unstable [75]. ROS generation is dependent on endogenous (mainly mitochondria) and exogenous factors (air pollutants and radiation) [76]. Reprogrammed metabolism as in the case of WE phenomenon can generate high intracellular ROS levels, possibly from increased respiration and also elevated amounts of protons [55,75]. ROS can interact with different cellular components to induce oxidative stress (lipids and DNA), proliferation, and apoptosis-related signaling pathways (proteins) and can cause activity changes in enzymes and transcription factors [55]. The produced species include hydrogen peroxide, superoxide anion, hypochlorous acid, singlet oxygen, and hydroxyl radical [75].

In various cancers, ROS has opposing roles based on the levels being produced. At low to moderate levels, ROS plays a role in signal transduction for cancer cell survival and aggressiveness [76]. However, high levels can cause cell toxicity and DNA damage-induced cell death [76]. To counteract the apoptotic effects of high intracellular ROS, cancer cells induce the transcription of antioxidant enzymes mainly through the transcription factor NRF2 [76]. One of the transcription factors that ROS induces is HIF1α in response to hypoxia; ROS also stabilizes HIF1α by preventing its degradation, resulting in the activation of angiogenesis factors and further promoting WE phenotype leading to cancer progression and invasion [55,77,78]. The produced ROS can cause mitochondrial DNA mutations, possibly leading to alterations in electron transport chain-related genes and consequently modifying ATP production [55].

Extracellular acidosis can induce mitochondrial ROS generation in which cancer cells adapt by shifting to the oxidative branch of the pentose phosphate pathway and inducing G6PD expression for NADPH generation and ROS neutralization [32,79]. This causes oxidative stress and DNA-double strand breaks that can contribute to genomic instability [80]. Similar to the ischemia/reperfusion model, which involves tissue acidosis and reducing equivalents buildup when blood supply is restricted, accompanied by ROS generation surges when blood flow is restored, there is spatial heterogeneity in oxygen tension in TME due to blood flow fluctuations [18]. This variation could similarly result in surges in ROS production in the tumor [18].

As with other TME conditions, nutrient deprivation in tumors results in oxidative stress due to the increased ROS production that primes cancer cells to adapt to the resulting stress and shift to a quiescent state [29]. In such conditions, autophagy is triggered as a protection response to prevent cell death [81]. Glucose deprivation increases ROS levels, leading to AMPk activation and promotion of catabolic pathways [82].

In summary, TME in solid tumors plays a pivotal role in reprogramming cellular metabolism, contributing significantly to cancer progression. The shift from hyperplasia to full tumor formation creates distinct microenvironmental conditions, including hypoxia, acidosis, and nutrient deprivation, driven by rapid cell proliferation and altered vasculature. These conditions foster metabolic rewiring, favoring the survival of adaptable cancer cell clones within this challenging ecosystem. The abnormal tumor microcirculation, characterized by limited vasculature and variously functioning new vasculature, further exacerbates hostile conditions like oxygen depletion, extracellular acidosis, high lactate levels, and fluctuating nutrient availability. We discussed some of the molecular mechanisms that cancer cells exploit to adapt to these novel variable conditions, such as HIF1 activation in response to hypoxia, which orchestrates metabolic changes such as increased glycolysis and altered glucose transporters, impacting glucose metabolism. HIF1 also influences pyruvate dehydrogenase kinase, leading to a shift away from oxidative phosphorylation and potentially affecting fatty acid synthesis and protein acetylation or activation of mTOR signaling complexes to enhance cancer cell survival under nutrient deprivation. This acidic microenvironment can be the ultimate side product of both hypoxia and nutrient deprivation through the WE and is toxic for the cells. Adaptation to acidic TME can be triggered through cellular adaptations, including alterations in amino acid and lipid metabolism. Transcription factors like p53, HIFs, and NF-κB play pivotal roles in mediating metabolic reprogramming within the acidic TME. Additionally, ROS generated during reprogrammed metabolism can influence cell survival, aggressiveness, and genomic stability. Collectively, the intricate interplay between microenvironment-induced metabolic changes, transcription factors, and ROS contributes to the complex landscape of cancer cell adaptation and progression in solid tumors.

Epigenetic and metabolic crosstalk in TME

The term epigenetics was first coined in 1942 by Conrad Waddington [83], and it's derived from the Greek word "epi" meaning over or on top of. It has been used to explain the emergence of phenotypes that can't be explained solely through genetic factors. Until recently, the role of epigenetic modifications in metabolic reprogramming and driving tumor progression has been recognized in several cancers [5]. As we discussed above, dynamic TME conditions can exert selection pressures on cancer cells, leading to the survival of the fittest clones that are undergoing metabolic changes. Epigenetic-driven adaptation is partly through heritable DNA modifications like DNA methylation and nonheritable modifications like chromatin accessibility alterations and noncoding RNA regulation, which are the main parts of these evolutionary adaptations that we will be discussing below.

DNA methylation

DNA methylation is a major epigenetic modification involved in regulating gene expression [84]. It consists of the transfer of a methyl group by the DNA methyltransferase (DNMT) enzyme family to the 5′ carbon position of the base cytosine in CpG islands, where DNMT1 is involved in the maintenance of DNA methylation during replication. Alternatively, DNMT3A, DNMT3B, and DNMT3L catalyze de novo DNA methylation [85,86]. DNA methylation patterns are significantly altered during cancer initiation and progression, leading to changes in major cellular pathways and metabolic reprogramming that rewires cancer cells and modifies their metabolome [5]. In many cancers, tumor suppressor genes like CDKN2A, MLH1, BRCA1, and VHL are primarily silenced through CpG island promoter hypermethylation [5]. This effect is mediated by hypoxic conditions that deregulate the activity of TET enzymes [87]. Consequently, methylation silencing of BRCA1 in breast cancer and VHL in clear cell renal cell carcinoma alters tumor cell metabolism by increasing glycolysis [88,89]. HIF1α stabilization increases the expression of the 5-methylcytosine (5mC) oxidases TET1/3 (ten-eleven translocation proteins 1/3). In three consecutive oxidation reactions, TET1/3 converts 5mC into 5-hydroxymethylcytosine (5hmC), 5-formylcytosine (5fC), and 5-carboxylcytosine (5caC), resulting in the removal of the methyl group and inhibition of its repressive effect [4]. Hypoxia-induced HIF1α alters DNA methylation status in neuroblastoma [90], which was shown to be TET1 driven, resulting in transcription activation of hypoxia response genes [91]. Hypoxia was shown to negatively affect TET enzyme activity, which resulted in hypermethylation in gene promoters and enhancers [87]. DNA hypomethylation affects glucose metabolism in liver cancer and glioblastoma multiforme by increasing the expression of the glycolytic enzyme hexokinase 2, which promotes glycolysis [92,93]. Recent studies have shown that diet effect on TME can also have effects on DNA methylation patterns [94]. Chronic acidosis in a colorectal cancer cell line showed expression changes related to DNA methylation [95]. However, direct effects of DNA methylation changes corresponding to TME acidosis and the correlation with metabolic reprogramming are not well studied and need more attention.

RNA methylation

Several chemical RNA modifications exist that play a role in different cellular processes. More attention has been paid to their role in tumor progression because of their regulatory function in vital biological pathways and the new evidence showing

RNA epigenetic pathway dysregulation controlled by RNA modification writers, erasers, and readers in cancer [96,97]. Several RNA modifications can alter RNA metabolism by modifying stability and splicing. The most common and well-studied modification is N^6-methyladenosine (m^6A), which involves adenosine methylation on position 6 and is catalyzed by the Methyltransferase-like (METTL) family of enzymes involved in RNA methylation. This modification is mainly found in mRNAs, long intergenic ncRNAs, primary miRNAs, and rRNAs [97]. m^6A mRNA plays a role in cancer cell metabolic reprogramming based on what target it's regulating. This could be through a direct regulation of metabolic enzymes and transporters in glucose, lipid, and glutamine metabolism, as shown in several cancers [98]. It can also alter metabolism indirectly by regulating oncogenes and metabolic signaling pathways [98]. In hypoxic environments, m^6A has different responses in different cancers. Global m^6A epitranscriptome reprogramming was noted in hepatocellular carcinoma under hypoxia that alters metabolism as a response, and m^6A mRNA demethylation was shown to be important in maintaining ATP levels under such stress [99]. In hepatocellular carcinoma, HIF1α induces the expression of an m^6A reader to upregulate autophagy-related genes as a hypoxic protective response [100]. In pancreatic cancer, hypoxia activates the demethylase ALKBH5 to decrease m^6A mRNAs, which promotes a glycolytic shift [101].

Chromatin modifications

Alterations in chromatin states (open vs closed chromatin) regulate gene transcription through changes in accessibility to transcription factors for transcriptional activation, which happens mainly through histone modifications and chromatin remodeling. Writer proteins add chemical marks on histones that reader proteins can recognize and can undergo specific modifications [102]. This primarily occurs through various histone modifications like methylation, acetylation, and phosphorylation catalyzed by different families of histone-modifying enzymes [103]. Such marks can be recognized by eraser proteins that can remove these modifications [102]. These modifications alter chromatin states differently and lead to regulation of transcription [102].

Chromatin remodeling

Perturbations in chromatin states occurring in cancers can be due to cancer cell metabolic changes, consequently altering gene expression [104]. It is widely known that several metabolites from metabolic pathways are cofactors for histone-modifying enzymes, which results in rapid and reversible changes in gene expression for metabolic adaptation [105]. Chromatin remodelers can also alter energy metabolism through ATP-dependent modifications of DNA-histone interactions and nucleosome composition [105]. In the WE-dependent cancer cells of clear cell renal cell carcinoma, mutations occur in the tumor suppressor gene VHL and the PBAF chromatin remodeling complex subunit PBRM1 in almost half of the cases [105]. This was shown to deregulate genes involved in the oxidative phosphorylation pathway

[105]. Although the INO80 remodeler complex has several oncogenic roles in cancers like proliferation and anchorage-independent growth, it could have metabolic reprogramming functions that were implied in yeast studies, which gives the possibility of happening in cancers indirectly [105]. Recently, chronic acidosis in a colorectal cancer cell line led to alterations in chromatin accessibility, which enhances tumor progression and metastasis [95].

Histone methylation

Histone methylation involves the addition of a methyl group to the basic residues arginine, lysine, and histidine of histones where 1–3 methyl groups can be added [106]. It has direct effects on gene expression patterns, chromatin compaction, and nucleosome dynamics and has the slowest turnover among all histone PTMs [106]. Though it was previously thought to be stable and irreversible, it was later shown that it can be dynamic, depending on the environmental cues [106]. Histone methylation can have both activating (H3K4me2/3) and repressing effects (H3K27me), depending on the site of methylation [107]. Various solid tumors show overexpression of different family members of the histone lysine demethylases KDMs that can regulate the metabolic shift to glycolysis [5]. MLH1 inactivation in colon cancer in response to hypoxia occurs through the action of the histone demethylase LSD1, and this epigenetic-induced silencing persists even after reverting to normoxic conditions [108]. Histone lysine demethylation enhances glycolysis by HIF1α coactivation in bladder cancer, which occurs through the recruitment of the demethylase JMJD1A to promoter regions of glycolytic genes; this demethylates H3K9me2 and activates the glycolytic pathway [109]. HIF1α coactivation by another demethylase, JMJD2C, promotes glycolysis and lung metastasis in breast cancer [110]. The demethylase (LSD1/KDM1A) was suggested to maintain glycolysis, inhibit mitochondrial metabolism, and alter fatty acid oxidation in hepatocellular carcinoma [111]. Similar effects on glycolysis and mitochondrial metabolism were noted in esophageal cancer [112]. Hypoxia-mediated HIF1α induction activates the demethylase JMJD2B [113,114], which is overexpressed in ER+ breast cancer and bladder cancer [115,116]. In turn, JMJD2B activation regulates the expression of cyclin-dependent kinase 6 (CDK6) and carbonic anhydrase 9 (CA9) to promote carcinogenesis [4]. In glutamine-deprived conditions, histone hypermethylation on H3K27 occurs due to the decrease in the histone demethylase cofactor (α-ketoglutarate), which renders melanoma cell line resistant to BRAF inhibitor treatment [117].

Histone acetylation

Acetylation is a reversible PTM of histones that is catalyzed by a family of histone acetyltransferases (HATs) on lysine residues. This modification is reverted through the action of histone deacetylases (HDACs) [107]. Acetylation alters chromatin structure to activate transcription by disrupting the interaction between histone tails and nucleosomal DNA [107].

Extracellular acidosis increases the activity of Sirtuin (SIRT) family of HDACs [4], which is accompanied by global histone deacetylation [50,118] and was suggested that this functions as a regulatory mechanism to modulate pHi for cellular survival; moreover, it was also reported to occur under acute starvation [118]. The histone deacetylation driven by an increase in NAD+ SIRT1-dependent activity increases HIF2α, which promotes reductive glutamine metabolism. This led to a decrease in HIF1α expression, causing the inhibition of glycolysis [50]. Chronic acidosis-mediated histone deacetylation, driven by SIRT1 and SIRT6, induces fatty acid metabolism [119].

Histone lactylation

The WE, as also the main route of lactate production in cancer, is connected to various cellular processes like angiogenesis, hypoxia, macrophage polarization, and T cell activation. Lactate, derived from pyruvate in tumor cells, is recognized as an energy source and byproduct. However, its nonmetabolic roles in physiology and disease are unclear. Recent research revealed lactate-driven histone lysine lactylation as an epigenetic change that directly boosts chromatin-based gene transcription [120]. They pinpointed 28 lactylation sites on core histones in human and mouse cells. Hypoxia and bacterial exposure trigger glycolysis-produced lactate, acting as a precursor for histone lactylation. In a model using M1 macrophages exposed to bacteria, it is demonstrated that distinct temporal dynamics of histone lactylation can be compared to acetylation [120]. During the later phase of M1 macrophage polarization, heightened histone lactylation prompts homeostatic genes like Arg1 linked to wound healing. These findings proposed an inherent "lactate clock" in bacterially challenged M1 macrophages that activate gene expression to foster homeostasis, suggesting histone lactylation and its role in cancer [120].

Noncoding RNA

Noncoding RNAs are functional RNA molecules that have major regulatory roles without being translated into functional proteins. Of those implicated in altering cancer evolution trajectory are long noncoding RNAs (lncRNAs) and short noncoding RNAs like microRNAs (miRNAs) [121]. Noncoding RNAs can act as tumor suppressors or oncogenes depending on the context and their targets that we will discuss here.

lncRNA

Cytoplasmic lncRNA has been shown to regulate signaling pathways that alter metabolism in cancer cells in response to the changes of TME [54,122–124]. Hypoxia triggers NF-kB Ca^{2+}-dependent signaling pathway activation due to increased cytosolic Ca^{2+} through activation of the kinase PCNK by the lncRNA CamK-A [123]. Tumor energy metabolic uptake, glycolysis, and TME remodeling are increased because of this activation [123]. Several studies have shown the major role of lncRNAs in regulating glucose metabolism in cancer [125]. In TNBC, HIF1α is stabilized, and the normoxic HIF1α signaling pathway is thus activated by the lncRNA LINK-A, which could have implications for metabolic alterations [124]. HIFAL, a HIF1α antisense lncRNA, promotes glycolysis through its regulatory role in HIF1α-driven transactivation in breast cancer [126]. BCAR4 expression, another lncRNA implicated in metabolic changes promoting breast cancer progression, was shown to be controlled by YAP, leading to activation of the Hedgehog signaling pathway and upregulation of the glycolytic enzymes HK2 and PFKFB3 [127]. The interaction between HIF1α and VHL is disrupted by the hypoxia-induced lincRNA-p21 (large intergenic ncRNA, a subclass of lncRNAs) to enhance glycolysis [128]. LncRNAs can also alter metabolism through translational repression or mRNA degradation of specific factors by acting as sponges for miRNAs and preventing their targeted gene silencing [125]. The lncRNA H19 alters glucose metabolism by targeting miR-let-7, which reduces glucose uptake and influences PKM2 overexpression [125]. H19 can also target miR-519D-3p to activate LDHA signaling [125]. Starvation conditions in tumors can regulate certain lncRNAs to activate different stress responses. Glucose deprivation can activate HOXC-AS3, leading to a metabolic switch [129]. Glutamine deprivation deregulates lncRNA GLS-AS, which normally inhibits glutaminase expression posttranscriptionally, through Myc induction to promote glutamine hydrolysis and provide TCA cycle precursors [130]. LncRIM promotes breast cancer progression by regulating the HIPPO-YAP signaling pathway and reprogramming iron metabolism [122]. This occurs by cytoplasmic localization of lncRIM and direct disruption of the interaction of the tumor suppressor NF2 and the kinase LATS1 [122]. Lipid metabolism was shown to be altered to maintain stemness in breast cancer by the lncRNA RPOM [131] or by MALAT1 for tumor growth in liver cancer [132]. Amino acid metabolism was also shown to be partly regulated by different lncRNAs to promote malignancy [125].

miRNA

miRNAs have also been shown to play a role in metabolic reprogramming during cancer progression. In several cancers, glucose metabolism can be altered at different points in the pathway by several miRNAs [133]. Hexokinase II, the glycolytic enzyme initiating the first step in glycolysis, can be negatively regulated by miR143, as shown in different cancers [134–137]. In a study done in breast cancer cell lines, miR200 loss showed an association with EMT and phosphoglucose isomerase upregulation, which increases NF-κB binding ability to promote the transition to a mesenchymal phenotype [138]. miR135 regulates another glycolytic enzyme, phosphofructokinase 1, which leads to aerobic glycolysis inhibition as an adaptation mechanism to glutamine deprivation [139]. The microRNAs miR-133a, miR-133b, miR326, and miR-122 were shown to regulate pyruvate kinase M2, which is upregulated in many cancers due to the downregulation of these miRNAs [140–142]. miR145 can suppress the WE by negatively regulating the KLF4/PTBP1/PKMs pathway in bladder cancer, impeding cancer cell growth [143]. Various miRNAs have also been shown to increase glucose uptake to compensate for the low ATP levels due to increased glycolysis in several cancers [54].

miRNAs were also implicated in amino acid and lipid metabolism regulation. In glutaminolysis, miR-23a/b regulates glutaminase to alter glutamine catabolism [67]. Glutaminase is also regulated by another miRNA (miR203) in temozolomide-resistant melanoma cells that are glutamine dependent [144]. The serine glycine one carbon pathway can also be altered by miRNA levels where miR193b, miR-198, and miR340 regulate serine hydroxymethyltransferase 2, serine hydroxymethyltransferase 1, and phosphoserine aminotransferase, respectively [133]. As previously discussed, lipid metabolism can be altered to promote cancer cell survival in harsh conditions. Cancer lipid homeostasis can be regulated by miR-122, miR-33, miR-27a/27b, miR-34a, miR-21, and miR-378 through different mechanisms [133]. In breast cancer, PPAR coactivator 1-alpha is inversely regulated by miR-217 [145]. Fatty acid oxidation is promoted for cancer progression by downregulation of miRNA-328-3p in breast cancer [146] and microRNA-377-3p in hepatocellular carcinoma [147].

The TME stressors that we discussed extensively can alter miRNA expression, and the effect and response differ among different cancers. Several miRNAs were shown to be regulated by hypoxia through HIF dependent and independent pathways in different cancers [148–151]. Extracellular acidosis and nutrient deprivation were also shown to have an effect on miRNA levels to target different pathways for cancer cell survival [139,152–156]. Many of the altered miRNAs in response to TME stressors can also play a role in metabolic reprogramming, as we explained above, which aids in tumor progression and aggressiveness.

Metabolic plasticity

As discussed in this section, several modifications at the epigenome level can occur to facilitate tumor adaptation to the harsh microenvironment, which leads to extensive metabolic reprogramming. Conversely, cellular metabolism can alter the epigenetic state of cancer cells mainly through the metabolites generated in different pathways (Fig. 2) [5]. This reciprocal interaction is one of the levels of plasticity that cancer cells acquire that makes them more aggressive (metabolic plasticity). Cancer cells need access to a variety of nutrient sources and alternative metabolic pathways to survive the different stressors through metabolic rewiring. It has been shown that several metabolites alter the epigenome through expression regulation, substrate inhibition, or acting as cofactors for epigenetic-modifying enzymes [5]. In the case of DNA/histone methylation, SAM/SAH ratio determines methylation status, where its increase leads to tumor suppressor hypermethylation and silencing, whereas the ratio decrease leads to oncogene promoter hypomethylation [5]. LSD1-driven histone methylation requires cofactor FAD+ reduction to FADH2 [5]. In terms of histone acetylation, one of the major metabolites that regulates it is acetyl-CoA as it supplies the acetyl group for histone acetylation [5]. However, acetyl-CoA levels are largely dependent on nutrient availability, which fluctuates in cancers [5]. Mutations in TCA cycle-associated enzymes lead to their abnormal production and consequently affect epigenetic modifications. An example of this is IDH1/2 mutations that favor 2-hydroxyglutarate synthesis due to the prevention of α-KG to isocitrate conversion [5]. 2-Hydroxyglutarate has been shown to inhibit DNA/histone methylation by

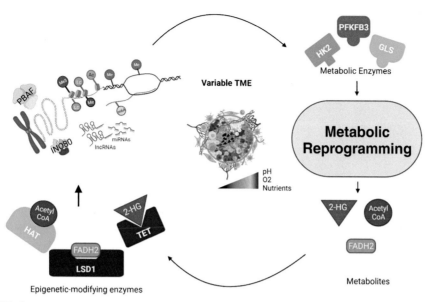

FIG. 2

Interplay between epigenetics and metabolism. Different epigenetic modifications under the influence of variable microenvironmental conditions can lead to metabolic reprogramming by altering chromatin accessibility and repression/activation marks for regulating metabolic factors. This produces different metabolites that can serve as cofactors or antagonists for epigenetic modifying enzymes, enabling epigenetic modifications. This interplay between epigenetic modifications and metabolism under the harsh TME is termed as metabolic plasticity.

Created with BioRender.com.

inhibiting TET and JmjC activity through its action as a competitive inhibitor of α-KG [5]. As a result of this bidirectional regulation of metabolism and epigenetics in cancer, a four-way crosstalk was suggested. (i) Cofactors for epigenetic modifying enzymes could have their levels altered by metabolic reprogramming. (ii) Mutations or metabolite level changes can provide oncometabolites, cofactors, and antagonists that can positively or negatively affect epigenetic enzymes, which shifts the epigenetic landscape. (iii) Conversely, epigenetic modifications can alter metabolic enzyme levels to alter metabolism. And (iv) this affects epigenetic modification status and signaling pathways that rewires cancer cells for adaptation [157].

Epigenetic modifications in shaping the TME

Waddington proposed the epigenetic landscape model to explain how the environment leads to the selection of certain phenotypes and cell states beyond genetic control [83]. Similarly, the variable microenvironmental stressors in TME can lead to

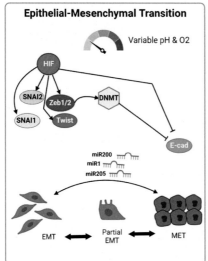
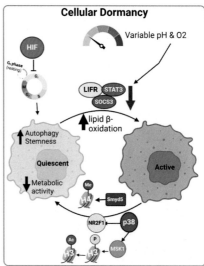

FIG. 3

Phenotypic plasticity under variable TME influence. The epigenetic state of cancer cells is remodeled when exposed to harsh metabolic conditions. As an adaption mechanism, cancer cells change their phenotype to enable their survival under the microenvironmental stressors. Phenotypes like EMT/MET and quiescence/active are not terminal, and cancer cells can switch bidirectionally to promote tumor progression.

Created with BioRender.com.

various epigenetic alterations that shift cell states or give rise to different phenotypes, making cancer cells more plastic to respond to a constantly changing niche (Fig. 3).

Epithelial-mesenchymal plasticity

Epithelial-mesenchymal transition (EMT) is a cellular reprogramming process that is essential for embryonic development and tissue repair [158]. However, in cancer, EMT has been implicated in facilitating tumor progression through invasion and metastasis. In the transition, there is a loss of cell-cell adhesion, abnormal apical-basal polarity, and cytoskeletal reorganization leading to the gain of mesenchymal characteristics like invasiveness and motility [159]. The transition to a mesenchymal phenotype can be regulated by several transcription factors and, more importantly, through noncoding RNAs and different epigenetic modifications [158]. Different sets of transcription factors stabilize the epithelial or mesenchymal states of cells: SNAI1, SNAI2, Zeb1/2, and Twist [160]. Cancer cells mostly undergo partial EMT, which enables them to spread and metastasize at distinct sites. This partial state transition facilitates cancer cell plasticity and contributes to tumor aggressiveness [161]. Consequently, cancer cells express markers of both states, and the level of each state-specific marker is regulated to switch to the required phenotype. This partial state allows cancer cells to revert back to an epithelial state to establish secondary tumors in suitable environments [162].

Extracellular acidosis and hypoxia have been shown to promote EMT due to morphological changes and EMT marker expression [163,164]. Hypoxia activates different signaling networks and transcription factors that promote the mesenchymal transition. This is mainly through hypoxia-driven HIF activation, which upregulates EMT transcription factors like SNAI1/2 and ZEB [164,165]. In colorectal cancer, HIF1 indirectly suppresses miR-200b to induce EMT, and the same miRNA can regulate HIF1 for MET reversion [165]. HIFs can also modulate signaling pathways for EMT promotion [165]. This was shown by HIF-mediated TGFα upregulation in lung cancer [166]. HIF1α also results in E-cadherin loss and TWIST activation, favoring EMT and enhancing tissue invasion [167].

The epigenome can play a vital role in regulating the transition between the two phenotypes, enabling their phenotypic plasticity [158]. Several miRNAs regulate the bidirectional transition between both phenotypes by regulating EMT transcription factor expression. Double negative feedback loops between miRNAs and EMT transcription factors exist to modulate the transitory state that cancer cells are shifting to, as in the case of miR-200 family/miR-205 and Zeb1/2 in addition to miR-200/miR1 and SNAI2 [158]. DNA methylation changes have also been shown to be one of the important regulators of EMT. Common among several cancers is the promoter methylation of CDH1, which inhibits the expression of one of the epithelial markers, E-cadherin [158]. Its methylation status has been shown to be controlled by ZEB1 through the recruitment of DNA methyltransferases [158]. In addition, specific histone methylation sites can be enhanced by lysine-specific demethylase-1 like H3K4me3 euchromatic and H3K36me3 transcription elongation marks for promoting cell migration in EMT [158].

Cancer cell dormancy

Cancer cells can enter a dormant state that has been found to occur early in the course of tumor formation. It's the main reason why metastasis occurs after long remission periods [165]. Dormant cancer cells can experience cell cycle arrest, low metabolic activity, and proliferation cessation to maintain a quiescent state [165]. The transition to a dormant state helps cancer cells survive harmful events from TME conditions, immune cell attacks, and therapy [165]. Hypoxia-induced HIF activation has been linked to cancer cell dormancy as its early response is cell cycle arrest [165]. Hypoxia-mediated dormancy occurs through different mechanisms in various cancer types. Cyclic hypoxia in breast cancer cells resulted in their survival in successive chronic hypoxia, leading to a G0/G1 arrest and entering a dormant state; such cells showed stem cell marker expression and increased autophagy, which was proposed to be a survival mechanism under such microenvironmental stress [168]. In pancreatic and colorectal cancer cell lines, a dormant state after chronic hypoxia results in metabolic suppression characterized by reduced ATP turnover and decreased Akt activity [169]. This state transition allowed the patient-derived colorectal cancer cell line to acquire a chemoresistant phenotype [169]. Primary lung cancer cells with mutated EGFR shift to dormancy in hypoxia despite constant EGFR activation, and this is facilitated by ERBB family RTK dimerization prevention; the altered heterodimer formation was mainly driven by MIG6 and was proposed to contribute to EGFR tyrosine kinase inhibitor resistance [169]. Hypoxia influences the fate of disseminated tumor cells in HNSCC and breast cancer by enabling a dormant state at metastatic sites, leading to chemotherapy resistance [170]. Despite the evidence showing hypoxia and HIF signaling playing a major role in dormancy, hypoxia can also activate the dormant disseminated tumor cells at metastatic sites in a HIF-independent manner [165]. Hypoxia downregulates the dormancy promoting LIFR/STAT3/SOCS3 signaling pathway in breast cancer and consequently activates dormant disseminated cells in the bone, leading to bone metastasis [171].

Though little is known about the metabolic status of dormant cancer cells, lipid metabolism has been suggested to be a facilitator of cancer dormancy escape despite the known fact that dormant cells slow their metabolic rate [172]. High expression of CD36, a fatty acid translocase, was found in metastatic human oral cancer cells and prostate cancer cells. This promotes lipid β-oxidation for efficient energy production that drives metastatic tumor growth [172].

Epigenetics can play an important role in dormancy transition and reactivation of cancer cells [173]. As recent studies have shown, disseminated cancer cells disperse at an early stage from their initial primary tumor site and show limited genomic divergence in metastatic sites [174–176]. This phenotypic plasticity allows the disseminated cancer cells to establish secondary tumors when the environment is suitable [173]. The stress-activated kinase p38 is one of the major players in tumor cell dormancy induction and was suggested to regulate a transcription factor network [177]. Of the transcription factors it was found to regulate was NR2F1, which is normally silenced by promoter hypermethylation in proliferative cancer cells [178]. NR2F1 activation was shown to induce a global repressive chromatin state by altering H3 PTMs that lead to quiescence and cell lineage commitment [178]. Screening using mouse models suggested that lung-disseminated breast cancer cells enter dormancy partially by the histone methyltransferase Smyd5, which is known to methylate H4 [179]. In ER+ breast cancer, the downstream p38 target MSK1 regulates promoter chromatin status of luminal cell differentiation genes by H3 phosphorylation at distinct sites, enabling H3 acetylation and dormancy maintenance [180]. Alternative splicing has also been implicated to facilitate dormancy transition. The inhibitor of differentiation Id1b isoform induces a G0/G1 cell cycle arrest with up-regulation of stemness markers, causing a quiescent state with self-renewal [181]. In hypoxic environments, the unfolded protein response (UPR) is activated by the X-box binding protein 1 isoform sXBP-1 to enhance dormant tumor cell stress tolerance and survival [173].

Intratumor heterogeneity leading to phenotypic variation

Tumor cell heterogeneity adds another level of complexity to their response to the variable TME. Tumor cells often exhibit a high degree of phenotypic and functional diversity, commonly referred to as intra-tumor heterogeneity. This heterogeneity arises due to genetic mutations, epigenetic modifications, microenvironmental influences, and the plasticity of cancer cells themselves. Some research proposed the presence of cancer stem cells and their differentiation into nontumorigenic progeny to further contribute to tumor cell diversity [182]. However, the precise prevalence of the stem-cell model in different cancers and its explanatory power for clinical behaviors remain uncertain and questionable. Advancements in techniques like lineage tracing and high-resolution deep sequencing offer potential insights into the validity of the cancer stem-cell model in the future. It's becoming increasingly clear that a single cancer cell's genome has the capacity to generate various phenotypic states, enabling cancer cells to transition between these states even without making significant alterations to their genomic makeup [183]. This notion underscores the significance of nongenetic factors and cellular plasticity in shaping the behavior of cancer cells and their responses to their constantly varying TME, challenging the traditional perspective that tumor evolution is primarily driven by genetic mutations. Fluctuating TME can impose stronger selective pressures on tumor cells, selecting certain cells with higher fitness to survive and thrive in these variable tumor-specific microenvironmental niches, leading to aggressive clonal domination across all the clones in a tumor population. These clones have distinct metabolic profiles, signaling pathways, and harsh TME resistance mechanisms with the flexibility to respond quickly to emerging changes. The ability of tumor cells to switch between different states or phenotypes in response to external cues is defined as phenotypic plasticity, allowing cancer cells to adapt to changing conditions. The heterogeneity in response can be defined as the plasticity of the population itself that can affect the tumor evolution intensively [184].

References

[1] D. Hanahan, R.A. Weinberg, The hallmarks of cancer, Cell 100 (1) (2000) 57–70.

[2] D. Hanahan, R.A. Weinberg, Hallmarks of cancer: the next generation, Cell 144 (5) (2011) 646–674.

[3] D. Hanahan, Hallmarks of cancer: new dimensions, Cancer Discov. 12 (1) (2022) 31–46.

[4] B. Ordway, et al., Causes and consequences of variable tumor cell metabolism on heritable modifications and tumor evolution, Front. Oncol. 10 (2020) 373.

[5] V. Miranda-Goncalves, et al., Metabolism and epigenetic interplay in cancer: regulation and putative therapeutic targets, Front. Genet. 9 (2018) 427.

[6] B. Arneth, Tumor microenvironment, Medicina (Kaunas) 56 (2019) 1.

[7] J.P. Etchegaray, R. Mostoslavsky, Interplay between metabolism and epigenetics: a nuclear adaptation to environmental changes, Mol. Cell 62 (5) (2016) 695–711.

[8] J. Winkler, et al., Concepts of extracellular matrix remodelling in tumour progression and metastasis, Nat. Commun. 11 (1) (2020) 5120.

[9] S. Cassim, J. Pouyssegur, Tumor microenvironment: a metabolic player that shapes the immune response, Int. J. Mol. Sci. 21 (1) (2019) 157.

[10] J. Li, et al., Targeting metabolism in cancer cells and the tumour microenvironment for cancer therapy, Molecules 25 (20) (2020) 4831.

[11] S.M. Fendt, C. Frezza, A. Erez, Targeting metabolic plasticity and flexibility dynamics for cancer therapy, Cancer Discov. 10 (12) (2020) 1797–1807.

[12] M. Damaghi, et al., The harsh microenvironment in early breast cancer selects for a Warburg phenotype, Proc. Natl. Acad. Sci. USA 118 (3) (2021) e2011342118.

[13] T. Soga, Cancer metabolism: key players in metabolic reprogramming, Cancer Sci. 104 (3) (2013) 275–281.

[14] M. Damaghi, J.W. Wojtkowiak, R.J. Gillies, pH sensing and regulation in cancer, Front. Physiol. 4 (2013) 370.

[15] P. Vaupel, Tumor microenvironmental physiology and its implications for radiation oncology, Semin. Radiat. Oncol. 14 (3) (2004) 198–206.

[16] M. Stubbs, et al., Causes and consequences of tumour acidity and implications for treatment, Mol. Med. Today 6 (1) (2000) 15–19.

[17] P. Vaupel, M. Hockel, Blood supply, oxygenation status and metabolic micromilieu of breast cancers: characterization and therapeutic relevance, Int. J. Oncol. 17 (5) (2000) 869–879.

[18] V.V. Khramtsov, R.J. Gillies, Janus-faced tumor microenvironment and redox, Antioxid. Redox Signal. 21 (5) (2014) 723–729.

[19] W. Al Tameemi, et al., Hypoxia-modified cancer cell metabolism, Front. Cell Dev. Biol. 7 (2019) 4.

[20] J. Pouyssegur, F. Dayan, N.M. Mazure, Hypoxia signalling in cancer and approaches to enforce tumour regression, Nature 441 (7092) (2006) 437–443.

[21] Z. Wu, et al., OMA1 reprograms metabolism under hypoxia to promote colorectal cancer development, EMBO Rep. 22 (1) (2021) e50827.

[22] A.A. Tirpe, et al., Hypoxia: overview on hypoxia-mediated mechanisms with a focus on the role of HIF genes, Int. J. Mol. Sci. 20 (24) (2019) 6140.

[23] Y.M. Woo, et al., Inhibition of aerobic glycolysis represses Akt/mTOR/HIF-1alpha axis and restores tamoxifen sensitivity in antiestrogen-resistant breast cancer cells, PLoS One 10 (7) (2015) e0132285.

[24] D. Wang, et al., Cisplatin-resistant NSCLC cells induced by hypoxia transmit resistance to sensitive cells through exosomal PKM2, Theranostics 11 (6) (2021) 2860–2875.

[25] Q. Hua, et al., Hypoxia-induced lncRNA-AC020978 promotes proliferation and glycolytic metabolism of non-small cell lung cancer by regulating PKM2/HIF-1alpha axis, Theranostics 10 (11) (2020) 4762–4778.

[26] R.A. Cairns, et al., Metabolic targeting of hypoxia and HIF1 in solid tumors can enhance cytotoxic chemotherapy, Proc. Natl. Acad. Sci. USA 104 (22) (2007) 9445–9450.

[27] M. Harachi, et al., mTOR complexes as a nutrient sensor for driving cancer progression, Int. J. Mol. Sci. 19 (10) (2018) 3267.

[28] K.H. Vousden, K.M. Ryan, p53 and metabolism, Nat. Rev. Cancer 9 (10) (2009) 691–700.

[29] E.Z. White, et al., Serum deprivation initiates adaptation and survival to oxidative stress in prostate cancer cells, Sci. Rep. 10 (1) (2020) 12505.

[30] D.G. Hardie, Molecular pathways: is AMPK a friend or a foe in cancer? Clin. Cancer Res. 21 (17) (2015) 3836–3840.

[31] E. Persi, et al., Systems analysis of intracellular pH vulnerabilities for cancer therapy, Nat. Commun. 9 (1) (2018) 2997.

[32] G. Lamonte, et al., Acidosis induces reprogramming of cellular metabolism to mitigate oxidative stress, Cancer Metab. 1 (1) (2013) 23.

[33] Z. Daverio, et al., How Warburg-associated lactic acidosis rewires cancer cell energy metabolism to resist glucose deprivation, Cancers (Basel) 15 (5) (2023) 1417.

[34] J.L. Chen, et al., The genomic analysis of lactic acidosis and acidosis response in human cancers, PLoS Genet. 4 (12) (2008) e1000293.

[35] J. Xie, et al., Beyond Warburg effect—dual metabolic nature of cancer cells, Sci. Rep. 4 (2014) 4927.

[36] H. Prado-Garcia, A. Campa-Higareda, S. Romero-Garcia, Lactic acidosis in the presence of glucose diminishes Warburg effect in lung adenocarcinoma cells, Front. Oncol. 10 (2020) 807.

[37] H. Wu, M. Ying, X. Hu, Lactic acidosis switches cancer cells from aerobic glycolysis back to dominant oxidative phosphorylation, Oncotarget 7 (26) (2016) 40621–40629.

[38] M.L. Marino, et al., Autophagy is a protective mechanism for human melanoma cells under acidic stress, J. Biol. Chem. 287 (36) (2012) 30664–30676.

[39] J.W. Wojtkowiak, et al., Chronic autophagy is a cellular adaptation to tumor acidic pH microenvironments, Cancer Res. 72 (16) (2012) 3938–3947.

[40] P. Vaupel, G. Multhoff, Revisiting the Warburg effect: historical dogma versus current understanding, J. Physiol. 599 (6) (2021) 1745–1757.

[41] T. Epstein, R.A. Gatenby, J.S. Brown, The Warburg effect as an adaptation of cancer cells to rapid fluctuations in energy demand, PLoS One 12 (9) (2017) e0185085.

[42] M.G. Vander Heiden, L.C. Cantley, C.B. Thompson, Understanding the Warburg effect: the metabolic requirements of cell proliferation, Science 324 (5930) (2009) 1029–1033.

[43] T. Chano, et al., Tumour-specific metabolic adaptation to acidosis is coupled to epigenetic stability in osteosarcoma cells, Am. J. Cancer Res. 6 (4) (2016) 859–875.

[44] Z. Dai, W. Zheng, J.W. Locasale, Amino acid variability, tradeoffs and optimality in human diet, Nat. Commun. 13 (1) (2022) 6683.

[45] P.Y. Tsai, et al., Adaptation of pancreatic cancer cells to nutrient deprivation is reversible and requires glutamine synthetase stabilization by mTORC1, Proc. Natl. Acad. Sci. USA 118 (10) (2021) e2003014118.

[46] C.M. Metallo, et al., Reductive glutamine metabolism by IDH1 mediates lipogenesis under hypoxia, Nature 481 (7381) (2011) 380–384.

[47] A.R. Mullen, et al., Reductive carboxylation supports growth in tumour cells with defective mitochondria, Nature 481 (7381) (2011) 385–388.

[48] S. Cameron, et al., Chronic hypoxia favours adoption to a castration-resistant cell state in prostate cancer, Oncogene 42 (21) (2023) 1693–1703.

[49] M.J. Epler, et al., Metabolic acidosis stimulates intestinal glutamine absorption, J. Gastrointest. Surg. 7 (8) (2003) 1045–1052.

[50] C. Corbet, et al., The SIRT1/HIF2alpha axis drives reductive glutamine metabolism under chronic acidosis and alters tumor response to therapy, Cancer Res. 74 (19) (2014) 5507–5519.

[51] J. Bralet, L. Schreiber, C. Bouvier, Effect of acidosis and anoxia on iron delocalization from brain homogenates, Biochem. Pharmacol. 43 (5) (1992) 979–983.

[52] W. Hassan, et al., Effects of acidosis and Fe (II) on lipid peroxidation in phospholipid extract: comparative effect of diphenyl diselenide and ebselen, Environ. Toxicol. Pharmacol. 28 (1) (2009) 152–154.

[53] L.J. Su, et al., Reactive oxygen species-induced lipid peroxidation in apoptosis, autophagy, and ferroptosis, Oxid. Med. Cell. Longev. 2019 (2019) 5080843.

[54] R.C. Shankaraiah, et al., Non-coding RNAs in the reprogramming of glucose metabolism in cancer, Cancer Lett. 419 (2018) 167–174.

[55] B. Perillo, et al., ROS in cancer therapy: the bright side of the moon, Exp. Mol. Med. 52 (2) (2020) 192–203.

[56] S. Suzuki, et al., Phosphate-activated glutaminase (GLS2), a p53-inducible regulator of glutamine metabolism and reactive oxygen species, Proc. Natl. Acad. Sci. USA 107 (16) (2010) 7461–7466.

[57] W. Hu, et al., Glutaminase 2, a novel p53 target gene regulating energy metabolism and antioxidant function, Proc. Natl. Acad. Sci. USA 107 (16) (2010) 7455–7460.

[58] M.F. Salama, et al., A novel role of sphingosine kinase-1 in the invasion and angiogenesis of VHL mutant clear cell renal cell carcinoma, FASEB J. 29 (7) (2015) 2803–2813.

[59] J. Liu, et al., Tumor suppressor p53 and metabolism, J. Mol. Cell Biol. 11 (4) (2019) 284–292.

[60] Y. Mao, P. Jiang, The crisscross between p53 and metabolism in cancer, Acta Biochim. Biophys. Sin. Shanghai 55 (6) (2023) 914–922.

[61] K.L. Eales, K.E. Hollinshead, D.A. Tennant, Hypoxia and metabolic adaptation of cancer cells, Oncogenesis 5 (1) (2016) e190.

[62] C. Duan, Hypoxia-inducible factor 3 biology: complexities and emerging themes, Am. J. Physiol. Cell Physiol. 310 (4) (2016) C260–C269.

[63] E.E. Wicks, G.L. Semenza, Hypoxia-inducible factors: cancer progression and clinical translation, J. Clin. Invest. 132 (11) (2022) e159839.

[64] J.H. Lim, et al., Sirtuin 1 modulates cellular responses to hypoxia by deacetylating hypoxia-inducible factor 1alpha, Mol. Cell 38 (6) (2010) 864–878.

[65] A. Valli, et al., Hypoxia induces a lipogenic cancer cell phenotype via HIF1alpha-dependent and -independent pathways, Oncotarget 6 (4) (2015) 1920–1941.

[66] J.D. Gordan, et al., HIF-2alpha promotes hypoxic cell proliferation by enhancing c-myc transcriptional activity, Cancer Cell 11 (4) (2007) 335–347.

[67] P. Gao, et al., c-Myc suppression of miR-23a/b enhances mitochondrial glutaminase expression and glutamine metabolism, Nature 458 (7239) (2009) 762–765.

[68] E.M. Dioum, et al., Regulation of hypoxia-inducible factor 2alpha signaling by the stress-responsive deacetylase sirtuin 1, Science 324 (5932) (2009) 1289–1293.

[69] S. Rodriguez-Enriquez, et al., Transcriptional regulation of energy metabolism in cancer cells, Cells 8 (10) (2019) 1225.

[70] K. Kawauchi, et al., p53 regulates glucose metabolism through an IKK-NF-kappaB pathway and inhibits cell transformation, Nat. Cell Biol. 10 (5) (2008) 611–618.

[71] Y. Xia, S. Shen, I.M. Verma, NF-kappaB, an active player in human cancers, Cancer Immunol. Res. 2 (9) (2014) 823–830.

[72] D. Capece, et al., NF-kappaB: blending metabolism, immunity, and inflammation, Trends Immunol. 43 (9) (2022) 757–775.

[73] X. Wang, et al., Alpha-ketoglutarate-activated NF-kappaB signaling promotes compensatory glucose uptake and brain tumor development, Mol. Cell 76 (1) (2019) 148–162e7.

[74] K. Lingappan, NF-kappaB in oxidative stress, Curr. Opin. Toxicol. 7 (2018) 81–86.

[75] H. Yang, et al., The role of cellular reactive oxygen species in cancer chemotherapy, J. Exp. Clin. Cancer Res. 37 (1) (2018) 266.

[76] H. Nakamura, K. Takada, Reactive oxygen species in cancer: current findings and future directions, Cancer Sci. 112 (10) (2021) 3945–3952.

[77] Y. Wang, et al., The intricate interplay between HIFs, ROS, and the ubiquitin system in the tumor hypoxic microenvironment, Pharmacol. Ther. 240 (2022) 108303.

[78] J. Kim, J. Kim, J.S. Bae, ROS homeostasis and metabolism: a critical liaison for cancer therapy, Exp. Mol. Med. 48 (11) (2016) e269.

[79] A. Riemann, et al., Acidic environment leads to ROS-induced MAPK signaling in cancer cells, PLoS One 6 (7) (2011) e22445.

[80] H.Y. Zhang, et al., In benign Barrett's epithelial cells, acid exposure generates reactive oxygen species that cause DNA double-strand breaks, Cancer Res. 69 (23) (2009) 9083–9089.

[81] M. Dodson, V. Darley-Usmar, J. Zhang, Cellular metabolic and autophagic pathways: traffic control by redox signaling, Free Radic. Biol. Med. 63 (2013) 207–221.

[82] Y. Zhao, et al., ROS signaling under metabolic stress: cross-talk between AMPK and AKT pathway, Mol. Cancer 16 (1) (2017) 79.

[83] U. Deichmann, Epigenetics: the origins and evolution of a fashionable topic, Dev. Biol. 416 (1) (2016) 249–254.

[84] L.D. Moore, T. Le, G. Fan, DNA methylation and its basic function, Neuropsychopharmacology 38 (1) (2013) 23–38.

[85] K. Skvortsova, C. Stirzaker, P. Taberlay, The DNA methylation landscape in cancer, Essays Biochem. 63 (6) (2019) 797–811.

[86] M. Trerotola, et al., Epigenetic inheritance and the missing heritability, Hum. Genomics 9 (1) (2015) 17.

[87] B. Thienpont, et al., Tumour hypoxia causes DNA hypermethylation by reducing TET activity, Nature 537 (7618) (2016) 63–68.

[88] M. Privat, et al., BRCA1 induces major energetic metabolism reprogramming in breast cancer cells, PLoS One 9 (7) (2014) e102438.

[89] G.L. Semenza, HIF-1 mediates the Warburg effect in clear cell renal carcinoma, J. Bioenerg. Biomembr. 39 (3) (2007) 231–234.

[90] F. Cimmino, et al., HIF-1 transcription activity: HIF1A driven response in normoxia and in hypoxia, BMC Med. Genet. 20 (1) (2019) 37.

[91] C.J. Mariani, et al., TET1-mediated hydroxymethylation facilitates hypoxic gene induction in neuroblastoma, Cell Rep. 7 (5) (2014) 1343–1352.

[92] A. Goel, S.P. Mathupala, P.L. Pedersen, Glucose metabolism in cancer. Evidence that demethylation events play a role in activating type II hexokinase gene expression, J. Biol. Chem. 278 (17) (2003) 15333–15340.

[93] A. Wolf, et al., Developmental profile and regulation of the glycolytic enzyme hexokinase 2 in normal brain and glioblastoma multiforme, Neurobiol. Dis. 44 (1) (2011) 84–91.

[94] C.D. Davis, E.O. Uthus, DNA methylation, cancer susceptibility, and nutrient interactions, Exp. Biol. Med. (Maywood) 229 (10) (2004) 988–995.

[95] Z.H. Zhou, et al., Chromatin accessibility changes are associated with enhanced growth and liver metastasis capacity of acid-adapted colorectal cancer cells, Cell Cycle 18 (4) (2019) 511–522.

[96] E. Wilkinson, Y.H. Cui, Y.Y. He, Roles of RNA modifications in diverse cellular functions, Front. Cell Dev. Biol. 10 (2022) 828683.

[97] I. Barbieri, T. Kouzarides, Role of RNA modifications in cancer, Nat. Rev. Cancer 20 (6) (2020) 303–322.

[98] X. Han, L. Wang, Q. Han, Advances in the role of m(6)A RNA modification in cancer metabolic reprogramming, Cell Biosci. 10 (2020) 117.

[99] Y.J. Wang, et al., Reprogramming of m(6)A epitranscriptome is crucial for shaping of transcriptome and proteome in response to hypoxia, RNA Biol. 18 (1) (2021) 131–143.

[100] Q. Li, et al., HIF-1alpha-induced expression of m6A reader YTHDF1 drives hypoxia-induced autophagy and malignancy of hepatocellular carcinoma by promoting ATG2A and ATG14 translation, Signal. Transduct. Target Ther. 6 (1) (2021) 76.

[101] X. Liu, et al., m6A methylation regulates hypoxia-induced pancreatic cancer glycolytic metabolism through ALKBH5-HDAC4-HIF1alpha positive feedback loop, Oncogene 42 (25) (2023) 2047–2060.

[102] T. Zhang, S. Cooper, N. Brockdorff, The interplay of histone modifications—writers that read, EMBO Rep. 16 (11) (2015) 1467–1481.

[103] T. Kouzarides, Chromatin modifications and their function, Cell 128 (4) (2007) 693–705.

[104] S. Zhao, C.D. Allis, G.G. Wang, The language of chromatin modification in human cancers, Nat. Rev. Cancer 21 (7) (2021) 413–430.

[105] A.J. Morrison, Cancer cell metabolism connects epigenetic modifications to transcriptional regulation, FEBS J. 289 (5) (2022) 1302–1314.

[106] E.L. Greer, Y. Shi, Histone methylation: a dynamic mark in health, disease and inheritance, Nat. Rev. Genet. 13 (5) (2012) 343–357.

[107] Z. Zhao, A. Shilatifard, Epigenetic modifications of histones in cancer, Genome Biol. 20 (1) (2019) 245.

[108] Y. Lu, et al., Silencing of the DNA mismatch repair gene MLH1 induced by hypoxic stress in a pathway dependent on the histone demethylase LSD1, Cell Rep. 8 (2) (2014) 501–513.

[109] W. Wan, et al., Histone demethylase JMJD1A promotes urinary bladder cancer progression by enhancing glycolysis through coactivation of hypoxia inducible factor 1alpha, Oncogene 36 (27) (2017) 3868–3877.

[110] W. Luo, et al., Histone demethylase JMJD2C is a coactivator for hypoxia-inducible factor 1 that is required for breast cancer progression, Proc. Natl. Acad. Sci. USA 109 (49) (2012) E3367–E3376.

[111] A. Sakamoto, et al., Lysine demethylase LSD1 coordinates glycolytic and mitochondrial metabolism in hepatocellular carcinoma cells, Cancer Res. 75 (7) (2015) 1445–1456.

[112] K. Kosumi, et al., Lysine-specific demethylase-1 contributes to malignant behavior by regulation of invasive activity and metabolic shift in esophageal cancer, Int. J. Cancer 138 (2) (2016) 428–439.

[113] L. Fu, et al., HIF-1alpha-induced histone demethylase JMJD2B contributes to the malignant phenotype of colorectal cancer cells via an epigenetic mechanism, Carcinogenesis 33 (9) (2012) 1664–1673.

[114] J.G. Kim, et al., Histone demethylase JMJD2B-mediated cell proliferation regulated by hypoxia and radiation in gastric cancer cell, Biochim. Biophys. Acta 1819 (11–12) (2012) 1200–1207.

[115] M. Kawazu, et al., Histone demethylase JMJD2B functions as a co-factor of estrogen receptor in breast cancer proliferation and mammary gland development, PLoS One 6 (3) (2011) e17830.

[116] G. Toyokawa, et al., The histone demethylase JMJD2B plays an essential role in human carcinogenesis through positive regulation of cyclin-dependent kinase 6, Cancer Prev. Res. (Phila.) 4 (12) (2011) 2051–2061.

[117] M. Pan, et al., Regional glutamine deficiency in tumours promotes dedifferentiation through inhibition of histone demethylation, Nat. Cell Biol. 18 (10) (2016) 1090–1101.

[118] M.A. McBrian, et al., Histone acetylation regulates intracellular pH, Mol. Cell 49 (2) (2013) 310–321.

[119] C. Corbet, et al., Acidosis drives the reprogramming of fatty acid metabolism in cancer cells through changes in mitochondrial and histone acetylation, Cell Metab. 24 (2) (2016) 311–323.

[120] D. Zhang, et al., Metabolic regulation of gene expression by histone lactylation, Nature 574 (7779) (2019) 575–580.

[121] H. Yan, P. Bu, Non-coding RNA in cancer, Essays Biochem. 65 (4) (2021) 625–639.

[122] X.Y. He, et al., LncRNA modulates Hippo-YAP signaling to reprogram iron metabolism, Nat. Commun. 14 (1) (2023) 2253.

[123] L.J. Sang, et al., LncRNA CamK-A regulates Ca(2+)-signaling-mediated tumor microenvironment remodeling, Mol. Cell 72 (1) (2018) 71–83 e7.

[124] A. Lin, et al., The LINK-A lncRNA activates normoxic HIF1alpha signalling in triple-negative breast cancer, Nat. Cell Biol. 18 (2) (2016) 213–224.

[125] A. Safi, et al., The role of noncoding RNAs in metabolic reprogramming of cancer cells, Cell. Mol. Biol. Lett. 28 (1) (2023) 37.

[126] F. Zheng, et al., The HIF-1alpha antisense long non-coding RNA drives a positive feedback loop of HIF-1alpha mediated transactivation and glycolysis, Nat. Commun. 12 (1) (2021) 1341.

[127] X. Zheng, et al., LncRNA wires up Hippo and Hedgehog signaling to reprogramme glucose metabolism, EMBO J. 36 (22) (2017) 3325–3335.

[128] F. Yang, et al., Reciprocal regulation of HIF-1alpha and lincRNA-p21 modulates the Warburg effect, Mol. Cell 53 (1) (2014) 88–100.

[129] W. Zhu, et al., Low glucose-induced overexpression of HOXC-AS3 promotes metabolic reprogramming of breast cancer, Cancer Res. 82 (5) (2022) 805–818.

[130] S.J. Deng, et al., Nutrient stress-dysregulated antisense lncRNA GLS-AS impairs GLS-mediated metabolism and represses pancreatic cancer progression, Cancer Res. 79 (7) (2019) 1398–1412.

[131] S. Liu, et al., A novel lncRNA ROPM-mediated lipid metabolism governs breast cancer stem cell properties, J. Hematol. Oncol. 14 (1) (2021) 178.

[132] H. Wang, et al., An integrated transcriptomics and proteomics analysis implicates lncRNA MALAT1 in the regulation of lipid metabolism, Mol. Cell. Proteomics 20 (2021) 100141.

[133] N. Suriya Muthukumaran, et al., MicroRNAs as regulators of cancer cell energy metabolism, J. Pers. Med. 12 (8) (2022) 1329.

[134] R. Fang, et al., MicroRNA-143 (miR-143) regulates cancer glycolysis via targeting hexokinase 2 gene, J. Biol. Chem. 287 (27) (2012) 23227–23235.

[135] A. Peschiaroli, et al., miR-143 regulates hexokinase 2 expression in cancer cells, Oncogene 32 (6) (2013) 797–802.

[136] S. Jiang, et al., A novel miR-155/miR-143 cascade controls glycolysis by regulating hexokinase 2 in breast cancer cells, EMBO J. 31 (8) (2012) 1985–1998.

[137] L.H. Gregersen, et al., MicroRNA-143 down-regulates Hexokinase 2 in colon cancer cells, BMC Cancer 12 (2012) 232.

[138] A. Ahmad, et al., Phosphoglucose isomerase/autocrine motility factor mediates epithelial-mesenchymal transition regulated by miR-200 in breast cancer cells, Cancer Res. 71 (9) (2011) 3400–3409.

[139] Y. Yang, et al., MiR-135 suppresses glycolysis and promotes pancreatic cancer cell adaptation to metabolic stress by targeting phosphofructokinase-1, Nat. Commun. 10 (1) (2019) 809.

[140] B. Kefas, et al., Pyruvate kinase M2 is a target of the tumor-suppressive microRNA-326 and regulates the survival of glioma cells, Neuro-Oncology 12 (11) (2010) 1102–1112.

[141] A.M. Liu, et al., miR-122 targets pyruvate kinase M2 and affects metabolism of hepatocellular carcinoma, PLoS One 9 (1) (2014) e86872.

[142] T.S. Wong, et al., Identification of pyruvate kinase type M2 as potential oncoprotein in squamous cell carcinoma of tongue through microRNA profiling, Int. J. Cancer 123 (2) (2008) 251–257.

[143] K. Minami, et al., MiR-145 negatively regulates Warburg effect by silencing KLF4 and PTBP1 in bladder cancer cells, Oncotarget 8 (20) (2017) 33064–33077.

[144] X. Chang, et al., Sensitization of melanoma cells to temozolomide by overexpression of microRNA 203 through direct targeting of glutaminase-mediated glutamine metabolism, Clin. Exp. Dermatol. 42 (6) (2017) 614–621.

[145] S. Zhang, et al., PGC-1 alpha interacts with microRNA-217 to functionally regulate breast cancer cell proliferation, Biomed. Pharmacother. 85 (2017) 541–548.

[146] F. Zeng, et al., Fatty acid beta-oxidation promotes breast cancer stemness and metastasis via the miRNA-328-3p-CPT1A pathway, Cancer Gene Ther. 29 (3–4) (2022) 383–395.

[147] T. Zhang, et al., MicroRNA-377-3p inhibits hepatocellular carcinoma growth and metastasis through negative regulation of CPT1C-mediated fatty acid oxidation, Cancer Metab. 10 (1) (2022) 2.

[148] G. Moriondo, et al., Effect of hypoxia-induced micro-RNAs expression on oncogenesis, Int. J. Mol. Sci. 23 (11) (2022) 6294.

[149] G. Shen, et al., Hypoxia-regulated microRNAs in human cancer, Acta Pharmacol. Sin. 34 (3) (2013) 336–341.

[150] M. Yamakuchi, et al., MicroRNA-22 regulates hypoxia signaling in colon cancer cells, PLoS One 6 (5) (2011) e20291.

[151] C. He, et al., Hypoxia-inducible microRNA-224 promotes the cell growth, migration and invasion by directly targeting RASSF8 in gastric cancer, Mol. Cancer 16 (1) (2017) 35.

[152] A. Riemann, S. Reime, O. Thews, Hypoxia-related tumor acidosis affects microRNA expression pattern in prostate and breast tumor cells, Adv. Exp. Med. Biol. 977 (2017) 119–124.

[153] J. Eismann, et al., Hypoxia- and acidosis-driven aberrations of secreted microRNAs in endometrial cancer in vitro, Oncol. Rep. 38 (2) (2017) 993–1004.

[154] J. Lu, et al., Starvation stress attenuates the miRNA-target interaction in suppressing breast cancer cell proliferation, BMC Cancer 20 (1) (2020) 627.

[155] K. Fite, L. Elkhadragy, J. Gomez-Cambronero, A repertoire of microRNAs regulates cancer cell starvation by targeting phospholipase D in a feedback loop that operates maximally in cancer cells, Mol. Cell. Biol. 36 (7) (2016) 1078–1089.

[156] Z. Su, et al., MicroRNAs in apoptosis, autophagy and necroptosis, Oncotarget 6 (11) (2015) 8474–8490.

[157] C.C. Wong, Y. Qian, J. Yu, Interplay between epigenetics and metabolism in oncogenesis: mechanisms and therapeutic approaches, Oncogene 36 (24) (2017) 3359–3374.

[158] W. Lu, Y. Kang, Epithelial-mesenchymal plasticity in cancer progression and metastasis, Dev. Cell 49 (3) (2019) 361–374.

[159] Y. Chen, et al., The role of histone methylation in the development of digestive cancers: a potential direction for cancer management, Signal. Transduct. Target Ther. 5 (1) (2020) 143.

[160] Z. Huang, et al., Epithelial-mesenchymal transition: the history, regulatory mechanism, and cancer therapeutic opportunities, MedComm 3 (2) (2020) e144.

[161] D. Senft, Z.E. Ronai, Adaptive stress responses during tumor metastasis and dormancy, Trends Cancer 2 (8) (2016) 429–442.

[162] O. Shuvalov, et al., Linking metabolic reprogramming, plasticity and tumor progression, Cancers (Basel) 13 (4) (2021) 762.

[163] M. Sadeghi, et al., Integrative analysis of breast cancer cells reveals an epithelial-mesenchymal transition role in adaptation to acidic microenvironment, Front. Oncol. 10 (2020) 304.

[164] J. Zhang, et al., Regulation of epithelial-mesenchymal transition by tumor microenvironmental signals and its implication in cancer therapeutics, Semin. Cancer Biol. 88 (2023) 46–66.

[165] J. Araos, J.P. Sleeman, B.K. Garvalov, The role of hypoxic signalling in metastasis: towards translating knowledge of basic biology into novel anti-tumour strategies, Clin. Exp. Metastasis 35 (7) (2018) 563–599.

[166] H. Dopeso, et al., PHD3 controls lung cancer metastasis and resistance to EGFR inhibitors through TGFalpha, Cancer Res. 78 (7) (2018) 1805–1819.

[167] G. Kroemer, J. Pouyssegur, Tumor cell metabolism: cancer's Achilles' heel, Cancer Cell 13 (6) (2008) 472–482.

[168] A. Carcereri de Prati, et al., Metastatic breast cancer cells enter into dormant state and express cancer stem cells phenotype under chronic hypoxia, J. Cell. Biochem. 118 (10) (2017) 3237–3248.

[169] H. Endo, et al., Dormancy of cancer cells with suppression of AKT activity contributes to survival in chronic hypoxia, PLoS One 9 (6) (2014) e98858.

[170] G. Fluegen, et al., Phenotypic heterogeneity of disseminated tumour cells is preset by primary tumour hypoxic microenvironments, Nat. Cell Biol. 19 (2) (2017) 120–132.

[171] R.W. Johnson, et al., Induction of LIFR confers a dormancy phenotype in breast cancer cells disseminated to the bone marrow, Nat. Cell Biol. 18 (10) (2016) 1078–1089.

[172] T.G. Phan, P.I. Croucher, The dormant cancer cell life cycle, Nat. Rev. Cancer 20 (7) (2020) 398–411.

[173] N.J. Robinson, K.A. Parker, W.P. Schiemann, Epigenetic plasticity in metastatic dormancy: mechanisms and therapeutic implications, Ann. Transl. Med. 8 (14) (2020) 903.

[174] Z. Hu, et al., Quantitative evidence for early metastatic seeding in colorectal cancer, Nat. Genet. 51 (7) (2019) 1113–1122.

[175] M.Q. Reeves, et al., Multicolour lineage tracing reveals clonal dynamics of squamous carcinoma evolution from initiation to metastasis, Nat. Cell Biol. 20 (6) (2018) 699–709.

[176] H. Hosseini, et al., Early dissemination seeds metastasis in breast cancer, Nature 540 (7634) (2016) 552–558.

[177] A.P. Adam, et al., Computational identification of a p38SAPK-regulated transcription factor network required for tumor cell quiescence, Cancer Res. 69 (14) (2009) 5664–5672.

[178] M.S. Sosa, et al., NR2F1 controls tumour cell dormancy via SOX9- and RARbeta-driven quiescence programmes, Nat. Commun. 6 (2015) 6170.

[179] H. Gao, et al., Forward genetic screens in mice uncover mediators and suppressors of metastatic reactivation, Proc. Natl. Acad. Sci. USA 111 (46) (2014) 16532–16537.

[180] S. Gawrzak, et al., MSK1 regulates luminal cell differentiation and metastatic dormancy in ER(+) breast cancer, Nat. Cell Biol. 20 (2) (2018) 211–221.

[181] I. Manrique, et al., The inhibitor of differentiation isoform Id1b, generated by alternative splicing, maintains cell quiescence and confers self-renewal and cancer stem cell-like properties, Cancer Lett. 356 (2 Pt B) (2015) 899–909.

[182] C.E. Meacham, S.J. Morrison, Tumour heterogeneity and cancer cell plasticity, Nature 501 (7467) (2013) 328–337.

[183] J.C. Marine, S.J. Dawson, M.A. Dawson, Non-genetic mechanisms of therapeutic resistance in cancer, Nat. Rev. Cancer 20 (12) (2020) 743–756.

[184] S. Boumahdi, F.J. de Sauvage, The great escape: tumour cell plasticity in resistance to targeted therapy, Nat. Rev. Drug Discov. 19 (1) (2020) 39–56.

Involvement of epigenetic modifications in cancer stem cells and chemoresistance

9

Prajakta Oak[a] and Chitra Thakur[b]

[a]*Biotech/Scientific Professional, Munich, Germany,* [b]*Stony Brook Cancer Center, Department of Pathology, Renaissance School of Medicine, Stony Brook University, Stony Brook, NY, United States*

Cancer, in a broad sense, is characterized as a group of diseases that is primarily caused by dysregulated cell growth and uncontrolled division. Over the years, researchers have been fighting cancer on various fronts, i.e., from developing new diagnostic strategies to detect tumors at initial stages, to discovering varied combinatorial treatments for fighting the rarest possible form of cancer (Fig. 1).

Despite such advancement in diagnostics and treatment, sometimes, a relapse is observed. Relapse is often associated with cancer drug resistance, rendering the therapeutic interventions ineffective. A review by Emran et al. summarizes the widely accepted mechanisms for drug resistance including overexpression of drug efflux transporters, reduced drug uptake, altered drug metabolism and targets, improved DNA repair mechanisms, increase in antiapoptotic survival pathways, and epigenetic changes as presented in Fig. 2 [1].

Tumor heterogeneity and drug resistance

Currently, drug resistance is the major threat to successful therapeutic interventions. As opposed to the earlier opinions, the theory of tumor heterogeneity is evaluated and is universally accepted. Over the course of cancer progression, the cellular population is subject to deviations and changes owing to genetic or nongenetic factors, bestowing unique characteristics to each cell population present in tumor.

Nongenetic factors such as phenotypic plasticity, primarily owing to interaction of the cells of a tumor to different microenvironments having varied blood pressure, neighboring somatic cells, infiltration of immune cells, and extracellular matrix composition, serve as some of the factors responsible for heterogenic population, hence giving rise to drug resistance as well as, in some cases, malignancy [2,3]. A study performed by Zlatian et al. on 50 colorectal cancer patients histologically

Cancer Epigenetics and Nanomedicine. **https://doi.org/10.1016/B978-0-443-13209-4.00019-2**
Copyright © 2024 Elsevier Inc. All rights are reserved, including those for text and data mining, AI training, and similar technologies.

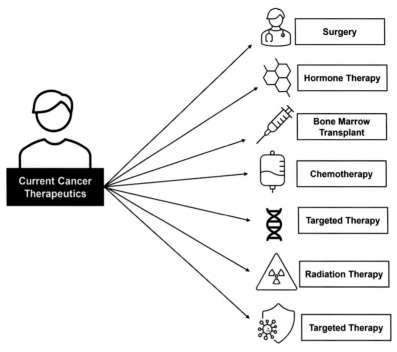

FIG. 1

Compilation of current cancer therapeutic strategies. This figure describes various treatments that are used to combat different forms of cancer. For a localized tumor, **Surgery,** i.e., surgical removal of the tumor with/without accompanying organs/tissues is the commonly used therapeutic intervention. When required this can be combined with certain treatments like **Hormonal therapy,** which targets and modulates hormonal secretion as well as function to interfere with tumor growth, or **Chemotherapy** utilizing chemical medication to target fast-growing cancer cells, or **Radiation therapy,** i.e., application of ionizing radiations to suppress rapidly dividing cancer cells. Doctors and researchers are currently inclined toward **Targeted therapy** approaches that utilize an array of compounds to deliver the treatment directly to the site, often with the help of biomarkers defining tumor or cancer. **Immunotherapy** is an emerging approach to trigger or regulate our own immune system so that these cells can target and diminish the tumor population.

confirmed different phenotypes, demonstrating tumoral heterogeneity causing different prognoses [4]. Similarly, Glöckner et al. confirms intertumoral heterogeneity in specimens collected from breast cancer patients [5]. Consequently, considering heterogeneity in tumor or metastatic cancer disease to tease apart differential cellular phenotypes leading to successful combinatorial treatment interventions is critical. Although "in vitro" two-dimensional (2D) cellular models generate considerable data supporting the evolution of tumors and efficacy of treatment strategies,

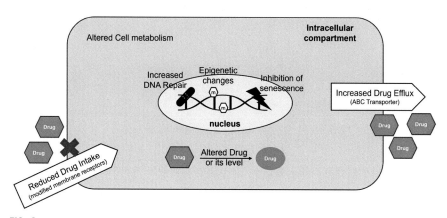

FIG. 2

Mechanisms of drug resistance in cancer. Drug resistance in cancer can be acquired by multiple processes as shown in this figure. The list ranges from upregulation of drug transporter proteins discharging the drug out of the cells and altering the drug for its ineffectiveness to upregulation of DNA repair mechanism with a reduction in genes regulating senescence. Additionally, genetic and epigenetic modifications hold a prime spot in this list. This figure needs to be revised for clarity.

three-dimensional (3D) "in vitro" cellular models are crucial in studying the heterogeneity of the tumor, its interactions with the microenvironment and, in turn, its response to different combinatorial treatment options [6–11].

This model also gained popularity with increasing ethical concerns and restrictions on animal models mirroring human disease in animal systems. Fig. 3 shows a comparable 3D spheroid model termed mammospheres based on heterogeneity of the tumor arising from cancer stem cells (CSCs). The two populations in mammospheres Her2^{low} with stem cell-like properties were targeted with drug Salinomycin and Her2^{high} were eliminated using the common drug-antibody Trastuzumab, hence proving the theory of understanding CSCs as one of the bases in efficient combinatorial treatments of cancer [6].

Cancer stem cells: A new dimension to drug resistance

Compelling evidence indicates that targeting a stubborn subset of the cancer, associated with relapse and malignancies, paves the way to modern treatment interventions. Often termed CSCs or Tumor initiating cells, they display distinct stem cell-like characteristics described as quiescence, anchorage-dependent growth with indefinite proliferative potential, self-renewal, pluripotency capabilities, and upregulation of multiple drug resistance (MDR) transporters like ATP-binding cassette (ABC) protein aiding in efflux of drugs. At present, CSCs are

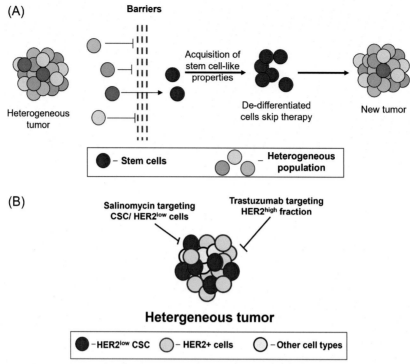

FIG. 3

3D "in vitro" models with breast cancer cells for screening combinatorial treatment strategies. (A) Depicts the presence of CSCs in heterogeneous tumors escaping the chemotherapeutics demonstrated through 3D spheroids of breast cancer cells known as mammosphere. These cells further differentiate into new tumors giving rise to relapse. (B) Use of mammospheres to screen combinatorial treatment (Trastuzumab and Salinomycin) targeting both rapidly proliferating Her2^{high} and quiescent CSC Her2^{low} populations.

widely identified and isolated based on their unique array of cell surface markers that often coincide with markers present on Totipotent or Pluripotent stem cells [12–16].

Together these characteristics differentiate tumorigenic CSC population from nontumorigenic population. Certain "in vivo" studies exhibited the development of tumors in animal models upon injection of a limited number of isolated CSCs, supporting the tumorigenic potential of this cancer subset (Fig. 4) [17–22].

As discussed earlier, CSC exhibits a set of cell surface markers that are uniquely associated with them. Studies done on liver carcinoma demonstrate a set of cell surface markers such as EPCAM, CD90, CD133, CD24, and CD13 associated with CSCs. On the contrary, Wilson et al. confirm in their study with human

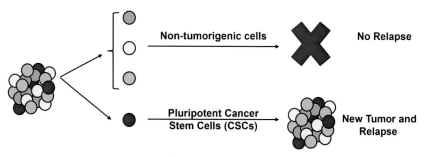

FIG. 4

Heterogeneity, cancer stem cells, and relapse. This model places CSCs at the top of hierarchy of a tumor. As opposed to other cells from tumor, CSC possesses capabilities like quiescence and pluripotency. Hence, they escape therapy and give rise to a new tumor, aiding in resistance to current therapeutics.

hepatocellular carcinoma (HCC) that the subset isolated using the known CSC markers failed to differentiate their protein profile utilizing immunohistochemical and western blotting techniques from the adjacent noncancerous tissue cells [23]. Hence, the usage of cell surface markers to distinguish CSCs is fading away, and studies are instead moving in the direction of identifying their functional characteristics and molecular mechanisms regulating CSCs [24]. Fig. 5 summarizes key factors inducing drug resistance in CSCs [25].

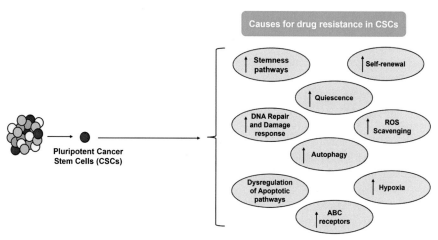

FIG. 5

Drug resistance in CSC. This illustration summarizes major CSC characteristics that aid in cell survival, aiding in drug resistance, and relapse.

Reprogramming of cancer stem cells and epigenetic modifications

A landmark study by Takahashi et al. identified that pluripotency can be induced by reprogramming the somatic cells from mouse embryonic and adult fibroblast cultures utilizing factors Oct4, Sox2, Klf4, and c-Myc [26]. Many sequential steps define such a reprogramming process including biding of stem cell-specific transcription factors to relevant DNA sites, blocking the differentiation factors, and modifications at genetic level [27,28]. Simultaneously, chromatin remodeling and methylation changes are essential to regulate the transition of differentiated somatic cells to undifferentiated stem cells. Such changes categorized under epigenetic mechanisms are defined as the processes that reversibly alter the gene expression without changing DNA sequence. Such mechanisms dictating cell fate without modification to DNA sequence comprise DNA methylations, histone modifications, and alterations in noncoding RNAs.

DNA methylation

The process involving the reversible transfer of methyl group from S-adenosyl methionine (SAM) to $5'$-position of cytosine residues of the CpG dinucleotides position is termed DNA methylation. This process is mediated by the group of enzymes known as DNA methyltransferases (DNMT1, DNMT3A, and DNMT3B). Hypomethylation of promoter regions aids in gene expression of the target genes, while hypermethylation shields the transcription process, suppressing the gene expression [29].

DNMT1 plays a major role in maintaining methylation patterns, especially during embryonic development [30]. DNMT3A and DNMT3B are known to interact and stimulate each other and mutually methylate promoters of OCT-4 and Nanog. Their diminished expression causes inadequate methylation and, hence, dysregulated expression of OCT-4 and Nanog, affecting embryonic development [31].

A study performed by Fouad et al. substantiates a significant impact of global methylation patterns in colorectal cancer patients on treatment outcomes and patient survival [32]. Another study on nonsmall cell lung (NSCL) cancer displays the association of KRAS mutation with elevated methylation, confirming an epigenetic basis [33]. In line with these studies, higher levels of DNMT1 correlate with CSCs from pancreatic ductal adenocarcinoma [34]. Association of differentially methylated genes is confirmed in CSCs isolated from esophageal squamous cell carcinoma cell lines and human primary esophageal cancer cells. Here, the CSCs were identified and isolated based on properties like side population and spheroid forming potential, and the methylation patterns coincided with significant biological processes [35]. An extensively studied model for association of DNA methylation to CSCs is breast cancer. Studies in breast and glioma CSCs exhibit that the methylation status of SMAD protein governs tumor suppressive or tumor-promoting effect of paracrine TGF-β signaling [36–38]. As reviewed by Veschi and Francesco et al., in addition to regulating DNA methylation, it is also involved in regulating the crosstalk between CSCs and neighboring microenvironments, leading to CSC maintenance, propagation, relapse, and metastasis [39]. Hence, DNA methylation pattern, especially in CSCs, is a prime event to explore and understand to gain knowledge on drug resistance.

Histone modifications

Modification of histones by methylation, demethylation, acetylation, deacetylation, phosphorylation, and ubiquitylation are considered significant epigenetic modifications. Such modifications on promoter or enhancer region of any gene alter the binding capability to protein, hence altering gene expression.

Histone methylation and demethylation

During histone methylation process, the methyl group binds to lysine (k) and arginine (R) residues with the help of histone methyltransferases. Occurring at three different levels, the methylation is either mono-, bi-, or tri-, and depending on target histone modifications, either results in activation or repression of the gene [40]. Histone H3 lysine 4 (H3K4), histone H3 lysine 36 (H3K36), and histone H3 lysine 79 (H3K79) are associated with gene activation, whereas histone H3 lysine 9 (H3K9), histone H3 lysine 27 (H3K27), and histone H4 lysine 20 (H4K20) are associated with gene repression [41]. Lysine-specific demethylase (LSD) is associated with many cancers including bladder, lung, colorectal, and acute myeloid leukemia (AML). Loss of LSD is affiliated with impairment in hematopoietic stem cells, suggesting its involvement in CSCs maintenance and progression. In line with this, studies have shown the involvement of histone methylation in regulating CSC self-renewal signaling pathways like Wnt, Notch, Hedgehog, etc. [42].

Histone acetylation and deacetylation

Another category of histone modifications is acetylation, and deacetylation that correlates with many diseases including cancer [43]. Histone acetyltransferases (HAT) play a major role in such modifications by adding the acetyl group to lysine residues of histones and nonhistone proteins. On the contrary, histone deacetylases (HDACs) remove the acetyl group, implying the contrasting functions of HAT that is responsible for enhancing the gene expression by relaxing the chromatin structure and HDAC diminishing gene expression by condensing the chromatin [43,44]. Disruption in balancing act of HAT and HDAC often affects certain critical pathways including the ones governing differentiation and self-renewal of CSCs [25,43].

The association of upregulated HDACs leading to differentiation and maintenance of CSCs is confirmed in breast and ovarian cancers [45,46]. P300, a member of HAT family, and CBP are coactivators of pathways such as Wnt/β-catenin and c-Myb that are associated with CSCs and drug resistance. In addition, this epigenetic modification of c-Myb governs the self-renewal and proliferation potential of CSCs in AML [47]. In agreement, the inhibition of HDAC11 abrogated Sox-2 signaling, prime to self-renewal and viability of the cells [48].

Noncoding RNAs

Noncoding RNAs do not translate into proteins and come across as paramount epigenetic regulators due to their role in regulating gene expression at posttranslational levels.

Micro-RNAs (miRNA)

Certain micro-RNAs (miRNAs) affiliate with genes supervising vital CSC functions in tumorigenesis such as stemness, differentiation, and epithelial-mesenchymal transition (EMT) [49]. For example, downregulation of miRNA34a in gastric cancer affects the formation of survival and proliferative proteins critical for CSCs, namely CD44, Oct-4, Bcl-2, Sox-2, and Notch [50]. On the other hand, oncogenic miRNA21 is found to be upregulated in pancreatic CSCs, leading to cell proliferation and chemoresistance [51].

Long noncoding RNAs (lncRNA)

Moreover, long noncoding RNAs (lncRNAs) play a pivotal role in maintaining stem cell-like phenotype including malignant transformations [52]. HOX transcript antisense RNA (HOTAIR) is a lncRNA that represses gene expression by recruiting chromatin modifiers, hence holding an important position among epigenetic modulators. HOTAIR is corroborated to acquisition of stemness by upregulation in $CD133^+/CD44^+$ CSC population of colon cancer. Here, the TGF-β treatment of these CSCs induces EMT and aids in their maintenance [53]. Also, in breast CSC pool, HOTAIR suppresses the tumor-inhibiting miRNA7 [54].

MALAT-1 is another widely studied lncRNA associated with breast, ovarian, and pancreatic CSCs governing and enhancing their properties like proliferation, invasion, colony formation, and EMT [55–58]. The foundations of noncoding RNAs that play an epigenetic role in regulating gene expression and maintaining CSCs in different cancers and metastasis are opening new avenues in the field of understanding drug resistance and cancer progression.

RNA methylation

MODOMICs database identifies seven times more presence of RNA methylation when compared with DNA Methylations [43]. It is a posttranslational modification, especially of mRNA and lncRNAs, impacting these modifications and RNA interactions with other cell components [59]. For example, demethylation of one of the commonly known RNA modifications, N6-methyladenosine (m6A), increases Nanog expression, rendering self-renewal and maintenance of breast CSC [60]. In line with this, m6A regulation holds importance in maintaining stemness of Glioblastoma CSCs [61]. Certain therapeutic interventions discussed later in this chapter highlight the importance of RNA methylation in drug resistance and CSCs.

Table 1 Epigenetic alterations in CSCs.

Cancer type	Epigenetic modifications	Type
Leukemia	PRMT1 (upregulation)	Methylase
	CBP/p300 (protein interactions)	Acetylases
	MOZ	Acetylases
	DNMT3A (downregulation)	Acetylases
	Tet2 (downregulation)	DNA methylases
Glioblastoma	KDMB1 (overexpression)	Demethylases
	METTL3 (m6A modifications)	RNA methyltransferase
	METTL14 (m6A modifications)	RNA methyltransferase
Breast cancer	KDMA1 (overexpression)	Demethylases
	DNMT1 (overexpression)	DNA methyltransferase
	HOTAIR (overexpression)	Long noncoding RNAs
	Linc00617 (upregulation)	Long noncoding RNAs
Pancreatic cancer	PRC1 (overexpression)	Chromatin remodelers
	HOTTIP (overexpression)	Long noncoding RNAs
	MALAT-1 (upregulation)	Long noncoding RNAs
Hepatocellular carcinoma	HDAC3 (overexpression)	Deacetylases
	InchPVT 1 (upregulation)	Long noncoding RNAs
	MALAT-1 (upregulation)	Long noncoding RNAs
Colorectal carcinoma	KDM3A (mRNA Stabilization)	Demethylases
	SIRT-1 (overexpression)	Deacetylases

"In total", all the epigenetic mechanisms described in this chapter assist in maintenance of CSC through pro-survival signaling, proliferation, differentiation, and self-renewal, hence acquiring drug resistance capabilities. Table 1 summarizes the major epigenetic alterations associated with CSCs [62].

Epigenetic involvement in drug resistance

Current therapeutics involving chemotherapy, radiation therapy, targeted, and immunotherapies have paved the way for modern age treatment options with prolonged survival rate of patients. Nevertheless, relapse and metastasis are still two major challenges in effective patient care. Evidence shows that well-studied genetic aberrations are central to explaining conventional and targeted therapeutic approaches, yet there is a need to explore beyond genetics to target the tumor subsets that otherwise lead to relapse [63–66].

Discovery of a stubborn subset of cells in heterogeneous tumors, i.e., CSCs possessing slow-growing, self-renewal capabilities with augmented drug transporters to escape conventional and targeted therapeutics, brought a new dimension to understanding drug resistance. In this chapter we have discussed how various epigenetic mechanisms control, to some extent, the stem cell-like characteristics of CSC that could be utilized as the bridge to fill the knowledge gap between present-day therapeutics and drug resistance.

Therapeutic targeting of epigenetic alterations in cancers
DNMT inhibitors

As discussed earlier, DNMTs hold a prime spot in governing the CSC status, hence making it an important target for therapeutic interventions. DNMT inhibitors (DNMTi) are widely studied therapeutic agents that inhibit DNMT activity and hence aid in combating cancer. At present two Azanucleosides (azacytidine and decitabine) have been approved by the US Food and Drug Administration (FDA) for the treatment of AML and myelodysplastic syndrome (MDS) [67]. Azacytidine (Aza) is a cytosine inhibitor covalently binding to the enzyme, rendering it ineffective [68]. Aza treatment has inhibitory effects on CSCs from gastric, prostate, and pancreatic cancers [69]. Besides, in a study of new DNMTi, Gaudecitabine SGI-110 treatment leads to reduced tumor-initiating ability and increased sensitivity of ovarian CSCs to platinum, hence introducing it as one of the drugs with combinatorial treatment potential [70]. Furthermore, Li et al. demonstrate that DNMTi targets colorectal CSCs through downregulation of Wnt/β-catenin pathway, confirming its ability to reduce stemness of CSCs [71]. Additionally, overexpression of DNMTs in Gastric cancer is associated with the abrogation of Tumor suppressor genes. Low doses of DNMTi administered for gastric cancer cells can reverse this phenomenon inducing drug sensitivity [72].

Histone deacetylase (HDAC) inhibitors

One of the processes through which histone modifications occur is acetylation catalyzed by HDAC. Therefore, studying HDAC inhibitors as potential drug targets for combinatorial treatments is recommended. FDA-approved HDAC inhibitors, Vorinostat and Romidepsin, are used in treatment of cutaneous T-cell lymphoma [73,74]. In addition, a few more HDAC inhibitors are undergoing clinical study evaluations and are gaining importance in this field [75,76]. HDAC inhibitors like valproic acid target CSCs from AML by inducing differentiation and demolishing their quiescent state, that otherwise is responsible to escape present-day therapeutics [77]. Also, Entinostat, a new HDAC inhibitor, has been reported to reverse EMT phenotype in triple-negative breast cancers (TNBCs) [78].

Histone methyltransferase inhibitors

Histone lysine methyltransferase (HKMT) inhibitors are recently gaining importance in combinatorial treatment strategies for resistant cancers. DOT1L is a HEK79 methyltransferase found in mixed lineage leukemia associated with overexpression of many critical target genes [79]. EPZ-5676 is a novel DOT1L inhibitor that minimizes tumors in MLL xenograft models and is currently in clinical trials for MLL and AML [80]. Furthermore, Kim et al. verify that BIX-01294, a HKMT inhibitor, induced dysfunction in euchromatic histone lysine methyltransferase 1 (EHMT) and enhances cell death in colon and breast cancers [81].

Combinatorial strategies for epigenetic therapeutics

Breast cancer is well-studied model for understanding CSCs, drug resistance, epigenetic involvement as well as therapeutic options. A study performed by Pathania et al. displays the effectiveness of combining two epigenetic modulators, DNMTi Azacytidine and HDAC inhibitor butyrate, in targeting CSC [82]. Furthermore, combining Azacytidine with Entinostat exhibits a positive response in patients during phase I/II trials of NSCL cancer [83]. Moreover, as described earlier SGI-110 drives ovarian CSC toward differentiation, hence rendering them sensitive to platinum therapy [70]. In line with this, Azacytidine treatment sensitized colon cancer cell lines to irinotecan therapy [84]. Breast CSCs can be targeted to inhibit tumor growth by utilizing nanoparticles packed with doxorubicin and decitabine, again confirming the effectiveness of the combination of an epigenetic modulator with a conventional drug [85]. Besides, DNMTi and HDACi reduce the resistance to immune therapy by modulating immune responses. Therefore, a combinatorial treatment strategy of epigenetic modulators with targeted therapies and immunotherapies has the potential to suppress drug resistance and minimize relapse [86].

References

[1] T.B. Emran, et al., Multidrug resistance in cancer: understanding molecular mechanisms, immunoprevention and therapeutic approaches, Front. Oncol. 12 (2022) 891652.

[2] A. Marusyk, K. Polyak, Tumor heterogeneity: causes and consequences, Biochim. Biophys. Acta 1805 (1) (2010) 105–117.

[3] C.C. Park, M.J. Bissell, M.H. Barcellos-Hoff, The influence of the microenvironment on the malignant phenotype, Mol. Med. Today 6 (8) (2000) 324–329.

[4] O.M. Zlatian, et al., Histochemical and immunohistochemical evidence of tumor heterogeneity in colorectal cancer, Rom. J. Morphol. Embryol. 56 (1) (2015) 175–181.

[5] S. Glöckner, et al., Marked intratumoral heterogeneity of c-myc and cyclinD1 but not of c-erbB2 amplification in breast cancer, Lab. Invest. 82 (10) (2002) 1419–1426.

[6] P.S. Oak, Development of novel combinatorial treatment strategies to overcome resistance in breast cancer, in: Faculty of Chemistry and Pharmacy, LMU München, 2012.

[7] C.R. Thoma, et al., 3D cell culture systems modeling tumor growth determinants in cancer target discovery, Adv. Drug Deliv. Rev. 69–70 (2014) 29–41.

[8] M. Zanoni, et al., 3D tumor spheroid models for in vitro therapeutic screening: a systematic approach to enhance the biological relevance of data obtained, Sci. Rep. 6 (2016) 19103.

[9] E.R. Boghaert, et al., The volume of three-dimensional cultures of cancer cells in vitro influences transcriptional profile differences and similarities with monolayer cultures and xenografted tumors, Neoplasia 19 (9) (2017) 695–706.

[10] E. Krawczyk, J. Kitlińska, Preclinical models of neuroblastoma-current status and perspectives, Cancers (Basel) 15 (13) (2023).

[11] S.M. Badr-Eldin, et al., Three-dimensional in vitro cell culture models for efficient drug discovery: progress so far and future prospects, Pharmaceuticals (Basel) 15 (8) (2022).

[12] M. Lee-Theilen, et al., Co-expression of CD34, CD90, OV-6 and cell-surface vimentin defines cancer stem cells of hepatoblastoma, which are affected by Hsp90 inhibitor 17-AAG, Cells 10 (10) (2021).

[13] L. Zhang, L. Shen, D. Wu, Clinical significance of cancer stem cell markers in lung carcinoma, Acta Biochim. Pol. 68 (2) (2021) 187–191.

[14] S. Goto, T. Kawabata, T.S. Li, Enhanced expression of ABCB1 and Nrf2 in CD133-positive cancer stem cells associates with doxorubicin resistance, Stem Cells Int. 2020 (2020) 8868849.

[15] R.P. Nagare, et al., ALDH1A1+ ovarian cancer stem cells co-expressing surface markers CD24, EPHA1 and CD9 form tumours in vivo, Exp. Cell Res. 392 (1) (2020) 112009.

[16] P. Xia, et al., Cancer stem cell markers for urinary carcinoma, Stem Cells Int. 2022 (2022) 3611677.

[17] I. Skidan, S.C. Steiniger, In vivo models for cancer stem cell research: a practical guide for frequently used animal models and available biomarkers, J. Physiol. Pharmacol. 65 (2) (2014) 157–169.

[18] J.E. Visvader, G.J. Lindeman, Cancer stem cells in solid tumours: accumulating evidence and unresolved questions, Nat. Rev. Cancer 8 (10) (2008) 755–768.

[19] A. Seno, et al., Cancer stem cell induction from mouse embryonic stem cells, Oncol. Lett. 18 (3) (2019) 2756–2762.

[20] S.B. Keysar, et al., Regulation of head and neck squamous cancer stem cells by PI3K and SOX2, J. Natl. Cancer Inst. 109 (1) (2017).

[21] F. Kokabi, et al., A reliable mouse model of liver and lung metastasis by injecting esophageal cancer stem cells (CSCs) through tail-vein injection, Mol. Biol. Rep. 50 (4) (2023) 3401–3411.

[22] E.J. Kilmister, S.T. Tan, Insights into vascular anomalies, cancer, and fibroproliferative conditions: the role of stem cells and the renin-angiotensin system, Front. Surg. 9 (2022) 868187.

[23] G.S. Wilson, et al., Efficacy of using cancer stem cell markers in isolating and characterizing liver cancer stem cells, Stem Cells Dev. 22 (19) (2013) 2655–2664.

[24] E.K. Chow, et al., Oncogene-specific formation of chemoresistant murine hepatic cancer stem cells, Hepatology 56 (4) (2012) 1331–1341.

[25] S. Keyvani-Ghamsari, et al., Current understanding of epigenetics mechanism as a novel target in reducing cancer stem cells resistance, Clin. Epigenetics 13 (1) (2021) 120.

[26] K. Takahashi, S. Yamanaka, Induction of pluripotent stem cells from mouse embryonic and adult fibroblast cultures by defined factors, Cell 126 (4) (2006) 663–676.

[27] E. Mosca, et al., Overlapping genes may control reprogramming of mouse somatic cells into induced pluripotent stem cells (iPSCs) and breast cancer stem cells, In Silico Biol. 10 (5-6) (2010) 207–221.

[28] J. Suzuka, et al., Rapid reprogramming of tumour cells into cancer stem cells on double-network hydrogels, Nat. Biomed. Eng. 5 (8) (2021) 914–925.

[29] S. Romero-Garcia, H. Prado-Garcia, A. Carlos-Reyes, Role of DNA methylation in the resistance to therapy in solid tumors, Front. Oncol. 10 (2020) 1152.

[30] C. Chen, et al., DNA methylation: from cancer biology to clinical perspectives, Front. Biosci. (Landmark, Ed.) 27 (12) (2022) 326.

[31] J.Y. Li, et al., Synergistic function of DNA methyltransferases Dnmt3a and Dnmt3b in the methylation of Oct4 and Nanog, Mol. Cell. Biol. 27 (24) (2007) 8748–8759.

[32] M.A. Fouad, et al., Impact of global DNA methylation in treatment outcome of colorectal cancer patients, Front. Pharmacol. 9 (2018) 1173.

[33] C.J. Marsit, et al., Genetic and epigenetic tumor suppressor gene silencing are distinct molecular phenotypes driven by growth promoting mutations in nonsmall cell lung cancer, J. Cancer Epidemiol. 2008 (2008) 215809.

[34] S. Zagorac, et al., DNMT1 inhibition reprograms pancreatic cancer stem cells via upregulation of the miR-17-92 cluster, Cancer Res. 76 (15) (2016) 4546–4558.

[35] X. Yu, et al., Genome-wide DNA methylation pattern of cancer stem cells in esophageal cancer, Technol. Cancer Res. Treat. 19 (2020) 1533033820983793.

[36] A. Bruna, et al., High TGFbeta-Smad activity confers poor prognosis in glioma patients and promotes cell proliferation depending on the methylation of the PDGF-B gene, Cancer Cell 11 (2) (2007) 147–160.

[37] A. Tufegdzic Vidakovic, et al., Context-specific effects of TGF-β/SMAD3 in cancer are modulated by the epigenome, Cell Rep. 13 (11) (2015) 2480–2490.

[38] E.N. Wainwright, P. Scaffidi, Epigenetics and cancer stem cells: unleashing, hijacking, and restricting cellular plasticity, Trends Cancer 3 (5) (2017) 372–386.

[39] V. Veschi, et al., Cancer stem cells in thyroid tumors: from the origin to metastasis, Front. Endocrinol. (Lausanne) 11 (2020) 566.

[40] T.B. Toh, J.J. Lim, E.K. Chow, Epigenetics in cancer stem cells, Mol. Cancer 16 (1) (2017) 29.

[41] T. Kouzarides, Chromatin modifications and their function, Cell 128 (4) (2007) 693–705.

[42] E. Ortiz-Sánchez, Overview: epigenetic regulation in cancer stem cells by methylation. Austin J cancer, Clin. Res. 4 (1) (2014) 1007.

[43] N. Liu, et al., Acetylation and deacetylation in cancer stem-like cells, Oncotarget 8 (51) (2017) 89315–89325.

[44] H. Wapenaar, F.J. Dekker, Histone acetyltransferases: challenges in targeting bi-substrate enzymes, Clin. Epigenetics 8 (2016) 59.

[45] C. Liu, et al., Histone deacetylase 3 participates in self-renewal of liver cancer stem cells through histone modification, Cancer Lett. 339 (1) (2013) 60–69.

[46] A.E. Witt, et al., Identification of a cancer stem cell-specific function for the histone deacetylases, HDAC1 and HDAC7, in breast and ovarian cancer, Oncogene 36 (12) (2017) 1707–1720.

[47] S. Uttarkar, et al., Small-molecule disruption of the Myb/p300 cooperation targets acute myeloid leukemia cells, Mol. Cancer Ther. 15 (12) (2016) 2905–2915.

[48] N. Bora-Singhal, et al., Novel HDAC11 inhibitors suppress lung adenocarcinoma stem cell self-renewal and overcome drug resistance by suppressing Sox2, Sci. Rep. 10 (1) (2020) 4722.

[49] T. Huang, et al., Noncoding RNAs in cancer and cancer stem cells, Chin. J. Cancer 32 (11) (2013) 582–593.

[50] M. Agostini, R.A. Knight, miR-34: from bench to bedside, Oncotarget 5 (4) (2014) 872–881.

[51] S. Bimonte, et al., The role of miRNAs in the regulation of pancreatic cancer stem cells, Stem Cells Int. 2016 (2016) 8352684.

[52] M. Schwerdtfeger, et al., Long non-coding RNAs in cancer stem cells, Transl. Oncol. 14 (8) (2021) 101134.

[53] C. Pádua Alves, et al., Brief report: the lincRNA Hotair is required for epithelial-to-mesenchymal transition and stemness maintenance of cancer cell lines, Stem Cells 31 (12) (2013) 2827–2832.

[54] H. Zhang, et al., MiR-7, inhibited indirectly by lincRNA HOTAIR, directly inhibits SETDB1 and reverses the EMT of breast cancer stem cells by downregulating the STAT3 pathway, Stem Cells 32 (11) (2014) 2858–2868.

[55] F. Jiao, et al., Long noncoding RNA MALAT-1 enhances stem cell-like phenotypes in pancreatic cancer cells, Int. J. Mol. Sci. 16 (4) (2015) 6677–6693.

[56] F. Jiao, et al., Elevated expression level of long noncoding RNA MALAT-1 facilitates cell growth, migration and invasion in pancreatic cancer, Oncol. Rep. 32 (6) (2014) 2485–2492.

[57] M. Korpal, et al., The miR-200 family inhibits epithelial-mesenchymal transition and cancer cell migration by direct targeting of E-cadherin transcriptional repressors ZEB1 and ZEB2, J. Biol. Chem. 283 (22) (2008) 14910–14914.

[58] M. Pa, et al., Long noncoding RNA MALAT1 functions as a sponge of MiR-200c in ovarian cancer, Oncol. Res. (2017).

[59] G. Romano, et al., RNA methylation in ncRNA: classes, detection, and molecular associations, Front. Genet. 9 (2018) 243.

[60] C. Zhang, et al., Hypoxia induces the breast cancer stem cell phenotype by HIF-dependent and ALKBH5-mediated m^{6}A-demethylation of NANOG mRNA, Proc. Natl. Acad. Sci. U. S. A. 113 (14) (2016) E2047–E2056.

[61] Q. Cui, et al., m(6)A RNA methylation regulates the self-renewal and tumorigenesis of glioblastoma stem cells, Cell Rep. 18 (11) (2017) 2622–2634.

[62] F. Verona, et al., Targeting epigenetic alterations in cancer stem cells, Front. Mol. Med. (2022) 2.

[63] S.V. Sharma, et al., A chromatin-mediated reversible drug-tolerant state in cancer cell subpopulations, Cell 141 (1) (2010) 69–80.

[64] B. Biehs, et al., A cell identity switch allows residual BCC to survive Hedgehog pathway inhibition, Nature 562 (7727) (2018) 429–433.

[65] S. Boumahdi, F.J. de Sauvage, The great escape: tumour cell plasticity in resistance to targeted therapy, Nat. Rev. Drug Discov. 19 (1) (2020) 39–56.

[66] A.N. Hata, et al., Tumor cells can follow distinct evolutionary paths to become resistant to epidermal growth factor receptor inhibition, Nat. Med. 22 (3) (2016) 262–269.

[67] A. Gnyszka, Z. Jastrzebski, S. Flis, DNA methyltransferase inhibitors and their emerging role in epigenetic therapy of cancer, Anticancer Res. 33 (8) (2013) 2989–2996.

[68] K. Dzobo, et al., Advances in therapeutic targeting of cancer stem cells within the tumor microenvironment, An Updated Review. Cells 9 (8) (2020).

[69] S. Talukdar, et al., Evolving strategies for therapeutically targeting cancer stem cells, Adv. Cancer Res. 131 (2016) 159–191.

[70] Y. Wang, et al., Epigenetic targeting of ovarian cancer stem cells, Cancer Res. 74 (17) (2014) 4922–4936.

[71] S. Li, et al., Inhibition of DNMT suppresses the stemness of colorectal cancer cells through down-regulating Wnt signaling pathway, Cell. Signal. 47 (2018) 79–87.

[72] S.E. Norollahi, et al., Therapeutic approach of cancer stem cells (CSCs) in gastric adenocarcinoma; DNA methyltransferases enzymes in cancer targeted therapy, Biomed. Pharmacother. 115 (2019) 108958.

[73] E.A. Olsen, et al., Phase IIb multicenter trial of vorinostat in patients with persistent, progressive, or treatment refractory cutaneous T-cell lymphoma, J. Clin. Oncol. 25 (21) (2007) 3109–3115.

[74] R.L. Piekarz, et al., Phase II multi-institutional trial of the histone deacetylase inhibitor romidepsin as monotherapy for patients with cutaneous T-cell lymphoma, J. Clin. Oncol. 27 (32) (2009) 5410–5417.

[75] N. Ahuja, H. Easwaran, S.B. Baylin, Harnessing the potential of epigenetic therapy to target solid tumors, J. Clin. Invest. 124 (1) (2014) 56–63.

[76] A.C. West, R.W. Johnstone, New and emerging HDAC inhibitors for cancer treatment, J. Clin. Invest. 124 (1) (2014) 30–39.

[77] G. Bug, et al., Effect of histone deacetylase inhibitor valproic acid on progenitor cells of acute myeloid leukemia, Haematologica 92 (4) (2007) 542–545.

[78] A. Schech, et al., Histone deacetylase inhibitor entinostat inhibits tumor-initiating cells in triple-negative breast cancer cells, Mol. Cancer Ther. 14 (8) (2015) 1848–1857.

[79] E. Bitoun, P.L. Oliver, K.E. Davies, The mixed-lineage leukemia fusion partner AF4 stimulates RNA polymerase II transcriptional elongation and mediates coordinated chromatin remodeling, Hum. Mol. Genet. 16 (1) (2007) 92–106.

[80] C.R. Klaus, et al., DOT1L inhibitor EPZ-5676 displays synergistic antiproliferative activity in combination with standard of care drugs and hypomethylating agents in MLL-rearranged leukemia cells, J. Pharmacol. Exp. Ther. 350 (3) (2014) 646–656.

[81] Y. Kim, et al., BIX-01294 induces autophagy-associated cell death via EHMT2/G9a dysfunction and intracellular reactive oxygen species production, Autophagy 9 (12) (2013) 2126–2139.

[82] R. Pathania, et al., Combined inhibition of DNMT and HDAC blocks the tumorigenicity of cancer stem-like cells and attenuates mammary tumor growth, Cancer Res. 76 (11) (2016) 3224–3235.

[83] A. Suraweera, K.J. O'Byrne, D.J. Richard, Combination therapy with histone deacetylase inhibitors (HDACi) for the treatment of cancer: achieving the full therapeutic potential of HDACi, Front. Oncol. 8 (2018) 92.

[84] H. Moro, et al., Epigenetic priming sensitizes gastric cancer cells to irinotecan and cisplatin by restoring multiple pathways, Gastric Cancer 23 (1) (2020) 105–115.

[85] S.Y. Li, et al., Combination therapy with epigenetic-targeted and chemotherapeutic drugs delivered by nanoparticles to enhance the chemotherapy response and overcome resistance by breast cancer stem cells, J. Controlled Release 205 (2015) 7–14.

[86] A. Majchrzak-Celińska, A. Warych, M. Szoszkiewicz, Novel approaches to epigenetic therapies: from drug combinations to epigenetic editing, Genes (Basel) 12 (2) (2021).

Cancer biomarkers: Where genetics meets epigenetics

10

Snehal Nirgude[a] and Jennifer M. Kalish[a,b]

[a]*Division of Human Genetics and Center for Childhood Cancer Research, Children's Hospital of Philadelphia, Philadelphia, PA, United States,* [b]*Departments of Pediatrics and Genetics, Perelman School of Medicine at the University of Pennsylvania, Philadelphia, PA, United States*

Epigenetics in cancer biology

Epigenetics is the study of stable, heritable changes that allow the transfer of gene function information from one cell generation to the next such that cellular identity and lineage fidelity are preserved, with no alterations in the underlying DNA sequence [1–3]. However, epigenetic changes are reversible in nature [4]. Epigenetic mechanisms that bring about gene regulation are DNA methylation, histone modifications, chromatin remodeling, and noncoding RNAs (Fig. 1). These mechanisms are interconnected and reversible and constitute the "epigenetic code" to modulate the gene expression pattern beyond the DNA sequence (Fig. 2) [2].

Cancer is a cell signaling disorder and the resulting outcome of heterogeneous genetic and epigenetic alterations that occur in cells through various stages of tumorigenesis. The cancer phenotype, including clinical outcome, tumor stage, tumor grade, etc., has been extensively corelated to gene expression [5]. However, this is an end point analysis. Epigenetic events are early events, and hence, epigenetic biomarkers can serve as better prognostic markers. Epigenetic deregulation is one of the major hallmarks of cancer and can lead to activation of oncogenes or silencing of tumor suppressor genes (TSGs) [6]. This chapter focuses on the connections between genetics and epigenetics as related to oncogenesis.

Histone modifications

Histones are the fundamental components of nucleosomes that constitute chromatin. Every nucleosome consists of a histone octamer comprising two copies of four histones—H2A, H2B, H3, and H4. The N-terminals of these histones, populated with basic lysine/arginine residues and hydroxyl group-containing Serine/Threonine/Tyrosine residues, undergo different covalent posttranslational modifications

Cancer Epigenetics and Nanomedicine. https://doi.org/10.1016/B978-0-443-13209-4.00006-4
Copyright © 2024 Elsevier Inc. All rights reserved, including those for text and data mining, AI training, and similar technologies.

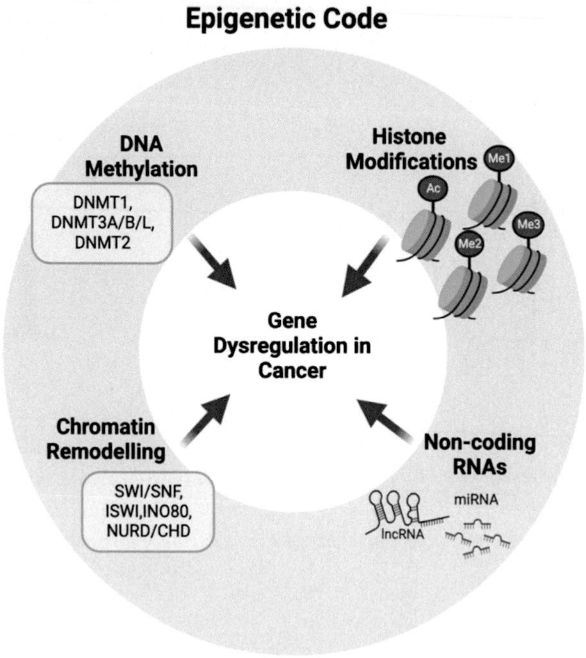

Epigenetic Code

DNA Methylation

DNMT1, DNMT3A/B/L, DNMT2

Histone Modifications

Me1, Ac, Me2, Me3

Gene Dysregulation in Cancer

Chromatin Remodelling

SWI/SNF, ISWI,INO80, NURD/CHD

Non-coding RNAs

miRNA

lncRNA

FIG. 1

The epigenetic code: the epigenetic code comprises four main components that regulate gene expression—DNA methylation, histone modifications, noncoding RNAs, and chromatin remodeling.

Epigenetic Deregulation in Cancer

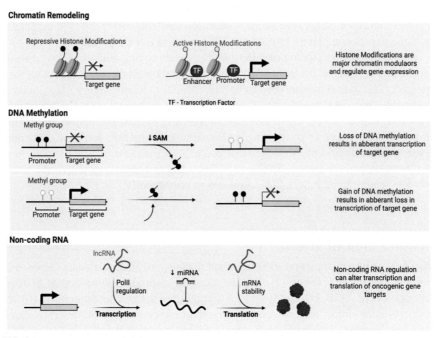

Chromatin Remodeling

Repressive Histone Modifications

Active Histone Modifications

Enhancer   Promoter   Target gene

Target gene

TF - Transcription Factor

Histone Modifications are major chromatin modulaors and regulate gene expression

DNA Methylation

Methyl group

Promoter   Target gene

↓ SAM

Loss of DNA methylation results in abberant transcription of target gene

Methyl group

Promoter   Target gene

Gain of DNA methylation results in abberant loss in transcription of target gene

Non-coding RNA

lncRNA

PolII regulation

Transcription

↓ miRNA

mRNA stability

Translation

Non-coding RNA regulation can alter transcription and translation of oncogenic gene targets

FIG. 2

Epigenetic mechanisms altered in cancer: epigenetic mechanisms that lead to aberrant gene expression or repression.

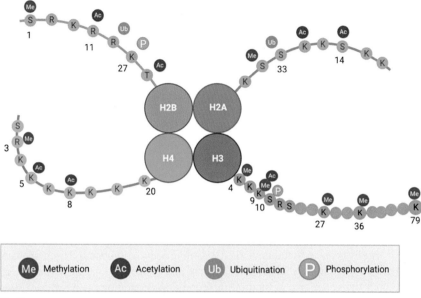

FIG. 3

Histone modifications: the histone modifications occur at the N-terminals of the histones, which are populated with basic lysine (K)/arginine (R) residues and hydroxyl group-containing Serine (S)/Threonine (T)/Tyrosine (Y) residues.

(PTMs) such as methylation, acetylation, phosphorylation, ubiquitination, and sumoylation when they protrude out of the nucleosome (Fig. 3) [7]. These modifications, either individually or in combination, encode distinct nucleosome functions such as gene transcription, X-chromosome inactivation, heterochromatin formation, mitosis, and DNA repair and replication [2] and form the "histone modification code." The presence or absence of these modifications can change the nucleosomal conformation, modulating chromatin structure and gene expression.

Appropriate histone modifications are required for gene expression, and aberrant alterations in PTMs can lead to tumorigenesis. Since alterations in histone modifications occur at early stages of carcinogenesis, understanding these patterns provides insights into early tumor development. Histone acetylation and methylation have been most extensively studied and are discussed in detail below.

Histone acetylation

Histone acetylation adds the acetyl group to the positive charge of lysine residues, which loosens the tight chromatin conformation, making it accessible to transcription factors and leading to gene activation. Histone acetylation occurring at lysine residues of histones H3 and H4 is regulated by two enzymes—histone acetyltransferases (HATs) that add acetyl groups and histone deacetylases (HDACs) that remove them. Both HATs (Gcn5/PCAF, p300/CBP, and the MYST families) and HDACs work in concert to maintain histone acetylation and are altered in cancer [8]. HATs are primarily involved in chromosomal translocations and, therefore, mainly implicated in hematological cancers, whereas HDACs silence the TSGs by aberrant binding [9]. Global loss of histone acetylation like H4K16ac [10] mediated by HDAC overexpression is observed in many cancers leading to gene repression [11].

Histone methylation

Histone methylation is regulated at lysine and arginine residues with the help of "writers," histone methyltransferases (HMTs), "readers," histone methylation-recognizing proteins, and "erasers," histone demethylases (HDMs). HMTs methylate the lysine and arginine residues on the histone tails with the help of *S*-adenosyl-methionine. Mono-, di-, or trimethylated states of lysine and mono- or dimethylated states of arginine can be found in vivo [12]. Unlike acetylation, methylation does not directly impact the histone-DNA interactions, and hence, histone methylation can lead to both transcriptional activation or repression depending on the methylation site and lysine/arginine residue. Both lysine HMTs (NSD1, SMYD3, and G9a) and arginine HMTs (PRMT1, PRMT5) are aberrantly expressed in cancer [9].

Histone readers are nonhistone proteins that bind to chromatin via their domains (bromo, chromo, and plant homeodomain) and affect their structure to regulate transcription, DNA repair, or replication [13]. Meanwhile, HDMs alter chromosome accessibility by deacetylation of histones. A classic example of HDMs is histone lysine-specific demethylase 1 (LSD1), which removes mono or dimethylated H3K4 and H3K9 and is overexpressed in many cancer types [14]. Thus, LSD1 inhibitors are being explored as anticancer drugs [14].

Simultaneous enrichment of activating (e.g., histone H3 lysine 4 monomethylation [H3K4me1] or trimethylation [H3K4me3]) and repressing (e.g., H3K27me3) chromatin modifications can coexist and are termed as "bivalent chromatin domains" [15]. These are mainly found in pluripotent embryonic stem cells in imprinted gene regions and differentiated cells [16]. Profiling bivalent domains can give insights into developmental cell states—bivalent domains are associated with developmental genes that are presently silent but poised for activation upon differentiation [15].

Histone PTMs as cancer biomarkers

Changes in histone modification patterns are also observed in cancer cells. PTMs have great potential as cancer biomarkers since they are found in both tumors and circulate in blood [13]. Various PTMs have been reported in different cancer forms, including breast, colorectal, esophageal, and lung, among others—Table 1 summarizes the histone acetylation, methylation modifications, their association with gene transcription, and their impact on the type of cancer.

Table 1 Histone modifications observed in cancer: the table summarizes the histone acetylation, methylation modifications, their association with gene transcription, and impact on type of cancer.

Modification	Site of modification	Effect on transcription	Impact on cancer type
Acetylated lysine	H3K9 (enhancers, promoters)	Activation	Breast [17] Lung [18]
	H3K27 (enhancers, promoters)	Activation	Colorectal [19]
	H3K18	Activation	Breast [17] Prostate [20] Pancreatic [21]
	H3K56		Colorectal [22]
	H3K14	Activation	
	H4K12	Activation	Breast [17]
	H4K 5/8/13/16		
	H2AK 5/9/13		
	H2BK 5/12/15/20		
Methylated arginine	H3R 17/23	Activation	
	H4R3	Activation	
	H4R2		Breast [17]
Methylated lysine	H3K4Me3 (promoter)	Activation	Hepatocellular [23]
	H3K4Me1 (enhancer)	Activation	Prostate [20] Breast [17] Pancreatic [21] Renal [24] Lung [24] Prostate [24]
	H3K 36/79 (transcribed region)	Repression	
	H3K9me3 (satellite repeats, telomeres, pericentromeres)	Repression	Colorectal [25] Gastric [26] Acute myeloid leukemia [27] Bladder [28]
	H3K27me3 (promoters, gene-rich regions)	Repression	Breast [29] Ovarian [29] Pancreatic [29] Hepatocellular [30] Colorectal [31] Nonsmall cell lung [32] Oral squamous cell [33]
	H4K20Me3	Repression	Breast [34] Colorectal [35]

Aberrant gene silencing is seen in cancer cells with alterations in H3K9 [36] and H3K27 [37] methylation patterns. The H3K27me3 mark is also associated with the Polycomb Group (PcG) domain. H3K27me3 is deposited by enhancer of zeste homolog 2 (EZH2) and is associated with gene repression in a cell-type-specific manner [38]. In cancer, permanent DNA methylation occurs at the H3K27me3 polycomb mark via an "epigenetic switching" mechanism (replacement of gene repression by the polycomb mark with long-term silencing through DNA methylation), leading to permanent silencing of regulatory genes [8]. Another regulator, DOT1L (disruptor of telomeric silencing 1-like), methylates H3K79 and has functional implications in telomeric silencing, transcriptional elongation, DNA repair, and cell cycle regulation. DOT1L plays a vital role in the development of breast, lung [39], ovarian [40] cancer, and mixed lineage leukemia [41]. Dysregulation of HMTs and lysine-specific demethylases are also known repressive marks that alter the cancer epigenome [8].

Epigenetic dysregulation mediated by histone modifications can lead to activation of oncogenes or silencing of TSGs, resulting in oncogenesis. These dynamic epigenomic mechanisms in cancer cells can be studied by utilizing histone profile approaches [42]. Such approaches not only reveal key chromatin signatures specific to cancer subtypes but also have the potential to identify novel actionable targets for treatment [43]. PTGER2 and KLF7 were discovered as biomarker genes in colorectal cancer by studying the changes in H3K37me3 and H3K4me3 histone marks [44]. Hence, the study of histone profiling in cancer can give insights into transcriptional states, which can guide therapeutic decisions [45].

DNA methylation

DNA methylation is a chemical covalent process that involves the addition of a methyl (CH_3) group at the fifth carbon in the cytosine ring, leading to a change in the structure of DNA and its interaction with the transcription machinery (Fig. 4) [4,46]. DNA methylation is not only species-specific but also tissue specific [47]. *S*-adenosyl-methionine is a methyl donor, and the reaction is catalyzed by the DNA methyl transferase (DNMT) family [2,46]. The DNMT enzymes are encoded by five genes—*DNMT1*, *DNMT2*, *DNMT3A*, *DNMT3B*, and *DNMT3L*. These enzymes carry out two important activities—de novo methylation (methylate unmethylated DNA) and maintenance (one that methylates hemimethylated sites—newly replicated DNA is hemimethylated with methyl groups only on the parental strands) [48,49]. During DNA replication, DNMT1 maintains the methylation pattern of newly synthesized DNA strands, while DNMT3A/3B is de novo methyltransferases that maintain de novo methylation during early development and gametogenesis [50]. DNMT3L is another member that belongs to the family of DNMT3, which binds to DNMT3A/B to increase their catalytic activity. However, the roles of maintenance and de novo methylation are not mutually exclusive [50]. DNMT2 (or tRNA cytosine-5-methyltransferase) is an RNA methyltransferase.

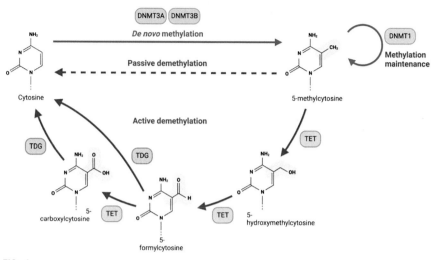

FIG. 4

DNA methylation process: the DNA methylation process leading to the conversion of cytosine to 5-methylcytosine by DNMTs. DNA demethylation is mainly catalyzed by the TET and TDG enzymes. *TDG*, thymine DNA glycosylase; *TET*, ten-eleven translocation.

Aberrant DNA methylation, a hallmark of cancer, can lead to transcription activation or inactivation depending upon the site of methylation [51]. In cancer, hypermethylation of promoter or enhancer of genes, including TSGs, is observed. This leads to TSG silencing. Whereas DNA hypomethylation is seen in high, moderate copy-repeats and in unique sequences involved in transcriptional control [52]. In carcinogenesis, these epigenetic mechanisms work synergistically with existing driver mutations, leading to worse clinical outcomes [53].

DNA methylation can inhibit gene transcription either by recruiting methyl-CpG-binding domain (MBD) proteins, which further recruit histone-modifying and chromatin-remodeling complexes, or prevent the recruitment of DNA-binding proteins from their target sites. In breast cancer, TSGs like BRCA1, E-cadherin, TMS1,14-3-3σ (also known as HME1) have been reported to be downregulated by promoter hypermethylation [50,54]. Genes like p16/CDKN2A [55], p15/CdkN2B [56], and p57KIP1 [57] have been shown to undergo repression due to DNA hypermethylation in cancer. However, methylation changes in gene promoters may not always correlate with its expression. For example, the Wilms' tumor suppressor 1 (*WT1*) gene is overexpressed in breast tumor tissue despite hypermethylation of its promoter [54].

Since the methylation marks are reversible, DNMT inhibitors (DNMTI) like azacitidine and decitabine have received US FDA approval for the treatment of hematological malignancies and patients with high-risk myelodysplastic syndrome (MDS) [50]. A Phase II study of combination therapy with DNMTI 5-azacitidine (5-AZA) and a histone deacetylase inhibitor (HDACI) Entinostat (MS-275) has been tried for estrogen receptor (ER) and progesterone receptor (PR) reexpression in advanced triple-negative breast cancer (TNBC—ER negative, PR negative, human epidermal growth factor receptor 2 [HER2] negative) [58]. The outcome of this study has shown robust efficacy in clinical trials [50]. Other DNMT inhibitors have also been developed and are tested for cancer treatment [59].

TET (ten-eleven translocation) proteins are iron-Fe(II) and 2-oxoglutarate-dependent dioxygenases that mediate DNA demethylation by oxidizing 5-methylcytosine (5mC) to 5-hydroxymethylcytosine (5hmC), 5-formylcytosine (5fC), and 5-carboxylcytosine (5caC) (Fig. 4) [60]. Mutations in TET genes are frequently observed in both solid and liquid malignancies, which lead to inactivation of the genes. Out of three TET family members (TET1, TET2, and TET3), TET1 and TET3 are known to have a role in breast tumor malignancy [61], while in hematopoietic malignancies, TET2 is most frequently mutated genes [62]. In addition, the TET enzymes are inhibited due to metabolic perturbations arising from mutations in genes encoding isocitrate dehydrogenase (IDH), fumarate hydratase (FH), or succinate dehydrogenase (SDH) [63].

Chromatin remodeling complexes

Another key mechanism that regulates gene expression is nucleosome occupancy. The ATP-dependent chromatin remodelers are DNA translocases that regulate nucleosome occupancy/repositioning and are grouped into four families—SWI/SNF (switch/sucrose nonfermenting), ISWI (imitation SWI), INO80 (inositol requiring 80), and NURD (nucleosome remodeling and deacetylation)/Mi2/CHD (chromatin helicase DNA binding) complexes [64]. In cancer, inactivating mutations, leading to loss of function in various subunits/components of chromatin modelers have been reported [65]. About 20% of all cancers display mutation in SWI/SNF chromatin remodeling complex [59]. Inactivating mutations in SNF5, a core subunit of SWI/SNF, have been reported in renal carcinomas, melanomas, and rhabdoid tumors [9]. Similarly, other members of the SWI/SNF complex, like ATPases (BRG1 or BRM) and core subunits (SNF5, BAF155, and BAF 170), have also been implicated to have accumulated mutations in cancer [9]. Members of NURD complexes like MTA1/2 [66] and MTA3 [67] are also implicated in carcinogenesis. These mutations alter the nucleosome occupancy pattern and lead to aberrant gene expression or repression.

Noncoding RNAs

The third important component of the epigenetic machinery is the noncoding RNAs, which include microRNAs (miRNAs), small interfering RNA (siRNAs), piwi-interacting RNA (piRNAs), and long noncoding RNAs (lncRNAs) RNA [68]. These noncoding RNAs play an important role in protein expression by modifying the sequence structure of expression of the mRNA [46]. LncRNAs are more than 200 nucleotides in length and interact with DNA, RNA, and proteins in the nucleus to regulate gene expression [69]. Though the specific mode of action of lncRNAs remains elusive, few lncRNAs are currently used as cancer biomarkers. For example, the prostate cancer antigen (PCA) lncRNA is used as an early diagnostic biomarker for prostate cancer [70]. Other lncRNAs like H19 for breast cancer [71], HOTAIR [72], and MALAT1 [73] for gastric cancer are being explored. lncRNAs need intensive study with respect to their mechanism of action, expression, and structure to use them as therapeutic targets.

miRNAs, one of the most studied noncoding RNAs, are ~22 nucleotides noncoding RNAs that regulate gene expression by RNA interference posttranscriptionally [3,46]. This regulation is based on the complementarity of miRNA with the $3'$ UTR region of target mRNA. However, miRNAs can also bind to the $5'$ UTR or coding region of target mRNA and activate translation [74]. miRNAs can modulate epigenetic machinery and reciprocally, their expression can be modulated by the epigenetic machinery [3].

miRNAs in cancer

miRNAs that are implicated in cancer can be divided into oncogenic miRNAs (oncomiRs)—overexpressed in cancers [75] and tumor suppressive miRNAs (TSmiRs) [76]—downregulated in cancers. Therapeutic strategies can be designed to downregulate oncomiRs and upregulate TSmiRs. In cancer, the miRNAs are known to affect the hallmark processes of invasion, metastasis, cell proliferation, apoptosis, drug resistance, energy metabolism, cell cycle, and angiogenesis (Fig. 5). Since miRNAs are known to target multiple genes, their role as oncomiRs or TSmiRs depends on the type of cancer.

Many miRNAs have been now categorized with their role in cancer, but the classic and well-studied ones are—miR-21 and the cluster miR-17-92 as oncomiRs; miR-34, miR-15/16, miR-200, and let-7 as TSmiRs [77,78]. miR-21, an oncomiR, is overexpressed in an array of cancers like breast, colorectal, lung, and pancreatic cancer; glioblastoma; neuroblastoma; leukemia; and lymphoma and regulates all the processes that lead to tumorigenesis [77]. The cluster miR-17-92 is composed of miRNAs 17, 18a, 19a, 20a, 19b-1, and 92a-1 and is overexpressed in lung cancer [79] and lymphoma [80]. V-myc avian myelocytomatosis viral oncogene homolog (c-Myc) regulates the apoptotic pathway by modulating miRNAs in cluster miR-17-92 [81]. The TSmiR miR-34a exhibits its inhibitory effect on cancer stem cells by targeting CD44 in lung [82] and prostate cancer [83]. Let-7 inhibits self-renewal and dedifferentiation of breast cancer stem cells by targeting RAS and HMGA2 [84]. miR-200c targets ZEB1 and E-cadherin in pancreatic cells and regulates epithelial-mesenchymal transition (EMT) [85]. miR-200b inhibits EMT, self-renewal and mammosphere formation in breast cancer [86].

The expression of miRNAs is also partially regulated by PTMs of histones, and the expression of epigenetic modifiers (DNMT1, DNMT3A, DNMT3B, EZH2) is regulated by miRNA expression. The promoter of miR-125b-1 is enriched with H3K27me3 and H3K9me3 marks in breast cancer, which also regulates its expression

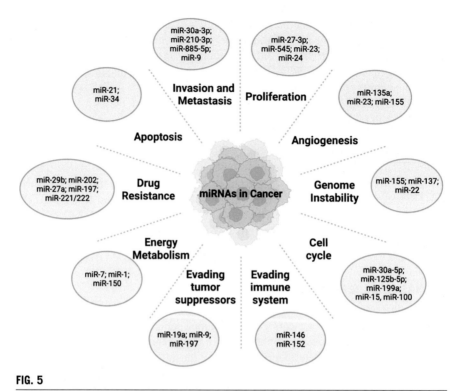

FIG. 5

miRNAs affecting the hallmarks of cancer—miRNAs are known to regulate various cellular processes (invasion and metastasis, proliferation, angiogenesis, cell cycle, energy metabolism apoptosis) via gene regulation and may lead to drug resistance and genome instability in cancer cells.

[87]. miR-29 family is reported to revert DNA methylation by targeting DNMT3A and DNMT3B in lung cancer [88]. Meanwhile, miR-101 is reported to modulate EZH2 expression in cancer cells [89,90]. These examples show an elegant interplay between epigenetic mechanisms to control the transcriptome of cancer cells.

miRNA-based therapeutic strategies

miRNAs are often deregulated in cancer. miRNAs modulate multiple genes, including pharmacogenes [91], and can regulate entire pathways directly or indirectly. Due to their unique expression profile and stability in biological samples, miRNAs have been explored as diagnostic predictors, cancer biomarkers, or therapeutic targets [92]. The current strategy to use miRNAs for therapeutic interventions is based on modulating the miRNA expression by either inhibiting oncomiRs/miRNA suppression therapy or reconstituting TSmiRs/miRNA replacement therapy (Fig. 6) [93].

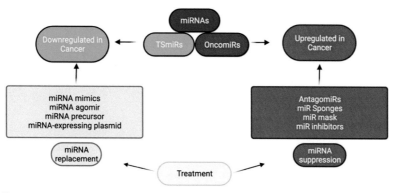

FIG. 6

miRNA-based therapeutic strategies for cancer: oncogenic miRNAs (oncomiRs) are overexpressed and can be targeted by using antogomiRs, miRsponges, miRNA masks, and miRNA inhibitors. Tumor suppressor miRNA (TSmiRs) are downregulated and can be overexpressed using miRNA mimics, miRNA agomir, miRNA precursor, and miRNA-expressing plasmids [27,30].

The miRNA suppression therapy uses antagomiRs/miRNA antagonists, which contain entire complementary sequences of targeted endogenous miRNA [94]. The antagomiRs are designed such that they have strong affinity toward their target miRNA with more resistance to nucleases and lower toxicity [95]. As shown in Fig. 6, miRNA antagonists can also be used in the form of miRNA sponges, miRNA masks, and miRNA inhibitors. miRNA inhibitors and miRNA masks are single-stranded RNAs with different chemical modifications, whereas miR sponges are usually copies of plasmid encoding binding sites complementary to the seed region of the target miRNA [93]. For example, miRNA sponges have been designed to inhibit miR-132 and miR-212 to treat cardiovascular diseases and to inhibit miR-550a in human breast cancer cells [96].

Decreased expression of certain miRNAs is observed in cancer which leads to loss of the miRNA inhibitory effect leading to oncogene activation. In miRNA replacement therapy, the target miRNAs are overexpressed or are replaced by transfection into the cells to restore the "normal" miRNA function. As shown in Fig. 6, this strategy consists of miRNA-mimics, miRNA-agomiR, miRNA-precursor, and miRNA-expressing plasmids. Mimics and agomirs are synthetic double-stranded miRNA-like RNA molecules with different chemical modifications that mimic endogenous mature miRNA molecules transiently. Whereas miRNA-precursors are chemically modified single-stranded RNA fragments that simulate mature miRNAs upon cleaved by Dicer enzyme [93]. Example for miRNA replacement therapy include artificial overexpression of miR-34a using NOV340 liposome in an orthotopic model of hepatocellular carcinoma, which showed promising anticancer results [97].

Stability, bioavailability, and therapeutic delivery are major challenges for nucleotide-based therapeutic approaches [98]. However, nusinersen, an antisense therapeutic, recently received FDA approval for the treatment of spinal muscular atrophy, suggesting the future utility of these approaches [99,100]. For in vivo applications of miR-based therapies, an efficient delivery system is essential like viral vectors or nonviral carriers, which include inorganic material-based delivery systems, lipid-based nanocarriers, polymeric vectors/dendrimer-based vectors, cell-derived membrane vesicles and 3D scaffold-based delivery systems [93]. Further work is needed in this area for cancer therapy.

Conclusion

The epigenetic machinery and cancer progression intersect in a variety of ways as epigenetic dysregulation feeds into oncogenesis. The epigenetic code comprising DNA methylation, histone modifications, chromatin remodelers, and noncoding RNAs represent a series of dynamic alterations that are critically involved in normal cellular function that can transition into carcinogenesis. With the help of advancements in technology, we can decipher the impact of chromatin organization on cancer development. However, there are many questions that remain unanswered within cancer epigenetics. For example, what is the hierarchy of the epigenetic events in gene expression or repression? The answer to this question will provide an array of diagnostic predictors/biomarkers in potential in the precancer to cancer transition. Further studies are still required at the mechanistic and clinical levels to understand the complexity of cancer epigenetics so that additional targeted therapies can be developed and then transitioned so that we can target the exact epigenetic modifiers and truly translate them from bench to bedside.

References

[1] A. Roberti, A.F. Valdes, R. Torrecillas, M.F. Fraga, A.F. Fernandez, Epigenetics in cancer therapy and nanomedicine, Clin. Epigenetics 11 (2019) 81.

[2] Q.W. Chen, X.Y. Zhu, Y.Y. Li, Z.Q. Meng, Epigenetic regulation and cancer (review), Oncol. Rep. 31 (2014) 523–532, https://doi.org/10.3892/or.2013.2913.

[3] Q. Yao, Y. Chen, X. Zhou, The roles of microRNAs in epigenetic regulation, Curr. Opin. Chem. Biol. 51 (2019) 11–17, https://doi.org/10.1016/j.cbpa.2019.01.024.

[4] P.M. Das, R. Singal, DNA methylation and cancer, J. Clin. Oncol. 22 (2004) 4632–4642, https://doi.org/10.1200/jco.2004.07.151.

[5] S. Narrandes, W. Xu, Gene expression detection assay for cancer clinical use, J. Cancer 9 (2018) 2249.

[6] N. Darwiche, Epigenetic mechanisms and the hallmarks of cancer: an intimate affair, Am. J. Cancer Res. 10 (2020) 1954.

[7] J. Qin, B. Wen, Y. Liang, W. Yu, H. Li, Histone modifications and their role in colorectal cancer (review), Pathol. Oncol. Res. 26 (2019) 2023–2033.

[8] S. Sharma, T.K. Kelly, P.A. Jones, Epigenetics in cancer, Carcinogenesis 31 (2010) 27.

[9] J.S. You, P.A. Jones, Cancer genetics and epigenetics: two sides of the same coin? Cancer Cell 22 (2012) 9.

[10] M.F. Fraga, E. Ballestar, A. Villar-Garea, M. Boix-Chornet, J. Espada, G. Schotta, et al., Loss of acetylation at Lys16 and trimethylation at Lys20 of histone H4 is a common hallmark of human cancer, Nat. Genet. 37 (2005) 391–400.

[11] Y. Li, E. Seto, HDACs and HDAC inhibitors in cancer development and therapy, Cold Spring Harb. Perspect. Med. 6 (2016), https://doi.org/10.1101/cshperspect.a026831.

[12] A.J. Bannister, T. Kouzarides, Histone Methylation: Recognizing the Methyl Mark, Methods in Enzymology, vol. 376, Academic Press, 2003, pp. 269–288. https://doi.org/10.1016/S0076-6879(03)76018-2. (ISSN 0076-6879, ISBN 9780121827809).

[13] P. McAnena, J.A.L. Brown, M.J. Kerin, Circulating nucleosomes and nucleosome modifications as biomarkers in cancer, Cancers 9 (2017), https://doi.org/10.3390/cancers9010005.

[14] Y.-C. Zheng, J. Ma, Z. Wang, J. Li, B. Jiang, W. Zhou, et al., A systematic review of histone lysine-specific demethylase 1 and its inhibitors, Med. Res. Rev. 35 (2015) 1032–1071.

[15] A.P. Aiden, M.N. Rivera, E. Rheinbay, M. Ku, E.J. Coffman, T.T. Truong, et al., Wilms tumor chromatin profiles highlight stem cell properties and a renal developmental network, Cell Stem Cell 6 (2010) 591.

[16] S.H. Bernhart, H. Kretzmer, L.M. Holdt, F. Jühling, O. Ammerpohl, A.K. Bergmann, et al., Changes of bivalent chromatin coincide with increased expression of developmental genes in cancer, Sci. Rep. 6 (2016) 1–18.

[17] S.E. Elsheikh, A.R. Green, E.A. Rakha, D.G. Powe, R.A. Ahmed, H.M. Collins, et al., Global histone modifications in breast cancer correlate with tumor phenotypes, prognostic factors, and patient outcome, Cancer Res. 69 (2009) 3802–3809.

[18] J.S. Song, Y.S. Kim, D.K. Kim, S.I. Park, S.J. Jang, Global histone modification pattern associated with recurrence and disease-free survival in non-small cell lung cancer patients, Pathol. Int. 62 (2012) 182–190.

[19] J. Karczmarski, T. Rubel, A. Paziewska, M. Mikula, M. Bujko, P. Kober, et al., Histone H3 lysine 27 acetylation is altered in colon cancer, Clin. Proteomics 11 (2014), https://doi.org/10.1186/1559-0275-11-24.

[20] D.B. Seligson, S. Horvath, T. Shi, H. Yu, S. Tze, M. Grunstein, et al., Global histone modification patterns predict risk of prostate cancer recurrence, Nature 435 (2005) 1262–1266.

[21] Q.A. Acton, Pancreatic Cancer: New Insights for the Healthcare Professional: 2011 Edition, ScholarlyEditions, 2012.

[22] A. Benard, I.J. Goossens-Beumer, A.Q. van Hoesel, H. Horati, W. de Graaf, H. Putter, et al., Nuclear expression of histone deacetylases and their histone modifications predicts clinical outcome in colorectal cancer, Histopathology 66 (2015) 270–282.

[23] C. He, J. Xu, J. Zhang, D. Xie, H. Ye, Z. Xiao, et al., High expression of trimethylated histone H3 lysine 4 is associated with poor prognosis in hepatocellular carcinoma, Hum. Pathol. 43 (2012) 1425–1435.

[24] D.B. Seligson, S. Horvath, M.A. McBrian, V. Mah, H. Yu, S. Tze, et al., Global levels of histone modifications predict prognosis in different cancers, Am. J. Pathol. 174 (2009) 1619–1628.

[25] U. Gezer, D. Ustek, E.E. Yörükcr, A. Cakiris, N. Abaci, G. Leszinski, et al., Characterization of H3K9me3- and H4K20me3-associated circulating nucleosomal DNA by high-throughput sequencing in colorectal cancer, Tumour Biol. 34 (2013) 329–336.

[26] Y.S. Park, M.Y. Jin, Y.J. Kim, J.H. Yook, B.S. Kim, S.J. Jang, The global histone modification pattern correlates with cancer recurrence and overall survival in gastric adenocarcinoma, Ann. Surg. Oncol. 15 (2008) 1968–1976.

[27] C. Müller-Tidow, H.-U. Klein, A. Hascher, F. Isken, L. Tickenbrock, N. Thoennissen, et al., Profiling of histone H3 lysine 9 trimethylation levels predicts transcription factor activity and survival in acute myeloid leukemia, Blood 116 (2010) 3564–3571.

[28] J. Ellinger, A. Bachmann, F. Göke, T.E. Behbahani, C. Baumann, L.C. Heukamp, et al., Alterations of global histone H3K9 and H3K27 methylation levels in bladder cancer, Urol. Int. 93 (2014) 113–118, https://doi.org/10.1159/000355467.

[29] A. Russo, S. Iacobelli, J. Iovanna, Diagnostic, Prognostic and Therapeutic Value of Gene Signatures, Springer Science & Business Media, 2011.

[30] M.-Y. Cai, J.-H. Hou, H.-L. Rao, R.-Z. Luo, M. Li, X.-Q. Pei, et al., High expression of H3K27me3 in human hepatocellular carcinomas correlates closely with vascular invasion and predicts worse prognosis in patients, Mol. Med. 17 (2011) 12–20.

[31] A. Benard, I.J. Goossens-Beumer, A.Q. van Hoesel, H. Horati, H. Putter, E.C.M. Zeestraten, et al., Prognostic value of polycomb proteins EZH2, BMI1 and SUZ12 and histone modification H3K27me3 in colorectal cancer, PLoS One 9 (2014) e108265.

[32] X. Chen, N. Song, K. Matsumoto, A. Nanashima, T. Nagayasu, T. Hayashi, et al., High expression of trimethylated histone H3 at lysine 27 predicts better prognosis in non-small cell lung cancer, Int. J. Oncol. 43 (2013) 1467–1480.

[33] Y.-W. Chen, S.-Y. Kao, H.-J. Wang, M.-H. Yang, Histone modification patterns correlate with patient outcome in oral squamous cell carcinoma, Cancer 119 (2013) 4259–4267.

[34] S. Badve, Y. Gökmen-Polar, Molecular Pathology of Breast Cancer, Springer, 2016.

[35] A. Benard, I.J. Goossens-Beumer, A.Q. van Hoesel, W. de Graaf, H. Horati, H. Putter, et al., Histone trimethylation at H3K4, H3K9 and H4K20 correlates with patient survival and tumor recurrence in early-stage colon cancer, BMC Cancer 14 (2014) 531.

[36] C.T. Nguyen, D.J. Weisenberger, M. Velicescu, F.A. Gonzales, J.C.Y. Lin, G. Liang, et al., Histone H3-lysine 9 methylation is associated with aberrant gene silencing in cancer cells and is rapidly reversed by 5-aza-2′-deoxycytidine, Cancer Res. 62 (2002) 6456–6461.

[37] M.E. Valk-Lingbeek, S.W.M. Bruggeman, M. van Lohuizen, Stem cells and cancer; the polycomb connection, Cell 118 (2004) 409–418.

[38] Y. Cai, Y. Zhang, Y.P. Loh, J.Q. Tng, M.C. Lim, Z. Cao, et al., H3K27me3-rich genomic regions can function as silencers to repress gene expression via chromatin interactions, Nat. Commun. 12 (2021) 1–22.

[39] W. Kim, R. Kim, G. Park, J.-W. Park, J.-E. Kim, Deficiency of H3K79 histone methyltransferase Dot1-like protein (DOT1L) inhibits cell proliferation, J. Biol. Chem. 287 (2012) 5588–5599.

[40] S. Chava, S. Bugide, Y.J.K. Edwards, R. Gupta, Disruptor of telomeric silencing 1-like promotes ovarian cancer tumor growth by stimulating pro-tumorigenic metabolic pathways and blocking apoptosis, Oncogenesis 10 (2021) 1–14.

[41] S.R. Daigle, E.J. Olhava, C.A. Therkelsen, C.R. Majer, C.J. Sneeringer, J. Song, et al., Selective killing of mixed lineage leukemia cells by a potent small-molecule DOT1L inhibitor, Cancer Cell 20 (2011) 53–65.

[42] Q.-Y. Zhao, P.-J. Lei, X. Zhang, J.-Y. Zheng, H.-Y. Wang, J. Zhao, et al., Global histone modification profiling reveals the epigenomic dynamics during malignant transformation in a four-stage breast cancer model, Clin. Epigenetics 8 (2016) 1–15.

[43] Y. Xi, J. Shi, W. Li, K. Tanaka, K.L. Allton, D. Richardson, et al., Histone modification profiling in breast cancer cell lines highlights commonalities and differences among subtypes, BMC Genomics 19 (2018), https://doi.org/10.1186/s12864-018-4533-0.

[44] S. Enroth, A. Rada-Iglesisas, R. Andersson, O. Wallerman, A. Wanders, L. Påhlman, et al., Cancer associated epigenetic transitions identified by genome-wide histone methylation binding profiles in human colorectal cancer samples and paired normal mucosa, BMC Cancer 11 (2011) 450.

[45] J. Zhuang, Q. Huo, F. Yang, N. Xie, Perspectives on the role of histone modification in breast cancer progression and the advanced technological tools to study epigenetic determinants of metastasis, Front. Genet. (2020), https://doi.org/10.3389/fgene.2020.603552.

[46] D. Pal, S. Ghatak, C.K. Sen, Epigenetic modification of microRNAs, in: MicroRNA in Regenerative Medicine, Academic Press, 2015, pp. 77–109, https://doi.org/10.1016/b978-0-12-405544-5.00003-4.

[47] J. Zhou, R.L. Sears, X. Xing, B. Zhang, D. Li, N.B. Rockweiler, et al., Tissue-specific DNA methylation is conserved across human, mouse, and rat, and driven by primary sequence conservation, BMC Genomics 18 (2017), https://doi.org/10.1186/s12864-017-4115-6.

[48] K.-W. Jair, K.E. Bachman, H. Suzuki, A.H. Ting, I. Rhee, R.-W.C. Yen, et al., De novo CpG island methylation in human cancer cells, Cancer Res. 66 (2006) 682–692.

[49] N. Petryk, S. Bultmann, T. Bartke, P.-A. Defossez, Staying true to yourself: mechanisms of DNA methylation maintenance in mammals, Nucleic Acids Res. 49 (2020) 3020–3032.

[50] J. Yu, J. Zayas, B. Qin, L. Wang, Targeting DNA methylation for treating triple-negative breast cancer, Pharmacogenomics 20 (16) (2019) 1151–1157, https://doi.org/10.2217/pgs-2019-0078 (accessed February 15, 2021).

[51] A. Nishiyama, M. Nakanishi, Navigating the DNA methylation landscape of cancer, Trends Genet. 37 (2021) 1012–1027.

[52] M. Ehrlich, DNA methylation in cancer: too much, but also too little, Oncogene 21 (2002) 5400–5413.

[53] D.M. Roy, L.A. Walsh, T.A. Chan, Driver mutations of cancer epigenomes, Protein Cell 5 (2014) 265.

[54] B.P. de Almeida, J.D. Apolónio, A. Binnie, P. Castelo-Branco, Roadmap of DNA methylation in breast cancer identifies novel prognostic biomarkers, BMC Cancer 19 (2019) 1–12.

[55] A. Merlo, J.G. Herman, L. Mao, D.J. Lee, E. Gabrielson, P.C. Burger, et al., 5′ CpG island methylation is associated with transcriptional silencing of the tumour suppressor p16/CDKN2/MTS1 in human cancers, Nat. Med. 1 (1995) 686–692.

[56] E.E. Cameron, K.E. Bachman, S. Myöhänen, J.G. Herman, S.B. Baylin, Synergy of demethylation and histone deacetylase inhibition in the re-expression of genes silenced in cancer, Nat. Genet. 21 (1999) 103–107.

[57] J.Y. Shin, H.S. Kim, J. Park, J.B. Park, J.Y. Lee, Mechanism for inactivation of the KIP family cyclin-dependent kinase inhibitor genes in gastric cancer cells, Cancer Res. 60 (2000) 262–265.

[58] R.M. Connolly, R.C. Jankowitz, E. Andreopoulou, J.B. Allred, S.C. Jeter, J. Zorzi, et al., OT3-01-06: a phase 2 study investigating the safety, efficacy and surrogate biomarkers of response of 5-azacitidine (5-AZA) and entinostat (MS-275) in patients with advanced breast cancer, Cancer Res. 71 (2011). OT3-01-06.

[59] J. Kaur, A. Daoud, S.T. Eblen, Targeting chromatin remodeling for cancer therapy, Curr. Mol. Pharmacol. 12 (2019) 215.

[60] A.R. Yun Huang, Connections between TET proteins and aberrant DNA modification in cancer, Trends Genet. 30 (2014) 464.

[61] M.-Z. Wu, S.-F. Chen, S. Nieh, C. Benner, L.-P. Ger, C.-I. Jan, et al., Hypoxia drives breast tumor malignancy through a TET–TNFα–p38–MAPK signaling axis, Cancer Res. 75 (2015) 3912–3924.

[62] K.D. Rasmussen, K. Helin, Role of TET enzymes in DNA methylation, development, and cancer, Genes Dev. 30 (2016) 733.

[63] L. Scourzic, E. Mouly, O.A. Bernard, TET proteins and the control of cytosine demethylation in cancer, Genome Med. 7 (2015) 1–16.

[64] L. Ho, G.R. Crabtree, Chromatin remodelling during development, Nature 463 (2010) 474–484, https://doi.org/10.1038/nature08911.

[65] G. Längst, L. Manelyte, Chromatin remodelers: from function to dysfunction, Genes 6 (2015) 299.

[66] G.G. Wang, C.D. Allis, P. Chi, Chromatin remodeling and cancer, part II: ATP-dependent chromatin remodeling, Trends Mol. Med. 13 (2007) 373–380.

[67] R.E. Mansel, O. Fodstad, W.G. Jiang, Metastasis of Breast Cancer, Springer Science & Business Media, 2007.

[68] J.-W. Wei, K. Huang, C. Yang, C.-S. Kang, Non-coding RNAs as regulators in epigenetics, Oncol. Rep. 37 (2017) 3–9, https://doi.org/10.3892/or.2016.5236.

[69] A. Khan, X. Zhang, Function of the long noncoding RNAs in hepatocellular carcinoma: classification, molecular mechanisms, and significant therapeutic potentials, Bioengineering (Basel) 9 (2022), https://doi.org/10.3390/bioengineering9080406.

[70] Y. Qian, L. Shi, Z. Luo, Long non-coding RNAs in cancer: implications for diagnosis, prognosis, and therapy, Front. Med. 7 (2020) 612393, https://doi.org/10.3389/fmed.2020.612393.

[71] K. Zhang, Z. Luo, Y. Zhang, L. Zhang, L. Wu, L. Liu, et al., Circulating lncRNA H19 in plasma as a novel biomarker for breast cancer, Cancer Biomark. 17 (2016) 187–194.

[72] M. Hajjari, A. Salavaty, HOTAIR: an oncogenic long non-coding RNA in different cancers, Cancer Biol. Med. 12 (2015) 1–9.

[73] H.-T. Zheng, D.-B. Shi, Y.-W. Wang, X.-X. Li, Y. Xu, P. Tripathi, et al., High expression of lncRNA MALAT1 suggests a biomarker of poor prognosis in colorectal cancer, Int. J. Clin. Exp. Pathol. 7 (2014) 3174–3181.

[74] U.A. Ørom, F.C. Nielsen, A.H. Lund, MicroRNA-10a binds the 5′UTR of ribosomal protein mRNAs and enhances their translation, Mol. Cell 30 (4) (2008) 460–471, https://doi.org/10.1016/j.molcel.2008.05.001. https://pubmed.ncbi.nlm.nih.gov/18498749/. (PMID: 18498749).

[75] A.A. Svoronos, D.M. Engelman, F.J. Slack, OncomiR or tumor suppressor? The duplicity of microRNAs in cancer, Cancer Res. 76 (2016) 3666.

[76] S. Nirgude, S. Desai, B. Choudhary, Curcumin alters distinct molecular pathways in breast cancer subtypes revealed by integrated miRNA/mRNA expression analysis, Cancer Rep. 5 (10) (2022) e1596.

[77] W. Tan, B. Liu, S. Qu, G. Liang, W. Luo, C. Gong, MicroRNAs and cancer: key paradigms in molecular therapy (review), Oncol. Lett. 15 (2018) 2735–2742.

[78] J. Hayes, P.P. Peruzzi, S. Lawler, MicroRNAs in cancer: biomarkers, functions and therapy, Trends Mol. Med. 20 (2014) 460–469.

[79] Z.-W. Zhang, Y. An, C.-B. Teng, The roles of miR-17-92 cluster in mammal development and tumorigenesis, Yi Chuan 31 (2009) 1094–1100 (in Chinese).

[80] H. Osada, T. Takahashi, Let-7 and miR-17-92: small-sized major players in lung cancer development, Cancer Sci. 102 (2011) 9–17, https://doi.org/10.1111/j.1349-7006.2010.01707.x.

[81] A. Rinaldi, G. Poretti, I. Kwee, E. Zucca, C.V. Catapano, M.G. Tibiletti, et al., Concomitant MYC and microRNA cluster miR-17-92 (C13orf25) amplification in human mantle cell lymphoma, Leuk. Lymphoma 48 (2007) 410–412.

[82] Y. Shi, C. Liu, X. Liu, D.G. Tang, J. Wang, The microRNA miR-34a inhibits non-small cell lung cancer (NSCLC) growth and the CD44hi stem-like NSCLC cells, PLoS One 9 (2014) e90022.

[83] X. Yan, B. Tang, B. Chen, Y. Shan, H. Yang, Reproducibility project: cancer biology. Replication study: the microRNA miR-34a inhibits prostate cancer stem cells and metastasis by directly repressing CD44, Elife (2019) 8, https://doi.org/10.7554/eLife.43511.

[84] F. Yu, H. Yao, P. Zhu, X. Zhang, Q. Pan, C. Gong, et al., Let-7 regulates self renewal and tumorigenicity of breast cancer cells, Cell 131 (2007) 1109–1123.

[85] C. Ma, Y.C. Ding, W. Yu, Q. Wang, B. Meng, T. Huang, MicroRNA-200c overexpression plays an inhibitory role in human pancreatic cancer stem cells by regulating epithelial-mesenchymal transition, Minerva Med. 106 (2015) 193–202.

[86] P.A. Gregory, A.G. Bert, E.L. Paterson, S.C. Barry, A. Tsykin, G. Farshid, et al., The miR-200 family and miR-205 regulate epithelial to mesenchymal transition by targeting ZEB1 and SIP1, Nat. Cell Biol. 10 (2008) 593–601.

[87] F. Cisneros-Soberanis, M.A. Andonegui, L.A. Herrera, miR-125b-1 is repressed by histone modifications in breast cancer cell lines, Springerplus 5 (2016) 959.

[88] M. Fabbri, R. Garzon, A. Cimmino, Z. Liu, N. Zanesi, E. Callegari, et al., MicroRNA-29 family reverts aberrant methylation in lung cancer by targeting DNA methyltransferases 3A and 3B, Proc. Natl. Acad. Sci. USA 104 (2007) 15805–15810.

[89] J.M. Friedman, G. Liang, C.-C. Liu, E.M. Wolff, Y.C. Tsai, W. Ye, et al., The putative tumor suppressor microRNA-101 modulates the cancer epigenome by repressing the polycomb group protein EZH2, Cancer Res. 69 (2009) 2623–2629.

[90] S. Varambally, Q. Cao, R.-S. Mani, S. Shankar, X. Wang, B. Ateeq, et al., Genomic loss of microRNA-101 leads to overexpression of histone methyltransferase EZH2 in cancer, Science 322 (2008) 1695–1699.

[91] W. Zhang, D.M. Eileen, Emerging role of microRNAs in drug response, Curr. Opin. Mol. Ther. 12 (2010) 695.

[92] S. Naidu, P. Magee, M. Garofalo, MiRNA-based therapeutic intervention of cancer, J. Hematol. Oncol. 8 (2015), https://doi.org/10.1186/s13045-015-0162-0.

[93] Y. Fu, J. Chen, Z. Huang, Recent progress in microRNA-based delivery systems for the treatment of human disease, ExRNA 1 (2019), https://doi.org/10.1186/s41544-019-0024-y.

[94] M.P. Czech, MicroRNAs as therapeutic targets, N. Engl. J. Med. 354 (2006), https://doi.org/10.1056/NEJMcibr060065.

[95] A.F. Christopher, R.P. Kaur, G. Kaur, A. Kaur, V. Gupta, P. Bansal, MicroRNA therapeutics: discovering novel targets and developing specific therapy, Perspect. Clin. Res. 7 (2016) 68.

[96] C. Diener, A. Keller, E. Meese, Emerging concepts of miRNA therapeutics: from cells to clinic, Trends Genet. 38 (2022) 613–626.

[97] A.G. Bader, miR-34—a microRNA replacement therapy is headed to the clinic, Front. Genet. 3 (2012), https://doi.org/10.3389/fgene.2012.00120.

[98] S. Bajan, G. Hutvagner, RNA-based therapeutics: from antisense oligonucleotides to miRNAs, Cells 9 (2020), https://doi.org/10.3390/cells9010137.

[99] D. Ramchandani, S.K. Lee, S. Yomtoubian, M.S. Han, C.H. Tung, V. Mittal, Nanoparticle delivery of miR-708 mimetic impairs breast cancer metastasis, Mol. Cancer Ther. 18 (2019), https://doi.org/10.1158/1535-7163.MCT-18-0702.

[100] E. Mercuri, B.T. Darras, C.A. Chiriboga, J.W. Day, C. Campbell, A.M. Connolly, et al., Nusinersen versus sham control in later-onset spinal muscular atrophy, N. Engl. J. Med. 378 (2018) 625–635.

Epigenetics approach in cancer treatment with focus on lung and breast cancer

11

Sayani Bhattacharjee

NanoString Technologies, Seattle, WA, United States

Introduction to epigenetics in breast and lung cancer

Early detection methods for breast cancer have substantially improved the mortality rate for millions of patients over the decades. Since 1990s, medical professionals have been equipped with a gamut of comprehensive treatment regimens. The World Health Organization reported 685,000 deaths globally from breast cancer and 1.8 million deaths from lung cancer in 2020. Breast and lung cancers occur in every country of the world. Women globally can develop breast cancer after puberty, with the chances of getting diagnosed increasing with age. Smoking and the use of pipes, cigars, and cigarettes are the leading causes of lung cancer. However, nonsmokers can also get the disease. In addition, hereditary cancer syndromes, air pollution, history of chronic lung diseases, secondhand smoke exposure, and exposure to chemicals, radon, and asbestos at work are risk factors, too [1].

Tumors comprise a heterogeneous population of cells [2,3] that adopt different approaches to proliferate, metastasize, and acquire resistance to therapy. Epigenetic alterations are a common approach that is adapted by cancer cells to develop breast and lung cancer. Chemical changes that impact the activation of genes in cancer cells are the main focus of epigenetic therapy. Targeting the normal expression of tumor suppressor genes, which normally prevent the proliferation of cancer cells, is the goal of epigenetic therapy in the treatment of various cancers [4].

In 1999, Masaki Okano et al. were the first to report an aberrant DNA methylation in mammalian cancer [5]. More precise cancer diagnostic and prognostic instruments are developed from the detection of mutations in the DNA methylation mechanism. The process of covalently adding a methyl group (CH3) to the cytosine $5'$-position, which is located before the guanine in the DNA sequence, is known as DNA methylation. Such methylation controls gene expression, which in turn controls the primary biological mechanism linked to cancer. The CpG dinucleotides are concentrated in enormous clusters known as the CpG islands [6–8]. Methylation

233

Cancer Epigenetics and Nanomedicine. https://doi.org/10.1016/B978-0-443-13209-4.00014-3
Copyright © 2024 Elsevier Inc. All rights reserved, including those for text and data mining, AI training, and similar technologies.

results in the formation of a 5-methylcytosine (5-mC) structure, which can stop the expression of methylated genes by engaging methyl binding domain proteins (MBDs) in conjunction with histone protein modification, or it can block transcription factors' access to the DNA's binding sites. When oncogenes are less methylated, it results in their abnormal activation, and when the promoters of important tumor suppressor genes are heavily methylation, it silences the genes [9,10].

Recently, there has been a great deal of research on epigenetic changes as potential biomarkers for early breast and lung cancer diagnosis, prognosis, and the direction of therapy choices. DNA cytosine methylation, miR alterations, and histone modifications have received particular attention [11–13]. There are various degrees of therapeutic usefulness and distinct testing procedures for each of these epigenetic modifications. The majority of epigenetic biomarkers for lung cancer are now in research and most likely won't be used in clinical settings for some time [13]; however, they present tremendous promise when combined with other therapies.

The primary attribute of epigenetic modifications is their nongenetic nature, which ensures that genomic information is not reprogrammed or altered. There are three primary processes that are understood: noncoding RNAs (ncRNAs), histone modification, and DNA methylation. They play a crucial role in controlling cellular immunity, which is mediated in certain cells and tissues via controlling transcription and gene expression [14]. The development and spread of tumors are significantly influenced by epigenetic changes. There are two main categories of epigenetic modifications that take place during carcinogenesis. The first involves covalent chromatin changes, such as histone marks and DNA methylation. Histone variations, ATP-dependent chromatin remodeling complexes, and ncRNAs like microRNAs (miRNAs) are included in the second, more diverse category [15].

DNA methylation in breast and lung cancer

A primary cause of breast cancer is epigenetic changes. The field of epigenetics investigates the chemicals and processes that maintain proper cell growth, development, and differentiation while maintaining alternate gene activity states within the same DNA. Development of the mammary gland requires a crosstalk between several signaling pathways and hormonal mechanisms with chromatin regulators. WNT and hedgehog pathways are two of the most highly studied pathways that have been reported to affect the development of embryonic mammary gland [16].

DNA methylation is a reversible phenomenon that is controlled by a particular class of enzymes known as DNA methyltransferases (DNMTs). The three DNMTs that are active are DNMT1, DNMT3A, and DNMT3B. DNMT1 is the most abundant of these three and is responsible for maintaining existing methylation. On the other hand, DNMT3A and DNMT3B are responsible for de novo methylation. An enzyme family known as ten-eleven translocation methylcytosine dioxygenases, or TETs, catalyzes the demethylation of DNA. Through the process of hydroxymethylation, TETs may convert 5-mC to 5-hydroxymethylcytosine (5-hmC). Three key enzymes,

TET1, TET2, and TET3, are involved in DNA demethylation, which recovers the silenced genes that were previously impacted by DNMTs. All of these factors work together to affect the transcriptional activation of critical genes involved in both genomic stability and tumorigenesis [5,17,18]. Apolipoprotein B mRNA editing catalytic polypeptide-like family (APOBEC), growth arrest and DNA-damage inducible protein (GADD45), and members of the cytidine deaminases family of proteins are among the other proteins that have DNA demethylase activities and are linked to breast cancer [19]. There is strong evidence linking GADD45A to both epigenetic gene regulation and DNA repair. The relationship between the GADD45 and BRCA1 genes has been proposed to impact the pathophysiology of breast cancer, most likely via inducing nucleotide excision repair processes [20]. It's interesting to note that breast cancer has aberrant methylation of GADD45A [21]. It has been demonstrated that activation-induced cytidine deaminase (AID) proteins participate in the deamination of 5-mC to thymine, which is a crucial step in active DNA demethylation [22]. Furthermore, in nontransformed mammary epithelial cells, AID is known to promote DNA demethylation and is necessary for the epithelial-mesenchymal transition (EMT) [23]. Additionally, it has been demonstrated that APOBEC mutagenesis influences the tumor progression in ER+/HER2-breast cancer, despite the fact that APOBEC1 contains DNA demethylase activity. Also, AID is known to facilitate DNA demethylation and is essential for the EMT in nontransformed mammary epithelial cells [24,25]. Most recently, it was demonstrated that via inducing immunogenic responses, APOBEC mutagenesis inhibited the development of breast cancers [26].

CpG island hypermethylation is present in multiple genes associated with breast cancer [27] and aberrant activity of DNMTs resulted in the hypermethylation and silencing of the tumor suppressor behavior genes HOXA5, TMS1, p16, RASSF1A, and BRCA1 in multiple cases [28–30]. Furthermore, E-cadherin, TMS1, GSTP1, and p16 are among the genes that are silenced as a result of promoter hypermethylation [31,32]. Major biological processes like proapoptosis (HOXA5, TMS1), cell cycle checkpoints (RASSF1A, p16), estrogen signaling, and DNA repair mechanisms (BRCA1) are all impacted by these genes. Although the BRCA1 gene is one of the best examples of a gene that predisposes people to breast cancer and is often silenced in random breast tumors, reports have shown that CpG hypermethylation of BRCA1 is linked to amplification of DNMT 3b. About 80% of breast tumors also show lowered expression of a different cell cycle inhibitor gene, p21/CIP1/WAF1, due to elevated methylation of the p21/CIP1/WAF1 gene. These findings are consistent with the loss of the cell cycle checkpoint gene p16INK4a in early stages of sporadic breast cancer caused by aberrant CpG promoter methylation [33].

A unique pattern in DNA methylation is also observed in various subtypes of breast cancer. For instance, it has been demonstrated that ER+/luminal breast cancer exhibits a higher frequency of DNA methylation than ER-/basal-like tumors [34,35]. Moreover, well-differentiated tumors have a lower degree of methylated CpG islands than poorly differentiated breast tumors, which show a higher degree of methylation. Likewise, it has been noted that PR-negative breast tumors exhibit elevated progesterone receptor gene promoter hypermethylation. Differential methylation patterns in the ER, PR, or HER2 gene can impact the expression of these receptors on breast tumors, which can in turn affect how responsive the tumors are to appropriate hormone and/or endocrine therapies. In total, 807 cancer-associated genes were examined in an effort to investigate the DNA methylation profiles of the three commonly recognized expression subtypes of breast cancer, namely luminal A, luminal B, and basal like. The results showed that each of the three subtypes has variable methylation profiles that differ from one another [36].

Changes in DNA methylation in healthy breast tissue or healthy tissues close to cancer may also provide indicators of the risk of developing breast cancer. It's interesting to note that there is evidence to show that certain cancer-related genes in normal breast tissues may have methylation variations that can be detected before breast cancer develops. Also, by utilizing their individual methylation patterns, different forms of breast cancer may be traced back to the particular progenitor population, which resolves any problems arising from their cell of origin or biological heterogeneity as seen in breast cancer [37]. Six CpG sites are proposed to predict patient survival, and seven breast cancer-specific methylation biomarkers have been found more recently by comparing breast cancer to normal breast. PRAC2, TDR10, and TMEM132C genes have been shown to be novel DNA methylation-gene indicators of diagnostic and prognostic value in breast cancer. These genes were identified by using a genome-wide strategy to evaluate the DNA methylation and expression patterns in breast cancer and normal breast [38]. Six global trends that impact the DNA methylation profiles of the breast were identified by a large-scale integrative analysis of the methylation profiles across 1538 METABRIC breast tumors with regard to transcriptional, genetic, and clinical aspects. "Immune and stromal cell contamination," "replication linked hypomethylation clock," "X chromosome dosage compensation," and "epigenetic instability at CpG islands" are the names of these trends. The most significant finding of this study was the identification of X inactivation as a potent dosage compensatory mechanism that may be responsible for the methylation of acquired X-associated loci in ER-negative tumors [39].

Normally, genomic DNA is highly methylated; nevertheless, lung cancer has extensive aberrant methylation of DNA, including both hypo- and hypermethylation. Changes in worldwide DNA methylation patterns are caused by dysregulated expression of several master epigenetic regulators [40]. Global DNA hypomethylation results in activation of oncogenes, microsatellite instability, or loss of imprinting [41]. On the other hand, hypermethylation of normally unmethylated CpG islands results in silencing of tumor suppressor genes and is an early event of lung carcinogenesis [42]. Therefore, it is important to devise therapeutic regimens that can target both of these events. High-resolution mapping in lung squamous cell carcinoma (LUSC) shows aberrant DNA methylation patterns in lung tumors when compared to matched normal lung tissue. Lung tumors demonstrated extensive DNA hypomethylation, but also gene-specific hypermethylation in most of the LUSC tumors evaluated [43]. Furthermore, several reports have found that malignant transformation and cancer progression upon aberrant methylation of genes involved in cell differentiation, EMT, and cell-cycle regulation (e.g., *CDKN2A/p16*, *APC*, *MGMT*, *RASSF1A*, *FHIT*, and *TSCL1*) [42,44].

Targeting DNMTs with epigenetic therapeutics may have the benefit of selectively targeting cancer cells that have aberrant epigenetic modifications rather than normal cells, which may reduce cytotoxicity. Both azacitidine and decitabine, the most researched DNMT inhibitors (DNMTi), have not shown promise when used alone to treat nonsmall cell lung cancer (NSCLC) [45,46]. DNMT1 expression is high in smoking-related lung cancer and is directly involved in the silencing of tumor suppressors during lung cancer pathogenesis [47]. There are studies reporting that knockdown of DNMT1 decreases growth of lung cancer cells both in vitro and in vivo [48]. This makes DNMT1 a popular target for epidrugs. DNMT3B overexpression on the other hand has been reported to accelerate carcinogen-induced transformation and is associated with poor prognosis [49,50]. Conversely, DNMT3A overexpression correlates with a more favorable prognosis, and deletion in a Kras-mutant mouse model promotes tumor growth and progression [51]. The fact that the dosages used in the prior clinical trials were excessive may have contributed to their failure; DNMTi may need to be used at a level that may cause DNA demethylation but is not harmful to healthy cells. Demethylating drugs are believed to stimulate cancer cells by reactivating DNA repair pathways or tumor suppressor genes when administered in conjunction with chemotherapy. Synergistic anticancer action on colony formation and on-target impact of DNA hypomethylation of tumor suppressor genes was shown when azacitidine was combined with either gemcitabine or cisplatin [52]. Treatment with azacitidine and trichostatin A reversed cisplatin resistance and restored candidate gene expression [53,54]. In order to determine whether azacitidine plus cytotoxic chemotherapy enhanced the response to adjuvant therapy, NCT01209520 was an initial trial that enrolled individuals who had hypermethylation in a specific set of genes (DAPK, RASSF1A, p16INKa, GATA-4, and APC). Unfortunately, due to poor accrual, this study was closed. DNMTi treatment resensitizes cancer cells to epidermal growth factor receptor tyrosine kinase inhibitors (EGFR-TKIs) in addition to chemoresistance, which they develop resistance to. One possible mechanism of acquired resistance to gefitinib is EGFR promoter methylation, and gefitinib and azacitidine combination therapy caused cancer cells to grow less rapidly and undergo apoptosis [55]. Immune checkpoint inhibition (ICI) in conjunction with DNMTi is also being investigated because azacitidine at low doses increases the expression of genes involved in immunomodulatory pathways, such as PD-L1, and the degree of induction is associated with methylation loss [56,57]. Clinical trials investigating DNMTi and ICI are underway, which include combinations of azacitidine with durvalumab (NCT02250326) and decitabine with nivolumab (NCT02664181).

DNA 5′-cytosine hypermethylation is an early lung carcinogenesis marker [41,58]. p16, PAK3, NISCH, KIF1A, OGDHL, BRMS1, FHIT, CTSZ, CCNA1, NRCAM, LOX, MGMT, DOK1, SOX15, TCF21, DAPK, RAR, RASSF1, CYGB, MSX1, BNC1, CTSZ, and CDKN2A are some commonly hypermethylated genes in lung cancer [59–63]. The probability of hypermethylation for each gene varies, with some like p16 and MGMT hypermethylated in 100% of patients with pulmonary squamous cell carcinoma up to 3 years before cancer diagnosis [64]. p16 inhibits cyclin-dependent kinases 4 and 6, which after binding cyclin D1, phosphorylates and inactivates the retinoblastoma tumor suppressor gene. This in effect blocks cell cycle progression. p16 is lost in ~70% of lung cancer cases; this loss is mostly attributed to promoter methylation, promoting the G_1 to S phase transition [42,65]. Interestingly, p16 methylation occurs in normal-appearing epithelium from smokers and precursor lesions and increases in frequency with the progression of the carcinogenic process [42]. Each gene hypermethylation event contributes to cancer through a different method, but most include the simultaneous activation of genes that promote cell growth and cycle advancement and the suppression of tumor suppressor genes.

Sputum samples, blood (plasma and serum), and bronchoscopic washings/brushings—all of which are less intrusive and less taxing on the patient than tumor biopsies—can all reveal DNA hypermethylation in lung cancer patients. Eventually, these technologies could also be helpful in identifying very early lung cancers or recently recurrent tumors that are invisible to existing methods [66]. 5′-Cytosine methylation is quantified predominantly by three different molecular methods:

- Methylation-sensitive restriction enzymes: Only a small percentage of restriction endonucleases can cut methylation DNA, whereas the majority do not. This analysis can take many different forms, but in general it compares the activities of endonucleases that cut or refuse to cut methylated DNA. To do this, it frequently makes use of the isoschizomers *Msp*I and *Hpa*II, which both recognize CCGG, with HpaII cutting being blocked by either methylated cytosine or methylated outer cytosine [67,68]. After being treated with endonuclease, DNA sequences that are methylated or unmethylated are selected and subjected to PCR or DNA sequencing analysis [66,67].
- Bisulfite conversion occurs when DNA is treated with sodium bisulfite under the right circumstances, which results in the deamination of unmethylated cytosine to uracil while leaving methylated cytosine unaltered. Through PCR amplification, a thymine is created from a deaminated cytosine (a uracil). Sequencing or mass spectrometry can then be used to examine the PCR products. Analysis of the methylcytosine content and particular methyl-cytosine moieties is possible by comparing DNA samples that are identical with and without bisulfite [69–71].
- Using either a tagged *E. coli* methyl-binding domain protein or a methylcytosine-specific antibody, affinity purification procedures allow for the immunoprecipitation of methylated DNA. Next-generation DNA sequencing is frequently used to evaluate the resultant immunoprecipitates [72,73].

Many studies have demonstrated that alteration in cytosine hypermethylation has diagnostic and prognostic value in lung cancer and in some cases appears to predict treatment responses. The methylation of 20 TSGs, for instance, was investigated by Zhang et al. [74] in 78 NSCLCs in comparison to 50 plasma samples that were matched from people without cancer. A five-gene set (*APC, RASSF1A, CHD13, KLK10*, and *DLEC1*) with a sensitivity of 83.64% and a specificity of 74.0% for cancer detection in the Chinese population demonstrated considerably greater methylation in lung cancer patients. According to the same study, patients with four or more concurrently methylated genes in a 14-gene panel (APC, CHD13, KLK13, DLEC1, RASSF1A, EFEMP1, SFRP1, RAR, p16INK4A, RUNX3, Hmlh1, DAPK, BRAC1, p14ARF) had a worse progression-free 2-year survival of 13.8 months compared to 17.8 months with fewer than four methylated genes. This data was based on a sample of 64 lung cancer patients. Research conducted by Salazar et al. [75] revealed that gene methylation may be helpful in predicting therapeutic responses, since lung cancer patients with unmethylated plasma CHFR genes reacted far better to EGFR tyrosine kinase inhibitors than those with methylated CHFR genes.

Chromatin remodeling and HDAC inhibition

Epigenetic regulation is complex, involving several levels. To fit into the nucleus, NA is coiled around histone proteins. Each individual histone octamer is made up of two copies of the H3/H4 tetramers and H2A/H2B dimer cores, which wrap around the DNA's 146 base pairs. Histone repeats, which together make up chromatin, are the building blocks of nucleosomes [76,77]. The N terminal tail of the histone octamer is unstructured and extends outward from the nucleosome at varying lengths. A variety of modifications, including the addition of chemical moieties, can be applied to this projecting amino terminal tail. Heterochromatin-wrapped DNA is either transcriptionally available or not depending on the addition of different chemical moieties or tags. The structure is transcriptionally silent, or heterochromatin, when the chromatin is tightly folded, blocking the DNA from being accessed by transcription factors. As opposed to euchromatin, which is also known as when the structure is less condensed and more relaxed, making it more accessible to transcription factors and maintaining transcriptional activity [78]. Tyrosine, arginine, serine, and lysine are the four amino acid residues that are prone to modification; over six different types of modifications are possible. Proline isomerization, ubiquitination, biotinylation, sumoylation, methylation, acetylation, and phosphorylation are a few of these. Heterochromatin states transition from euchromatin to heterochromatin, and this process ultimately regulates gene expression. The various patterns of histone modifications are also known as the histone code [79]. Unmethylated DNA has a more open conformation, whereas methylated DNA causes the genomic DNA to wind tightly around the histone proteins H2A, H2B, H3, and H4, creating a nucleosome. Transcriptional repression or activation is determined by conformational changes or chromatin remodeling. DNA is packed and unpacked into chromatin by chromatin remodeling complexes.

BRCA1 plays a role in many histone modifications that affect chromatin function. The most frequent ones are as follows: deacetylation of H2A and H3, interactions with HDAC1 that lead to deacetylation of DNA repair genes (e.g., KDM5B, Ku70 pathway genes), histone H2A ubiquitination [80]. Furthermore, BRCA1 interacts with two structurally similar HATs, CBP, and p300. The BRCA1 gene interacts with the catalytic subunits of the deacetylase complex histone, which is how Zheng et al. [81] explained the mechanism of estrogen receptor suppression. Trichostatin A, an HDAC inhibitor, significantly restores ERα suppression that is reliant on BRCA1. It has been demonstrated that HDAC monotherapy positively affects the induction of apoptosis, growth arrest, and differentiation in breast cancer [82–84]. Several studies have revealed a number of histone changes that are characteristic of breast cancer; nevertheless, the efficacy of inhibitor monotherapy has not yet been conclusively demonstrated. The results of sensitizing cancer cells to radiation and traditional anti-cancer medications are far more encouraging [85]. Valproic acid, trichostatin A, and entinostat have been shown to be beneficial in overcoming medication resistance, including HER2-targeted therapy [86].

In both NSCLC and SCLC, there is frequent mutation in components of the SWI/SNF chromatin remodeling complex [47,87]. The chromatin regulators SMARCA4/BRG1 and ARID1A are among the most commonly mutated genes in lung adenocarcinoma and play a pivotal role in lung carcinogenesis [88]. The loss of BRG1/SMARCA4 causes extensive chromatin remodeling and nucleosome positioning alterations, which in turn reduce the expression of downstream tumor-suppressor genes [89]. SMARCA4 functions as an oncogene in some situations but is mostly a tumor suppressor. Concurrent mutations in SMARCA4 and SMARCA2, another chromatin remodeler, are associated with a worse prognosis in NSCLC patients since the illness is typically resistant to treatment [90,91]. It has been shown by recent preclinical research that cancers lacking SMARCA4 may be particularly sensitive to therapies that target alternative pathways. When BRD4 and HER3 were targeted with bromodomain and extraterminal motif protein (BET) inhibitors, the proliferation of NSCLC cells lacking SMARCA4 was reduced. Similarly, cyclin D1 deficiency and subsequent sensitivity to CDK4/6 inhibitors are caused by SMARCA4 loss in NSCLC cells [92,93].

Targeting both pathways at once may lead to therapeutic synergism and increased TSG expression, even if targeting each process separately has had unsatisfactory results for lung cancer [94]. The combination of decitabine and TSA (an HDAC inhibitor) treatment, as shown by Cameron et al. [95], results in a synergistic reactivation of TSG expression in colon cancer, but neither medication alone affects the transcription of TSG. Analogously, Boivin et al. [96] showed that AZA plus the HDAC inhibitor phenylbutyrate inhibited DNA synthesis in lung cancer cell lines more than either drug did on its own. Zhu et al. [97] discovered that pretreated lung cancer cell lines with decitabine further increased histone acetylation and augmented the apoptosis induced by HDAC inhibitors. In a similar vein, p16, p21, and the pro-apoptotic gene PRC2 were revealed to have been reexpressed in an orthotopic mouse model of lung cancer treated with AZA plus the HDAC inhibitor entinostat. The scientific rationale behind combining hypomethylating agents with HDAC inhibitors in patients with advanced lung cancer is strengthened by these findings [97,98].

Initial clinical trials (decitabine and valproic acid, Chu et al. [99]; 5-AZA and sodium phenylbutyrate, Lin et al. [100]; Hydralazine and magnesium valproate, Candelaria et al. [101]; Decitabine and vorinostat, Stathis et al. [102]) using a combined approach failed to show significant response in patients with lung cancer. On the other hand, a more current clinical trial that combined entinostat and AZA in highly pretreated advanced NSCLC has rekindled interest in the combinatory strategy.

Remarkably, a median survival of 6.4 months was achieved overall. Of the 34 evaluable patients, 10 had stable disease for a minimum of 12 weeks, 1 had a complete response (CR) that lasted for 14 months, and 1 had a partial response that lasted for 8 months [94].

Vorinostat has not demonstrated the same level of HDAC inhibitory activity or capacity to suppress lung cancer cell line survival as the innovative cyclic amide-bearing hydroxamic acid-based HDAC inhibitors SL142 and SL325. These tiny compounds significantly increase caspase-3 activity, suggesting that they may trigger apoptosis in lung cancer [103]. Another novel HDAC inhibitor, N-hydroxy-4-(4-phenylbutyryl-amino) benzamide (HTPB), significantly suppressed the growth of lung cancer cells by causing cell cycle arrest, mitochondrial-mediated apoptosis, disruption of F-actin dynamics, and inhibition of MMP2 and MMP9. It was observed both in vivo and in vitro [104]. CG0006 is a newly synthesized HDAC inhibitor that was assessed in an NCI-60 cancer cell panel and induced cell death by amplifying the expression of p21 and p27 [105]. Other novel agents such as MGCD0103, OSU-HDAC 44, CI-944, MS-275, and LAQ824 were tested and showed significant cytotoxic effects on lung cancer cells [106–109].

In the last decade, it has become increasingly evident that HDAC inhibitors exhibit a more pronounced effect when combined with other medications. When paired with paclitaxel and carboplatin for advanced lung cancer, vorinostat has demonstrated a notable therapeutic benefit. Nonsmall cell lung carcinoma cells underwent caspase-mediated AIF-dependent apoptotic cell death upon receiving a combination of TSA and etoposide therapy. When combined with TSA, genistein and beta-carotene as dietary components improved the cell growth arrest effect on A549 NSCLC cells [110]. When 5-FU drug-mediated cytotoxicity was combined with low-dose vorinostat, the outcomes were synergistic, particularly in 5-FU-resistant NSCLC cells. Through histone acetylation at the promoter of p21waf1/cip1, vorinostat can upregulate the expression of that gene and downregulate thymidylate synthase, potentially circumventing 5-FU resistance. In order to facilitate future clinical investigations of vorinostat plus chemotherapy in patients with NSCLC, this is the first report demonstrating that vorinostat increased 5-FU sensitivity through the modulation of 5-FU metabolism in lung cancer cells [111].

Epigenetic targeted therapy may be guided by alterations to histones and variations in the expression patterns of HATs and HDACs, which may be useful in early tumor diagnosis and prognostication [112–114]. Although histone modifications, HATs, and HDACs are being employed to treat lung cancer, it will take some time before they are used clinically as lung cancer biomarkers or to direct therapy [94,95,103,108,115].

Role of miRNAs as epigenetic biomarkers

A unique class of small (18–26 nucleotide) ncRNA molecules that have been evolutionarily conserved are called miRNAs. They play a role in the development of diseases and in the proper development and maintenance of tissue homeostasis through the posttranscriptional regulation of gene expression. miRNAs act as both oncogenes and tumor suppressor genes, which provides them with the power to modulate a gamut of genomic processes while also acting as biomarkers. Although there is a great deal of research on the significance and promise of miRs in oncology, the majority of breast cancer clinical trials are still observational. Their objective is to find miRs that affect how cancer cells react to particular medications or to examine the connection between the miRs they have chosen and the efficiency of adjuvant and neoadjuvant chemotherapy. It has been able to find miRs that may be indicators of medication resistance or predictors of hormone sensitivity in both scientific and clinical studies, as well as molecules linked to the possibility of experiencing side effects from treatment.

One of the most extensively studied is the suppressor miR-34a [116]. One of the key players in the control of the cell cycle and apoptosis is miR-34a. According to a number of research studies, breast cancer frequently has mutated or reduced miR-34a. When miR-34a is added to cancer cells, it inhibits their ability to proliferate, invade, migrate, and induce apoptosis. This is how miR-34a is used in breast cancer treatment. According to studies, miR-34a can also improve the way chemotherapy works for breast cancer patients. For instance, in one study, 5-fluorouracil (5-FU), a chemotherapy medication frequently used to treat breast cancer, was combined with synthetic miR-34a to treat breast cancer cells. The outcomes demonstrated that, in comparison to treatment with 5-FU alone, the combination of miR-34a with 5-FU resulted in higher suppression of cell growth and enhanced apoptosis. The advantages of miR-34a replacement treatment in slowing the development of orthotopic and subcutaneous transplanted tumors were shown by Adams et al. That has been demonstrated experimentally in senescence. Furthermore, they reported that dasatinib sensitization of cancer cells is impacted by a negative feedback loop between miR-34a and c-SRC [117]. According to Li et al., MiR-34a also affects the chemotherapeutic drug 5-fluorouracil [118]. They found that there was no suppression of cancer cell invasion or death as a result of the substantial decrease in miR-34a levels in breast cancer cell lines and tissues found in their investigation. MiR-34's targeting of Bcl-2 and SIRT1 produced the positive effects, including sensitization of cells to 5-FU after treatment. As a possible therapeutic agent for patients with breast cancer [119] and other forms of cancer, these investigations validated the effectiveness of the mimic miR-34a (MXR34) [120–122]. Li et al. [123] found a substantial reduction in miR-34a expression in tissues and drug-resistant cell lines, which is connected with multidrug resistance (MDR) in breast cancer. The scientists observed that individuals with reduced expression of miR-34a had reduced overall survival as well as disease-free survival; the introduction of mimic miR-34a in vitro resulted in a partial reversal of MDR. The targets of this miR are Bcl-2, CCND1, and NOTCH1, according to the authors, who also point out that miR-34a has no direct impact on the expression of HER-2, TP53, or TOP-2a. The issue of transporting miRNA to cancer cells is one of the difficulties in using miR-34a as a breast cancer treatment. In an effort to increase the efficiency of miRNA delivery to cancer cells, a variety of miRNA transport techniques, including lipid nanoparticles, viral vectors, and vector-based nanoparticles, are currently being researched.

miRs taken from sputum and blood may be useful lung cancer biomarkers [66,124]. They are useful for the early diagnosis of lung cancer and are very stable in human plasma. A test based on the miR-34 group was created by Bianchi et al., and it can identify lung cancer in 80% of asymptomatic high-risk smokers who are otherwise healthy [125,126]. Interestingly, this class of miRs has shown value in predicting lung cancer relapse, where low expression of these miRs was highly predictive of relapse [127]. A poor clinical outcome, as well as events like increased lymph node metastasis and larger tumor size, are predicted by low levels of miR-30a, miR-107, miR-138, miR-204, miR-32, miR-148b, miR-145, miR-224, miR-200c, miR-125b, and miR-375. Conversely, high levels of miR-126, miR-21, miR-197, mi-150, and miR-141 also indicate a poor outcome [127–131].

It has also been demonstrated that miRs are useful for forecasting treatment outcomes. For instance, Zhao et al. discovered that circulating miRs might be useful in forecasting the patient's prognosis, gefitinib sensitivity, and EGFR mutation [132]. Lastly, increased levels of miRs-33a and miR-124 suppress the EMT transition and tumor metastasis, respectively, suggesting that they may have prognostic significance in lung cancer [133]. The usual method for quantifying miRs is PCR amplification. It will take many more years to produce trustworthy miR panels for clinical application in lung cancer diagnosis, prognosis, and therapy. Currently, alterations in miRs are seldom employed in clinical settings [66].

Scope of epidrugs

Epidrugs are therapies designed against epigenetic alterations. The advantage of epidrugs over traditional therapies against genetic mutations comes from the reversible nature of these epigenetic changes. Some common targets for epidrugs include, but are not limited to, enzymes like DNMTs and histone deacetylases. Millward et al. [134] investigated advanced solid tumors, including NSCLC cells, in combination with vorinostat and the new bicyclic proteasome inhibitor marizomib; they discovered a very synergistic anticancer effect. RECIST criteria did not show any response, although 61% of evaluable patients had stable disease, and 39% had decreased tumor measures [134]. Vorinostat and arsenic trioxide (ATO) work together to improve the in vitro and in vivo mortality of H1299 NSCLC cells, as demonstrated by Chien et al. [135]. Suboptimal dosages of the NSAID (non-steroidal anti-inflammatory drug) sulindac in combination with vorinostat were used by Seo et al. to restrict the development of A549 human NSCLC cells, mainly by increased MMP breakdown, cytochrome C release and caspase activation [136].

It's interesting to note that demethylation of four epigenetically repressed genes linked to lung cancer (APC, RASSF1a, CDH13, and CDKN2A) was linked to better overall and progression-free survival (PFS) in serial plasma circulating DNA samples from these patients [94]. Another interesting finding from this research was that many of the patients had a noteworthy clinical response to the next anticancer therapies (anti-PD1 monoclonal antibody and cytotoxic chemotherapy) and a durable clinical response after stopping epigenetic therapy. Following failure of epigenetic treatment, 2 patients survived for 44 and 52 months, respectively, and 4 out of the 19 patients who underwent salvage therapy afterward showed a large objective response [56]. An intriguing theory has been brought forth by this observation—epigenetic therapy might rewire cancer cells to make them more receptive to later therapies. The aforementioned results highlight epigenetic priming, a novel paradigm in cancer treatment. It entails pretreating with epigenetic modulators before treating with anti-neoplastic agents. Numerous clinical trials are currently exploring this intriguing idea. Patients with pretreated NSCLC are presently being randomly assigned in an ongoing trial to receive second-line chemotherapy alone or to receive priming with 5-AZA and entinostat before receiving second-line chemotherapy. In patients with advanced NSCLC, nivolumab, a monoclonal antibody inhibitor of PD-1, is being studied in another phase II trial to see if it is effective after pretreatment with 5-AZA and entinostat. Based on recent research, this ongoing trial aims to determine whether treatment with AZA increases the expression of PD-L1, which could potentially increase the efficacy of anti-PD1 therapy [56].

5-AZA and decitabine are catabolized by cytidine deaminase in the liver following subcutaneous or intravenous injection, which lowers the drug's bioavailability in the lung. These medications may reach greater quantities in the lung tissue by aerosol administration, which avoids the hepatic first pass. A third of the equivalent effective systemic dosage was required for aerosolized 5-AZA delivery to significantly reduce the burden of lung tumors and induce worldwide DNA demethylation, according to pharmacokinetic mice model results [137].

The possibility for combined low-dose epigenetic treatment has been investigated because of the limited efficacy of single-agent epigenetic therapy and the side effects linked to DNMT inhibitors at cytotoxic dosages, such as persistent cytopenias and ensuing loss of dose intensity [94]. Forty-five extensively pretreated advanced NSCLC patients were enrolled in a phase I/II research using the combination of azacytidine and etinostat. Phase II dose recommendations for the combination were as follows: $40 \, mg/m^2$ for azacytidine on days 1–6 and 8, and 7 mg of etinostat taken orally on days 3 and 10 of a 28-day cycle. Fatigue and transitory hematologic toxicity were the most frequent grade 3–4 toxicities, observed in 28% of patients. In addition, 10 patients experienced stable illness for at least 12 weeks. Two patients experienced objective responses, including a CR that lasted 14 months and a partial response that lasted 8 months. The median survival was 6.4 months, and the median PFS was 7.4 weeks. Notably, the patient who underwent extended continuous radiation therapy had three prior chemotherapy regimens during which her tumor progressed quickly, and methylation of a potential candidate gene was found in her tumor. About 25% of the study's patients, who had previously shown no response to standard systemic therapy, responded objectively to immediate poststudy therapy (which included immunotherapy and chemotherapy directed against the programmed death-1 (PD1) immune checkpoint). This finding supports the theory that combination epigenetic therapy may alter the tumors' susceptibility to systemic therapy [56].

Future directions

The advent of epigenetic medications in cancer treatment begs the question of potential adverse consequences. Since epitherapeutics are thought to largely target rapidly dividing cells, there shouldn't be much of a harmful effect on normal cells. There are current clinical trials for second-line advanced NSCLC using the theory that epidrugs may epigenetically trigger NSCLC tumors to respond to systemic therapy [138]. While monotherapies have not yielded the most promising results, using epidrugs in combination with other therapies has shown synergistic effects for both breast and lung cancers. Another trial is aiming to investigate the efficacy of 5-azacytidine/entinostat or azacytidine alone for four cycles as a first epigenetic treatment for second- and third-line advanced NSCLC. The trial will be followed with nivolumab, an antiprogrammed death-1 antibody [139]. 5-Azacytidine may upregulate a number of immune-related tumor genes, such as programmed death-ligand 1 (PD-L1), one of PD1's two ligands and a target of multiple immune checkpoint inhibitors undergoing clinical development, according to recent studies in NSCLC cell lines [56].

A phase I trial of inhaled azacytidine in patients with advanced NSCLC and a combination study of tetrahydrouridine and 5-flouro-2-deoxycytidine for advanced solid tumors, including NSCLC, are two more active clinical research routes [140,141]. Translation of recent findings concerning the role of miRNAs and long ncRNAs in NSCLC into clinical trials is another promising avenue of investigation [12]. However, a different strategy is being aggressively pursued to create nonnucleoside drugs like SGI-1027, RG108, and MG98 that may, for example, efficiently prevent DNA methylation without being integrated into DNA [142–144]. These compounds work by either inhibiting the catalytic or cofactor binding sites of DNMT or by specifically targeting their regulatory messenger RNA regions. Natural nonnucleoside DNMTs such polyphenols and epigallocatechin-3-gallate are also examined [145,146]. These drugs have demonstrated various effects, including VEGF inhibition, apoptotic induction, and ESR1 reexpression. However, the ability of medications based on nonnucleoside chemicals to suppress proliferation is not up to par. As native cellular constituents, miRNAs have the benefit of not being poisonous or causing side effects; further research has demonstrated the minimal antigenicity and great efficacy of this type of treatment. But there is still a lot of research to be done before miRs can be used clinically to treat breast cancer. This includes improving therapeutic manipulation techniques, delivering the molecules to target cells, getting past immune system defenses, and preserving the long-term function of nanoconstructs [147].

Features of the epigenome can be utilized to categorize patients into risk groups and can be significant in predicting prognosis. It is also useful in determining whether individuals with breast cancer are susceptible to or resistant to a particular treatment drug, or who are likely to respond favorably to neoadjuvant and adjuvant chemotherapy. Keeping an eye on certain epimutations or circulating miRNAs may help patients respond better to hormone and chemotherapy treatments.

Epigenetic medicines cannot be introduced as monotherapy according to current breast cancer therapeutic procedures. Since this therapy is still in its early stages, it is important to carefully consider the advantages for patients, any possible side effects, how it interacts with other medications, and the precise processes by which it affects the cancer cell and causes it to develop resistance. The prospects of combining epi-drugs with targeted treatments and chemotherapeutics to boost or regain sensitivity to these medications are far more encouraging.

References

[1] World Health Organization, Breast Cancer, World Health Organization, 2023.

[2] S. Bhattacharjee, et al., PARP inhibitors chemopotentiate and synergize with cisplatin to inhibit bladder cancer cell survival and tumor growth, BMC Cancer 22 (1) (2022) 312.

[3] J.P. Pletcher, et al., The emerging role of poly (ADP-ribose) polymerase inhibitors as effective therapeutic agents in renal cell carcinoma, Front. Oncol. 11 (2021) 5–7.

[4] J. Szczepanek, et al., Harnessing epigenetics for breast cancer therapy: the role of DNA methylation, histone modifications, and microRNA, Int. J. Mol. Sci. 24 (8) (2023) 4–11.

[5] M. Okano, et al., DNA methyltransferases Dnmt3a and Dnmt3b are essential for de novo methylation and mammalian development, Cell 99 (3) (1999) 247–257.

[6] J.G. Herman, S.B. Baylin, Gene silencing in cancer in association with promoter hyper-methylation, N. Engl. J. Med. 349 (21) (2003) 2042–2054.

[7] M. Kulis, M. Esteller, 2—DNA methylation and cancer, in: Z. Herceg, T. Ushijima (Eds.), Advances in Genetics, Academic Press, 2010, pp. 27–56.

[8] N. Ahuja, A.R. Sharma, S.B. Baylin, Epigenetic therapeutics: a new weapon in the war against cancer, Annu. Rev. Med. 67 (1) (2016) 73–89.

[9] P.A. Jones, S.B. Baylin, The epigenomics of cancer, Cell 128 (4) (2007) 683–692.

[10] A.P. Feinberg, Phenotypic plasticity and the epigenetics of human disease, Nature 447 (7143) (2007) 433–440.

[11] J. Li, et al., Particulate matter-induced epigenetic changes and lung cancer, Clin. Respir. J. 11 (5) (2017) 539–546.

[12] M. Boeri, et al., MicroRNA signatures in tissues and plasma predict development and prognosis of computed tomography detected lung cancer, Proc. Natl. Acad. Sci. 108 (9) (2011) 3713–3718.

[13] T. Liloglou, et al., Epigenetic biomarkers in lung cancer, Cancer Lett. 342 (2) (2014) 200–212.

[14] A. Kim, et al., Epigenetic regulation in breast cancer: insights on epidrugs, Epigenomes 7 (1) (2023) 1–5.

[15] V. Ortiz-Barahona, R.S. Joshi, M. Esteller, Use of DNA methylation profiling in trans-lational oncology, Semin. Cancer Biol. 83 (2022) 523–535.

[16] H. Macias, L. Hinck, Mammary gland development, Wiley Interdiscip. Rev. Dev. Biol. 1 (4) (2012) 533–557.

[17] M.S. Kareta, et al., Reconstitution and mechanism of the stimulation of de novo meth-ylation by human DNMT3L, J. Biol. Chem. 281 (36) (2006) 25893–25902.

[18] K. Williams, J. Christensen, K. Helin, DNA methylation: TET proteins—guardians of CpG islands? EMBO Rep. 13 (1) (2012) 28–35.

[19] A. Schäfer, Gadd45 proteins: key players of repair-mediated DNA demethylation, in: D. A. Liebermann, B. Hoffman (Eds.), Gadd45 Stress Sensor Genes, Springer New York, New York, NY, 2013, pp. 35–50.

[20] S. Pietrasik, et al., Interplay between BRCA1 and GADD45A and its potential for nucleotide excision repair in breast cancer pathogenesis, Int. J. Mol. Sci. 21 (3) (2020) 870.

[21] W. Wang, et al., Analysis of methylation-sensitive transcriptome identifies GADD45a as a frequently methylated gene in breast cancer, Oncogene 24 (16) (2005) 2705–2714.

[22] J. Jeschke, E. Collignon, F. Fuks, Portraits of TET-mediated DNA hydroxymethylation in cancer, Curr. Opin. Genet. Dev. 36 (2016) 16–26.

[23] D.P. Muñoz, et al., Activation-induced cytidine deaminase (AID) is necessary for the epithelial–mesenchymal transition in mammary epithelial cells, Proc. Natl. Acad. Sci. 110 (32) (2013) E2977–E2986.

[24] H.D. Morgan, et al., Activation-induced cytidine deaminase deaminates 5-methylcytosine in DNA and is expressed in pluripotent tissues: implications for epigenetic reprogramming, J. Biol. Chem. 279 (50) (2004) 52353–52360.

[25] J.U. Guo, et al., Hydroxylation of 5-methylcytosine by TET1 promotes active DNA demethylation in the adult brain, Cell 145 (3) (2011) 423–434.

[26] A.V. DiMarco, et al., APOBEC mutagenesis inhibits breast cancer growth through induction of T cell-mediated antitumor immune responses, Cancer Immunol. Res. 10 (1) (2022) 70–86.

[27] D.C. Koboldt, et al., Comprehensive molecular portraits of human breast tumours, Nature 490 (7418) (2012) 61–70.

[28] T. Fujikane, et al., Genomic screening for genes upregulated by demethylation revealed novel targets of epigenetic silencing in breast cancer, Breast Cancer Res. Treat. 122 (3) (2010) 699–710.

[29] M. Esteller, et al., Promoter hypermethylation and BRCA1 inactivation in sporadic breast and ovarian tumors, JNCI J. Natl. Cancer Inst. 92 (7) (2000) 564–569.

[30] R. Radpour, et al., Integrated epigenetics of human breast cancer: synoptic investigation of targeted genes, microRNAs and proteins upon demethylation treatment, PLoS One 6 (11) (2011) e27355.

[31] S.A. Shargh, et al., Downregulation of E-cadherin expression in breast cancer by promoter hypermethylation and its relation with progression and prognosis of tumor, Med. Oncol. 31 (11) (2014) 250.

[32] D.T. Butcher, D.I. Rodenhiser, Epigenetic inactivation of BRCA1 is associated with aberrant expression of CTCF and DNA methyltransferase (DNMT3B) in some sporadic breast tumours, Eur. J. Cancer 43 (1) (2007) 210–219.

[33] M. Askari, et al., Aberrant promoter hypermethylation of p21 (WAF1/CIP1) gene and its impact on expression and role of polymorphism in the risk of breast cancer, Mol. Cell. Biochem. 382 (1) (2013) 19–26.

[34] K. Holm, et al., Molecular subtypes of breast cancer are associated with characteristic DNA methylation patterns, Breast Cancer Res. 12 (3) (2010) R36.

[35] B. Győrffy, et al., Aberrant DNA methylation impacts gene expression and prognosis in breast cancer subtypes, Int. J. Cancer 138 (1) (2016) 87–97.

[36] C. Thakur, et al., Epigenetics and environment in breast cancer: new paradigms for anti-cancer therapies, Front. Oncol. 12 (2022) 4.

[37] S. Dedeurwaerder, et al., DNA methylation profiling reveals a predominant immune component in breast cancers, EMBO Mol. Med. 3 (12) (2011) 726–741.

[38] B.P. de Almeida, et al., Roadmap of DNA methylation in breast cancer identifies novel prognostic biomarkers, BMC Cancer 19 (1) (2019) 219.

[39] R.N. Batra, et al., DNA methylation landscapes of 1538 breast cancers reveal a replication-linked clock, epigenomic instability and cis-regulation, Nat. Commun. 12 (1) (2021) 5406.

[40] Z. Yang, et al., An integrative pan-cancer-wide analysis of epigenetic enzymes reveals universal patterns of epigenomic deregulation in cancer, Genome Biol. 16 (1) (2015) 140.

[41] E. Brzeziańska, A. Dutkowska, A. Antczak, The significance of epigenetic alterations in lung carcinogenesis, Mol. Biol. Rep. 40 (1) (2013) 309–325.

[42] S.A. Belinsky, Gene-promoter hypermethylation as a biomarker in lung cancer, Nat. Rev. Cancer 4 (9) (2004) 707–717.

[43] G.P. Pfeifer, T.A. Rauch, DNA methylation patterns in lung carcinomas, Semin. Cancer Biol. 19 (3) (2009) 181–187.

[44] S.M. Langevin, R.A. Kratzke, K.T. Kelsey, Epigenetics of lung cancer, Transl. Res. 165 (1) (2015) 74–90.

[45] S. Liu, et al., Epigenetic therapy in lung cancer, Front. Oncol. 3 (2013) 1–4.

[46] M. Duruisseaux, M. Esteller, Lung cancer epigenetics: from knowledge to applications, Semin. Cancer Biol. 51 (2018) 116–128.

[47] J.A. Biegel, T.M. Busse, B.E. Weissman, SWI/SNF chromatin remodeling complexes and cancer, Am. J. Med. Genet. C: Semin. Med. Genet. 166 (3) (2014) 350–366.

[48] Q. Lai, et al., The loss-of-function of DNA methyltransferase 1 by siRNA impairs the growth of non-small cell lung cancer with alleviated side effects via reactivation of RASSF1A and APC in vitro and vivo, Oncotarget 8 (35) (2017) 2–5.

[49] I. Rhee, et al., DNMT1 and DNMT3b cooperate to silence genes in human cancer cells, Nature 416 (6880) (2002) 552–556.

[50] I. Teneng, et al., Global identification of genes targeted by DNMT3b for epigenetic silencing in lung cancer, Oncogene 34 (5) (2015) 621–630.

[51] R.E. Husni, et al., DNMT3a expression pattern and its prognostic value in lung adenocarcinoma, Lung Cancer 97 (2016) 59–65.

[52] M. Füller, et al., 5-Azacytidine enhances efficacy of multiple chemotherapy drugs in AML and lung cancer with modulation of CpG methylation, Int. J. Oncol. 46 (3) (2015) 1192–1204.

[53] I. Ibanez de Caceres, et al., IGFBP-3 hypermethylation-derived deficiency mediates cisplatin resistance in non-small-cell lung cancer, Oncogene 29 (11) (2010) 1681–1690.

[54] Y.-W. Zhang, et al., Integrated analysis of DNA methylation and mRNA expression profiling reveals candidate genes associated with cisplatin resistance in non-small cell lung cancer, Epigenetics 9 (6) (2014) 896–909.

[55] X.-Y. Li, et al., Blockade of DNA methylation enhances the therapeutic effect of gefitinib in non-small cell lung cancer cells, Oncol. Rep. 29 (5) (2013) 1975–1982.

[56] J. Wrangle, et al., Alterations of immune response of non-small cell lung cancer with azacytidine, Oncotarget 4 (11) (2013) 2–7.

[57] H. Li, et al., Immune regulation by low doses of the DNA methyltransferase inhibitor 5-azacitidine in common human epithelial cancers, Oncotarget 5 (3) (2014) 3–7.

[58] I. Balgkouranidou, T. Liloglou, E.S. Lianidou, Lung cancer epigenetics: emerging biomarkers, Biomark. Med 7 (1) (2013) 49–58.

[59] D.S. Shames, et al., A genome-wide screen for promoter methylation in lung cancer identifies novel methylation markers for multiple malignancies, PLoS Med. 3 (12) (2006) e486.

[60] J.E. Bailey-Wilson, et al., A major lung cancer susceptibility locus maps to chromosome 6q23–25, Am. J. Hum. Genet. 75 (3) (2004) 460–474.

[61] L.T. Smith, et al., Epigenetic regulation of the tumor suppressor gene TCF21 on 6q23-q24 in lung and head and neck cancer, Proc. Natl. Acad. Sci. 103 (4) (2006) 982–987.

[62] K.E. Schuebel, et al., Comparing the DNA hypermethylome with gene mutations in human colorectal cancer, PLoS Genet. 3 (9) (2007) e157.

[63] M. Wang, et al., Identification of a novel tumor suppressor gene p34 on human chromosome 6q25.1, Cancer Res. 67 (1) (2007) 93–99.

[64] R.A. Weinberg, The retinoblastoma protein and cell cycle control, Cell 81 (3) (1995) 323–330.

[65] R.E. Shackelford, W.K. Kaufmann, R.S. Paules, Cell cycle control, checkpoint mechanisms, and genotoxic stress, Environ. Health Perspect. 107 (Suppl. 1) (1999) 5–24.

[66] S.A. Belinsky, et al., Aberrant methylation of p16(INK4a) is an early event in lung cancer and a potential biomarker for early diagnosis, Proc. Natl. Acad. Sci. USA 95 (20) (1998) 11891–11896.

[67] C. Korch, P. Hagblom, In-vivo-modified gonococcal plasmid pJD1. A model system for analysis of restriction enzyme sensitivity to DNA modifications, Eur. J. Biochem. 161 (3) (1986) 519–524.

[68] C. Waalwijk, R.A. Flavell, MspI, an isoschizomer of hpaII which cleaves both unmethylated and methylated hpaII sites, Nucleic Acids Res. 5 (9) (1978) 3231–3236.

[69] J. Tost, I.G. Gut, Analysis of gene-specific DNA methylation patterns by pyrosequencing technology, Methods Mol. Biol. 373 (2007) 89–102.

[70] M. Ehrich, et al., Cytosine methylation profiles as a molecular marker in non-small cell lung cancer, Cancer Res. 66 (22) (2006) 10911–10918.

[71] M. Ehrich, et al., Quantitative high-throughput analysis of DNA methylation patterns by base-specific cleavage and mass spectrometry, Proc. Natl. Acad. Sci. USA 102 (44) (2005) 15785–15790.

[72] M. Jung, et al., MIRA-seq for DNA methylation analysis of CpG islands, Epigenomics 7 (5) (2015) 695–706.

[73] S.H. Cross, et al., Purification of CpG islands using a methylated DNA binding column, Nat. Genet. 6 (3) (1994) 236–244.

[74] Y. Zhang, et al., Methylation of multiple genes as a candidate biomarker in non-small cell lung cancer, Cancer Lett. 303 (1) (2011) 21–28.

[75] F. Salazar, et al., First-line therapy and methylation status of CHFR in serum influence outcome to chemotherapy versus EGFR tyrosine kinase inhibitors as second-line therapy in stage IV non-small-cell lung cancer patients, Lung Cancer 72 (1) (2011) 84–91.

[76] K. Luger, et al., Crystal structure of the nucleosome core particle at 2.8 Å resolution, Nature 389 (6648) (1997) 251–260.

[77] G.A. Bentley, et al., Crystal structure of the nucleosome core particle at 16 Å resolution, J. Mol. Biol. 176 (1) (1984) 55–75.

[78] V.G. Allfrey, R. Faulkner, A.E. Mirsky, Acetylation and methylation of histones and their possible role in the regulation of RNA synthesis, Proc. Natl. Acad. Sci. 51 (5) (1964) 786–794.

[79] A.J. Bannister, T. Kouzarides, Regulation of chromatin by histone modifications, Cell Res. 21 (3) (2011) 381–395.

[80] Q. Zhu, et al., BRCA1 tumour suppression occurs via heterochromatin-mediated silencing, Nature 477 (7363) (2011) 179–184.

[81] L. Zheng, et al., BRCA1 mediates ligand-independent transcriptional repression of the estrogen receptor, Proc. Natl. Acad. Sci. USA 98 (17) (2001) 9587–9592.

[82] F.F. Cai, et al., Epigenetic therapy for breast cancer, Int. J. Mol. Sci. 12 (7) (2011) 4465–4487.

[83] F. Falahi, et al., Current and upcoming approaches to exploit the reversibility of epigenetic mutations in breast cancer, Breast Cancer Res. 16 (4) (2014) 412.

[84] T. Beckers, et al., Distinct pharmacological properties of second generation HDAC inhibitors with the benzamide or hydroxamate head group, Int. J. Cancer 121 (5) (2007) 1138–1148.

[85] S. Shankar, et al., Suberoylanilide hydroxamic acid (zolinza/vorinostat) sensitizes TRAIL-resistant breast cancer cells orthotopically implanted in BALB/c nude mice, Mol. Cancer Ther. 8 (6) (2009) 1596–1605.

[86] X. Huang, et al., HDAC inhibitor SNDX-275 enhances efficacy of trastuzumab in erbB2-overexpressing breast cancer cells and exhibits potential to overcome trastuzumab resistance, Cancer Lett. 307 (1) (2011) 72–79.

[87] E.A. Collisson, et al., Comprehensive molecular profiling of lung adenocarcinoma, Nature 511 (7511) (2014) 543–550.

[88] D.M. Walter, et al., Systematic in vivo inactivation of chromatin-regulating enzymes identifies Setd2 as a potent tumor suppressor in lung adenocarcinoma, Cancer Res. 77 (7) (2017) 1719–1729.

[89] T. Orvis, et al., BRG1/SMARCA4 inactivation promotes non-small cell lung cancer aggressiveness by altering chromatin organization, Cancer Res. 74 (22) (2014) 6486–6498.

[90] D.N. Reisman, et al., Loss of BRG1/BRM in human lung cancer cell lines and primary lung cancers: correlation with poor prognosis, Cancer Res. 63 (3) (2003) 560–566.

[91] O.A. Romero, et al., MAX inactivation in small cell lung cancer disrupts MYC–SWI/SNF programs and is synthetic lethal with BRG1, Cancer Discov. 4 (3) (2014) 292–303.

[92] T. Shorstova, et al., SWI/SNF-compromised cancers are susceptible to bromodomain inhibitors, Cancer Res. 79 (10) (2019) 2761–2774.

[93] Y. Xue, et al., SMARCA4 loss is synthetic lethal with CDK4/6 inhibition in non-small cell lung cancer, Nat. Commun. 10 (1) (2019) 557.

[94] R.A. Juergens, et al., Combination epigenetic therapy has efficacy in patients with refractory advanced non-small cell lung cancer, Cancer Discov. 1 (7) (2011) 598–607.

[95] E.E. Cameron, et al., Synergy of demethylation and histone deacetylase inhibition in the re-expression of genes silenced in cancer, Nat. Genet. 21 (1) (1999) 103–107.

[96] A.-J. Boivin, et al., Antineoplastic action of 5-aza-2′-deoxycytidine and phenylbutyrate on human lung carcinoma cells, Anti-Cancer Drugs 13 (8) (2002) 869–874.

[97] W.G. Zhu, et al., DNA methyltransferase inhibition enhances apoptosis induced by histone deacetylase inhibitors, Cancer Res. 61 (4) (2001) 1327–1333.

[98] M.I. Niesen, G. Blanck, Rescue of major histocompatibility-DR surface expression in retinoblastoma-defective, non-small cell lung carcinoma cells by the MS-275 histone deacetylase inhibitor, Biol. Pharm. Bull. 32 (3) (2009) 480–482.

[99] B.F. Chu, et al., Phase I study of 5-aza-2'-deoxycytidine in combination with valproic acid in non-small-cell lung cancer, Cancer Chemother. Pharmacol. 71 (1) (2013) 115–121.

[100] J. Lin, et al., A phase I dose-finding study of 5-azacytidine in combination with sodium phenylbutyrate in patients with refractory solid tumors, Clin. Cancer Res. 15 (19) (2009) 6241–6249.

[101] M. Candelaria, et al., A phase II study of epigenetic therapy with hydralazine and magnesium valproate to overcome chemotherapy resistance in refractory solid tumors, Ann. Oncol. 18 (9) (2007) 1529–1538.

[102] A. Stathis, et al., Phase I study of decitabine in combination with vorinostat in patients with advanced solid tumors and non-Hodgkin's lymphomas, Clin. Cancer Res. 17 (6) (2011) 1582–1590.

[103] S. Han, et al., Anti-tumor effect in human lung cancer by a combination treatment of novel histone deacetylase inhibitors: SL142 or SL325 and retinoic acids, PLoS One 5 (11) (2010) e13834.

[104] J.M. Shieh, et al., Mitochondrial apoptosis and FAK signaling disruption by a novel histone deacetylase inhibitor, HTPB, in antitumor and antimetastatic mouse models, PLoS One 7 (1) (2012) e30240.

[105] J.J. Hwang, et al., A novel histone deacetylase inhibitor, CG0006, induces cell death through both extrinsic and intrinsic apoptotic pathways, Anti-Cancer Drugs 20 (9) (2009) 815–821.

[106] K.C. Cuneo, et al., Histone deacetylase inhibitor NVP-LAQ824 sensitizes human non-small cell lung cancer to the cytotoxic effects of ionizing radiation, Anti-Cancer Drugs 18 (7) (2007) 793–800.

[107] M. Fournel, et al., MGCD0103, a novel isotype-selective histone deacetylase inhibitor, has broad spectrum antitumor activity in vitro and in vivo, Mol. Cancer Ther. 7 (4) (2008) 759–768.

[108] J. Gray, et al., Combination of HDAC and topoisomerase inhibitors in small cell lung cancer, Cancer Biol. Ther. 13 (8) (2012) 614–622.

[109] Y.A. Tang, et al., A novel histone deacetylase inhibitor exhibits antitumor activity via apoptosis induction, F-actin disruption and gene acetylation in lung cancer, PLoS One 5 (9) (2010) e12417.

[110] R.-J. Shiau, et al., Genistein and β-carotene enhance the growth-inhibitory effect of trichostatin A in A549 cells, Eur. J. Nutr. 49 (1) (2010) 19–25.

[111] N. Komatsu, et al., SAHA, a HDAC inhibitor, has profound anti-growth activity against non-small cell lung cancer cells, Oncol. Rep. 15 (1) (2006) 187–191.

[112] D.B. Seligson, et al., Global levels of histone modifications predict prognosis in different cancers, Am. J. Pathol. 174 (5) (2009) 1619–1628.

[113] H. Sasaki, et al., Histone deacetylase 1 mRNA expression in lung cancer, Lung Cancer 46 (2) (2004) 171–178.

[114] H. Ozdağ, et al., Differential expression of selected histone modifier genes in human solid cancers, BMC Genomics 7 (2006) 90.

[115] M. Esteller, Cancer epigenetics for the 21st century: what's next? Genes Cancer 2 (6) (2011) 604–606.

[116] S. Imani, et al., The diagnostic role of microRNA-34a in breast cancer: a systematic review and meta-analysis, Oncotarget 8 (14) (2017) 23177–23187.

[117] B.D. Adams, et al., miR-34a silences c-SRC to attenuate tumor growth in triple-negative breast cancer, Cancer Res. 76 (4) (2016) 927–939.

[118] L. Li, et al., MiR-34a inhibits proliferation and migration of breast cancer through down-regulation of Bcl-2 and SIRT1, Clin. Exp. Med. 13 (2) (2013) 109–117.

[119] M. Pichler, G.A. Calin, MicroRNAs in cancer: from developmental genes in worms to their clinical application in patients, Br. J. Cancer 113 (4) (2015) 569–573.

[120] D.S. Hong, et al., Phase 1 study of MRX34, a liposomal miR-34a mimic, in patients with advanced solid tumours, Br. J. Cancer 122 (11) (2020) 1630–1637.

[121] G. Lucibello, et al., PD-L1 regulation revisited: impact on immunotherapeutic strategies, Trends Mol. Med. 27 (9) (2021) 868–881.

[122] B. Smith, P. Agarwal, N.A. Bhowmick, MicroRNA applications for prostate, ovarian and breast cancer in the era of precision medicine, Endocr. Relat. Cancer 24 (5) (2017) R157–r172.

[123] Z.H. Li, et al., miR-34a expression in human breast cancer is associated with drug resistance, Oncotarget 8 (63) (2017) 106270–106282.

[124] F. Ozsolak, et al., Chromatin structure analyses identify miRNA promoters, Genes Dev. 22 (22) (2008) 3172–3183.

[125] F. Bianchi, et al., Circulating microRNAs: next-generation biomarkers for early lung cancer detection, Ecancermedicalscience 6 (2012) 246.

[126] P.S. Mitchell, et al., Circulating microRNAs as stable blood-based markers for cancer detection, Proc. Natl. Acad. Sci. USA 105 (30) (2008) 10513–10518.

[127] E. Gallardo, et al., miR-34a as a prognostic marker of relapse in surgically resected non-small-cell lung cancer, Carcinogenesis 30 (11) (2009) 1903–1909.

[128] R. Tang, et al., Downregulation of MiR-30a is associated with poor prognosis in lung cancer, Med. Sci. Monit. 21 (2015) 2514–2520.

[129] W. Guo, et al., Decreased expression of miR-204 in plasma is associated with a poor prognosis in patients with non-small cell lung cancer, Int. J. Mol. Med. 36 (6) (2015) 1720–1726.

[130] H. Ge, et al., MicroRNA-148b is down-regulated in non-small cell lung cancer and associated with poor survival, Int. J. Clin. Exp. Pathol. 8 (1) (2015) 800–805.

[131] Y. Bai, et al., Expression of miR-32 in human non-small cell lung cancer and its correlation with tumor progression and patient survival, Int. J. Clin. Exp. Pathol. 8 (1) (2015) 824–829.

[132] Q. Zhao, et al., Circulating miRNAs is a potential marker for gefitinib sensitivity and correlation with EGFR mutational status in human lung cancers, Am. J. Cancer Res. 5 (5) (2015) 1692–1705.

[133] Y. Zhang, et al., Down-regulation of microRNA-124 is correlated with tumor metastasis and poor prognosis in patients with lung cancer, Int. J. Clin. Exp. Pathol. 8 (2) (2015) 1967–1972.

[134] M. Millward, et al., Phase 1 clinical trial of the novel proteasome inhibitor marizomib with the histone deacetylase inhibitor vorinostat in patients with melanoma, pancreatic and lung cancer based on in vitro assessments of the combination, Investig. New Drugs 30 (6) (2012) 2303–2317.

[135] C.-W. Chien, et al., Enhanced suppression of tumor growth by concomitant treatment of human lung cancer cells with suberoylanilide hydroxamic acid and arsenic trioxide, Toxicol. Appl. Pharmacol. 257 (1) (2011) 59–66.

[136] S.-K. Seo, et al., Combined effects of sulindac and suberoylanilide hydroxamic acid on apoptosis induction in human lung cancer cells, Mol. Pharmacol. 73 (3) (2008) 1005–1012.

[137] M.D. Reed, et al., Aerosolised 5-azacytidine suppresses tumour growth and reprogrammes the epigenome in an orthotopic lung cancer model, Br. J. Cancer 109 (7) (2013) 1775–1781.

[138] Available from: www.clinicaltrials.gov: Identifier NCT01935947.

[139] Available from: www.clinicaltrials.gov: Identifier NCT01928576.

[140] Available from: www.clinicaltrials.gov: Identifier NCT00978250.

[141] Available from: www.clinicaltrials.gov: Identifier NCT02009436.

[142] R.J. Amato, Inhibition of DNA methylation by antisense oligonucleotide MG98 as cancer therapy, Clin. Genitourin. Cancer 5 (7) (2007) 422–426.

[143] C. Hu, et al., DNA methyltransferase inhibitors combination therapy for the treatment of solid tumor: mechanism and clinical application, Clin. Epigenetics 13 (1) (2021) 166.

[144] D.M. Roy, L.A. Walsh, T.A. Chan, Driver mutations of cancer epigenomes, Protein Cell 5 (4) (2014) 265–296.

[145] C. Braicu, et al., Epigallocatechin-3-gallate (EGCG) inhibits cell proliferation and migratory behaviour of triple negative breast cancer cells, J. Nanosci. Nanotechnol. 13 (1) (2013) 632–637.

[146] Y. Li, et al., Synergistic epigenetic reactivation of estrogen receptor-α (ERα) by combined green tea polyphenol and histone deacetylase inhibitor in ERα-negative breast cancer cells, Mol. Cancer 9 (2010) 274.

[147] J. Szczepanek, M. Skorupa, A. Tretyn, MicroRNA as a potential therapeutic molecule in cancer, Cells 11 (6) (2022) 8–9.

Dietary components as epigenetic modifiers and their roles in cancer prevention

12

Chitra Thakur[a] and Uttara Saran[b]

[a]*Stony Brook Cancer Center, Department of Pathology, Renaissance School of Medicine, Stony Brook University, Stony Brook, NY, United States,* [b]*Department of Genomic Medicine, The University of Texas MD Anderson Cancer Center, Houston, TX, United States*

Introduction

Cancer is a major burden on public health worldwide. Uncontrolled cell proliferation is one of the most common phenotypes of all cancer cells. Such a rapid growth of cancer cells requires metabolic adaptations for its sustenance and survival owing to the hypoxic and nutrient-deprived stressful tumor microenvironmental conditions.

During tumorigenesis, the interplay between the tumor cells and its microenvironment is inevitable. External and internal stimuli such as oxygen supply, nutrients, and oncogenic signals impact the metabolism of cancer cells [1]. Hence, an altered metabolism in cancer cells contributes to tumorigenesis, malignancy, and stemness, where cancer metabolism is closely interlinked with epigenetic regulation in cancer development and progression [2].

In recent years, cancer metabolism and epigenetics have gained widespread attention owing to their critical involvement in the process of carcinogenesis. The term epigenetics implies "above the genes." It is defined by inherited somatic changes that are not linked with any changes in the DNA sequence. A gene can be turned ON or OFF through various epigenetics mechanisms, predominately grouped under the categories of DNA methylation, histones covalent modifications, chromatin structure, and noncoding RNAs [3]. Interestingly, epigenetic changes are dynamic and reversible in nature and influence the expression of genes without changing their sequence. Notably, epigenetic marks are less stable and are sensitive to external and internal stimuli such as exposure to nutrients, toxins, and other environmental factors. In this chapter, we will discuss how dietary components affect the epigenome, as well as their importance in chemoprevention and epigenetic regulation.

Cancer Epigenetics and Nanomedicine. https://doi.org/10.1016/B978-0-443-13209-4.00010-6
Copyright © 2024 Elsevier Inc. All rights are reserved, including those for text and data mining, AI training, and similar technologies.

Epigenetic mechanisms and its importance in cancer

Gene regulation is a complex process, where the methylation of DNA is a vital step governing whether the genes will be expressed or not. DNA methylation involves the addition of a methyl group to the 5-carbon (C^5) position of a cytosine, i.e., when a methyl group is transferred from a methyl precursor S-adenosyl methionine (SAM), to the cytosines existing in the CpG islands [4]. Such a process of methyl group transfers is catalyzed by a group of enzymes called DNA methyltransferases (DNMTs), where hypermethylation of the CpG dinucleotides results in transcriptional gene silencing. Similarly, demethylation of DNA occurs due to a group of enzymes called DNA demethylases, resulting in the transcriptional activation of the gene [5]. In fact, hypermethylation of tumor suppressor genes and hypomethylation of oncogenes is a known phenomenon in cancer, where global hypomethylation is linked with almost all human neoplasias [6,7]. In addition, altered expression of DNMTs has a major role in cancer development and progression [8].

Within a cell, DNA does not exist as a naked molecule; rather it is spooled around a group of specialized chromosomal proteins called histones. Such a chromosomal packaging, also termed chromatin, can impact the gene's activity. While a compact packaging of histones, also called heterochromatin, hinders the accessibility of DNA to the other gene regulatory/binding proteins, preventing gene expression, a loose packaging of histones, also called euchromatin, facilitates gene expression. Such a modification to the histone proteins happens as posttranslational modifications occurring at the N-terminal of histones and includes the processes of acetylation, methylation, phosphorylation, biotinylation, and ubiquitination [9]. Modification to histone proteins is mediated by a group of enzymes that catalyzes the addition or removal of methyl groups to the lysine or arginine residues and are called histone methyltransferases (HMTs) and histone demethylases (HDMs), respectively; and the enzymes that catalyze the addition or removal of acetyl groups to the lysine residues of the histones are called histone acetyltransferases (HATs) and histone deacetylases (HDACs), respectively [10].

Thus, DNA methylation, modification of histones, and the different chromatin states altogether impact gene regulation and are implicated in human cancer development and malignant progression. As already stated, global hypomethylation in the DNA accompanied by hypermethylation at other sites is a frequent phenomenon in cancers [7]; epigenetic marks can serve as vital clues in cancer diagnosis and therapeutic design. For example, detection of aberrant methylation patterns associated with cancer formation, utilizing the targeted methylation sequencing tools. Likewise, detection of abnormal histone modifications can serve as a prominent epigenetic biomarker in cancer diagnosis, as well as in the prediction of clinical outcomes. For example, in prostate, kidney, and lung cancers, decreased levels of histone modification mark H3K4me2 are linked with poor prognosis [11]. Interestingly, epigenetic marks can help in the diagnostic differentiation of cancer tissues with and without malignancy. In prostate cancer, acetylation of histone H3 and demethylation of histone H3 at lysine 9 position (H3K9) can determine the difference between prostate cancer and the prostate tissue of nonmalignant features. In addition, trimethylation of histone H3 at lysine 4 position (H3K4) is able to serve as a key predictor of the recurrence of prostate cancer [12]. In other cancers such as prostate, endometrial, and breast cancers, the expression of Enhancer of zeste homolog 2 (EZH2), a histone-lysine N-methyltransferase enzyme, serves as a discrete diagnostic marker of malignancy [13]. Because epigenetic mechanisms are reversible and regulate cancer-associated gene expression and signaling pathways, they can be exploited in the development of treatment and monitoring strategies in cancers [14–16].

Environment plays a major role in shaping up the various trajectories adopted by a cell's epigenome owing to the fact that epigenetic processes are responsive to many factors that include but are not limited to development, aging, pathological context, and environmental factors [17,18]. Here, we will shed light on dietary components, which are among the many other factors influencing epigenetics.

Crosstalk between dietary components and metabolism in epigenetic regulation

Consumption of food is critical for sustaining essential life processes, where good nutrition is an important determinant of an individual's health and well-being. For example, diets rich in fruits and vegetables have been shown to lower the risk of cancer, mainly because of their influence on the expression of oncogenes and tumor suppressors [19]. Moreover, dietary components influence epigenetic modifications, where metabolism and epigenetics are closely associated [2].

Altered metabolism in cancer cells is crucial for establishing specific epigenetic programs instrumental for tumorigenesis and malignant progression of the disease. Aerobic Glycolysis, The Pentose Phosphate Pathway, The PI3K Pathway, Reactive Oxygen Species, Glutamine, etc., are some of the major components of metabolic rewiring in cancer cells and have been well described. Metabolic alterations in the cancer cells influence the epigenetic landscape by at least three distinct cellular operations. First is the reprogramming of the metabolic pathways where the metabolite levels are altered. Noteworthy, many of these metabolites serve as key cofactors or substrates of the essential enzymes catalyzing the epigenetic modifications. Second is the process of nuclear translocation of the metabolites by the enzymes involved in the act, and third involves the generation of oncometabolites, which in turn modulate the activity of several epigenetic enzymes, where accumulated oncometabolites in cancer cells is crucial for propelling the progression of tumors [2].

To further understand how dietary components influence epigenetic processes, it is imperative to understand the metabolic control of DNA and histone methylation (Fig. 1). The epigenetic process of methylation reaction requires the transfer of a methyl group from SAM, resulting in the formation of S-adenosylhomocysteine (SAH), which in turn is recycled back into the methionine cycle. SAM serves as a universal methyl donor in mammals and is generated from methionine and adenosine

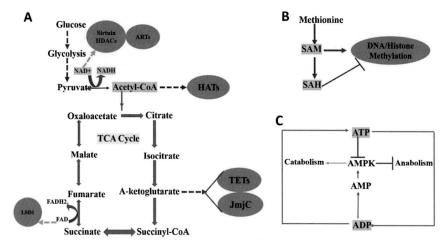

FIG. 1

Metabolites serve as cellular rheostats and regulate the epigenetic processes [2]. Variations in the concentration of several metabolites that act as either substrate or cofactors for key epigenetic enzymes influence chromatin modification and also by a feedback mechanism that dynamically regulates the entire process. (A) The tricarboxylic acid (TCA) generates metabolites that link energy pathways with epigenetic chromatin modifications, highlighted in orange. Glycolysis generates acetyl-CoA that feeds itself into the TCA cycle further and serves as a substrate for histone acetyltransferases (HATs). Pyruvate to acetyl-CoA conversion generates nicotinamide adenine dinucleotide (NAD+), which is needed by the sirtuin histone deacetylases (HDACs; histone deacetylation) and ADP-ribosyltransferases (ARTs). α-Ketoglutarate and flavin adenine dinucleotide (FAD) serve as cofactors for DNA ten-eleven translocations (TETs) and histone demethylases (Jumonji C domain containing JmjC), LSD1. (B) Product metabolite *S*-adenosyl methionine (SAM) generated via one carbon cycle acts as a methyl donor to the histone-modifying enzymes, histone methyltransferases (HMTs) and DNA methyltransferases (DNMTs), thereby facilitating histone and DNA methylation. On the contrary, *S*-adenosylhomocysteine (SAH) negatively regulates this process, indicating that the SAM/SAH ratio is essential in regulating DNA and histone methylation. (C) Cellular ATP/ADP ratio has a physiological role where the conversion of adenosine triphosphate (ATP) to adenosine diphosphate (ADP) aids in the anabolic process. Catabolism, however, relies on ADP to ATP conversion, where activation of AMP-activated protein kinase (AMPK) is critical in regulating this balance. Therefore, within the cellular environment, NAD+/NADH, acetyl-CoA/Co-A, SAM/SAH, and ATP/ADP ratio act as sensory signals (highlighted in *green*) governing the various epigenetic processes.

triphosphate (ATP). The enzymes catalyzing the reaction are the DNMTs and the HMTs for DNA and histone methylation, respectively. Hence, the availability of SAM is directly going to influence the methylation status of DNA and histones. Moreover, SAH is antagonistic toward methyltransferases which renders the cellular SAM/SAH ratio to be a pivotal determinant of the methylation potential of a cell [2,20]. On the contrary, demethylation of DNA and histone is brought about by demethylases.

HDMs can belong to the family of lysine-specific demethylases—LSD1 and LSD2, or the JmjC family of proteins; both of these are flavin adenine dinucleotide (FAD)-dependent oxidase enzymes. Here, a-ketoglutarate (aKG) serves as a cofactor for demethylases of the JmjC family for their enzymatic activity. Importantly, the catalytic cofactors FAD and αKG are released as an intermediary metabolite from the tricarboxylic acid (TCA) metabolic pathway occurring in mitochondria [20].

Another epigenetic mechanism is histone acetylation, which is dynamically mediated by HATs and HDACs. Oxidative phosphorylation is an energy-producing anabolic process where acetyl-CoA delivers the acetyl group to the TCA cycle to be oxidized for energy production [21]. Interestingly, acetyl-CoA serves as a substrate for the HATs, where the enzyme transfers the acetyl moiety of acetyl-CoA to the lysine residues of histone proteins, resulting in transcriptional activation [22,23]. Hence, differential levels of cellular acetyl-CoA strongly impact the HATs-mediated acetylation of histones. Therefore, a good balance between the HAT and HDAC enzymatic activities determines the acetylation, where the existence of many other cellular metabolites of antagonistic features toward HDACs has been reported. Butyrate is one such metabolite that hinders the HDACs I, II, and IV enzymatic activities [24] and is generated by commensal bacteria that ferments the dietary fibers and undigested carbohydrates.

Types of dietary components and their role in epigenetics and chemoprevention

Bioactive food components can have important implications in altering the DNA methylation profiles in human cancers as they serve as methyl donors or cofactors in the key enzymatic processes involved in methylation. These food components that act as methyl donors and cofactors fall under the category of micronutrients such as choline, betaine, folate, vitamin B12, and other B vitamin families [25]. The reason these nutrients influence the epigenetic enzymatic reactions is due to their engagement in the "one-carbon metabolism" cycle, where they transfer one-carbon groups from the relevant donors to the DNA and proteins undergoing methylation [26,27]. Hence, the balance between SAM and SAH can be modulated by the availability of methyl donors arising from the nutrients, which in turn affect the enzymatic activity of methyl transferases. Studies have reported that certain dietary components such as epigallocatechin-gallate (EGCG), green tea polyphenol, genistein, or soy isoflavone are able to inhibit the activities of DNMTs in a direct and competitive manner [27]. On the other hand, demethylation enzymes such as the TETs are responsive to nutrients containing aKG [28]. Altogether, this indicates the importance of dietary components that can directly or indirectly impact the methylation status of the cells and hence are pivotal in cancer development and progression.

Some of the prominent dietary components with their roles in epigenetic regulation and cancer have been summarized in Table 1.

Table 1 Epigenetic and chemopreventive roles of dietary components.

Bioactive component	Dietary source	Epigenetic modulation	Cancer type	Anticancer effect	Reference study
Apigenin	Nuts, onion, oranges, vegetables, celery, artichoke, parsley, oregano, lettuce	DNMT ↓ HDAC ↓	Skin Prostate	Induction of apoptosis and autophagy Induction of apoptosis Inhibition of proliferative	[29]
Allicin	Garlic	HDAC ↓	Colon, liver, prostate, erythroleukemia	Decreased proliferation and angiogenesis	[30–33]
Butyrate	Fiber-rich food	HDAC ↓	Colon	Decreased proliferation and increased apoptosis	[34–37]
Curcumin	Turmeric	DNMT ↓ HDAC ↓	Acute myeloid leukemia, prostate, colon	Decreased proliferation, tumorigenesis, and increased apoptosis	[38–43]
Daidzein	Soy-based foods	DNMT ↓ HDAC ↓	Prostate kidney	Decreased proliferation	[44–46]
Epigallocatechin gallate	Tea (green, black), cocoa	DNMT ↓ HDAC ↓	Squamous cell, colon, cervix, prostate, skin, breast	Increased apoptosis Decreased proliferation and cell invasion	[47–53]
Genistein	Soy-based foods	DNMT ↓ HDAC ↓	Breast, prostate	Decreased proliferation and tumorigenesis	[54–57]
Indole-3 carbinol diindolylmethane	Cruciferous veggies	HDAC ↓	Prostate, breast, colon	Increased apoptosis Decreased proliferation and inflammation	[58–60]

Table 1 Epigenetic and chemopreventive roles of dietary components. *Continued*

Bioactive component	Dietary source	Epigenetic modulation	Cancer type	Anticancer effect	Reference study
Lycopene	Tomatoes, watermelon, grapefruit	DNMT ↓	Breast	Decreased proliferation	[55]
Piceatannol	Grapes, passion fruit, berries	HDAC ↓	Renal fibrosis	Increased apoptosis Decreased proliferation and inflammation	[61,62]
Quercetin	Citrous fruits, apples, dark berries, cherries	HDAC ↓	Liver, leukemia	Increased apoptosis Decreased proliferation, angiogenesis, and cell invasion	[63–65]
Resveratrol	Grapes, red wine, berries	DNMT ↓ HDAC ↓	Breast, prostate, hepatoblastoma	Decreased proliferation and increased apoptosis	[66–70]
Sulforaphane	Cruciferous veggies	DNMT ↓ HDAC ↓	Breast, prostate, colorectal	Decreased proliferation, increased apoptosis, and elevated immune response	[71–77]

Modified and adapted from M. Montgomery, A. Srinivasan, Epigenetic gene regulation by dietary compounds in cancer prevention, Adv. Nutr. 10(6) (2019) 1012–1028.

Green leafy vegetables, beans, lentils, certain fruits such as lemons, bananas, and melons, certain fortified cereals, and breads are rich sources of naturally occurring **folate** [78] where several studies suggested an increase in DNA methylation upon folate supplementation. While an increase in DNA methylation of two proto-oncogenes estrogen receptor alpha (ER-α) and secreted frizzled-related protein-1 (SFRP-1) in colorectal mucosa, was observed upon folate addition in a clinical trial study [79], an inverse association between folate intake and the risk of colon cancer has been reported [80,81]. **Vitamin B**, naturally occurring in certain food items such as meat, eggs, dairy products, legumes, and some dark leafy vegetables and fruits [82], has been associated with human neoplasia where increased consumption of vitamin B2, B6, and B12 was inversely correlated with prostate cancer [83], esophageal cancer [84], cervical intraepithelial neoplasia [85], and colorectal cancer [86]. Also, in lung and breast cancers, vitamin B12 levels were associated with global DNA methylation [87,88]. Choline and Betaine serve as methyl donors and alter the bioavailability of homocysteine, where they are suggested to influence the methylation status of genes, locally and globally [25]. Foods such as fish, eggs, dairy products, and cruciferous vegetables are rich sources of choline. Within the cellular system, irreversible oxidation of choline produces betaine, which is a direct methyl donor to homocysteine, in turn converting the homocysteine to methionine [89]. In fact, diet with less choline was found to elevate the SAH levels in the livers of rodents, where a high incidence of liver cancer development and decreased DNA methylation and DNMT activity was reported [90,91]. This is indeed suggestive of chemoprevention features of choline, where the protective roles of dietary betaine and choline against cancers of the breast, lung, and nasopharynx were suggested in a metaanalysis consisting of 11 epidemiological studies [92]. As widely accepted, diet and nutrition are vital for maintaining good health and life in general; it has been understood that epigenetic processes are vulnerable to environmental factors, where diet plays a major role [93,94]. This also implies that prenatal and/or early postnatal windows are crucial phases that set up the epigenome of an individual, which is also responsive to environmental factors, such as nutrition, in this context [95].

Dietary polyphenols

Plants are abundant in phytochemicals, and polyphenols are the most important group of phytochemicals occurring as secondary plant metabolites. The existence of polyphenols is the reason behind the bitterness, flavor, odor, astringency, and color of the food. They serve as dietary antioxidants and are implicated in human health and diseases [96]. Flavonoids and nonflavonoids comprise the two major types of plant polyphenols. While flavonoids are a structure of 15 carbon skeletons consisting of two phenyl rings in addition to a heterocyclic ring, nonflavonoids constitute an aromatic ring with one or more hydroxyl groups. Flavanols, flavonols, anthocyanidins, flavones, flavanones, and chalcones belong to the family of flavonoids, and stilbene, phenolic acids, saponin, curcumin, and tannins belong to nonflavonoid group of polyphenols [97]. Dietary polyphenols have significant roles in oxidative stress-induced human diseases and have major implications in the prevention and treatment of cancers [98–100]. Oxidative stress due to the production of increased reactive oxygen species (ROS) plays an important role in causing DNA damage and is implicated in human cancers [101]. Dietary polyphenols, owing to their antioxidant properties, serve as a protective entity against many cancers as they act on free radicals, thereby scavenging ROS and alleviating oxidative damage [102]. They modulate the epigenetic processes in cancers and have chemopreventive roles [103]. Apart from their chemoprotective features, dietary polyphenols are also implicated in influencing the epigenetics and gene regulation in noncommunicable chronic diseases, where they mitigate inflammation and oxidative stress [104].

Flavonoids have been widely studied and are known for their antiobesity, antidiabetic, antiinflammatory, and antioxidative features [105–109]. In cancer, flavonoids are reported to suppress proliferation and angiogenesis and facilitate cytotoxicity and apoptotic cell death [110,111]. Frequently occurring polyphenols are the EGCG present in green tea, curcumin, and resveratrol found in grapes [112]. Green tea and chocolates are also rich in catechin group of flavanols, whereas fruits such as apples, berries, pears, peaches, and grapes are laden with cyanidin, delphinidin, malvidin, pelargonidin, peonidin, and petunidin group of anthocyanins [113].

Epigallocatechin-gallate

EGCG is the most abundant and biologically active catechins group of polyphenols abundantly found in green tea and has anticancer properties [114–116]. Animal studies utilizing rodents have shown that consumption of EGCG and green tea extract in drinking water impeded carcinogenesis in several organs [117]. In humans, studies suggested that green tea intake can minimize the risk of several cancers, such as the cancers of the lung, breast, stomach, prostate, bladder, pancreas, intestinal tract, and esophagus, again attesting the importance of green tea in chemoprotective roles [118].

Molecular studies on the green tea component EGCG have shown its direct binding to the enzymatic substrate of DNMT3b and HDAC1, eventually resulting in its suppression. This led to the restoration of retinoic acid receptor β, cadherin1, and death-associated protein kinase-1, some of the prominent tumor suppressors [50].

Moreover, reduced activity of DNMT was observed in esophageal cancer cells treated with EGCG, and consequently, the hypermethylation of p16, RARβ, hMLH1, and MGMT tumor suppressor genes was reversed in a time and dose-dependent fashion upon EGCG administration [119]. Similarly, when A431 skin cancer cells were treated with EGCG, global DNA methylation was reduced along with the reduction in DNMT activity (decreased level of DNMT1, DNMT3a, and DNMT3b) and

5-methyl-cytosine. Such a reduction in DNA methylation led to the reexpression of p16(INK4a) and p21/Cip1 [52]. In pulmonary cells, EGCG treatment was able to cause the demethylation of the promoter of Wnt oncogene [120]. As epigenetic control of Wnt/β-catenin signaling pathway has major roles in human carcinogenesis [121], the impact of green tea component EGCG on Wnt/β-catenin pathway has also been recognized [122,123].

Sulforaphane

Sulforaphane is a sulfur-based nutrient found in vegetables such as broccoli, cauliflower, Brussels sprouts, etc., and is implicated in chemoprevention [124]. Interestingly, sulforaphane has been identified to strengthen the suppressive activity of EGCG on DNMT1, simultaneously facilitating the restraining of nTERT [125]. In fact, EGCG-mediated suppression of hTERT is brought about by DNMTs and HATs activity, thereby executing the hypomethylation of DNA and promoter deacetylation, respectively [48]. In this context, studies have recognized the modulating effect of EGCG on most of the enzymes of HATs category, where it served as an inhibitory factor for HATs [126].

In triple-negative breast cancer cells MDA-MB-23, combinatorial application of EGCG and an inhibitor of HDAC, trichostatin A (TSA), resulted in the reactivation of estrogen receptor-α (ER-α) by epigenetic mechanisms of histone modifications. Furthermore, cell proliferation was impeded, and chemosensitivity to tamoxifen was facilitated for ER-α-negative breast cancer cells upon combinatorial treatment of EGCG with sulforaphane [127,128].

Resveratrol

Resveratrol is a nonflavonoid polyphenol found to occur naturally in plants such as grapes, berries, pines, and peanuts, which aids against infections caused by pathogens [129]. Resveratrol is a health-giving phytochemical with multiple benefits having antioxidative, antiinflammatory, antiaging, and anticancer properties [130,131]. Resveratrol is involved in several biological operations pertaining to cell growth, apoptosis, angiogenesis, and metastasis spread, where chemopreventive and therapeutic repercussions of resveratrol have been suggested [132–134]. In vitro and in vivo studies have highlighted the potency of resveratrol used in the treatment of cancer [135]. In this context, inhibitory actions of resveratrol have been found in many cancer cells such as cancer of the breast, stomach, colon, liver, and leukemia [133,136]. In prostate cancer, resveratrol was found to restore the PTEN tumor suppressor gene by targeting the metastasis-associated protein 1 (MTA1)/HDACs, which in turn revoked negative regulation on the epigenetic machinery of histone modifications in cancer cells [137]. Moreover, it was shown that resveratrol facilitated the p53 acetylation, where it mediated the downregulation of MTA1 in prostate cancer cells [69]. In vitro studies in breast cancer revealed antimetastasis features of resveratrol where TGF-β1-mediated epithelial matrix transformation was reversed [138]. Also, epigenetic silencing of tumor suppressor BRCA1 was obstructed by resveratrol [139]. Suppression of proliferation and induction of cell death was observed in breast cancer cell lines treated with resveratrol and in combination with pterostilbene [140]. At epigenetic level, the influence of resveratrol on global DNA methylation was observed in breast cancer [141]. NAD-dependent deacetylase sirtuin-1 (SIRT1) was also impacted by resveratrol, where studies have shown resveratrol-mediated activation of SIRT1 [68]; consequently, the negative regulation of an antiapoptotic protein survivin was identified with an underlying mechanism of H3K9 deacetylation within its gene promoter [142,143]. In colon cancer, SIRT1, which is otherwise downregulated, has been found to be reversed by resveratrol [144], and, such an overexpressed SIRT1 exhibited antiproliferative features in colon cancer cell lines [145]. By SIRT1 suppression and hyperacetylation of p53/FOXO3a, resveratrol fostered apoptosis in Hodgkin lymphoma cells [146]. Altogether, several in vitro and in vivo studies showed the epigenetic regulation of resveratrol on the HDAC pathway as the underlying mechanism on suppressing the growth of tumors. Moreover, this growth suppressive feature of resveratrol can be attributed to its engagement in several biological pathways such as PI3K/AKT, Wnt, NF-κB, and Notch signaling [147].

Curcumin

Curcumin is the most typical polyphenol component isolated from the roots of *Curcuma longa* (also known as turmeric) and has many health benefits where it exerts antiinflammatory, antioxidant, and anticancer activities. Hence, it is utilized as a curative agent in Chinese and Indian medicine [148,149] and has been widely studied in human cancers [150]. Chemopreventive action of curcumin is primarily enabled by NF-κB and PI3K/AKT signaling pathways known for stimulating cell cycle cessation and cell death/apoptosis [151]. Moreover, curcumin exerts its regulation on the methylation of DNA and modification of histones. Curcumin-mediated abrogation of cell proliferation and stimulation of apoptotic cell death in cancers is executed by its inhibitory activities on DNMT and HDACs [152]. Studies have shown the inhibitory function of curcumin on HDAC and HAT, hence serving as a histone modifying agent [153], where several in vitro model systems have suggested the epigenetic regulation of curcumin on the activities of HDAC and HAT. By inhibiting DNMT, curcumin reduces DNA hypermethylation and hence alleviates cancer development by facilitating the expression of some tumor suppressors. For example, by dwindling the levels of DNMT1, curcumin decreased the hypermethylation of DLC1 promoter. This resulted in the expression of DLC1, which further attenuated the cell growth of human breast cancer cells [154]. Also, global hypomethylation in leukemia cells has been detected upon curcumin administration [40]. In fact, using in vivo and ex vivo models of acute myeloid leukemia, studies have shown the downregulation of DNMT upon curcumin treatment, where curcumin mediated the rescue of p15INK4b via hypomethylating its promoter, eventually facilitating cell cycle halt and apoptosis. Hence, curcumin hampered tumor growth by epigenetic mechanisms [40]. In vitro and in vivo studies in breast cancer too revealed curcumin's inhibitory effect on DNMT1, thereby rescuing RASSF1A function and impairing the growth of breast cancer cells [155]. No wonder curcumin has been suggested to serve as a great nontoxic hypomethylating candidate for therapy in breast cancer settings [156,157].

Curcumin-mediated gene silencing has also been attributed to the promoter acetylation of histone proteins. For example, in brain cancer cells, curcumin caused histone acetylation and apoptotic cell death, which was linked with the functionality of poly(ADP-ribose) polymerase (PARP) enzyme [153]. Curcumin-mediated hypoacetylation of histone H3 and H4 has been observed where it suppressed the activity of an enzyme p300 in TREM-1 promoter region, hence regulating the expression of TREM-1 gene [158]. Interestingly, several studies also identified the inhibitory feature of curcumin on p300/CBP activity [159,160]. Curcumin has been well described for its regulation of DNA methylation and histone modification in a variety of human cancers, suggesting its therapeutic significance [152]. Thus, research on curcumin's anticancer properties holds great potential and is still on its way where extensive clinical trials are surely warranted [161].

Quercetin

Quercetin is a plant pigment and a potent antioxidant flavonoid found in citrus fruits, berries, grapes, cherries, broccoli, onions, red wine, and green tea. It has multiple health benefits, where its positive role in heart health and digestive health has been recognized along with its antitumor, antiviral, antiinflammatory, antidiabetic, antihypertensive, and antiallergy features [162]. Several prominent cellular signaling pathways have been implicated in quercetin-mediated anticancer activity, and these include the Wnt/β-catenin, mitogen-activated protein kinase (MAPK), p53, nuclear factor kappa B (NF-κB), phosphoinositide 3-kinase (PI3K)/protein kinase B (AKT), and Janus kinase (JAK)/signal transducer and transcription activator (STAT) pathways [163,164]. Human cervical cells exhibited a dose-dependent fashion of decrease in DNMT, HDAC, and HMT upon Quercetin treatment [165]. Antagonistic roles of quercetin on DNMT1 and DNMT3a have also been identified, and as an epigenetic regulator, quercetin's role in cancer is well discussed [165–167].

Genistein

Polyphenolic isoflavone genistein belongs to flavonoid and naturally occurs in plants such as soybeans and fava beans. Dietary intake of genistein has been shown to decrease the risk of several cancers in epidemiological studies [168]. Through its regulation of DNA methylation and histone modification, genistein can switch on the tumor suppressor genes and hence influence the growth of cancer cells [169]. By its influence on histone modifications, genistein was shown to suppress early breast tumorigenesis by epigenetically regulating the p21 and p16 genes [170].

A polyphenolic and organosulfur enriched bioactive component, **garlic** (*Allium sativum*) has multiple health benefits due to its antiprotozoal, antiviral, antibacterial, antifungal, antiinflammatory, and antioxidant features [171,172]. Several preclinical studies have justified the antitumor properties of garlic in a variety of human cancers [173,174]. Moreover, garlic-derived compounds have potent antioxidant and anticancer properties and hence have cancer-preventive roles, where studies revealed an augmented CpG demethylation or histone acetylation activities by garlic-derived compounds [175].

Conclusion

Cancer development and malignant progression is a complex phenomenon with an integration of genetic and epigenetic events. Environmental factors have major roles in influencing the epigenetic processes, where dietary components not only modulate the epigenetic mechanisms but are also implicated in chemoprevention roles. Growing body of evidence suggests the rationale for studying nutrient epigenetic modifiers, and hence, the term "epigenetic diet" beneficial for health and wellness deserves further investigation in the context of tumorigenesis. Dietary bioactive compounds, in combination with chemotherapeutic agents, can exert synergistic effects, where research regarding their bioavailability, toxicity, and efficacy is warranted.

References

[1] L. Hui, Y. Chen, Tumor microenvironment: sanctuary of the devil, Cancer Lett. 368 (1) (2015) 7–13.

[2] C. Thakur, F. Chen, Connections between metabolism and epigenetics in cancers, Semin. Cancer Biol. 57 (2019) 52–58.

[3] T.K. Kelly, D.D. De Carvalho, P.A. Jones, Epigenetic modifications as therapeutic targets, Nat. Biotechnol. 28 (10) (2010) 1069–1078.

[4] L.D. Moore, T. Le, G. Fan, DNA methylation and its basic function, Neuropsychopharmacology 38 (1) (2013) 23–38.

[5] P.H. Tate, A.P. Bird, Effects of DNA methylation on DNA-binding proteins and gene expression, Curr. Opin. Genet. Dev. 3 (2) (1993) 226–231.

[6] M. Ehrlich, DNA hypomethylation in cancer cells, Epigenomics 1 (2) (2009) 239–259.

[7] A.P. Feinberg, B. Vogelstein, Hypomethylation distinguishes genes of some human cancers from their normal counterparts, Nature 301 (5895) (1983) 89–92.

[8] W. Zhang, J. Xu, DNA methyltransferases and their roles in tumorigenesis, Biomark. Res. 5 (1) (2017) 1.

[9] A.J. Bannister, T. Kouzarides, Regulation of chromatin by histone modifications, Cell Res. 21 (3) (2011) 381–395.

[10] R. Marmorstein, R.C. Trievel, Histone modifying enzymes: structures, mechanisms, and specificities, Biochim. Biophys. Acta 1789 (1) (2009) 58–68.

[11] M.E. Figueroa, et al., DNA methylation signatures identify biologically distinct subtypes in acute myeloid leukemia, Cancer Cell 17 (1) (2010) 13–27.

[12] J. Ellinger, et al., Global levels of histone modifications predict prostate cancer recurrence, Prostate 70 (1) (2010) 61–69.

[13] I.M. Bachmann, et al., EZH2 expression is associated with high proliferation rate and aggressive tumor subgroups in cutaneous melanoma and cancers of the endometrium, prostate, and breast, J. Clin. Oncol. 24 (2) (2006) 268–273.

[14] Y. Cheng, et al., Targeting epigenetic regulators for cancer therapy: mechanisms and advances in clinical trials, Signal Transduct. Target. Ther. 4 (1) (2019) 62.

[15] K. Nepali, J.-P. Liou, Recent developments in epigenetic cancer therapeutics: clinical advancement and emerging trends, J. Biomed. Sci. 28 (1) (2021) 27.

[16] Â. Sousa, et al., Editorial: epigenetic therapy against cancer: toward new molecular targets and technologies, Front. Cell Dev. Biol. 11 (2023) 1218986, https://doi.org/10.3389/fcell.2023.1218986.

[17] M. Jung, G.P. Pfeifer, Aging and DNA methylation, BMC Biol. 13 (2015) 7.

[18] K.A. Lillycrop, G.C. Burdge, Epigenetic mechanisms linking early nutrition to long term health, Best Pract. Res. Clin. Endocrinol. Metab. 26 (5) (2012) 667–676.

[19] S. Lévesque, et al., Trial watch: dietary interventions for cancer therapy, Oncoimmunology 8 (7) (2019) 1591878.

[20] C. Chen, Z. Wang, Y. Qin, Connections between metabolism and epigenetics: mechanisms and novel anti-cancer strategy, Front. Pharmacol. 13 (2022) 935536, https://doi.org/10.3389/fphar.2022.935536.

[21] F. Pietrocola, et al., Acetyl coenzyme A: a central metabolite and second messenger, Cell Metab. 21 (6) (2015) 805–821.

[22] L.A. Racey, P. Byvoet, Histone acetyltransferase in chromatin. Evidence for in vitro enzymatic transfer of acetate from acetyl-coenzyme A to histones, Exp. Cell Res. 64 (2) (1971) 366–370.

[23] L. Cai, et al., Acetyl-CoA induces cell growth and proliferation by promoting the acetylation of histones at growth genes, Mol. Cell 42 (4) (2011) 426–437.

[24] E.P. Candido, R. Reeves, J.R. Davie, Sodium butyrate inhibits histone deacetylation in cultured cells, Cell 14 (1) (1978) 105–113.

[25] S. Zeisel, Choline, other methyl-donors and epigenetics, Nutrients 9 (5) (2017) 445, https://doi.org/10.3390/nu9050445.

[26] S. Friso, et al., One-carbon metabolism and epigenetics, Mol. Asp. Med. 54 (2017) 28–36.

[27] O.S. Anderson, K.E. Sant, D.C. Dolinoy, Nutrition and epigenetics: an interplay of dietary methyl donors, one-carbon metabolism and DNA methylation, J. Nutr. Biochem. 23 (8) (2012) 853–859.

[28] E. Tamanaha, et al., Distributive processing by the Iron(II)/α-ketoglutarate-dependent catalytic domains of the TET enzymes is consistent with epigenetic roles for oxidized 5-methylcytosine bases, J. Am. Chem. Soc. 138 (30) (2016) 9345–9348.

[29] X. Paredes-Gonzalez, et al., Apigenin reactivates Nrf2 anti-oxidative stress signaling in mouse skin epidermal JB6 P+ cells through epigenetics modifications, AAPS J. 16 (2014) 727–735.

[30] H. Nian, et al., Allyl mercaptan, a garlic-derived organosulfur compound, inhibits histone deacetylase and enhances Sp3 binding on the P21WAF1 promoter, Carcinogenesis 29 (9) (2008) 1816–1824.

[31] N. Druesne, et al., Diallyl disulfide (DADS) increases histone acetylation and p21 waf1/cip1 expression in human colon tumor cell lines, Carcinogenesis 25 (7) (2004) 1227–1236.

[32] M.A. Lea, V.M. Randolph, Induction of histone acetylation in rat liver and hepatoma by organosulfur compounds including diallyl disulfide, Anticancer Res. 21 (4A) (2001) 2841–2845.

[33] H. Nian, et al., Modulation of histone deacetylase activity by dietary isothiocyanates and allyl sulfides: studies with sulforaphane and garlic organosulfur compounds, Environ. Mol. Mutagen. 50 (3) (2009) 213–221.

[34] J.R. Davie, Inhibition of histone deacetylase activity by butyrate, J. Nutr. 133 (7) (2003) 2485S–2493S.

[35] J. Encarnação, et al., Revisit dietary fiber on colorectal cancer: butyrate and its role on prevention and treatment, Cancer Metastasis Rev. 34 (2015) 465–478.

[36] A. McIntyre, P. Gibson, G. Young, Butyrate production from dietary fibre and protection against large bowel cancer in a rat model, Gut 34 (3) (1993) 386.

[37] D.L. Zoran, et al., Wheat bran diet reduces tumor incidence in a rat model of colon cancer independent of effects on distal luminal butyrate concentrations, J. Nutr. 127 (11) (1997) 2217–2225.

[38] T.O. Khor, et al., Pharmacodynamics of curcumin as DNA hypomethylation agent in restoring the expression of Nrf2 via promoter CpGs demethylation, Biochem. Pharmacol. 82 (9) (2011) 1073–1078.

[39] L. Shu, et al., Epigenetic CpG demethylation of the promoter and reactivation of the expression of Neurog1 by curcumin in prostate LNCaP cells, AAPS J. 13 (2011) 606–614.

[40] J. Yu, et al., Curcumin down-regulates DNA methyltransferase 1 and plays an anti-leukemic role in acute myeloid leukemia, PLoS One 8 (2) (2013) e55934.

[41] Y. Chen, et al., Curcumin, both histone deacetylase and p300/CBP-specific inhibitor, represses the activity of nuclear factor kappa B and Notch 1 in Raji cells, Basic Clin. Pharmacol. Toxicol. 101 (6) (2007) 427–433.

[42] Y. Guo, et al., Curcumin inhibits anchorage-independent growth of HT29 human colon cancer cells by targeting epigenetic restoration of the tumor suppressor gene DLEC1, Biochem. Pharmacol. 94 (2) (2015) 69–78.

[43] H.-I. Liu, et al., Curcumin, a potent anti-tumor reagent, is a novel histone deacetylase inhibitor regulating B-NHL cell line Raji proliferation, Acta Pharmacol. Sin. 26 (5) (2005) 603–609.

[44] M. Adjakly, et al., DNA methylation and soy phytoestrogens: quantitative study in DU-145 and PC-3 human prostate cancer cell lines, Epigenomics 3 (6) (2011) 795–803.

[45] A. Vardi, et al., Soy phytoestrogens modify DNA methylation of GSTP1, RASSF1A, EPH2 and BRCA1 promoter in prostate cancer cells, In Vivo 24 (4) (2010) 393–400.

[46] T. Hong, et al., Isoflavones stimulate estrogen receptor-mediated core histone acetylation, Biochem. Biophys. Res. Commun. 317 (1) (2004) 259–264.

[47] J.B. Berletch, et al., Epigenetic and genetic mechanisms contribute to telomerase inhibition by EGCG, J. Cell. Biochem. 103 (2) (2008) 509–519.

[48] K. Kato, et al., Effects of green tea polyphenol on methylation status of RECK gene and cancer cell invasion in oral squamous cell carcinoma cells, Br. J. Cancer 99 (4) (2008) 647–654.

[49] E. Navarro-Perán, et al., Effects of folate cycle disruption by the green tea polyphenol epigallocatechin-3-gallate, Int. J. Biochem. Cell Biol. 39 (12) (2007) 2215–2225.

[50] M.A. Khan, et al., (−)-Epigallocatechin-3-gallate reverses the expression of various tumor-suppressor genes by inhibiting DNA methyltransferases and histone deacetylases in human cervical cancer cells, Oncol. Rep. 33 (4) (2015) 1976–1984.

[51] Y. Li, et al., Synergistic epigenetic reactivation of estrogen receptor-α (ERα) by combined green tea polyphenol and histone deacetylase inhibitor in ERα-negative breast cancer cells, Mol. Cancer 9 (2010) 274.

[52] V. Nandakumar, M. Vaid, S.K. Katiyar, (−)-Epigallocatechin-3-gallate reactivates silenced tumor suppressor genes, Cip1/p21 and p16INK4a, by reducing DNA methylation and increasing histones acetylation in human skin cancer cells, Carcinogenesis 32 (4) (2011) 537–544.

[53] M. Pandey, S. Shukla, S. Gupta, Promoter demethylation and chromatin remodeling by green tea polyphenols leads to re-expression of GSTP1 in human prostate cancer cells, Int. J. Cancer 126 (11) (2010) 2520–2533.

[54] M.Z. Fang, et al., Reversal of hypermethylation and reactivation of p16INK4a, RARβ, and MGMT genes by genistein and other isoflavones from soy, Clin. Cancer Res. 11 (19) (2005) 7033–7041.

[55] A. King-Batoon, J.M. Leszczynska, C.B. Klein, Modulation of gene methylation by genistein or lycopene in breast cancer cells, Environ. Mol. Mutagen. 49 (1) (2008) 36–45.

[56] S. Majid, et al., Genistein reverses hypermethylation and induces active histone modifications in tumor suppressor gene B-cell translocation gene 3 in prostate cancer, Cancer 116 (1) (2010) 66–76.

[57] S. Majid, et al., Genistein induces the p21WAF1/CIP1 and p16INK4a tumor suppressor genes in prostate Cancer cells by epigenetic mechanisms involving active chromatin modification, Cancer Res. 68 (8) (2008) 2736–2744.

[58] P.B. Busbee, M. Nagarkatti, P.S. Nagarkatti, Natural indoles, indole-3-carbinol and 3,3′-diindolylmethane, inhibit T cell activation by staphylococcal enterotoxin B through epigenetic regulation involving HDAC expression, Toxicol. Appl. Pharmacol. 274 (1) (2014) 7–16.

[59] Y. Li, X. Li, B. Guo, Chemopreventive agent 3,3′-diindolylmethane selectively induces proteasomal degradation of class I histone deacetylases, Cancer Res. 70 (2) (2010) 646–654.

[60] E.G. Rogan, The natural chemopreventive compound indole-3-carbinol: state of the science, In Vivo 20 (2) (2006) 221–228.

[61] S.Y. Choi, et al., Piceatannol attenuates renal fibrosis induced by unilateral ureteral obstruction via downregulation of histone deacetylase 4/5 or p38-MAPK signaling, PLoS One 11 (11) (2016) e0167340.

[62] M.A. Seyed, et al., A comprehensive review on the chemotherapeutic potential of piceatannol for cancer treatment, with mechanistic insights, J. Agric. Food Chem. 64 (4) (2016) 725–737.

[63] W.J. Lee, Y.R. Chen, T.H. Tseng, Quercetin induces FasL-related apoptosis, in part, through promotion of histone H3 acetylation in human leukemia HL-60 cells, Oncol. Rep. 25 (2) (2011) 583–591.

[64] G. Lou, et al., The p53/miR-34a/SIRT1 positive feedback loop in quercetin-induced apoptosis, Cell. Physiol. Biochem. 35 (6) (2015) 2192–2202.

[65] R.V. Priyadarsini, et al., The flavonoid quercetin modulates the hallmark capabilities of hamster buccal pouch tumors, Nutr. Cancer 63 (2) (2011) 218–226.

[66] W. Qin, et al., Methylation and miRNA effects of resveratrol on mammary tumors vs. normal tissue, Nutr. Cancer 66 (2) (2014) 270–277.

[67] A. Bednarek, et al., Comparative effects of retinoic acid, vitamin D and resveratrol alone and in combination with adenosine analogues on methylation and expression of phosphatase and tensin homologue tumour suppressor gene in breast cancer cells, Br. J. Nutr. 107 (6) (2012) 781–790.

[68] M.T. Borra, B.C. Smith, J.M. Denu, Mechanism of human SIRT1 activation by resveratrol, J. Biol. Chem. 280 (17) (2005) 17187–17195.

[69] L. Kai, S.K. Samuel, A.S. Levenson, Resveratrol enhances p53 acetylation and apoptosis in prostate cancer by inhibiting MTA1/NuRD complex, Int. J. Cancer 126 (7) (2010) 1538–1548.

[70] S. Venturelli, et al., Resveratrol as a pan-HDAC inhibitor alters the acetylation status of histone [corrected] proteins in human-derived hepatoblastoma cells, PLoS One 8 (8) (2013) e73097.

[71] S.M. Meeran, S.N. Patel, T.O. Tollefsbol, Sulforaphane causes epigenetic repression of hTERT expression in human breast cancer cell lines, PLoS One 5 (7) (2010) e11457.

[72] Z.Y. Su, et al., Requirement and epigenetics reprogramming of Nrf2 in suppression of tumor promoter TPA-induced mouse skin cell transformation by sulforaphane, Cancer Prev. Res. (Phila.) 7 (3) (2014) 319–329.

[73] C.P. Wong, et al., Effects of sulforaphane and 3,3′-diindolylmethane on genome-wide promoter methylation in normal prostate epithelial cells and prostate cancer cells, PLoS One 9 (1) (2014) e86787.

[74] M.C. Myzak, et al., Sulforaphane inhibits histone deacetylase activity in BPH-1, LnCaP and PC-3 prostate epithelial cells, Carcinogenesis 27 (4) (2006) 811–819.

[75] M.C. Myzak, et al., A novel mechanism of chemoprotection by sulforaphane: inhibition of histone deacetylase, Cancer Res. 64 (16) (2004) 5767–5774.

[76] M.C. Myzak, et al., Sulforaphane retards the growth of human PC-3 xenografts and inhibits HDAC activity in human subjects, Exp. Biol. Med. (Maywood) 232 (2) (2007) 227–234.

[77] M. Schwab, et al., The dietary histone deacetylase inhibitor sulforaphane induces human beta-defensin-2 in intestinal epithelial cells, Immunology 125 (2) (2008) 241–251.

[78] J.G. Donnelly, Folic acid, Crit. Rev. Clin. Lab. Sci. 38 (3) (2001) 183–223.

[79] K. Wallace, et al., Association between folate levels and CpG Island hypermethylation in normal colorectal mucosa, Cancer Prev. Res. (Phila.) 3 (12) (2010) 1552–1564.

[80] E. Giovannucci, et al., Folate, methionine, and alcohol intake and risk of colorectal adenoma, J. Natl. Cancer Inst. 85 (11) (1993) 875–884.

[81] L.J. Su, L. Arab, Nutritional status of folate and colon cancer risk: evidence from NHANES I epidemiologic follow-up study, Ann. Epidemiol. 11 (1) (2001) 65–72.

[82] Institute of Medicine Standing Committee on the Scientific Evaluation of Dietary Reference, I., O.B.V. its Panel on Folate, and Choline, The national academies collection: reports funded by National Institutes of Health, in: Dietary Reference Intakes for Thiamin, Riboflavin, Niacin, Vitamin B(6), Folate, Vitamin B(12), Pantothenic Acid, Biotin, and Choline, National Academies Press (US), Washington, DC, 1998.

[83] J. Hultdin, et al., Plasma folate, vitamin B12, and homocysteine and prostate cancer risk: a prospective study, Int. J. Cancer 113 (5) (2005) 819–824.

[84] Y. Qiang, et al., Intake of dietary one-carbon metabolism-related B vitamins and the risk of esophageal Cancer: a dose-response meta-analysis, Nutrients 10 (7) (2018) 835, https://doi.org/10.3390/nu10070835.

[85] C.J. Piyathilake, et al., Folate and vitamin B12 may play a critical role in lowering the HPV 16 methylation-associated risk of developing higher grades of CIN, Cancer Prev. Res. (Phila.) 7 (11) (2014) 1128–1137.

[86] T. Otani, et al., Folate, vitamin B6, vitamin B12, and vitamin B2 intake, genetic polymorphisms of related enzymes, and risk of colorectal cancer in a hospital-based case-control study in Japan, Nutr. Cancer 53 (1) (2005) 42–50.

[87] C.J. Piyathilake, et al., Localized folate and vitamin B-12 deficiency in squamous cell lung cancer is associated with global DNA hypomethylation, Nutr. Cancer 37 (1) (2000) 99–107.

[88] G.L. Johanning, D.C. Heimburger, C.J. Piyathilake, DNA methylation and diet in cancer, J. Nutr. 132 (12) (2002) 3814s–3818s.

[89] S.H. Zeisel, Choline: an essential nutrient for humans, Nutrition 16 (7–8) (2000) 669–671.

[90] K.A. da Costa, et al., Accumulation of 1,2-sn-diradylglycerol with increased membrane-associated protein kinase C may be the mechanism for spontaneous hepatocarcinogenesis in choline-deficient rats, J. Biol. Chem. 268 (3) (1993) 2100–2105.

[91] K.A. da Costa, et al., Effects of prolonged (1 year) choline deficiency and subsequent re-feeding of choline on 1,2-sn-diradylglycerol, fatty acids and protein kinase C in rat liver, Carcinogenesis 16 (2) (1995) 327–334.

[92] S. Sun, et al., Choline and betaine consumption lowers cancer risk: a meta-analysis of epidemiologic studies, Sci. Rep. 6 (2016) 35547.

[93] B.T. Heijmans, et al., Persistent epigenetic differences associated with prenatal exposure to famine in humans, Proc. Natl. Acad. Sci. USA 105 (44) (2008) 17046–17049.

[94] H. Landecker, Food as exposure: nutritional epigenetics and the new metabolism, BioSocieties 6 (2) (2011) 167–194.

[95] F. Indrio, et al., Epigenetic matters: the link between early nutrition, microbiome, and long-term health development, Front. Pediatr. 5 (2017) 178, https://doi.org/10.3389/fped.2017.00178.

[96] K.B. Pandey, S.I. Rizvi, Plant polyphenols as dietary antioxidants in human health and disease, Oxidative Med. Cell. Longev. 2 (5) (2009) 270–278.

[97] R.K. Singla, et al., Natural polyphenols: chemical classification, definition of classes, subcategories, and structures, J. AOAC Int. 102 (5) (2019) 1397–1400.

[98] Y. Zhou, et al., Natural polyphenols for prevention and treatment of cancer, Nutrients 8 (8) (2016) 515, https://doi.org/10.3390/nu8080515.

[99] A.N. Panche, A.D. Diwan, S.R. Chandra, Flavonoids: an overview, J. Nutr. Sci. 5 (2016) e47.

[100] M. Rudrapal, et al., Dietary polyphenols and their role in oxidative stress-induced human diseases: insights into protective effects, antioxidant potentials and mechanism(s) of action, Front. Pharmacol. 13 (2022) 806470, https://doi.org/10.3389/fphar.2022.806470.

[101] T.B. Kryston, et al., Role of oxidative stress and DNA damage in human carcinogenesis, Mutat. Res. 711 (1) (2011) 193–201.

[102] H. Zhang, R. Tsao, Dietary polyphenols, oxidative stress and antioxidant and anti-inflammatory effects, Curr. Opin. Food Sci. 8 (2016) 33–42.

[103] M. Adelipour, M. Cheraghzadeh, M. Rashidi, Polyphenols as epigenetic modulators in treating or preventing of cancers, Gene Rep. 29 (2022) 101710.

[104] F.T. Borsoi, et al., Dietary polyphenols and their relationship to the modulation of non-communicable chronic diseases and epigenetic mechanisms: a mini-review, Food Chem.: Mol. Sci. 6 (2023) 100155.

[105] A. Mahboob, et al., Role of flavonoids in controlling obesity: molecular targets and mechanisms, Front. Nutr. 10 (2023) 1177897, https://doi.org/10.3389/fnut.2023.1177897.

[106] A.K.S. Oliveira, et al., Anti-obesity properties and mechanism of action of flavonoids: a review, Crit. Rev. Food Sci. Nutr. 62 (28) (2022) 7827–7848.

[107] X. Yi, et al., Flavonoids improve type 2 diabetes mellitus and its complications: a review, Front. Nutr. 10 (2023).

[108] J. Xiao, Recent advances in dietary flavonoids for management of type 2 diabetes, Curr. Opin. Food Sci. 44 (2022) 100806.

[109] P.-G. Pietta, Flavonoids as antioxidants, J. Nat. Prod. 63 (7) (2000) 1035–1042.

[110] M.K. Chahar, et al., Flavonoids: a versatile source of anticancer drugs, Pharmacogn. Rev. 5 (9) (2011) 1.

[111] M.L. Falcone Ferreyra, S.P. Rius, P. Casati, Flavonoids: biosynthesis, biological functions, and biotechnological applications, Front. Plant Sci. 3 (2012) 222.

[112] G. Williamson, The role of polyphenols in modern nutrition, Nutr. Bull. 42 (3) (2017) 226–235.

[113] A.H. Waheed Janabi, et al., Flavonoid-rich foods (FRF): a promising nutraceutical approach against lifespan-shortening diseases, Iran J. Basic Med. Sci. 23 (2) (2020) 140–153.

[114] G.J. Du, et al., Epigallocatechin gallate (EGCG) is the most effective cancer chemopreventive polyphenol in green tea, Nutrients 4 (11) (2012) 1679–1691.

[115] K.J. Min, T.K. Kwon, Anticancer effects and molecular mechanisms of epigallocatechin-3-gallate, Integr. Med. Res. 3 (1) (2014) 16–24.

[116] I. Rady, et al., Cancer preventive and therapeutic effects of EGCG, the major polyphenol in green tea, Egypt. J. Basic Appl. Sci. 5 (1) (2018) 1–23.

[117] C.S. Yang, et al., Cancer prevention by tea: animal studies, molecular mechanisms and human relevance, Nat. Rev. Cancer 9 (6) (2009) 429–439.

[118] Z. Cheng, et al., A review on anti-cancer effect of green tea catechins, J. Funct. Foods 74 (2020) 104172.

[119] M.Z. Fang, et al., Tea polyphenol (−)-epigallocatechin-3-gallate inhibits DNA methyltransferase and reactivates methylation-silenced genes in cancer cell lines, Cancer Res. 63 (22) (2003) 7563–7570.

[120] Z. Gao, et al., Promoter demethylation of WIF-1 by epigallocatechin-3-gallate in lung cancer cells, Anticancer Res. 29 (6) (2009) 2025–2030.

[121] A. Sharma, R. Mir, S. Galande, Epigenetic regulation of the Wnt/β-catenin signaling pathway in cancer, Front. Genet. 12 (2021) 681053, https://doi.org/10.3389/fgene.2021.681053.

[122] S. Oh, et al., Green tea polyphenol EGCG suppresses Wnt/β-catenin signaling by promoting GSK-3β- and PP2A-independent β-catenin phosphorylation/degradation, Biofactors 40 (6) (2014) 586–595.

[123] J. Kim, et al., Suppression of Wnt signaling by the green tea compound (−)-epigallocatechin 3-gallate (EGCG) in invasive breast cancer cells: requirement of the transcriptional repressor HBP1, J. Biol. Chem. 281 (16) (2006) 10865–10875.

[124] D.B. Nandini, et al., Sulforaphane in broccoli: the green chemoprevention!! Role in cancer prevention and therapy, J. Oral Maxillofac. Pathol. 24 (2) (2020) 405.

[125] E. Ferrari, S. Bettuzzi, V. Naponelli, The potential of epigallocatechin gallate (EGCG) in targeting autophagy for cancer treatment: a narrative review, Int. J. Mol. Sci. 23 (11) (2022) 6075, https://doi.org/10.3390/ijms23116075.

[126] K.C. Choi, et al., Epigallocatechin-3-gallate, a histone acetyltransferase inhibitor, inhibits EBV-induced B lymphocyte transformation via suppression of RelA acetylation, Cancer Res. 69 (2) (2009) 583–592.

[127] Y. Li, et al., Synergistic epigenetic reactivation of estrogen receptor-α (ERα) by combined green tea polyphenol and histone deacetylase inhibitor in ERα-negative breast cancer cells, Mol. Cancer 9 (1) (2010) 1–12.

[128] Y. Li, S.M. Meeran, T.O. Tollefsbol, Combinatorial bioactive botanicals re-sensitize tamoxifen treatment in ER-negative breast cancer via epigenetic reactivation of ERα expression, Sci. Rep. 7 (1) (2017) 9345.

[129] B. Salehi, et al., Resveratrol: a double-edged sword in health benefits, Biomedicines 6 (3) (2018) 91, https://doi.org/10.3390/biomedicines6030091.

[130] X. Meng, et al., Health benefits and molecular mechanisms of resveratrol: a narrative review, Foods 9 (3) (2020) 340, https://doi.org/10.3390/foods9030340.

[131] J.H. Ko, et al., The role of resveratrol in cancer therapy, Int. J. Mol. Sci. 18 (12) (2017) 2589, https://doi.org/10.3390/ijms18122589.

[132] A. Bishayee, et al., Suppression of the inflammatory cascade is implicated in resveratrol chemoprevention of experimental hepatocarcinogenesis, Pharm. Res. 27 (6) (2010) 1080–1091.

[133] L.G. Carter, J.A. D'Orazio, K.J. Pearson, Resveratrol and cancer: focus on in vivo evidence, Endocr. Relat. Cancer 21 (3) (2014) R209–R225.

[134] D. Vervandier-Fasseur, N. Latruffe, The potential use of resveratrol for cancer prevention, Molecules 24 (24) (2019) 4506, https://doi.org/10.3390/molecules24244506.

[135] B. Ren, et al., Resveratrol for cancer therapy: challenges and future perspectives, Cancer Lett. 515 (2021) 63–72.

[136] L. Huminiecki, J. Horbańczuk, The functional genomic studies of resveratrol in respect to its anti-cancer effects, Biotechnol. Adv. 36 (6) (2018) 1699–1708.

[137] S. Dhar, et al., Resveratrol regulates PTEN/Akt pathway through inhibition of MTA1/HDAC unit of the NuRD complex in prostate cancer, Biochim. Biophys. Acta 1853 (2) (2015) 265–275.

[138] Y. Sun, et al., Resveratrol inhibits the migration and metastasis of MDA-MB-231 human breast cancer by reversing TGF-β1-induced epithelial-mesenchymal transition, Molecules 24 (6) (2019) 1131.

[139] A.J. Papoutsis, et al., Resveratrol prevents epigenetic silencing of BRCA-1 by the aromatic hydrocarbon receptor in human breast cancer cells, J. Nutr. 140 (9) (2010) 1607–1614.

[140] R. Kala, T.O. Tollefsbol, A novel combinatorial epigenetic therapy using resveratrol and pterostilbene for restoring estrogen receptor-α (ERα) expression in ERα-negative breast cancer cells, PLoS One 11 (5) (2016) e0155057.

[141] R. Medina-Aguilar, et al., Methylation landscape of human breast cancer cells in response to dietary compound resveratrol, PLoS One 11 (6) (2016) e0157866.

[142] R.H. Wang, et al., Interplay among BRCA1, SIRT1, and survivin during BRCA1-associated tumorigenesis, Mol. Cell 32 (1) (2008) 11–20.

[143] W. Stünkel, et al., Function of the SIRT1 protein deacetylase in cancer, Biotechnol. J. 2 (11) (2007) 1360–1368.

[144] E.K. Vernousfaderani, et al., Resveratrol and colorectal cancer: a molecular approach to clinical researches, Curr. Top. Med. Chem. 21 (29) (2021) 2634–2646.

[145] R. Firestein, et al., The SIRT1 deacetylase suppresses intestinal tumorigenesis and colon cancer growth, PLoS One 3 (4) (2008) e2020.

[146] R. Frazzi, et al., Resveratrol-mediated apoptosis of hodgkin lymphoma cells involves SIRT1 inhibition and FOXO3a hyperacetylation, Int. J. Cancer 132 (5) (2013) 1013–1021.

[147] S. Ghafouri-Fard, et al., Disease-associated regulation of gene expression by resveratrol: special focus on the PI3K/AKT signaling pathway, Cancer Cell Int. 22 (1) (2022) 298.

[148] R.K. Maheshwari, et al., Multiple biological activities of curcumin: a short review, Life Sci. 78 (18) (2006) 2081–2087.

[149] A. Goel, B.B. Aggarwal, Curcumin, the golden spice from Indian saffron, is a chemosensitizer and radiosensitizer for tumors and chemoprotector and radioprotector for normal organs, Nutr. Cancer 62 (7) (2010) 919–930.

[150] A. Giordano, G. Tommonaro, Curcumin and cancer, Nutrients 11 (10) (2019) 2376, https://doi.org/10.3390/nu11102376.

[151] S. Reuter, et al., Modulation of anti-apoptotic and survival pathways by curcumin as a strategy to induce apoptosis in cancer cells, Biochem. Pharmacol. 76 (11) (2008) 1340–1351.

[152] T. Ming, et al., Curcumin: an epigenetic regulator and its application in cancer, Biomed. Pharmacother. 156 (2022) 113956.

[153] S.K. Kang, S.H. Cha, H.G. Jeon, Curcumin-induced histone hypoacetylation enhances caspase-3-dependent glioma cell death and neurogenesis of neural progenitor cells, Stem Cells Dev. 15 (2) (2006) 165–174.

[154] X. Zhou, et al., Curcumin inhibits the growth of triple-negative breast cancer cells by silencing EZH2 and restoring DLC1 expression, J. Cell. Mol. Med. 24 (18) (2020) 10648–10662.

[155] L. Du, et al., Reactivation of RASSF1A in breast cancer cells by curcumin, Nutr. Cancer 64 (8) (2012) 1228–1235.

[156] U. Kumar, U. Sharma, G. Rathi, Reversal of hypermethylation and reactivation of glutathione S-transferase pi 1 gene by curcumin in breast cancer cell line, Tumour Biol. 39 (2) (2017). 1010428317692258.

[157] V. Zoi, et al., The role of curcumin in cancer treatment, Biomedicines 9 (9) (2021).

[158] Z. Yuan, et al., Curcumin mediated epigenetic modulation inhibits TREM-1 expression in response to lipopolysaccharide, Int. J. Biochem. Cell Biol. 44 (11) (2012) 2032–2043.

[159] M.G. Marcu, et al., Curcumin is an inhibitor of p300 histone acetylatransferase, Med. Chem. 2 (2) (2006) 169–174.

[160] K. Balasubramanyam, et al., Curcumin, a novel p300/CREB-binding protein-specific inhibitor of acetyltransferase, represses the acetylation of histone/nonhistone proteins

and histone acetyltransferase-dependent chromatin transcription, J. Biol. Chem. 279 (49) (2004) 51163–51171.

[161] C. de Waure, et al., Exploring the contribution of curcumin to cancer therapy: a systematic review of randomized controlled trials, Pharmaceutics 15 (4) (2023) 1275, https://doi.org/10.3390/pharmaceutics15041275.

[162] P. Lakhanpal, D.K. Rai, Quercetin: a versatile flavonoid, Int. J. Med. Update 2 (2) (2007) 22–37.

[163] F. Khan, et al., Molecular targets underlying the anticancer effects of quercetin: an update, Nutrients 8 (9) (2016) 529.

[164] P. Asgharian, et al., Potential mechanisms of quercetin in cancer prevention: focus on cellular and molecular targets, Cancer Cell Int. 22 (1) (2022) 257.

[165] M. Kedhari Sundaram, et al., Quercetin modifies 5'CpG promoter methylation and reactivates various tumor suppressor genes by modulating epigenetic marks in human cervical cancer cells, J. Cell. Biochem. 120 (10) (2019) 18357–18369.

[166] J. Zhu, et al., Epigenetic regulation by quercetin: a comprehensive review focused on its biological mechanisms, Crit. Rev. Food Sci. Nutr. 63 (2023) 1–20.

[167] A. Bouyahya, et al., Natural bioactive compounds targeting histone deacetylases in human cancers: recent updates, Molecules 27 (8) (2022) 2568, https://doi.org/10.3390/molecules27082568.

[168] H. Naeem, et al., Anticancer perspectives of genistein: a comprehensive review, Int. J. Food Prop. 26 (2) (2023) 3305–3341.

[169] Y. Zhang, H. Chen, Genistein, an epigenome modifier during cancer prevention, Epigenetics 6 (7) (2011) 888–891.

[170] Y. Li, et al., Epigenetic regulation of multiple tumor-related genes leads to suppression of breast tumorigenesis by dietary genistein, PLoS One 8 (1) (2013) e54369.

[171] G. El-Saber Batiha, et al., Chemical constituents and pharmacological activities of garlic (Allium sativum L.): a review, Nutrients 12 (3) (2020) 872, https://doi.org/10.3390/nu12030872.

[172] J. Ansary, et al., Potential health benefit of garlic based on human intervention studies: a brief overview, Antioxidants (Basel) 9 (7) (2020) 619, https://doi.org/10.3390/antiox9070619.

[173] E. Dorant, et al., Garlic and its significance for the prevention of cancer in humans: a critical view, Br. J. Cancer 67 (3) (1993) 424–429.

[174] S. Tanaka, et al., Aged garlic extract has potential suppressive effect on colorectal adenomas in humans, J. Nutr. 136 (3 Suppl) (2006) 821s–826s.

[175] H. Zhang, et al., Garlic-derived compounds: epigenetic modulators and their antitumor effects, Phytother. Res. 38 (3) (2024) 1329–1344.

Nanomedicine targeting epigenetic machinery in cancer therapy

Harnessing plant-derived biosynthetic nanomaterials for epigenetic modulation in cancer therapy

13

Ritu Karwasra[a], Kushagra Khanna[b], Shivani Bhardwaj[c], Nitin Sharma[d], Ashok K. Janakiraman[b], Ramkanth Sundarapandian[e], and Surender Singh[f]

[a]*Central Council for Research in Unani Medicine, Ministry of Ayush, Govt of India, New Delhi, India,* [b]*Faculty of Pharmaceutical Sciences, UCSI University, UCSI Highest, Kuala Lumpur, Malaysia,* [c]*ICAR—Central Institute for Research on Buffaloes Hisar, Haryana, India,* [d]*Department of Pharmaceutics, ISF College of Pharmacy, Moga, Punjab, India,* [e]*Department of Pharmaceutics, Karpagam College of Pharmacy, Coimbatore, Tamil Nadu, India,* [f]*Department of Pharmacology, All India Institute of Medical Sciences, New Delhi, India*

Introduction

Cancer is a complex and multifactorial disease characterized by uncontrolled cell growth and the ability to invade surrounding tissues. It is a leading cause of death worldwide and poses a significant challenge to public health [1]. It is associated with multiple etiological factors. Some of the known risk factors include genetic predisposition, exposure to carcinogens (such as tobacco smoke and certain chemicals), radiation exposure, chronic inflammation, certain infections (like human papillomavirus and hepatitis viruses), unhealthy lifestyle choices (such as poor diet, lack of physical activity, and excessive alcohol consumption), and hormonal imbalances [2]. The pathophysiology of cancer involves the uncontrolled growth and division of cells. Normal cells have a regulated life cycle, with the ability to undergo programmed cell death (apoptosis) when necessary. In cancer, mutations or epigenetic alterations disrupt the balance between cell growth and cell death, leading to uncontrolled proliferation. These alterations can affect various cellular processes, including growth signaling pathways, cell cycle control, DNA repair mechanisms, angiogenesis, invasion and metastasis [3]. Mutations in genes such as proto-oncogenes (e.g., Ras, HER2) can lead to abnormal activation of growth signaling pathways, promoting cell growth and division. DNA repair mechanisms. Mutations in genes like tumor suppressor genes (e.g., p53, RB) can result in the loss of cell cycle regulation, leading to uncontrolled cell division. Defects in DNA repair genes (e.g., BRCA1, BRCA2) can impair the cell's ability to repair DNA damage, leading to the

279

Cancer Epigenetics and Nanomedicine. https://doi.org/10.1016/B978-0-443-13209-4.00016-7
Copyright © 2024 Elsevier Inc. All rights reserved, including those for text and data mining, AI training, and similar technologies.

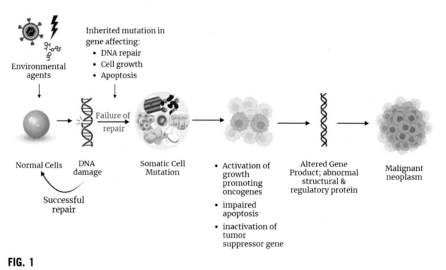

FIG. 1

Pathogenesis involved in the cancer.

accumulation of genetic mutations. Cancer cells can stimulate the formation of new blood vessels (angiogenesis) to ensure a nutrient supply, enabling tumor growth and metastasis. Cancer cells can acquire the ability to invade surrounding tissues and spread to distant sites through the bloodstream or lymphatic system, forming metastases (Fig. 1) [4].

Diagnosing cancer involves a combination of approaches, including medical history and physical examination, imaging tests, laboratory tests, and biopsy. Evaluating symptoms and risk factors and conducting a thorough physical examination, as well as techniques such as X-rays, computed tomography (CT), magnetic resonance imaging (MRI), ultrasound, and positron emission tomography (PET) scans, can help visualize tumors and their extent. Blood tests, tumor markers, and genetic testing can provide additional information about the presence and characteristics of cancer. The removal of a sample of tissue for microscopic examination confirms the presence of cancer and provides information about its type, grade, and molecular characteristics [5]. Over the years, extensive research has focused on understanding the molecular mechanisms underlying cancer development and progression, leading to the identification of various therapeutic targets. Cancer treatment approaches depend on the type and stage of cancer, as well as individual patient factors. Treatment modalities include surgery, radiation therapy, chemotherapy, targeted therapy, immunotherapy, hormone therapy, precision medicine, and palliative care [6]. Surgical removal of tumors and affected tissues is often used for localized cancers. The use of high-energy radiation to kill cancer cells or shrink tumors.

Table 1 Common medications used for cancer treatment.

Medication	Mechanism of action	Indications
Paclitaxel	Microtubule inhibitor	Breast, ovarian, lung, and other cancers
Cisplatin	DNA-damaging agent	Testicular, ovarian, bladder, and others
Trastuzumab	HER2-targeted monoclonal antibody	HER2-positive breast and gastric cancer
Imatinib	Tyrosine kinase inhibitor	Chronic myeloid leukemia, gastrointestinal stromal tumors
Rituximab	CD20-targeted monoclonal antibody	Non-Hodgkin lymphoma
Bevacizumab	VEGF-targeted monoclonal antibody	Colorectal, lung, kidney, and other cancers
Pembrolizumab	PD-1 checkpoint inhibitor	Melanoma, lung, bladder, and others
Tamoxifen	Selective estrogen receptor modulator	Breast cancer
Bortezomib	Proteasome inhibitor	Multiple myeloma, mantle cell lymphoma
Enzalutamide	Androgen receptor inhibitor	Prostate cancer

Administration of drugs that kill or inhibit the growth of cancer cells, either systemically or locally. Drugs that specifically target molecular alterations in cancer cells to block specific signaling pathways or promote immune responses. Immunotherapy involves stimulating or enhancing the body's immune system to recognize and attack cancer cells. Hormone therapy blocks or suppressing hormones that promote the growth of hormone-sensitive cancers, such as breast or prostate cancer. Precision medicine utilizes genetic profiling and molecular testing to identify specific mutations or alterations in cancer cells and select targeted therapies based on individual characteristics. Palliative care focuses on relieving symptoms, improving quality of life, and providing supportive care for patients with advanced or incurable cancers (Table 1) [7].

The authors described the small selection of medications used in cancer treatment, and there are numerous other drugs and treatment options available, depending on the specific cancer type and individual patient characteristics. The current landscape of cancer treatment calls for the exploration and development of novel therapeutic modalities that can effectively target the underlying molecular mechanisms driving tumorigenesis. Epigenetics, as a rapidly advancing field, offers a promising avenue for the discovery of innovative treatment strategies. By understanding and harnessing the intricate epigenetic modifications occurring in cancer cells, researchers have the potential to unlock new therapeutic targets and avenues for intervention. Traditional cancer therapies such as surgery, chemotherapy, and radiation primarily target rapidly dividing cells without specific consideration for the underlying molecular drivers. In contrast, epigenetic therapies hold the potential to achieve more precise and targeted interventions by addressing the root causes of the disease [8]. Epigenetics refers to heritable changes in gene expression patterns that do not involve alterations in the DNA sequence itself. These changes are mediated by various epigenetic mechanisms, including DNA methylation, histone modifications, and noncoding RNA molecules. Epigenetic modifications play a crucial role in normal cellular development and differentiation, as they regulate gene expression by turning genes "on" or "off" without modifying the underlying DNA sequence [9]. In cancer, aberrant epigenetic modifications can disrupt the normal regulation of gene expression, leading to uncontrolled cell growth and tumor formation. Epigenetic alterations are now recognized as key drivers of cancer development, progression, and metastasis. Prominent examples include hypermethylation of tumor suppressor gene promoters, leading to their silencing, and global hypomethylation, resulting in genomic instability. Understanding the role of epigenetics in cancer has opened up new avenues for therapeutic interventions. Epigenetic modulators, such as DNA methyltransferase inhibitors and histone deacetylase (HDAC) inhibitors, have shown promising results in reactivating silenced tumor suppressor genes and inhibiting cancer cell growth [8]. However, there is a need for innovative approaches to enhance the efficacy and specificity of epigenetic therapies.

Biosynthetic nanomaterials derived from plants have garnered significant interest in various fields, including cancer research and therapy. These nanomaterials possess unique physicochemical properties and are derived from renewable and biocompatible sources. Plant-based nanomaterials can be synthesized from plant extracts, loaded with phytochemicals, or derived from plant-derived exosomes. These biosynthetic nanomaterials offer several advantages in cancer treatment. First, they can target cancer cells specifically, minimizing off-target effects and reducing systemic toxicity. Second, they can penetrate tumor tissues efficiently due to their small size and surface properties, enhancing drug delivery to cancer cells. Third, these nanomaterials can modulate epigenetic processes in cancer cells, enabling precise and targeted manipulation of aberrant gene expression [10]. Plant-based nanomaterials have shown promise in epigenetic modulation by influencing DNA methylation, histone modifications, and noncoding RNA regulation. They can act as carriers for epigenetic drugs or phytochemicals with epigenetic modulatory properties. Additionally, these nanomaterials can be engineered to enhance their stability, bioavailability, and targeting ability. The use of biosynthetic nanomaterials from plants in cancer treatment holds great potential for overcoming drug resistance, improving therapeutic outcomes, and reducing adverse effects (Fig. 2) [11].

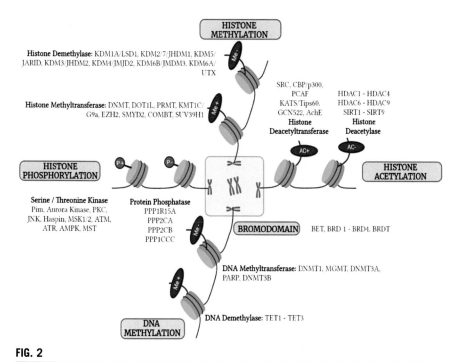

FIG. 2

Epigenetic modification during cancer.

Epigenetic modulation in cancer

Epigenetic modifications are chemical alterations to the DNA and associated proteins that can influence gene expression without changing the underlying DNA sequence. These modifications include DNA methylation, histone modifications, and noncoding RNA molecules. They act as regulatory marks that can turn genes on or off, controlling their expression levels and ultimately impacting cellular functions. DNA methylation involves the addition of a methyl group to the DNA molecule, typically occurring at cytosine residues within CpG dinucleotides. Methylation of gene promoters is generally associated with gene silencing, as it hinders the binding of transcription factors and other regulatory proteins, preventing gene expression. Histones are proteins that help package DNA into a compact structure called chromatin. Various chemical modifications, such as acetylation, methylation, phosphorylation, and ubiquitination, can occur on histone tails. These modifications can alter the chromatin structure, influencing the accessibility of DNA to the transcriptional machinery and thus affecting gene expression. Noncoding RNAs, including microRNAs (miRNAs) and long noncoding RNAs (lncRNAs), play crucial roles

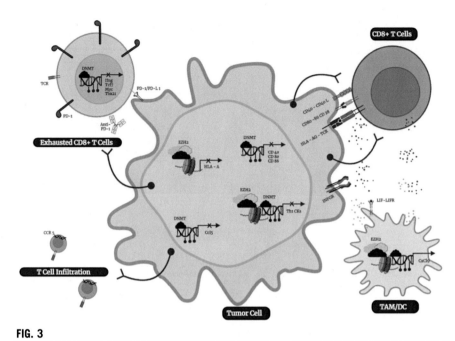

FIG. 3

Mechanism of epigenetic modulation in cancer cells.

in gene regulation. miRNAs can bind to messenger RNAs (mRNAs) and inhibit their translation or promote their degradation, leading to reduced protein expression. lncRNAs can interact with DNA, RNA, or proteins, influencing gene expression through diverse mechanisms (Fig. 3) [12].

Epigenetic dysregulation is a hallmark of cancer and contributes to tumor initiation, progression, and metastasis. Aberrant epigenetic modifications can result in the activation of oncogenes or the inactivation of tumor suppressor genes, disrupting normal cellular functions. Hypermethylation of gene promoter regions, particularly of tumor suppressor genes, can lead to their silencing, preventing the control of cell growth and promoting tumor development. Conversely, global DNA hypomethylation, which leads to genomic instability, can facilitate the activation of oncogenes and the loss of imprinting. Histone modifications can affect chromatin structure and gene expression. For example, decreased levels of histone acetylation and increased methylation of specific histone residues are often associated with gene silencing in cancer. These alterations can affect critical genes involved in cell cycle control, DNA repair, and apoptosis, promoting tumorigenesis. Aberrant expression of noncoding RNAs is frequently observed in cancer. Dysregulated miRNAs can target tumor suppressor genes or oncogenes, disrupting normal gene expression patterns. Additionally, altered expression of lncRNAs can influence chromatin structure, transcriptional regulation, and signaling pathways involved in cancer development [13].

Current approaches for epigenetic modulation in cancer therapy

Given the importance of epigenetic alterations in cancer, targeting these modifications has emerged as a potential therapeutic strategy. Several approaches have been developed to modulate epigenetic changes in cancer cells including DNA methylation inhibitors, HDAC inhibitors, and noncoding RNA modulators. Drugs such as 5-azacytidine and decitabine can reverse DNA hypermethylation and reactivate silenced tumor suppressor genes, restoring normal cellular functions and inhibiting tumor growth. HDAC inhibitors, including vorinostat and romidepsin, block the removal of acetyl groups from histones, leading to increased histone acetylation, relaxed chromatin structure, and reactivation of silenced genes [14]. Strategies targeting dysregulated noncoding RNAs, such as miRNA mimics or inhibitors, aim to restore normal miRNA expression patterns or block the function of oncogenic miRNAs, respectively. Additionally, lncRNA-targeting therapies are being explored to manipulate the expression and function of specific lncRNAs involved in cancer progression. These approaches hold promise in cancer therapy, either as standalone treatments or in combination with conventional therapies. However, challenges remain, including the need for increased specificity, understanding of resistance mechanisms, and optimization of delivery methods to ensure effective and safe epigenetic modulation in cancer patients (Fig. 4) [15].

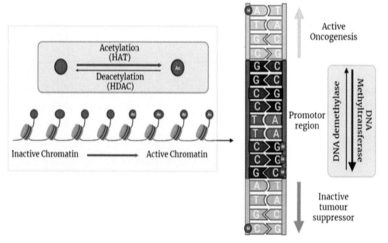

FIG. 4

Current approaches for epigenetic modulation in cancer cells.

Biosynthetic nanomaterials from plants

Biosynthetic nanomaterials derived from plants are a rapidly advancing field in nanotechnology and have gained considerable attention due to their unique properties and potential applications. These nanomaterials are synthesized using plant-derived biomolecules, such as proteins, polysaccharides, and polyphenols, either extracted directly from plants or produced through biotechnological methods. Biosynthetic nanomaterials offer the advantage of being derived from renewable and sustainable plant sources. Plants provide a vast array of biomolecules with diverse structures and functionalities, making them ideal for the synthesis of nanomaterials. Plant-derived nanomaterials exhibit inherent biocompatibility and low toxicity compared to synthetic counterparts. This characteristic is particularly important for biomedical applications, as it reduces the risk of adverse effects and enhances the biocompatibility of these nanomaterials in living systems. The synthesis of biosynthetic nanomaterials from plants often involves environmentally friendly and cost-effective methods. Plant-based extraction techniques and bioprocessing methods minimize the use of harsh chemicals and energy-intensive processes, making them more sustainable and eco-friendly [16]. Plant-derived nanomaterials can be easily customized and functionalized to meet specific requirements. They can be modified by incorporating targeting ligands, drugs, or imaging agents onto their surfaces, enabling precise targeting, controlled release, and multimodal therapeutic approaches. Biosynthetic nanomaterials from plants possess unique physicochemical properties, including size, shape, surface charge, and stability, which can be tailored by adjusting the synthesis parameters. These properties influence their behavior in biological systems, such as cellular uptake, biodistribution, and therapeutic efficacy. Many plant-based nanomaterials exhibit excellent biodegradability, allowing them to be metabolized and eliminated from the body over time. This characteristic reduces concerns regarding long-term accumulation and potential toxicity associated with persistent nanomaterials [17]. The advantages of biosynthetic nanomaterials from plants make them highly promising for various applications, including drug delivery, imaging, diagnostics, and tissue engineering. Their biocompatibility, customizability, and eco-friendly nature contribute to their growing popularity as alternatives to synthetic nanomaterials for biomedical and environmental applications.

Plant-based nanomaterials used in cancer research

Plant-derived nanoparticles

Plant-derived nanoparticles are nanoparticles synthesized using plant extracts or plant-based materials. These nanoparticles can be obtained from a variety of plants and offer unique properties for cancer research and therapy.

(a) *Gold nanoparticles*: Gold nanoparticles derived from plant extracts exhibit excellent biocompatibility and stability. They can be functionalized with targeting ligands or loaded with therapeutic agents for targeted drug delivery or imaging applications in cancer.

(b) *Silver nanoparticles*: Silver nanoparticles synthesized from plant extracts have shown antimicrobial and anticancer properties. They can be used for localized delivery of anticancer agents or as therapeutic agents themselves.

(c) *Iron oxide nanoparticles*: Iron oxide nanoparticles derived from plants have attracted attention for their potential applications in cancer diagnosis and therapy. They can be utilized as contrast agents in MRI or for hyperthermia treatment of tumors [18].

Plant secondary metabolites

Plant secondary metabolites are bioactive compounds produced by plants that play a role in their defense mechanisms. These metabolites have shown promising anticancer properties and can be utilized in cancer research.

(a) *Phytochemicals*: Phytochemicals, such as curcumin from turmeric, resveratrol from grapes, and quercetin from fruits and vegetables, have demonstrated anticancer activities. They can modulate various cellular processes, including apoptosis, cell cycle arrest, and inflammation, making them potential candidates for cancer treatment.

(b) *Flavonoids*: Flavonoids are a class of plant secondary metabolites that exhibit antioxidant and anticancer properties. They can inhibit tumor cell proliferation, induce apoptosis, and modulate cellular signaling pathways involved in cancer development.

Plant-based polymeric nanoparticles

Plant-based polymeric nanoparticles are nanoparticles composed of natural polymers derived from plants. These nanoparticles offer advantages such as biocompatibility, biodegradability, and tunable properties for cancer research.

(a) *Chitosan nanoparticles*: Chitosan, derived from the chitin found in crustacean shells or fungal cell walls, can be formulated into nanoparticles for drug delivery in cancer therapy. Chitosan nanoparticles possess mucoadhesive properties, allowing enhanced drug absorption and sustained release at the tumor site.

(b) *Cellulose-based nanoparticles*: Nanoparticles derived from cellulose, a natural polymer abundant in plant cell walls, have been explored for various biomedical applications, including cancer treatment. They can be surface-modified for targeted drug delivery or functionalized with imaging agents for cancer diagnosis (Table 2) [19].

These plant-based nanomaterials offer a diverse range of properties and functionalities for cancer research. They provide potential solutions for targeted drug delivery, imaging, and therapeutic interventions while harnessing the benefits of natural

Table 2 Plant-based nanomaterials used in cancer research.

Plant-based nanomaterials	Properties and applications
Plant-derived nanoparticles	
Gold nanoparticles	– Biocompatible, stable
	– Targeted drug delivery
	– Imaging agents
Silver nanoparticles	– Antimicrobial and anticancer properties
	– Localized drug delivery
	– Therapeutic agents
Iron oxide nanoparticles	– Used in cancer diagnosis and therapy
	– Contrast agents for MRI
	– Hyperthermia treatment
Plant secondary metabolites	
Phytochemicals	– Curcumin, resveratrol, quercetin, etc.
	– Anticancer activities
	– Modulate apoptosis, cell cycle, inflammation
Flavonoids	– Antioxidant and anticancer properties
	– Inhibit tumor cell proliferation
	– Induce apoptosis, modulate signaling pathways
Plant-based polymeric nanoparticles	
Chitosan nanoparticles	– Biocompatible, biodegradable
	– Mucoadhesive properties
	– Enhanced drug absorption
	– Sustained release at tumor site
Cellulose-based nanoparticles	– Biocompatible, versatile
	– Surface modification for targeted drug delivery
	– Functionalized with imaging agents

compounds derived from plants. They hold great potential for advancing cancer research and improving cancer diagnosis, treatment, and therapeutic outcomes.

Epigenetic modulation by biosynthetic nanomaterials

Biosynthetic nanomaterials derived from plants can modulate epigenetic processes through various mechanisms, allowing for potential epigenetic modulation in cancer. Some of the mechanisms of action include enhanced cellular uptake, targeted delivery, controlled release, intracellular localization, and synergistic effects. Biosynthetic nanomaterials can improve the cellular uptake of epigenetic modifiers, such as DNA methyltransferase inhibitors or HDAC inhibitors. The nanomaterials can encapsulate or carry these modifiers, facilitating their internalization into target cells and increasing their efficacy. Plant-derived nanoparticles can be functionalized with targeting ligands or antibodies specific to cancer cells or their receptors.

This enables specific delivery of epigenetic modifiers to tumor cells, minimizing off-target effects and enhancing the therapeutic potential [20]. Plant-based polymeric nanoparticles can provide sustained release of epigenetic drugs, ensuring a prolonged exposure to the modifiers at the target site. This controlled release allows for continuous modulation of epigenetic processes and long-lasting effects. Biosynthetic nanomaterials can facilitate the intracellular localization of epigenetic modifiers to specific subcellular compartments, such as the nucleus or chromatin regions. This localization enables direct interaction with the epigenetic machinery and more efficient modulation of gene expression. Combining biosynthetic nanomaterials with other therapeutic agents, such as chemotherapy drugs or targeted therapies, can result in synergistic effects. These combinations can enhance the effectiveness of epigenetic modulation and improve overall cancer treatment outcomes [21].

Plant-derived nanoparticles for targeted delivery of epigenetic modifiers

Gold nanoparticles are functionalized with epigenetic modifiers, such as DNA methylation inhibitors, for targeted delivery to cancer cells.

Plant-derived silver nanoparticles loaded with HDAC inhibitors for selective epigenetic modulation in tumors.

Plant secondary metabolites as natural epigenetic modulators

Curcumin, a phytochemical from turmeric, has been shown to modulate DNA methylation and histone modifications, exerting epigenetic effects in cancer cells.

Resveratrol, a natural compound found in grapes and berries, has demonstrated epigenetic activity by influencing histone modifications and DNA methylation patterns.

Plant-based polymeric nanoparticles for sustained release of epigenetic drugs

Chitosan nanoparticles are encapsulating DNA methyltransferase inhibitors for sustained release and targeted epigenetic modulation in cancer cells.

Cellulose-based nanoparticles loaded with HDAC inhibitors for controlled release and prolonged epigenetic modulation in tumors.

These examples illustrate the potential of biosynthetic nanomaterials derived from plants for epigenetic modulation in cancer. By utilizing the advantages of plant-based nanomaterials, such as targeted delivery, controlled release, and natural epigenetic modulatory properties, these nanomaterials hold promise for novel strategies in cancer epigenetics research and therapy [22].

Experimental evidence and preclinical studies

Several in vitro studies have provided evidence for the effectiveness of biosynthetic nanomaterials in epigenetic modulation for cancer treatment. These studies have explored various plant-derived nanomaterials and their ability to modulate epigenetic processes. In vitro studies have demonstrated that gold nanoparticles functionalized with epigenetic modifiers, such as DNA methyltransferase inhibitors or HDAC inhibitors, can effectively target cancer cells and induce epigenetic changes. These nanomaterials have shown promising results in reversing DNA hypermethylation or histone deacetylation, leading to reexpression of silenced tumor suppressor genes and inhibition of cancer cell growth. Natural compounds derived from plants, such as curcumin and resveratrol, have been extensively studied for their epigenetic modulatory effects [23–25]. In vitro experiments using cancer cell lines have shown that these plant secondary metabolites can influence DNA methylation patterns, histone modifications, and expression of epigenetic regulatory enzymes. They have demonstrated the ability to reprogram cancer cells toward a less aggressive phenotype and enhance sensitivity to other anticancer therapies [26]. In vitro studies utilizing plant-based polymeric nanoparticles, such as chitosan or cellulose-based nanoparticles, have shown their potential in delivering epigenetic modifiers to cancer cells. These nanoparticles can efficiently encapsulate or conjugate epigenetic drugs and release them in a sustained manner. The studies have demonstrated enhanced cellular uptake, improved stability, and increased therapeutic efficacy of the loaded epigenetic modifiers [27].

Preclinical studies involving animal models have provided valuable insights into the therapeutic potential of biosynthetic nanomaterials for cancer treatment. These studies have focused on assessing the safety, efficacy, and mechanism of action of these nanomaterials in vivo [28]. Preclinical studies using plant-derived nanoparticles have shown successful targeted delivery of epigenetic modifiers to tumor sites. These nanomaterials accumulate in the tumor microenvironment, resulting in effective modulation of epigenetic marks and subsequent inhibition of tumor growth [29]. Tumor regression and improved survival rates have been observed in animal models treated with these nanomaterials. Preclinical studies have explored the potential of combining biosynthetic nanomaterials with other anticancer therapies. Combining plant-based nanomaterials with chemotherapy drugs, radiation therapy, or targeted therapies has demonstrated synergistic effects, enhancing therapeutic outcomes. The combination approaches have shown improved tumor regression, reduced side effects, and prolonged survival in animal models [30].

Biosynthetic nanomaterials offer targeted delivery, improved stability, and sustained release of epigenetic modifiers, enhancing their therapeutic efficacy. In vitro studies provide valuable insights into the molecular mechanisms of action and demonstrate the potential of these nanomaterials to modulate epigenetic processes. Preclinical studies using animal models allow for the assessment of safety, efficacy, and therapeutic outcomes, providing a bridge between in vitro findings and future clinical applications [31].

Despite promising results in vitro and in preclinical models, the translation of biosynthetic nanomaterials to clinical settings is still in its early stages, and more research is needed to establish their safety and efficacy in humans. The complexity of the tumor microenvironment and interpatient variability pose challenges in designing effective treatment strategies using biosynthetic nanomaterials. Long-term effects and potential off-target effects of these nanomaterials require further investigation. Standardization of experimental protocols, dosage optimization, and comprehensive toxicity studies are necessary for the successful development and translation of biosynthetic nanomaterials. The experimental evidence from in vitro studies and preclinical investigations suggests the potential of biosynthetic nanomaterials derived from plants in epigenetic modulation for cancer treatment. However, further research and rigorous preclinical and clinical studies are necessary to validate their effectiveness, optimize their therapeutic strategies, and ensure their safety for human use [32].

Clinical potential and future directions

Biosynthetic nanomaterials derived from plants hold significant clinical potential in the field of epigenetic modulation for cancer treatment. Some key points highlighting their clinical potential include targeted therapy, personalized medicine, combination therapies, and noninvasive diagnostics. Biosynthetic nanomaterials can facilitate targeted delivery of epigenetic modifiers to tumor sites, minimizing off-target effects and enhancing therapeutic efficacy. This targeted approach has the potential to improve treatment outcomes and reduce systemic toxicity. Biosynthetic nanomaterials can be functionalized with targeting ligands or antibodies specific to cancer cells or their receptors. This opens avenues for personalized medicine, allowing tailored treatments based on individual patient characteristics and tumor profiles. These nanomaterials can be integrated with other therapeutic strategies, such as chemotherapy drugs, radiation therapy, or targeted therapies [33]. Combination therapies have the potential to synergistically enhance treatment efficacy, overcome drug resistance, and improve patient outcomes. Plant-based nanoparticles can also serve as imaging agents, aiding in noninvasive diagnostics for cancer detection and monitoring of treatment response. This can improve early detection, enable real-time monitoring of therapeutic effects, and guide treatment decisions (Fig. 5).

While biosynthetic nanomaterials show promise for clinical applications, there are several challenges and considerations that need to be addressed for their successful translation into clinical practice. Comprehensive studies on the safety profile and potential toxicities of biosynthetic nanomaterials are crucial. Understanding their pharmacokinetics, biodistribution, and long-term effects is essential for ensuring patient safety. The scalability and reproducibility of biosynthetic nanomaterial production need to be optimized to meet clinical demands. Consistency in manufacturing processes and quality control is vital

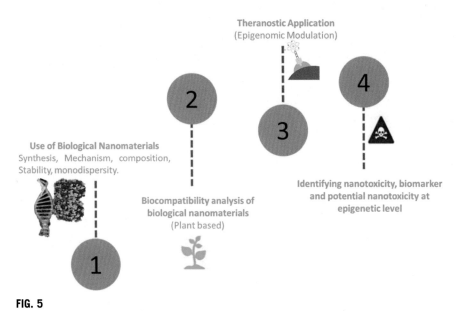

FIG. 5

Future directions for epigenetic modulation in cancer cells.

for clinical translation. The regulatory landscape surrounding the use of nanomaterials in clinical settings needs to be navigated. Complying with regulatory guidelines and obtaining necessary approvals are important for progressing toward clinical trials. The cost-effectiveness of biosynthetic nanomaterials must be considered for their widespread clinical adoption. Developing efficient and cost-effective manufacturing processes will be crucial in making these technologies accessible to patients [34].

The field of biosynthetic nanomaterials for epigenetic modulation in cancer treatment is still evolving, and there are several areas of further research and future directions to explore. Conducting well-designed clinical trials to evaluate the safety, efficacy, and therapeutic potential of biosynthetic nanomaterials in human cancer patients is critical. Clinical trials will provide valuable data for optimizing treatment strategies, identifying patient populations that would benefit the most, and establishing the clinical value of these nanomaterials. Investigating the synergistic effects of combining biosynthetic nanomaterials with other treatment modalities, such as immunotherapy or gene therapy, can further enhance therapeutic outcomes. Understanding the mechanisms underlying these synergistic effects will be important for developing effective combination regimens. Identifying predictive biomarkers that can help select patients likely to respond to biosynthetic nanomaterial-based therapies is crucial for personalized medicine [35]. Developing biomarkers that reflect epigenetic alterations or responses to treatment will aid in patient stratification and treatment optimization. Continual research on enhancing targeting efficiency, cellular uptake, and intracellular localization of biosynthetic nanomaterials will contribute to their improved efficacy. Designing smart delivery systems that respond to specific cues within the tumor microenvironment can further enhance targeting precision. Conducting long-term follow-up studies to assess the durability of epigenetic modulation and potential late toxicities is essential. Monitoring the effects of biosynthetic nanomaterials on normal tissues and their impact on overall patient well-being will contribute to their safe clinical implementation.

By addressing these research areas, refining the technologies, and overcoming the associated challenges, biosynthetic nanomaterials have the potential to revolutionize epigenetic modulation in cancer treatment and pave the way for more personalized and effective therapies in the future.

Conclusion

In conclusion, biosynthetic nanomaterials derived from plants offer a promising approach for epigenetic modulation in cancer treatment. These nanomaterials demonstrate various advantages, including targeted delivery, controlled release, and natural epigenetic modulatory properties. Plant-derived nanoparticles, plant secondary metabolites, and plant-based polymeric nanoparticles have shown efficacy in modulating epigenetic processes in cancer cells. In vitro studies and preclinical investigations have provided evidence of their effectiveness in reversing epigenetic dysregulation, inhibiting tumor growth, and enhancing treatment outcomes.

The research on biosynthetic nanomaterials in epigenetic modulation for cancer has significant future implications. It holds the potential to revolutionize cancer treatment by providing targeted and personalized therapies that can reprogram the epigenetic landscape of tumor cells. By exploiting the advantages of biosynthetic nanomaterials, such as their natural origin, biocompatibility, and tunable properties, we can overcome challenges associated with conventional epigenetic therapies. Moreover, the integration of biosynthetic nanomaterials with other treatment modalities, such as chemotherapy or immunotherapy, offers opportunities for synergistic effects and combinatorial approaches. This research also opens doors for noninvasive diagnostics and monitoring of treatment response. However, it is crucial to address the challenges of safety, scalability, and regulatory considerations to ensure successful translation into clinical practice. Further research is needed to conduct well-designed clinical trials, identify predictive biomarkers, and optimize delivery strategies. Long-term studies are also necessary to assess the durability and potential long-term effects of these nanomaterials.

Nutshell biosynthetic nanomaterials from plants present a promising avenue for epigenetic modulation in cancer, offering novel therapeutic possibilities that can transform the landscape of cancer treatment and improve patient outcomes in the future.

References

[1] R. Kumari, N. Sharma, R. Karwasra, K. Khanna, Colon cancer and their targeting approaches through nanocarriers: a review, Asian Pac. J. Trop. Biomed. 13 (3) (2023) 104.

[2] C.B. Blackadar, Historical review of the causes of cancer, World J. Clin. Oncol. 7 (1) (2016) 54.

[3] L. Maiorino, J. Daßler-Plenker, L. Sun, M. Egeblad, Innate immunity and cancer pathophysiology, Annu. Rev. Pathol.: Mech. Dis. 17 (2022) 425–457.

[4] E.R. Nelson, C.-y. Chang, D.P. McDonnell, Cholesterol and breast cancer pathophysiology, Trends Endocrinol. Metab. 25 (12) (2014) 649–655.

[5] M. Ambroggi, C. Biasini, C. Del Giovane, F. Fornari, L. Cavanna, Distance as a barrier to cancer diagnosis and treatment: review of the literature, Oncologist 20 (12) (2015) 1378–1385.

[6] A. Bhatia, Y. Kumar, Cellular and molecular mechanisms in cancer immune escape: a comprehensive review, Expert Rev. Clin. Immunol. 10 (1) (2014) 41–62.

[7] G.P. Dunn, C.M. Koebel, R.D. Schreiber, Interferons, immunity and cancer immunoediting, Nat. Rev. Immunol. 6 (11) (2006) 836–848.

[8] M. Esteller, Epigenetics in cancer, N. Engl. J. Med. 358 (11) (2008) 1148–1159.

[9] A.P. Feinberg (Ed.), The Epigenetics of Cancer Etiology. Seminars in Cancer Biology, Elsevier, 2004.

[10] P. Prasher, M. Sharma, M. Mehta, S. Satija, A.A. Aljabali, M.M. Tambuwala, et al., Current-status and applications of polysaccharides in drug delivery systems, Colloid Interface Sci. Commun. 42 (2021) 100418.

[11] J.T. Jordan, K.P. Singh, J.E. Cañas-Carrell, Carbon-based nanomaterials elicit changes in physiology, gene expression, and epigenetics in exposed plants: a review, Curr. Opin. Environ. Sci. Health 6 (2018) 29–35.

[12] J.S. You, P.A. Jones, Cancer genetics and epigenetics: two sides of the same coin? Cancer Cell 22 (1) (2012) 9–20.

[13] G. Cheng, Circulating miRNAs: roles in cancer diagnosis, prognosis and therapy, Adv. Drug Delivery Rev. 81 (2015) 75–93.

[14] M. Gjerstorff, J.S. Burns, O. Nielsen, M. Kassem, H. Ditzel, Epigenetic modulation of cancer-germline antigen gene expression in tumorigenic human mesenchymal stem cells: implications for cancer therapy, 175 (1) (2009) 314–323.

[15] H.P. Mohammad, O. Barbash, C.L. Creasy, Targeting epigenetic modifications in cancer therapy: erasing the roadmap to cancer, Nat. Med. 25 (3) (2019) 403–418.

[16] A. Arora, N. Sharma, D. Kakkar, Natural polysaccharides for ulcerative colitis: a general overview, Asian Pac. J. Trop. Biomed. 13 (5) (2023) 185.

[17] A. Plucinski, Z. Lyu, B.V. Schmidt, Polysaccharide nanoparticles: from fabrication to applications, J. Mater. Chem. B 9 (35) (2021) 7030–7062.

[18] V. Mohammadzadeh, M. Barani, M.S. Amiri, M.E.T. Yazdi, M. Hassanisaadi, A. Rahdar, et al., Applications of plant-based nanoparticles in nanomedicine: a review, Sustain. Chem. Pharm. 25 (2022) 100606.

[19] M. Mughees, S. Wajid, Herbal based polymeric nanoparticles as a therapeutic remedy for breast cancer, Anti-Cancer Agents Med. Chem. (Form. Curr. Med. Chem.-Anti-Cancer Agents) 21 (4) (2021) 433–444.

[20] S. Suchanti, A. Singh, R. Mishra, Epigenetic modulation by biosynthetic nanomaterials from plants in cancer, Mater. Today: Proc. 43 (2021) 3197–3199.

[21] S. Shyamasundar, C.T. Ng, L.Y. Lanry Yung, S.T. Dheen, B.H. Bay, Epigenetic mechanisms in nanomaterial-induced toxicity, Epigenomics 7 (3) (2015) 395–411.

[22] M. Vrânceanu, D. Galimberti, R. Banc, O. Dragoş, A. Cozma-Petruţ, S.-C. Hegheş, et al., The anticancer potential of plant-derived nutraceuticals via the modulation of gene expression, Plan. Theory 11 (19) (2022) 2524.

[23] N.-H. Nam, Naturally occurring NF-κB inhibitors, Mini-Rev. Med. Chem. 6 (8) (2006) 945–951.

[24] L.G. Carter, J.A. D'Orazio, K.J. Pearson, Resveratrol and cancer: focus on in vivo evidence, Endocr.-Relat. Cancer 21 (3) (2014) R209–R225.

[25] J.-H. Ko, G. Sethi, J.-Y. Um, M.K. Shanmugam, F. Arfuso, A.P. Kumar, et al., The role of resveratrol in cancer therapy, Int. J. Mol. Sci. 18 (12) (2017) 2589.

[26] A.A.G. Salido, S.B.I. Assanga, L.M.L. Luján, D.F. Ángulo, C.L.L. Espinoza, ALA SA., Composition of secondary metabolites in Mexican plant extracts and their antiproliferative activity towards cancer cell lines, Int. J. Sci. 5 (2016) 63–77.

[27] E.A. El-Alfy, M.K. El-Bisi, G.M. Taha, H.M. Ibrahim, Preparation of biocompatible chitosan nanoparticles loaded by tetracycline, gentamycin and ciprofloxacin as novel drug delivery system for improvement the antibacterial properties of cellulose based fabrics, Int. J. Biol. Macromol. 161 (2020) 1247–1260.

[28] B. Mahitha, B.D.P. Raju, G. Dillip, C.M. Reddy, K. Mallikarjuna, L. Manoj, et al., Biosynthesis, characterization and antimicrobial studies of AgNPs extract from *Bacopa monniera* whole plant, Dig. J. Nanomater. Biostruct. 6 (2) (2011) 587–594.

[29] E.-A. Moacă, C.G. Watz, C. Păcurariu, L.B. Tudoran, R. Ianoş, V. Socoliuc, et al., Biosynthesis of iron oxide nanoparticles: physico-chemical characterization and their in vitro cytotoxicity on healthy and tumorigenic cell lines, NANO 12 (12) (2022) 2012.

[30] C. Jiang, Z. Jiang, S. Zhu, J. Amulraj, V.K. Deenadayalan, J.A. Jacob, et al., Biosynthesis of silver nanoparticles and the identification of possible reductants for the assessment of in vitro cytotoxic and in vivo antitumor effects, J. Drug Deliv. Sci. Technol. 63 (2021) 102444.

[31] A. Mohmed, S. Hassan, A. Fouda, M. Elgamal, S. Salem, Extracellular biosynthesis of silver nanoparticles using aspergillus sp. and evaluation of their antibacterial and cytotoxicity, J. Appl. Life Sci. Int. 11 (2) (2017) 1–12.

[32] A. Van de Walle, A. Plan Sangnier, A. Abou-Hassan, A. Curcio, M. Hémadi, N. Menguy, et al., Biosynthesis of magnetic nanoparticles from nano-degradation products revealed in human stem cells, Proc. Natl. Acad. Sci. 116 (10) (2019) 4044–4053.

[33] M. Verma, Personalized medicine and cancer, J. Personal. Med. 2 (1) (2012) 1–14.

[34] A. Patsalias, Z. Kozovska, Personalized medicine: stem cells in colorectal cancer treatment, Biomed. Pharmacother. 141 (2021) 111821.

[35] K. Jain, Role of nanobiotechnology in developing personalized medicine for cancer, Technol. Cancer Res. Treat. 4 (6) (2005) 645–650.

Nanotechnology-enhanced immunotherapy for cancer 14

Akshata R. Naik

Foundational Medical Studies, Oakland University William Beaumont School of Medicine,
Rochester, MI, United States

Introduction

"Immunotherapy" is a broad term that encompasses treatment methodologies that leverage one's own body's immune system to combat cancer. There have been several milestones in terms of identifying potential targets within the body's immune system. However, to understand immunotherapy, we first need to know the fundamentals of the immune system in addition to its role in cancer progression. The body's immune system is highly complex, comprising several cell types with highly specific functions. Each of these specialized functions provides an avenue for targeting cancers, thus leading to several sub-fields within cancer immunotherapy.

The role of immune cells in dampening cancer was first shown by William Coley when he administered extracts of heat-inactivated *Streptococcus pyogenes* and *Serratia marcescens* which he termed as "Coley's toxins" into patients with cancer that resulted in favorable prognosis. Immunotherapy has come a long way since this discovery and can be of several types as we will discuss in this chapter. It is also significant to know that cancer immunology is quite the opposite of infection and that we need our immune systems to be effectively active. Immune cells must respond differently toward tumors and not the usual way they respond to pathogens. Pathogens are foreign, while cancer cells are self that need to be perceived as foreign. Therefore, this chapter is focused on the way the immune responses are modified and enhanced to combat tumors. Although the body's immune system itself is trained to conduct tumor surveillance, it is not enough! They need to outperform tumors as cancer cells are very smart and escape surveillance by modifying or expressing certain cell surface markers to disguise as self. As we will see in this chapter, immunotherapy mainly targets tumors either by enhancing the activating immune signals or by inhibiting the immune checkpoints.

Cancer Epigenetics and Nanomedicine. https://doi.org/10.1016/B978-0-443-13209-4.00001-5
Copyright © 2024 Elsevier Inc. All rights are reserved, including those for text and data mining, AI training, and similar technologies.

The fundamentals of the immune system

If and when a foreign antigen surpasses the physiological and mechanical barriers of the human body and manages to enter inside, it is encountered by the body's immunological response provided by the immune system. The immune system, as we all know, is the body's internal defense system with two major arms: (1) innate immunity and (2) adaptive immunity [1]. The innate immune system is the first line of defense and provides a quick yet nonspecific immune response against pathogenic antigens. However, the adaptive immune response, which is much slower to respond, is antigen-specific and retain long-term antigenic memory.

A common precursor population of pluripotent hematopoietic stem cells (HSCs) within the bone marrow that express the cell surface marker CD34+ generate the common myeloid progenitors (CMP) and the common lymphoid progenitors (CLP) [2]. Almost all cells of the innate response except the natural killer (NK) cells are derived from the CMP. The cells of the adaptive immune response, including the NK cells, are derived from the CLP. Macrophages, neutrophils, basophils, eosinophils, NK cells, dendritic cells, and mast cells are the cell types that belong to the innate immune system. The innate immune system also includes the "complement system" that comprise myriad plasma proteins, which in various combinations of structured and regulated interactions facilitate susceptibility of foreign pathogens to "phagocytosis" by inducing a series of inflammatory responses [3]. On the other hand, the cells, T- and B-lymphocytes, belong to the adaptive immune system. The T-cells are responsible for the cell-mediated immune response, and their development occurs within the environment of the thymus. Two types of T-cells are eventually produced: CD4+ T-cells, which bind to major histocompatibility complex (MHC) Class II molecules, and CD8+ T-cells, which bind to MHC Class I molecules. The B-cells are responsible for the humoral immune response, and their development occurs within the bone marrow as immature B-cells, which then enter the spleen for their final maturation. Historically, the two major arms of the immune system, innate and adaptive, were thought to be distinct from each other. However, recent evidence suggests that they interact with each other to produce a cohesive and effective immune response to surmount an infection [4].

Although we will not discuss this in great detail, we first need to understand the basics of T-cell and B-cell production. For the purpose of this chapter, we will discuss T-cell ontogeny as it will help better understand the recent work on cancer immunotherapy.

T-cell ontogeny

T-cell development and maturation take place in the thymus, an organ located in the chest area. Once the lymphoid progenitors are formed in the bone marrow, they then migrate to the thymus to be programmed into mature T-cells, which then identify various types of foreign pathogens and neoantigens while tolerating self-antigens

[5]. The progenitor cells at this stage within the thymus do not express any cell surface markers such as the T-cell receptor (TCR) or the coreceptors CD4 or CD8 that are needed for mounting an antigenic response and hence are termed as double negative (DN) cells which is stage DN1. The thymus consists of the outer cortical region and the inner medullary region, which provide a crucial environment for the T cells to develop. Once the lymphoid progenitors enter the cortico-medullary region, they become committed to follow the T-cell lineage and shut off their pathways to become either B-cells or NK cells. Based on various combinations of expression of cell surface markers such as CD44 and CD25, T-cells range from DN1 to DN4. Stage DN4 is when the T-cells express the mature TCR and proceed to express both, CD8 and CD4 to become double positive (DP) [6]. To understand the process of $\alpha\beta$ TCR maturation, we will begin at stage DN3, where cells express the pre-TCR.

TCRs can be of two different types: the $\alpha\beta$ TCRs or the $\gamma\delta$ TCRs. The T-cells that recognize antigenic presentation are the $\alpha\beta$ cell surface receptors of T-cells [7]. These cells will then express the pre-TCR α after expressing a series of other cell surface markers that form the DN3 stage. The β chain is then loaded onto the cell surface after rearrangement of the recombinant activating genes (RAGs), RAG1, and RAG2 genes into various permutations and combinations that provide specificity against various antigenic peptides. Thus, the pre-Tα pairs with the pre-Tβ on the cell surface. Further maturation of T-cells requires active signaling of the pre-TCR complex to release intracellular secondary messengers that stimulate the expression of key enzymes, genes of which are otherwise inactive. This is the stage of β selection and the loss of pre-Tα to produce a mature α chain of the TCR complex. Post this stage, these cells, which are now in the late DN3 or early DN4 stage, undergo 6–8 divisions to produce the mature $\alpha\beta$ chains along with CD3/ç. This is when the cells begin to express the coreceptors CD8 first and then CD4. At this point, cells are still residing within the thymus and are DP, expressing both CD8 and CD4 along with the mature $\alpha\beta$ TCR, although the cells themselves are yet to mature further into naïve T-cells.

Next, the TCR complex on the double positive T-cells engage with self-peptide MHC ligands for differentiation into either CD4 or CD8 lineages. About 5% of total DP thymocyte cells that engage with just enough intensity produce a cell survival signal. More than 90% of DP thymocytes that engage with self-peptide MHC complexes produce too weak a signal and die by apoptosis due to their inability to initiate a cell survival signal and die by neglect. The other 5% of DP thymocytes produce a signal so strong that a self-correcting apoptotic signal is induced. The cells that interact way too strongly are detrimental to the host and can cause issues with autoimmunity. The expression of either CD4 or CD8 coreceptor on the T-cells is dependent on the interaction of TCR with either MHC Class II or MHC Class I molecules, respectively, to become single positive T-cells. The TCRs of T-cells that have a strong enough interaction with MHC Class II molecules differentiate into CD4+ cells, while the ones with a strong enough interaction with MHC Class II molecules differentiate into CD8+ T-cells. Although the underlying cell signaling behind the differentiation of T-cells, either into CD4+ or CD8+ single positive cells, is well delineated, there is still debate about how the T-cells achieve this fate of differentiation. Two models, "stochastic" and "instruction" models, have been proposed [8]. Further maturation of T-cells occurs in the medulla where T-cells that react strongly toward self-antigens are negatively selected and routed for apoptosis, although sometimes recognition of self-antigens can also have different fate for the T-cells such as maturation into regulatory T-cells (Tregs). The naïve T-cells that are developed are now ready for screening pathogens in the secondary lymphoid tissues. The CD4+ T-cells develop a helper role that further differentiate into several subtypes, while the CD8+ T-cells develop a cytotoxic role. For a detailed understanding of positive and negative selection of T-cells, please refer to the review in Ref. [9] here.

Once these naïve T-cells are ready, they:

(a) Need to be activated to initiate an immune response which is cell mediated.
(b) Need to undergo differentiation and multiply into effector cells in order to combat a pathogenic infection.

T-cells that differentiate and proliferate from naïve T-cells are capable of performing effector functions. Naïve T-cells identify antigens presented to them by dendritic cells in secondary peripheral lymphoid organs, after which they release the cytokine IL-2, which then initiates a signaling cascade for some of the naïve T-cells to differentiate and proliferate into effector T-cells that are specific to the antigen presented. The majority of the effector T-cells then migrate via circulation to the site of infection to rid them of the pathogens. Some effector T-cells stay back in the lymphoid organs to signal B-cells to produce antibodies. After the pathogen is cleared, most of the effector T-cells undergo apoptosis, although few of them become memory T-cells that retain memory toward the specific antigens.

T-cell activation signals

Now, let us understand very briefly the activation signals that are required for the T-cells to differentiate and proliferate. Although the mechanisms are far more detailed [10] than what is listed here, I am covering only the basics of it as this activation signal, along with the regulatory checkpoints of T-cell activation, are crucial for the understanding of immunotherapy. T-cell activation involves engaging several membrane receptors on the T-cells with their respective ligands on the antigen-presenting cells (APCs). The first step, as we saw above, is the T-cell recognition of the antigen presented by the dendritic cells, which are the APCs that activate the T-cell. T-cells with CD4 coreceptors recognize antigenic peptides presented by MHC Class II, while those with CD8 coreceptors engage with MHC Class I ligands. This initial engagement is strengthened by adhesion molecules and is required for stimulating the series of signals that then activate T-cells. It is especially important for bringing the signaling enzymes closer to the CD3 and ζ tails and phosphorylate them to trigger the activation signals. There are other ligands on the APC, such as the B7-1/B7-2, that bind to CD28 receptors on T-cells, which are important

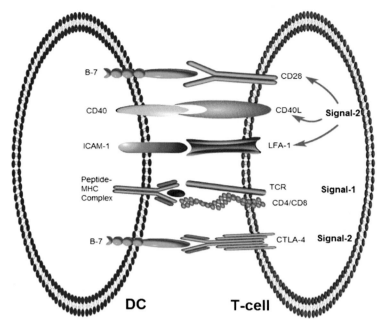

FIG. 1

Naïve T-cell activation signals leading to T-cell activation and proliferation to perform effector functions [12]. An antigen presented to T-cells via MHC complex is recognized by the TCR, which is "signal 1." The costimulation, "signal 2," is provided by various molecule pairs as listed in the figure above. These are CD40-CD40L, CTLA4-B7 ligand, and ICAM-1-LFA-1.

for costimulation [11]. Post costimulation, many cytokines are recruited to this site, where they bind to receptors on T-cells, which further set in motion intracellular signals. All the signals eventually work toward differentiating T-cells into effector cells, which proliferate to migrate to the site of infection (Fig. 1).

Tumor immunology

Tumor surveillance function by the immune system also occurs. However, tumor cells often evade the immune system and develop into malignancies easily. Tumor cells express certain proteins that are recognized by the immune system as tumor antigens. Research is now focused on understanding these tumor antigens and how our immune system recognizes them. More importantly, knowing the mechanism behind how tumor cells evade the antigenic response helps identify potential targets for cancer immunotherapy. This section will describe the various tumor antigens, their recognition by the immune system, and the mechanism that our immune system tries to prevent malignancy formation. Additionally, the focus is also on the process tumor cells follow to evade body's defense mechanisms. Tumor antigens can be generated by various mechanisms, which are then recognized mainly by CD8+ cytotoxic T lymphocytes as they are processed and presented by class I MHC molecules. Activation and proliferation of CD8+ T-cells often need help from CD4+ T-cells.

The most common type of tumor antigens is termed "neoantigens," as they are newly generated proteins by the tumor cells which are normally not present in healthy cells. These neoantigens are usually processed and presented by the host's MHC system, thus initiating a response by the host's adaptive immune system. The neoantigens do not play any role in tumor transformation and are expressed only after a cell has been transformed; hence, they are termed "passenger" mutations. On the contrary, there are "driver" mutations that are actually involved in driving the transformation of a healthy cell into a cancerous cell. The product proteins of these mutations can also be perceived as foreign tumor antigens [13].

Other types of proteins that qualify as tumor antigens are the proteins whose expressions are irregular. It means that the protein itself is unmutated but its level of expression is changed. For example, if a certain protein is usually expressed during embryological stages, but its expression goes up during adulthood, then it is most likely due to its expression on tumors. Note that the expression levels of these proteins change due to a mutation of the epigenetic mechanisms that control its expression, such as in the promoter regions of a gene. A classic example of such a tumor antigen is the HER2 protein expression on breast cancer cells. Several tumors are also caused by viruses in which case the viral antigens serve as tumor antigens.

Immune responses against tumors

Most of the tumor antigens are processed by MHC class I molecules and, hence, are recognized by CD8+ T-cells. Once these cells are activated they need to differentiate and proliferate into effector cytotoxic T lymphocytes to mount an immune response against the tumor. Several studies have noted favorable outcomes for tumors with increased CTL infiltration. However, MHC class I molecules lack the ability of costimulation for CTL activation and proliferation. Therefore, tumor antigens are also processed and presented by MHC class II molecules to CD4+ T-cells, which aid in the proliferation and activation of CTLs, as we discussed in our previous section. The effector CTLs then migrate to the site of tumor and kill the tumor cells, which express the respective antigens that the CTLs are primed against [14].

Despite such robust immune mechanisms in place, tumors evade the body's immune mechanism mainly by T-cell exhaustion, which is defined as the lowered ability of T-cells to produce cytokines and proliferate. T-cell exhaustion is a result of prolonged antigenic stimulation, which sets off a series of responses facilitated by the immune checkpoint receptors, thus reducing T-cell responses [15]. The most common immune checkpoints that have been studied with respect to cancer are CTLA-4, PD-1, T-cell Ig and mucin-domain containing (TIM)-3, and lymphocyte-activating gene 3 (LAG3). Other mechanisms by which tumors evade immune response are either by mutating or completely stopping the expression of MHC class I molecules.

Alternatively, tumors may also upregulate Treg, immune inhibitory B cells, and myeloid-derived suppressor cells (MDSCs) by number and/or function within the tumor microenvironment as they have immunosuppressive properties.

Adoptive T-cell therapy for combating cancers

As you saw above, T-cells have the capacity and ability to mount an immune response against tumor-specific antigens when presented by MHC. However, certain mechanisms that are adapted by tumor cells lead to evasion of these responses. Adoptive T-cell therapy has been successful to a large extent in superseding such evasive responses by tumor cells and, killing these tumors. The grounding principle of adoptive cell therapy is to increase T-cell numbers and fortify its ability to kill tumor cells by enhancing its recognition ability of tumor-specific antigens [16,17]. T-cells are isolated from the patient's blood or the tumor microenvironment and are cultured ex vivo to proliferate. The proliferated T-cells are then reinfused into the patients to attack the tumor along with lymphodepletion induced via chemotherapy. Lymphodepletion aids the reinfused T-cells to enhance their anticancer response as it depletes immunosuppressive processes such as Tregs and coinhibitory molecules.

A step above this is that the isolated T-cells can be genetically engineered to express a TCR highly specific to a particular tumor antigen along with the necessary costimulatory molecules that can recognize antigenic peptides that are unprocessed and do not need presentation via MHC complexes. These T-cells are referred to as "chimeric antigen receptor T-cell" (CAR-T) cells. CAR-T cells have demonstrated favorable outcomes for hematologic malignancies, although not for solid tumors. Adoptive cell therapies have shifted the paradigm in creating treatment approaches to combat cancer, and currently, various targeting methods are being researched to not just kill tumor cells but also to prevent relapse [18].

Adoptive T-cell therapy can be further enhanced by conjugating with immunotherapy-loaded nanoparticles termed "backpacks" on their cell surface. These backpacks can be used to carry cytokines that modify the tumor microenvironment and make it more conducive for the T-cells that carry these backpacks to enhance their activity. A big advantage of T-cells being the carriers instead of engineered nanoparticles is that T-cells migrate down chemokine gradients and are thus specific against the targeted tumor [19].

Immune checkpoints and their role in cancer immunotherapy

As T-cell activation occurs via the TCR and CD-28 costimulatory receptor, there are also mechanisms in place that are triggered to regulate T-cell activation signals, which function as a way to reduce autoimmune responses and adverse immune reactions that can be caused by prolonged T-cell activation. The most well-established inhibitory receptors that bring about this regulation are the cytotoxic T lymphocyte antigen 4 (CTLA-4) and the programmed cell death protein 1 (PD-1), which are referred to as "coinhibitors."

CTLA-4

CTLA-4 is a B7 ligand binding protein that is constitutively expressed on regulatory T-cells, and its expression on activated T-cells is transiently increased upon T-cell activation. CTLA-4 on T-cells competes for the B7 ligand on APCs, thus preventing the B7 ligand's engagement with CD28, which leads to inhibition of costimulation and, therefore, limits further activation of T-cells. CTLA-4 has a much higher affinity to B7 than CD28, and hence, it binds to B7 even at lower B7 expressions, which is true under conditions when either self-antigens are presented or some tumor antigens are presented, although not during pathogenic antigens. At higher B7 expression conditions, such as presentation of pathogenic antigens, even if some CTLA-4 binds to B7, there are enough B7 for the CD28 to bind and still induce costimulation [20,21]. During conditions pertaining to lower B7 expression, specifically in tumor antigen presentation, most of the B7 that are available are occupied by CTLA-4 on T-cells, thus attenuating the T-cell response against tumor antigens. Therefore, CTLA-4 makes a promising therapeutic target to combat cancer, and indeed, monoclonal antibodies such as anti-CTLA-4 are shown to not only induce better immune responses against cancers but also help in limiting Treg function and proliferation as these cells constitutively express CTLA-4, thus reducing the immunosuppressive activity of Tregs. Ipilimumab and tremelimumab are FDA-approved anti-CTLA-4 monoclonal antibodies that are used to treat skin cancer and nonsmall cell lung cancers, respectively, in combination with traditional nonimmune cancer therapies [20].

PD-1/PD-L1 pathway

PD-1, the other coinhibitory molecule, is present on both CD4 and CD8 T-cells and binds to the PD-1 ligand (PD-L1) found on APCs. Similar to CTLA-4, it functions to inhibit T-cell activation as a way to prevent hyperactivation and proliferation of T-cells. PD-1 expression on T-cells increases upon activation, and PD-L1 expression on PACs increases due to cytokine production during inflammation. PD-1/PD-L1 engagement initiates an intracellular downstream signaling cascade within T-cells that inhibits downstream signals from the TCR and the CD28 costimulation in T-cells [22]. PD-1 receptors are also present in other cells, such as B-cells, NK, and APCs, as well as in tumor cells. Similarly, PD-L1 is also expressed in several immune cells including T-cells and tumor cells. PD-L2 is another ligand with a higher affinity for PD-1 receptors than PD-L1. Interestingly, several tumor cells also express PD-1 and PD-L1. The PD-L1 expressing tumor cells become resistant to cytotoxic T lymphocyte killing and cellular apoptosis when they bind to PD-1 receptors on the T-cells. Several monoclonal antibodies, such as atezolizumab, avelumab, and durvalumab, which block PD-L1, and pembrolizumab, nivolumab, and cemiplimab that block PD-L1 are FDA approved [22] (Fig. 2).

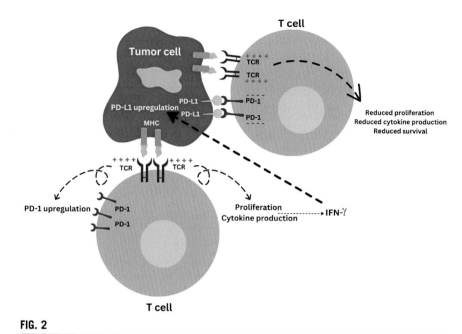

FIG. 2

T-cell inhibition and reduced proliferation via PD-1/PD-L1 pathway. Tumor cells exhibit PD-L1, which binds to PD-1 on T-cells, thus inhibiting T-cell activation.

TIGIT

TIGIT stands for T-cell immunoglobin and ITIM domain and is a T-cell coinhibitory receptor that is expressed on CD4+ memory and Tregs, CD8+ T-cells, and NK cells. TIGIT has ligands such as CD155, CD112, and CD113, and upon their engagement with TIGIT, they induce suppression of CD4+ T-cell activation via upregulation of antiinflammatory cytokine production by dendritic cells. However, TIGIT engagement on Tregs enhances its immunosuppressive activity. Since TIGIT is also expressed on CD8+ cytotoxic T-cells along with PD-1 therapies have targeted a combined blockade of TIGIT and PD-1 and seems to be promising in terms of increasing T-cell activation and proliferation [23].

LAG3

Lymphocyte activation gene (LAG) 3 is another coinhibitory molecule expressed on activated CD4+, CD8+, and NK cells, which suppresses T-cell activation and proliferation. LAG3 has ligands on tumor cells which, when engaged, suppresses T-cell function and helps in the proliferation of tumor cells. Thus, antibodies blocking LAG3 are a therapeutic cancer immunotherapy target [24].

Other therapies

Since the advent of immunotherapy several targets have been and are currently being researched and identified at every step of immune activation. Therapies range from supplementing cytokines to administering cancer vaccines. Several T-cell costimulatory molecules are also currently being targeted. However, we focused on some of the important ones in this chapter, and discussing them in greater detail is out of the scope of this chapter.

Nanotechnological advances in immunotherapy

Even though immunotherapies are promising and are able to combat cancers they have several side effects in terms of immune adverse reactions. The adverse reactions are a result of off-targets not specific to tumor microenvironment and due to systemic release of immune modulators. Nanotechnology has demonstrated the potential in reducing such adverse reactions. Some of the advantages of nanoparticle drug delivery are local retention, reduced systemic leakage, enhanced immune responses, and engineering immune cells [25].

We discussed immune checkpoint blockade previously for T-cell activation and proliferation to combat cancer. However, this activation is beneficial when the T-cell activity is local to tumor microenvironment, and there is lowered dissipation of checkpoint inhibitors in circulation. Therapies have focused on conjugating ICI antibodies with peptides that have a high affinity toward extracellular matrix proteins so that they are locally retained, thus reducing systemic side effects. Another advantage of using nanoparticles is to provide a safer and more effective administration, where a study demonstrates safer and more effective administration of immune checkpoint blockade proteins when conjugated with collagen [26].

References

[1] R. Warrington, et al., An introduction to immunology and immunopathology, Allergy Asthma Clin. Immunol. 7 (1) (2011) S1.

[2] S. Huang, L.W. Terstappen, Lymphoid and myeloid differentiation of single human CD34+, HLA-DR+, CD38- hematopoietic stem cells, Blood 83 (6) (1994) 1515–1526.

[3] J.R. Dunkelberger, W.-C. Song, Complement and its role in innate and adaptive immune responses, Cell Res. 20 (1) (2010) 34–50.

[4] R. Clark, T. Kupper, Old meets new: the interaction between innate and adaptive immunity, J. Invest. Dermatol. 125 (4) (2005) 629–637.

[5] J.E. Smith-Garvin, G.A. Koretzky, M.S. Jordan, T cell activation, Annu. Rev. Immunol. 27 (2009) 591–619.

[6] B.V. Kumar, T.J. Connors, D.L. Farber, Human T cell development, localization, and function throughout life, Immunity 48 (2) (2018) 202–213.

[7] C.A. Janeway Jr., P. Travers, M. Walport, et al., Antigen recognition by T cells, in: Immunobiology: The Immune System in Health and Disease, Garland Science, New York, 2001.

[8] R.N. Germain, T-cell development and the CD4–CD8 lineage decision, Nat. Rev. Immunol. 2 (5) (2002) 309–322.

[9] L. Klein, et al., Positive and negative selection of the T cell repertoire: what thymocytes see (and don't see), Nat. Rev. Immunol. 14 (6) (2014) 377–391.

[10] J.-R. Hwang, et al., Recent insights of T cell receptor-mediated signaling pathways for T cell activation and development, Exp. Mol. Med. 52 (5) (2020) 750–761.

[11] L. Chen, D.B. Flies, Molecular mechanisms of T cell co-stimulation and co-inhibition, Nat. Rev. Immunol. 13 (4) (2013) 227–242.

[12] Y. Tai, et al., Molecular mechanisms of T cells activation by dendritic cells in autoimmune diseases, Front. Pharmacol. 9 (2018) 642.

[13] J.R. Pon, M.A. Marra, Driver and passenger mutations in cancer, Annu. Rev. Pathol.: Mech. Dis. 10 (1) (2015) 25–50.

[14] D. Ostroumov, et al., CD4 and CD8 T lymphocyte interplay in controlling tumor growth, Cell. Mol. Life Sci. 75 (4) (2018) 689–713.

[15] C.U. Blank, et al., Defining 'T cell exhaustion', Nat. Rev. Immunol. 19 (11) (2019) 665–674.

[16] Z. Wang, Y.J. Cao, Adoptive cell therapy targeting neoantigens: a frontier for cancer research, Front. Immunol. 11 (2020) 176.

[17] K. Perica, et al., Adoptive T cell immunotherapy for cancer, Rambam Maimonides Med. J. 6 (1) (2015) e0004.

[18] S. Stock, et al., Enhanced chimeric antigen receptor T cell therapy through co-application of synergistic combination partners, Biomedicines 10 (2) (2022) 307.

[19] H. Lin, et al., Engineering novel multi-cytokine backpacks for manufacturing functionally improved CAR T cell products, Blood 140 (Suppl. 1) (2022) 10245–10246.

[20] N. Sobhani, et al., CTLA-4 in regulatory T cells for cancer immunotherapy, Cancers 13 (6) (2021) 1440.

[21] S.C. Wei, C.R. Duffy, J.P. Allison, Fundamental mechanisms of immune checkpoint blockade therapy, Cancer Discov. 8 (9) (2018) 1069–1086.

[22] Y. Han, D. Liu, L. Li, PD-1/PD-L1 pathway: current researches in cancer, Am. J. Cancer Res. 10 (3) (2020) 727–742.

[23] X. Chu, et al., Co-inhibition of TIGIT and PD-1/PD-L1 in cancer immunotherapy: mechanisms and clinical trials, Mol. Cancer 22 (1) (2023) 93.

[24] J.L. Huo, et al., The promising immune checkpoint LAG-3 in cancer immunotherapy: from basic research to clinical application, Front. Immunol. 13 (2022) 956090.

[25] M.S. Goldberg, Improving cancer immunotherapy through nanotechnology, Nat. Rev. Cancer 19 (10) (2019) 587–602.

[26] J. Ishihara, et al., Targeted antibody and cytokine cancer immunotherapies through collagen affinity, Sci. Transl. Med. 11 (487) (2019).

Nanoparticles in metastatic cancer treatment

15

K.R. Manu[a], Ananya Kar[a], Pushparathinam Gopinath[b], Garima Gupta[c], Amirhossein Sahebkar[d,e], Prashant Kesharwani[f], and Rambabu Dandela[a]

[a]*Department of Industrial and Engineering Chemistry, Institute of Chemical Technology, Bhubaneswar, Odisha, India,* [b]*Department of Chemistry, Faculty of Engineering and Technology, SRM Institute of Science and Technology, Kattankulathur, Tamil Nadu, India,* [c]*School of Allied Medical Sciences, Lovely Professional University, Phagwara, Punjab, India,* [d]*Biotechnology Research Center, Pharmaceutical Technology Institute, Mashhad University of Medical Sciences, Mashhad, Iran,* [e]*Applied Biomedical Research Center, Mashhad University of Medical Sciences, Mashhad, Iran,* [f]*Department of Pharmaceutics, School of Pharmaceutical Education and Research, Jamia Hamdard, New Delhi, India*

Introduction

Metastatic cancer, the intricate process by which cancer cells disseminate from a primary tumor to establish secondary lesions in distant anatomical sites, remains a paramount challenge within contemporary oncology. It often unfolds insidiously, with over 80% of lung cancer patients already harboring metastases at the time of diagnosis. Surgical interventions offer limited curative potential, and traditional therapeutic approaches frequently falter in the face of the complex, multifaceted nature of metastatic cancer [1].

The limitation of conventional treatments lies in their inability to effectively target metastatic sites, leaving them largely impervious primarily. This incongruity has galvanized the quest for innovative approaches that transcend the constraints of established treatment modalities. Nanotechnology, with its ever-expanding capabilities in precision targeting, early detection, and intracellular drug delivery, stands as a beacon of hope in the relentless pursuit of effective metastatic cancer management [2].

While not without challenges, nanotechnology has found its place in clinical medicine. Notably, liposome-encapsulated doxorubicin has become a mainstay in the treatment of Karposi's sarcoma and ovarian cancer, benefiting more than 300,000 patients annually while mitigating cardiotoxicity. Protein nanoparticles (NPs) containing paclitaxcl have gained approval for metastatic breast cancer treatment, demonstrating enhanced drug uptake in tumor tissues. Iron oxide NPs, like ferumoxytol, originally designed for anemia caused by iron deficiency, have

Cancer Epigenetics and Nanomedicine. https://doi.org/10.1016/B978-0-443-13209-4.00013-1
Copyright © 2024 Elsevier Inc. All rights are reserved, including those for text and data mining, AI training, and similar technologies.

309

exhibited efficacy in early metastasis staging for prostate and testicular cancers. With more than 40 nanotherapeutics now in clinical practice, the future promises innovations, including heightened precision in attacking metastatic areas. Improved imaging methods have also enabled effective early detection [3].

This chapter seeks to provide a comprehensive exploration of the pivotal role of NPs in the treatment of metastatic cancer. It delves deeply into the intricate design principles governing NPs, their multifaceted mechanisms of action, and their transformative potential in oncology. Rooted in scientific rigor and clinical relevance, this examination strives to impart a profound understanding of how nanotechnology may reshape the landscape of metastatic cancer management, ultimately leading to improved patient outcomes. Through this meticulous analysis, we endeavor to illuminate the transformative capacity of NPs in the context of metastatic cancer, offering a ray of hope to those confronting the challenges of this formidable disease [4].

Understanding metastasis in cancer

Metastasis, a complex and critical facet of cancer progression, involves the spreading of cancer cells from the original tumor to produce secondary growths in different anatomical places. This process is characterized by a sequence of well-orchestrated events commencing with the invasion of cancer cells. These cells, equipped with enhanced migratory and invasive properties due to the epithelial-mesenchymal transition (EMT), can break away from the primary tumor. Subsequent intravasation involves their entry into blood or lymphatic vessels, followed by extravasation, during which they exit from these vessels at distant sites. Once established at these secondary sites, metastatic cells must create microenvironments conducive to their survival and uncontrolled proliferation. Understanding the complexities of metastasis is paramount for the development of effective interventions. It furnishes valuable insights into the vulnerabilities of metastatic cancer cells, potential therapeutic targets, and strategies to disrupt the metastatic process. Contemporary research has illuminated various aspects, including the pivotal role of the tumor microenvironment. The interactions between cancer cells and the host tissues are dynamic and multifaceted, playing a central role in the metastatic cascade. The intricate mechanisms driving metastasis include genetic and molecular underpinnings, and the tumor microenvironment acts as a dynamic stage where these events unfold. Fig. 1 represents how NPs could be directed to certain tissues, subcellular sections, or cancer cells in the bloodstream.

Traditionally, this metastatic cascade has been conceptualized as consisting of several sequential steps, each presenting unique physiological barriers that cancer cells must overcome to successfully metastasize [5–7]. These steps include:

- EMT and basement membrane breach: The cascade begins with EMT, a process in which cancer cells lose their epithelial characteristics and acquire mesenchymal traits. This transformation enables these cells to breach the primary tumor's basement membrane.

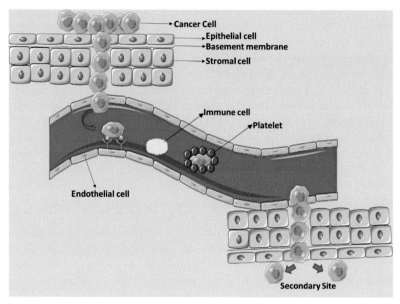

FIG. 1

The stages of metastasis and therapy strategies.

- Dissociation of tumor cells: Following EMT, cancer cells detach from the bulk of the primary tumor.
- Invasion of neighboring tissues: The detached tumor cells invade neighboring tissues, effectively infiltrating healthy tissue structures.
- Intravasation: Some tumor cells successfully enter preexisting blood or lymph vessels, positioning themselves for transport to distant sites.
- Transport through vessels: These circulating tumor cells navigate the bloodstream or lymphatic system, potentially traveling over considerable distances.
- Extravasation: Upon reaching secondary sites, tumor cells exit the blood or lymphatic vessels, marking a crucial step in establishing secondary tumors.
- Establishment of disseminated cells: The disseminated cancer cells can establish themselves in secondary anatomical sites, where they may be in a dormant state for extended periods.
- The outgrowth of metastases: Dormant cells may eventually reawaken, proliferate, and give rise to micrometastases and macrometastases, or secondary tumors.

It's essential to recognize that each step of this cascade presents specific challenges and barriers that cancer cells must overcome to continue their journey. Successfully metastasizing tumor cells need to navigate a complex series of obstacles and micro-environments [8,9].

Recent research has introduced an intriguing addition to the metastatic cascade, denoted as step "0." This novel step involves the creation of a premetastatic niche at the target site even before the arrival of the tumor cells. This niche is conducive to establishing secondary tumors and may significantly affect the metastatic process. Studies have demonstrated that the presence of a distant tumor can mobilize bone marrow-derived cells, leading to their accumulation in the lungs. These cells subsequently alter the local microenvironment, preparing it for the arrival of tumor cells. The precise timing of premetastatic niche formation remains a topic of investigation [10].

Intriguingly, inflammation and chemokines have been identified as factors that attract tumor cells to the lungs. The presence of distant tumors induces increased levels of proinflammatory chemokines in the tumor-bearing mice's lungs. These chemokines, such as S100A8 and S100A9, attract tumor cells to the lungs through a serum amyloid toll-like receptor (TLR4)-mediated positive feedback loop. While these findings hold promise, their translation to human cancer progression remains a subject of ongoing research. Nevertheless, they open possibilities for therapeutic interventions to disrupt the signaling networks essential for premetastatic niche formation, potentially preventing the establishment and outgrowth of distant metastases. Metastasis involves a range of biological complexities, including breaching the basement membrane, resisting anoikis (cell death resulting from a loss of cell adhesion), orchestrating intravasation and extravasation, and promoting angiogenesis. These processes are driven by the intricate molecular and cellular mechanisms that govern tumor cell migration, the role of proteases in remodeling the extracellular matrix, and the involvement of immune cells and macrophages in guiding tumor cells to blood vessels [11].

Understanding metastasis remains a scientific challenge, as the progression model, which suggests genetic instability leads to the generation of diverse cellular clones and subsequent selection of the fittest population, must fully account for clinical and experimental observations. Additionally, the exact source of selection pressure for metastasis within the primary tumor is unclear. Metastasis is an exceptionally complex process with intricate molecular and cellular mechanisms that continue to be the focus of extensive research and exploration. Gaining a comprehensive understanding of these mechanisms is crucial for developing effective strategies to combat cancer metastasis [12,13].

NPs for drug delivery

Nanotechnology has brought about a transformative paradigm shift in drug delivery. Its applications encompass the site-specific and temporally controlled administration of a broad spectrum of therapeutic agents, ranging from conventional small molecules to more intricate compounds such as peptides, proteins, and nucleic acids like DNA and RNA. This field has garnered substantial attention and research endeavors in recent years, owing to its immense potential in advancing drug delivery strategies to new horizons [14].

Fundamentals and rationale for using NPs in cancer treatment

Pharmaceutical nanotechnology primarily revolves around developing therapeutic substances in biocompatible nanostructures, including conjugates, micellar systems, NPs, and nanocapsules. These nanoscale drug delivery systems offer multiple advantages, with a primary focus on enhancing the safety and efficacy of medications. Notably, they can significantly boost drug bioavailability, extend the duration of drug activity within the target tissue, and enhance the stability of therapeutic agents, making them more resilient to enzymatic or chemical degradation. Furthermore, these nanostructures empower precise drug delivery to specific sites, thereby minimizing the risk of off-target effects. These remarkable benefits are a direct consequence of the minute scale of these drug delivery systems. NPs, typically ranging in size from 10 to 1000 nm, can be produced through a variety of techniques, allowing drugs to be encapsulated, entrapped, or bonded to a NP matrix. Within this category, nanospheres involve the uniform dispersion of the drug within a spherical matrix. At the same time, nanocapsules feature a cavity that confines the drug and is enveloped by a boundary structure, often constructed from polymers. Additionally, a diverse range of nanomaterials has been explored for their potential in drug delivery, encompassing magnetic NPs, inorganic NPs, dendrimers, ferrofluids, nanostructured lipid carriers, quantum dots, solid lipid NPs, biodegradable polymeric micelles, nanoliposomes, polymeric NPs, and lipid-drug conjugates [15–17].

Nanochemistry plays a crucial role in the pharmaceutical domain, profoundly influencing the pharmacokinetics and the absorption, distribution, metabolism, and excretion (or ADME) processes of therapeutic agents. A standout feature of nanotechnology is targeted drug delivery, which holds transformative potential, particularly in cancer treatment. By precisely targeting specific organs or body parts, it becomes possible to minimize the impact of drugs on nontargeted areas, thereby reducing the incidence of side effects and the required drug dosage.

Furthermore, various types of nanodrug delivery vehicles have been engineered to enhance drug permeability through formidable barriers within the human body, including the notoriously impermeable blood-brain barrier (BBB). These nano drug carriers also enhance drug solubility in diverse biological and nonbiological media. In the evolving domain of gene therapy, nanocarriers have emerged as a significant breakthrough, offering ideal platforms for the delivering of genetic materials, enzymes, drugs, nucleotides, and more. These nanostructures can directly transport these agents to the cell nucleus or even specific organelles within the cell. Additionally, magnetic nanomaterials have witnessed recent developments, enabling controlled NPs with trackable movements from external sources and facilitating new possibilities in diagnostics and drug delivery [18–20].

In summary, the field of NPs holds immense potential to revolutionize the medical and pharmaceutical sectors. It is poised to shape the future of drug delivery and related therapeutic approaches, offering a promising pathway toward safer, more effective, and precisely targeted treatments. As research continues to advance, the marriage of nanotechnology with pharmaceutical science opens up new vistas treating a myriad of diseases, especially those that have hitherto posed substantial challenges. The development of tailored drug delivery systems on a nanoscale is poised to redefine the landscape of medicine and usher in a new era of precision and efficacy [21,22].

Applications of NPs for drug deliverance

Nanoscale delivery vehicles have emerged as powerful tools to target various biological mechanisms and combat the disease in cancer treatment. These versatile carriers are sourced from diverse origins, including biological, organic, and inorganic materials, offering distinct advantages and applications. Predominantly, lipid-based and polymeric materials have taken the forefront due to their adaptability for incorporating targeting moieties, controlled degradation under certain conditions, and the ability to efficiently transport a wide range of therapeutic agents. However, the landscape of nanomaterials for cancer therapy has expanded significantly, presenting an exciting yet challenging array of options for researchers and engineers [23,24].

Polymeric materials, a major category of drug carriers, exhibit notable diversity. Within this category, core-shell particles are utilized, wherein a surrounding material encapsulates the drug payload through noncovalent interactions. An exemplary case is using poly(lactic-co-glycolic acid) (PLGA) NPs constructed from FDA-approved materials to transport hydrophobic drugs. Polymeric micelles, formed by block copolymers, spontaneously encapsulate hydrophobic drugs effectively. Further innovation has led to polymeric NPs with precisely controlled sizes and shapes, enabling cell attachment and facilitating the externalization of drug payloads, effectively turning cells into "backpacks" for drug transport. Notably, long-circulating polymers have shown promise in targeting circulating tumor cells, providing an innovative approach to combat metastatic cancer [25].

Hydrogel NPs, or nanogels, are hydrophilic polymer networks that undergo expansion upon exposure to water in aqueous environments. These nanogels are highly customizable, allowing for the covalent or noncovalent binding of drugs and targeting ligands. Their responsiveness to external factors like pH and temperature makes them an attractive option for controlled drug release. Lipid-based carriers are versatile platforms for precise drug delivery, including liposomes, micelles, and lipoplexes. These carriers can be tailored to transport both water-soluble and insoluble therapeutics. For instance, by combining liposomes with specific targeting ligands, for example, integrin-binding peptides, they may get collected in tumor vasculature through angiogenesis, enabling the efficient delivery of therapeutic payloads. The development of pH and temperature-sensitive formulations offers fine-tuned control over drug release, enhancing the precision of cancer treatment [26].

Gold NPs have emerged as valuable tools in thermoablative therapies. These NPs react to near-IR light by emitting heat energy, inducing the coagulation of tumor vasculature. This property can enhance the therapeutic efficacy of different therapies when used cooperatively. Moreover, gold NPs can serve as scaffolds for attaching multiple ligands, expanding their potential applications in metastatic cancer treatment. Additionally, different nanomaterial types, including Fe-NPs and carbon nanotubes (CNTs) or spherical NPs, are being explored for drug delivery purposes. Their specific characteristics determine whether drugs are bound to their outer surfaces or encapsulated within their interiors, making them versatile tools in the fight against metastatic cancer. The diverse array of nanocarriers reflects ongoing innovation in the field, offering tailored solutions to address the multifaceted challenges of metastatic cancer treatment [27,28].

NPs with intrinsic anticancer properties are opening new avenues in the field of cancer therapy. Among these innovations, a particularly remarkable one involves a bioinorganic NP constructed from a polyelectrolyte albumin complex and MnO_2. These NPs are an ingenious method for generating oxygen within the hypoxic tumor microenvironment. They accomplish this feat by reacting with hydrogen peroxide (H_2O_2), a substance produced by cancer cells in low-oxygen conditions. The result is a significant increase in the tumor's pH, shifting it from 6.7 to 7.2. When these NPs are combined with ionizing radiation, the synergy yields remarkable outcomes. It significantly inhibits the growth of breast tumors, induces a higher frequency of DNA double-strand ruptures, and promotes increased death of tumor cells in comparison to simple radiation therapy. Furthermore, serum protein-coated gold nanorods have demonstrated their potential to block the migratory movement and invasion of breast cancer cells both in laboratory and live subjects. In-depth analyses, including quantitative proteomics and real-time PCR arrays, have unveiled the underlying mechanism behind this inhibition. The gold nanorods achieve this by effectively down-regulating the expression of various genes related to energy generation [29,30].

In the realm of antimetastasis properties, a noteworthy NP containing Gd (gadolinium) has emerged. These metallofullerenol NPs exhibit the capacity to hinder the production of matrix metalloproteinase (MMP) enzymes, effectively interfering with the invasive behavior of cancer cells in laboratory settings. What's particularly intriguing is the observation that these NPs, when applied to primary invasive tumors in animal models, lead to significantly fewer metastases at ectopic sites while concurrently reducing the expression of MMPs. The creation of a fibrous cage-like structure is also noteworthy, as it potentially serves as a physical barrier that hampers the cancer cells and tumor-causing macrophages, which are the source of MMP enzymes. Importantly, these inherently active NPs circumvent the need for drug cargo, offering a potential solution to circumvent the systemic toxicity commonly associated with traditional drug therapies [31].

In the domain of breast cancer gene therapy, the application of small interfering RNA (siRNA) has shown immense promise. siRNA is a synthetic RNA duplex specifically designed to target and degrade mRNA within the cell's cytoplasm, offering therapeutic benefits. Overcoming the challenges of in vivo siRNA delivery, primarily related to its short circulation time and proneness to degradation, nanotechnology-mediated RNA interference has come to the forefront. Researchers have delved into various siRNA targets, including protease-activated receptor 1, surviving, and many more. These targets are pivotal in cancer metastasis, angiogenesis, proliferation, apoptosis, and other critical processes. To facilitate the effective delivery of siRNA molecules aimed at these specific targets, nonviral nanocarriers have been meticulously investigated. These carriers, including poly(amidoamine) dendrimers, β-cyclodextrin-based polymers, polyethyleneimine-polyethylene glycol (PEG) copolymers, gold NPs, and polysaccharide-based NPs, are characterized by their significant cationic charges, enabling effective interaction with RNA strands.

As a result, siRNA-loaded NPs are efficiently taken up by cells, leading to the successful downregulation of target genes. In murine tumor models, this innovative approach has demonstrated significant potential in inhibiting tumor growth, suppressing invasion and migration, and ultimately impeding breast cancer progression. This multipronged approach represents a promising frontier in the quest for highly effective anticancer therapeutics that harness the unique capabilities of nanomaterials [32–34].

Targeted drug delivery methodologies

Targeted drug delivery is a critical facet of contemporary pharmaceuticals, seeking to administer medications with precision to their intended locations in the body, thereby enhancing their effectiveness while minimizing potential side effects. In the past, direct techniques like injections, catheters, and gene guns were employed for specific drug delivery. While these methods provide accuracy, they often necessitate invasive procedures, proving inconvenient for patients and financially burdensome to administer [35].

To address these limitations, researchers have devoted their efforts to the formation of targeted drug delivery systems (TDDS). These systems utilize biological, chemical, and physical modifications, sometimes with the inclusion of carriers, to enhance drug targeting. Several approaches have been explored to improve drug precision [36].

One approach involves studying the structure-activity relationships of drugs to optimize their characteristics. For instance, drugs with small molecule structures designed for brain delivery can be chemically modified to enhance their abilities to get across the BBB, especially if they are small. Prodrugs represent another avenue, where compounds are rendered pharmacologically inactive and become active drugs only after reaching their target site, thus improving the pharmacokinetics of the drug. Conjugating drugs with ligands such as antibodies, peptides, aptamers, or folic acid is another strategy. These ligands facilitate targeted drug delivery to specific cells or tissues, increasing precision [37].

Nanocarriers and nanosystems have emerged as highly efficient drug delivery platforms. These systems encompass a variety of carriers, including nanogels, liposomes, polymer-drug conjugates, polymeric micelles, polymeric NPs, and CNTs. A significant advantage of such structures is that the pharmacokinetics of drug-packed nanocarriers depend mainly on the nanosystems themselves, providing a means of control and further targeting.

This drug delivery approach operates based on two primary modes of targeting: passive and active targeting. Passive targeting exploits the physiological characteristics of the target site. For instance, nanocarriers are designed to leverage the enhanced permeability and retention (EPR) effect commonly observed in tumor tissues. This phenomenon results from the faulty vasculature and weak drainage system of lymph in tumors, enabling drug-loaded nanocarriers to accumulate selectively at these sites. Active targeting, on the contrary, involves the modification of drug carriers with specific ligands or molecules that bind to receptors or antigens found at the target site. This approach allows for precise and active drug delivery to specific cells or tissues, ultimately enhancing the therapeutic outcome [38,39].

The formation of TDDS has transformed drug therapy. Researchers are continuously exploring innovative strategies to enhance drug targeting, including chemical modifications, prodrugs, and the utilization of nanosystems. These advancements have paved the way for both passive and active targeting, offering a more precise and effective drug delivery.

Passive targeting: EPR effect (enhanced permeability and retention)

Passive targeting is a fundamental principle present in the human body, where natural substances like neurotransmitters, hormones, and growth factors have an inherent tendency to target specific receptors at their intended sites of action. This concept can be extended to drug delivery, where the accumulation of drugs or drug-carrier structures at their desired sites is achieved passively through physicochemical and physiological factors.

In various disease conditions, specific tissues undergo physiological modifications that could be leveraged for passive targeting using nanocarriers. For instance, leaking vasculature having significant gaps in blood vessel epithelial layers allows appropriately sized nanocarriers to passively target and extravasate into the target tissue in cases of inflammation, as seen in conditions such as inflammatory bowel disease, tumor tissues, and inflammatory rheumatoid arthritis. The treatment of inflammatory illnesses can benefit from passive targeting, even in tumor areas with inadequate lymphatic outflow. Targeting liver illnesses is made possible by the accumulation of nanocarriers in the liver caused by extensive fenestrations. The EPR effect is the name given to this phenomenon of nanocarrier accumulation in sick tissues due to leaky fenestrations and poorly organized lymphatic drainage [40].

Mononuclear phagocytes and macrophages comprise the reticuloendothelial system (RES), which performs a significant part in the destiny of nanocarriers. With this information, illnesses affecting the RES, such as leishmaniasis and malaria, can be treated by passively targeting macrophages, lymph nodes, and the spleen. Modifications like PEG attachment to nanocarriers are used to improve passive targeting. This makes the nanocarriers long-circulating and evades the RES, allowing them to accumulate in large amounts at target areas [41,42].

Additionally, intrinsic triggers seen in diseased tissues—such as redox systems and pH variations, such as the low pH in the tumor microenvironment—benefit passive targeting (using high glutathione levels in cancer). Medicine targeting systems that are sensitive to stimuli are engineered to react to said stimuli by releasing the medicine only at the designated target site, thereby protecting surrounding healthy tissues. Stimuli-responsive devices have been the subject of extensive research and offer intriguing opportunities to improve medicine delivery precision while minimizing negative effects [43,44].

The EPR effect initially discovered about three decades ago, has become a subject of extensive research and application in drug delivery systems, especially for cancer therapy. It involves the selective accumulation of macromolecules and colloidal drug carriers near tumor sites. However, recent studies have uncovered the intricate and multifaceted nature of the EPR effect, demonstrating its crucial role in enhancing the effectiveness of cancer treatments [45].

Traditionally, tumor growth follows a pattern where solid masses form due to cell proliferation. The inside cells of tumors experience nutrition shortage as they enlarge, which causes cell death and the release of growth factors that cause the tumor's blood arteries to sprout. Notably, these newly formed blood vessels within tumor tissues often lack a basal membrane, creating fenestrations ranging from 200 to 2000 nm. These gaps allow for the extravasation of macromolecules, including drug-loaded carriers, into the tumor microenvironment. This aspect of the EPR effect is primarily associated with enhanced permeation. Simultaneously, tumors exhibit irregular lymphatic drainage patterns and face substantial physical stress due to their rapid expansion. This compromised drainage and increased pressure play a role in retaining macromolecules within the tumor tissue, contributing to the retaining component of the EPR effect [46,47].

The EPR effect is driven by a sequence of events involving the extravasation of macromolecules via the blood vessels, following their movement within the tumor microenvironment through mechanisms like diffusion and convection. Several factors influence the EPR effect. These include the architecture of the vasculature within the tumor, the composition of the interstitial fluid, the nature of the extracellular matrix, the presence of phagocytes, the existence of necrotic regions within the tumor, and characteristics of colloidal drug carriers. Such carrier-related characteristics encompass particle shape, surface charge, blood circulation time, particle size, and any surface modifications like the bonding of PEG to enable stealth characteristics for evading the RES [48,49].

The EPR effect is a dynamic interplay of complex physiological and biochemical processes that influence the accumulation and distribution of drug carriers within tumor tissues. Understanding and harnessing the EPR effect has become pivotal in the design of targeted drug deliverance systems, with the ultimate goal of improving the efficacy of cancer therapeutics.

Active targeting

In drug delivery it relates to the binding of specialized marker components to colloid carrier systems, allowing them to be selectively recognized by the intended target, whether it's an organelle or an organ. This targeting involves molecular targets, such as surface receptors overexpressed on tumor cells, and employs various ligands, including dietary ligands (e.g., carbohydrates, folate), monoclonal antibodies, non-antibody ligands (peptidic ligands), and more.

In accordance with the degree of penetration, it can be divided into three levels: organ, cellular, and subcellular. But the fundamental feature of a targeting ligand is its precision which must be steady in physiological settings regardless of the target site. Additionally, the binding affinity of these targeting ligands is crucial and must remain unchanged. In some cases, powerful binding affinities are necessary for effective targeting, particularly assuming colloidal carrier mobility in physiological circumstances [50].

Even though passive targeting has produced notable outcomes, active targeting techniques have been the subject of much research due to the desire for more control over precise drug delivery. Drugs or drug carriers can be made more selective toward specific receptors or markers on cells, tissues, or organs by modifying and functionalizing them. The disease's etiology, the target organ, and the existence of targetable components impact the targeting moiety selection. The usage of ligands like sugars, lectins, peptides, antibodies, and more may be necessary for these alterations. This tactic prevents nonspecific accumulations and associated adverse effects, and the medication or drug carriers are guaranteed to effectively reach their targeted sites of action [51].

Nanocarriers can be exposed to external stimuli, including magnetic fields and ultrasound, to facilitate drug release, imaging, and targeting of the desired point of action. The advantages of this active targeting strategy include simultaneous imaging and therapy, the capacity to target deep-seated tissues, real-time targeting, and the ability to integrate several external stimuli for improved efficiency and targeting [52].

Magnetic nanoparticles (MNP) have been extensively researched for applications such as hyperthermia, magnetic drug targeting, and imaging therapy. Superparamagnetic iron oxide nanoparticles (SPIONs) are a common choice for biomedical applications due to their nontoxic nature and the ability to be functionalized with different targeting coatings. Optimization of both the MNP and the external magnet is essential to ensure that MNP can overcome blood flow and reach the target area [53].

Drug delivery via ultrasound has been investigated in great detail and has been used for contrast imaging. Drug-loaded carriers may be disrupted by ultrasound-mediated targeting, resulting in drug release. Additionally, it can perforate intravascular endothelium layers, which opens up the target tissue's extracellular space to drug entry. Temperature-sensitive nanocarriers and ultrasound can be used to create targeted hyperthermia, which increases the cytotoxic effect on tumor cells. Applications for this method include thrombosis, cardiovascular disorders, tumor treatment, and imaging of tumors. It provides the ability to image and initiate medication release simultaneously, and for even greater advantages, it can be coupled with magnetic field applications.

A range of physical techniques has been investigated in order to maximize the capacity for localizing anticancer drugs, specifically near tumor sites. These physical indicators for drug targeting may be either endogenous, originating from within the body, or exogenous, involving external forces and technologies. The tumor microenvironment offers intrinsic cues that can be leveraged for physical drug targeting. Notably, this microenvironment tends to be slightly acidic and may exhibit mild hyperthermia, offering unique endogenous stimuli. Drug localization at the tumor sight is significantly enhanced by utilizing external forces, such as magnets or ultrasound energy.

These approaches have demonstrated distinct advantages in drug delivery. For example, they have led to higher tumor levels of drugs, like doxorubicin, delivered through polymeric micelles when compared to the drug-free counterpart. The primary goal of these physical targeting strategies is to selectively and precisely manipulate drug carriers and their payloads. These methods use both endogenous and exogenous stimuli to maximize drug delivery to tumor sites while minimizing exposure to normal tissues. This innovative approach holds great promise in the field of drug delivery for cancer treatment and other diseases, offering the potential for more effective and targeted therapies [54,55].

Intracellular/intramolecular targeted therapies

Chronic tissue damage and cellular dysregulation can have far-reaching consequences on the intricate signaling systems governing the cell cycle, eventually giving rise to cancer. Recognizing how certain molecules or even specific molecular sites can serve incredibly varied roles in both healthy and cancerous cells adds a layer of complexity and intrigue to the field of cancer research. To address these complexities and challenges, molecular targeted therapies have emerged as a promising approach to combat the aberrant cell cycle and molecular pathways associated with cancer [56].

The cell cycle, a fundamental process in cellular biology, consists of four distinct phases: G1, S, G2, and M. During the G1 phase, cells make critical decisions regarding whether to advance to the S phase, undergo programmed cell death (apoptosis), or enter a quiescent state (G0). The S phase is characterized by DNA synthesis, a pivotal step followed by the G2 phase, preparing the cell for the M phase, during which cell division occurs. The precise orchestration of these phases is maintained via the regulation of a family of proteins abbreviated as CDKs (cyclin-dependent kinases) [57].

CDKs play a crucial role in governing the cell cycle, and various checkpoints ensure the accuracy and integrity of these processes. These checkpoints cover essential aspects such as detecting DNA damage, monitoring events preceding cell division (antephase), and overseeing spindle assembly, which is essential for proper chromosome segregation. Dysfunction in any of these regulatory mechanisms can result in abnormal cell proliferation and, in many cases, tumorigenesis [58,59].

Tumorigenesis is a multifaceted process characterized by complex conditions where genetic aberrations and cell cycle dysregulation contribute significantly to cancer development. In addition to the reduction of genes that suppress tumors like TP53, BRCA1, and BRCA2, deviations in the cell cycle abnormalities play a similarly crucial role in tumor growth. Multiple mediators, including events like telomere issues, bridge the gap between cell cycle dysregulation and genetic instability. Moreover, the reduction of the retinoblastoma tumor suppressor protein (pRb2) is a defining feature of tumor cells, enabling them to bypass the S-phase checkpoint. This phenomenon is associated with the CDK/p16INK4A/pRb pathway.

Another crucial cell cycle surveillance pathway is the p53/HDM2/p14ARF pathway, which responds to various stressful signals like hypoxia and DNA damage. Within this pathway, the E3 ubiquitin ligase plays a pivotal role in the ubiquitylation and proteasomal degradation of p53, which subsequently leads to significant transcriptional changes and the establishment of negative feedback loops. Inhibiting CDKs is a significant focus within the molecular targeted therapies. Strategic CDK inhibitors could be made to compete by attaching to ATP binding regions or increasing natural CDK inhibitors. Despite the many cyclins recognized so far, cyclin D and E frequently emerge as overexpressed factors in a wide range of malignancies [60–63].

Molecular targeted therapies represent a nuanced approach to cancer treatment, categorized into three generations of agents. The first generation of therapies primarily impacts cancer cells by inducing DNA damage or interfering with DNA synthesis. These agents may target tubulins, affecting processes like microtubule assembly. However, the first-generation drugs can pose challenges, such as the risk of secondary cancers in patients who have survived childhood cancers or testicular carcinomas, as well as harming instantly replicating typical cells, including follicles for hair, hematopoietic cells, and gastrointestinal tract lining. Additionally, they may harm postmitotic components like peripheral nervous systems and cardiac muscles.

Some of the side effects of traditional chemotherapy are intended to be addressed by the second generation of molecularly targeted anticancer therapies. Oncogene addiction, which encompasses both direct and indirect gene changes, is the focus of this generation. These changes may be caused by mutations that result in function loss or gain, gene amplification, or overexpression of oncogenes that include p53, Rb, and MYC. According to the current study, around 20% of kinases possess a key role in tumor development. This insight sparked the creation of several targeted medications, including Gleevac (imatinib), a potent tyrosine kinase inhibitor approved for the therapy of chronic myeloid leukemia.

Many pharmaceutical compounds have since been approved, such as ruxolitinib (Janus kinases); tivatinib (hepatocyte growth factor receptor); vemurafenib (B-Raf); gefitinib (epidermal growth factor receptor); lapatinib (HER2 and epidermal growth factor receptor); vismodegib (Hedgehog signaling pathway); and sorafenib, sunitinib, and pazopanib (targeting multiple tyrosine kinases). Another class of medicines in this second generation is monoclonal antibodies, which will be covered in greater detail later in this chapter. Other drugs in this class target mTOR and checkpoint kinases, two nononcogene addiction pathways.

Over time, resistance may arise even though these medicines primarily target oncoprotein vulnerabilities and are more unlikely to cause toxicity in normal cells. The third generation of targeted therapies represents an evolving frontier characterized by agents that alter processes within cells relevant to cancer progression, including chromatin variations, protein chaperones, and proteasome blockers. This generation holds the potential to minimize side effects while maximizing effectiveness in cancer treatment [64–68].

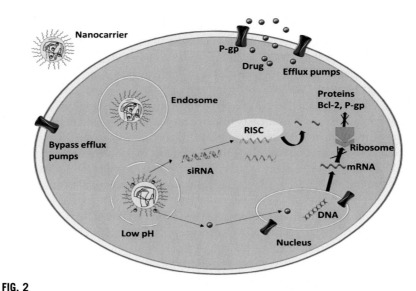

FIG. 2

A schematic depiction of the pathways linked to multidrug resistance and siRNA interference.

Hence, molecular-targeted therapies offer a highly specific approach to treating cancer, focusing on the molecular mechanisms underlying tumor growth. By disrupting the proliferation and survival of cancer cells while sparing normal cells, these therapies promise more precise and less harmful cancer therapies. However, the intricate nature of cancer and the development of drug resistance pose ongoing challenges and opportunities in this field. As our understanding of cancer biology deepens, so does the potential for innovative targeted therapies to improve patient outcomes. Multidrug resistance is caused by cancer cells modified genetically in order to expel anticancer drugs, which are then recycled and enter the circulation, as seen in Fig. 2.

Applications in metastatic cancer treatment

Efforts to target NPs to sites of metastasis involve two steps: primary and secondary targeting. Primary targeting entails guiding NPs to specific organs where metastases reside, while secondary targeting directs these NPs to cancerous cells along with particular subcellular sites inside those cells. Primary targeting factors include surface charge, mechanical properties, particle size, chemistry, and the route of administration, all of which significantly influence NP localization. For example, particle size determines whether particles can exit or enter fenestrated vessels in the liver endothelium or the tumor microenvironment [69].

Primary targeting is a critical step in the deployment of NPs for the treatment of metastatic cancer. It involves a complex interplay of factors that significantly

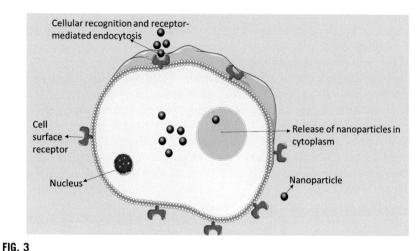

FIG. 3

Systematic representation of active cellular targeting.

influence the precise localization of these NPs. Several key considerations in primary targeting include particle size, surface charge, mechanical properties, chemical composition, and the chosen route of administration. Each of these parameters is critical in evaluating the efficacy of primary targeting and the subsequent success of NP-based therapies [70]. Fig. 3 represents the other aspects that are crucial to the NP's performance including the mode of administration, physicochemical characteristics such as ligand density, and NP size.

Particle size is a fundamental determinant in NP behavior. In the context of metastatic cancer, the size of NPs profoundly impacts their ability to navigate through the intricate network of blood vessels and tissues. Larger NPs may encounter challenges in exiting or entering specific anatomical structures, such as the liver endothelium or the tumor microenvironment. Understanding the optimal size range for effective targeting is essential for successfully applying NP therapeutics. Surface charge is another critical consideration in primary targeting. The electrical charge of NPs influences their interactions with biological environments. Depending on their charge, NPs can either facilitate or impede their journey to target organs, with important implications for biodistribution [71].

Material composition is an inherent feature of NPs that significantly dictates their fate within the body. Certain types of NPs, including lipid complexes, tend to collect preferentially in specific organs, such as the liver, impacting their distribution to other critical sites. As a result, careful consideration of material composition is essential in primary targeting strategies. The mechanical properties and chemical characteristics of NPs, including their rigidity, flexibility, and chemical makeup, are also important factors in determining their ability to navigate biological barriers and reach their intended destinations. These properties can significantly impact the success of primary targeting strategies, necessitating tailored approaches. The chosen route of administration is a critical decision in primary targeting. The selected route, whether intravenous, intraperitoneal, or another method, profoundly affects NP biodistribution and its ultimate localization. Selecting the most appropriate route is crucial in optimizing primary targeting [72,73].

When considering metastatic cancer treatment, a focus on life-threatening metastases that frequently affect organs like the lymph nodes, brain, bone, liver, and lungs becomes paramount. Targeting these challenging sites requires innovative strategies that overcome substantial barriers to effective primary targeting.

The brain poses particular difficulties due to the presence of the BBB, which is frequently cited as the organ that is hardest to target with intravenously administered NPs. Only particular materials are allowed to pass through this barrier, which is made up of tightly bound endothelial cells, through blood circulation entering the cerebrospinal fluid. On the other hand, disorders affecting the central nervous system, such as metastases and brain tumors, can compromise the functionality of the BBB, changing its permeability and permitting therapeutic access. Studies show that the most efficient way for NPs to pass the BBB is if they are smaller than 15 nm.

Nonetheless, particles with a diameter of 15–100 nm have the potential to enter the brain, though their effectiveness decreases with increasing size. It has been demonstrated that adding lipophilic moieties and decreasing surface charge to NPs improves their ability to pass through the BBB. This is especially true for NPs that are decorated with apolipoprotein E (ApoE), which opens up a possible treatment option for brain metastases [74–76].

To enhance the uptake of NPs into the brain parenchyma, novel approaches like conjugating monoclonal antibodies to NPs have been investigated, apart from alterations in size and surface. This method takes advantage of these antibodies' particular binding to BBB receptors, which increases their capacity to enter the brain. It has also been demonstrated that circulating cells can take up NPs and transport them to the brain. Leukocytes and macrophages, for example, have the ability to phagocytose sugar-coated NPs and are found to congregate near regions of BBB deterioration associated with the disease. These cells have the ability to enter the brain and release NPs where they are most needed. This approach makes use of cells' capacity to penetrate biological membranes, enter deep tissues, and settle on disease sites, which renders them desirable carriers [77,78].

Another problem that arises when NPs enter their intended organs is directing them toward cancerous cells within the intricate tissue microenvironment. To solve this problem, several approaches have been developed, each with unique benefits and drawbacks. One method uses external driving forces to assemble iron oxide NPs or uses acoustical waves to cause the localization of microbubbles. An additional novel strategy using an activated nanosignaling framework, whereby a single target nanomaterial initiates a biological cascade locally, attracting additional therapeutic NPs to the site of disease. Amplifying a local signal has great potential for accurately identifying and managing metastatic lesions [27].

Furthermore, researchers have developed self-propelled NPs capable of autonomous navigation, which may prove instrumental in directing NPs with unprecedented precision to specific subcellular locations within malignant cells or the intricate microenvironments associated with metastatic cancer. This autonomous navigation represents a highly promising avenue for enhancing primary targeting precision. In essence, primary targeting strategies in metastatic cancer treatment represent a multidimensional field of research and innovation, with each factor, whether particle size, surface charge, mechanical properties, chemical composition, or route of administration, playing a critical role in the successful deployment of NPs. Understanding the specific challenges posed by metastases in various organs and developing tailored approaches for primary targeting is pivotal to realizing NPs' potential in treating metastatic cancer [79].

One of the most important aspects of treating metastatic cancer is secondary targeting, which is precisely directing drugs or NPs toward particular cancer cells, either within noncancerous cell populations or in transit from the primary tumor. To achieve precise targeting, NPs must possess a certain degree of chemical specificity that allows them to attach to distinct molecular signatures that are displayed by cancerous cells. These cells frequently display unique cell-surface components and secretion factors and can additionally produce proteins that are generally linked to the embryo's development. Additionally, metastatic cells retain surface proteins from their original location, differentiating them from cells at the implantation site. These unique characteristics serve as handles for investigators to target cancer cells effectively and minimize potential side effects associated with targeting noncancerous cell types [80,81].

Strategies for secondary targeting differ from those employed in primary targeting, necessitating consideration of binding affinity, specificity, and immunological effects. Conjugated antibodies, whether carrying drugs, polymers, or radioisotopes, have found clinical applications in cancer targeting. For example, tositumomab is a combination therapy that targets follicular B-cell lymphoma using a radiolabeled CD20-specific antibody. Targeting ligands based on antibodies has also been applied to a variety of nanodelivery systems. Similarly, short peptides have been added to NPs to improve their ability to attach to certain kinds of cells within tissues. These peptides contain integrin-binding domains, such as arginine-glycine-aspartic acid (RGD) peptides and isoleucine-lysine-valine-alanine-valine (IKVAV) peptide sequence [82,83].

Modern strategies use high-throughput techniques to discover new targeted ligands including peptides, antibodies, and nucleic acid-based ligands like aptamers. These techniques include ribosome display, phage display, in vitro evolution, and in vitro screening. Aptamers, like pegaptanib, have been approved for noncancer treatments, but they are not yet approved for use as cancer therapies. Because of their strong affinity for complementary DNA strands, peptide nucleic acids (PNAs) can be modified covalently by targeting ligands and fluorophores, which enables them to bind to and suppress the expression of prometastatic genes [84].

The folate receptor, which is overexpressed in a number of cancers, is one example of a small-molecule-binding domain that has shown affinity for folic acid-coated NPs. Notably, substances like dextran that resemble the lipopolysaccharides found on the surface of bacteria can be used to target specific cells like macrophages, which actively phagocytose particles. However, since phagosomes and lysosomes frequently fuse, causing the contents to degrade, these strategies must also include mechanisms to regulate the uptake pathway.

It is possible to engineer the pathway by which NPs enter a cell to influence the cellular compartment where drugs are released. Tertiary targeting is a new field that will become important. For example, the well-known uptake pathway known as clathrin-dependent endocytosis frequently directs particles into the lysosomal pathway, where the contents are enzymatically degraded and sequestered. NPs can be tailored to evade lysosomes by eluding endosomes or entering the cell via nonlysosomal routes. A technique that has been suggested uses the proton sponge effect, in which cationic surface-grouping NPs cause osmotic lysis when endosomes are acidified. An additional route that circumvents lysosomes is caveolin-dependent endocytosis, which can be facilitated by albumin, cholesterol, or folic acid-coated NPs [85].

In essence, secondary targeting strategies in metastatic cancer treatment require a high degree of precision, involving the development of NPs or drugs that can selectively bind to cancer cells, avoiding noncancerous cells and minimizing potential side effects. These strategies harness the unique molecular characteristics of cancer cells to guide NPs or drugs to their intended destinations within the complex tumor microenvironment.

Nanotechnology has revolutionized the landscape of metastatic cancer treatment by emphasizing advanced imaging and diagnostics as crucial components. Nanoscale imaging agents, such as quantum dots, are particularly noteworthy due to their highly photostable and tunable properties, unlocking several possibilities in cancer diagnosis and treatment. In the realm of magnetic resonance imaging (MRI), SPIONs, primarily made of iron oxide, have emerged as superior alternatives to conventional gadolinium-based contrast agents. They offer higher contrast at lower concentrations, especially when coated with dextran or the RGD peptide. SPIONs are being extensively researched for their ability to detect nodal tumors and image integrin $\alpha V\beta 3$-positive tumor neovasculature. Moreover, innovative NP designs enhance the efficacy and pharmacokinetics of gadolinium-based contrast agents [86–88].

Contrast agents for computed tomography (CT) have historically been composed of tiny molecules with short half-lives in the human body. These agents' residence time is extended when encapsulated in NPs, which lowers the dosage needed and improves clinical flexibility. Furthermore, low-sensitivity methods such as single photon emission computed tomography (SPECT) are being optimized by NPs [89].

In the field of surgical resection, nanomaterials have been pivotal, aiding surgeons in identifying tumor margins, thus contributing to more precise and effective tumor removal. Moreover, nanomaterials have been instrumental in detecting cancer cells within the bloodstream and identifying unique regions within tumors. Quantum dots, for instance, have demonstrated their utility in tracking metastatic cells and distinguishing between heterogeneous tumor subpopulations in vivo [90].

The era of nanoscale sensors, which have enormous potential for early cancer detection, has also been ushered in by nanotechnology. These sensors' distinct electrical and optical characteristics enable sensitivity lower to the single-molecule levels. To measure specific reactive oxygen species (ROS) and the real-time concentrations of chemotherapy drugs, for instance, single-walled nanotubes of carbon are utilized with remarkable precision. By modifying surface electrons, localized surface plasmon resonance (LSPR) nanowires and NPs can identify proteins and cancer markers with remarkable sensitivity. To enable precise biomarker detection, new strategies employing NPs were created and designed to quench a fluorophore until a particular protein binds [91,92].

Conclusion and future perspectives

In summary, metastatic cancer remains a formidable clinical challenge, often regarded as incurable with existing therapeutic approaches. However, nanomaterials have emerged as a promising avenue to address this complex problem. While most nanotechnology-based cancer treatments have primarily focused on primary tumors, there is a growing recognition of the potential of nanotechnology to tackle each step of the metastatic process. Metastasis involves a series of intricate biological mechanisms, including tumor cell circulation, angiogenesis, extravasation, intravasation, and the establishment of secondary locations. NP therapies hold great potential for precisely targeting and intervening at these specific stages. The very factors that make an environment conducive to metastasis can serve as specific targets for tailored therapeutic interventions. Despite encouraging progress, there is an ongoing need for further research and development to refine NP targeting methods, especially for challenging sites like the bone, brain, and microenvironment of tumors. With our deepening understanding of cancer biology, interdisciplinary collaboration between clinicians, biologists, and engineers is becoming increasingly critical. These collaborations are instrumental in generating innovative ideas for diagnostics and treatments for metastatic cancer. The development of NP therapies that are finely tuned to address the specific needs of patients at different stages of metastasis can significantly enhance clinical outcomes.

Looking ahead, advancing NP-based strategies, perfecting their targeting mechanisms, and broadening their applications to various metastatic sites are of paramount importance. Additionally, integrating cutting-edge diagnostic tools and real-time monitoring techniques will empower us to detect and treat metastatic cancer at earlier and more manageable phases. As our knowledge of metastasis continues to expand, the synergistic relationship between research, technology, and clinical implementation offers the promise of more effective therapies and improved prognoses for patients facing the challenges of this disease. This ongoing journey represents a beacon of hope in the quest to combat metastatic cancer comprehensively and effectively.

Acknowledgments

The authors acknowledge ICT-IOC, Bhubaneswar, for providing necessary support. Rambabu Dandela thanks DST-SERB for Ramanujan Fellowship (SB/S2/RJN-075/2016), Core Research Grant (CRG/2018/000782), and ICT-IOC startup grant.

References

[1] A. Schroeder, D.A. Heller, M.M. Winslow, J.E. Dahlman, G.W. Pratt, R. Langer, T. Jacks, D.G. Anderson, Treating metastatic cancer with nanotechnology, Nat. Rev. Cancer 12 (1) (2011) 39–50.

[2] P.H. Lizotte, A.M. Wen, M.R. Sheen, J. Fields, P. Rojanasopondist, N.F. Steinmetz, S. Fiering, In situ vaccination with cowpea mosaic virus nanoparticles suppresses metastatic cancer, Nat. Nanotechnol. 11 (3) (2015) 295–303.

[3] D.S. Spencer, A.S. Puranik, N.A. Peppas, Intelligent nanoparticles for advanced drug delivery in cancer treatment, Curr. Opin. Chem. Eng. 7 (2015) 84–92.

[4] Q. Mu, H. Wang, M. Zhang, Nanoparticles for imaging and treatment of metastatic breast cancer, Expert Opin. Drug Deliv. 14 (1) (2017) 123–136.

[5] S. Turajlic, C. Swanton, Metastasis as an evolutionary process, Science 352 (6282) (2016) 169–175.

[6] G.P. Gupta, J. Massagué, Cancer metastasis: building a framework, Cell 127 (4) (2006) 679–695.

[7] C.L. Chaffer, R.A. Weinberg, A perspective on cancer cell metastasis, Science 331 (6024) (2011) 1559–1564.

[8] A. Mantovani, Inflaming metastasis, Nature 457 (7225) (2009) 36–37.

[9] E.C. Woodhouse, R.F. Chuaqui, Skeletal complications of malignancy mors-including breast, prostate, and lung-frequently metastasize, Cancer 80 (1997) 1529–1566.

[10] P.S. Steeg, Targeting metastasis, Nat. Rev. Cancer 16 (4) (2016) 201–218.

[11] K.W. Hunter, N.P.S. Crawford, J. Alsarraj, Mechanisms of metastasis, Breast Cancer Res. 10 (1) (2008) 1–10, https://doi.org/10.1186/bcr1988.

[12] T.R. Geiger, D.S. Peeper, Metastasis mechanisms, Biochim. Biophys. Acta Rev. Cancer 1796 (2) (2009) 293–308.

[13] S. Kraljevic Pavelic, M. Sedic, H. Bosnjak, S. Spaventi, K. Pavelic, Metastasis: new perspectives on an old problem, Mol. Cancer 10 (1) (2011) 1–14.

[14] J. Kreuter, Application of nanoparticles for the delivery of drugs to the brain, Int. Congr. Ser. 1277 (2005) 85–94.

[15] G. Han, P. Ghosh, V.M. Rotello, Multi-functional gold nanoparticles for drug delivery, Adv. Exp. Med. Biol. 620 (2007) 48–56.

[16] Y. Diebold, M. Calonge, Applications of nanoparticles in ophthalmology, Prog. Retin. Eye Res. 29 (6) (2010) 596–609.

[17] X. Wu, R.H. Guy, Applications of nanoparticles in topical drug delivery and in cosmetics, J. Drug Deliv. Sci. Technol. 19 (6) (2009) 371–384.

[18] W.H. De Jong, P.J.A. Borm, Drug delivery and nanoparticles: applications and hazards, Int. J. Nanomedicine 3 (2) (2008) 133–149.

[19] M. Namdeo, S. Saxena, R. Tankhiwale, M. Bajpai, Y.M. Mohan, S.K. Bajpai, Magnetic nanoparticles for drug delivery applications, J. Nanosci. Nanotechnol. 8 (7) (2008) 3247–3271.

[20] A. Baeza, D. Ruiz-Molina, M. Vallet-Regí, Recent advances in porous nanoparticles for drug delivery in antitumoral applications: inorganic nanoparticles and nanoscale metal-organic frameworks, Expert Opin. Drug Deliv. 14 (6) (2017) 783–796.

[21] S.A.A. Rizvi, A.M. Saleh, Applications of nanoparticle systems in drug delivery technology, Saudi Pharm. J. 26 (1) (2018) 64–70.

[22] Y. Malam, J. Lim, E., and M. Seifalian, A., Current trends in the application of nanoparticles in drug delivery, Curr. Med. Chem. 18 (7) (2011) 1067–1078.

[23] Y. Zhu, L. Liao, Applications of nanoparticles for anticancer drug delivery: a review, J. Nanosci. Nanotechnol. 15 (7) (2015) 4753–4773.

[24] W. Park, K. Na, Advances in the synthesis and application of nanoparticles for drug delivery, Wiley Interdiscip. Rev. Nanomed. Nanobiotechnol. 7 (4) (2015) 494–508.

[25] D.S. Kohane, Microparticles and nanoparticles for drug delivery, Biotechnol. Bioeng. 96 (2) (2007) 203–209.

[26] M. Hamidi, A. Azadi, P. Rafiei, Hydrogel nanoparticles in drug delivery, Adv. Drug Deliv. Rev. 60 (15) (2008) 1638–1649.

[27] B. Haley, E. Frenkel, Nanoparticles for drug delivery in cancer treatment, Urol. Oncol. Semin. Orig. Investig. 26 (1) (2008) 57–64.

[28] M. Arruebo, R. Fernández-Pacheco, M.R. Ibarra, J. Santamaría, Magnetic nanoparticles for drug delivery, Nano Today 2 (3) (2007) 22–32.

[29] S.J. Douglas, S.S. Davis, L. Illum, Nanoparticles in drug delivery, Crit. Rev. Ther. Drug Carrier Syst. 3 (3) (1987) 233–261.

[30] P. Couvreur, Nanoparticles in drug delivery: past, present and future, Adv. Drug Deliv. Rev. 65 (1) (2013) 21–23.

[31] M.J. Mitchell, M.M. Billingsley, R.M. Haley, M.E. Wechsler, N.A. Peppas, R. Langer, Engineering precision nanoparticles for drug delivery, Nat. Rev. Drug Discov. 20 (2) (2020) 101–124.

[32] J. Dobson, Magnetic nanoparticles for drug delivery, Drug Dev. Res. 67 (1) (2006) 55–60.

[33] K. Cho, X. Wang, S. Nie, Z. Chen, D.M. Shin, Therapeutic nanoparticles for drug delivery in cancer, Clin. Cancer Res. 14 (5) (2008) 1310–1316.

[34] A.Z. Wilczewska, K. Niemirowicz, K.H. Markiewicz, H. Car, Nanoparticles as drug delivery systems, Pharmacol. Rep. 64 (5) (2012) 1020–1037.

[35] S.P. Vyas, V. Sihorkar, V. Mishra, Controlled and targeted drug delivery strategies towards intraperiodontal pocket diseases, J. Clin. Pharm. Ther. 25 (1) (2000) 21–42.

[36] J. Bar, R.S. Herbst, A. Onn, Targeted drug delivery strategies to treat lung metastasis, Expert Opin. Drug Deliv. 6 (10) (2009) 1003–1016.

[37] Z. Wang, F. Meng, Z. Zhong, Emerging targeted drug delivery strategies toward ovarian cancer, Adv. Drug Deliv. Rev. 178 (2021) 113969.

[38] M.T. Manzari, Y. Shamay, H. Kiguchi, N. Rosen, M. Scaltriti, D.A. Heller, Targeted drug delivery strategies for precision medicines, Nat. Rev. Mater. 6 (4) (2021) 351–370.

[39] X. Wei, X. Chen, M. Ying, W. Lu, Brain tumor-targeted drug delivery strategies, Acta Pharm. Sin. B 4 (3) (2014) 193–201.

[40] J.R. Upponi, V.P. Torchilin, Passive vs. Active Targeting: An Update of the EPR Role in Drug Delivery to Tumors, Nano-Oncologicals: New Targeting and Delivery Approaches, Springer International Publishing, 2014, pp. 3–45.

[41] T. Tanaka, S. Shiramoto, M. Miyashita, Y. Fujishima, Y. Kaneo, Tumor targeting based on the effect of enhanced permeability and retention (EPR) and the mechanism of receptor-mediated endocytosis (RME), Int. J. Pharm. 277 (1–2) (2004) 39–61.

[42] H. Maeda, Enhanced permeability and retention (EPR) effect: basis for drug targeting to tumor, in: V. Muzykantov, V. Torchilin (Eds.), Biomedical Aspects of Drug Targeting, Springer, Boston, MA, 2002, pp. 211–228.

[43] E.A. Azzopardi, E.L. Ferguson, D.W. Thomas, The enhanced permeability retention effect: a new paradigm for drug targeting in infection, J. Antimicrob. Chemother. 68 (2) (2013) 257–274.

[44] H. Maeda, The enhanced permeability and retention (EPR) effect in tumor vasculature: the key role of tumor-selective macromolecular drug targeting, Adv. Enzym. Regul. 41 (1) (2001) 189–207.

[45] D. Kalyane, N. Raval, R. Maheshwari, V. Tambe, K. Kalia, R.K. Tekade, Employment of enhanced permeability and retention effect (EPR): nanoparticle-based precision tools for targeting of therapeutic and diagnostic agent in cancer, Mater. Sci. Eng. C 98 (2019) 1252–1276.

[46] J.M. Chan, P.M. Valencia, L. Zhang, O.C.F. Robert Langer, Polymeric nanoparticles for drug delivery Juliana, J. Cancer Sci. Ther. 4 (1) (2012) 163–175.

[47] V.R. Shinde, N. Revi, S. Murugappan, S.P. Singh, A.K. Rengan, Enhanced permeability and retention effect: a key facilitator for solid tumor targeting by nanoparticles, Photodiagn. Photodyn. Ther. 39 (2022) 102915.

[48] J. Wu, The enhanced permeability and retention (EPR) effect: the significance of the concept and methods to enhance its application, J. Pers. Med. 11 (8) (2021) 771.

[49] G. Onzi, S.S. Guterres, A.R. Pohlmann, L.A. Frank, Active targeting of nanocarriers, in: The ADME Encyclopedia: A Comprehensive Guide on Biopharmacy and Pharmacokinetics, Springer International Publishing, 2021, pp. 1–13.

[50] L. Basile, R. Pignatello, C. Passirani, Active targeting strategies for anticancer drug nanocarriers, Curr. Drug Deliv. 9 (3) (2012) 255–268.

[51] C.S. Kue, A. Kamkaew, K. Burgess, L.V. Kiew, L.Y. Chung, H.B. Lee, Small molecules for active targeting in cancer, Med. Res. Rev. 36 (3) (2016) 494–575.

[52] F. Salahpour Anarjan, Active targeting drug delivery nanocarriers: ligands, Nano-Struct. Nano-Objects 19 (2019) 100370.

[53] A. Béduneau, P. Saulnier, J.P. Benoit, Active targeting of brain tumors using nanocarriers, Biomaterials 28 (33) (2007) 4947–4967.

[54] J.D. Byrne, T. Betancourt, L. Brannon-Peppas, Active targeting schemes for nanoparticle systems in cancer therapeutics, Adv. Drug Deliv. Rev. 60 (15) (2008) 1615–1626.

[55] R. Bazak, M. Houri, S. El Achy, S. Kamel, T. Refaat, Cancer active targeting by nanoparticles: a comprehensive review of literature, J. Cancer Res. Clin. Oncol. 141 (5) (2015) 769–784.

[56] P. Zou, Y. Yu, Y.A. Wang, Y. Zhong, A. Welton, C. Galbán, S. Wang, D. Sun, Superparamagnetic iron oxide nanotheranostics for targeted cancer cell imaging and pH-dependent intracellular drug release, Mol. Pharm. 7 (6) (2010) 1974–1984.

[57] P. Verderio, P. Bonetti, M. Colombo, L. Pandolfi, D. Prosperi, Intracellular drug release from curcumin-loaded PLGA nanoparticles induces G2/M block in breast cancer cells, Biomacromolecules 14 (3) (2013) 672–682.

[58] A. Kopp, S. Hofsess, T.M. Cardillo, S.V. Govindan, J. Donnell, G.M. Thurber, Antibody-drug conjugate Sacituzumab Govitecan drives efficient tissue penetration and rapid intracellular drug release, Mol. Cancer Ther. 22 (1) (2023) 102–111.

[59] W. Wang, H. Sun, F. Meng, S. Ma, H. Liu, Z. Zhong, Precise control of intracellular drug release and anti-tumor activity of biodegradable micellar drugs via reduction-sensitive shell-shedding, Soft Matter 8 (14) (2012) 3949–3956.

[60] R.S. Navath, Y.E. Kurtoglu, B. Wang, S. Kannan, R. Romero, R.M. Kannan, Dendrimer-drug conjugates for tailored intracellular drug release based on glutathione levels, Bioconjug. Chem. 19 (12) (2008) 2446–2455.

[61] L. Liu, Y. Bi, M. Zhou, X. Chen, X. He, Y. Zhang, T. Sun, C. Ruan, Q. Chen, H. Wang, C. Jiang, Biomimetic human serum albumin nanoparticle for efficiently targeting therapy to metastatic breast cancers, ACS Appl. Mater. Interfaces 9 (8) (2017) 7424–7435.

[62] J. Choi, S. Kim, T. Tachikawa, M. Fujitsuka, T. Majima, PH-induced intramolecular folding dynamics of i-motif DNA, J. Am. Chem. Soc. 133 (40) (2011) 16146–16153.

[63] Y. Sheng, J. Hu, J. Shi, L.J. Lee, Stimuli-responsive carriers for controlled intracellular drug release, Curr. Med. Chem. 26 (13) (2019) 2377–2388.

[64] J. Huang, C. Zong, H. Shen, Y. Cao, B. Ren, Z. Zhang, Tracking the intracellular drug release from graphene oxide using surface-enhanced Raman spectroscopy, Nanoscale 5 (21) (2013) 10591–10598.

[65] P. Sun, D. Zhou, Z. Gan, Novel reduction-sensitive micelles for triggered intracellular drug release, J. Control. Release 155 (1) (2011) 96–103.

[66] H.Y. Min, H.Y. Lee, Molecular targeted therapy for anticancer treatment, Exp. Mol. Med. 54 (10) (2022) 1670–1694.

[67] H. Sun, F. Meng, R. Cheng, C. Deng, Z. Zhong, Reduction-responsive polymeric micelles and vesicles for triggered intracellular drug release, Antioxid. Redox Signal. 21 (5) (2014) 755–767. https://home.liebertpub.com/ars.

[68] Y. Liu, W. Wang, J. Yang, C. Zhou, J. Sun, pH-sensitive polymeric micelles triggered drug release for extracellular and intracellular drug targeting delivery, Asian J. Pharm. Sci. 8 (3) (2013) 159–167.

[69] P. Rychahou, F. Haque, Y. Shu, Y. Zaytseva, H.L. Weiss, E.Y. Lee, W. Mustain, J. Valentino, P. Guo, B.M. Evers, Delivery of RNA nanoparticles into colorectal cancer metastases following systemic administration, ACS Nano 9 (2) (2015) 1108–1116.

[70] A.C. Anselmo, S. Mitragotri, Nanoparticles in the clinic: an update, Bioeng. Transl. Med. 4 (3) (2019) e10143.

[71] W. Park, Y.J. Heo, D.K. Han, Local CTLA4 blockade effectively restrains experimental pancreatic adenocarcinoma growth in vivo, Onco Targets Ther 3 (1) (2014) e27614.

[72] A. Shafei, W. El-Bakly, A. Sobhy, O. Wagdy, A. Reda, O. Aboelenin, A. Marzouk, K. El Habak, R. Mostafa, M.A. Ali, M. Ellithy, A review on the efficacy and toxicity of different doxorubicin nanoparticles for targeted therapy in metastatic breast cancer, Biomed. Pharmacother. 95 (2017) 1209–1218.

[73] J. Lee, D.K. Chatterjee, M.H. Lee, S. Krishnan, Gold nanoparticles in breast cancer treatment: promise and potential pitfalls, Cancer Lett. 347 (1) (2014) 46–53.

[74] S. Marrache, J.H. Choi, S. Tundup, D. Zaver, D.A. Harn, S. Dhar, Immune stimulating photoactive hybrid nanoparticles for metastatic breast cancer, Integr. Biol. 5 (1) (2013) 215–223.

[75] A.C. Anselmo, S. Mitragotri, C. Samir Mitragotri, Nanoparticles in the clinic, Bioeng. Transl. Med. 1 (1) (2016) 10–29.

[76] C. Hu, M. Niestroj, D. Yuan, S. Chang, J. Chen, Treating cancer stem cells and cancer metastasis using glucose-coated gold nanoparticles, Int. J. Nanomedicine 10 (2015) 2065–2077.

[77] C. Hu, T. Lei, Y. Wang, J. Cao, X. Yang, L. Qin, R. Liu, Y. Zhou, F. Tong, C.S. Umeshappa, H. Gao, Phagocyte-membrane-coated and laser-responsive nanoparticles control primary and metastatic cancer by inducing anti-tumor immunity, Biomaterials 255 (2020) 120159.

[78] J. Jose, R. Kumar, S. Harilal, G.E. Mathew, D.G.T. Parambi, A. Prabhu, M.S. Uddin, L. Aleya, H. Kim, B. Mathew, Magnetic nanoparticles for hyperthermia in cancer treatment: an emerging tool, Environ. Sci. Pollut. Res. 27 (16) (2020) 19214–19225.

[79] S. Gavas, S. Quazi, T.M. Karpiński, Nanoparticles for cancer therapy: current progress and challenges, Nanoscale Res. Lett. 16 (1) (2021) 1–21.

[80] S.R. Grobmyer, G. Zhou, L.G. Gutwein, N. Iwakuma, P. Sharma, S.N. Hochwald, Nanoparticle delivery for metastatic breast cancer, Nanomedicine 8 (Suppl. 1) (2012) S21–S30.

[81] M. Zhou, W. Lai, G. Li, F. Wang, W. Liu, J. Liao, H. Yang, Y. Liu, Q. Zhang, Q. Tang, C. Hu, J. Huang, R. Zhang, Platelet membrane-coated and VAR2CSA malaria protein-functionalized nanoparticles for targeted treatment of primary and metastatic cancer, ACS Appl. Mater. Interfaces 13 (22) (2021) 25635–25648.

[82] J. Han, Q. Wang, Z. Zhang, T. Gong, X. Sun, Cationic bovine serum albumin based self-assembled nanoparticles as siRNA delivery vector for treating lung metastatic cancer, Small 10 (3) (2014) 524–535.

[83] K. Lee, H. Lee, K.H. Bae, T.G. Park, Heparin immobilized gold nanoparticles for targeted detection and apoptotic death of metastatic cancer cells, Biomaterials 31 (25) (2010) 6530–6536.

[84] T. Kang, Q. Zhu, D. Wei, J. Feng, J. Yao, T. Jiang, Q. Song, X. Wei, H. Chen, X. Gao, J. Chen, Nanoparticles coated with neutrophil membranes can effectively treat cancer metastasis, ACS Nano 11 (2) (2017) 1397–1411.

[85] Z. Zhang, H. Wang, T. Tan, J. Li, Z. Wang, Y. Li, Rational design of nanoparticles with deep tumor penetration for effective treatment of tumor metastasis, Adv. Funct. Mater. 28 (40) (2018) 1801840.

[86] M.M. Yallapu, B.K. Gupta, M. Jaggi, S.C. Chauhan, Fabrication of curcumin encapsulated PLGA nanoparticles for improved therapeutic effects in metastatic cancer cells, J. Colloid Interface Sci. 351 (1) (2010) 19–29.

[87] R. Awasthi, A. Roseblade, P.M. Hansbro, M.J. Rathbone, K. Dua, M. Bebawy, Nanoparticles in cancer treatment: opportunities and obstacles, Curr. Drug Targets 19 (14) (2018) 1696–1709.

[88] W. Zhang, F. Wang, C. Hu, Y. Zhou, H. Gao, J. Hu, The progress and perspective of nanoparticle-enabled tumor metastasis treatment, Acta Pharm. Sin. B 10 (11) (2020) 2037–2053.

[89] D.P. Cormode, P.C. Naha, Z.A. Fayad, Nanoparticle contrast agents for computed tomography: a focus on micelles, Contrast Media Mol. Imaging 9 (1) (2014) 37–52.

[90] G. Mariani, L. Bruselli, T. Kuwert, E.E. Kim, A. Flotats, O. Israel, M. Dondi, N. Watanabe, A review on the clinical uses of SPECT/CT, Eur. J. Nucl. Med. Mol. Imaging 37 (10) (2010) 1959–1985.

[91] E. Hutter, J.H. Fendler, Exploitation of localized surface plasmon resonance, Adv. Mater. 16 (19) (2004) 1685–1706.

[92] K.M. Mayer, J.H. Hafner, Localized surface plasmon resonance sensors, Chem. Rev. 111 (6) (2011) 3828–3857.

Amine-terminated dendrimers: A novel method for diagnose, control and treatment of cancer

16

Yeganeh Modirrousta[a] and Somaye Akbari[b]

[a]Polymer & Color Engineering Department, Amirkabir University of Technology, Tehran, Iran,
[b]Textile Engineering Department, Amirkabir University of Technology, Tehran, Iran

Introduction

Cancer is one of the most dangerous human diseases and is the second leading cause of death worldwide after medical diseases [1]. Common drugs used in cancer treatment often include chemotherapy, surgery, and radiation therapy (RT) [2]. Chemotherapy is the most common treatment for many types of cancer, but this strategy is often unsatisfactory due to tumor resistance. Chemotherapy doses are limited due to undesirable levels of tissue toxicity in the body and are difficult to detect due to non-specific sedation injections. The harmful effects of these substances may be due to the low solubility of many anticancer drugs in water, their low concentrations, their targeted biodistribution in the body, and their apparent adverse effects on organs and solid tissues [3,4]. Drug carriers are being developed to overcome the obstacles posed by chemotherapeutic agents [5–7]. The use of systems has several advantages, such as ensuring that the drug reaches the desired point, does not damage other tissues, has greater permeability and durability, and allows for controlled release of the drug. In addition, combination therapy aimed at achieving a synergistic effect often uses several chemotherapy drugs. Effective and high-quality delivery of chemotherapy drugs to the internal organs of cancer cells and various tumors in a manner specific to normal tissues and organs may be the highlight of therapy and help overcome tumor "multidrug resistance" (MDR) [8,9]. Various nanostructures such as liposomes, polymer nanoparticles, micelles, strong lipid nanoparticles, nanocages, gold nanoparticles, nanocrystals, graphene oxide, carbon nanotubes, and dendrimers have been used as nanocarriers. All of these agents have been studied for their drug delivery and different properties to target different infections, especially cancer [10–18].

Cancer Epigenetics and Nanomedicine. https://doi.org/10.1016/B978-0-443-13209-4.00021-0

Copyright © 2024 Elsevier Inc. All rights are reserved, including those for text and data mining, AI training, and similar technologies.

Among these nanosystems, dendrimers are a class of engineered macromolecules that have a branched and tree-like structure whose rearranged monomers are linked to each other and the central core in a layered manner by covalent bonds. The word dendrimer is derived from dendron, which means tree in Greek. Each layer of the dendrimer is called a generation, and the numbering of the generations starts from the central core (G0) and increases as the layers expand [18–20]. The dendrimer structure contains an interior space and various end groups for drug imaging and storage. The precise morphology of the dendrimer depends on its molecular chemical composition [19,21]. Compared to straight and branched polymers, dendrimers have many differences, such as the ability to adjust the size at the nanoscale, control the degree of aggregation, the structure and atomic weight of dendrimers and their production for a specific purpose [22,23], circular morphology, controllable lipophilicity, and, as a result, the ability to penetrate cell divisions [24] and the ability to modify with different strategies [22]. This incredible compatibility of dendrimers makes them a suitable drug carrier with attractive properties [22,25]. These advantages make dendrimers into nanoscale multimolecular drug/gene devices [26]. Dendrimer-encapsulated drugs with interesting features such as long half-life, greater stability, better water solubility, and reduced potential to stimulate antibacterial drug responses [27] have made dendrimers popular in the biomedical field [20,28–32]. Many reports have shown that dendrimers are more efficient than viral vectors, liposomes, and direct polymers for the delivery of various types of biomolecules [33,34]. Among dendrimers, the largest group is amino dendrimers, which have different types, including peptide dendrimers poly(propylene imine) (PPI), poly-L-lysine (PLL) dendrimers, polyamidoamine (PAMAM) dendrimers, poly(ethylene imine) (PEI), organosilicon dendrimers, etc. [35,36]. Among these, the most widely used dendrimers in the field of drug carriers and quality treatments are PAMAM and PPI [26].

In this chapter, after a brief introduction of amine-terminated dendrimers, their application in drug/gene delivery systems and codelivery systems will be reviewed, and an overview of their effectiveness in cancer diagnosis, control, and treatment in recent years will be made.

A summary of amine-terminated dendrimers

Different types of nanoparticles (such as silica nanoparticles, polymers, liposomes, micelles, and dendrimers) have demonstrated the ability to deliver drugs to specific sites and target specific cancer cells [37,38]. Dendrimers have gained popularity over the years because these nanoparticles are ideal therapeutic substrates, not only due to their intrinsic properties but also due to their ability to bind to drug molecules associated with cancer cells, such as cell-penetrating peptides, antibodies, folic acid, or glucose [39,40]. In addition, there are various dendrimers with different amino groups, including PAMAM, PPI, PLL, and PEI, which are used in pharmaceutical applications. Among them, two widely used dendrimers in the field of biomedicine are PPI and PAMAM, which have a great future as drug or gene carriers.

The famous PAMAM dendrimers, synonymous with "Starburst" and "arborols," were the first dendritic structures to be characterized and studied from the 1970s to 1990s [21]. PAMAM dendrimers have several advantages [26,41]. Their hydrophilicity, biocompatibility, pharmacological, and nonimmunogenic properties; explain their advantageous utility in sedative use. Ethylenediamine, diaminododecane, diaminohexane, and diaminobutane are the most common centers of PAMAM dendrimers [21,42,43]. Their branched units are based on methyl acrylate and ethylenediamine and have amino groups (in full ring form) and carboxyl groups (in half ring form) [44]. PAMAM dendrimers have the most important biomedical applications among dendrimers. This dendrimer has antibacterial, antiviral, and antioxidant properties and has been widely used as a drug/gene carrier, in addition to MRI imaging and protein focusing [45].

One-step dendrimers (OS-PAMAM) have stood out from other dendrimers in recent years due to their unique properties such as speed, high loading capacity, and low-cost synthesis [46]. The Organosilicon-amidoamine (OS-PAMAM) dendrimer was the first commercial silicon-containing dendrimer. Its inner part is composed of hydrophilic and nucleophilic PAMAM, its outer part is made of hydrophobic organic silicon (OS), and its structure is composed of reversible unimolecular micelles. These dendrimers are valuable precursor particles for programming honeycomb systems with nanometer-sized PAMAM and OS voids [47–49]. Moosolubilizing hydrophobic drugs can physically interact with the inner or outer recess of the PAMAM dendrimer. This molecular capsule promotes water solubility and incorporates controlled discharge capabilities. The physical interaction between PAMAM and drugs in liquid complexes can be controlled by a variety of noncovalent interactions, such as hydrogen retention, electrostatic interactions, steric hindrance, and direct hydrophobicity. The sedative type of secretion is controlled by pH in some cases. For example, because the pH of the tumor vascular microenvironment is acidic, amino groups become protonated, and their composition changes. Acidic pH may be a suitable stimulus for drug release. Therefore, drug release from PAMAM dendrimers is pH sensitive and faster in acidic environments [26,35,36,50–54].

PPI dendrimer was the first dendrimer described by Buhleier et al. [55], and it is called "atomic waterfall." With PAMAM, this type of dendrimer has also been extensively studied. The PPI dendrimer contains 1,4-diaminobutane (contact) in the central position but can be synthesized from the ethylenediamine center and other atoms by Michael expansion reaction. Propyleneimine monomer is used as branching unit. Therefore, they contain tripropylene tertiary amines inside, and their surface ends consist of essential amines [56]. The proximity of the alkyl chains in the branched units gives them a more hydrophobic inner layer than PAMAM dendrimers (containing amide groups extending to the alkyl chains) of similar age [57]. In the 5th century, PPI dendrimers were commercialized and widely used in materials science and engineering. These dendrimers are commercially available under the brand name Astramol [47–49]. The "waterfall" structure of amines was proposed by Buhleier and coworkers in 1978 [55]. Regardless, a larger-scale synthesis of PPI dendrimers 15 was presented shortly thereafter in partitioning reflections by Malhaupt and Meijer using a modified Voetle strategy [58]. The term "polypropylene imine dendrimer" (PPI) refers to dendrimers that contain a diaminobutane (Niz) center and 1, 2, 3, 4, or 5 rings of propylene imine beads attached to it. Since spot is the center of the PPI, they are also called DAB dendrimers [59]. Dosed drugs can be noncovalently encapsulated in PPI dendrimers. The total number of intertwined guest atoms is proportional to the shape and size of the particles, as well as the total shape and size of the internal dendrimer cavities. PPI dendrimers can also electrostatically attach a large number of oppositely charged drug atoms to amino groups on their surface [60]. These dendrimers are widely used as natural particle carriers in research settings and in vivo conditions [61]. To reduce the toxic quality of PPI dendrimers, their surface groups were specifically modified using carbohydrate compounds [62].

PLL dendrimers are a type of peptide dendrimers that are combined with oligonucleotides as a quality product in most cases due to their long thickness. These dendrimers are biocompatible, water soluble, biodegradable, and compatible. Unlike other dendrimers, peptide bonds are present in their structure, and their core unit and segments are often based on the amino acid lysine [63]. PLL dendrimers contrast with the common concept of PAMAM and PPI dendrimers because they are predominantly disordered. In all respects, these are precise atoms that attach a controlled number of centrally branched lysine groups and terminal amine groups to their structure [63]. In summary, PLL contains two main amines that are regularly monitored and regulated to provide superior organic performance [64,65].

PEI is one of the commercially available and valuable cationic polyamines and has been widely used as an efficient drug carrier, a gene delivery system, and an adhesive component for wood. Yemul et al. synthesized amine-terminated PEI dendrimers up to the third generation using EDA as core via the divergent synthesis method. Strong fluorescence of PEI dendrimers was observed under acidic conditions. The emission intensity increased with increasing dendrimer production from G1 to G3 and time [66].

The application of amine-terminated dendrimers in cancer Diagnose

To analyze and treat cancer using molecular imaging (MI) and chemotherapy, it is necessary to find a multifunctional nanoplatform that can be used as a combination of prodrugs and antidrugs. The developed multifunctional nanoparticles can be used as contrast agents for molecular imaging applications and as therapeutic agents under certain conditions when anticancer drugs are not available [67,68]. On the other hand, nanoparticles can be combined with imaging agents for molecular imaging applications and anticancer drugs for chemotherapy applications [69]. Among the many available nanoplatforms, dendrimers, especially PAMAM dendrimers, have received much attention [18,70,71]. Dendrimers are long mono-disperse, branched in cavities, and have many useful surface groups [28]. These properties allow them to covalently bind to experts in concentrating, molecular imaging, and transforming anticancer drugs to target drug delivery applications [18,72,73]. However, there are few reports on the simultaneous integration of imaging components and anticancer drugs into nanoplatforms based on anticancer therapy [74–76]. Over the past decade, MI has made it possible to obtain in vitro and in vivo physiological data with high sensitivity and specificity [77]. MI strategies include optical imaging [78], computed tomography (CT) [79], magnetic resonance imaging (MRI) [80], positron emission tomography [81], and computed tomography single-photon computing [82]. Among the MI methods, CT and MRI have shown their superiority over other imaging strategies. These methods are more advantageous when appropriate MI probes are used. Further advances in nanotechnology show that multifunctional nanomaterials can be used as MI probes that go beyond atom and drug transport capabilities to focus on detection and treatment [83] but can also provide distinct imaging modalities based on tissue composition. For accurate cancer identification and confirmation, it is essential to combine dual-mode and multimode imaging capabilities in a single nanoparticle (NP) framework so that increased blood clearance pressures can be avoided, added by arranging multiple measurements [84]. Due to limitations of the CT discriminators used, such as short imaging time, nephrotoxicity at often high concentrations, and nonspecificity, NP-based mineral operators have been developed. For example, gold nanoparticles (Au-NPs) [79,85] capable of long-term X-ray absorption have been used as CT discriminators due to their favorable biocompatibility after functionalization. Surface, long circulation, and their simple surface biological function, and the relatively hydrophobic interior of the dendrimer allows for attractive visualization of hydrophobic anticancer drugs [16,24–27]. By extension, the main strengths of dendrimers could make them reasonable scaffolds or stabilizers for the arrangement of dendrimer-encapsulated gold nanoparticles (Au-DENP) or stabilized gold nanoparticles using dendrimer in CT imaging. On the other hand, gadolinium (Gd)-based contrast agents, which are currently widely used as MRI contrast agents for clinical findings, have disadvantages such as short open time (T1), lifetime in the blood is short, and Gd is unstable. Tailoring the chelate/Gd complexes for MRI imaging (in fact, for dendrimers with a Go generation number, e.g., generation 2) and ensuring PEGylation around the dendrimer also improves the arrangement of Au-DENP for CT imaging [86,87]. Corrosive (III)/diethylenetriaminepentaacetic acid (DTPA) complexes, which can cause nephrogenic systemic fibrosis [88,89], have been developed as operants for molecular discrimination by MR. These macromolecular specialists possess promising properties such as well-defined structures, favorable pharmacokinetics, and long in vivo open times [90,91]. However, there are very few distinct operators that can be used for MRI and CT imaging. These multimodal imaging experiments, such as iohexolgadoteridol [92], Gd-G8 dendrimer [93], Gd AuNP tracer [94,95], and FePt nanoparticles [96], yielded little effect, efficiency, stability, or implementation time. Therefore, programming a stable dual-mode differentiated tissue while allowing tactile MRI and CT imaging remains a major challenge. The surface of PAMAM dendrimers can be modified with various useful peripherals, allowing them to be used in various biomedical applications, such as conjugated adsorbents for MR contrast agents [97] or drug and nucleic acid delivery [98,99]. Broadly speaking, the inherent properties of dendrimers allow them to be used as templates or stabilizers to program inorganic nanoparticles such as gold and silver. Previous considerations [79,100–102] suggest that fifth-generation gold nanoparticles (G5) encapsulated in PAMAM dendrimers (AuDENP) can be used as an operator to differentiate CT angiography or as a cancer-specific CT carrier. In a 2013 review [103], Gd-loaded Au-DENP (Gd-AuDENP), using facile dendrimer chemistry, demonstrated dual-mode MR/CT imaging of the heart, liver, kidney, and bladder of mice were held. Dendrimers can be useful for demonstration purposes because they act as dual-mode discriminators, comparable to MR/fluorescence discriminators and MR/CT discriminators [71]. In this case, the hydroxyl-terminated PAMAM dendrimer is capable of generating blue fluorescence with high quantum efficiency through the direct oxidation group [104]. Furthermore, Wang and Imae [105] described fluorescence under acidic conditions from PAMAM and PPI dendrimers. Recently, Tsai et al. [106] demonstrated that natural fluorescent PAMAM dendrimers can be used as high-quality nanocarriers and probes for the delivery of nuclear caustics. Huang et al. [107] described the simple combination of MTX (a cytotoxic drug), folic acid (pro-focus), and fluorescein (imaging pro) with PAMAM (G3) dendrimer using the press does not contain chemical copper. Manufacturers report cyclooctane release levels to vary from batch to batch. This stage step is performed using g-azido functionalized MTX. The efficiency of the complex is 90%. The response from the copper-free press was effective and loud. Talanov and coworkers [108] described the development of a PAMAM dendrimer-based nanoprobe with MR and fluorescence (Fl) strategies. Gd (III) is covalently bonded to the dendrimer to create an untapped macromolecular discrimination operator for MRI. They used 1B4M-DTPA and Cy5.5 as dual adsorbents. PAMAM dendrimers were covalently linked to Gd (III)-DTP chelates and Cy5.5 near-infrared (NIR) fluorescent dye units to form dual MRI-FI operators. The manufacturers organized 9 separate batches and selected 1 batch for evaluation that contained 1.25 atoms of Cy dye and 145 atoms of 1B4M-Gd. Therefore, this dual-labeled dendrimer differentiation tissue performs MRI and IF simultaneously.

Per research conducted by Shi et al. [109], it appears that Au-DENP can be covalently linked by concentrating the ligands and imaging particles onto target and imaged cancer cells. Au-DENP configured with several corrosive folic acid (FA) and fluorescein isothiocyanate (FI) atoms is water soluble, stable, and biocompatible. FA and FI-modified Au-DENP appear to bind specifically to KB cells (a human epithelial carcinoma cell line) by binding to FA receptors with high affinity within 2h, mainly in cell lysosomes goals are internalized. These results report a simple approach to using Au-DENP as a substrate to concentrate and image cancer cells.

Following a thought, Li and his group [110] took full advantage of Apts, dendrimers, and QDs, prepared Apt dendrimer-conjugated QD nanoprobes (Apt-dQDs) and investigated the possibility of using Apt-dQDs nanoprobes in selective detection and visualization of tumor cells. It appears that the ordered nanoprobes can target and image U251 glioblastoma cells under research facility conditions. These data are an initial step to encourage the clinical application of the Apt-dQD nanoprobe in imaging-focused glioblastoma.

Magnetic resonance imaging (MRI) has become one of the most powerful imaging tools in modern clinical decision-making [111,112]. Atomic resonance imaging is a developing strategy for detecting cancer at the atomic level [113] and typically requires intra- or extra-atomic testing that includes focusing on the ligand and signaling components present and can be detected by MRI. The first type is often very specific to a particular tumor type or its microenvironment. The last-mentioned mode can change the alignment of attractive dipoles, which is used to establish a comparative relationship between flagellar differentiation and tumor atom preparation, in particular, for robust tumor detection [114,115]. Vascular endothelial growth factor receptors (VEGFRs) are expressed in many tumor tissues [116–118], being almost undetectable in normal tissues, which provides a theoretical basis for the synthesis of probes that can specifically bind to the tumor. Currently, the most popular MRI contrast agents in cancer imaging are gadolinium chelating compounds [119], but clinically, they have several disadvantages, including short half-lives (several hours) due to low hydrophilic properties. Since the 1990s, superparamagnetic oxide nanoparticles (SPIONPs) have been used as an extremely stable imager for in vitro atomic and cellular MRI applications [120] since the MRI flag movement opened [121]. Dendrimer-lysine (DGL) conjugate structure has outstanding biological activity, biocompatibility, nonimmunogenicity, biodegradability, and excellent water solubility. This construct has been widely used due to its multifunctional nature [122]. The design and association of SPIONP-DGL nanoparticles (NPs) between species can be considered an MRI contrast for better circulation [71]. More importantly, the MRI detection flag can be obtained by directly substituting SPIONP-DGL composite nanoparticles for single Gd particles because the flag produced by single Gd particles is very weak [123], but if DGL dendrimers are used as skeleton-decorated magnetic nanoparticles (MNPs), the active amino groups on its surface are largely blocked, which prevents both conjugation with specific targeting ligands such as peptides and drug loading. Shen et al., to ensure free amino groups on the DGL surface [124], designed and described a modern assay of heterogeneous peptide dimers attached to nanosized PLL-Fe_3O_4 dendrimers for early detection and treatment of liver cancer. The binding of PLL dendrimer to NPs provides enough space for the expansion of DOX accumulation. In vitro cytotoxicity, apoptosis assessment, and serial cell imaging demonstrated the ability of this assay to specifically enhance HepG2 cells among three selected cell types. Atomic composition analysis showed that MNP-DGL-RGD-GX1-DOX nanoparticles accelerated apoptosis through the receptor pathway. In vivo, diffusion and MRI data confirmed that the nanoprobe successfully binds to the tumor using $\alpha v \beta 3$ dual integrin receptors on the vascular endothelium. The high tumor inhibition rate firmly confirmed its anticancer effect. Overall, the composite nanoprobes have the potential for good tissue discrimination and unusual nanodevices.

Langereis et al. [125] described the incorporation of a 5–6 nm PPI dendrimer complex containing corrosive gadolinium-diethylenetriaminepentaacetic acid (PPI-Gd-DTPA) as an MRI discriminator. Transmission electron microscopy (TEM) showed that these dendrimers did not self-assemble. The adequacy of these dendritic discriminators was measured by MRI, correlating with longitudinal (r1) and horizontal (r2) openings at 208°C and 1.5T. Compliance with r1 and r2 increases as the number of dendritic frames increases. Kobayashi et al. [126] used PPI-DAB dendrimer as a tissue-specific carrier (B4M-Gd1) in MRI imaging. Synthesis of PPI dendrimer 1B4M-Gd-flag expanded Gd(III) in rat liver with superior differentiation compared to GdDTPA (diethylenetriaminepentaacetic acid). Then, PPI-B4M-Gd1 may be a valuable discriminator for detecting liver micrometastases.

Saad and his group [127] compared the use of direct polymers, liposomes, and dendrimers for tumor-centered treatment and imaging. They used PAMAM-type star dendrimers to prepare paclitaxel and/or Cy5.5. LHRH was used as a semitarget because LHRH receptors are overexpressed in the plasma layer of cancer cells.

RT is one of the most common and suitable strategies for the treatment of malignant tumors. However, proximal hypoxia in solid tumors leads to RT resistance in tumors [128,129] and significantly reduces the beneficial effects, thereby discouraging the RT strategy. Due to the undeniable characteristics of hypoxia, which are fundamentally different from normal tissues, it has been proposed as one of the main targets for the development of a separate and useful group of experts [130,131]. Nanomaterials, including components with high nuclear numbers and enhanced photovoltaic effects, have long been of great interest to increase the performance of RT [132]. Several types of nanomaterials with long nuclear components (such as gold, titanium, etc.) have been used as "sensitizers" to increase the sensitivity of cancer cells to radiation. To form composite nanostructures with long core components, polymers such as highly branched polymers and dendrimers have been used to incorporate mineral clusters or nanoparticles (NPs) and fabricate hybrid nanomaterials. This nanohybrid has higher water solubility, freezing, and chemical performance than nonpolymer inorganic nanomaterials [133–135]. In this case, PAMAM dendrimers are used as a format for the in situ fabrication of dendrimer-encapsulated nanoparticles (DENPs), allowing the dendrimer, as a stabilizer, to trap one or more metal nanoparticles at depth [109]. Due to its deeply branched internal structure and multi-level chemistry capabilities, PAMAM dendrimers can be used as nanoreactors to trap various particles (such as gold, copper, platinum, etc.) and produce functional nanohybrids that can be used for treatment or imaging applications in the field of oncology [70,135,136]. Furthermore, an attractive approach to reduce tumor radioresistance is to construct a complete nanosystem with significant radiosensitization and additional imaging capabilities capable of improving response, radiotherapy response, screening hypoxic tumors, and providing real-time data [71].

Fan et al. [137], addressing hypoxia-sensitive RT detection of tumors that can be simultaneously imaged with high precision, developed guided multifunctional dendrimer-based nanosensors by CT/MR imaging. Using the smart dendrimer platform technology, the CT imaging agent of gold nanoparticles and the MR imaging agent of Gd(III)-chelator complexes can be easily incorporated into the dendrimer platform, while the tumor hypoxia-sensitive agent Nit can be coated on the surface. The dendrimer was designed to enable effective targeting of hypoxic cancer cells in vitro and tumor hypoxia in vivo. In addition to the good dual-mode CT/MR imaging performance of tumor hypoxia applied by the designed dendrimer nanohybrids,

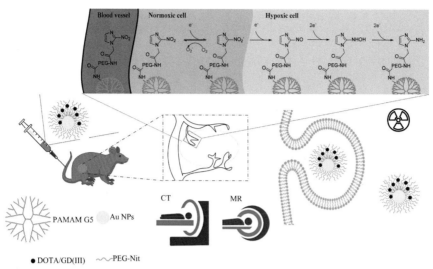

FIG. 1

Schematic illustration of the application of Gd-Au DENPs-Nit for dual-mode CT/MR imaging and sensitized RT of tumors. The Gd-Au DENPs-Nit were tail vein injected, accumulated at tumor site, bioreduced in hypoxic cells, and endocytosed by the cells for sensitized RT of tumors.

they can also act as effective nanohybrids to enhance the RT response of tumor hypoxia by increasing intracellular ROS production, enhancing DNA damage, and preventing DNA repair is used (the schematic can be seen in Fig. 1).

Shi and his group [102] investigated PAMAM dendrimeric gold nanoparticles modified with FA and FI for cancer treatment and imaging. Flow cytometry analysis showed that folic acid modification had significant mean fluorescence emission in imaging and supported targeted drug delivery; the mean fluorescence emission of the unmodified dendrimer carrier at a concentration of 50 nM is 25, while this coefficient is for the dendrimer carrier modified with folate. This acid has the same concentration of 425. Kavousi and coworkers [138] developed an aptamer-containing PAMAM dendrimer with gold nanoparticles and prostate-specific antigen (PSA) as a biosensor to detect cancer cells of prostate cancer. The Nyquist plot shows that the dendrimer combined with PSA (27 μA) has a higher conductivity than the dendrimer without PSA (14 μA). This type of sensor features safety, reproducibility, stability, and high sensitivity for prostate cancer cells.

Treatment

A successful drug delivery system consists of two parts: loading and releasing. In this section, the use of amine dendrimers in both sections is investigated.

Drug loading

Anticancer drug molecules can be covalently attached to the end groups of dendrimers or trapped in the core by hydrogen bonds, hydrophobic interactions, or electrostatic interactions [139]. Dendrimer production quantity affects drug loading (DL) capacity. The relatively high production quantity provides more space for the client drug and more functional groups on the surface for drug incorporation. PPI, PAMAM, PLL, polypeptide, polyester, polyether dendrimers, and PEG or carbohydrate dendrimers are mainly used as anticancer drug carriers [136,140].

Overall, PAMAM dendritic constructs with higher generations (four generations or more) exhibited better efficacy and higher DL rates than constructs with lower generations. This may be due to greater physical or chemical interactions, as higher-generation dendrimers provide more space in the dendritic cavities, where tertiary amines can more easily interact with other molecules [43,141]. The same is true for chemical conjugation, as the number of modifiable surface groups conjugated to the drug increases as production increases [43].

In the report presented by Abedi and group [142], tetramethylscutellarein (TMScu), a flavonoid with low solubility and relevant anticancer properties, was encapsulated by the EDTA core of PAMAM-G4 dendrimer to improve solubility and efficiency of encapsulation. Drug loading and release increase specificity in vitro [142]. The above research results show that PAMAM-G4 dendrimer can increase the solubility of the drug in water, and the release rate of TMScu from the TMScu/PAMAM-G4 complex is highest under acidic conditions (pH 4.0).

In one study by Zhang et al. [143], the effects of end groups on PAMAM-G5 drug release kinetics and cancer cell inhibition were evaluated, and the anticancer drug doxorubicin (DOX) was encapsulated in PAMAM-G5 dendrimer. Various groups, including acetyl (PAMAM-G5-NHAc), glycidol hydroxyl (PAMAM-G5-NGlyOH), and carboxyl (PAMAM-G5-SAH), are used as terminals (surface groups) of the dendrimer, and according to as a result, all three types of groups were functionally effective in encapsulating DOX. Additionally, the DOX/PAMAM-G5 complex showed significant therapeutic effects by inhibiting cancer cell growth [143].

Photodynamic therapy (PDT) is a treatment that uses photosensitizers or photosensitizers as drugs along with some type of light (usually from a laser source). PDT, which uses functionalized nanoparticles that can selectively localize to diseased tissues or cells, is a promising approach to precisely treat disease at specific sites. The action of PDT involves the selective binding of photosensitive (PS) molecules to patient tissues. Irradiation of tissues at certain wavelengths of light activates PS, leading to ROS production in tissues and cell death [144]. Using PEGylated dendrimers, Kojima and his group [145] prepared nanocapsules containing photosensitizers, including rose bengal (RB) and protoporphyrin IX (PpIX), for use in PDT. The authors synthesized two PEG-linked PAMAM-G4 dendrimers (PEG-PAMAM-G4) and (PEG-PPI-G5), each dendrimer containing 64 terminators. The results showed that fewer PpIX molecules were surrounded by two PEG-attached dendrimers and were more stable than free RB under the same physiological conditions. Spyropoulos-Antonakakis and colleagues [146] prepared a combination of PAMAM nanomedicine and PAMAM-ZnPc for use as PDT in the effective treatment of atherosclerosis. Using atomic force microscopy (AFM), the authors studied the aggregation of PAMAM-G0 as a drug carrier as well as the ability of PAMAM(G0) dendrimer combined with ZnPc photosensitizer to target carotid artery tissues in symptomatic and asymptomatic humans. Addition of PAMAM-G0 or the Zn-Pc/PAMAM-G0 pair to carotid tissues, healthy or atherosclerotic, significantly altered the properties of human carotid tissue with exercise responses in different combinations of nanoparticles. The results showed deposition in atherosclerotic tissues with different accumulation characteristics and opposite effects on healthy tissues.

Buczkowski and coworkers [147] studied the increased solubility of 5-FU by PAMAM dendrimers. There was a linear relationship between solubility and dendrimer concentration between 2.5 and 50 mM. The authors concluded that the drug molecules not only bind to the active sites on the surface but also occupy the space of the dendrimer.

DOX is a drug widely used in the treatment of many types of cancer, including malignant leukemia and soft tissue sarcoma [148]. Similar to PTX, DOX drug delivery has been widely reported and studied using PAMAM and other dendrimers. However, due to its water solubility, loading DOX into dendrimers has several advantages over other drugs. DOX also has its fluorescence properties, making it a useful drug for studying the potential of dendrimers in anticancer drug delivery. Drug loading efficiency can be influenced by many different factors, including functional group, size, chemical structure, number of generations, degree of binding of PAMAM to PEG (pegylation), molecular weight loaded drug molecule, pH, solvent type, and temperature. The number and length of polyethylene glycol (PEG) chains attached to the surface of PAMAM dendrimers can influence drug encapsulation efficiency. For example, PEG2000 added to the PAMAM-G4 surface can maximize the trapping of DOX molecules on each PAMAM dendrimer (about 6.5 times), while the same delivery system can trap 26 methotrexate (MTX) molecule [149]. Methotrexate, an anticancer drug used in chemotherapy, is a folate analog and dihydrofolate reductase (DHFR) inhibitor, which catalyzes the conversion of dihydrofolate (DHF) to tetrahydrofolate (THF) and is essential for the biosynthesis of purine and pyrimidine bases and, as a consequence, the production of DNA and RNA [150–153].

MTX is an antimetabolite drug used in the treatment of cancers, autoimmune diseases, ectopic pregnancy, and medical abortion. MTX was one of the first anticancer drugs developed using dendrimers. van Dongen and coworkers [154] synthesized and characterized the MTX-G5 *PAMAM* dendrimer conjugate using G5-(COGMTX)n and G5-(MFCO-MTX)n as molecular linkers. In addition to the above pair, the dimers G5-G5(D), D-(COGMTX)n, and D-(MFCO-MTX)n were also prepared. The monomeric G5-(COG-MTX)n compounds exhibited rapid reversible and weak binding to folate binding protein (FBP), similar to the binding observed with the monovalent binding of MTX. The next conjugate, D-(COGMTX)n, exhibits a slow-onset tight binding mechanism in which MTX first binds to FBP and then induces a conformational rearrangement of the protein. MTX concentration directly affects the rate of irreversible binding.

Kirkpatrick and coworkers [155] designed different half-generation PAMAM dendrimers as active CDDP carriers and observed that DL and release behavior depended on dendrimer size. As the size of the half-generation dendrimer increases, the DL and release capacity also increase. The antitumor activity of dendrimer-CDDP compounds was studied in ovarian cancer cell lines A2780, A2780cis, and A2780cp and in vivo studies against A2780 xenografts.

The high density of functional groups, such as amine and carboxyl groups on the dendrimer surface, has potential applications to increase the solubility of hydrophobic drugs through electrostatic interactions. For example, consider the PAMAM-G3 dendrimer with an ammonia core. Compared with conventional linear polymers, its amino group density is much higher. Nonsteroidal antiinflammatory drugs containing a carboxyl group, including ibuprofen, ketoprofen, diflunisal, naproxen, and indomethacin, have been extensively complexed into dendrimers through electrostatic interactions. Some anticancer and antibacterial drugs are also combined on this basis. The common feature of these drug molecules is that they are weakly acidic and contain a carboxyl group [156].

In general, cancer cells have an accelerated metabolism and high glucose requirement, known as the "Warburg effect," which is one of the hallmarks of cancer [157]. Therefore, cells express a series of glucose transporters (GLUTs) to meet their energy needs. At least six GLUT transporters are overexpressed in breast cancer cells [158–160]. Benefits of treatment with MTX-containing glycosylated dendrimers include improved permeability and affinity to cross the blood-brain barrier with glucose and increased drug delivery in glioma tumors (U87 MG) [161]. For this reason, glycosylation in PAMAM may play an important role in increasing drug uptake in cancer cells and creates a need to improve this system with inexpensive dendrimers with high loading capacity. Therefore, Torres-Perez and colleagues developed a system based on "276" nanoparticles consisting of a one-step PAMAM dendrimer conjugated to MTX and glucose (OS-PAMAM-MTX-GLU pair) as a targeted therapy for cells. In this study, TNBC cells (MDA-MB-231) and noncancerous cells (HaCaT) were exposed to OS-PAMAM-MTX-GLU to evaluate their effects on the ability of cell existence. The OS-PAMAM-MTX-GLU drug delivery system targets tumor cells and shows the highest killing capacity compared to free MTX within 4 h without significant toxic effects on HaCaT cells. OS-PAMAM-FITC-MTX-GLU achieved peak cellular uptake within 2 h, and its amount in MDA-MD-231 cells was twice that of HaCaT cells. Iron oxide nanoparticles stabilized with arginine-based peptide dendrimers have been reported to effectively deliver DOX to cancer cells [162]. Glutamic acid-based peptide dendrimer composites, loaded with the drug nattokinase, exhibited very favorable thrombolytic effects in vitro and in vivo [163,164].

In another study, BC was studied in MDA-MB-231 and MCF-7 cell lines in vitro and in Balb/c mice in vivo by synthesizing nanoparticles modified with thioaptamer targeting CD44 (TA). In this study, thioaptamer-conjugated polyethylene glycol-PAMAM nanoparticles containing miRNA-145 were prepared. With the prepared delivery system, accumulation was observed only in cancerous tissues and absorption efficiency was high with positively charged cells. Although no significant gene silencing was observed in MCF-7, MDA-MB-231 showed excellent gene silencing ability. This system has also been reported to reduce invasion and metastasis [165]. In a study by Liu and colleagues [166], phospholipid-modified PAMAM-siMDR1 dendriplexes were loaded with siRNA and targeted the multidrug resistance gene (MDR1 gene) in MCF-7/ADR breast cancer cells. With this drug delivery system, cellular drug uptake and gene silencing are both increased. Observations suggest that by reducing P-gp expression, doxorubicin increases cell accumulation and reduces tumor cell migration.

Shao and coworkers [57] compared the DL capacity, release properties, and cytotoxicity of PPI-G4 with PAMAM-G3 dendrimer. Despite having the same number of surface amine groups in these two dendrimers, PAMAM-G3 performed better than PPI-G4 in solubilizing and releasing phenylbutazone molecules, and the PPI-G4-phenylbutazone complex showed stability is less effective in aqueous solution than PAMAM-G3-phenylbutazone and was 50 times more toxic than PAMAM-G3 dendrimer to MCF-7 and A549 cells. These results indicate that PPI-G4 dendrimer requires modification of surface groups to improve drug stability, loading capacity, release, and toxicity [57].

The effect of dendrimer quantity on toxicity and drug delivery efficiency under laboratory conditions was studied by Kesharwani and colleagues [167]. After loading PPI dendrimers of different generations (3, 4, and 5G) with the chemotherapeutic drug melphalan (M), this group studied noncovalent interactions such as hydrogen bonding and hydrophobic interactions between melphalan dendrimer and PPI. Their observations showed that the number of charged particles increased with dendrimer production, which may be due to the expansion of the internal cavity. The in vitro release of melphalan from all PPI dendrimers followed a nonlinear trend characterized by a relatively faster initial release during the first 3–4 h. The authors suggest that PPI-G4-M is superior to third- and fifth-generation PPIs in terms of therapeutic potential and biocompatibility because as production increases, the unique factor increases exponentially. The cause is toxicity while increasing loading and release. Sustained and effective targeting is meaningless and can be overlooked.

Consistent with studies in the field of surface modification, Szulc et al. [168] proposed that PPI dendrimers modified with surface maltose could be used as drug carriers for cytidine-5′-triphosphate (CTP). PPI dendrimers form highly effective complexes with CTP, making them a suitable choice for drug delivery systems. Mannosylated (mannose-modified) PPI dendrimer increased cellular uptake of efavirenz (an HIV drug) at 48 h compared to the free drug [169].

Drug delivery
Compared to other nanodrug delivery systems, dendrimer derivatives (PAMAM) have shown great promise as a nanodrug delivery system due to their molecular structure, intracellular size, and biocompatibility and their tight control [170,171].

For example, a PEGylated PAMAM dendrimer synthesized with Dox effectively killed A549 cells and was used as an in vitro model of alveolar adenocarcinoma [172]. Matai et al. [173] reported a simple method to prepare AG-G5 hybrid nanogels chemically cross-linked with alginate (AG) and poly(amidoamine) G5.0 via carbodiamine chemistry, which exhibits antibacterial effects for cancer. Based on the results of the above study, PAMAM may be ideal for use as a drug delivery system. Furthermore, the design of drug nanocarriers with active tumor-targeting activity is another important factor influencing anticancer effects [174]. For effective drug delivery to the tumor site, active tumor-targeting ligands are typically linked to drug nanocarriers using a covalent/noncovalent approach. Among these ligands, hyaluronic acid (HA) [175,176] is supposed to recognize and interact with CD44, which is transforming in various types of solid tumors, including pancreatic, lung, and breast cancer [177–179]. Indeed, BP has become a new biomarker for early detection of recurrences and monitoring of prognostic conditions for effective treatment in breast cancer patients [180,181]. Nanodrug delivery systems based on HA-modified polymers have also been shown to improve system continuity [182]. Therefore, HA was used as the target group for PAMAM nanoparticles.

Considering the above, in the study of Guo and his group [183], a very promising nanocarrier-enhanced PAMAM.G4.0 dendrimer was developed. In this study, a new type of PAMAM dendrimer derivative was created. HA was used as the target group, and PAMAM was coated with Pt and Dox by covalent reaction, which was found to be highly stable, biocompatible, and have antibreast cancer potential. This scheme allows for the synthetic destruction of breast cancer cells. HA-PAMAM-Pt-Dox was found to contain two highly stable drugs and enter cells through a lysosome-mediated pathway. Cytotoxicity studies were performed on MCF-7 and MDA-MB-231 breast cancer cells, showing that HA-PAMAM-Pt-Dox has a stronger anticancer effect than the monomer. In vivo, tissue distribution studies of HA-PAMAM showed that HA-PAMAM significantly increased drug accumulation in tumor tissue compared to free drug solution. Furthermore, drug distribution studies showed that after 24 h virtually no drug was observed in the heart and kidneys, suggesting that HA-PAMAM may reduce side effects and enhance anticancer effects. In vivo, antitumor data using MDA-MB-231 tumor-bearing BALB/c mice showed that HA-PAMAM-Pt-Dox has a stronger antitumor effect than other drug formulations. The present study demonstrated coadministration of cisplatin with DOX to achieve highly effective synergy in breast cancer cells and may extend this approach to other anticancer drugs.

Dendrimeric anticancer drug pairs have demonstrated intracellular drug delivery and improved bioavailability of loaded molecules. Cisplatin is a widely used anticancer drug, and at least 50 cisplatin molecules are required to be effective. The cisplatin-dendrimer complex showed a reduction in the cytotoxicity of healthy cells and, conversely, a significant lethality of tumors [184]. It has been suggested that "encapsulation of complexes via modulatory controlled liposome release system (MLCRS)" is one of the effective methods to control the drug release rate from the environment drug distribution. In 2005, Papagiannaros and coworkers [185] successfully encapsulated DOX into PAMAM-G4 dendrimers and then encapsulated the formed DOX/PAMAM-G4 complex into a liposome using the MLCRS system. This hybrid method increases DOX loading efficiency and release time. An approach to developing dendrimers as anticancer drug carriers is to exploit their multivalent properties to covalently attach drug molecules to the dendrimer environment. Covalent conjugation of drugs with PAMAM dendrimers has been used to increase efficacy and solubility, reduce nonspecific toxicity, and stabilize drug release [26,97]. The surface groups of the PAMAM dendrimer provide a flexible attachment point for incorporating therapeutic agents, ranging from anticancer drugs to imaging probes, in solution without losing the spherical shape of the PAMAM dendrimer. As shown in Fig. 1, anticancer drugs can be attached to the PAMAM surface by "direct coupling" or through a "separable interface." Several chemotherapeutic drugs, such as DOX, MTX, paclitaxel, and cisplatin, are attached to the PAMAM surface by direct conjugation [45,186,187].

Biotin is an essential micronutrient with high expression levels in rapidly proliferating cells, such as cancer cells. Assuming that the synthesis of PAMAM dendrimers with biotin molecules could help improve the specific uptake by cancer cells, these dendrimers were biotinylated using sulfoNHS-LC-biotin and had a specific structure which is characterized by ^{1}H NMR and ionization by matrix-assisted laser desorption. The production efficiency and cellular uptake mechanism of biotin PAMAMG4 in ovarian (OVCAR-3) and human embryonic kidney (HEK 293T) cancer cells were studied by fluorescence microscopy and cytometry. The results obtained showed that the cellular uptake of biotin-PAMAM in OVCAR-3 cells was significantly higher than in HEK 293T cells ($P < .05$). Meanwhile, the presence of free biotin or colchicine significantly reduced biotin absorption from PAMAM-G4 at lower concentrations (0.1 μM). Based on the evidence, biotinylated PAMAM was internalized by biotin receptor-mediated endocytosis and cargo-mediated endocytosis, and the cytotoxicity of biotinylated PAMAM-G4 in cytotoxicity of biotinylated PAMAM-G4 in HEK 293T cells was comparable to that of the parental PAMAM dendrimers. As a result, biotinylated PAMAM dendrimers were as effective as nanocarriers in targeted drug delivery [188].

Jin and coworkers [189] developed a pH-responsive dendrimer nanocarrier using PAMAM-G4 dendrimer with a poly[2-(N,N-diethylamino)ethyl methacrylate] (PDEA) core, which was modified with PEG, to release 5-fluorouracil (5-FU). PEG increases drug circulation, and PDEA is responsible for its pH sensitivity. The authors reported that drug release was much faster at pH = 6.5 than at pH = 7.4 because the PDEA chains were hydrophilic at acidic pH and hydrophobic at high pH, that is, 7.4. They also reported increased antitumor activity against H22 cells due to faster diffusion and targeted drug delivery due to low pH at the tumor site.

Zhu and his group [190] studied the influence of the degree of PEGylation on the release rate and anticancer activity of drugs by using semi-PEGYlated PAMAM for targeted delivery of DOX. Acid-sensitive and acid-insensitive succinic cis-aconite bonds were created between DOX and the polymer to give PEG-PAMAM-cis aconite-DOX (PPCD) and PEG-PAMAM-succinic-DOX (PPCD) conjugates. PPCD showed increased cytotoxicity against mouse B16 cells, but cellular uptake decreased with increasing levels of PEGylation. Although PPSD showed more DOX accumulation in tumors at the same level of PEGylation, PPCD showed higher antitumor activity due to the pH-dependent release of doxorubicin and the amount of free drug at the same time inside the tumor. In general, increasing the level of PEGylation will increase the anticancer activity of PPCD.

Duncan and colleagues [45,191] prepared PAMAM-cisplatin dendrimer pairs, which form complexes with increased water solubility, reduced systemic toxicity, and selective accumulation in solid tumors. In addition, the dendrimer-cisplatin complex in the treatment of subcutaneous B16F10 melanoma showed greater efficacy than cisplatin alone. Alpha-tocopheryl succinate (α-TOS) is a vitamin E-derived compound with anticancer activity and low water solubility that is attached to the surface of PAMAM dendrimers by direct grafting [74,116,192]. Zheng and his team combined α-TOS with PAMAM-G5-NH2 via an amide bond and obtained a multifunctional compound (PAMAM-G5-NHAcn-α-Tos-FI-FA), soluble in water and stable within the corresponding pH range and can completely inhibit the growth of cancer cells. In addition, this formulation can also inhibit [72]. Kurtoglu and group [193] directly conjugated ibuprofen to PAMAM-NH2-G4 and PAMAM-OH-G4 dendrimers by establishing amide and ester bonds, respectively. The results of this study show that esterase and cathepsin B enzymes in plasma are not capable of hydrolyzing amide or ester bonds. Additionally, ibuprofen bound to PAMAM-NH2-G4 (with amide linkage) showed no significant release at different pH ranges (1.2, 5.0, 7.4, and 8.5). On the other hand, the direct combination of ibuprofen ester with PAMAM-OH-G4 was released at different pH values, and at pH $= 5$ and pH $= 8.5$, the release of ibuprofen was equal at 3% and 38%, respectively. The stability of the ester bond against enzymatic hydrolysis suggests that the dendrimers attached to PAMAM-G4 block enzyme activity. Creating a steric barrier on the PAMAM surface, by directly combining drugs and species with separable interfaces, prevents drug release. Furthermore, the unfavorable stability of directly conjugated drugs, especially those conjugated via an amide linkage, under various conditions may be a limiting factor for drug binding to the dendrimer surface [69,94]. In a study by Gao et al. [194], poorly water-soluble compounds, such as ursolic acid (UA) and formic acid (FA), were covalently linked to PAMAM-G3 and G5 dendrimers via an acid-sensitive ester bond. This study showed that the cytotoxicity of the drug against Hela cells was significantly increased. Additionally, because the linker is ester type, the release of UA from the FA-PAMAM-G3-UA complex is pH sensitive, and UA exhibits a biphasic release pattern, with rapid initial release, followed by a sustained release phase [194]. Dendrimer IPP can increase the solubility of acidic, basic, and amphoteric drugs (such as amphotericin B, famotidine, and indomethacin). The increase in solubility depends on the chemical nature of the drug and the pH [195].

Biswal and his group [196] studied controlled drug delivery to the HeLa229 cell line using fourth-generation PAMAM dendrimers as drug carriers and methotrexate and doxorubicin as two anticancer drugs. The PAMAM drug combination showed better cytotoxicity and delayed drug release in vitro compared to control trials (drug alone), which is necessary to reduce side effects and increase the treatment index. More importantly, the intrinsic fluorescence properties of dendrimers and drug molecules are effectively used to image cell lineages using fluorescence microscopy. In summary, the experimental results presented in this study show that the PAMAM drug complex delivers MTX and DOX in a controlled manner, compared to the case without dendrimer. Cytotoxicity studies also showed a higher rate of cell death in the presence of the drug-dendrimer combination. The formation of a complex between the drug and the PAMAM dendrimer leads to a decrease in the rate of exit from the cell, which then increases the local concentration of the dendrimer-drug complex inside the cell. As a result, the intracellular drug content, as well as the intrinsic fluorescence of the PAMAM dendrimer, increased, which was effectively used to image HeLa 229 cells.

The results show that the size and surface charge of PAMAM dendrimers can regulate their tumor accumulation and penetration behavior. Bugno and coworkers [197] used PAMAM dendrimers with suitable and controlled size ($<10\,$nm) and surface charge to explore how the physical properties of nanoparticles govern the behavior of bacteria that accumulate and invade their tumors. The results show that the penetration and aggregation ability of PAMAM dendrimers in MCTS depends greatly on their physical properties. However, the penetration efficiency of smaller dendrimers in MCTS was higher than that of larger dendrimers but caused overall tumor accumulation. In contrast, while larger cationic dendrimers rapidly accumulate on tumors, their penetration is limited to the outermost surface of MCTS. The results show that in terms of cell interactions, there is a delicate balance between the accumulation of dendrimers in the tumor and their ability to penetrate the cell mass. Despite the progress made in the development of MMP-2/9 inhibitors, adverse side effects and pharmacokinetic issues remain major challenges hindering their clinical success in cancer treatment. However, new targeting methods have reinvigorated research in the field of MMPs. One such approach is the use of novel s-triazine-based dendrimers, which have intrinsic inhibitory potential for MMP-2/9 and, as a targeted therapeutic, can bind to cancer cell-specific ligands and effectors through biodegradable agents. The anticancer connection. The designed dendrimer substrate is formulated with zinc-binding (hydrazide) and terminal branching (carboxylic acid and hydrazide) linkers that increase potency against MMP-2/9. Preliminary cytotoxicity screening and MMP-2/9 inhibition assay on free dendrimers showed promising activity at safe doses (MMP-9; IC50$=0.35$–$0.57\,\mu$M, MMP-2; IC50$=0.39$–$0.77\,\mu$M) (EC15$=4.4$ EC150$\,\mu$M). Dendrimer hydrazide is comparable to NNGH and superior to the carboxylic acid analog. MTT test results showed that free dendrimer had superior advantages over the reference anticancer agent honokiol. Their anticancer potency is enhanced by HK conjugation, ligand assembly, and pegylation, for example, by conjugation to hydrazide dendrimer (TPG3) [198].

To improve drug accumulation in lung tumors, Zhong et al. [199] investigated the ability of the PAMAM-G4-DOX conjugate to reduce the burden of lung metastases in locoregions. DOX was attached to the dendrimer surface via acid-sensitive hydrazone linkages, and mouse B16-F10 melanoma cells were used as a model for lung metastasis. Injection of the DOX-dendrimer pair into the lungs showed a reduction in tumor burden, sustained drug accumulation in the lungs, and drug distribution into cardiac tissue, or, in other words, a reduction in the systemic toxicity of the drug. Creating acid-sensitive hydrazone linkage with DOX may be a way to induce stimulus-responsive transporters that specifically release their cargo after exposure to the acidic conditions of the tumor or bacterial environment [200]. Pan et al. [201] studied the possibility of reducing MDR by reducing the expression of P-gp gene and protein in two MDR cancer cell lines, adding PEG2k to PAMAM-G4 dendrimer and transforming with phospholipid DOPE, a compound called G4—produces PAMAM-PEG2k-DOPE with a micelle structure and is called dendrimer mixed micelle or MDM. The resulting complex was loaded with DOX and a medicinal siRNA called siMDR-1. In this complex, PAMAM dendrimer plays an important role in the binding of siRNA to DOX (complex), facilitating cell interaction and facilitating intracellular escape. The PEG fragments also protect the cationic charge and homogenize the nanostructure. A balance between cell interactions and cytotoxicity is essential to maximize treatment effectiveness. As reported by this group, the molar ratio of PAMAM-PEG2k-DOPE and PEG5k-DOPE in MDM, 1:10, is the most promising substrate for the simultaneous delivery of nucleic acids with hydrophobic DOX in MDM,1:10, reduces the amount of membrane-bound P-gp and also limits its function, leading to a reversal of MDR. In addition to the successful delivery of siMDR-1 to MDR cancer cells, a synergistic anticancer effect was also achieved through the codelivery of DOX and siMDR-1 in dendrimer-based nanocomposites.

PAMAM dendrimer has also been used for combination chemotherapy. In one study, Guo et al. [183] studied fourth-generation PAMAM dendrimer nanoparticles modified with hyaluronic acid to provide a systemic synthesis of cisplatin and doxorubicin, synergistic drug effects, and the possibility of minimal drug dosing for cancer treatment in combination clinical chemotherapy. The results showed that HA-PAMAM-Pt-Dox has a high potential to enhance the effectiveness of cisplatin and doxorubicin chemotherapy in breast cancer. The antagonistic nature of drugs, variable solubility, and limited tumor targeting of drugs are major treatment problems. Considering the advantages of dendrimers, such as molecular weight and size control, bioavailability, and biosafety, the PAMAM-G4 dendrimer has been improved into a drug carrier by covalent linkage BP treatment. Observations show that the HA-PAMAM-Pt-Dox system can effectively kill breast cancer cells in vitro and in vivo and produce favorable synergistic effects.

Zhang and colleagues [202] studied multifunctional PAMAM dendrimers combined with doxorubicin for pH-responsive drug delivery and targeted chemotherapy to cancer cells. Fifth-generation acetylated PAMAM dendrimer modified with folic acid (FA) via pH-sensitive cis-aconite linkage was used to form G5NHAc-FA-DOX adducts. The addition of FA to dendrimers triggered the overexpression of FA receptors in cancer cells and targeted G5NHAc-FA-DOX complexes to demonstrate their effectiveness in cancer treatment.

Yao and Ma [203] investigated the enhancement of the therapeutic effect of paclitaxel by increasing its cellular uptake in cancer cells and the subsequent reduction of its cytotoxic effect. To achieve these goals, biotinylated PAMAM dendrimer complexes with paclitaxel were prepared using the biotinylation method. The degree of biotinylation of PAMAM with the NH2 terminal group was the main parameter evaluated by the HABA assay. The initial integrity of the complex was studied by DSC. Drug release (DR) and DL parameters were also investigated for the biotinylated PAMAM-PTX dendrimer complex. Cellular uptake studies in OVCAR-3 and HEK293T cells were performed using fluorescence techniques. The results obtained by the HABA method showed complete biotinylation of the PAMAM dendrimer. The DSC study demonstrated the integrity of the complex compared to the pure drug and its physical mixture. The highest amounts of DL (12.09%) and DR (70%) were observed at 72 h in the biotinylated complex containing 20 mg of the drug. The special feature of OVCAR-3 (cancer) cells compared to HEK293T (normal) cells is the stronger cellular uptake of the complex. Experimental and statistical evaluations confirmed that the biotinylated PTX-PAMAM-NH2 dendrimer complex not only enhances cellular uptake but also prolongs drug release up to 72 h while reducing cellularity toxicity.

Li and colleagues [130] studied gastric cancer (GC) as the second leading cause of cancer-related death. Cancer stem cells (CSCs) with the CD44 marker play an important role in GC. The drug rMETase has been used as a chemotherapy option in polymer-based nanoparticle drug delivery against GC. Injection of PAMAM-G5-Au-METase-HA into nude mice reduced the number of CD44+ cancer cells and inhibited tumor growth.

Human epidermal growth factor receptor 2 (HER2) is one of the promising target molecules in immunotherapy. HER2 protein expression has been observed in various tumors, including breast and ovarian cancer [204]. Overexpression of the HER2 receptor in tumor cells provides an opportunity for the development of drug delivery systems targeting HER2. Additionally, possession of an extracellular domain makes the HER2 receptor an ideal target for receptor-mediated drug delivery in tumors. Monoclonal antibodies against HER2 offer a potential strategy to specifically target HER2. Trastuzumab (Herceptin) is a recombinant human IG1 monoclonal antibody reported to selectively bind to human epidermal growth factor receptor 2 (EGFR2) with nanomolar affinity [205–210]. By binding to subdomain IV of the extracellular domain of HER2, trastuzumab blocks it and prevents excessive proliferation of HER2+ cancer cells by stopping the cell cycle in G1 phase [211]. Preclinical studies have shown that HER2 overexpression occurs in more than 20% of breast cancers and is associated with resistance to anticancer drugs such as paclitaxel and docetaxel [212]. Such studies have also reported synergistic effects of trastuzumab and taxanes [213]. The combination of trastuzumab and taxane is a first-line treatment for many different types of cancer, including lung cancer, ovarian cancer, and metastatic breast cancer (MBC). In patients with HER2+ breast cancer, three weekly doses of docetaxel (2100 mg/m) plus trastuzumab (at a loading dose of 4 mg/kg, followed by 2 mg/kg once weekly) resulted in an increased overall survival rate. Tumor response rate (ORR), overall survival, duration of response, time to progression, time to treatment failure (TTF), and toxicity of the drug combination were slightly increased compared with docetaxel alone [214]. In the same way, paclitaxel, according to the National Comprehensive Cancer Network (NCCN) guidelines, is the preferred single chemotherapy agent for MBC [215], as, combined with trastuzumab (at a loading dose of 4 mg/kg, then 2 mg/kg weekly), compared to paclitaxel alone, it improved progression-free survival (PFS) in HER2+ patients at a dose of 80 mg/m^2/week [216]. In vitro studies by Miyano and coworkers [217] also confirmed the effectiveness of monoclonal antibodies added to dendrimers. The PAMAM-G6 dendrimer was modified with two amino acids, lysine and glutamic acid (K-G6-E), and then trastuzumab and the fluorescent dye AlexaFlour 488 were attached to it. The results confirm that the KG6E-trastuzumab pair binds specifically and dose-dependently to SKBR-3 (HER2+) cells and with low affinity to MCF-7 (HER2−) cells. Furthermore, the obtained placenta was significantly taken up by SKBR-3 cells and then transported to lysosomes. The application of anti-HER2 mAb-PAMAM dendrimer conjugates as targeted drug delivery vehicles was investigated. Dendrimer antibody conjugates have been used to target prostate-specific membrane antigen (PMSA) [218] and CD14 antigen [219], in boron transfer [220], and in mass imaging applications [221]. There is growing interest in the synthesis of anti-HER2 mAb conjugates for gene delivery [222], tumor targeting [223], and imaging applications [224]. PAMAM dendrimers are biocompatible [225], nonimmunostimulatory [226], water soluble, and attached to many biological molecules such as proteins, synthetic drugs, and small molecules [227,228]. In the study by Shukla et al., an anti-HER2 mAb dendrimer complex was synthesized with a fifth-generation PAMAM dendrimer, and an Alexa Fluor 488 fluorescent tag was used to label it. Confocal microscopy and flow cytometry results showed comparable binding and uptake of immunodendrimer complexes with free antibodies [229]. In one study, Marcinkowska et al. [230] successfully synthesized two pairs of dendrimer-trastuzumab conjugates serving as docetaxel and paclitaxel drug carriers to target HER2-overexpressing cells. Analysis of the cytotoxicity, cellular uptake, and internalization of the conjugates revealed them to be promising carriers for selective and targeted drug delivery to HER2-expressing tumor tissues. These dendrimer-drug complexes exhibit potent toxicity to HER2+ cells and negligible toxicity to HER2− cells and demonstrate strong selective binding to HER2+ cells. This selective binding is a result of both the use of trastuzumab in the dendrimer structure that binds and blocks HER2 and the presence of pH-sensitive binding structures that help the dendrimer enter cells and release medicine.

Tiu and colleagues improved the low permeability of soluble paclitaxel by using third-generation PAMAM dendrimers as drug carriers. Cytotoxicity studies showed that the addition of lauryl chains and paclitaxel to dendrimer G3 significantly increased ($P < .05$) the cytotoxicity of the drug to the human Caco-2 cell line as well as with primary porcine brain endothelial cells (PBEC). The resulting compound showed approximately 12-fold higher permeability in basal and apical cell monolayers compared to free paclitaxel [177]. Paclitaxel was also attached to

PAMAM-G4 dendrimer with hydroxyl polymer and bisPEG to increase drug solubility and anticancer activity. The cytotoxicity of the PAMAM-succinic acid-paclitaxel complex on A2780 human ovarian cancer cells was increased 10-fold compared to the free, unconjugated drug [176].

Soto-Castro and coworkers [231] reported a one-step synthesis of targeting nanodevices based on the PAMAM framework for MTX drug delivery. They prepared four different water-soluble compounds, named F1 to F4, with or without folic acid. Compounds F3 (lacking folic acid) and F4 (containing folic acid) were selected for testing. The antitumor activity of MTX in human lymphoma cells inhibited their growth by up to 80%.

Zhang and colleagues [229] reported enhanced DOX targeting by conjugation to RGD-modified PEGylated PAMAM dendrimers via acid-sensitive cis-aconite linkages (RGD-PPCD), then binds to integrins overexpressed on tumor cells. The authors observed a controlled release of DOX in weakly acidic lysosomes. To further investigate these systems as a treatment for glioma, DOX was conjugated to PAMAM via an acid-sensitive succinic bond and then modified to form RGD PPCD. For comparative studies, DOX was conjugated to PEG PAMAM by acid-insensitive cross-linking to produce PPSD.

He and his group [232] modified the PAMAM dendrimer surface with transferrin (Tf) and wheat germ agglutinin (WGA) and loaded it with doxorubicin. The effectiveness of the obtained dendrimer (PAMAM-PEG-WGA-Tf) in crossing the blood-brain barrier and its ability to target glioma tumors was investigated. The results showed that WGA and Tf had a positive effect on the accumulation of DOX at the tumor site in the body and increased drug release, as well as crossing the blood-brain barrier and reducing the toxicity of DOX to normal cells.

Chang and his group [76] reported novel pH-responsive water-soluble nanocarriers for DOX delivery. The authors conjugated DOX with PAMAM, which was then attached to superparamagnetic iron oxide NPs (IONPs). Dendrimer PEG-PAMAM G2.5 was used to immobilize IONPs. DOX is attached to IONP by a hydrazone bond, which is acid cleavable. The diameter of the conjugate after loading was 13.0 nm. Multidrug-resistant tumor cells have specific drug detoxification/inactivation mechanisms. The terminal amino groups of polyamidoamine (PAMAM-NH2), which induce death in tumor-sensitive cells, may not be cytotoxic in tumor-resistant cells by a mechanism different from the tumor-sensitive mechanism. Zhang and his group [233] studied the cytotoxic effects of PAMAM-G4-NH2 on multidrug-resistant human breast cancer cells (MCF-7/ADR cells) and determined the mechanisms molecules can be cytotoxic. Within 48 h, the viability of MCF-7/ADR cells after treatment with PAMAM-G4-NH2 was significantly higher than that of MCF-7 cells at a concentration range of 200 to 500 μg/mL ($P < .05$). The viability of MCF-7/ADR cells treated with PAMAM-G4-OH and PAMAM-G4-COOH for 48 and 72 h was much higher than that of MCF-7/ADR cells treated with PAMAM-G4-NH2. After treatment with high concentration (1000 μg/mL) PAMAM-G4-NH2 for 24 h, apoptosis rate, ROS levels, and caspase 3 and 9 activities were increased in MCF-7 and MCF-7/ADR cells, while MMP expression decreased and cells were arrested in

G0/G1 phase. In summary, PAMAM-G4-NH2, instead of PAMAM-G4-OH and PAMAM-G4-COOH, exhibits cytotoxicity in MCF 7/ADR cells, which can mechanically induce apoptosis in MCF-7 cells. Mechanism similar to that of tumor ADR cells is induced in a concentration-dependent, mitochondria-mediated manner and arrests the G0/G1 phase. Research results show that PAMAM-G4-NH2 can be used as a carrier to deliver anticancer drugs through reasonable design and also can activate multiple apoptotic pathways to increase drug effectiveness. In multidrug-resistant breast cancer, a drug delivery system based on PAMAM-G4-NH2 is expected to provide significant improvements in tumor treatment.

Guo and coworkers [183] reported the construction of a dual complex of DOX and cisplatin attached to PAMAM dendrimers to accelerate cancer treatment. The drug release study showed that the hyaluronic acid-modified PAMAM dendrimer carrier (40% in 24 h) was released faster than the unmodified PAMAM dendrimer carrier (38% in 24 h) at pH = 7.4. Similarly, at pH = 5.5, PAMAM was modified with hyaluronic acid (58% after 24 h) and released the drug faster than the unmodified PAMAM dendrimer carrier (52% after 24 h). In vivo tissue distribution studies showed that PAMAM dendrimer carrier modified with hyaluronic acid increased drug accumulation in cancer cells compared to free drug solution.

PPI dendrimers, especially their quaternary ammonium derivatives and sugars, are promising gene carriers that can be used to target the liver and avoid the lungs [234]. Agashe [235], in 2007, studied the biodistribution of PPI dendrimers coated with mannose or lactose in mice to determine their drug-carrying capacity. The sugar-modified dendrimers were significantly distributed in the liver, indicating their usefulness in liver targeting. Shah and colleagues [236] synthesized modified PPI dendrimers as drug carriers and conjugated them with a synthetic analog of luteinizing hormone-releasing hormone (LHRH) as a tumor-targeting molecule, the drug paclitaxel, and siRNA made from CD44 mRNA [236]. They observed a significant accumulation of nontargeted dendrimers in the tumor. Dendrimer targeting of tumor cells by LHRH peptide significantly increased PPI dendrimer accumulation in the tumor, and this complex significantly enhanced antitumor activity. Many PPI dendrimers, with different conjugations, have been tested as gene transfer vectors and artificial gene delivery in vivo, and their obvious effects in increasing gene transfer efficiency have been demonstrated. According to research by Ross and his team, increasing the number of dendrimer generations increases the expression level of tumor genes, and for dendriplexes with PPI-G3, the level of gene expression in tumor tissue is 12 times higher than that with dendriplexes with PPI-G3 [237]. In summary, PPI dendrimers and their derivatives are good candidates for drug and gene delivery systems. However, their effectiveness and potential applications depend on the type, number of generations, and toxicity of the dendrimer.

The study by Birdhariya and his group [238] aimed to evaluate and compare the effects of surface coatings with different groups (OH, COOH, and NH2) on the tumor-targeting ability of folate-linked PPI dendrimers (F-PPI). The formulation was formulated to trap the drug and release it under laboratory conditions, and its hemolytic and cytotoxic effects against HeLa and SiHa cell lines were evaluated by MTT assay. The use of all surface coating formulations increased MTX loading. However, the MTX release rate was reduced compared to the unmodified formulation. Additionally, F-COOH-PPI showed the highest tumor-targeting ability compared to other formulations.

Pistolis et al. [239] studied the effect of varying the pH of the dendrimer medium on the solubility, binding, and release of pyrene encapsulated in DAB-PPI dendrimers with 32 or 64 type 1 amine end groups (DAB-32 or DAB-64). The results of their study showed that the solubility of pyrene is proportional to the respective molecular weights of the two dendrimers. Pyrene is enclosed in dendrimer molecules and occupies a position near the dendrimer core. Acidic environments stimulate the release of pyrene, and in alkaline environments, its mixing with dendrimers occurs better. These results are important for controlled drug release. Sideratou and coworkers [240] prepared a variety of quaternary PPI dendrimers and studied their performance as pH-sensitive controlled release systems; Quaternion PPI dendrimers are interesting nonviral vectors for the delivery of genetic materials, including DNA [236], antisense oligonucleotides [241], and small interfering RNA (siRNA) [242]. The displacement effect of PPI dendrimers has also been studied [236,243]. Kabanov and coworkers [244] found that all protonated dendrimeric amine groups can form ion pairs with carboxylate or sulfonate polyanion groups. However, this does not happen for rigid and negatively charged DNA double helices. The PPI dendrimer interacts only with the primary surface amines of DNA without the involvement of internal amine groups [244]. A ternary complex of cationic PPI-DAB dendrimer, cucurbituril (CB), and DNA was produced by Lim et al. [241] and presented as an example of a gene carrier. This complex can transfer genes to mammalian cells with high efficiency, and its cytotoxicity is relatively low. The second-generation PPI dendrimer appended with arginine (PPI2-R) was also investigated for gene transfer systems by Kim and coworkers [245], which showed its low toxicity and high efficiency in gene transfer. Guanidinylation of the PPI-G4 dendrimer also led to a significant increase in its transfection efficiency, which was dependent on the number of guanidine groups in each dendrimer and the cell line used [246]. In evaluating PPI-DAB dendrimers as gene delivery systems, Zinselmeyer et al. [247] found that second- and third-generation PPIs had high transfection efficiency and low cytotoxicity, whereas fourth- and fifth-generation PPIs showed excessive cytotoxicity. They are not suitable for use during blood transfusions.

In the studies performed by Golshan et al. [203], the aim was to synthesize dendrimer-modified gold nanoparticles (Au-G4A) of the fourth generation of PPI as nanocarriers of doxorubicin and to study drug release kinetics under laboratory conditions from nanoparticles in different areas. Based on this, AuNPs were modified by reducing chloroauric acid (HAuCl4) solution with synthetic trisodium citrate and with cysteamine to obtain amine-functionalized nanoparticles (Au-NH2). Au-NH2 nanoparticles are used as multifunctional cores and participate in the addition of acrylonitrile by Michael reaction and reduction with lithium aluminum hydride (LAH) to synthesize Au-G4A nanoparticles. In addition, the peripheral primary amino groups of Au-G4A are conjugated with folic acid. The synthesized dendritic structure demonstrated the release properties of the Higuchi and Korsmeyer-Pepps model due to better drug solubility in the release medium due to the presence of dendrimer pores and drug release through the polymer matrix. Gold nanoparticles with a diameter of about 15 nm were synthesized and attached to fourth-generation PPI dendrimers. Then, the peripheral amino groups were conjugated with folic acid, and the effect of bioconjugation on the drug release behavior was studied. UV-visible spectroscopy, AFM, TEM, FT-IR, and TGA results demonstrated the successful synthesis of hybrid nanoparticles. Au-G4A and Au-G4F samples containing DOX were subjected to pH changes to study the drug release behavior. The drug content of Au-G4A and Au-G4F nanoparticles is 0.033 and 0.045 (mg drug/mg dendrimer), respectively. As a result, the DL rate for Au-G4F nanoparticles was significantly higher than that of Au-G4A nanoparticles due to the incorporation of FA on the surface of dendrons. Also, at different pH values, nonadjuvanted structures show cumulative drug release compared to FA-adjuvanted. Also, the release kinetics were investigated through different models. As a result, both Higuchi and Kors-Meirpepas models were implemented on the data to describe the DOX release kinetics from Au/ dendritic hybrid nanostructures.

Tietze and his group [248] reported that small interfering RNA (siRNA) has great potential in the treatment of incurable diseases or metastatic cancers. They report a novel modular polyplex carrier system for targeted siRNA delivery based on knockdown transfection with maltose-modified PPI (mal-PPI) dendrimers fused to single-strand variants (scFvs). The results suggest that mal-PPI-based polyplexes provide a promising tool to improve cancer siRNA therapy and a novel strategy for modular bioconjugation of protein ligands into nanoparticles.

Toxicity of dendrimers

Although dendrimer applications are increasingly common and growing, the risk of human exposure to them is inevitable. On the other hand, studies investigating the potential risks of dendrimer exposure are inconsistent and remain rare. Most data on dendrimer toxicity come from cytotoxicity assays and some from in vivo mammalian studies [47,249]. Regardless of the widespread application of amine-terminated dendrimers, their intrinsic toxicity caused by the presence of these amine groups has limited the use of cationic dendrimers. This toxicity is thought to be due to the interaction between the positive charge of the surface groups and the negative charge of the biofilm. The intensity of toxicity is directly related to the number of amino groups, which increases with the number of generations of each dendrimer [47]. Dendrimers such as PPI, PAMAM, and PLL exert significant cytotoxicity in vitro due to their surface cationic groups [250,251]. However, the evidence regarding dendrimer safety is conflicting [226]. There are reports of concentration-dependent production and toxicity of environmentally free amine groups.

Based on studies [252], anionic or neutral dendrimers, such as carboxylic acid or hydroxyl-terminated PAMAMs, showed no or very little toxicity. However, studies showed that the toxicity of cationic dendrimers such as NH2-terminated PAMAM dendrimers as well as PPI dendrimers increases with increasing generation number [253,254]. Mechanisms of toxicity include cell membrane destabilization and increased ROS, which can lead to apoptosis [255].

Recent findings show that exposure to PAMAM dendrimers (G3.0 and G4.0) affects the transcriptome of 48-h zebrafish embryos similar to bacterial infection, thus indicating activation of the innate immune response [256]. Therefore, Bowdoin and colleagues investigated the toxicity of several commercially available cationic PAMAMs and PPIs, as well as anionic PAMAM dendrimers, in a study using the 96-h fish embryo toxicity (FET) test as an in vivo model and two human cancer cell lines. His laboratory systems have shown that FET provides acute toxicity results that are comparable to adult fish tests and allows for cheap and easy testing while complying with EU Directive 2010/2010 (63/63). It is not considered an animal experiment. In addition, it offers many possibilities to include intermediate toxicity endpoints to assess systemic and specific effects. The results of the two test systems indicated that previous data on the toxicity of PAMAM dendrimers and PPIs may not provide a complete picture of possible adverse effects associated with exposure to dendrimers. In this study, findings suggest that cytotoxicity data underestimate the true toxicity of dendrimers, as cellular sensitivity was lower on average compared to whole-organism toxicity of zebrafish embryos. The charge of the end groups of the cationic dendrimers seems to be the main reason. Fish embryos and toxicity in vitro, although the trends were opposite, indicating that there are different modes of action in cells versus whole embryos. Corion was an important influencing factor in the size and, consequently, the production of dendrimers. Anionic PAMAM dendrimers showed little toxicity on embryos and fish cells at tested concentrations, but adverse effects on aquatic organisms at concentrations higher than 50 µM cannot be ruled out. These results indicate that concern about the use of dendrimers is justified, and more data are needed to confirm their effects on humans and the environment [257].

PPI dendrimers, especially the fifth generation, are the most studied dendrimers, and their extreme toxicity has been demonstrated in several of these studies. Kesharwani and his team [258], to explore the tumor-targeting potential of fourth-generation PPI dendrimers and improve them as an alternative to fifth-generation PPIs, treated these dendrimers by incorporating folate and modifying the surface, then the anticancer drug melphalan. Hemolytic toxicity, cytotoxicity, cellular uptake, and fluorescence uptake studies showed that the developed PPI-G4-folate dendrimer has less inherent toxicity due to the use of folic acid as the target ligand and surface modification compounds.

Kesharwani and coworkers studied PPI dendrimers of different generations and their surface modifications [25,259]. Melphalan was encapsulated in third-, fourth-, and fifth-generation PPIs and showed enhanced tumor growth inhibition and increased survival in BALB/c mice injected with MCF-7 cells, specifically for G4 and G5. The hemolytic toxicity of these dendrimers increases with increasing yield [109]. When dendrimers were modified with folic acid to increase cancer targeting, biocompatibility was improved, possibly because folate protects certain cationic groups. However, G5 has lower biocompatibility compared to G3 and G4. Further-more, folate-modified dendrimers showed enhanced inhibition of tumor growth in BALB/c mice bearing MCF-7 tumors [25].

The ability of immunodendrimers to improve drug delivery conditions through the dendrimer and reduce their nonspecific toxicity was evaluated in studies by Jain and colleagues [260]. To increase tumor specificity and thus increase the effective-ness of breast cancer treatment, they tested the ability to target tumors by loading PTX inside a half-generation (G4–5) PPI dendrimer grafted with the primary mono-clonal antibody makB1. The resulting conjugate pair (mAbK1-PPI-PTX), targets mesothelin protein receptors that are overexpressed in uterine cancer. The in vitro evaluation of immunodendrimers in the ovarian cell line OVCAR-3 showed that compared to PPI-PTX and free PPI-PTX dendrimers, hepatotoxicity, nephrotoxicity, and hemolytic toxicity were significantly lower.

In 2016, Szulc and colleagues [261] reported a promising strategy for the treat-ment of leukemia. Cytarabine (Ara-C) has limited effectiveness due to drug resis-tance, poor drug absorption, and accumulation in cancer cells, and it must be converted into active triphosphate compounds. PPI dendrimers form complexes with Ara-C triphosphate (Ara-CTP) nucleotide forms. In this study, PPI glycodendrimers were used as drug-delivery devices to facilitate the delivery of activated cytarabine to cancer cells. An in vitro study was performed using leukemia cell lines 1301 and HL-60 as well as peripheral blood mononuclear cells. The results indicate that this com-pound may be a versatile candidate for chemotherapy (the schematic is shown in Fig. 2).

Chen and his group [156] reported the cytotoxicity of cationic melamine dendri-mers with surface groups such as amine, guanidine, carboxylate, sulfonate, or phos-phonate and concluded that cationic dendrimers were much more toxic than anionic or PEGylated dendrimers.

Jain and colleagues [262] reported a PPI dendrimer to selectively target folate ligand-conjugated doxorubicin. They reported selective drug targeting and antitumor

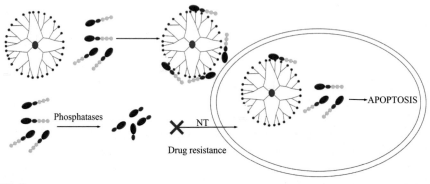

FIG. 2

Schematic of strategy for the treatment of leukemia.

effects for anticancer agents. The drug release rate is higher under acidic pH conditions, and the developed dendrimer has high biocompatibility and low toxicity. Several lysine-based dendrimers have been reported and show promising properties in terms of safety, efficacy, and toxicity compared with others.

Cytotoxicity

Jevprasesphant and colleagues studied the cytotoxicity of PAMAM dendrimers in Caco-2 cell lines and observed significant toxicity with these dendrimers [263].

Khandare et al. [264] reported the combination of the drug PTX with bis-PEG-modified linear dendrimers, one with and one with a hydroxyl-terminated PAMAM-G4 dendrimer. The authors reported that the in vitro cytotoxic activity of the conjugates against A2780 human ovarian cancer cells was 10 times higher for the PTX-dendrimer-succinic acid conjugate but 25 times for the linear PEG-PTX conjugate.

Agashe and colleagues [250] studied the cytotoxicity of simple carbohydrate-coated, amino acid-protected PPI-G5 dendrimers in HepG2 and COS-7 cell lines as well as the effects of terminal function, concentration, and incubation period. It has been observed in cytotoxicity. For PPI-G5, cell viability was studied using different dendrimer concentrations at 24, 48, and 72 h incubation times. Cell survival decreased with increasing concentration and incubation time. The toxicity of PPI-G5 is concentration dependent as well as time dependent and is thought to be due to the presence of free primary amine groups in PPI-G5 and their associated positive charge. The COS-7 cell line showed higher cell viability than HepG2 at all concentration points and during the incubation period.

Stasko et al. [264] evaluated cytotoxicity and membrane disruption by PPI dendrimers, conjugated PPI dendrimers, and PPI dendrimers with peripheral neutral acetamide groups on human umbilical vein endothelial cells (HUVECs) and found that single PPI dendrimers increased plasma membrane permeability and significant cytotoxicity showed changes over time.

Hemolytic toxicity

Teow and coworkers [265] investigated PAMAM-G3 dendrimer-based delivery of PTX as a means to overcome cellular barriers. The authors attached lauryl chains as permeability enhancers and glutaric anhydride as binding agents to the dendrimer surface. Free PAMAM-G3 dendrimers showed no cytotoxicity, while lauryl chains containing PAMAM-G3 dendrimers showed cytotoxicity against Caco-2 cells and primary PBEC.

Lai and coworkers [266] reported the photochemical internalization of DOX-PAMAM conjugate as an anticancer drug. DOX was conjugated to PAMAM dendrimer via pH-sensitive and pH-insensitive linkers, then combined with different photochemical internalization (PCI) strategies. "After-light" PCI treatment was effective in releasing DOX from the PAMAM-hyd-DOX conjugate, leading to increased DOX accumulation and increased cell death through a synergistic effect. Contrast is observed in "front light" PCI treatment. Neither PCI method improved the cytotoxicity of PAMAM amide-DOX.

Yellepeddi and coworkers [267] prepared biotinylated PAMAM dendrimers for intracellular delivery of CDDP to ovarian cancer cells. The authors used PAMAM-G4-NH2 and PAMAM G3.5-COOH, in which 22 and 19 biotin molecules were attached to the dendrimer by biotinylation, respectively. The obtained compounds had sizes ranging from 20 to 40 nm, and drug encapsulation rates were 5.33% to 21.10%. The authors found that biotinylated PAMAM-G4-NH2 had the highest CDDP loading, while biotinylated PAMAM-G3.5-COOH had the lowest loading. The IC50 value of the desiccant-CDDP complex was significantly lower than that of free CDDP in OVCAR-3, SKOV-3, and CP70 cell lines.

Bhadra and colleagues developed the PAMAM-G4 dendrimer for delivery of the anticancer drug 5-FU and found hemolytic toxicity to be 15.3%–17.3% [268]. Asthana and his group [269] also evaluated the hemolytic toxicity of these dendrimers and observed hemolytic toxicity up to 18%, close to the value reported by Bhadra et al. [268].

The free cationic end groups of dendrimers cause hemolysis due to interactions with red blood cells and affect blood parameters related to the polycationic properties of uncoated dendrimers. The effects of PPI dendrimers on various blood parameters, including white blood cells (WBC), red blood cells (RBC), hemoglobin (Hb), hematocrit (HCT), and mean corpuscular hemoglobin (MCH), were determined using an Erma particle counter by measuring Erma particles (Agashe et al. [250]). The authors observed a significant decrease in red blood cell count, a significant increase in white blood cell count, and a decrease in Hb content and MCH content, as well as a significant difference between the HCT values of PPIs dendrimer and control. RBC counts, hemoglobin values, HCT, and MCH were significantly reduced during treatment with PPI-G5.

In a study by Jain and his group [270], the effects of different generations of PPI dendrimers on human erythrocytes were reported, and it was found that the toxicity of PPI dendrimers increased with hyperplasia. Agashe and his group [250] also studied the hemolytic toxicity of PPI-G5 dendrimer. They observed hemolysis rates of $34.2 \pm 0.2\%$, $51.6 \pm 0.3\%$, and $86.2 \pm 0.6\%$ with PPI-G5 dendrimer at a concentration of 1 mg/mL after incubation for 1, 2, and 4 h, respectively. Bhadra and colleagues [271] compared the effects of primaquine phosphorus-containing dendrimers on various hematological parameters in male albino rats (Sprague-Dawley strain) and found that red blood cell counts were $1.1 \times 1.1 \times 0.05 \times 106 \pm 0.05$. per liter, and the increase in white blood cell count is lower than the normal value compared to uncoated PPI dendrimer.

Dendrimer PLL was also found to induce hemolysis in vitro [272]. They found a hemolysis rate of $14.1 \pm 1.02\%$ with PLL-G4 dendrimer. Current reports suggest that dendrimers with higher generation numbers may have higher hemolytic toxicity, which may be due to higher total cationic charge. Agrawal and his group [272] also observed a significant increase in white blood cell count and a decrease in red blood cell count from PLL-G4 dendrimer in their 2007 study. Red blood cell count containing PLL-G4 dendrimer decreased to $7.5 \times 106 \pm 0.3$/L, and white blood cell count increased to 15.2 ± 0.4/L. From these studies, it can be concluded that cationic dendrimers can cause significant disturbances in blood parameters, which means a significant increase in white blood cell count and a decrease in red blood cell count, Hb value, HCT, and MCH. And that requires a strategy that demonstrates their compatibility.

Toxicity of dendrimers in the body

In vivo toxicity studies are necessary to demonstrate the safety of any drug delivery study. Few scientists have conducted a systematic study of the in vivo toxicity of dendrimers. Roberts and colleagues [226] studied the in vivo toxicity of generation 3, 5, and 7 PAMAM dendrimers in Swiss-Webster mice, in which only generation 7 PAMAM dendrimers were capable of causing biological effects. The authors ultimately concluded that dendrimers do not have properties that would prevent their use in biological applications. Rajananthanan and colleagues [273] also studied the immunological properties of next-generation dendrimer polymer-based molecular formulations and found that the formulation was nontoxic to mice and induced antibacterial responses. Malik and his group [263] studied the biodistribution of marker 125I in vivo. The PAMAM cationic dendrimer was labeled to characterize the toxicity of this polymer carrier. In this study, the authors observed that following parenteral and intravenous (IP and IV) administration, the PAMAM cationic dendrimer was rapidly cleared from the circulation, only 0.1% to 1.0% of the current administered dose present in the blood 1 h after administration.

In their study, Torres-Pérez and his group [46] (shown in Fig. 3) developed a single-step PAMAM dendrimer of methotrexate and glucose (OS-PAMAM-MTX-GLU) and evaluated the efficacy of the OS-PAMAM-MTX-GLU conjugate using triple-negative BC cells (MDA MB-231) evaluated. In this study, it is believed that the use of methotrexate (MTX), which has antimetabolite activity, with a nanosized drug delivery system would be beneficial due to its side effects such as hepatotoxicity, inflammation, mouth ulcers, and decreased white blood cell count. In addition, glucose incorporation into PAMAM dendrimer was also achieved due to the high glucose demand of cancer cells and overexpression of GLUT. According to the cytotoxicity study performed using the MTT method, OS-PAMAM-MTX-GLU was shown to reduce the viability of MDA-MB-231 cells by 20%. Cancer cell specific toxicity in MDA MB-231 cells, MTX alone was reduced by 70%, OS-PAMAM-MTX conjugate by 45%, OS-PAMAM-MTX-GLU conjugate by 20%, and OS-PAMAM-MTX-GLU decreased by 20%. The reduced viability of MDA-MB-231 was attributed to increased glucose uptake due to glucose incorporation. The addition of glucose increases its uptake into cancer cells and supports the results of cytotoxicity studies. The PAMAM dendrimer and MTX/glucose combination shows promise in the treatment of triple-negative BC, as it increases accumulation in tumor cells and provides targeted therapy [46].

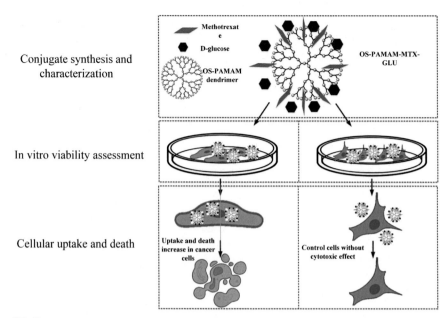

FIG. 3

Schematic of synthesis, assessment, and cellular uptake and death.

Lai and his group reported PAMAM dendrimer conjugate containing DOX for cancer treatment. DOX was conjugated to dendrimer via amide and hydrazone as coupling molecules.   The DR study showed that at pH 4.5 (47% in 24 h), the prepared PAMAM-hyd-DOX nanocarrier released the drug faster than at pH 7.4 (8% in 24 h). It also showed the release of PAMAM-amide-DOX comparing the drug with PAMAM-hyd-DOX at pH 4.5. Cytotoxicity also confirmed that PAMAM-hyd-DOX nanocarriers were more toxic to cancer cells than PAMAM-amide-DOX nanocarriers [266].

Conclusion and future trend

Drug delivery systems can be listed as follows: dendrimer, liposome, phytosome, transfersome, polymeric micelles, nanosuspension, nano/microemulsion, and nano/microparticles. In recent years, dendrimers have become leaders in the field of drug delivery due to advantages such as DL capacity, ease of synthesis, stability, convenient operation, controllable size, and efficiency, as well as proactive targeting [41]. In addition, dendrimers have high solubility, miscibility, and reactivity due to their multiple chain terminations. These drug delivery systems are soluble in many solvents [47,131,274]. Therefore, in this chapter of the book, amine-containing dendrimers and their applications in drug delivery and cancer control have been discussed.

References

[1] P. Kesharwani, L. Xie, S. Banerjee, G. Mao, S. Padhye, F.H. Sarkar, et al., Hyaluronic acid-conjugated polyamidoamine dendrimers for targeted delivery of 3, 4-difluorobenzylidene curcumin to CD44 overexpressing pancreatic cancer cells, Colloids Surf. B: Biointerfaces 136 (2015) 413–423.

[2] B. Xiao, L. Ma, D. Merlin, Nanoparticle-mediated co-delivery of chemotherapeutic agent and siRNA for combination cancer therapy, Expert Opin. Drug Deliv. 14 (1) (2017) 65–73.

[3] T. Iwamoto, Clinical application of drug delivery systems in cancer chemotherapy: review of the efficacy and side effects of approved drugs, Biol. Pharm. Bull. 36 (5) (2013) 715–718.

[4] C.N. Ellis, M.B. Ellis, W.S. Blakemore, Effect of adriamycin on heart mitochondrial DNA, Biochem. J. 245 (1) (1987) 309–312.

[5] M. Eskandani, J. Barar, J. Ezzati Nazhad Dolatabadi, H. Hamishehkar, H. Nazemiyeh, Formulation, characterization, and geno/cytotoxicity studies of galbanic acid-loaded solid lipid nanoparticles, Pharm. Biol. 53 (10) (2015) 1525–1538.

[6] J.E.N. Dolatabadi, Y. Omidi, Solid lipid-based nanocarriers as efficient targeted drug and gene delivery systems, TrAC Trends Anal. Chem. 77 (2016) 100–108.

[7] A. Alibakhshi, F.A. Kahaki, S. Ahangarzadeh, H. Yaghoobi, F. Yarian, R. Arezumand, et al., Targeted cancer therapy through antibody fragments-decorated nanomedicines, J. Control. Release 268 (2017) 323–334.

[8] T. Ciuleanu, C.-M. Tsai, C.-J. Tsao, J. Milanowski, D. Amoroso, D. Heo, et al., A phase II study of erlotinib in combination with bevacizumab versus chemotherapy plus bevacizumab in the first-line treatment of advanced non-squamous non-small cell lung cancer, Lung Cancer 82 (2) (2013) 276–281.

[9] J. Shen, Q. Wang, Q. Hu, Y. Li, G. Tang, P.K. Chu, Restoration of chemosensitivity by multifunctional micelles mediated by P-gp siRNA to reverse MDR, Biomaterials 35 (30) (2014) 8621–8634.

[10] A.M. Jhaveri, V.P. Torchilin, Multifunctional polymeric micelles for delivery of drugs and siRNA, Front. Pharmacol. 5 (2014) 77.

[11] A.Z. Wang, R. Langer, O.C. Farokhzad, Nanoparticle delivery of cancer drugs, Annu. Rev. Med. 63 (2012) 185–198.

[12] L. Sercombe, T. Veerati, F. Moheimani, S.Y. Wu, A.K. Sood, S. Hua, Advances and challenges of liposome assisted drug delivery, Front. Pharmacol. 6 (2015) 286.

[13] M.D.C. Jasmine, V.V. Prabhu, Polymeric nanoparticles—the new face in drug delivery and cancer therapy, Malaya J. Biosci. 1 (2014) 1–7.

[14] N. Rahmanian, H. Hamishehkar, J.E.N. Dolatabadi, N. Arsalani, Nano graphene oxide: a novel carrier for oral delivery of flavonoids, Colloids Surf. B: Biointerfaces 123 (2014) 331–338.

[15] J. Ezzati Nazhad Dolatabadi, H. Hamishehkar, H. Valizadeh, Development of dry powder inhaler formulation loaded with alendronate solid lipid nanoparticles: solid-state characterization and aerosol dispersion performance, Drug Dev. Ind. Pharm. 41 (9) (2015) 1431–1437.

[16] Z. Bakhtiary, J. Barar, A. Aghanejad, A.A. Saei, E. Nemati, J. Ezzati Nazhad Dolatabadi, et al., Microparticles containing erlotinib-loaded solid lipid nanoparticles for treatment of non-small cell lung cancer, Drug Dev. Ind. Pharm. 43 (8) (2017) 1244–1253.

[17] J.E.N. Dolatabadi, H. Valizadeh, H. Hamishehkar, Solid lipid nanoparticles as efficient drug and gene delivery systems: recent breakthroughs, Adv. Pharm. Bull. 5 (2) (2015) 151–159.

[18] J. Zhu, X. Shi, Dendrimer-based nanodevices for targeted drug delivery applications, J. Mater. Chem. B 1 (34) (2013) 4199–4211.

[19] P. Tripathi, A. Khopade, S. Nagaich, S. Shrivastava, S. Jain, N. Jain, Dendrimer grafts for delivery of 5-fluorouracil, Die Pharm. 57 (4) (2002) 261–264.

[20] D.A. Tomalia, Birth of a new macromolecular architecture: dendrimers as quantized building blocks for nanoscale synthetic polymer chemistry, Prog. Polym. Sci. 30 (3–4) (2005) 294–324.

[21] D.M. Watkins, Y. Sayed-Sweet, J.W. Klimash, N.J. Turro, D.A. Tomalia, Dendrimers with hydrophobic cores and the formation of supramolecular dendrimer–surfactant assemblies, Langmuir 13 (12) (1997) 3136–3141.

[22] H. Wang, Q. Huang, H. Chang, J. Xiao, Y. Cheng, Stimuli-responsive dendrimers in drug delivery, Biomater. Sci. 4 (3) (2016) 375–390.

[23] S.G. Sampathkumar, K.J. Yarema, Dendrimers in cancer treatment and diagnosis, in: Nanotechnologies for the Life Sciences (Online), Wiley, 2007.

[24] M. Kalomiraki, K. Thermos, N.A. Chaniotakis, Dendrimers as tunable vectors of drug delivery systems and biomedical and ocular applications, Int. J. Nanomedicine 11 (2016) 1.

[25] P. Kesharwani, R.K. Tekade, N.K. Jain, Generation dependent safety and efficacy of folic acid conjugated dendrimer based anticancer drug formulations, Pharm. Res. 32 (2015) 1438–1450.

[26] J.B. Wolinsky, M.W. Grinstaff, Therapeutic and diagnostic applications of dendrimers for cancer treatment, Adv. Drug Deliv. Rev. 60 (9) (2008) 1037–1055.

[27] G. Pasut, F. Veronese, Polymer–drug conjugation, recent achievements and general strategies, Prog. Polym. Sci. 32 (8–9) (2007) 933–961.

[28] J.M. Frechet, D.A. Tomalia, Dendrimers and Other Dendritic Polymers, John Wiley & Sons, Ltd, 2001.

[29] G.R. Newkome, C.N. Moorefield, F. Vögtle, F. Vögtle, F. Vögtle, G. Chemist, Dendrimers and Dendrons: Concepts, Syntheses, Applications, Wiley Online Library, 2001.

[30] M. Najlah, D. Emanuele, A., Synthesis of dendrimers and drug-dendrimer conjugates for drug delivery, Curr. Opin. Drug Discov. Devel. 10 (6) (2007) 756.

[31] F. Vögtle, G. Richardt, N. Werner, Dendrimer Chemistry: Concepts, Syntheses, Properties, Applications, John Wiley & Sons, 2009.

[32] R. Hourani, A. Kakkar, Advances in the elegance of chemistry in designing dendrimers, Macromol. Rapid Commun. 31 (11) (2010) 947–974.

[33] M. Ionov, Z. Garaiova, I. Waczulikova, D. Wróbel, E. Pędziwiatr-Werbicka, R. Gomez-Ramirez, et al., siRNA carriers based on carbosilane dendrimers affect zeta potential and size of phospholipid vesicles, Biochim. Biophys. Acta, Biomembr. 1818 (9) (2012) 2209–2216.

[34] M. Ionov, D. Wróbel, K. Gardikis, S. Hatziantoniou, C. Demetzos, J.-P. Majoral, et al., Effect of phosphorus dendrimers on DMPC lipid membranes, Chem. Phys. Lipids 165 (4) (2012) 408–413.

[35] S. Mignani, J. Rodrigues, H. Tomas, M. Zablocka, X. Shi, A.-M. Caminade, et al., Dendrimers in combination with natural products and analogues as anti-cancer agents, Chem. Soc. Rev. 47 (2) (2018) 514–532.

[36] B.K. Nanjwade, H.M. Bechra, G.K. Derkar, F. Manvi, V.K. Nanjwade, Dendrimers: emerging polymers for drug-delivery systems, Eur. J. Pharm. Sci. 38 (3) (2009) 185–196.

[37] L. Brannon-Peppas, J.O. Blanchette, Nanoparticle and targeted systems for cancer therapy, Adv. Drug Deliv. Rev. 56 (11) (2004) 1649–1659.

[38] D. Peer, J.M. Karp, S. Hong, O.C. Farokhzad, R. Margalit, R. Langer, Nanocarriers as an emerging platform for cancer therapy, in: Nano-Enabled Medical Applications, Jenny Stanford Publishing, 2020, pp. 61–91.

[39] J. Liu, W.D. Gray, M.E. Davis, Y. Luo, Peptide- and saccharide-conjugated dendrimers for targeted drug delivery: a concise review, Interface Focus 2 (3) (2012) 307–324.

[40] S. Franzen, A comparison of peptide and folate receptor targeting of cancer cells: from single agent to nanoparticle, Expert Opin. Drug Deliv. 8 (3) (2011) 281–298.

[41] S. Svenson, D.A. Tomalia, Dendrimers in biomedical applications—reflections on the field, Adv. Drug Deliv. Rev. 64 (2012) 102–115.

[42] H. Chang, H. Wang, N. Shao, M. Wang, X. Wang, Y. Cheng, Surface-engineered dendrimers with a diaminododecane core achieve efficient gene transfection and low cytotoxicity, Bioconjug. Chem. 25 (2) (2014) 342–350.

[43] R. Esfand, D.A. Tomalia, Poly (amidoamine)(PAMAM) dendrimers: from biomimicry to drug delivery and biomedical applications, Drug Discov. Today 6 (8) (2001) 427–436.

[44] S. Zhu, M. Hong, L. Zhang, G. Tang, Y. Jiang, Y. Pei, PEGylated PAMAM dendrimer-doxorubicin conjugates: in vitro evaluation and in vivo tumor accumulation, Pharm. Res. 27 (2010) 161–174.

[45] N. Malik, E.G. Evagorou, R. Duncan, Dendrimer-platinate: a novel approach to cancer chemotherapy, Anti-Cancer Drugs 10 (8) (1999) 767–776.

[46] S.A. Torres-Pérez, R.-G.M. del Pilar, E. Ramón-Gallegos, Glycosylated one-step PAMAM dendrimers loaded with methotrexate for target therapy in breast cancer cells MDA-MB-231, J. Drug Deliv. Technol. 58 (2020) 101769.

[47] K. Jain, P. Kesharwani, U. Gupta, N. Jain, Dendrimer toxicity: let's meet the challenge, Int. J. Pharm. 394 (1–2) (2010) 122–142.

[48] B. Noriega-Luna, L.A. Godínez, F.J. Rodríguez, A. Rodríguez, G.Z.-L. Larrea, C. Sosa-Ferreyra, et al., Applications of dendrimers in drug delivery agents, diagnosis, therapy, and detection, J. Nanomater. 2014 (2014) 39.

[49] Y.-Q. Ma, Theoretical and computational studies of dendrimers as delivery vectors, Chem. Soc. Rev. 42 (2) (2013) 705–727.

[50] Y. Wang, X. Cao, R. Guo, M. Shen, M. Zhang, M. Zhu, et al., Targeted delivery of doxorubicin into cancer cells using a folic acid–dendrimer conjugate, Polym. Chem. 2 (8) (2011) 1754–1760.

[51] Y. Wang, R. Guo, X. Cao, M. Shen, X. Shi, Encapsulation of 2-methoxyestradiol within multifunctional poly (amidoamine) dendrimers for targeted cancer therapy, Biomaterials 32 (12) (2011) 3322–3329.

[52] F. Fu, Y. Wu, J. Zhu, S. Wen, M. Shen, X. Shi, Multifunctional lactobionic acid-modified dendrimers for targeted drug delivery to liver cancer cells: investigating the role played by PEG spacer, ACS Appl. Mater. Interfaces 6 (18) (2014) 16416–16425.

[53] X. He, C.S. Alves, N. Oliveira, J. Rodrigues, J. Zhu, I. Bányai, et al., RGD peptide-modified multifunctional dendrimer platform for drug encapsulation and targeted inhibition of cancer cells, Colloids Surf. B: Biointerfaces 125 (2015) 82–89.

[54] J. Zhu, Z. Xiong, M. Shen, X. Shi, Encapsulation of doxorubicin within multifunctional gadolinium-loaded dendrimer nanocomplexes for targeted theranostics of cancer cells, RSC Adv. 5 (38) (2015) 30286–30296.

[55] E. Buhleier, W. Wehner, F. Vögtle, Cascade" and "nonskid-chain-like" syntheses of molecular cavity topologies, Synthesis 2 (1978) 155–158.

[56] S. Bae, J. Park, J.-S. Kim, Cas-OFFinder: a fast and versatile algorithm that searches for potential off-target sites of Cas9 RNA-guided endonucleases, Bioinformatics 30 (10) (2014) 1473–1475.

[57] N. Shao, Y. Su, J. Hu, J. Zhang, H. Zhang, Y. Cheng, Comparison of generation 3 polyamidoamine dendrimer and generation 4 polypropylenimine dendrimer on drug loading, complex structure, release behavior, and cytotoxicity, Int. J. Nanomedicine 6 (2011) 3361–3372.

[58] R.A. Bapat, S. Dharmadhikari, T.V. Chaubal, M.C.I.M. Amin, P. Bapat, B. Gorain, et al., The potential of dendrimer in delivery of therapeutics for dentistry, Heliyon 5 (10) (2019) e02544.

[59] M. Chai, Y. Niu, W.J. Youngs, P.L. Rinaldi, Structure and conformation of DAB dendrimers in solution via multidimensional NMR techniques, J. Am. Chem. Soc. 123 (20) (2001) 4670–4678.

[60] E. Kohli, H.-Y. Han, A.D. Zeman, S.V. Vinogradov, Formulations of biodegradable Nanogel carriers with 5′-triphosphates of nucleoside analogs that display a reduced cytotoxicity and enhanced drug activity, J. Control. Release 121 (1–2) (2007) 19–27.

[61] W.-D. Jang, K.K. Selim, C.-H. Lee, I.-K. Kang, Bioinspired application of dendrimers: from bio-mimicry to biomedical applications, Prog. Polym. Sci. 34 (1) (2009) 1–23.

[62] B. Klajnert, D. Appelhans, H. Komber, N. Morgner, S. Schwarz, S. Richter, et al., The influence of densely organized maltose shells on the biological properties of poly (propylene imine) dendrimers: new effects dependent on hydrogen bonding, Chem. A Eur. J. 14 (23) (2008) 7030–7041.

[63] B.P. Roberts, M.J. Scanlon, G.Y. Krippner, D.K. Chalmers, Molecular dynamics of poly (l-lysine) dendrimers with naphthalene disulfonate caps, Macromolecules 42 (7) (2009) 2775–2783.

[64] J.S. Choi, K. Nam, J.-y. Park, J.-B. Kim, J.-K. Lee, J.-s. Park, Enhanced transfection efficiency of PAMAM dendrimer by surface modification with L-arginine, J. Control. Release 99 (3) (2004) 445–456.

[65] L.M. Kaminskas, V.M. McLeod, D.B. Ascher, G.M. Ryan, S. Jones, J.M. Haynes, et al., Methotrexate-conjugated PEGylated dendrimers show differential patterns of deposition and activity in tumor-burdened lymph nodes after intravenous and subcutaneous administration in rats, Mol. Pharm. 12 (2) (2015) 432–443.

[66] O. Yemul, T. Imae, Synthesis and characterization of poly (ethyleneimine) dendrimers, Colloid Polym. Sci. 286 (2008) 747–752.

[67] Z. Zhou, B. Kong, C. Yu, X. Shi, M. Wang, W. Liu, et al., Tungsten oxide nanorods: an efficient nanoplatform for tumor CT imaging and photothermal therapy, Sci. Rep. 4 (1) (2014) 3653.

[68] J. Li, Y. Hu, J. Yang, P. Wei, W. Sun, M. Shen, et al., Hyaluronic acid-modified Fe3O4@ Au core/shell nanostars for multimodal imaging and photothermal therapy of tumors, Biomaterials 38 (2015) 10–21.

[69] D. Kim, Y.Y. Jeong, S. Jon, A drug-loaded aptamer–gold nanoparticle bioconjugate for combined CT imaging and therapy of prostate cancer, ACS Nano 4 (7) (2010) 3689–3696.

[70] M. Shen, X. Shi, Dendrimer-based organic/inorganic hybrid nanoparticles in biomedical applications, Nanoscale 2 (9) (2010) 1596–1610.

[71] Z. Qiao, X. Shi, Dendrimer-based molecular imaging contrast agents, Prog. Polym. Sci. 44 (2015) 1–27.

[72] Y. Zheng, F. Fu, M. Zhang, M. Shen, M. Zhu, X. Shi, Multifunctional dendrimers modified with alpha-tocopheryl succinate for targeted cancer therapy, MedChemComm. 5 (7) (2014) 879–885.

[73] J.F. Kukowska-Latallo, K.A. Candido, Z. Cao, S.S. Nigavekar, I.J. Majoros, T.P. Thomas, et al., Nanoparticle targeting of anticancer drug improves therapeutic response in animal model of human epithelial cancer, Cancer Res. 65 (12) (2005) 5317–5324.

[74] J. Zhu, L. Zheng, S. Wen, Y. Tang, M. Shen, G. Zhang, et al., Targeted cancer theranostics using alpha-tocopheryl succinate-conjugated multifunctional dendrimer-entrapped gold nanoparticles, Biomaterials 35 (26) (2014) 7635–7646.

[75] L. Zheng, J. Zhu, M. Shen, X. Chen, J.R. Baker, S.H. Wang, et al., Targeted cancer cell inhibition using multifunctional dendrimer-entrapped gold nanoparticles, MedChemComm. 4 (6) (2013) 1001–1005.

[76] Y. Chang, X. Meng, Y. Zhao, K. Li, B. Zhao, M. Zhu, et al., Novel water-soluble and pH-responsive anticancer drug nanocarriers: doxorubicin–PAMAM dendrimer conjugates attached to superparamagnetic iron oxide nanoparticles (IONPs), J. Colloid Interface Sci. 363 (1) (2011) 403–409.

[77] R. Weissleder, M.J. Pittet, Imaging in the era of molecular oncology, Nature 452 (7187) (2008) 580–589.

[78] M.M. Van Schooneveld, E. Vucic, R. Koole, Y. Zhou, J. Stocks, D.P. Cormode, et al., Improved biocompatibility and pharmacokinetics of silica nanoparticles by means of a lipid coating: a multimodality investigation, Nano Lett. 8 (8) (2008) 2517–2525.

[79] R. Guo, H. Wang, C. Peng, M. Shen, M. Pan, X. Cao, et al., X-ray attenuation property of dendrimer-entrapped gold nanoparticles, J. Phys. Chem. C 114 (1) (2010) 50–56.

[80] L.S. Karfeld-Sulzer, E.A. Waters, N.E. Davis, T.J. Meade, A.E. Barron, Multivalent protein polymer MRI contrast agents: controlling relaxivity via modulation of amino acid sequence, Biomacromolecules 11 (6) (2010) 1429–1436.

[81] T.H. Schindler, H.R. Schelbert, A. Quercioli, V. Dilsizian, Cardiac PET imaging for the detection and monitoring of coronary artery disease and microvascular health, JACC Cardiovasc. Imaging 3 (6) (2010) 623–640.

[82] K.R. Bhushan, P. Misra, F. Liu, S. Mathur, R.E. Lenkinski, J.V. Frangioni, Detection of breast cancer microcalcifications using a dual-modality SPECT/NIR fluorescent probe, J. Am. Chem. Soc. 130 (52) (2008) 17648–17649.

[83] J.A. Barreto, W. O'Malley, M. Kubeil, B. Graham, H. Stephan, L. Spiccia, Nanomaterials: applications in cancer imaging and therapy, Adv. Mater. 23 (12) (2011) H18–H40.

[84] A. Louie, Multimodality imaging probes: design and challenges, Chem. Rev. 110 (5) (2010) 3146–3195.

[85] E. Boisselier, D. Astruc, Gold nanoparticles in nanomedicine: preparations, imaging, diagnostics, therapies and toxicity, Chem. Soc. Rev. 38 (6) (2009) 1759–1782.

[86] Y. Cao, Y. He, H. Liu, Y. Luo, M. Shen, J. Xia, et al., Targeted CT imaging of human hepatocellular carcinoma using low-generation dendrimer-entrapped gold nanoparticles modified with lactobionic acid, J. Mater. Chem. B 3 (2) (2015) 286–295.

[87] H. Liu, H. Wang, Y. Xu, M. Shen, J. Zhao, G. Zhang, et al., Synthesis of PEGylated low generation dendrimer-entrapped gold nanoparticles for CT imaging applications, Nanoscale 6 (9) (2014) 4521–4526.

[88] H.H. Abujudeh, R. Kaewlai, A. Kagan, L.B. Chibnik, R.M. Nazarian, W.A. High, et al., Nephrogenic systemic fibrosis after gadopentetate dimeglumine exposure: case series of 36 patients, Radiology 253 (1) (2009) 81–89.

[89] P. Caravan, J.J. Ellison, T.J. McMurry, R.B. Lauffer, Gadolinium (III) chelates as MRI contrast agents: structure, dynamics, and applications, Chem. Rev. 99 (9) (1999) 2293–2352.

[90] J. Lim, B. Turkbey, M. Bernardo, L.H. Bryant Jr., M. Garzoni, G.M. Pavan, et al., Gadolinium MRI contrast agents based on triazine dendrimers: relaxivity and in vivo pharmacokinetics, Bioconjug. Chem. 23 (11) (2012) 2291–2299.

[91] G. Ratzinger, P. Agrawal, W. Körner, J. Lonkai, H.M. Sanders, E. Terreno, et al., Surface modification of PLGA nanospheres with Gd-DTPA and Gd-DOTA for high-relaxivity MRI contrast agents, Biomaterials 31 (33) (2010) 8716–8723.

[92] J. Zheng, J. Liu, M. Dunne, D.A. Jaffray, C. Allen, In vivo performance of a liposomal vascular contrast agent for CT and MR-based image guidance applications, Pharm. Res. 24 (2007) 1193–1201.

[93] C.A.S. Regino, S. Walbridge, M. Bernardo, K.J. Wong, D. Johnson, R. Lonser, et al., A dual CT-MR dendrimer contrast agent as a surrogate marker for convection-enhanced delivery of intracerebral macromolecular therapeutic agents, Contrast Media Mol. Imaging 3 (1) (2008) 2–8.

[94] C. Alric, J. Taleb, G. Le Duc, C. Mandon, C. Billotey, A. Le Meur-Herland, et al., Gadolinium chelate coated gold nanoparticles as contrast agents for both X-ray computed tomography and magnetic resonance imaging, J. Am. Chem. Soc. 130 (18) (2008) 5908–5915.

[95] M.N. Sk, H.-K. Kim, J. Park, Y.-M. Chang, T.-J. Kim, Gold nanoparticles coated with Gd-chelate as a potential CT/MRI bimodal contrast agent, Bull. Korean Chem. Soc. 31 (5) (2010) 1177–1181.

[96] S.-W. Chou, Y.-H. Shau, P.-C. Wu, Y.-S. Yang, D.-B. Shieh, C.-C. Chen, In vitro and in vivo studies of FePt nanoparticles for dual modal CT/MRI molecular imaging, J. Am. Chem. Soc. 132 (38) (2010) 13270–13278.

[97] A.R. Menjoge, R.M. Kannan, D.A. Tomalia, Dendrimer-based drug and imaging conjugates: design considerations for nanomedical applications, Drug Discov. Today 15 (5–6) (2010) 171–185.

[98] D. Chandrasekar, R. Sistla, F.J. Ahmad, R.K. Khar, P.V. Diwan, The development of folate-PAMAM dendrimer conjugates for targeted delivery of anti-arthritic drugs and their pharmacokinetics and biodistribution in arthritic rats, Biomaterials 28 (3) (2007) 504–512.

[99] Y. Cheng, J. Wang, T. Rao, X. He, T. Xu, Pharmaceutical applications of dendrimers: promising nanocarriers for drug delivery, Front. Biosci. 13 (4) (2008) 1447–1471.

[100] C. Peng, L. Zheng, Q. Chen, M. Shen, R. Guo, H. Wang, et al., PEGylated dendrimer-entrapped gold nanoparticles for in vivo blood pool and tumor imaging by computed tomography, Biomaterials 33 (4) (2012) 1107–1119.

[101] H. Wang, L. Zheng, C. Peng, R. Guo, M. Shen, X. Shi, et al., Computed tomography imaging of cancer cells using acetylated dendrimer-entrapped gold nanoparticles, Biomaterials 32 (11) (2011) 2979–2988.

[102] X. Shi, S. Wang, S. Meshinchi, M.E. Van Antwerp, X. Bi, I. Lee, J.R. Baker Jr., Dendrimer-entrapped gold nanoparticles as a platform for cancer-cell targeting and imaging, Small 3 (7) (2007) 1245–1252.

[103] S. Wen, K. Li, H. Cai, Q. Chen, M. Shen, Y. Huang, et al., Multifunctional dendrimer-entrapped gold nanoparticles for dual mode CT/MR imaging applications, Biomaterials 34 (5) (2013) 1570–1580.

[104] W.I. Lee, Y. Bae, A.J. Bard, Strong blue photoluminescence and ECL from OH-terminated PAMAM dendrimers in the absence of gold nanoparticles, J. Am. Chem. Soc. 126 (27) (2004) 8358–8359.

[105] D. Wang, T. Imae, Fluorescence emission from dendrimers and its pH dependence, J. Am. Chem. Soc. 126 (41) (2004) 13204–13205.

[106] Y.-J. Tsai, C.-C. Hu, C.-C. Chu, T. Imae, Intrinsically fluorescent PAMAM dendrimer as gene carrier and nanoprobe for nucleic acids delivery: bioimaging and transfection study, Biomacromolecules 12 (12) (2011) 4283–4290.

[107] B. Huang, A. Desai, H. Zong, S. Tang, P. Leroueil, J.R. Baker Jr., Copper-free click conjugation of methotrexate to a PAMAM dendrimer platform, Tetrahedron Lett. 52 (13) (2011) 1411–1414.

[108] V.S. Talanov, C.A.S. Regino, H. Kobayashi, M. Bernardo, P.L. Choyke, M.W. Brechbiel, Dendrimer-based nanoprobe for dual modality magnetic resonance and fluorescence imaging, Nano Lett. 6 (7) (2006) 1459–1463.

[109] X. Shi, S. Wang, S. Meshinchi, M.E. Van Antwerp, X. Bi, I. Lee, et al., Dendrimer-entrapped gold nanoparticles as a platform for cancer-cell targeting and imaging, Small 3 (7) (2007) 1245–1252.

[110] Z. Li, P. Huang, R. He, J. Lin, S. Yang, X. Zhang, et al., Aptamer-conjugated dendrimer-modified quantum dots for cancer cell targeting and imaging, Mater. Lett. 64 (3) (2010) 375–378.

[111] T. Hussain, Q.T. Nguyen, Molecular imaging for cancer diagnosis and surgery, Adv. Drug Deliv. Rev. 66 (2014) 90–100.

[112] X. Li, J. Wei, K.E. Aifantis, Y. Fan, Q. Feng, F.Z. Cui, et al., Current investigations into magnetic nanoparticles for biomedical applications, J. Biomed. Mater. Res. A 104 (5) (2016) 1285–1296.

[113] K. Li, S. Wen, A.C. Larson, M. Shen, Z. Zhang, Q. Chen, et al., Multifunctional dendrimer-based nanoparticles for in vivo MR/CT dual-modal molecular imaging of breast cancer, Int. J. Nanomedicine 8 (2013) 2589–2600.

[114] R.E. Jacobs, S.R. Cherry, Complementary emerging techniques: high-resolution PET and MRI, Curr. Opin. Neurobiol. 11 (5) (2001) 621–629.

[115] T.F. Massoud, S.S. Gambhir, Molecular imaging in living subjects: seeing fundamental biological processes in a new light, Genes Dev. 17 (5) (2003) 545–580.

[116] Y. Zheng, S. Ji, A. Czerwinski, F. Valenzuela, M. Pennington, S. Liu, FITC-conjugated cyclic RGD peptides as fluorescent probes for staining integrin $\alpha v \beta 3 / \alpha v \beta 5$ in tumor tissues, Bioconjug. Chem. 25 (11) (2014) 1925–1941.

[117] A. Massaguer, A. González-Cantó, E. Escribano, S. Barrabés, G. Artigas, V. Moreno, et al., Integrin-targeted delivery into cancer cells of a Pt (IV) pro-drug through conjugation to RGD-containing peptides, Dalton Trans. 44 (1) (2015) 202–212.

[118] S. Takahashi, Vascular endothelial growth factor (VEGF), VEGF receptors and their inhibitors for antiangiogenic tumor therapy, Biol. Pharm. Bull. 34 (12) (2011) 1785–1788.

[119] M.-F. Bellin, MR contrast agents, the old and the new, Eur. J. Radiol. 60 (3) (2006) 314–323.

[120] M. Mahmoudi, S. Sant, B. Wang, S. Laurent, T. Sen, Superparamagnetic iron oxide nanoparticles (SPIONs): development, surface modification and applications in chemotherapy, Adv. Drug Deliv. Rev. 63 (1–2) (2011) 24–46.

[121] F.J.A.T. Gilbert, Dynamic contrast-enhanced MRI in cancer, Imaging Med. 1 (2009) 173–186.

[122] A. Ibrahim, K. Da, V.C. Kašička, C.M. Faye, H. Cottet, Effective charge determination of dendrigraft poly-L-lysine by capillary isotachophoresis, Macromolecules 46 (2) (2013) 533–540.

[123] M. Rohrer, H. Bauer, J. Mintorovitch, M. Requardt, H.-J. Weinmann, Comparison of magnetic properties of MRI contrast media solutions at different magnetic field strengths, Investig. Radiol. 40 (11) (2005) 715–724.

[124] J.-M. Shen, X.-X. Li, L.-L. Fan, X. Zhou, J.-M. Han, M.-K. Jia, et al., Heterogeneous dimer peptide-conjugated polylysine dendrimer-Fe3O4 composite as a novel nanoscale molecular probe for early diagnosis and therapy in hepatocellular carcinoma, Int. J. Nanomedicine 12 (2017) 1183.

[125] S. Langereis, Q.G. De Lussanet, M.H. Van Genderen, W.H. Backes, E. Meijer, Multivalent contrast agents based on gadolinium–diethylenetriaminepentaacetic acid-terminated poly (propylene imine) dendrimers for magnetic resonance imaging, Macromolecules 37 (9) (2004) 3084–3091.

[126] H. Kobayashi, T. Saga, S. Kawamoto, N. Sato, A. Hiraga, T. Ishimori, et al., Dynamic micro-magnetic resonance imaging of liver micrometastasis in mice with a novel liver macromolecular magnetic resonance contrast agent DAB-Am64-(1B4M-Gd) 64, Cancer Res. 61 (13) (2001) 4966–4970.

[127] M. Saad, O.B. Garbuzenko, E. Ber, P. Chandna, J.J. Khandare, V.P. Pozharov, et al., Receptor targeted polymers, dendrimers, liposomes: which nanocarrier is the most efficient for tumor-specific treatment and imaging? J. Control. Release 130 (2) (2008) 107–114.

[128] C. Peitzsch, R. Perrin, R.P. Hill, A. Dubrovska, I. Kurth, Hypoxia as a biomarker for radioresistant cancer stem cells, Int. J. Radiat. Biol. 90 (8) (2014) 636–652.

[129] H.E. Barker, J.T. Paget, A.A. Khan, K.J. Harrington, The tumour microenvironment after radiotherapy: mechanisms of resistance and recurrence, Nat. Rev. Cancer 15 (7) (2015) 409–425.

[130] Y.-F. Li, H.-T. Zhang, L. Xin, Hyaluronic acid-modified polyamidoamine dendrimer G5-entrapped gold nanoparticles delivering METase gene inhibits gastric tumor growth via targeting CD44+ gastric cancer cells, J. Cancer Res. Clin. Oncol. 144 (2018) 1463–1473.

[131] G.-Z. Qiu, M.-Z. Jin, J.-X. Dai, W. Sun, J.-H. Feng, W.-L. Jin, Reprogramming of the tumor in the hypoxic niche: the emerging concept and associated therapeutic strategies, Trends Pharmacol. Sci. 38 (8) (2017) 669–686.

[132] G. Song, L. Cheng, Y. Chao, K. Yang, Z. Liu, Emerging nanotechnology and advanced materials for cancer radiation therapy, Adv. Mater. 29 (32) (2017) 1700996.

[133] Z. Cai, H. Zhang, Y. Wei, F. Cong, Hyaluronan-inorganic nanohybrid materials for biomedical applications, Biomacromolecules 18 (6) (2017) 1677–1696.

[134] D.-H. Park, S.-J. Hwang, J.-M. Oh, J.-H. Yang, J.-H. Choy, Polymer–inorganic supramolecular nanohybrids for red, white, green, and blue applications, Prog. Polym. Sci. 38 (10–11) (2013) 1442–1486.

[135] H. Yang, J. Zhao, C. Wu, C. Ye, D. Zou, S. Wang, Facile synthesis of colloidal stable MoS2 nanoparticles for combined tumor therapy, Chem. Eng. J. 351 (2018) 548–558.

[136] Y. Fan, J. Zhang, M. Shi, D. Li, C. Lu, X. Cao, et al., Poly (amidoamine) dendrimer-coordinated copper (II) complexes as a theranostic nanoplatform for the radiotherapy-enhanced magnetic resonance imaging and chemotherapy of tumors and tumor metastasis, Nano Lett. 19 (2) (2019) 1216–1226.

[137] Y. Fan, W. Tu, M. Shen, X. Chen, Y. Ning, J. Li, et al., Targeted tumor hypoxia dual-mode CT/MR imaging and enhanced radiation therapy using dendrimer-based nanosensitizers, Adv. Funct. Mater. 30 (13) (2020) 1909285.

[138] B. Kavosi, A. Salimi, R. Hallaj, F. Moradi, Ultrasensitive electrochemical immunosensor for PSA biomarker detection in prostate cancer cells using gold nanoparticles/PAMAM dendrimer loaded with enzyme linked aptamer as integrated triple signal amplification strategy, Biosens. Bioelectron. 74 (2015) 915–923.

[139] T.A. Cavell, L.C. Elledge, K.T. Malcolm, M.A. Faith, J.N. Hughes, Relationship quality and the mentoring of aggressive, high-risk children, J. Clin. Child Adolesc. Psychol. 38 (2) (2009) 185–198.

[140] W.B. Turnbull, J.F. Stoddart, Design and synthesis of glycodendrimers, Rev. Mol. Biotechnol. 90 (3–4) (2002) 231–255.

[141] M. Markowicz, P. Szymański, M. Ciszewski, A. Kłys, E. Mikiciuk-Olasik, Evaluation of poly (amidoamine) dendrimers as potential carriers of iminodiacetic derivatives using solubility studies and 2D-NOESY NMR spectroscopy, J. Biol. Phys. 38 (2012) 637–656.

[142] F. Abedi-Gaballu, G. Dehghan, M. Ghaffari, R. Yekta, S. Abbaspour-Ravasjani, B. Baradaran, et al., PAMAM dendrimers as efficient drug and gene delivery nanosystems for cancer therapy, Appl. Mater. Today 12 (2018) 177–190.

[143] M. Zhang, R. Guo, M. Keri, I. Banyai, Y. Zheng, M. Cao, et al., Impact of dendrimer surface functional groups on the release of doxorubicin from dendrimer carriers, J. Phys. Chem. B 118 (6) (2014) 1696–1706.

[144] C. Peng, Y. Li, H. Liang, J. Cheng, Q. Li, X. Sun, et al., Detection and photodynamic therapy of inflamed atherosclerotic plaques in the carotid artery of rabbits, J. Photochem. Photobiol. B Biol. 102 (1) (2011) 26–31.

[145] C. Kojima, Y. Toi, A. Harada, K. Kono, Preparation of poly (ethylene glycol)-attached dendrimers encapsulating photosensitizers for application to photodynamic therapy, Bioconjug. Chem. 18 (3) (2007) 663–670.

[146] N. Spyropoulos-Antonakakis, E. Sarantopoulou, P.N. Trohopoulos, A.L. Stefi, Z. Kollia, V.E. Gavriil, et al., Selective aggregation of PAMAM dendrimer nanocarriers and PAMAM/ZnPc nanodrugs on human atheromatous carotid tissues: a photodynamic therapy for atherosclerosis, Nanoscale Res. Lett. 10 (1) (2015) 210.

[147] A. Buczkowski, S. Sekowski, A. Grala, D. Palecz, K. Milowska, P. Urbaniak, et al., Interaction between PAMAM-NH2 G4 dendrimer and 5-fluorouracil in aqueous solution, Int. J. Pharm. 408 (1–2) (2011) 266–270.

[148] K.M. Laginha, S. Verwoert, G.J. Charrois, T.M. Allen, Determination of doxorubicin levels in whole tumor and tumor nuclei in murine breast cancer tumors, Clin. Cancer Res. 11 (19) (2005) 6944–6949.

[149] C. Kojima, K. Kono, K. Maruyama, T. Takagishi, Synthesis of polyamidoamine dendrimers having poly (ethylene glycol) grafts and their ability to encapsulate anticancer drugs, Bioconjug. Chem. 11 (6) (2000) 910–917.

[150] B.N. Cronstein, The mechanism of action of methotrexate, Rheum. Dis. Clin. N. Am. 23 (4) (1997) 739–755.

[151] M.N. Levine, V.H. Bramwell, K.I. Pritchard, B.D. Norris, L.E. Shepherd, H. Abu-Zahra, et al., Randomized trial of intensive cyclophosphamide, epirubicin, and fluorouracil chemotherapy compared with cyclophosphamide, methotrexate, and fluorouracil in premenopausal women with node-positive breast cancer. National Cancer Institute of Canada Clinical Trials Group, J. Clin. Oncol. 16 (8) (1998) 2651–2658.

[152] M. Colleoni, A. Rocca, M. Sandri, L. Zorzino, G. Masci, F. Nole, et al., Low-dose oral methotrexate and cyclophosphamide in metastatic breast cancer: antitumor activity and correlation with vascular endothelial growth factor levels, Ann. Oncol. 13 (1) (2002) 73–80.

[153] R. Gorlick, J.R. Bertino, Clinical pharmacology and resistance to dihydrofolate reductase inhibitors, in: Antifolate Drugs in Cancer Therapy, Humana Press, 1999, pp. 37–57.

[154] M.A. van Dongen, R. Rattan, J. Silpe, C. Dougherty, N.L. Michmerhuizen, M. Van Winkle, et al., Poly (amidoamine) dendrimer–methotrexate conjugates: the mechanism of interaction with folate binding protein, Mol. Pharm. 11 (11) (2014) 4049–4058.

[155] G.J. Kirkpatrick, J.A. Plumb, O.B. Sutcliffe, D.J. Flint, N.J. Wheate, Evaluation of anionic half generation 3.5–6.5 poly (amidoamine) dendrimers as delivery vehicles for the active component of the anticancer drug cisplatin, J. Inorg. Biochem. 105 (9) (2011) 1115–1122.

[156] H.-T. Chen, M.F. Neerman, A.R. Parrish, E.E. Simanek, Cytotoxicity, hemolysis, and acute in vivo toxicity of dendrimers based on melamine, candidate vehicles for drug delivery, J. Am. Chem. Soc. 126 (32) (2004) 10044–10048.

[157] R.K. Tekade, X. Sun, The Warburg effect and glucose-derived cancer theranostics, Drug Discov. Today 22 (11) (2017) 1637–1653.

[158] L. Szablewski, Expression of glucose transporters in cancers, Biochim. Biophys. Acta Rev. Cancer 1835 (2) (2013) 164–169.

[159] M.L. Macheda, S. Rogers, J.D. Best, Molecular and cellular regulation of glucose transporter (GLUT) proteins in cancer, J. Cell. Physiol. 202 (3) (2005) 654–662.

[160] A. Krzeslak, K. Wojcik-Krowiranda, E. Forma, P. Jozwiak, H. Romanowicz, A. Bienkiewicz, et al., Expression of GLUT1 and GLUT3 glucose transporters in endometrial and breast cancers, Pathol. Oncol. Res. 18 (2012) 721–728.

[161] R.S. Dhanikula, A. Argaw, J.-F. Bouchard, P. Hildgen, Methotrexate loaded polyethercopolyester dendrimers for the treatment of gliomas: enhanced efficacy and intratumoral transport capability, Mol. Pharm. 5 (1) (2008) 105–116.

[162] S. Nigam, D. Bahadur, Dendrimer-conjugated iron oxide nanoparticles as stimuli-responsive drug carriers for thermally-activated chemotherapy of cancer, Colloids Surf. B: Biointerfaces 155 (2017) 182–192.

[163] S.F. Zhang, S. Lü, C. Gao, J. Yang, X. Yan, T. Li, et al., Multiarm-polyethylene glycol-polyglutamic acid peptide dendrimer: design, synthesis, and dissolving thrombus, J. Biomed. Mater. Res. A 106 (6) (2018) 1687–1696.

[164] M. Huang, et al., A nano polymer conjugate for dual drugs sequential release and combined treatment of colon cancer and thrombotic complications, Mater. Sci. Eng. C 110 (2020) 110697.

[165] W. Fan, X. Wang, B. Ding, H. Cai, X. Wang, Y. Fan, et al., Thioaptamer-conjugated CD44-targeted delivery system for the treatment of breast cancer in vitro and in vivo, J. Drug Target. 24 (4) (2016) 359–371.

[166] J. Liu, J. Li, N. Liu, N. Guo, C. Gao, Y. Hao, et al., In vitro studies of phospholipid-modified PAMAM-siMDR1 complexes for the reversal of multidrug resistance in human breast cancer cells, Int. J. Pharm. 530 (1–2) (2017) 291–299.

[167] P. Kesharwani, R.K. Tekade, N.K. Jain, Generation dependent cancer targeting potential of poly (propyleneimine) dendrimer, Biomaterials 35 (21) (2014) 5539–5548.

[168] A. Szulc, M. Signorelli, A. Schiraldi, D. Appelhans, B. Voit, M. Bryszewska, et al., Maltose modified poly (propylene imine) dendrimers as potential carriers of nucleoside analog 5′-triphosphates, Int. J. Pharm. 495 (2) (2015) 940–947.

[169] T. Dutta, H.B. Agashe, M. Garg, P. Balasubramanium, M. Kabra, N.K. Jain, Poly (propyleneimine) dendrimer based nanocontainers for targeting of efavirenz to human monocytes/macrophages in vitro, J. Drug Target. 15 (1) (2007) 89–98.

[170] D. Luong, P. Kesharwani, R. Deshmukh, M.C.I.M. Amin, U. Gupta, K. Greish, et al., PEGylated PAMAM dendrimers: enhancing efficacy and mitigating toxicity for effective anticancer drug and gene delivery, Acta Biomater. 43 (2016) 14–29.

[171] A.K. Sharma, A. Gothwal, P. Kesharwani, H. Alsaab, A.K. Iyer, U. Gupta, Dendrimer nanoarchitectures for cancer diagnosis and anticancer drug delivery, Drug Discov. Today 22 (2) (2017) 314–326.

[172] Q. Zhong, S.R. da Rocha, Poly (amidoamine) dendrimer–doxorubicin conjugates: in vitro characteristics and pseudosolution formulation in pressurized metered-dose inhalers, Mol. Pharm. 13 (3) (2016) 1058–1072.

[173] I. Matai, P. Gopinath, Chemically cross-linked hybrid nanogels of alginate and PAMAM dendrimers as efficient anticancer drug delivery vehicles, ACS Biomater. Sci. Eng. 2 (2) (2016) 213–223.

[174] B. Bahmani, I. Vohra, N. Kamaly, R. Abdi, Active targeted delivery of immune therapeutics to lymph nodes, Curr. Opin. Organ Transplant. 23 (1) (2018) 8.

[175] M. Herrera, B. Bussolati, S. Bruno, L. Morando, G. Mauriello-Romanazzi, F. Sanavio, et al., Exogenous mesenchymal stem cells localize to the kidney by means of CD44 following acute tubular injury, Kidney Int. 72 (4) (2007) 430–441.

[176] G. Mattheolabakis, L. Milane, A. Singh, M.M. Amiji, Hyaluronic acid targeting of CD44 for cancer therapy: from receptor biology to nanomedicine, J. Drug Target. 23 (7–8) (2015) 605–618.

[177] S. Kumar, J.R. Inigo, R. Kumar, A.K. Chaudhary, J. O'Malley, S. Balachandar, et al., Nimbolide reduces CD44 positive cell population and induces mitochondrial apoptosis in pancreatic cancer cells, Cancer Lett. 413 (2018) 82–93.

[178] I. Morath, C. Jung, R. Leveque, C. Linfeng, R.-A. Toillon, A. Warth, et al., Differential recruitment of CD44 isoforms by ErbB ligands reveals an involvement of CD44 in breast cancer, Oncogene 37 (11) (2018) 1472–1484.

[179] V. Jeannot, C. Gauche, S. Mazzaferro, M. Couvet, L. Vanwonterghem, M. Henry, et al., Anti-tumor efficacy of hyaluronan-based nanoparticles for the co-delivery of drugs in lung cancer, J. Control. Release 275 (2018) 117–128.

[180] T.J. Key, P.K. Verkasalo, E. Banks, Epidemiology of breast cancer, Lancet Oncol. 2 (3) (2001) 133–140.

[181] R.S. Yahya, A.A. El-Bindary, H.A. El-Mezayen, H.M. Abdelmasseh, M.A. Eissa, Biochemical evaluation of hyaluronic acid in breast cancer, Clin. Lab. 60 (7) (2014) 1115–1121.

[182] J.-H. Park, H.-J. Cho, H.Y. Yoon, I.-S. Yoon, S.-H. Ko, J.-S. Shim, et al., Hyaluronic acid derivative-coated nanohybrid liposomes for cancer imaging and drug delivery, J. Control. Release 174 (2014) 98–108.

[183] X.-L. Guo, X.-X. Kang, Y.-Q. Wang, X.-J. Zhang, C.-J. Li, Y. Liu, et al., Co-delivery of cisplatin and doxorubicin by covalently conjugating with polyamidoamine dendrimer for enhanced synergistic cancer therapy, Acta Biomater. 84 (2019) 367–377.

[184] K. Jain, P. Kesharwani, U. Gupta, N.K. Jain, A review of glycosylated carriers for drug delivery, Biomaterials 33 (16) (2012) 4166–4186.

[185] A. Papagiannaros, K. Dimas, G.T. Papaioannou, C. Demetzos, Doxorubicin–PAMAM dendrimer complex attached to liposomes: cytotoxic studies against human cancer cell lines, Int. J. Pharm. 302 (1–2) (2005) 29–38.

[186] H.J. Hsu, J. Bugno, L. Sr, S. Hong, Dendrimer-based nanocarriers: a versatile platform for drug delivery, Wiley Interdiscip. Rev. Nanomed. Nanobiotechnol. 9 (1) (2017) e1409.

[187] G. Wu, R.F. Barth, W. Yang, S. Kawabata, L. Zhang, K. Green-Church, Targeted delivery of methotrexate to epidermal growth factor receptor–positive brain tumors by means of cetuximab (IMC-C225) dendrimer bioconjugates, Mol. Cancer Ther. 5 (1) (2006) 52–59.

[188] V.K. Yellepeddi, A. Kumar, S. Palakurthi, Biotinylated poly (amido) amine (PAMAM) dendrimers as carriers for drug delivery to ovarian cancer cells in vitro, Anticancer Res. 29 (8) (2009) 2933–2943.

[189] Y. Jin, X. Ren, W. Wang, L. Ke, E. Ning, L. Du, et al., A 5-fluorouracil-loaded pH-responsive dendrimer nanocarrier for tumor targeting, Int. J. Pharm. 420 (2) (2011) 378–384.

[190] S. Zhu, M. Hong, G. Tang, L. Qian, J. Lin, Y. Jiang, et al., Partly PEGylated polyamidoamine dendrimer for tumor-selective targeting of doxorubicin: the effects of PEGylation degree and drug conjugation style, Biomaterials 31 (6) (2010) 1360–1371.

[191] N. Malik, et al., Dendrimers: relationship between structure and biocompatibility in vitro, and preliminary studies on the biodistribution of 125I-labelled polyamidoamine dendrimers in vivo, J. Control. Release 65 (1–2) (2000) 133–148.

[192] J. Zhu, F. Fu, Z. Xiong, M. Shen, X. Shi, Dendrimer-entrapped gold nanoparticles modified with RGD peptide and alpha-tocopheryl succinate enable targeted theranostics of cancer cells, Colloids Surf. B: Biointerfaces 133 (2015) 36–42.

[193] Y.E. Kurtoglu, M.K. Mishra, S. Kannan, R.M. Kannan, Drug release characteristics of PAMAM dendrimer–drug conjugates with different linkers, Int. J. Pharm. 384 (1–2) (2010) 189–194.

[194] Y. Gao, Z. Li, X. Xie, C. Wang, J. You, F. Mo, et al., Dendrimeric anticancer prodrugs for targeted delivery of ursolic acid to folate receptor-expressing cancer cells: synthesis and biological evaluation, Eur. J. Pharm. Sci. 70 (2015) 55–63.

[195] U. Gupta, H.B. Agashe, N.K. Jain, Polypropylene imine dendrimer mediated solubility enhancement: effect of pH and functional groups of hydrophobes, J. Pharm. Pharm. Sci. 10 (3) (2007) 358–367.

[196] B.K. Biswal, M. Kavitha, R. Verma, E. Prasad, Tumor cell imaging using the intrinsic emission from PAMAM dendrimer: a case study with HeLa cells, Cytotechnology 61 (2009) 17–24.

[197] J. Bugno, H.-J. Hsu, R.M. Pearson, H. Noh, S. Hong, Size and surface charge of engineered poly (amidoamine) dendrimers modulate tumor accumulation and penetration: a model study using multicellular tumor spheroids, Mol. Pharm. 13 (7) (2016) 2155–2163.

[198] H.H. Khalil, H.A. Osman, M. Teleb, A. Darwish, M.M. Abu-Serie, S.N. Khattab, et al., Engineered s-triazine-based dendrimer-honokiol conjugates as targeted MMP-2/9 inhibitors for halting hepatocellular carcinoma, ChemMedChem 16 (24) (2021) 3701–3719.

[199] Q. Zhong, E.R. Bielski, L.S. Rodrigues, M.R. Brown, J.J. Reineke, S.R. da Rocha, Conjugation to poly (amidoamine) dendrimers and pulmonary delivery reduce cardiac accumulation and enhance antitumor activity of doxorubicin in lung metastasis, Mol. Pharm. 13 (7) (2016) 2363–2375.

[200] A.A. Kale, V.P. Torchilin, Design, synthesis, and characterization of pH-sensitive PEG–PE conjugates for stimuli-sensitive pharmaceutical nanocarriers: the effect of substitutes at the hydrazone linkage on the pH stability of PEG–PE conjugates, Bioconjug. Chem. 18 (2) (2007) 363–370.

[201] J. Pan, L.P. Mendes, M. Yao, N. Filipczak, S. Garai, G.A. Thakur, et al., Polyamidoamine dendrimers-based nanomedicine for combination therapy with siRNA and chemotherapeutics to overcome multidrug resistance, Eur. J. Pharm. Biopharm. 136 (2019) 18–28.

[202] M. Zhang, J. Zhu, Y. Zheng, R. Guo, S. Wang, S. Mignani, et al., Doxorubicin-conjugated PAMAM dendrimers for pH-responsive drug release and folic acid-targeted cancer therapy, Pharmaceutics 10 (3) (2018) 162.

[203] M. Golshan, M. Salami-Kalajahi, M. Mirshekarpour, H. Roghani-Mamaqani, M. Mohammadi, Synthesis and characterization of poly (propylene imine)-dendrimer-grafted gold nanoparticles as nanocarriers of doxorubicin, Colloids Surf. B: Biointerfaces 155 (2017) 257–265.

[204] D.J. Slamon, W. Godolphin, L.A. Jones, J.A. Holt, S.G. Wong, D.E. Keith, et al., Studies of the HER-2/neu proto-oncogene in human breast and ovarian cancer, Science 244 (4905) (1989) 707–712.

[205] M.A. Olayioye, R.M. Neve, H.A. Lane, N.E. Hynes, The ErbB signaling network: receptor heterodimerization in development and cancer, EMBO J. 19 (13) (2000) 3159–3167.

[206] H.-S. Cho, K. Mason, K.X. Ramyar, A.M. Stanley, S.B. Gabelli, D.W. Denney Jr., et al., Structure of the extracellular region of HER2 alone and in complex with the Herceptin Fab, Nature 421 (6924) (2003) 756–760.

[207] J. Park, K. Hong, P. Carter, H. Asgari, L. Guo, G. Keller, et al., Development of anti-p185HER2 immunoliposomes for cancer therapy, Proc. Natl. Acad. Sci. 92 (5) (1995) 1327–1331.

[208] P. Carter, L. Presta, C.M. Gorman, J. Ridgway, D. Henner, W. Wong, et al., Humanization of an anti-p185HER2 antibody for human cancer therapy, Proc. Natl. Acad. Sci. 89 (10) (1992) 4285–4289.

[209] J. Baselga, D. Tripathy, J. Mendelsohn, S. Baughman, C.C. Benz, L. Dantis, et al., Phase II study of weekly intravenous trastuzumab (Herceptin) in patients with HER2/neu-overexpressing metastatic breast cancer, in: Seminars in Oncology, 1999, pp. 78–83.

[210] C. Vogel, M. Cobleigh, D. Tripathy, J. Gutheil, L. Harris, L. Fehrenbacher, et al., First-line, single-agent Herceptin®(trastuzumab) in metastatic breast cancer: a preliminary report, Eur. J. Cancer 37 (2001) 25–29.

[211] T. Hurrell, K. Outhoff, The in vitro influences of epidermal growth factor and heregulin-β1 on the efficacy of trastuzumab used in Her-2 positive breast adenocarcinoma, Cancer Cell Int. 13 (1) (2013) 1–9.

[212] F. Ciardiello, R. Caputo, G. Pomatico, M. De Laurentiis, S. De Placido, A.R. Bianco, et al., Resistance to taxanes is induced by c-erbB-2 overexpression in human MCF-10A mammary epithelial cells and is blocked by combined treatment with an antisense oligonucleotide targeting type I protein kinase A, Int. J. Cancer 85 (5) (2000) 710–715.

[213] D.J. Slamon, B. Leyland-Jones, S. Shak, H. Fuchs, V. Paton, A. Bajamonde, et al., Use of chemotherapy plus a monoclonal antibody against HER2 for metastatic breast cancer that overexpresses HER2, N. Engl. J. Med. 344 (11) (2001) 783–792.

[214] M. Marty, F. Cognetti, D. Maraninchi, R. Snyder, L. Mauriac, M. Tubiana-Hulin, et al., Randomized phase II trial of the efficacy and safety of trastuzumab combined with docetaxel in patients with human epidermal growth factor receptor 2-positive metastatic breast cancer administered as first-line treatment: the M77001 study group, J. Clin. Oncol. 23 (19) (2005) 4265–4274.

[215] P.E. Clark, N. Agarwal, M.C. Biagioli, M.A. Eisenberger, R.E. Greenberg, H.W. Herr, et al., National comprehensive cancer N (2013) bladder cancer, J. Natl. Compr. Canc. Netw. 11 (2013) 446e75.

[216] F. Datko, G. D'Andrea, M. Dickler, M. Theodoulou, S. Goldfarb, D. Lake, et al., Abstract P5-18-20: phase II study of pertuzumab, trastuzumab, and weekly paclitaxel in patients with metastatic HER2-overexpressing metastatic breast cancer, Cancer Res. 72 (24_Supplement) (2012). P5-18-20-P5-18-20.

[217] T. Miyano, W. Wijagkanalan, S. Kawakami, F. Yamashita, M. Hashida, Anionic amino acid dendrimer–trastuzumab conjugates for specific internalization in HER2-positive cancer cells, Mol. Pharm. 7 (4) (2010) 1318–1327.

[218] A.K. Patri, A. Myc, J. Beals, T.P. Thomas, N.H. Bander, J.R. Baker, Synthesis and in vitro testing of J591 antibody–dendrimer conjugates for targeted prostate cancer therapy, Bioconjug. Chem. 15 (6) (2004) 1174–1181.

[219] T.P. Thomas, A.K. Patri, A. Myc, M.T. Myaing, J.Y. Ye, T.B. Norris, et al., In vitro targeting of synthesized antibody-conjugated dendrimer nanoparticles, Biomacromolecules 5 (6) (2004) 2269–2274.

[220] G. Wu, R.F. Barth, W. Yang, M. Chatterjee, W. Tjarks, M.J. Ciesielski, et al., Site-specific conjugation of boron-containing dendrimers to anti-EGF receptor monoclonal antibody cetuximab (IMC-C225) and its evaluation as a potential delivery agent for neutron capture therapy, Bioconjug. Chem. 15 (1) (2004) 185–194.

[221] H. Kobayashi, K. Reijnders, S. English, A.T. Yordanov, D.E. Milenic, A.L. Sowers, et al., Application of a macromolecular contrast agent for detection of alterations of tumor vessel permeability induced by radiation, Clin. Cancer Res. 10 (22) (2004) 7712–7720.

[222] S.-J. Chiu, N.T. Ueno, R.J. Lee, Tumor-targeted gene delivery via anti-HER2 antibody (trastuzumab, Herceptin®) conjugated polyethylenimine, J. Control. Release 97 (2) (2004) 357–369.

[223] H. Wartlick, K. Michaelis, S. Balthasar, K. Strebhardt, J. Kreuter, K. Langer, Highly specific HER2-mediated cellular uptake of antibody-modified nanoparticles in tumour cells, J. Drug Target. 12 (7) (2004) 461–471.

[224] J.A. Copland, M. Eghtedari, V.L. Popov, N. Kotov, N. Mamedova, M. Motamedi, et al., Bioconjugated gold nanoparticles as a molecular based contrast agent: implications for imaging of deep tumors using optoacoustic tomography, Mol. Imaging Biol. 6 (5) (2004) 341–349.

[225] R. Duncan, L. Izzo, Dendrimer biocompatibility and toxicity, Adv. Drug Deliv. Rev. 57 (15) (2005) 2215–2237.

[226] J.C. Roberts, M.K. Bhalgat, R.T. Zera, Preliminary biological evaluation of polyamidoamine (PAMAM) Starburst™ dendrimers, J. Biomed. Mater. Res. 30 (1) (1996) 53–65.

[227] U. Boas, P.M. Heegaard, Dendrimers in drug research, Chem. Soc. Rev. 33 (1) (2004) 43–63.

[228] A.K. Patri, I.J. Majoros, J.R. Baker Jr., Dendritic polymer macromolecular carriers for drug delivery, Curr. Opin. Chem. Biol. 6 (4) (2002) 466–471.

[229] L. Zhang, S. Zhu, L. Qian, Y. Pei, Y. Qiu, Y. Jiang, RGD-modified PEG–PAMAM–DOX conjugates: in vitro and in vivo studies for glioma, Eur. J. Pharm. Biopharm. 79 (2) (2011) 232–240.

[230] M. Marcinkowska, M. Stanczyk, A. Janaszewska, E. Sobierajska, A. Chworos, B. Klajnert-Maculewicz, Multicomponent conjugates of anticancer drugs and monoclonal antibody with PAMAM dendrimers to increase efficacy of HER-2 positive breast cancer therapy, Pharm. Res. 36 (2019) 1–17.

[231] D. Soto-Castro, J.A. Cruz-Morales, M.T.R. Apan, P. Guadarrama, Solubilization and anticancer-activity enhancement of methotrexate by novel dendrimeric nanodevices synthesized in one-step reaction, Bioorg. Chem. 41 (2012) 13–21.

[232] H. He, Y. Li, X.-R. Jia, J. Du, X. Ying, W.-L. Lu, et al., PEGylated poly (amidoamine) dendrimer-based dual-targeting carrier for treating brain tumors, Biomaterials 32 (2) (2011) 478–487.

[233] J. Zhang, Z. Wu, S. Zhan, M. Li, Y. Wang, H. Xu, et al., Nano-carrier polyamidoamine dendrimer G4 induces mitochondrialdependent apoptosis in human multidrug-resistant breast cancer cells through G0/G1 phase arrest, Curr. Pharm. Biotechnol. 24 (4) (2022) 589–598.

[234] A.G. Schatzlein, B.H. Zinselmeyer, A. Elouzi, C. Dufes, Y.T.A. Chim, C.J. Roberts, et al., Preferential liver gene expression with polypropylenimine dendrimers, J. Control. Release 101 (1–3) (2005) 247–258.

[235] H.B. Agashe, A.K. Babbar, S. Jain, R.K. Sharma, A.K. Mishra, A. Asthana, et al., Investigations on biodistribution of technetium-99m-labeled carbohydrate-coated poly (propylene imine) dendrimers, Nanomed. Nanotechnol. Biol. Med. 3 (2) (2007) 120–127.

[236] V. Shah, O. Taratula, O.B. Garbuzenko, O.R. Taratula, L. Rodriguez-Rodriguez, T. Minko, Targeted nanomedicine for suppression of CD44 and simultaneous cell death induction in ovarian cancer: an optimal delivery of siRNA and anticancer drug targeted suppression of CD44 protein and cell death induction, Clin. Cancer Res. 19 (22) (2013) 6193–6204.

[237] V. Russ, M. Günther, A. Halama, M. Ogris, E. Wagner, Oligoethylenimine-grafted polypropylenimine dendrimers as degradable and biocompatible synthetic vectors for gene delivery, J. Control. Release 132 (2) (2008) 131–140.

[238] B. Birdhariya, P. Kesharwani, N.K. Jain, Effect of surface capping on targeting potential of folate decorated poly (propylene imine) dendrimers, Drug Dev. Ind. Pharm. 41 (8) (2015) 1393–1399.

[239] G. Pistolis, A. Malliaris, D. Tsiourvas, C.M. Paleos, Poly (propyleneimine) dendrimers as pH-sensitive controlled-release systems, Chem. A Eur. J. 5 (5) (1999) 1440–1444.

[240] Z. Sideratou, D. Tsiourvas, C. Paleos, Quaternized poly (propylene imine) dendrimers as novel pH-sensitive controlled-release systems, Langmuir 16 (4) (2000) 1766–1769.

[241] Y.-B. Lim, T. Kim, J.W. Lee, S.-M. Kim, H.-J. Kim, K. Kim, et al., Self-assembled ternary complex of cationic dendrimer, cucurbituril, and DNA: noncovalent strategy in developing a gene delivery carrier, Bioconjug. Chem. 13 (6) (2002) 1181–1185.

[242] E. Pedziwiatr-Werbicka, M. Ferenc, M. Zaborski, B. Gabara, B. Klajnert, M. Bryszewska, Characterization of complexes formed by polypropylene imine dendrimers and anti-HIV oligonucleotides, Colloids Surf. B: Biointerfaces 83 (2) (2011) 360–366.

[243] C.L. Gebhart, A.V. Kabanov, Evaluation of polyplexes as gene transfer agents, J. Control. Release 73 (2–3) (2001) 401–416.

[244] V. Kabanov, A. Zezin, V. Rogacheva, Z.G. Gulyaeva, M. Zansochova, J. Joosten, et al., Interaction of Astramol poly (propyleneimine) dendrimers with linear polyanions, Macromolecules 32 (6) (1999) 1904–1909.

[245] T.-I. Kim, J.-U. Baek, C.Z. Bai, J.-S. Park, Arginine-conjugated polypropylenimine dendrimer as a non-toxic and efficient gene delivery carrier, Biomaterials 28 (11) (2007) 2061–2067.

[246] L.-A. Tziveleka, A.-M.G. Psarra, D. Tsiourvas, C.M. Paleos, Synthesis and characterization of guanidinylated poly (propylene imine) dendrimers as gene transfection agents, J. Control. Release 117 (1) (2007) 137–146.

[247] B.H. Zinselmeyer, S.P. Mackay, A.G. Schatzlein, I.F. Uchegbu, The lower-generation polypropylenimine dendrimers are effective gene-transfer agents, Pharm. Res. 19 (2002) 960–967.

[248] S. Tietze, I. Schau, S. Michen, F. Ennen, A. Janke, G. Schackert, et al., A poly (propyleneimine) dendrimer-based polyplex-system for single-chain antibody-mediated targeted delivery and cellular uptake of SiRNA, Small 13 (27) (2017) 1700072.

[249] M. Labieniec-Watala, C. Watala, PAMAM dendrimers: destined for success or doomed to fail? Plain and modified PAMAM dendrimers in the context of biomedical applications, J. Pharm. Sci. 104 (1) (2015) 2–14.

[250] H.B. Agashe, T. Dutta, M. Garg, N. Jain, Investigations on the toxicological profile of functionalized fifth-generation poly (propylene imine) dendrimer, J. Pharm. Pharmacol. 58 (11) (2006) 1491–1498.

[251] R.B. Kolhatkar, K.M. Kitchens, P.W. Swaan, H. Ghandehari, Surface acetylation of polyamidoamine (PAMAM) dendrimers decreases cytotoxicity while maintaining membrane permeability, Bioconjug. Chem. 18 (6) (2007) 2054–2060.

[252] O.L. Padilla De Jesús, H.R. Ihre, L. Gagne, J.M. Fréchet, F.C. Szoka, Polyester dendritic systems for drug delivery applications: in vitro and in vivo evaluation, Bioconjug. Chem. 13 (3) (2002) 453–461.

[253] N. Feliu, P. Kohonen, J. Ji, Y. Zhang, H.L. Karlsson, L. Palmberg, et al., Next-generation sequencing reveals low-dose effects of cationic dendrimers in primary human bronchial epithelial cells, ACS Nano 9 (1) (2015) 146–163.

[254] P.C. Naha, M. Davoren, A. Casey, H.J. Byrne, An ecotoxicological study of poly (amidoamine) dendrimers-toward quantitative structure activity relationships, Environ. Sci. Technol. 43 (17) (2009) 6864–6869.

[255] A. Janaszewska, K. Mączyńska, G. Matuszko, D. Appelhans, B. Voit, B. Klajnert, et al., Cytotoxicity of PAMAM, PPI and maltose modified PPI dendrimers in Chinese hamster ovary (CHO) and human ovarian carcinoma (SKOV3) cells, New J. Chem. 36 (2) (2012) 428–437.

[256] E. Oliveira, M. Casado, M. Faria, A.M. Soares, J.M. Navas, C. Barata, et al., Transcriptomic response of zebrafish embryos to polyaminoamine (PAMAM) dendrimers, Nanotoxicology 8 (sup1) (2014) 92–99.

[257] L. Bodewein, F. Schmelter, S. Di Fiore, H. Hollert, R. Fischer, M. Fenske, Differences in toxicity of anionic and cationic PAMAM and PPI dendrimers in zebrafish embryos and cancer cell lines, Toxicol. Appl. Pharmacol. 305 (2016) 83–92.

[258] P. Kesharwani, R.K. Tekade, N.K. Jain, Formulation development and in vitro–in vivo assessment of the fourth-generation PPI dendrimer as a cancer-targeting vector, Nanomedicine 9 (15) (2014) 2291–2308.

[259] K.T. Al-Jamal, W.T. Al-Jamal, J.T.-W. Wang, N. Rubio, J. Buddle, D. Gathercole, et al., Cationic poly-L-lysine dendrimer complexes doxorubicin and delays tumor growth in vitro and in vivo, ACS Nano 7 (3) (2013) 1905–1917.

[260] N.K. Jain, M.S. Tare, V. Mishra, P.K. Tripathi, The development, characterization and in vivo anti-ovarian cancer activity of poly (propylene imine)(PPI)-antibody conjugates containing encapsulated paclitaxel, Nanomedicine 11 (1) (2015) 207–218.

[261] A. Szulc, L. Pulaski, D. Appelhans, B. Voit, B. Klajnert-Maculewicz, Sugar-modified poly (propylene imine) dendrimers as drug delivery agents for cytarabine to overcome drug resistance, Int. J. Pharm. 513 (1–2) (2016) 572–583.

[262] K. Jain, U. Gupta, N.K. Jain, Dendronized nanoconjugates of lysine and folate for treatment of cancer, Eur. J. Pharm. Biopharm. 87 (3) (2014) 500–509.

[263] R. Jevprasesphant, J. Penny, R. Jalal, D. Attwood, N. McKeown, A. D'Emanuele, The influence of surface modification on the cytotoxicity of PAMAM dendrimers, Int. J. Pharm. 252 (1–2) (2003) 263–266.

[264] J.J. Khandare, S. Jayant, A. Singh, P. Chandna, Y. Wang, N. Vorsa, et al., Dendrimer versus linear conjugate: influence of polymeric architecture on the delivery and anticancer effect of paclitaxel, Bioconjug. Chem. 17 (6) (2006) 1464–1472. N.A. Stasko, C.B. Johnson, M.H. Schoenfisch, T.A. Johnson, E.L. Holmuhamedov, Cytotoxicity of polypropylenimine dendrimer conjugates on cultured endothelial cells, Biomacromolecules 8 (12) (2007) 3853–3859.

[265] H.M. Teow, Z. Zhou, M. Najlah, S.R. Yusof, N.J. Abbott, A. D'Emanuele, Delivery of paclitaxel across cellular barriers using a dendrimer-based nanocarrier, Int. J. Pharm. 441 (1–2) (2013) 701–711.

[266] P.-S. Lai, P.-J. Lou, C.-L. Peng, C.-L. Pai, W.-N. Yen, M.-Y. Huang, et al., Doxorubicin delivery by polyamidoamine dendrimer conjugation and photochemical internalization for cancer therapy, J. Control. Release 122 (1) (2007) 39–46.

[267] V.K. Yellepeddi, A. Kumar, D.M. Maher, S.C. Chauhan, K.K. Vangara, S. Palakurthi, Biotinylated PAMAM dendrimers for intracellular delivery of cisplatin to ovarian cancer: role of SMVT, Anticancer Res. 31 (3) (2011) 897–906.

[268] D. Bhadra, S. Bhadra, S. Jain, N. Jain, A PEGylated dendritic nanoparticulate carrier of fluorouracil, Int. J. Pharm. 257 (1–2) (2003) 111–124.

[269] A. Asthana, A.S. Chauhan, P.V. Diwan, N.K. Jain, Poly (amidoamine)(PAMAM) dendritic nanostructures for controlled site specific delivery of acidic anti-inflammatory active ingredient, AAPS PharmSciTech 6 (2005) E536–E542.

[270] V. Mishra, U. Gupta, N. Jain, Influence of different generations of poly (propylene imine) dendrimers on human erythrocytes, Die Pharm. 65 (12) (2010) 891–895.

[271] D. Bhadra, A. Yadav, S. Bhadra, N. Jain, Glycodendrimeric nanoparticulate carriers of primaquine phosphate for liver targeting, Int. J. Pharm. 295 (1–2) (2005) 221–233.

[272] P. Agrawal, U. Gupta, N. Jain, Glycoconjugated peptide dendrimers-based nanoparticulate system for the delivery of chloroquine phosphate, Biomaterials 28 (22) (2007) 3349–3359.

[273] P. Rajananthanan, G.S. Attard, N.A. Sheikh, W.J.W. Morrow, Evaluation of novel aggregate structures as adjuvants: composition, toxicity studies and humoral responses, Vaccine 17 (7–8) (1999) 715–730.

[274] T. Imae, Physicochemical properties of dendrimers and dendrimer complexes, in: Y. Cheng (Ed.), Dendrimer-Based Drug Delivery Systems: From Theory to Practice, John Wiley & Sons, Inc, 2012, pp. 55–92.

Nanomedicine and epigenome: Possible health risks, benefits, and future perspectives

17

Nitin Verma[a], Komal Thapa[a], Neha Kanojia[a], Parul Sood[a], Jatin Kumar[a], and Kamal Dua[b]

[a]*Chitkara University School of Pharmacy, Chitkara University, Himachal Pradesh, India,*
[b]*Discipline of Pharmacy, Graduate School of Health, University of Technology Sydney, Broadway, NSW, Australia*

Introduction

There are several toxicants in our environment, both natural and human made. The air, water, food, houses, workplaces, and possessions are just a few of the areas where these toxicants have a foothold in our daily lives. After toxicants enter the human body, they are very difficult to detoxify and eliminate, which causes a variety of syndromic symptoms to appear. When these toxicants are exposed, they can lead to serious illnesses, diseases, disability, or even death. Chemical substances like heavy metals, hydrocarbons, and pesticides are a few of the prevalent environmental toxins. Due to their widespread usage in our culture, so many of these chemical substances have the potential to cause cancer [1–3]. Rapid industrialization and disorganized turmoil have a significant impact on the increase in soil pollution and air and water [4–7]. ENMs are discharged into the environment as a result of their extensive use, production, and disposal, making accidental intake inevitable. Epigenetic changes have been found to have a significant impact on human development in recent years. In personalized medicine, a significant number of ENMs are utilized as drug carriers for both diagnosis and medication delivery. When compared to drug molecules diffusing freely, these medications significantly improve drug delivery to targeted cells [8–23].

Cancer Epigenetics and Nanomedicine. https://doi.org/10.1016/B978-0-443-13209-4.00003-9
Copyright © 2024 Elsevier Inc. All rights are reserved, including those for text and data mining, AI training, and similar technologies.

Therapeutic implications of nanomaterial in nanomedicine

The use of nanotechnology's knowledge and instruments in medicine opens up new avenues for medicine including imaging, diagnosis, drug development imaging and diagnosis, implantable materials for the treatment of cancer, and the regeneration of tissue. More than 50 nondrugs have gotten approval from US Food and Drug Administration (US FDA) and are currently in clinical use.

Diagnostic applications
Molecular imaging
Both anatomical and molecular imaging are possible with NMs, a brand-new and fascinating family of imaging agents Endorem (also known as Feridex in the United States), Sinerem (Combidex), and Resovist (Ferucarbotran), while a number of others are undergoing clinical research. Nevertheless, despite the advantages of adequate superparamagnetic characteristics, magnetic saturation, and colloidal stability, several of these innovative contrast agents have been stopped and are no longer produced [24–26]. Concerns about their safety profile, particularly those pertaining to possible toxicity and the possibility of fatal anaphylactic reactions, were the main factors in this decision. Other NMs have been created and used in various optical imaging techniques as contrast enhancers. Absolutely, optical techniques utilizing various nanomaterials have shown promise for cell tracking and visualization including carbon dots, carbonaceous nanomaterials, quantum dots (QDs), noble metal NMs (such as silver and gold nanoparticles), and organically modified fluorescent doped silica nanoparticles [27–29].

Medical biosensors
An intriguing use of nanotechnology in medicine is nano biosensors for molecular diagnosis. The development of "omics" technology and molecular biology has made it possible to identify important molecules that play a promising role in the pathogenesis of numerous diseases. Many other nano biosensors are currently being developed to detect specific biomarkers such as CA15-3, HER2, EGFR, PSA, CEA, etc.). Currently, many nanobiosensors using (AuNPs) or nanowires silicon are available for cardiovascular diseases [30,31].

Regenerative medicine
The goal of regenerative medicine is to bring damaged, aging, or missing cells and tissues as closely as possible to their original condition of structure and function. Tissue engineering applications and stem cell-based therapeutics are examples of regenerative strategies. NMs can be used to nanopattern 3D scaffold as an implant surface that imitates cells' natural environments to promote cell adhesion, differentiation, and mobility [32–34]. The adhesion and proliferation of chondrocytes have been

demonstrated to be accelerated by nanostructured poly(lactic-*co*-glycolic acid) (PLGA) surfaces, while endothelial cell functions have been enhanced by titanium surfaces [35].

Bone tissue engineering

Polymers derived from natural sources such as collagen, gelatin, silk, and alginates, as well as those derived synthetically like polylactic acid, hydroxyapatite, polylactoglycolic acid, and polyvinyl alcohol, have been employed in bone tissue engineering applications to develop scaffolds and matrices that support bone regeneration. Additionally, metal composites, ceramics, and carbon nanostructures-reinforced composites are other materials used for bone tissue engineering. It has been demonstrated that nanofibrous matrices promote osteogenic differentiation, bone formation, and tissue regeneration [36–42].

Cartilage reformation

There are currently few reconstructive possibilities for the regeneration of cartilage as it is a specialized avascular connective tissue made up of chondrocytes responsible for maintaining collagen and extracellular matrix (ECM) that is composed of proteoglycans and collagens. According to Li et al. (2005), the majority of tissue engineering techniques use a matrix that has been supported with either chondrocytes. 3D exogenous ECMs have been created using biomaterials like alginate, hyaluronic acid, fibrin, collagen, chitosan, and polyesters to direct the reformation of cartilage. Bacterial adherence to implants is a typical issue with prostheses. Nanostructured titanium surfaces may be used to inhibit pathogen adherence [43–46].

Therapy

Many different nanoscale therapeutic responses have been created over the past few decades, and some of them have been used in clinical diagnosis and treatment. In comparison to traditional chemotherapeutic treatments, they have a greater blood circulation half-life, improved medication absorption, fewer adverse effects, and better synergistic outcomes, which has increased interest in them [47].

Drug delivery

According to Peng et al., nanocarriers can be classified as polymeric-based, lipid-based, and inorganic formulations. Any type of polymer-based nanocarrier particularly nanocapsules and nanospheres are collectively referred to as polymer-based nanocarriers. Poly(alkyl cyanoacrylate), PLGA, PLA, polyglycolic acid, and poly(ε-caprolactone) are examples of synthetic biodegradable polymeric NMs. Chitosan, gelatin, and dextran ester are examples of natural polymers [48]. However, compared to synthetic polymers, natural polymers may have limitations in terms of purity and reproducibility. FDA-approved biodegradable and biocompatible Nms have been shown to promise in human cancer applications. Furthermore, the approval of

Abraxane—a notable example of a protein-based drug delivery vehicle that utilizes albumin as a carrier for the chemotherapy drug paclitaxel by the US FDA—has shown enhanced effect in the synthesis of protein-based nanocarriers formulations for cancer management. Patients with advanced solid tumors are now participating in phase 1 clinical trials with a (NCT00103791) polymeric NM formulation of docetaxel. For nanocarrier fabrication, natural polysaccharides like chitosan have been employed extensively for the transport of numerous therapeutically active substances such as proteins, genes, and medicines [49–54].

Phototherapy

Photodynamic and photothermal therapy, a promising therapeutic approach for cancer treatment has recently been revealed: phototherapy, a new noninvasive procedure. The basic idea behind this therapeutic approach is to use singlet oxygen (photodynamic therapy, PDT) heat (photothermal therapy, PTT) produced from irradiation light to effectively kill cancer cells. Local hyperthermia, achieved by raising the temperature of cells above 42°C through light irradiation, has been observed to selectively induce cell death while causing minimal damage to the surrounding cellular components and normal tissue. On the other hand, temperatures higher than 45°C directly cause cell death by the process of thermal ablation. PTT agents used for cancer treatment require specific properties to efficiently absorb light and convert it into heat [55–58].

Immunotherapy

Research and development in the use to target the immune system are quite active. A revolutionary strategy for treating autoimmune disorders, as well as regenerative medicine and cancer therapies, is NM-based immunotherapy.

Cancer disease immunotherapy

It is well known that tumors not only evade immune monitoring but also take advantage of it to spread locally and grow far. A potential method in the multimodal therapy of various cancers is the vaccination of dendritic cells, which entails the effective and targeted delivery of costimulatory and immunomodulatory chemicals to antigen-presenting cells utilizing NMs. Lipid- and polymer-based nanocarriers, as well as silica and Au NMs, are the most often employed nanocarriers [59–65].

Potential role of epigenetics in nanomedicine

Epigenetic modifications are changes in gene expression that don't depend on a gene's DNA sequence. These changes could affect epigenetic inheritance, epigenetic cancer development, or any other disease connected to changes in an organism. Through numerous somatic cell divisions, the epigenetic modifications and/or information are transmitted transgenerationally to daughter cells. The epigenome refers to the modifications that might occur to an organism's genome as a result of different chemical substances or species in the biological system. Epigenetic alterations may result from adjustments to a biological system's internal and external environments, including nitrosative stress and oxidative as well as dietary changes [66–69]. The genotype of an organism might show phenotypic variation brought on by the interaction of several environmental factors. The most advantageous form of this capacity, known as plasticity, happens throughout development to improve an organism's chances of survival and reproductive success [3]. Since the topic of epigenetics was first discovered a century ago, it has grown to be among the most alluring areas of study in the present landscape of biomedical research [70–73].

Types of epigenetic modifications

By interacting regulative noncoding RNAs, DNA methylation, and histone modifications, epigenetics enables sophisticated tissue and time-specific expression of genes influencing both pathologically as well as healthy advancement. Generally reversible, epigenetic marks can be affected by the environment [74–78] (Fig. 1).

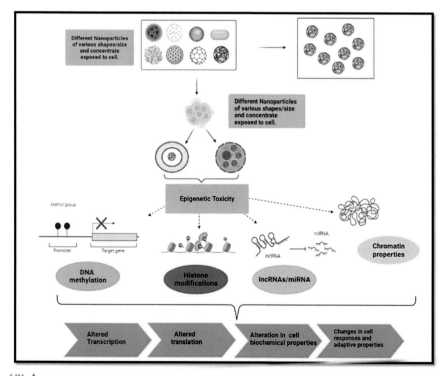

FIG. 1

Epigenetic toxicity of nanomaterials.

Despite the fact that numerous research has looked into the toxicity of epigenetic alterations brought on by the environment, only a small number have shown a rationalistic connection between various environmental exposures, epigenetic modifications, and unfavorable health outcomes. The study by Marczylo et al. was focused on investigating the potential link between environmental exposures and epigenetic alterations in the human epidemiological cohort [79,80]. These findings support links between different forms of environmental exposure, changed epigenetic processes, the emergence of behavioral abnormalities and childhood asthma, Alzheimer's disease, lung cancer, skin abnormalities, chromosomal abnormalities, and chronic obstructive pulmonary disease (COPD). Many substances—mostly heavy metals—have been designated as epimutations. According to Cheng et al. (2012), they have been demonstrated to affect histone alterations and DNA methylation. In 2008 the first study indicated that NMs can significantly cause epigenetic toxicity [81–83]. The epigenetic consequences of NM exposure were initially summarized by Stoccoro and colleagues in 2013. They showed that NM caused alterations in DNA methylation, histone acetylation, and methylation as well as expression of miRNA. It has also been demonstrated that some nanomedicines can hinder the gene expressions responsible for the methylation of DNA, resulting in significant universal changes in the epigenetic landscape. While the number of human studies on NM-induced epigenetic changes is limited, ongoing in vitro and animal studies are helping to expand our knowledge and providing a more comprehensive advancement of nanomedicine-induced epigenetic alterations. Various epigenetic modifications are outlined in Fig. 2 [84–87].

DNA methylation

One of the most thoroughly researched epigenetic alterations is DNA methylation. Target gene transcription factor binding is prevented by DNA methylation in promoters [88–93].

The integrity of the genome is maintained in part by global DNA methylation. The occurrence of cancer and increased chromosomal instability have been linked to global DNA hypomethylation.

A number of enzymes are essential to DNA methylation. The mechanics of DNA demethylation have been clarified by the identification of ten-eleven translocation (TET) proteins [94–97]. It has been demonstrated that the 5-mC hydroxylases of the TET family are involved in DNA methylation reprogramming, cancer suppression, and transcriptional activation and repression. They have a particular domain called MBD, which connects to other domains related to chromatin. Chromatin remodeling and transcription repression are caused by the interplay between DNA methylation and histone changes. It is well known that abnormal DNA methylation plays a part in complicated and rare diseases, but it is still unclear how environmental exposure to certain substances causes epigenetic modifications that lead to disease phenotypes [98].

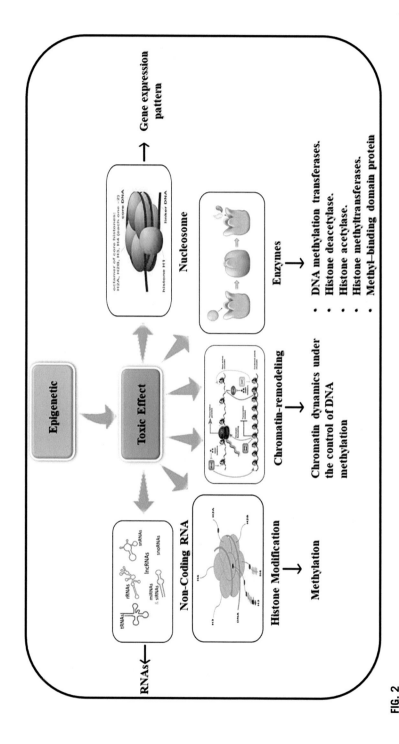

FIG. 2

Types of epigenetic modifications.

Histone modifications

The alterations that histone proteins undergo during epigenetic processes are the most varied when compared to DNA methylation. DNA is wrapped around histone proteins, which are octameric proteins, forming nucleosomes. A number of covalent modifications, including acetylation, ATP ribosylation, methylation, phosphorylation, ubiquitylation, and others, are responsible to cause distinct effects on chromatin structure and transcriptional regulation [99–102]. Recent genome-wide investigations have shown that areas that are actively transcribed or that are transcriptionally repressed have a particular pattern of alteration. They may have abnormal functions that affect transcription factors' access to DNA and the regulation of chromatin shape and activity [103,104]. Based on their extensive roles, histone-modifying enzymes can be categorized into different classes. HDACs or histone lysine demethylases (KDMs) are examples of epigenetic erasers that remove epigenetic marks that have been added by epigenetic writers (e.g., HATs, HMTs). Histone alterations are significant molecular targets for many types of NMs, according to numerous studies. Depending on the region of the chromatin that is impacted, the accessibility of nanomedicines into the nucleus of the cell can alter a variety of cellular processes [105–109].

Noncoding RNAs

The posttranscriptional process of gene expression is regulated by a number of kinds of regulatory noncoding RNAs (ncRNAs). It has been demonstrated that both short noncoding RNAs (200 nucleotides) contribute to the development of heterochromatin, DNA methylation-targeting, and histone modifications [110,111]. Three kinds of short noncoding RNAs (ncRNAs) aren't translated into proteins. Evolutionarily conserved, 20- to 24-nucleotide-long, small single-stranded molecules known as microRNAs (miRNAs) make up the class that has received the most research. miRNA deregulation has been linked to disorders of the nervous system, heart, development, and other conditions in addition to cancer. Piwi-interacting RNAs (piRNAs) are short noncoding RNAs (ncRNAs) of 24–31 nucleotides in length, whose main job is to control chromatin and reduce transposon activity. PiRNAs work largely in the nucleus and interact with PIWI proteins, in contrast to miRNAs [112–115]. The least understood ncRNA species are long ncRNAs (lncRNAs). They perform a variety of regulatory tasks by participating in the activation and repression of genes as signals or decoys. By directing the catalytic activity of chromatin-modifying proteins to particular genomic locations, they can operate as regulators of gene expression. They serve as building blocks for chromatin remodeling or control histone marks. Epigenetic processes control a cell's response to a variety of internal or external stimuli because of their plasticity and ability to engage in dynamic interactions [116–120].

In vitro and in vivo epigenetic modifications

An essential class of NMs is metal particles. DNA damage was once believed to be a mediator of metal toxicity. According to recent studies, exposure to metals has been linked to long-lasting changes in the epigenome. Although heavy metals' epigenetic targets have been extensively reviewed, research on these substances' effects at the nanoscale has been sparse. Polymeric nanoformulations (or other biodegradable devices) have been investigated even less than inorganic NMs despite being the most promising for pharmacological uses [121]. The fact that the components utilized to create polymer NMs are regarded as harmless is the key factor contributing to the lack of interest. However, a material's characteristics and behavior at the nanoscale might be different from what is seen at the macroscopic level. Given that the carriers' primary function in a significant number of applications is to reduce toxicity, special attention should be paid to their toxicity. The key conclusions of studies look at how exposure to NM affects various cell types and tissues' epigenetic processes in vitro and in vivo [122,123].

Silver

As antibacterial agents, silver nanoparticles (AgNPs) are employed in a range of applications, including the treatment of infected wounds and catheter dressings. In placental tissues, maternal exposure to AgNPs resulted in hypomethylation of the ZAC1 promoter and activation of the ZAC1 gene. Imprinted gene ZAC1 is essential for regulating embryonic development [124].

Cadmium telluride quantum dots

Human carcinogens cadmium (Cd) compounds are thought to act through epigenetic pathways. In 2005, the first study indicating that CdTe-QDs can alter epigenetic processes was released. Membrane blebbing and chromatic condensation are two characteristics of QD-induced cytotoxicity, according to research by Lovric and colleagues. Human breast cancer MCF-7 cells experienced decreased gene expression and global histone H3 hypoacetylation after being exposed to CdTe-QDs for 4 or 24h [125].

Titanium

Implanted medical devices like spinal fixation, cardiovascular stents, joint replacements, and dental implants frequently employ titanium. The World Health Organization/International Agency for Research on Cancer (IARC) classified titanium dioxide nanoparticles (TiO2NPs) as a Group 2B (probably carcinogenic) substance. TiO_2NPs exposure led to hypermethylation of the PARP1 promoter, which was brought on by oxidative stress. The study conducted by Ghosh et al. in 2017 investigated the effects of different crystal phases of TiO_2 nanoparticles (anatase, rutile, and a combination of anatase and rutile) on bronchial epithelial (16-HBE) cells. The findings of the study revealed that epigenetic alterations occurred even at subcytotoxic and subgenotoxic concentrations of the TiO_2 nanoparticles [126].

Iron

The effectiveness of supermagnetic iron oxide nanoparticles as effective MRI diagnostic tools and as CNS-specific drug delivery systems is widely acknowledged. Significant alteration in the expression pattern of miRNA after 24-h exposure in PC12 rat pheochromocytoma neuroendocrine cells, despite the fact the specific epigenetic mechanisms underlying the observed changes in miRNA expression were not extensively explored in this study. In NIH/3 T3 cells, a 24-h exposure to iron oxide nanoparticles (Fe_2O_3NPs) altered the expression of 167 miRNAs. The lipid biosynthesis route and cellular lipid metabolism are just two of the KEGG pathways and GO keywords that were considerably impacted [126,127].

Cobalt

Cobalt ferrite NM, a type of cobalt used in medicine, has applications in drug delivery, MRI, magnetic separation, and hyperthermia therapy. Cobalt oxide nanoparticles (Co_3O_4NP), primarily utilized in industrial applications, temporarily altered the expression of miR-21 and miR-30a despite not yet having been investigated for their capacity to affect epigenetic alterations. After 2 h, there was an increase in miR-155 expression, which decreased at longer exposure times. The autophagy pathway, which has a potential role in carcinogenesis, was the main consideration when choosing miRNA for the investigation. However, the Co_3O_4NPs-induced oxidative stress limited the body's capacity to detoxify and repair the harm that resulted, eliminating the induction of autophagy.

Role of epigenetic alterations in the safety assessment of nanomaterials

The field of nanotoxicology has been rapidly growing to understand and assess the potential toxicity of nanomaterials and nanoparticles. With increased data collection from experimental and epidemiological research, epigenetic changes have emerged as a potential mechanism to detect and predict toxicity produced by engineered NMs and especially to anticipate it in preclinical evaluations. Numerous experimental studies conducted both in vitro and in vivo have provided evidence of a link between toxicity and epigenetic changes resulting from exposure to specific NMs and NPs. This implies that epigenetic changes may serve as useful markers of the toxicity of NMs and NPs as well as promising translational biomarkers for identifying the negative effects of nanomaterials in people [127–129].

Additionally, most of the current studies merely provide a snapshot of the epigenetic modifications brought on by exposure. Due to all these factors, it can be challenging to determine the significance of epigenetic abnormalities in the mechanisms of NMs and NPs toxicity.

Conclusion and future perspectives

Despite mounting evidence that suggests NM exposure poses a genuine risk to human health, particularly in the context of nanomedicine, this issue is still debatable. Despite the impact of NM exposure on global DNA methylation, changes have been observed in a few studies. However, many reports do not establish a link between these methylation changes and alteration in gene expression, making it challenging to determine their potential functional implications. There have been numerous reports of NM-induced chromatin reorganization alterations, changed HDAC and TET activity, and a general epigenomic response. After two out of three NM exposures, several miRNAs were coregulated, which shows that many NMs have comparable epigenetic effects. The lack of overlay between in vivo and in vitro investigations is frequently brought on by the minimal number of studies. The link between NM exposure and epigenetic alterations is still physiologically tenable despite discrepancies in published data and difficulties in epigenomic research. It is important to distinguish between pathogenic changes and the natural reaction of the cells to the exposure. Most of the in vitro and animal experiments are used to support the epigenetic toxicity of NMs. Transposing results from controlled laboratory settings to the realm of epidemiology may be very difficult.

References

[1] F. Janku, I. Garrido-Laguna, L.B. Petruzelka, D.J. Stewart, R. Kurzrock, Novel therapeutic targets in non-small cell lung cancer, J. Thorac. Oncol. 6 (2011) 1601–1612.

[2] A. Jemal, R. Siegel, J. Xu, E. Ward, Cancer statistics, 2010, CA Cancer J. Clin. 60 (2010) 277–300.

[3] H.G. Russnes, N. Navin, J. Hicks, A.L. Borresen-Dale, Insight into the heterogeneity of breast cancer through next-generation sequencing, J. Clin. Invest. 121 (2011) 3810–3818.

[4] M. Blaxter, Genetics. Revealing the dark matter of the genome, Science 330 (2010) 1758–1759.

[5] A. Ashworth, C.J. Lord, J.S. Reis-Filho, Genetic interactions in cancer progression and treatment, Cell 145 (2011) 30–38.

[6] K.D. Hansen, W. Timp, H.C. Bravo, S. Sabunciyan, B. Langmead, O.G. McDonald, B. Wen, H. Wu, Y. Liu, D. Diep, E. Briem, K. Zhang, R.A. Irizarry, A.P. Feinberg, Increased methylation variation in epigenetic domains across cancer types, Nat. Genet. 43 (2011) 768–775.

[7] R.K. Thomas, A.C. Baker, R.M. Debiasi, W. Winckler, T. Laframboise, W.M. Lin, M. Wang, W. Feng, T. Zander, L. MacConaill, J.C. Lee, R. Nicoletti, C. Hatton, M. Goyette, L. Girard, K. Majmudar, L. Ziaugra, K.K. Wong, S. Gabriel, R. Beroukhim, M. Peyton, J. Barretina, A. Dutt, C. Emery, H. Greulich, K. Shah, H. Sasaki, A. Gazdar, J. Minna, S.A. Armstrong, I.K. Mellinghoff, F.S. Hodi, G. Dranoff, P.S. Mischel, T.F. Cloughesy, S.F. Nelson, L.M. Liau, K. Mertz, M.A. Rubin, H. Moch, M. Loda, W. Catalona, J. Fletcher, S. Signoretti, F. Kaye, K.C. Anderson, G.D. Demetri, R. Dummer, S. Wagner, M. Herlyn, W.R. Sellers, M. Meyerson, L. A. Garraway, High-throughput oncogene mutation profiling in human cancer, Nat. Genet. 39 (2007) 347–351.

[8] S. Liu, T. Shen, L. Huynh, M.I. Klisovic, L.J. Rush, J.L. Ford, J. Yu, B. Becknell, Y. Li, C. Liu, T. Vukosavljevic, S.P. Whitman, K.S. Chang, J.C. Byrd, D. Perrotti, C. Plass, G. Marcucci, Interplay of RUNX1/MTG8 and DNA methyltransferase 1 in acute myeloid leukemia, Cancer Res. 65 (2005) 1277–1284.

[9] J.Q. Guo, J.Y. Lian, Y.M. Xian, M.S. Lee, A.B. Deisseroth, S.A. Stass, R.E. Champlin, M. Talpaz, J.Y. Wang, R.B. Arlinghaus, BCR-ABL protein expression in peripheral blood cells of chronic myelogenous leukemia patients undergoing therapy, Blood 83 (1994) 3629–3637.

[10] M. Talpaz, N.P. Shah, H. Kantarjian, N. Donato, J. Nicoll, R. Paquette, J. Cortes, S. O'Brien, C. Nicaise, E. Bleickardt, M.A. Blackwood-Chirchir, V. Iyer, T.T. Chen, F. Huang, A.P. Decillis, C.L. Sawyers, Dasatinib in imatinib-resistant Philadelphia chromosome-positive leukemias, N. Engl. J. Med. 354 (2006) 2531–2541.

[11] C.J. Klein, M.V. Botuyan, Y. Wu, C.J. Ward, G.A. Nicholson, S. Hammans, K. Hojo, H. Yamanishi, A.R. Karpf, D.C. Wallace, M. Simon, C. Lander, L.A. Boardman, J.M. Cunningham, G.E. Smith, W.J. Litchy, B. Boes, E.J. Atkinson, S. Middha, BDPJ, Parisi JE, Mer G, Smith DI, Dyck PJ., Mutations in DNMT1 cause hereditary sensory neuropathy with dementia and hearing loss, Nat. Genet. 43 (2011) 595–600.

[12] T.J. Ley, L. Ding, M.J. Walter, M.D. McLellan, T. Lamprecht, D.E. Larson, C. Kandoth, J.E. Payton, J. Baty, J. Welch, C.C. Harris, C.F. Lichti, R.R. Townsend, R.S. Fulton, D.J. Dooling, D.C. Koboldt, H. Schmidt, Q. Zhang, J.R. Osborne, L. Lin, M. O'Laughlin, J.F. McMichael, K.D. Delehaunty, S.D. McGrath, L.A. Fulton, V.J. Magrini, T.L. Vickery, J. Hundal, L.L. Cook, J.J. Conyers, G.W. Swift, J.P. Reed, P.A. Alldredge, T. Wylie, J. Walker, J. Kalicki, M.A. Watson, S. Heath, W.D. Shannon, N. Varghese, R. Nagarajan, P. Westervelt, M.H. Tomasson, D.C. Link, T.A. Graubert, J. F. DiPersio, E.R. Mardis, R.K. Wilson, DNMT3A mutations in acute myeloid leukemia, N. Engl. J. Med. 363 (2010) 2424–2433.

[13] Y. Kanai, S. Ushijima, Y. Nakanishi, M. Sakamoto, S. Hirohashi, Mutation of the DNA methyltransferase (DNMT) 1 gene in human colorectal cancers, Cancer Lett. 192 (2003) 75–82.

[14] S. Liu, L.C. Wu, J. Pang, R. Santhanam, S. Schwind, Y.Z. Wu, C.J. Hickey, J. Yu, H. Becker, K. Maharry, M.D. Radmacher, C. Li, S.P. Whitman, A. Mishra, N. Stauffer, A.M. Eiring, R. Briesewitz, R.A. Baiocchi, K.K. Chan, P. Paschka, M. A. Caligiuri, J.C. Byrd, C.M. Croce, C.D. Bloomfield, D. Perrotti, R. Garzon, G. Marcucci, Sp1/NFkappaB/HDAC/miR-29b regulatory network in KIT-driven myeloid leukemia, Cancer Cell 17 (2010) 333–347.

[15] K.M. Kerr, Personalized medicine for lung cancer: new challenges for pathology, Histopathology (2011) (26. Swanton C, Caldas C. Molecular classification of solid tumours: towards pathway-driven therapeutics. British journal of cancer. 2009; 100:1517–1522).

[16] C. Oakman, L. Santarpia, A. Di Leo, Breast cancer assessment tools and optimizing adjuvant therapy, Nat. Rev. Clin. Oncol. 7 (2010) 725–732.

[17] E.A. Perez, Breast cancer management: opportunities and barriers to an individualized approach, Oncologist 16 (Suppl 1) (2011) 20–22.

[18] R.E. Laing, P. Hess, Y. Shen, J. Wang, S.X. Hu, The role and impact of SNPs in pharmacogenomics and personalized medicine, Curr. Drug Metab. 12 (2011) 460–486.

[19] A. Khare, I. Singh, P. Pawar, K. Grover, Design and evaluation of voriconazole loaded solid lipid nanoparticles for ophthalmic application, J. Drug Deliv. (2016) 2016.

[20] M.T. Landi, N. Chatterjee, N.E. Caporaso, M. Rotunno, D. Albanes, M. Thun, W. Wheeler, A. Rosenberger, H. Bickeboller, A. Risch, Y. Wang, V. Gaborieau, T. Thorgeirsson, D. Gudbjartsson, P. Sulem, M.R. Spitz, H.E. Wichmann, T. Rafnar, K. Stefansson, R.S. Houlston, P. Brennan, GPC5 rs2352028 variant and risk of lung cancer in never smokers, Lancet Oncol. 11 (2010) 714–716 (author reply 716).

[21] M. Ingelman-Sundberg, S.C. Sim, A. Gomez, C. Rodriguez-Antona, Influence of cytochrome P450 polymorphisms on drug therapies: pharmacogenetic, pharmacoepigenetic and clinical aspects, Pharmacol. Ther. 116 (2007) 496–526.

[22] K. Breving, A. Esquela-Kerscher, The complexities of microRNA regulation: mirandering around the rules, Int. J. Biochem. Cell Biol. 42 (2010) 1316–1329.

[23] B.M. Ryan, A.I. Robles, C.C. Harris, Genetic variation in microRNA networks: the implications for cancer research, Nat. Rev. Cancer 10 (2010) 389–402.

[24] C.M. McBride, S.H. Alford, R.J. Reid, E.B. Larson, A.D. Baxevanis, L.C. Brody, Putting science over supposition in the arena of personalized genomics, Nat. Genet. 40 (2008) 939–942. PubMed: 18665132 (35. Vasudevan S, Tong Y, Steitz JA. Switching from repression to activation: microRNAs can upregulate translation. Science. 2007; 318:1931–1934.).

[25] C.H. Lawrie, S. Gal, H.M. Dunlop, B. Pushkaran, A.P. Liggins, K. Pulford, A.H. Banham, F. Pezzella, J. Boultwood, J.S. Wainscoat, C.S. Hatton, A.L. Harris, Detection of elevated levels of tumour associated microRNAs in serum of patients with diffuse large B-cell lymphoma, Br. J. Haematol. 141 (2008) 672–675.

[26] P.S. Mitchell, R.K. Parkin, E.M. Kroh, B.R. Fritz, S.K. Wyman, E.L. Pogosova-Agadjanyan, A. Peterson, J. Noteboom, K.C. O'Briant, A. Allen, D.W. Lin, N. Urban, C.W. Drescher, B.S. Knudsen, D.L. Stirewalt, R. Gentleman, R.L. Vessella, P.S. Nelson, D.B. Martin, M. Tewari, Circulating microRNAs as stable blood-based markers for cancer detection, Proc. Natl. Acad. Sci. U. S. A. 105 (2008) 10513–10518.

[27] B.E. Bernstein, A. Meissner, E.S. Lander, The mammalian epigenome, Cell 128 (2007) 669–681.

[28] J.H. Sakamoto, A.L. van de Ven, B. Godin, E. Blanco, R.E. Serda, A. Grattoni, A. Ziemys, A. Bouamrani, T. Hu, S.I. Ranganathan, E. De Rosa, J.O. Martinez, C.A. Smid, R.M. Buchanan, S.Y. Lee, S. Srinivasan, M. Landry, A. Meyn, E. Tasciotti, X. Liu, P. Decuzzi, M. Ferrari, Enabling individualized therapy through nanotechnology, Pharmacol. Res. 62 (2010) 57–89.

[29] A.P. Feinberg, R.A. Irizarry, D. Fradin, M.J. Aryee, P. Murakami, T. Aspelund, G. Eiriksdottir, T.B. Harris, L. Launer, V. Gudnason, M.D. Fallin, Personalized epigenomic signatures that are stable over time and covary with body mass index, Sci. Transl. Med. 2 (2010) 49–67.

[30] J.N. Andersen, S. Sathyanarayanan, A. Di Bacco, A. Chi, T. Zhang, A.H. Chen, B. Dolinski, M. Kraus, B. Roberts, W. Arthur, R.A. Klinghoffer, D. Gargano, L. Li, I. Feldman, B. Lynch, J. Rush, R.C. Hendrickson, P. Blume-Jensen, C.P. Paweletz, Pathway-based identification of biomarkers for targeted therapeutics: personalized oncology with PI3K pathway inhibitors, Sci. Transl. Med. 2 (2010) 43–55.

[31] R.J. Leary, I. Kinde, F. Diehl, K. Schmidt, C. Clouser, C. Duncan, A. Antipova, C. Lee, K. McKernan, F.M. De La Vega, K.W. Kinzler, B. Vogelstein, L.A. Diaz Jr., V.E. Velculescu, Development of personalized tumor biomarkers using massively parallel sequencing, Sci. Transl. Med. 2 (2010) 2014.

[32] A. Meno, W.A. Messersmith, F.R. Hirsch, W.A. Franklin, S.G. Eckhardt, KRAS mutations and sensitivity to epidermal growth factor receptor inhibitors in colorectal cancer: practical application of patient selection, J. Clin. Oncol. Off. J. Am. Soc. Clin. Oncol. 27 (2009) 1130–1136.

[33] A. Sharma, V. Puri, P. Kumar, I. Singh, Biopolymeric, nanopatterned, fibrous carriers for wound healing applications, Curr. Pharm. Des. 26 (38) (2020) 4894–4908.

[34] M. Kaur, A. Sharma, V. Puri, G. Aggarwal, P. Maman, K. Huanbutta, M. Nagpal, T. Sangnim, Chitosan-based polymer blends for drug delivery systems, Polymers 15 (9) (2023) 2028.

[35] E.R. Mardis, The $1,000 genome, the $100,000 analysis? Genome Med. 2 (2010) 84.

[36] W.C. Hahn, R.A. Weinberg, Modelling the molecular circuitry of cancer, Nat. Rev. Cancer 2 (2002) 331–341.

[37] L. Liotta, E. Petricoin, Molecular profiling of human cancer, Nat. Rev. Genet. 1 (2000) 48–56 (49. Petricoin EF, Zoon KC, Kohn EC, Barrett JC, Liotta LA. Clinical proteomics: translating benchside promise into bedside reality. Nature reviews Drug discovery. 2002; 1:683–695.).

[38] K.K. Jain, Advances in the field of nanooncology, BMC Med. 8 (2010) 83.

[39] S.M. Moghimi, A.C. Hunter, J.C. Murray, Nanomedicine: current status and future prospects, FASEB J 19 (3) (2005) 311–330, https://doi.org/10.1096/fj.04-2747rev. [PMID: 15746175].

[40] A. Schroeder, D.A. Heller, M.M. Winslow, J.E. Dahlman, G.W. Pratt, R. Langer, T. Jacks, D.G. Anderson, Treating metastatic cancer with nanotechnology, Nat. Rev. Cancer 12 (2012) 39–50.

[41] P.E. Boukany, A. Morss, W.C. Liao, B. Henslee, H. Jung, X. Zhang, B. Yu, X. Wang, Y. Wu, L. Li, K. Gao, X. Hu, X. Zhao, O. Hemminger, W. Lu, G.P. Lafyatis, L.J. Lee, Nanochannel electroporation delivers precise amounts of biomolecules into living cells, Nat. Nanotechnol. 6 (2011) 747–754.

[42] D. Peer, J.M. Karp, S. Hong, O.C. Farokhzad, R. Margalit, R. Langer, Nanocarriers as an emerging platform for cancer therapy, Nat. Nanotechnol. 2 (2007) 751–760.

[43] R.R. Arvizo, S. Rana, O.R. Miranda, R. Bhattacharya, V.M. Rotello, P. Mukherjee, Mechanism of antiangiogenic property of gold nanoparticles: role of nanoparticle size and surface charge, Nanomedicine 7 (2011) 580–587.

[44] R.R. Arvizo, O.R. Miranda, M.A. Thompson, C.M. Pabelick, R. Bhattacharya, J.D. Robertson, V.M. Rotello, Y.S. Prakash, P. Mukherjee, Effect of nanoparticle surface charge at the plasma membrane and beyond, Nano Lett. 10 (2010) 2543–2548.

[45] R.S. Gaster, D.A. Hall, C.H. Nielsen, S.J. Osterfeld, H. Yu, K.E. Mach, R.J. Wilson, B. Murmann, J.C. Liao, S.S. Gambhir, S.X. Wang, Matrix-insensitive protein assays push the limits of biosensors in medicine, Nat. Med. 15 (2009) 1327–1332.

[46] E.I. Galanzha, E.V. Shashkov, T. Kelly, J.W. Kim, L. Yang, V.P. Zharov, In vivo magnetic enrichment and multiplex photoacoustic detection of circulating tumour cells, Nat. Nanotechnol. 4 (2009) 855–860.

[47] W.R. Sanhai, J.H. Sakamoto, R. Canady, M. Ferrari, Seven challenges for nanomedicine, Nat. Nanotechnol. 3 (2008) 242–244.

[48] M.E. Davis, J.E. Zuckerman, C.H. Choi, D. Seligson, A. Tolcher, C.A. Alabi, Y. Yen, J.D. Heidel, A. Ribas, Evidence of RNAi in humans from systemically administered siRNA via targeted nanoparticles, Nature 464 (2010) 1067–1070.

[49] Z. Chen, H. Meng, G. Xing, C. Chen, Y. Zhao, G. Jia, T. Wang, H. Yuan, C. Ye, F. Zhao, Z. Chai, C. Zhu, X. Fang, B. Ma, L. Wan, Acute toxicological effects of copper nanoparticles in vivo, Toxicol. Lett. 163 (2006) 109–120.

[50] S.M. Hussain, A.K. Javorina, A.M. Schrand, H.M. Duhart, S.F. Ali, J.J. Schlager, The interaction of manganese nanoparticles with PC-12 cells induces dopamine depletion, Toxicol. Sci. 92 (2006) 456–463.

[51] K.K. Jain, Applications of nanobiotechnology in clinical diagnostics, Clin. Chem. 53 (2007) 2002–2009.

[52] P. Debbage, Targeted drugs and nanomedicine: present and future, Curr. Pharm. Des. 15 (2009) 153–172.

[53] D.F. Emerich, C.G. Thanos, The pinpoint promise of nanoparticle-based drug delivery and molecular diagnosis, Biomol. Eng. 23 (2006) 171–184.

[54] S.D. Caruthers, P.M. Winter, S.A. Wickline, G.M. Lanza, Targeted magnetic resonance imaging contrast agents, Methods Mol. Med. 124 (2006) 387–400.

[55] A.H. Schmieder, P.M. Winter, S.D. Caruthers, T.D. Harris, T.A. Williams, J.S. Allen, E. K. Lacy, H. Zhang, M.J. Scott, G. Hu, J.D. Robertson, S.A. Wickline, G.M. Lanza, Molecular MR imaging of melanoma angiogenesis with alphanubeta3-targeted paramagnetic nanoparticles, Mag. Reson. Med. 53 (2005) 621–627.

[56] P. Blume-Jensen, T. Hunter, Oncogenic kinase signalling, Nature 411 (2001) 355–365.

[57] B. Vogelstein, K.W. Kinzler, Cancer genes and the pathways they control, Nat. Med. 10 (2004) 789–799.

[58] J.A. Engelman, J. Luo, L.C. Cantley, The evolution of phosphatidylinositol 3-kinases as regulators of growth and metabolism, Nat. Rev. Genet. 7 (2006) 606–619.

[59] J. Huang, B.D. Manning, A complex interplay between Akt, TSC2 and the two mTOR complexes, Biochem. Soc. Trans. 37 (2009) 217–222.

[60] H.M. Abdolmaleky, J.R. Zhou, S. Thiagalingam, C.L. Smith, Epigenetic and pharmacoepigenomic studies of major psychoses and potentials for therapeutics, Pharmacogenomics 9 (2008) 1809–1823.

[61] M.D. Anway, A.S. Cupp, M. Uzumcu, M.K. Skinner, Epigenetic transgenerational actions of endocrine disruptors and male fertility, Science 308 (2005) 1466–1469. PubMed: 15933200.

[62] B.T. Heijmans, E.W. Tobi, A.D. Stein, H. Putter, G.J. Blauw, E.S. Susser, P.E. Slagboom, L.H. Lumey, Persistent epigenetic differences associated with prenatal exposure to famine in humans, Proc. Natl. Acad. Sci. U. S. A. 105 (2008) 17046–17049.

[63] P.O. McGowan, A. Sasaki, A.C. D'Alessio, S. Dymov, B. Labonte, M. Szyf, G. Turecki, M.J. Meaney, Epigenetic regulation of the glucocorticoid receptor in human brain associates with childhood abuse, Nat. Neurosci. 12 (2009) 342–348.

[64] S.L. Schreiber, B.E. Bernstein, Signaling network model of chromatin, Cell 111 (2002) 771–778.

[65] B.M. Turner, Defining an epigenetic code, Nat. Cell Biol. 9 (2007) 2–6.

[66] H.T. Bjornsson, M.I. Sigurdsson, M.D. Fallin, R.A. Irizarry, T. Aspelund, H. Cui, W. Yu, M.A. Rongione, T.J. Ekstrom, T.B. Harris, L.J. Launer, G. Eiriksdottir, M.F. Leppert, C. Sapienza, V. Gudnason, A.P. Feinberg, Intra-individual change over time in DNA methylation with familial clustering, JAMA 299 (2008) 2877–2883.

[67] B. Li, M. Carey, J.L. Workman, The role of chromatin during transcription, Cell 128 (2007) 707–719.

[68] S.L. Berger, T. Kouzarides, R. Shiekhattar, A. Shilatifard, An operational definition of epigenetics, Genes Dev. 23 (2009) 781–783.

[69] R. Garzon, S. Liu, M. Fabbri, Z. Liu, C.E. Heaphy, E. Callegari, S. Schwind, J. Pang, J. Yu, N. Muthusamy, V. Havelange, S. Volinia, W. Blum, L.J. Rush, D. Perrotti, M. Andreeff, C.D. Bloomfield, J.C. Byrd, K. Chan, L.C. Wu, C.M. Croce, G. Marcucci, MicroRNA-29b induces global DNA hypomethylation and tumor suppressor gene reexpression in acute myeloid leukemia by targeting directly DNMT3A and 3B and indirectly DNMT1, Blood 113 (2009) 6411–6418.

[70] M. Fabbri, R. Garzon, A. Cimmino, Z. Liu, N. Zanesi, E. Callegari, S. Liu, H. Alder, S. Costinean, C. Fernandez-Cymering, S. Volinia, G. Guler, C.D. Morrison, K.K. Chan,

G. Marcucci, G.A. Calin, K. Huebner, C.M. Croce, MicroRNA-29 family reverts aberrant methylation in lung cancer by targeting DNA methyltransferases 3A and 3B, Proc. Natl. Acad. Sci. U. S. A. 104 (2007) 15805–15810.

[71] T. Kouzarides, Chromatin modifications and their function, Cell 128 (2007) 693–705.

[72] C.D. Allis, S.L. Berger, J. Cote, S. Dent, T. Jenuwien, T. Kouzarides, L. Pillus, D. Reinberg, Y. Shi, R. Shiekhattar, A. Shilatifard, J. Workman, Y. Zhang, New nomenclature for chromatin-modifying enzymes, Cell 131 (2007) 633–636.

[73] F. Mohn, D. Schubeler, Genetics and epigenetics: stability and plasticity during cellular differentiation, Trends Genet.: TIG 25 (2009) 129–136.

[74] O. Witt, H.E. Deubzer, T. Milde, I. Oehme, HDAC family: what are the cancer relevant targets? Cancer Lett. 277 (2009) 8–21.

[75] M. Dokmanovic, C. Clarke, P.A. Marks, Histone deacetylase inhibitors: overview and perspectives, Mol. Cancer Res.: MCR 5 (2007) 981–989. PubMed: 17951399.

[76] W. Weichert, HDAC expression and clinical prognosis in human malignancies, Cancer Lett. 280 (2009) 168–176.

[77] K. Liu, Y.F. Wang, C. Cantemir, M.T. Muller, Endogenous assays of DNA methyltransferases: evidence for differential activities of DNMT1, DNMT2, and DNMT3 in mammalian cells in vivo, Mol. Cell. Biol. 23 (2003) 2709–2719.

[78] J.G. Herman, S.B. Baylin, Gene silencing in cancer in association with promoter hypermethylation, N. Engl. J. Med. 349 (2003) 2042–2054.

[79] A.H. Ting, K.W. Jair, H. Suzuki, R.W. Yen, S.B. Baylin, K.E. Schuebel, CpG island hypermethylation is maintained in human colorectal cancer cells after RNAi-mediated depletion of DNMT1, Nat. Genet. 36 (2004) 582–584.

[80] I. Rhee, K.E. Bachman, B.H. Park, K.W. Jair, R.W. Yen, K.E. Schuebel, H. Cui, A.P. Feinberg, C. Lengauer, K.W. Kinzler, S.B. Baylin, B. Vogelstein, DNMT1 and DNMT3b cooperate to silence genes in human cancer cells, Nature 416 (2002) 552–556.

[81] A. Tsumura, T. Hayakawa, Y. Kumaki, S. Takebayashi, M. Sakaue, C. Matsuoka, K. Shimotohno, F. Ishikawa, E. Li, H.R. Ueda, J. Nakayama, M. Okano, Maintenance of self-renewal ability of mouse embryonic stem cells in the absence of DNA methyltransferases Dnmt1, Dnmt3a and Dnmt3b, Genes Cells 11 (2006) 805–814.

[82] M.F. Robert, S. Morin, N. Beaulieu, F. Gauthier, I.C. Chute, A. Barsalou, A.R. MacLeod, DNMT1 is required to maintain CpG methylation and aberrant gene silencing in human cancer cells, Nat. Genet. 33 (2003) 61–65.

[83] K. Williams, J. Christensen, M.T. Pedersen, J.V. Johansen, P.A. Cloos, J. Rappsilber, K. Helin, TET1 and hydroxymethylcytosine in transcription and DNA methylation fidelity, Nature 473 (2011) 343–348.

[84] S. Ito, L. Shen, Q. Dai, S.C. Wu, L.B. Collins, J.A. Swenberg, C. He, Y. Zhang, Tet proteins can convert 5-methylcytosine to 5-formylcytosine and 5-carboxylcytosine, Science 333 (2011) 1300–1303.

[85] M. Tahiliani, K.P. Koh, Y. Shen, W.A. Pastor, H. Bandukwala, Y. Brudno, S. Agarwal, L.M. Iyer, D.R. Liu, L. Aravind, A. Rao, Conversion of 5-methylcytosine to 5-hydroxymethylcytosine in mammalian DNA by MLL partner TET1, Science 324 (2009) 930–935.

[86] M.E. Figueroa, O. Abdel-Wahab, C. Lu, P.S. Ward, J. Patel, A. Shih, Y. Li, N. Bhagwat, A. Vasanthakumar, H.F. Fernandez, M.S. Tallman, Z. Sun, K. Wolniak, J.K. Peeters, W. Liu, S.E. Choe, V.R. Fantin, E. Paietta, B. Lowenberg, J.D. Licht, L.A. Godley,

R. Delwel, P.J. Valk, C.B. Thompson, R.L. Levine, A. Melnick, Leukemic IDH1 and IDH2 mutations result in a hypermethylation phenotype, disrupt TET2 function, and impair hematopoietic differentiation, Cancer Cell 18 (2010) 553–567.

[87] M. Esteller, Epigenetics in cancer, N. Engl. J. Med. 358 (2008) 1148–1159.

[88] A.P. Feinberg, B. Tycko, The history of cancer epigenetics, Nat. Rev. Cancer 4 (2004) 143–153.

[89] P. Chi, C.D. Allis, G.G. Wang, Covalent histone modifications—miswritten, misinterpreted and miserased in human cancers, Nat. Rev. Cancer 10 (2010) 457–469.

[90] S. Mizuno, T. Chijiwa, T. Okamura, K. Akashi, Y. Fukumaki, Y. Niho, H. Sasaki, Expression of DNA methyltransferases DNMT1, 3A, and 3B in normal hematopoiesis and in acute and chronic myelogenous leukemia, Blood 97 (2001) 1172–1179.

[91] I. Girault, S. Tozlu, R. Lidereau, I. Bieche, Expression analysis of DNA methyltransferases 1, 3A, and 3B in sporadic breast carcinomas, Clin. Cancer Res. 9 (2003) 4415–4422.

[92] S.E. Goelz, B. Vogelstein, S.R. Hamilton, A.P. Feinberg, Hypomethylation of DNA from benign and malignant human colon neoplasms, Science 228 (1985) 187–190.

[93] S.B. Baylin, J.E. Ohm, Epigenetic gene silencing in cancer—a mechanism for early oncogenic pathway addiction? Nat. Rev. Cancer 6 (2006) 107–116.

[94] S.A. Belinsky, Gene-promoter hypermethylation as a biomarker in lung cancer, Nat. Rev. Cancer 4 (2004) 707–717.

[95] M. Rodriguez-Paredes, M. Esteller, Cancer epigenetics reaches mainstream oncology, Nat. Med. 17 (2011) 330–339.

[96] P.A. Jones, S.B. Baylin, The fundamental role of epigenetic events in cancer, Nat. Rev. Genet. 3 (2002) 415–428.

[97] D. Iliopoulos, G. Guler, S.Y. Han, D. Johnston, T. Druck, K.A. McCorkell, J. Palazzo, P.A. McCue, R. Baffa, K. Huebner, Fragile genes as biomarkers: epigenetic control of WWOX and FHIT in lung, breast and bladder cancer, Oncogene 24 (2005) 1625–1633.

[98] M. Fabbri, D. Iliopoulos, F. Trapasso, R.I. Aqeilan, A. Cimmino, N. Zanesi, S. Yendamuri, S.Y. Han, D. Amadori, K. Huebner, C.M. Croce, WWOX gene restoration prevents lung cancer growth in vitro and in vivo, Proc. Natl. Acad. Sci. U. S. A. 102 (2005) 15611–15616.

[99] M. Suzuki, N. Sunaga, D.S. Shames, S. Toyooka, A.F. Gazdar, J.D. Minna, RNA interference mediated knockdown of DNA methyltransferase 1 leads to promoter demethylation and gene reexpression in human lung and breast cancer cells, Cancer Res. 64 (2004) 3137–3143.

[100] J.R. Melki, P.C. Vincent, S.J. Clark, Concurrent DNA hypermethylation of multiple genes in acute myeloid leukemia, Cancer Res. 59 (1999) 3730–3740.

[101] H.T. Bjornsson, M.D. Fallin, A.P. Feinberg, An integrated epigenetic and genetic approach to common human disease, Trends Genet.: TIG 20 (2004) 350–358. PubMed: 15262407 (123. Mateo Leach I, van der Harst P, de Boer RA. Pharmacoepigenetics in heart failure. Current heart failure reports. 2010; 7:83–90.).

[102] M.O. Hoque, S. Begum, O. Topaloglu, A. Chatterjee, E. Rosenbaum, W. Van Criekinge, W.H. Westra, M. Schoenberg, M. Zahurak, S.N. Goodman, D. Sidransky, Quantitation of promoter methylation of multiple genes in urine DNA and bladder cancer detection, J. Natl. Cancer Inst. 98 (2006) 996–1004.

[103] S.A. Belinsky, K.C. Liechty, F.D. Gentry, H.J. Wolf, J. Rogers, K. Vu, J. Haney, T.C. Kennedy, F.R. Hirsch, Y. Miller, W.A. Franklin, J.G. Herman, S.B. Baylin, P.A. Bunn,

T. Byers, Promoter hypermethylation of multiple genes in sputum precedes lung cancer incidence in a high-risk cohort, Cancer Res. 66 (2006) 3338–3344.

[104] W.H. Lee, R.A. Morton, J.I. Epstein, J.D. Brooks, P.A. Campbell, G.S. Bova, W.S. Hsieh, W.B. Isaacs, W.G. Nelson, Cytidine methylation of regulatory sequences near the pi-class glutathione S-transferase gene accompanies human prostatic carcinogenesis, Proc. Natl. Acad. Sci. U. S. A. 91 (1994) 11733–11737.

[105] M.O. Hoque, O. Topaloglu, S. Begum, R. Henrique, E. Rosenbaum, W. Van Criekinge, W.H. Westra, D. Sidransky, Quantitative methylation-specific polymerase chain reaction gene patterns in urine sediment distinguish prostate cancer patients from control subjects, J. Clin. Oncol. Off. J. Am. Soc. Clin. Oncol. 23 (2005) 6569–6575.

[106] L. Richiardi, V. Fiano, L. Vizzini, L. De Marco, L. Delsedime, O. Akre, A.G. Tos, F. Merletti, Promoter methylation in APC, RUNX3, and GSTP1 and mortality in prostate cancer patients, J. Clin. Oncol. Off. J. Am. Soc. Clin. Oncol. 27 (2009) 3161–3168.

[107] I.P. Ioshikhes, M.Q. Zhang, Large-scale human promoter mapping using CpG islands, Nat. Genet. 26 (2000) 61–63.

[108] J.F. Costello, M.C. Fruhwald, D.J. Smiraglia, L.J. Rush, G.P. Robertson, X. Gao, F.A. Wright, J.D. Feramisco, P. Peltomaki, J.C. Lang, D.E. Schuller, L. Yu, C.D. Bloomfield, M.A. Caligiuri, A. Yates, R. Nishikawa, H. Su Huang, N.J. Petrelli, X. Zhang, M.S. O'Dorisio, W.A. Held, W.K. Cavenee, C. Plass, Aberrant CpG-island methylation has non-random and tumour-type-specific patterns, Nat. Genet. 24 (2000) 132–138.

[109] M. Esteller, P.G. Corn, S.B. Baylin, J.G. Herman, A gene hypermethylation profile of human cancer, Cancer Res. 61 (2001) 3225–3229.

[110] T.K. Kelly, D.D. De Carvalho, P.A. Jones, Epigenetic modifications as therapeutic targets, Nat. Biotechnol. 28 (2010) 1069–1078.

[111] Y. Oki, J.P. Issa, Epigenetic mechanisms in AML—a target for therapy, Cancer Treat. Res. 145 (2010) 19–40.

[112] J.G. Herman, J. Jen, A. Merlo, S.B. Baylin, Hypermethylation-associated inactivation indicates a tumor suppressor role for p15INK4B, Cancer Res. 56 (1996) 722–727.

[113] J.P. Issa, B.A. Zehnbauer, C.I. Civin, M.I. Collector, S.J. Sharkis, N.E. Davidson, S.H. Kaufmann, S.B. Baylin, The estrogen receptor CpG island is methylated in most hematopoietic neoplasms, Cancer Res. 56 (1996) 973–977.

[114] J.P. Issa, H.M. Kantarjian, P. Kirkpatrick, Azacitidine, Nat. Rev. Drug Discov. 4 (2005) 275–276.

[115] W. Blum, S. Schwind, S.S. Tarighat, S. Geyer, A.K. Eisfeld, S. Whitman, A. Walker, R. Klisovic, J.C. Byrd, R. Santhanam, H. Wang, J.P. Curfman, S.M. Devine, S. Jacob, C. Garr, C. Kefauver, D. Perrotti, K.K. Chan, C.D. Bloomfield, M.A. Caligiuri, M.R. Grever, R. Garzon, G. Marcucci, Clinical and pharmacodynamic activity of bortezomib and decitabine in acute myeloid leukemia, Blood 119 (2012) 6025–6031.

[116] P.A. Marks, Epigenetic targeted anti-cancer drugs: an unfolding story, Oncology (Williston Park) 25 (231) (2011) 235. PubMed: 21548466 (160. Boumber Y, Issa JP. Epigenetics in cancer.).

[117] J.P. Issa, H.M. Kantarjian, Targeting DNA methylation, Clin. Cancer Res. 15 (2009) 3938–3946.

[118] C.B. Yoo, S. Jeong, G. Egger, G. Liang, P. Phiasivongsa, C. Tang, S. Redkar, P.A. Jones, Delivery of 5-aza-2′-deoxycytidine to cells using oligodeoxynucleotides, Cancer Res. 67 (2007) 6400–6408.

[119] C.I. Muller, B. Ruter, H.P. Koeffler, M. Lubbert, DNA hypermethylation of myeloid cells, a novel therapeutic target in MDS and AML, Curr. Pharm. Biotechnol. 7 (2006) 315–321.

[120] K. Ghoshal, J. Datta, S. Majumder, S. Bai, H. Kutay, T. Motiwala, S.T. Jacob, 5-Aza-deoxycytidine induces selective degradation of DNA methyltransferase 1 by a proteasomal pathway that requires the KEN box, bromo-adjacent homology domain, and nuclear localization signal, Mol. Cell. Biol. 25 (2005) 4727–4741.

[121] S. Liu, Z. Liu, Z. Xie, J. Pang, J. Yu, E. Lehmann, L. Huynh, T. Vukosavljevic, M. Takeki, R.B. Klisovic, R.A. Baiocchi, W. Blum, P. Porcu, R. Garzon, J.C. Byrd, D. Perrotti, M.A. Caligiuri, K.K. Chan, L.C. Wu, G. Marcucci, Bortezomib induces DNA hypomethylation and silenced gene transcription by interfering with Sp1/NF-kappaB-dependent DNA methyltransferase activity in acute myeloid leukemia, Blood 111 (2008) 2364–2373.

[122] M. Flasshove, D. Strumberg, L. Ayscue, B.S. Mitchell, C. Tirier, W. Heit, S. Seeber, J. Schutte, Structural analysis of the deoxycytidine kinase gene in patients with acute myeloid leukemia and resistance to cytosine arabinoside, Leukemia 8 (1994) 780–785.

[123] A.P. Stegmann, M.W. Honders, A. Hagemeijer, B. Hoebee, R. Willemze, J.E. Landegent, In vitro induced resistance to the deoxycytidine analogues cytarabine (AraC) and 5-aza-2′-deoxycytidine (DAC) in a rat model for acute myeloid leukemia is mediated by mutations in the deoxycytidine kinase (dck) gene, Ann. Hematol. 71 (1995) 41–47.

[124] S. Koscielny, Why most gene expression signatures of tumors have not been useful in the clinic, Sci. Transl. Med. 2 (2010). 14ps12 (169. Szyf M. Toward a discipline of pharmacoepigenomics. Current Pharmacogenomics. 2004; 2:357–3).

[125] B. Wang, Y. Li, C. Shao, Y. Tan, L. Cai, Cadmium and its epigenetic effects, Curr. Med. Chem. 19 (16) (2012) 2611–2620, https://doi.org/10.2174/092986712800492913. [PMID: 22471978].

[126] J.P. Issa, H.M. Kantarjian, Targeting DNA methylation, Clin. Cancer Res. 15 (2009) 3938–3946.

[127] C.B. Yoo, S. Jeong, G. Egger, G. Liang, P. Phiasivongsa, C. Tang, S. Redkar, P.A. Jones, Delivery of 5-aza-2′-deoxycytidine to cells using oligodeoxynucleotides, Cancer Res. 67 (2007) 6400–6408.

[128] C.I. Muller, B. Ruter, H.P. Koeffler, M. Lubbert, DNA hypermethylation of myeloid cells, a novel therapeutic target in MDS and AML, Curr. Pharm. Biotechnol. 7 (2006) 315–321.

[129] K. Ghoshal, J. Datta, S. Majumder, S. Bai, H. Kutay, T. Motiwala, S.T. Jacob, 5-Aza-deoxycytidine induces selective degradation of DNA methyltransferase 1 by a proteasomal pathway that requires the KEN box, bromo-adjacent homology domain, and nuclear localization signal, Mol. Cell. Biol. 25 (2005) 4727–4741.

Smart cancer nanomedicine: Challenges and future opportunities

18

Moumita Roy

Mechanical Engineering, Texas Tech University, Lubbock, TX, United States

Introduction
Cancer treatment challenges

Cancer is a highly heterogeneous and one of the deadliest diseases. Despite the global efforts on numerous cancer therapies over time, including chemotherapy, radiotherapy, and tumor surgical resection, they could not attain a complete cure for the disease [1].

Moreover, traditional anticancer treatments are responsible for compromised lifestyle of the patient, and they have significant toxic side effects [2]. Combating cancer is a battle against complexities and intricacies due to the metastatic nature of cancer cells, mutations, drug resistance, lack of early detection techniques, and the inability of scientific community to solve many cancer-related problems [3–6]. During cancer treatment, primary challenges are toxicity of chemotherapies and anticancer drugs and poor efficacy due to blood-brain barrier in several cancers like glioblastoma, brain tumors, etc. [7–9]. Conventional chemotherapy mainly kills cancer cells by blocking mitosis, preventing DNA synthesis of cancer cells, and killing them are the basic strategies of conventional cancer therapy. The fatal and toxic side effects mainly occur when chemotherapeutic drugs target healthy tissues [10].

Recently, the global pandemic COVID-19 further aggravated the problem. Also, the majority of global cancer patients face several challenges including missing dosages of chemotherapy therapies, along with the immunosuppressed status of some cancer patients (whether caused by the disease itself or the treatment) increases their risk of infection and hospitalization compared with the general population [11,12]. So, in this context, smart nanotherapy can be an ideal solution from the context of early diagnosis and treatment.

Cancer Epigenetics and Nanomedicine. **https://doi.org/10.1016/B978-0-443-13209-4.00015-5**
Copyright © 2024 Elsevier Inc. All rights reserved, including those for text and data mining, AI training, and similar technologies.

Nanotherapy and its challenges

Multidisciplinary emerging areas dealing with physics, biochemistry, material science, chemistry, biology, medicine, informatics, and engineering and involved in nanotherapy developments [13,14]. Interestingly, nanotechnology finds wide applications in early cancer and other disease diagnosis, medicine detection, veterinary medicine, food science, marine science, environmental chemistry, agriculture, and in several other industries [15–17]. The nanomaterials are typically small and range between 0.1 and 100 nm in size, and they exhibit extraordinary capabilities due to a higher surface-to-volume ratio [18]. The use of nanotechnology-based approaches and nanomaterials in oncology can lead to early diagnosis, drug development, targeted drug delivery, and efficient anticancer therapies [19]. Cancer nanotherapeutics have overcome multiple shortcomings of conventional therapies, including low water solubility, poor bioavailability, toxicity of traditional therapies in higher dosage, and nonspecific biodistribution. NP-based drug delivery systems have higher efficacy when compared with traditional drug delivery systems due to the increased half-life of vulnerable drugs and proteins, improved solubility of hydrophobic drugs, and the ability to control and target drug release in diseased sites [20].

Additionally, the smart artificially engineered nanomaterials exhibit targeted tumor site delivery with more specificity and higher cellular uptake, as compared with conventional materials, and they can also be extensively used to increase the therapeutic drug loading capacity and controlled sustained release of drugs, as well as selective and specific biodistribution by engineering their composition, synthesis methods, size, morphology, and surface chemistry. Artificially engineered smart nanomaterials can easily penetrate across biological barriers; enable pH, thermal, and light-based targeting of malignant cells; and prevent pharmaceuticals from being degraded by enzymes, enhance drug half-life in vivo responses, and improve anticancer drug biodistribution [21]. Nanomaterials also help in delivery of multiple drugs at single platform, reducing drug resistance and the sustained release of anticancer drugs by targeting the cancer sites.

Tumor microenvironment and nanotherapy action while targeting tumor physiology

The hallmarks of cancer consist of several critical mechanisms—inducing angiogenesis, resisting cell death, sustaining proliferative signals, evading growth suppressors, activating invasion and metastasis, and enabling replicative immortality. Malignant tumors, the most dreaded killers that threaten human life, and effective therapeutic strategies are thus urgently needed. Tumor microenvironment (TME) is composed of a heterogeneous mass composed of various cell subtypes, namely immune cells, endothelial and inflammatory cells, fibroblasts, and lymphocytes surrounded by the extracellular matrix (ECM), stroma, and vasculature, as well as chemokines, organelles, and secreted [22–25]. TME refers to the exterior of malignant/ benign cell's surrounding tumor components comprising of ECM, blood vessels,

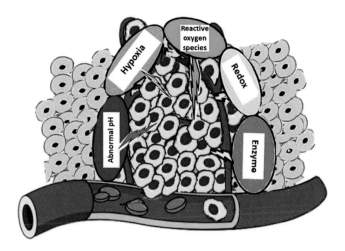

FIG. 1

Schematic of tumor microenvironment.

signaling molecules, fibroblasts, tumor vasculature, secreted factors, and lymphatics (Fig. 1). TME plays a critical role in tumorigenesis, tumor invasion, and metastasis as the malignant cells invade the local tissues during carcinogenesis by releasing pro-tumorigenic factors, which are responsible for the formation of TME, characterized by angiogenesis and hypoxia, redox potential alteration [26], nutrient and oxygen uptake (hypoxia conditions) changes [26–30], and blood flow alteration [29]. During tumor development, rapid replication and growth of cancer cells and aberrant blood vasculature results in hypoxia caused by a reduced insufficient oxygen supply [23]. Tumor hypoxia-induced different responses include altered gene expression, suppressing apoptosis, or promoting autophagy [26,27]. Several unique characteristics are present within TME, e.g., such as acidic pH [28–32] and hypoxia [28–32]. Parallelly, at all stages of carcinogenesis, nonmalignant cells of TME have tumor-promoting and dynamic functions [31].

The TME serves as a multidrug-resistant center for tumors during chemotherapy treatment and a physiological barrier against the penetration of various therapeutic nanoparticles (NPs). The acidic pH, hypoxic condition, and oxidative stress conditions exist in the TME. The TME acts as heterogeneous area in terms of gradients of solutes and nutrients (nano- to microscale) as well as differences in pH and cell viability due to hypoxia (microscale) and causes a significant effect on therapeutic outcomes.

Hypoxia causes the recruitment of immune cells to the tissue while prompting the release of cytokines and chemokines (molecular (nano-) scale) that affect cell-to-cell interactions (microscale). Primarily, TME heterogeneity and three-dimensionality represent a significant barrier to systemically administered therapeutics, including nanotherapeutics, and as a result, in vitro efficiencies of anticancer drugs (especially those shown in 2D cultures) do not correlate well with potencies observed in vivo

[32,33]. Another reason is that other cells in the TME such as endothelial cells, macrophages, and other cells of the immune system, and fibroblasts/myofibroblasts actively interact with the tumor cells in most solid tumors and affect cancer cell proliferation, survival, polarity, and invasive capacity. While the normal cellular microenvironment can inhibit or even prevent the growth of tumor cells, the changes that happen in the TME synergistically support tumor growth, and nanotherapy often overcomes these challenging problems. Tumors shape their respective microenvironment, promoting the growth of not only malignant cells but also nonmalignant TME or stromal cells. There are many mechanisms that still need to be elucidated in the tumor-stroma interactions, although the importance of an altered TME in the process of tumorigenesis is no longer questioned.

To achieve therapeutic responses in solid tumors, drug molecules primarily need to overcome multiple barriers at different physical scales. The TME includes several scale/mechanistic events. They are:

(a) Molecular (nano-) scale, including up- and down-regulation of various proteins that can signal tumor growth or drug-efflux mechanisms.
(b) Nano- to microscale, which incorporates gradients of cell nutrients and oxygen, growth factors, and other means of cell-to-cell communication.
(c) Microscale, in which interactions between cells occur in the acellular stroma compartment of the tumor.
(d) Micro- to macroscale, which incorporates the organ architecture, blood supply, lymphatics, and other physiological factors.

While these barriers span several orders of magnitude, they are intricately linked and cross-communicated. As an example, the architecturally/anatomically irregular and functionally impaired tumor neovasculature (micro- to macroscale) is characterized by reduced oxygen tension, oscillating flow, constricted blood vessels, and other abnormal features (Fig. 1).

Another predominant component of TME is that it contributes to all cancer stages. Activated fibroblasts are known as cancer-associated fibroblasts (CAFs) [34]. CAFs act directly on reconverting the antitumorigenic milieus into prometastatic environments via stroma-derived factors and it also increases myeloid-derived suppressor cells (MDSCs) activity through CXCL12, thus enhancing cancer progression and hypoxia status along with shape the TME by building large portions of the (ECM) and enhance tumorigenesis and angiogenesis through cytokines, growth factors, and matrix metalloproteinases (MMPs), which induce TME remodeling [35,36]. CAFs silence cytotoxic T cells and recruit inflammatory lymphocytes that promote tumor progression [37]. CAFs can also reconvert antitumorigenic milieus into prometastatic environments via stroma-derived factors.

The significant abnormalities in TME like acidic pH, altered redox potential, hyperthermia, and up-regulated expression of selected proteins (e.g., metalloproteases and others) and enzymes have drawn the interest of employing stimulus-responsive nanomaterials in cancer diagnosis and therapy [34] (Table 1).

Table 1 Smart nanoparticle-based strategies for targeting tumor microenvironment.

Cancer treated	Nanomaterial used	Antitumor agent	Stimuli	Characteristic
MDA-MB-231 breast cancer cells	HA/HAase/CS/liposome/shRNA (HCLR) nanocarrier	Inhibitor of apoptosis survivin-shRNA	Redox	Stable during blood circulation due to negative charge of hyaluronic acid [35]
Ovarian cancer cells (A2780), prostate cancer cells (PC-3), breast cancer cells (MCF7), colorectal cancer cells (HCT116), lung cancer cells (A549 and H460)	Platinum nanoparticles (platinum (IV) prodrug self-assembled with lipid-PEG)	Platinum	Glutathione	Targeted controlled drug release at tumor site [36]
4T1 breast cancer cells, OVCAR-3 ovarian cancer cells	Gold nanovesicles, nanoemulsion composed of perfluoropolyether, catalase, and photosensitizer IR780	Tirapazamine, near-infrared light activatable photosensitizer IR780	Hydrogen peroxide	Stable in water, cell culture media, and plasma of rat up to 3 weeks. No change in diameter or precipitation in cell culture media after 48h incubation at 25°C and 37°C. Can be stored at 4°C for 15months [37]
Glioblastoma, C6 cells	Low-molecular-weight protamine (LMWP) conjugated to poly(ethylene glycol)-poly (ε-caprolactone) nanoparticles	Paclitaxel	Matrix metalloproteinases enzyme	Demonstrated excellent pharmacokinetics and biodistribution profile [38]
4T1 breast cancer cells	Janus PEGylated dendrimer prodrug-based nanoparticles	Paclitaxel	Cathepsin B enzyme	Prodrug self-assembled in nanoscale range with negative surface charge, compact morphology, and appropriate size [39]
HCT116 human colorectal cancer cells	Nanodrug composed of lauric acid, mPEG, lecithin BSO-DOX	Doxorubicin	Hydrogen sulfide	Fluorescent prodrug possesses colorectal cancer-specific photocontrollable synergistic therapeutic effect [40]
HepG2 liver cancer cells	ATP-coated silver nanoparticles	Silver nanoparticles	Phosphatase enzyme	Excellent stability in physiological condition [41]

Different recent strategies of NP-based therapies help in overcoming the therapeutic challenges of TMEs including liposomal formulations and noble metal NPs, e.g., gold nanoparticle (AuNP)-based therapies (Table 2). This approach enables the synthesis of nanomaterial that responds to endogenous and/or exogenous stimuli like pH, temperature, magnetism, light, and enzymes to improve drug targeting and internalization. The stimulus-responsive nanomaterial possesses several interesting characteristics, which include (Fig. 2):

  (i) inhibiting tumor growth by enabling the tumor or TME targeting,
 (ii) facilitating the accumulation of drugs in altered TME, and
(iii) improving the therapeutic ability.

Table 2 Tumor microenvironment-responsive nanoparticles.

TME stimuli	Nanoparticle type	Functionalities	References
pH and redox	Gold nanoparticles	Drug release controlled by pH and disassembly mediated by GSH	[42]
pH	Gold nanocluster	pH-sensitive drug release [43]	[43]
Redox	Heparosan- and deoxycholic acid-conjugated micelle	GSH-responsive drug release and degradation	[44]
Reactive oxygen species (ROS)	Methoxy (polyethylene glycol) thioketal-poly (ε-caprolactone) (mPEG-TK-PCL) micelles	ROS-responsive drug release	[45]
Enzyme	His-tagged fluorescent fusion protein chimera and $NiFe_2O_4$-based magnetic nanoparticles	MMP-2 enzyme cleavable peptide linker	[46]
Hypoxia	Polyethyleneimine (PEI) conjugated alkylated 2-nitroimidazole (NI) and hyaluronic acid (HA) conjugated chlorin e6 (Ce6)	Light and hypoxia-triggered release of anticancer drug	[47]
pH/H_2O_2	Human serum albumin nanoparticle	pH-dependent degradation of nanoparticles into smaller polymer-drug conjugates	[48]
Hypoxia	Hollow mesoporous titanium dioxide nanoparticles	Hypoxic microenvironment creation via ultrasound irradiation and hypoxia-triggered release of anticancer drug release of drug by hypoxia	[49]

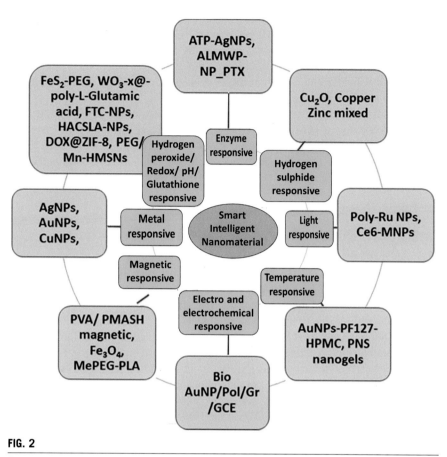

FIG. 2

Smart nanotechnology strategies in combating cancer.

pH-sensitive smart nanoparticles for targeting TME

In recent decades, several pH-sensitive NPs have been designed, especially those that became active by a pH-dependent structural transformation while reaching the acidic microenvironment in tumors. The acidic environment at the tumor site triggers the protonation of pH-sensitive moieties, in turn causing structural transformation and thereby disrupting the hydrophilic-hydrophobic equilibrium within the NP and the release of therapeutic cargo loaded inside the tumors. For the fabrication of these NPs fabricated acid-sensitive linkers or ionizable groups are used [50].

Different pH-sensitive smart NPs were synthesized for delivery of cancer drug doxorubicin [50–53]. The pH-induced destabilization of the NP enables the controlled release of DOX, followed by a dose-dependent cytotoxicity in murine cancer cells. pH-responsive NPs have also been developed by conjugating nanocarriers with acid-labile linkage, such as hydrazone [54,55], orthoester [56], imine [57], and phosphoramidate [58], whose hydrolysis ensures rapid the release of the drug. An interesting NP fabrication of TME responsive theragnostic with a pH-dependent fluorescence turn-on/off property was reported by Kang et al. [59].

Another interesting one was reported by Liao et al. [60], where the synthesis of pH-responsive hyaluronic acid-hydrazone linkage-doxorubicin (HA-hyd-DOX) self-assemble NPs for efficient DOX for tumor targeting.

Like other varieties, one of the major drawbacks of pH-responsive NPs is the non-responsive behavior of pH-responsive NPs in the perivascular region because the acidic pH is needed for responsiveness, and it is found in regions far away from the blood vessels. Moreover, the difference in pH between normal and tumor tissues is not significant enough for generating responsiveness in all instances.

Smart GSH, ROS, and Hypoxia-sensitive nanoparticles

The popular chemodynamic therapy (CDT) uses the Fenton reaction to elevate intracellular oxidative stress by converting intratumoral or intracellular hydrogen peroxide (H_2O_2) into hydroxyl radicals ($\cdot OH$) to kill cancer cells [61–68].

The acidic nature (pH $\sim$6.0–6.5) of the TME [61,62] and the overproduction of H_2O_2 ($\sim$50–100 μM) due to mitochondrial dysfunction [63] can activate the Fenton reaction. Therefore, the short half-life and high oxidation ability of $\cdot OH$ induced via Fenton reaction only generates and performs effective damage at the tumor site, avoiding side effects to surrounding tissues. Glucose oxidase (GOx) can selectively catalyze the oxidation of glucose into gluconic acid and H_2O_2 with high efficiency [61,62], which is the perfect characteristic for improving acidity and H_2O_2 levels in tumors and, thus, improving the CDT via the Fenton reaction [63,64]. Due to Warburg effect, cancer cells express an exceeding desire for glucose to supply energy for proliferation, which are more sensitive to changes in glucose concentration than normal cells [64–66]. The depletion of intratumoral glucose by GOx can effectively consume the energy for tumor growth and starve them to death while also improving the effects of CDT [67]. Supramolecular NPs constructed via noncovalent interactions act in the field of drug delivery due to their simple synthesis procedure, reversibility, and switchable structures [68]. These variety of NPs are sensitive to stimuli, with notable responsiveness [69,70]. The TME (high GSH and ROS)-responsive supramolecular NPs were designed and constructed via the host-guest interactions of water-soluble pillar [6] arene, which are the fifth generation of supramolecule, can act as hosts and bind with the specific functional group of various guests via hydrogen bonding, covalent bonding, π-π stacking interaction, electrostatic interaction, and ionic interaction [71–83]. The encapsulation of GOx in the NPs not only depletes glucose to starve cancer cells but also improves acidity and H_2O_2 levels in tumors, thereby improving the CDT to produce hydroxyl radicals with high oxidation ability for killing cancer cells. One near-infrared (NIR) fluorescent probe-based GSH-responsive NP was developed by Yuan et al., where the fluorescent probe consisted of nitroazo-aryl-ether (GSH-responsive unit) and tumor targeting unit.

GSH cleaved the nitroazo-aryl-ether group connecting fluorescence and the fluorescence quenching unit, which turned on the fluorescence [84]. Furthermore, manganese dioxide (MnO_2) nanosheets-based GSH-responsive nanoprobe has been used as magnetic resonance imaging (MRI)-based dual imaging system [85]. The MnO_2 nanosheets act as a fluorescence quencher, a GSH-activated MRI contrast agent, and a DNA nanocarrier. Upon endocytosis in tumor cells, cellular GSH acts on MnO_2 nanosheets, which leads to its disintegration and produces a high amount of Mn^{2+} ions for MRI.

The nanocarrier comprised of ROS-responsive poly(β-amino ester) ((PBAEROS)-based nanocarrier where the thioketal groups act on monomer structure) is used for the controlled release of DOX (in NIR photosensitizer IR780) to achieve the synergistic combined anticancer effect of PTT/PDT and chemotherapy [86]. Further, NPs were loaded with marine sulfated polysaccharide, known as poly(β-amino ester) PPID (photothermal/photodynamic (PTT/PDT) IR and DOX loaded) NPs, which have the capacity to respond to ROS and release DOX in a regulated way. ROS-responsive liposome nanocarrier shows their synergistic antitumor effect in breast cancer cells with no cardiotoxicity or side effects to normal cells [87].

Enzyme-responsive nanomaterials

Enzyme-responsive nanomaterials consist of nanomaterials like inorganic materials, polymers, and phospholipids, and the advantage of using them in biomedical field due to several advantages like high sensitivity and selectivity, catalytic efficacy, biorecognition, mild reaction conditions, and easy decomposition [88,89]. The enzyme-responsive NP is designed to respond to MMPs, which are proteases upregulated in the progression of certain cancers [90–92] and other diseases in tissue of interest, making it possible to deliver therapeutic cargo [93,94] or imaging agent. The ER-NPs act when functionalized with MMP-responsive peptides on the NP shell, and when they are exposed to MMPs, the peptides are cleaved at their recognition sequences, thereby the NP structure and induces a nano- to microscale morphology change in it.

Role of metal nanoparticles in cancer therapy

Metal NPs are useful as they provide multiplexed measurement capacity and high sensitivity and specificity [25]. Different varieties of metals, including gold, silver, iron and/or iron oxide, zinc, titanium, cerium oxide, nickel, copper, magnesium, barium, calcium, and bismuth-based metal NPs, have been reported as a cancer treatment. Gold NPs are among the leading, followed by silver and magnetic NPs action in cancer diagnosis and therapy. Noble metal NPs, especially of gold and silver, have been rigorously utilized in artwork for centuries based on their expressing vivacious colors through interaction with visible light. Recent studies on optoelectronic properties of gold and silver nanoparticles (AgNPs) have shown strong correlations with their size, shape, surface chemistry, aggregation behavior, and environment. Additionally, these two noble metal NPs have attracted intense scientific and technical interest due to retaining the unusual optical, electronic, and thermal properties; facile synthesis and surface bioconjugation; and feasibility in clinical diagnostics and therapeutics [25,95–100].

Gold nanoparticle

AuNPs have extensively been employed as drug delivery vehicles for breast and prostate cancers. Due to lower systemic toxicity, faster kidney clearance, and higher tumor accumulation, ultrasmall AuNPs (<10 nm in diameter) have been proven to be promising in several biomedical applications including modern medicine advanced applications like targeted antibodies or drug products and photothermal cancer therapy and cancer diagnosis [95–98]. AuNPs were found to prevent the cross-talk between cancer cells and CAF. Additionally, AuNPs decreased the enhancement effect of CAFs on PCCs' proliferation, migration, and invasion, as well as the fibrogenic response in pancreatic stellate cells (PSCs) [99].

Silver nanoparticle

AgNPs are becoming increasingly popular due to the wide range of applications in biomedical field including medical imaging, filters, drug delivery, nanocomposites, cell electrodes, and antimicrobial products [100]. AgNPs have attracted significant attention from researchers because of their large number of applications [101]. Primarily, the AgNPs' functions include ROS, oxidative stress, and DNA damage and apoptosis-mediated cancer cell death. ROS are essential for the survival of cells since they help to keep their internal balance in check [101]. The main difference between AgNPs and conventional small molecular drugs lies within the "nano" nature of AgNPs, along with the enhanced permeability and retention (EPR) effect, which has been exploited for drug design in the nanomedicine field which ultimately helps to reduce the severity of undesired side effects [100,101]. Also release of silver from the silver ions in the cytosol following endocytosis of AgNPs and their breakdown in an acidic environment from AgNPs have been linked to an increased risk of cancer and cell death due to their ability to interfere with cell's basic metabolic and cell cycle pathways [100–117]. The organic anticancer drug paclitaxel with inorganic AgNPs as tumor-targeting agents. Drug nanocrystals coated with NR1/AgNP demonstrated dramatically improved cellular absorption efficiency, in vitro anticancer activity, and an antimigration effect against a range of cancer cells [100,110–115].

Platinum nanoparticles

All around the world platinum-based drugs like cisplatin, carboplatin, and oxaliplatin are used, but the adverse effect of drug resistance often happens due to its lack of specificity [116,117]. The ultrasmall platinum NPs were disseminated in chitosan loaded across zinc-doped mesoporous silica nanocarriers, and doxorubicin molecules were loaded by the zinc species often used more efficiently into the tumor's acidic microenvironment for platinum-based nanotherapies [117].

Palladium nanoparticles

Palladium NPs are used in theragnostic applications for prodrug activators, photothermal agents, and anticancer and/or antibacterial therapy [118].

Nonnoble metal nanoparticle

Different nonnoble nanoparticles, e.g., copper nanoparticle, zinc nanoparticle, magnesium nanoparticle, titanium nanoparticle, cerium nanoparticle, act on smart cancer therapy.

Copper nanoparticle: The chitin-based silver and copper nanocomposite acts against human breast cancer (MCF-7) cells [119]. Several studies revealed an increase in ROS production, decreased antioxidant enzyme activity, and membrane integrity degradation, confirming the cellular cytotoxic effect of the copper-silver NPs-based nanocomposite [119].

Zinc nanoparticle: The CUR-loaded zinc oxide NPs and egg albumin-based zinc oxide NPs act as anticancerous agents [120,121].

Magnesium nanoparticles: Bionanocomposites and superparamagnetic magnesium ferrite-based NP systems have been used to combat several cancers like blood cancer and breast cancer [122–124].

Titanium nanoparticle: Biogenic titanium dioxide NPs have a unique size, shape, and biochemical functional corona that execute therapeutic effects at the molecular level, such as anticancer, antibacterial, antioxidant, larvicidal, and photocatalysis and for the photothermal therapy for a melanoma cancer model [125–127].

Conclusion

The NP-based therapy especially using smart NPs in treatment of cancer metastasis is highly challenging and newer avenues of research involve multiple advantages over traditional chemotherapies. Different stimulus-based smart NPs efficiently modulate the TME and efficiently act as anticancer treatment by altering the metastasis cascade.

Acknowledgments

I would like to sincerely acknowledge Dr. Kaushik Ghose, Research Scientist, IGCAST, Department of Plant and Soil Science, Texas Tech University/BASF Seed and Innovation Centre, for his help in preparing the images and tables in this chapter.

References

[1] M. Arruebo, N. Vilaboa, B. Sáez-Gutierrez, J. Lambea, A. Tres, M. Valladares, A. González-Fernández, Assessment of the evolution of cancer treatment therapies, Cancers (Basel) 3 (3) (2011) 3279–3330.

[2] J. Feliu, V. Heredia-Soto, R. Gironés, B. Jiménez-Munarriz, J. Saldaña, C. Guillén-Ponce, M.J. Molina-Garrido, Management of the toxicity of chemotherapy and targeted therapies in elderly cancer patients, Clin. Transl. Oncol. 22 (4) (2020) 457–467.

[3] G. Housman, S. Byler, S. Heerboth, K. Lapinska, M. Longacre, N. Snyder, S. Sarkar, Drug resistance in cancer: an overview, Cancers (Basel) 6 (3) (2014) 1769–1792.

[4] B. Mansoori, A. Mohammadi, S. Davudian, S. Shirjang, B. Baradaran, The different mechanisms of cancer drug resistance: a brief review, Adv Pharm. Bull. 7 (3) (2017) 339–348.

[5] J. Jin, X. Wu, J. Yin, M. Li, J. Shen, J. Li, Y. Zhao, Q. Zhao, J. Wu, Q. Wen, C.H. Cho, T. Yi, Z. Xiao, L. Qu, Identification of genetic mutations in cancer: challenge and opportunity in the new era of targeted therapy. Front, Oncologia 9 (2019) 263.

[6] G. Mendiratta, E. Ke, M. Aziz, et al., Cancer gene mutation frequencies for the U.S. population, Nat. Commun. 12 (2021) 5961.

[7] A. Bhowmik, R. Khan, M.K. Ghosh, Blood brain barrier: a challenge for effectual therapy of brain tumors, Biomed. Res. Int. 2015 (2015) 320941.

[8] A. Shergalis, A. Bankhead 3rd, U. Luesakul, N. Muangsin, N. Neamati, Current challenges and opportunities in treating glioblastoma, Pharmacol. Rev. 70 (3) (2018) 412–445.

[9] E.K. Noch, R. Ramakrishna, R. Magge, Challenges in the treatment of glioblastoma: multisystem mechanisms of therapeutic resistance, World Neurosurg. 116 (2018) 505–517.

[10] S. Hossen, M.K. Hossain, M.K. Basher, et al., Smart nanocarrier-based drug delivery systems for cancer therapy and toxicity studies: a review, J. Adv. Res. 15 (2019) 1–18.

[11] O.M. Al-Quteimat, A.M. Amer, The impact of the COVID-19 pandemic on cancer patients, Am. J. Clin. Oncol. 43 (6) (2020) 452–455.

[12] W. Liang, W. Guan, R. Chen, et al., Cancer patients in SARS-CoV-2 infection: a nationwide analysis in China, Lancet Oncol. 21 (2020) 335–337.

[13] M. Chidambaram, R. Manavalan, K. Kathiresan, Nanotherapeutics to overcome conventional cancer chemotherapy limitations, J. Pharm. Pharm. Sci. 14 (1) (2011) 67–77.

[14] P. Navya, et al., Current trends and challenges in cancer management and therapy using designer nanomaterials, Nano Converg. 6 (1) (2019) 1–30.

[15] A. Kaphle, et al., Nanomaterials for agriculture, food and environment: applications, toxicity and regulation, Environ. Chem. Lett. 16 (1) (2018) 43–58.

[16] C.O. Adetunji, et al., Nanomaterials from marine environments: an overview, in: O.V. Kharissova, L.M.T. Martínez, B.I. Kharisov (Eds.), Handbook of Nanomaterials and Nanocomposites for Energy and Environmental Applications, Springer International Publishing, Cham, 2020.

[17] F.S. Youssef, et al., Application of some nanoparticles in the field of veterinary medicine, Int. J. Vet. Sci. Med. 7 (1) (2019) 78–93.

[18] A. Sharma, A.K. Goyal, G. Rath, Recent advances in metal nanoparticles in cancer therapy, J. Drug Target. 26 (8) (2018) 617–632.

[19] Z. Cheng, et al., Nanomaterials for cancer therapy: current progress and perspectives, J. Hematol. Oncol. 14 (1) (2021) 1–27.

[20] M.J. Mitchell, M.M. Billingsley, R.M. Haley, et al., Engineering precision nanoparticles for drug delivery, Nat. Rev. Drug Discov. 20 (2021) 101–124.

[21] R. Liao, et al., Enzymatic protection and biocompatibility screening of enzyme-loaded polymeric nanoparticles for neurotherapeutic applications, Biomaterials 257 (2020) 120238.

[22] T. Wu, Y. Dai, Tumor microenvironment and therapeutic response, Cancer Lett. 387 (2017) 61–68.

[23] M. Yang, J. Li, P. Gu, X. Fan, The application of nanoparticles in cancer immunotherapy: targeting tumor microenvironment, Bioact. Mater. 6 (2021) 1973–1987.

[24] S. Guo, C.X. Deng, Effect of stromal cells in tumor microenvironment on metastasis initiation, Int. J. Biol. Sci. 14 (2018) 2083–2093.

[25] J.J. Xu, W.C. Zhang, Y.W. Guo, X.Y. Chen, Y.N. Zhang, Metal nanoparticles as a promising technology in targeted cancer treatment, Drug Delivery 29 (1) (2022) 664–678.

[26] L. Wang, et al., Tumor microenvironment-enabled nanotherapy, Adv. Healthc. Mater. 7 (8) (2018) e1701156.

[27] D.F. Quail, J.A. Joyce, Microenvironmental regulation of tumor progression and metastasis, Nat. Med. 19 (2013) 1423–1437.

[28] N.W. Coles, R.M. Johnstone, Glutamine metabolism in Ehrlich ascites carcinoma cells, Biochem. J. 83 (1962) 284–291.

[29] W.J. Richtsmeier, R. Dauchy, L.A. Sauer, In vivo nutrient uptake by head and neck cancers, Cancer Res. 47 (19) (1987) 5230–5233.

[30] P. Vaupel, F. Kallinowski, P. Okunief, Blood flow, oxygen and nutrient supply, and metabolic microenvironment of human tumors: a review, Cancer Res. 49 (23) (1989) 6449–6465.

[31] D. Hanahan, L.M. Coussens, Accessories to the crime: functions of cells recruited to the tumor microenvironment, Cancer Cell 21 (3) (2012) 309–322.

[32] G. Agiostratidou, I. Sgouros, E. Galani, A. Voulgari, N. Chondrogianni, E. Samantas, et al., Correlation of in vitro cytotoxicity and clinical response to chemotherapy in ovarian and breast cancer patients, Anticancer Res. 21 (2001) 455–459.

[33] J.P. Fruehauf, In vitro assay-assisted treatment selection for women with breast or ovarian cancer, Endocr.-Relat. Cancer 9 (2002) 171–182.

[34] T. Murata, E. Mekada, R.M. Hofman, Reconstitution of a metastatic-resistant tumor microenvironment with cancer-associated fibroblasts enables metastasis, Cell Cycle 16 (2017) 533–535.

[35] H. Chen, et al., Stimuli-responsive polysaccharide enveloped liposome for targeting and penetrating delivery of survivin-shRNA into breast tumor, ACS Appl. Mater. Interfaces 12 (2020) 22074–22087.

[36] R. Iyer, et al., Glutathione-responsive biodegradable polyurethane nanoparticles for lung cancer treatment, J. Control. Release 321 (2020) 363–371.

[37] L. Hong, et al., Development of a hydrogen peroxide-responsive and oxygen-carrying nanoemulsion for photodynamic therapy against hypoxic tumors using phase inversion composition method, J. Innov. Opt. Health Sci. 14 (02) (2021) 2150003.

[38] G. Gu, et al., PEG-co-PCL nanoparticles modified with MMP-2/9 activatable low molecular weight protamine for enhanced targeted glioblastoma therapy, Biomaterials 34 (1) (2013) 196–208.

[39] N. Li, et al., Enzyme-sensitive and amphiphilic PEGylated dendrimer-paclitaxel prodrug-based nanoparticles for enhanced stability and anticancer efficacy, ACS Appl. Mater. Interfaces 9 (8) (2017) 6865–6877.

[40] J. Zhou, et al., Lectin-gated, mesoporous, photofunctionalized glyconanoparticles for glutathione-responsive drug delivery, Chem. Commun. (Camb.) 51 (48) (2015) 9833–9836.

[41] L.P. Datta, et al., Enzyme responsive nucleotide functionalized silver nanoparticles with effective antimicrobial and anticancer activity, N. J. Chem. 41 (4) (2017) 1538–1548.

[42] Q.S. Feng, et al., Self-assembly of gold nanoparticles shows microenvironment-mediated dynamic switching and enhanced brain tumor targeting, Theranostics 7 (2017) 1875–1889.

[43] F. Xia, et al., pH-responsive gold nanoclusters-based nanoprobes for lung cancer targeted near-infrared fluorescence imaging and chemophotodynamic therapy, Acta Biomater. 68 (2018) 308–319.

[44] C. Sun, X. Li, X. Du, T. Wang, Redox-responsive micelles for triggered drug delivery and effective laryngopharyngeal cancer therapy, Int. J. Biol. Macromol. 112 (2018) 65–73.

[45] C. Sun, et al., A ROS-responsive polymeric micelle with a π-conjugated thioketal moiety for enhanced drug loading and efficient drug delivery, Org. Biomol. Chem. 15 (2017) 9176–9185.

[46] L. Sun, et al., Cell-permeable, MMP-2 activatable, nickel ferrite and his-tagged fusion protein self-assembled fluorescent nanoprobe for tumor magnetic targeting and imaging, ACS Appl. Mater. Interfaces 9 (39) (2017) 209–222.

[47] H. He, et al., Selective cancer treatment via photodynamic sensitization of hypoxia-responsive drug delivery, Nanoscale 10 (2017) 2856–2865.

[48] Q. Chen, L. Feng, J. Liu, W. Zhu, Z. Dong, Y. Wu, Z. Liu, Intelligent albumin MnO_2 nanoparticles as pH-/H_2O_2-responsive dissociable nanocarriers to modulate tumor hypoxia for effective combination therapy, Adv. Mater. (Deerfield Beach, FL) 30 (2018) 7129–7136.

[49] Q. Feng, et al., Hypoxia-specific therapeutic agents delivery nanotheranostics: a sequential strategy for ultrasound mediated on-demand tritherapies and imaging of cancer, J. Controlled Release 275 (2018) 192–200.

[50] J.V. John, S. Uthaman, R. Augustine, H.Y. Chen, I.K. Park, I. Kim, pH/redox dual stimuli-responsive sheddable nanodaisies for efficient intracellular tumour triggered drug delivery, J. Mater. Chem. B 5 (2017) 5027–5036.

[51] R.P. Johnson, et al., Glutathione and endosomal pH-responsive hybrid vesicles fabricated by zwitterionic polymer block poly(L-aspartic acid) as a smart anticancer delivery platform, React. Funct. Polym. 119 (2017) 47–56.

[52] R.P. Johnson, et al., Poly(PEGA)-b-poly(L-lysine)-b-poly(L-histidine) hybrid vesicles for tumoral pH-triggered intracellular delivery of doxorubicin hydrochloride, ACS Appl. Mater. Interfaces 7 (2015) 21770–21779.

[53] M. Zhang, et al., Ingenious pH-sensitive dextran/mesoporous silica nanoparticles based drug delivery systems for controlled intracellular drug release, Int. J. Biol. Macromol. 98 (2017) 691–700.

[54] S. Zhu, D.S. Lansakara-P, X. Li, Z. Cui, Lysosomal delivery of a lipophilic gemcitabine prodrug using novel acid-sensitive micelles improved its antitumor activity, Bioconjugate Chem. 239 (2012) 966–980.

[55] T. Thambi, V.G. Deepagan, C.K. Yoo, J.H. Park, Synthesis and physicochemical characterization of amphiphilic block copolymers bearing acid-sensitive orthoester linkage as the drug carrier, Polymer 52 (2011) 4753–4759.

[56] Q. Zha, X. Wang, X. Cheng, S.X. Fu, G.Q. Yang, W.J. Yao, R.P. Tang, Acid degradable carboxymethyl chitosan nanogels via an ortho ester linkage mediated improved penetration and growth inhibition of 3-D tumor spheroids in vitro, Mater. Sci. Eng. C Mater. 78 (2017) 246–257.

[57] S. Belali, A.R. Karimi, M. Hadizadeh, Cell-specific and pH-sensitive nanostructure hydrogel based on chitosan as a photosensitizer carrier for selective photodynamic therapy, Int. J. Biol. Macromol. 110 (2018) 437–448.

[58] Y.C. Tao, S.W. Liu, Y. Zhang, Z.G. Chi, J.R. Xu, A pH-responsive polymer based on dynamic imine bonds as a drug delivery material with pseudo target release behavior, Polym. Chem. UK 9 (2018) 878–884.

[59] E.B. Kang, J.E. Lee, Z.A.I. Mazrad, I. In, J.H. Jeong, S.Y. Park, pH-responsible fluorescent carbon nanoparticles for tumor selective theranostics via pH turn on/off fluorescence and photothermal effect in vivo and in vitro, Nanoscale 10 (2018) 2512–2523.

[60] J.H. Liao, et al., Tumor-targeting and pH-responsive nanoparticles from hyaluronic acid for the enhanced delivery of doxorubicin, Int. J. Biol. Macromol. 113 (2018) 737–747.

[61] C. Zhang, W. Bu, D. Ni, S. Zhang, Q. Li, Z. Yao, J. Zhang, H. Yao, Z. Wang, J. Shi, Synthesis of iron nanometallic glasses and their application in cancer therapy by a localized Fenton reaction, Angew. Chem. Int. Ed. Engl. X 55 (2018) 2101–2106.

[62] Z. Tang, Y. Liu, M. He, W. Bu, Chemodynamic therapy: tumour microenvironment-mediated Fenton and Fenton-like reactions, Angew. Chem., Int. Ed. Engl. 58 (2019) 946–956.

[63] Z. Tang, P. Zhao, H. Wang, Y. Liu, W. Bu, Biomedicine meets Fenton chemistry, Chem. Rev. 121 (2021) 1981–2019.

[64] Q. Chen, L. Feng, J. Liu, W. Zhu, Z. Dong, Y. Wu, Z. Liu, Intelligent albumin-MnO_2 nanoparticles as pH-/H_2O_2-responsive dissociable nanocarriers to modulate tumor hypoxia for effective combination therapy, Adv. Mater. X 28 (2021) 7129–7136.

[65] H. Ranji-Burachaloo, F. Karimi, K. Xie, Q. Fu, P.A. Gurr, D.E. Dunstan, G.G. Qiao, MOF-mediated destruction of cancer using the cell's own hydrogen peroxide, ACS Appl. Mater. Interfaces 9 (2017) 33599–33608.

[66] J. Li, W. Ke, L. Wang, M. Huang, W. Yin, P. Zhang, Q. Chen, Z. Ge, Self-sufficing H_2O_2-responsive nanocarriers through tumor-specific H_2O_2 production for synergistic oxidation-chemotherapy, J. Control. Release 225 (2016) 64–74.

[67] T. He, H. Xu, Y. Zhang, S. Yi, R. Cui, S. Xing, C. Wei, J. Lin, P. Huang, Glucose oxidase-instructed traceable self-oxygenation/hyperthermia dually enhanced cancer starvation therapy, Theranostics 10 (2020) 1544–1554.

[68] L.H. Fu, C. Qi, J. Lin, P. Huang, Catalytic chemistry of glucose oxidase in cancer diagnosis and treatment, Chem. Soc. Rev. 47 (2018) 6454–6472.

[69] C.A. Lyssiotis, A.C. Kimmelman, Metabolic interactions in the tumor microenvironment, Trends Cell Biol. 11 (2017) 863–875.

[70] C. Bowei, et al., Reactive oxygen species-responsive nanoparticles based on thioketal-containing poly(β-amino ester) for combining photothermal/photodynamic therapy and chemotherapy, Polym. Chem. 10 (2019).

[71] N.N. Pavlova, C.B. Thompson, The emerging hallmarks of cancer metabolism, Cell Metab. 1 (2016) 27–47.

[72] J. Swierczynski, A. Hebanowska, T. Sledzinski, Role of abnormal lipid metabolism in development, progression, diagnosis and therapy of pancreatic cancer, World J. Gastroenterol. 20 (2014) 2279–3035.

[73] M.G. Vander Heiden, L.C. Cantley, C.B. Thompson, Understanding the Warburg effect: the metabolic requirements of cell proliferation, Science 5930 (2016) 1029–1033.

[74] N. Song, X.Y. Lou, L. Ma, H. Gao, Y.W. Yang, Supramolecular nanotheranostics based on pillarenes, Theranostics 9 (2016) 3075–3093.

[75] M.J. Webber, R. Langer, Drug delivery by supramolecular design, Chem. Soc. Rev. 46 (9) (2017) 6600–6620.

[76] H.T. Feng, Y. Li, X. Duan, X. Wang, C. Qi, J.W.Y. Lam, D. Ding, B.Z. Tang, Substitution activated precise phototheranostics through supramolecular assembly of AIEgen and calixarene, J. Am. Chem. Soc. 142 (2017) 15966–15974.

[77] B. Li, et al., A pH responsive complexation-based drug delivery system for oxaliplatin, Chem. Sci. 8 (2017) 4458–4464.

[78] Z. Qi, K. Achazi, R. Haag, S. Dong, C.A. Schalley, Supramolecular hydrophobic guest transport system based on pillar[5]arene, Chem. Commun. 51 (2015) 10326–10329.

[79] T. Kakuta, T.A. Yamagishi, T. Ogoshi, Stimuli-responsive supramolecular assemblies constructed from pillar[n]arenes, Acc. Chem. Res. 51 (2018) 1656–1666.

[80] L. Shao, J. Zhou, B. Hua, G. Yu, A dual-responsive supra-amphiphile based on a water-soluble pillar[7]arene and a naphthalene diimide-containing guest, Chem. Commun. 51 (2017) 7215–7218.

[81] M. Zuo, W. Qian, Z. Xu, W. Shao, X.Y. Hu, D. Zhang, J. Jiang, X. Sun, L. Wang, Multi-responsive supramolecular theranostic nanoplatform based on pillar[5]arene and diphenylboronic acid derivatives for integrated glucose sensing and insulin delivery, Small 14 (2018) e1801942.

[82] X. Lv, D. Xia, Y. Zuo, X. Wu, X. Wei, P. Wang, Gemini-type supramolecular amphiphile based on a water-soluble pillar[5]arene and an Azastilbene guest and its application in stimuli-responsive self-assemblies, Langmuir 35 (2018) 8383–8388.

[83] C. Luo, et al., Self-assembled redox dual-responsive prodrug-nanosystem formed by single thioether-bridged paclitaxel-fatty acid conjugate for cancer chemotherapy, Nano Lett. 16 (2018) 5401–5408.

[84] Z. Yuan, et al., GSH-activated light-up near-infrared fluorescent probe with high affinity to alphavbeta3 integrin for precise early tumor identification, ACS Appl. Mater. Interfaces 10 (37) (2018) 30994–31007.

[85] D. Yuan, et al., MRI/fluorescence bimodal amplification system for cellular GSH detection and tumor cell imaging based on manganese dioxide nanosheet, Sci. Rep. 8 (1) (2018) 1747.

[86] B. Chen, et al., Reactive oxygen species-responsive nanoparticles based on a thioketal-containing poly(β-amino ester) for combining photothermal/photodynamic therapy and chemotherapy, Polym. Chem. 10 (2019) 4746–4757.

[87] H. Yi, et al., ROS-responsive liposomes with NIR light-triggered doxorubicin release for combinatorial therapy of breast cancer, J. Nanobiotechnol. 19 (2018) 134.

[88] Y. Ding, et al., A dual-functional implant with an enzyme-responsive effect for bacterial infection therapy and tissue regeneration, Biomater. Sci. 8 (2020) 1840–1854.

[89] K. Ling, et al., Alginate/chitosan microparticles for gastric passage and intestinal release of therapeutic protein nanoparticles, J. Control. Release 295 (2019) 174–186.

[90] M. Egeblad, Z. Werb, New functions for the matrix metalloproteinases in cancer progression, Nat. Rev. Cancer 2 (2002) 161–174.

[91] C. Gialeli, A.D. Theocharis, N.K. Karamanos, Roles of matrix metalloproteinases in cancer progression and their pharmacological targeting, FEBS J. 278 (2011) 16–27.

[92] K. Kessenbrock, V. Plaks, Z. Werb, Matrix metalloproteinases: regulators of the tumor microenvironment, Cell 141 (1) (2010) 52–67.

[93] J.E. Rundhaug, Matrix metalloproteinases, angiogenesis, and cancer: commentary re: A. C. Lockhart et al., Reduction of wound angiogenesis in patients treated with Enzyme-Responsive Nanoparticles 237 BMS-275291, a broad-spectrum matrix metalloproteinase inhibitor, Clin. Cancer Res. 9 (2003) 9551–9554.

[94] C.E. Callmann, C.V. Barback, M.P. Thompson, D.J. Hall, R.F. Mattrey, N.C. Gianneschi, Therapeutic enzyme-responsive nanoparticles for targeted delivery and accumulation in tumors, Adv. Mater. 27 (31) (2015) 4611–4615.

[95] W.H. Chen, et al., Therapeutic nanomedicine based on dual-intelligent functionalized gold nanoparticles for cancer imaging and therapy in vivo, Biomaterials 34 (2013) 8798–8807.

[96] M. Fan, Y. Han, S. Gao, H. Yan, L. Cao, Z. Li, X.J. Liang, J. Zhang, Ultrasmall gold nanoparticles in cancer diagnosis and therapy, Theranostics 31 (10) (2020) 4944–4957.

[97] P. Singh, S. Pandit, V.R.S.S. Mokkapati, A. Garg, V. Ravikumar, I. Mijakovic, Gold nanoparticles in diagnostics and therapeutics for human cancer, Int. J. Mol. Sci. 19 (7) (2018) 1979.

[98] A.R. Fernandes, P.V. Baptista, Gene silencing using multifunctionalized gold nanoparticles for cancer therapy, Methods Mol. Biol. 1530 (2017) 319–336.

[99] Y. Zhang, C.K. Elechalawar, M.N. Hossen, E.R. Francek, A. Dey, S. Wilhelm, R. Bhattacharya, P. Mukherjee, Gold nanoparticles inhibit activation of cancer-associated fibroblasts by disrupting communication from tumor and microenvironmental cells, Bioact. Mater. 6 (2020) 326–332.

[100] V. De Matteis, et al., Negligible particle-specific toxicity mechanism of silver nanoparticles: the role of Ag^+ ion release in the cytosol, Nanomedicine 11 (2015) 731–739.

[101] D. Kovács, N. Igaz, M.K. Gopisetty, M. Kiricsi, Cancer therapy by silver nanoparticles: fiction or reality? Int. J. Mol. Sci. 23 (2022) 839.

[102] W. Chen, W. Yang, P. Chen, et al., Disulfiram copper nanoparticles prepared with a stabilized metal ion ligand complex method for treating drug-resistant prostate cancers, ACS Appl. Mater. Interfaces 10 (2018) 41118–41128.

[103] J. Choi, G. Kim, S. Bin Cho, H.J. Im, Radiosensitizing high-Z metal nanoparticles for enhanced radiotherapy of glioblastoma multiforme, J. Nanobiotechnol. 18 (2020) 122.

[104] I.M. Chung, et al., Green synthesis of copper nanoparticles using *Eclipta prostrata* leaves extract and their antioxidant and cytotoxic activities, Exp. Ther. Med. 14 (2017) 18–24.

[105] Y. Dang, J. Guan, Nanoparticle-based drug delivery systems for cancer therapy, Smart Mater. Med. 1 (2020) 10–19.

[106] S. Dhanavel, E.A.K. Nivethaa, V. Narayanan, A. Stephen, In vitro cytotoxicity study of dual drug loaded chitosan/palladium nanocomposite towards HT-29 cancer cells, Mater. Sci. Eng. C Mater. Biol. Appl. 75 (2017) 1399–1410.

[107] R.P. Dhavale, et al., Chitosan coated magnetic nanoparticles as carriers of anticancer drug telmisartan: pH-responsive controlled drug release and cytotoxicity studies, J. Phys. Chem. Solids 148 (2021) 109749.

[108] Y. Huai, M.N. Hossen, S. Wilhelm, R. Bhattacharya, P. Mukherjee, Nanoparticle interactions with the tumor microenvironment, Bioconjug. Chem. 30 (2019) 2247–2263.

[109] A.C. Burduşel, O. Gherasim, A.M. Grumezescu, L. Mogoantă, A. Ficai, E. Andronescu, Biomedical applications of silver nanoparticles: an up-to-date overview, Nanomater. (Basel) 8 (9) (2018) 681.

[110] N.R. Chowdhury, M. MacGregor-Ramiasa, P. Zilm, P. Majewski, K. Vasilev, 'Chocolate' silver nanoparticles: synthesis, antibacterial activity and cytotoxicity, J. Colloid Interface Sci. 482 (2016) 151–158.

[111] K. Kejlová, V. Kašpárková, D. Krsek, D. Jírová, H. Kolářová, M. Dvořáková, K. Tománková, V. Mikulcová, Characteristics of silver nanoparticles in vehicles for biological applications, Int. J. Pharm. 496 (2015) 878–885.

[112] H. Maeda, H. Nakamura, J. Fang, The EPR effect for macromolecular drug delivery to solid tumors: improvement of tumor uptake, lowering of systemic toxicity, and distinct tumor imaging in vivo, Adv. Drug Deliv. Rev. 65 (2013) 71–79.

[113] N. Jain, P. Jain, D. Rajput, U.K. Patil, Green synthesized plant-based silver nanoparticles: therapeutic prospective for anticancer and antiviral activity, Micro Nano Syst. Lett. 9 (2021) 1–24.

[114] D. Kalyane, N. Raval, R. Maheshwari, V. Tambe, K. Kalia, R.K. Tekade, Employment of enhanced permeability and retention effect (EPR): nanoparticle-based precision tools for targeting of therapeutic and diagnostic agent in cancer, Mater. Sci. Eng. 98 (2019) 1252–1276, https://doi.org/10.1016/j.msec.2019.01.066.

[115] N. Muhammad, et al., Silver nanoparticles functionalized paclitaxel nanocrystals enhance overall anti-cancer effect on human cancer cells, Nanotechnology 32 (2021) 85105.

[116] Y. Mochida, H. Cabral, K. Kataoka, Polymeric micelles for targeted tumor therapy of platinum anticancer drugs, Expert Opin. Drug Deliv. 14 (2017) 1423–1438.

[117] A. Abed, M. Derakhshan, M. Karimi, M. Shirazinia, M. Mahjoubin-Tehran, M. Homayonfal, M.R. Hamblin, S.A. Mirzaei, H. Soleimanpour, S. Dehghani, F.F. Dehkordi, H. Mirzaei, Platinum nanoparticles in biomedicine: preparation, anti-cancer activity, and drug delivery vehicles, Front. Pharmacol. 13 (2022) 797804.

[118] M. Al-Fakeh, et al., Characterization, antimicrobial and anticancer properties of palladium nanoparticles biosynthesized optimally using Saudi propolis, NANO 11 (2021) 2666.

[119] D. Solairaj, P. Rameshthangam, G. Arunachalam, Anticancer activity of silver and copper embedded chitin nanocomposites against human breast cancer (MCF-7) cells, Int. J. Biol. Macromol. 105 (2017) 608–619.

[120] W.P.T.D. Perera, et al., Curcumin loaded zinc oxide nanoparticles for activity-enhanced antibacterial and anticancer applications, RSC Adv. 10 (2020) 30785–30795.

[121] T.S. Vijayakumar, et al., Facile synthesis and biophysical characterization of egg albumen-wrapped zinc oxide nanoparticles: a potential drug delivery vehicle for anticancer therapy, J. Drug Deliv. Sci. Technol. 60 (2020) 102015.

[122] S. Ansari Moghaddam, F. Rahmani, N. Delirezh, Investigating the effects of magnesium oxide nanoparticle toxicity on K562 blood type cancer cells, Armaghane Danesh 22 (2017) 584–594.

[123] B. Mangalampalli, N. Dumala, P. Grover, Toxicity assessment of magnesium oxide nano and microparticles on cancer and non-cancer cell lines, Nucleus 62 (2019) 227–241.

[124] I.K. Kgosiemang, R. Lefojane, P. Direko, et al., Green synthesis of magnesium and cobalt oxide nanoparticles using *Euphorbia tirucalli*: characterization and potential application for breast cancer inhibition, Inorg. Nano-Metal Chem. 50 (2020) 1070–1080.

[125] M. Ikram, et al., Therapeutic potential of biogenic titanium dioxide nanoparticles: a review on mechanistic approaches, Nanomedicine 16 (2021) 1429–1446.

[126] M.A. Behnam, F. Emami, Z. Sobhani, A.R. Dehghanian, The application of titanium dioxide (TiO_2) nanoparticles in the photo-thermal therapy of melanoma cancer model, Iran. J. Basic Med. Sci. 21 (2018) 1133.

[127] P.R. Prasad, S. Kanchi, E.B. Naidoo, In-vitro evaluation of copper nanoparticles cytotoxicity on prostate cancer cell lines and their antioxidant, sensing and catalytic activity: one-pot green approach, J. Photochem. Photobiol. B 161 (2016) 375–382.

Index

Note: Page numbers followed by *f* indicate figures and *t* indicate tables.

Printed in the United States
by Baker & Taylor Publisher Services